- [ ] Galápagos Islands, Ecuador
- [ ] Galle, Sri Lanka
- [ ] Gap of Dunloe, Ireland
- [ ] Gaspe Peninsular, Canada
- [ ] Gdaƒsk, Poland
- [ ] Geneva, Switzerland
- [ ] Giant Redwoods, USA
- [ ] Giant's Causeway, UK 394
- [ ] Giza Pyramids, Egypt
- [ ] God's Pocket, Canada
- [ ] Gondar, Ethiopia
- [ ] Gorée, Isle of, Senegal
- [ ] Gorges de Verdon, France
- [ ] Gorges due Tarn, France
- [ ] Grand Bazaar, Turkey
- [ ] Grand Canyon, USA
- [ ] Grand Erg Occidental Desert, Algeria
- [ ] Grand Palace, Bangkok, Thailand
- [ ] Graz, Austria
- [ ] Great Barrier Reef, Australia
- [ ] Great Lakes, Canada
- [ ] Great Masurian Lakes, Poland
- [ ] Great Ocean Road, Victoria, Australia
- [ ] Great Wall, China
- [ ] Great Zimbabwe Ruins, Zimbabwe
- [ ] Grunwald, Poland
- [ ] Gubbio, Italy
- [ ] Guggenheim Museum, Spain
- [ ] Guilin, China
- [ ] Gwalior, India

- [ ] Hadrian's Villa, Italy
- [ ] Hagia Sophia, Turkey
- [ ] Hakone, Japan
- [ ] Hateruma Island, Japan
- [ ] Havana, Cuba
- [ ] Herculaneum, Italy
- [ ] Himachal Pradesh, India
- [ ] Himeji, Japan
- [ ] Hoggar, Algeria
- [ ] Hoi An, Vietnam
- [ ] Hollywood, USA
- [ ] Hong Kong, China
- [ ] Horus, Temple of, Egypt
- [ ] Houses of Parliament, UK
- [ ] Huang Long Valley, China
- [ ] Hue, Vietnam

- [ ] Hvar Island, Croatia

- [ ] Iguazú Falls, Argentina
- [ ] Ilha Grande, Brazil
- [ ] Imperial Palaces of Beijing, China
- [ ] Ironbridge Gorge, UK
- [ ] Isejingu, Shima Hanto, Japan
- [ ] Isfahan, Iran
- [ ] Ivanovo, rock-hewn churches of, Bulgaria
- [ ] Izumo Taisha, Japan

- [ ] Jain Temples, India
- [ ] Jaisalmer, India
- [ ] Jerba Island, Tunisia
- [ ] Jericoacoara, Brazil
- [ ] Jerusalem, Israel
- [ ] Juffureh, Gambia
- [ ] Jungfrau mountain, Switzerland

- [ ] Kailasa, Tibet
- [ ] Kairouan, Tunisia
- [ ] Kakadu National Park, Australia
- [ ] Kanazawa, Japan
- [ ] Kandy, Sri Lanka
- [ ] Karapinar Crater Lakes, Turkey
- [ ] Karen Blixen Museum, Denmark
- [ ] Kauai, USA
- [ ] Kekova, Turkey
- [ ] Kelimutu, Indonesia
- [ ] Ketrzyn, Poland
- [ ] Keukenhof Gardens, Netherlands
- [ ] Kiev Pechersk Lavra, Ukraine
- [ ] Killary Harbour, Ireland
- [ ] Kochi, India
- [ ] Komodo National Park, Indonesia
- [ ] Korcula Island, Croatia
- [ ] Kotor, Montenegro
- [ ] Krak des Chevaliers, Syria
- [ ] Kraków, Poland
- [ ] Kremlin, Russia
- [ ] Kyoto, Japan

- [ ] La Scala, Italy
- [ ] Lake Arenal, Costa Rica

- [ ] Lake Baikal, Russia
- [ ] Lake District, UK
- [ ] Lake Maggiore, Italy–Switzerland
- [ ] Lake Malawi, Malawi
- [ ] Lake Manyara, Tanzania
- [ ] Lake Nakuru National Park, Kenya
- [ ] Lake Pichola, India
- [ ] Lake Tahoe, USA
- [ ] Lake Toba, Indonesia
- [ ] Lake Trasimeno, Italy
- [ ] Lake Turkana, Kenya
- [ ] Lalibela, Ethiopia
- [ ] Lamu Island, Kenya
- [ ] Las Vegas, USA
- [ ] Laurentians, Canada
- [ ] Lavenham, UK
- [ ] Leaning Tower of Pisa, Italy
- [ ] Leptis Magna, Libya
- [ ] Les Calanques, France
- [ ] Levoãa, Slovakia
- [ ] Lhasa, Tibet
- [ ] Lisbon, Portugal
- [ ] Livingstonia, Malawi
- [ ] Lixus, Morocco
- [ ] Lofoten Islands, Norway
- [ ] Loire Valley, France
- [ ] Los Cabos, Mexico
- [ ] Los Jameos del Agua, Spain
- [ ] Louvre, France
- [ ] Luang Prabang, Laos
- [ ] Luangwa, Zambia
- [ ] Lübeck, Germany
- [ ] Lumbini, Nepal
- [ ] Lushan National Park, China

- [ ] Machu Picchu, Peru
- [ ] Makalu, Nepal–Tibet border
- [ ] Manado Bay, Indonesia
- [ ] Mandalay, Myanmar
- [ ] Marienburg Castle, Poland
- [ ] Marquesa Islands, French Polynesia
- [ ] Marrakesh, Morocco
- [ ] Marseille, France
- [ ] Masai Mara Game Reserve, Kenya
- [ ] Matmata, Tunisia
- [ ] Matobo National Park, Zimbabwe
- [ ] Matsumoto, Japan

# 501

## MUST-VISIT DESTINATIONS

# 501
## MUST-VISIT DESTINATIONS

THUNDER BAY
P·R·E·S·S

San Diego, California

**Publisher:** Polly Manguel

**Project Editor:** Emma Beare

**Contributing Editor:** Cathy Lowne

**Publishing Assistant:** Jo Archer

**Designer:** Ron Callow/Design 23

**Picture Researchers:** Jennifer Veall, Sophie Delpech

**Production Manager:** Neil Randles

**Production Assistant:** Pauline LeNavenec

Thunder Bay Press
An imprint of the Baker & Taylor Publishing Group
10350 Barnes Canyon Road, San Diego, CA 92121
www.thunderbaybooks.com

Copyright © Octopus Publishing Group 2006

All notations of errors or omissions should be addressed to Thunder Bay Press, Editorial Department, at the above address. All other correspondence (author inquiries, permissions) concerning the content of this book should be addressed to Bounty Books, Octopus Publishing Group Ltd, 2-4 Heron Quays, London E14 4JP

ISBN-13: 978-1-60710-089-8
ISBN-10: 1-60710-089-4

Library of Congress Cataloging-in-Publication Data available upon request.

Printed in China

1 2 3 4 5 13 12 11 10 09

# Contents

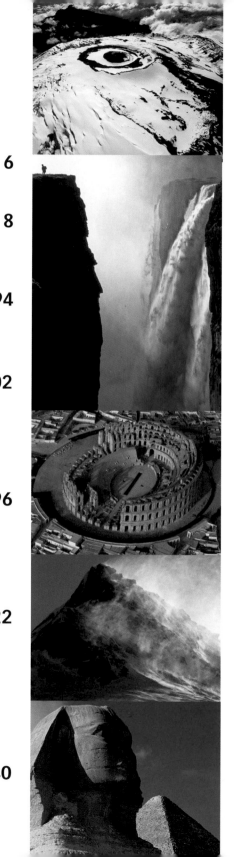

# Introduction

Fifty or sixty years ago travelling abroad for most people was an unrealizable dream. Only the wealthy with a lot of time on their hands could afford to travel to a foreign country for a holiday and even for them the idea of going to South America, Africa or Asia would have been pretty much unthinkable.

The development of air transport over the past few decades has changed all that. Today your often-dreamed-of trip to Cambodia or Uganda or Bolivia or even Antarctica can so easily become reality. More and more people from many different countries and of all age groups are catching the travel bug all the time.

The most remote places on earth are today accessible to the intrepid traveller. Whether it be the remarkable Yemeni island of Socotra in the Indian Ocean or Lake Baikal in Siberia, or Aitutaki in the South Pacific, none of the destinations in this book should be much more than two days' total travelling time from a major airport – provided you have the determination, energy and money to go there, of course. Truly the world now is your oyster.

Some of the must-visit destinations featured are great wonders of nature, but the majority are creations of human beings – towns and cities, cathedrals, castles, museums, gardens and markets – all testament to the industry, ingenuity and perseverance of mankind. Some of them, like the Great Wall of China, the Taj Mahal or the Acropolis, are famous throughout the world but many are little known. Were you to visit the spectacular lagoon at Dakhla or the beautiful temple of Wat Tham Paplong for example there is still every chance that you would be the only tourist there.

It is likely that some – or maybe even all – of your own favourite destinations are not included in this book. So it needs to be stressed that the 501 destinations chosen are just a selection from the many thousands of beautiful and interesting places in this wonderful world of ours.

Undoubtedly travel and tourism can have a damaging effect as visitors to some of the world's most famous cities and monuments can readily testify. Some particularly popular places, the city of Venice or Egypt's Valley of the Kings for example, can at certain times of year be – and feel – almost overwhelmed by the sheer number of visitors and your pleasure at finally reaching your eagerly awaited must-visit destination can be marred by the presence of just too many human beings. Sometimes you can dramatically improve the experience if you simply avoid making your trip during the busiest time of the year. Venice or Florence are still beautiful in the winter months. The Valley of the Kings is equally amazing in August – though admittedly the weather will be hot.

There are also many positive and important benefits from international travel and tourism – probably now the world's biggest single business. Some of these, like tourists' spending and the provision of employment are quite obvious. Yet others are arguably just as important if not so readily apparent – the breaking down of national barriers, understanding other people's habits, thinking and cultures, a shared pride in the fruits of the endeavours of one's fellow man.

Of course the travelling to your must-visit destination can often be as interesting and as much fun as the arriving there. The people you meet, the hotels you stay at, the meals you eat, the trips you take on the local trains, buses or taxis – once you return home your memories of your visit will be of the journey and the whole experience and not just of the destination itself.

If you are the proverbial armchair traveller who, for whatever reason, travels in your mind rather than in fact, this book should help your fantasies. However if you have ever remotely considered visiting the destinations of your dreams, stop resisting. Take the plunge and go. Your mind and your life will be enriched by the experience.

# AFRICA

# Gondar – Fasil Ghebbi

**WHEN TO GO**
September, October and November
are the best times to visit
**HOW TO GET THERE**
Gondar lies on the historical route in
north-west Ethiopia, north of Lake
Tana.
**WHAT IS THERE TO SEE**
The ancient capital of Ethiopia.

In the sixteenth and seventeenth centuries, the fortress city of Gondar – the Royal Enclosure – served as the residence of the Ethiopian emperor, Fasilides, who moved his capital here in 1636 AD. By the late 1640s he had built a great castle here, the recently restored Fasilades Palace. With its huge towers and looming battlement walls, it seems as if a piece of medieval Europe has been transported to Ethiopia.

Recognised as a UNESCO World Heritage site in 1979, the palace, surrounded by an impressive 900-m (2,953-ft) wall, stands in a compound filled with juniper and wild olive trees, amid Enqulal Gemb, or Egg Castle, named after its domed roof, the royal archive, many impressive churches and monastaries and a stable. These exemplify architecture that is marked by both Hindu and Arab influences, subsequently transformed by the Baroque style that the Jesuit missionaries brought to Gondar, and have earned the city the nickname 'The Ethiopian Camelot'.

Beyond the city to the north-west, by the Qaha River, are the Fasilades Baths. A two-storeyed, rustic battlement sits on the steps leading to a rectangular pool, while the bathing pavilion stands on pier arches and contains several rooms that may be reached via a stone bridge, part of which could be raised for defence in times of battle.

*Castle of Emperor Fasilides and his descendants.*

# Churches at Lalibela

Lalibela is Ethiopia's equivalent of Petra in Jordan. Surrounded on all sides by rugged and forbidding mountains to the north of the modern province of Wollo, Lalibela gives the impression that you've landed in a kingdom centuries past. The 11 medieval, monolithic churches of this thirteenth-century 'New Jerusalem' are Ethiopia's top attraction, and they inspire awe, regardless of whether you are interested in religion or religious architecture. Perched at 2,630 m (8,629 ft), the monastic settlement of Lalibela is a desolate, isolated place, a centre of pilgrimage to its many annual visitors.

Located in the heart of Ethiopia near a traditional village with circular dwellings, the churches of Lalibela are cut straight from bedrock so their roofs are at ground level. All 11 churches were built within a century – according to legend, with the help of angels

Close examination is required to appreciate the full extent of this achievement as some lie almost completely hidden in deep trenches, while others stand in open quarried caves. A complex labyrinth of tunnels and narrow passageways with offset crypts, grottoes and galleries connects them all. It's a damp and silent subterranean world, apart from the echoing sounds of the chanting faithful, that needs to be experienced to be fully understood.

Once the thriving and populous capital city of a medieval dynasty, the passing centuries have reduced Lalibela to a village. The churches have been kept alive by generations of priests who guard their treasures of ornamented crosses, illuminated Bibles and illustrated manuscripts. From the road below, it remains nearly invisible against a horizon dominated by the 4,200-m (13,780-ft) peak of Mount Abuna Joseph.

*Christians entering one of the rock-hewn churches.*

**WHAT IS THERE TO SEE**
11 monolithic churches built in the thirteenth century.
**WHEN SHOULD I VISIT**
September, October and November are the best times to visit.
**WHERE IS IT**
In the former province of Wollo.
**WHY IS IT IMPORTANT**
It is one of modern Ethiopia's holiest cities.

*Ancient site of stelae and monoliths.*

**WHAT IS IT**
Ethiopia's holiest city.
**WHY IS IT IMPORTANT**
Christianity was declared the national religion here in the fourth century.
**WHAT IS THERE TO SEE**
One of the possible resting places of the Ark of the Convenant, in which the Ten Commandments are held.
**WHERE IS IT**
In north-eastern Ethiopia on the horn of Africa.

# Aksum – ruins of ancient city

Aksum is considered the holiest city in Ethiopia. Christianity was declared the national religion here in the fourth century by the ruler, Ezana, who constructed much of the monumental architecture and converted much of the Axumite Kingdom's population to Christianity around 330 AD after his own conversion. Once a prosperous kingdom on the Tigray Plateau, it was close to the Blue Nile basin and the Afar depression and accessible to the port of Adulis on the Red Sea coast, which allowed it to maintain trade relations with many nations including Egypt, India, the Sudan and Arabia.

At its peak, Aksum controlled territories as far as southern Egypt, east to the Gulf of Aden, south to the Omo River and west to the Cushite Kingdom of Meroe. The South Arabian kingdom of the Himyarites was also under its power.

The modern city of Aksum is located in the north-eastern portion of what is now Ethiopia, on the horn of Africa. It lies high on a plateau 2,195 m (7,200 ft) above sea level. According to the Ethiopian Orthodox Church, Aksum is where the original Ark of the Covenant, containing the Ten Commandments, is located. The Ark is supposed to be in the seventeenth-century church of Our Lady Mary of Zion, but only its guardian may look at it. The church's museum has a small but impressive collection of bibles, crosses and crowns.

Just past the museum is Aksum's ancient stelae field. These are enormous carved pillars made from single granite blocks, the highest of those still standing is a looming 24 m (79 ft) tall.

Just outside of town you will find the ruins of King Kaleb's Tomb, the Queen of Sheba's Palace and the Pentalewon Monastery. Women are not allowed inside the monastary, but the views from here are worth the somewhat arduous walk up the hill.

# Simien National Park

Massive erosion over the years on the Ethiopian plateau has created one of the most spectacular landscapes in the world. The Simien National Park, a UNESCO World Heritage Site, consists of a rocky massif – cut through by streams and gorges – which slopes dramatically down to grasslands and wide valleys. The pinnacle of the Simien Mountains, Ras Dejen 4,620 m (15,157 ft), is the highest point in Ethiopia and the fourth highest peak on the continent.

The national park has three general botanical regions; the lower slopes for cultivation and grazing, the forested alpine regions and the higher mountain grasslands growing fescue grasses and heathers, splendid red hot pokers as well as giant lobelia.

**WHAT IS IT**
A World Heritage Site with dramatic scenery.
**WHY IS IT IMPORTANT**
For its spectacular scenery, flora and fauna.
**NOTABLE GEOGRAPHY**
It is the home of Ras Dejen, the highest point in Ethiopia and the fourth highest peak in Africa.
**WHERE IS IT**
The Simien Mountains are in north-west Ethiopia, east of the highway from Gondar to Aksum.

Not only are the views from the mountains breathtaking, but the park is also home to some extremely rare animals such as the gelada (bleeding heart) baboons with their distinctive red breasts, the obscure Simien fox, Ethiopian wolves and large birds of prey including the lammergeier. The park was created primarily to protect the 1,000 walia ibex, a type of wild goat found nowhere else in the world, which also live in the park.

Trekking in the Simiens is excellent and the park is easily accessible from Debareq, 101 km (63 mi) from Gondar. The infrastructure is good: equipment, provisions and guides are available. Although not too far from the equator, snow and ice commonly appear on the highest points of the Simien Mountains and temperatures at night often fall below 0 °C (32 °F) so it is important to be prepared for all conditions.

*The Simien Mountains.*

# Amboseli National Reserve

Amboseli National Reserve, formerly known as Amboseli National Park, has been under the control of the Olkejiado County Council, rather than the Kenyan Wildlife Service, since September 2005. This change means that revenue generated by the park now benefits the local Masai communities.

Amboseli is one of Kenya's most popular and is renowned for its population of an estimated 650 elephants, as well as its large herds of wildebeest, zebra, impala and, if you're lucky, the endangered black rhino and elusive cheetah. The backdrop of the snow-capped peak of Mount Kilimanjaro, just 40 km (25 mi) away and rising majestically above the clouds, dominates the reserve.

Designated an international biosphere reserve and national park in 1974, Amboseli covers a mere 392 sq km (244 sq mi), but despite its small size and the fragility of its ecosystem, it manages to support a wide range of mammals. More than 50 of the larger species of mammals and over 400 species of birds can be found throughout the area.

With its rugged landscape and the romantic, mystical atmosphere of the great mountain looming above, it is no wonder that Amboseli inspired the big-game-hunting tales of Ernest Hemingway and Robert Ruark.

The volcanic ash from Kilimanjaro's last eruption thousands of years ago gives many areas of the reserve a dusty appearance, yet a continuous supply of water from the mountain's melted snow flows in underground streams creating the bold contrast of lush green areas. Various springs, swamps and marshes in the park provide havens for wildlife.

Keep an eye out for the arid lakebed that produces mirages in the sweltering heat and be sure to enjoy the views afforded by Observation Hill.

*A herd of African Elephants in front of Mount Kilimanjaro, Amboseli National Park.*

# Lamu Island

**WHERE IT IS**
Off the coast of Kenya.
**HOW TO GET THERE**
The best way to get to Lamu is to fly.
The road to Lamu is rough and while
there are buses, the journey is tedious
and sometimes dangerous.
**WHAT TO SEE**
At the centre of town is Sultan's Fort,
built by the Omanis in 1808, and now
a museum.
**WHAT TO DO**
Relax and enjoy.
**CULTURAL ETIQUETTE**
Lamu is strictly Islamic so be sensitive
as to how you dress.

Lamu has been called 'enchanting' and it is no great surprise that this is the word used to describe it. Its long, white sandy beaches framed by rolling dunes are as unspoiled today as they were when the land was settled in the fourteenth century as a Swahili trading post.

Lamu town is Kenya's oldest and it has had a colourful history. In its day it served as a thriving port for the export of timber, ivory and amber as well a major outpost for the then thriving slave trade. After the abolition of slavery, Lamu's economy suffered, and has never fully recovered. Tourism arrived in the 1960s when the sleepy island turned into a hippy heaven, rivalled only by Katmandu.

The island has, however, managed to retain its distinctive character and charm. The simple lines of the Swahili architecture, built in coral and mangrove wood and featuring porches and rooftop patios, allows the friendly locals every opportunity to gather and enjoy the sweeping ocean views in the afternoon breeze.

Donkeys – the main mode of transport – wander through labyrinthine streets the width of an average pavement. Children's laughter echoes in the courtyards as they play in the dappled sunlight while men chat in groups in the street and women wearing their black buibui veils scamper around behind the heavy carved wooden doors for which the island is famous – offering another snapshot of paradise.

*The minaret of the Friday or Juma Mosque at Shela village on Lamu Island.*

# Lake Turkana

*Volcano on Lake Turkana.*

Appearing mirage-like in the middle of a vast, lunar landscape of extinct volcanoes and lava beds is the world's largest desert lake. A World Heritage Site, Lake Turkana, the most northerly of Kenya's Rift Valley Lakes, is extraordinary to behold. Also known as the Jade Sea for the array of blue and green hues produced by the algae it contains, Lake Turkana is fed by the Omo River in Ethiopia and, having no outlet, its levels fluctuate with the rainfall of Ethiopia.

The 'Jurrassic-like setting' of the lake, made all the more spectacular by its drastic contrast to the barren surroundings, is steeped in prehistory.

The lake was first discovered by westerners in 1888 when an Austrian explorer found human skulls and bones here and 80 years later was made famous by Richard Leakey's discovery of fossil remains dating back three million years at his excavation at Koobi Fora. It is widely believed that this is where man first walked upright.

Today, visitors are attracted to the lake to see its population of 22,000 Nile crocodiles in addition to hippos, venomous snakes, Grevy's and plains zebras, reticulated giraffes, camels and more than 40 different species of fish. There are also plentiful numbers of migrating waterfowl, including flocks of flamingos, to be seen.

**WHAT TO SEE**
More than 22,000 crocodiles, large herds of hippos and over 40 different species of fish – if you dare to try catching one!

**WHEN TO GO**
October–April offers the best viewing of migratory birds, the crocodiles hatch in April and May.

**HOW TO FIND IT**
Located roughly 750 km (466 mi) by road north of Nairobi.

**HISTORICAL SIGNIFICANCE**
It is widely believed to be where man first walked upright.

**ALSO KNOWN AS**
'The Jade Sea' for its water's myriad hues of blues and greens.

17

*Giraffes, with their young, on the savanna, Masai Mara.*

# Masai Mara Game Reserve

A call comes over your guide's walkie talkie, a crackling message that lions have been sighted and the jeep speeds off in a puff of dust in hot pursuit. It is just another hazy afternoon in the Masai Mara Game Reserve. As you approach the pride of lions basking lazily in the belting sun, you understand why this park with its abundance of wildlife, rolling plains and grasslands, was chosen as the location for making the film *Out of Africa*.

The park is in the south-western corner of Kenya, close to the Tanzanian border and roughly 275 km (171 mi) from Nairobi. Opened in 1974, the Masai Mara National Reserve comprises 1,510 sq km (938 sq mi) of plains and woodlands and is Africa's richest, and most visited, wildlife reserve.

'The Mara' is home to an incredibly rich and varied wildlife, and is renowned as the only reserve where you can view the 'Big Five' in a single morning's game drive. From July to October you can also witness the amazing annual migration of more than 1.3 million wildebeest, zebras and gazelles from the Serengeti, quickly followed by lions, leopards, cheetahs and hyenas, together with the opportunistic vultures hovering above.

Hot-air ballooning is a favourite way to witness the majestic scenery and wildlife, particularly at sunrise. The experience of hovering above a seemingly endless parade of animals is an experience that will not quickly be forgotten. Afterwards, you can celebrate with a glass of champagne toasting your spectacular surroundings!

Traditional Masai villages, or manyattas, consisting of mud-covered straw huts are located in the north of the park. Here you may walk around, take photographs and talk to the hospitable locals, who are dressed in bright red and adorned with colourful beads and jewellery.

**WHY VISIT**
The reserve is known for the diversity and high density of easily observable wildlife.
**WHEN TO GO**
From July to October you can witness the annual migration of wildlife coming from the Serengeti.
**WORTH THE SPLURGE**
Take a sunrise balloon ride for an unforgettable sight of the vast plains.
**WHERE TO STAY**
Various types of accommodation are available, ranging from stone lodges to luxury tented camps and private camps for small groups seeking a traditional safari experience.

# The Rift Valley

Some 20 million years ago, the earth's crust weakened and tore itself apart, causing a jagged rift, thousands of kilometres long across the African continent. The land on either side then erupted, creating great volcanic mountains, while the valley floor gradually sank into a low flat plain. This geologic phenomenon, called the Great Rift Valley by the Scottish explorer John Walter Gregory, divides Kenya down the length of the country, essentially separating east from west. Today's Rift Valley is characterised by uninhabitable desert and fertile farmland, flat arid plains and steep escarpments.

In some places this natural divide is up to 100 km (60 mi) wide, and at its narrowest point, just north of Nairobi, a mere 45 km (28 mi) wide. The valley floor is at its lowest near Lake Turkana where there is virtually no distinction between the Great Rift and the surrounding desert. As it heads south, however, the valley walls form sheer cliffs rising up to 1,900 m (6,232 ft) at Lake Naivasha. From there the valley descends further to 580 m (1,902 ft) at the Tanzanian border.

The Rift Valley is currently home to 30 active and semi-active volcanoes and a countless number of hot springs. This string of lakes and boiling springs north-west of Nairobi includes Lake Baringo, Lake Bogoria, Lake Nakuru, Lake Elementaita, Lake Naivasha and Lake Magadi in the south. These lakes are unique for their water composition of highly concentrated sodium carbonate caused by the high alkalinity in the surrounding volcanic rocks coupled with poor drainage outlets because of the steep sides of the valley. The sodium carbonate content creates an ideal breeding ground for algae in which several species of fish, tilapia in particular, thrive. As a result, millions of birds flock to these soda lakes to feast on the abundant food supply.

**WHAT IS IT**
A natural geological phenomenon caused by the weakening of the earth's crust followed by volcanic eruptions.
**WHERE IS IT**
West of Mount Kenya in the Kenyan highlands.
**WHAT TO SEE**
Volcanoes, hot springs and millions of birds!

*Ravines in the Rift Valley.*

# Lake Nakuru National Park

Few words can accurately describe the awe-inspiring vision of a seemingly endless pink blanket of feathers laying at your feet. This is the astonishing beauty that greets you at Lake Nakuru National Park.

Designated a bird sanctuary in 1960 and established as a national park in June 1968, Lake Nakuru National Park was created for the protection of its huge flocks of greater and lesser flamingoes. Tens of thousands of these flamingoes descend upon the shores of this shallow alkaline lake, which is also known as a soda lake.

Located 157 km (98 mi) from Nairobi, at an elevation of 1,200–1,800 m (4,000–6,000 ft) above sea level, the park covers 188 sq km (117 sq mi) of land and encompasses a range of superb habitats for wildlife – from the lake itself to, bush, grassland, steep bare ridges and woodland.

The park is an important site for both white and black rhinos, brought back from from the brink through a successful breeding effort after poaching had nearly destroyed the populations here. Around the lake zebras and Bohor's reedbuck can be seen, while clawless otters and hippos can be found in the lake itself or on its shores and klipspringers and rock hyraxes live on the steep cliffs.

Other wildlife highlights include grazing animals such as buffaloes, Rothschild's giraffes, eland, impala, Chandler's reedbuck and steinbok as well as the lions and leopards that prey on them.

*Flamingoes feeding on Lake Nakuru.*

# Tsavo National Park

After a very long, rough and bumpy bus ride, it is the endless expanse of dry grassland and the rich, dark red clay earth that makes the first impression on a traveller entering the Tsavo National Park.

The Park is divided into two areas – Tsavo East and Tsavo West – by the Nairobi–Mombasa highway. It is the largest game park in Kenya, and one of the largest in the world, and is the most popular destination in Africa for safaris.

Known for its high concentration of elephants and lions, Tsavo National Park offers a stunning assortment of animals able to survive in the unforgiving arid, volcanic landscape – including the famed 'Big Five'.

From one hotel, formerly a sisal plantation, you can watch massive elephants through floor-to-ceiling glass windows as you dine by candlelight. It is like living in a wildlife programme as you witness these, and other animals, drink from an isolated pond within arms' length. The views of the various animals caught in the dim torch-lit night as you watch them from your luxurious grass-covered hut, which is perched on stilts, are incredible.

Tsavo East is less visited and only the southern area of the park, below the Galana River, is open to visitors. Sightings of elephants are virtually guaranteed here except in the wetter months of May, June and November, when the larger animals disperse. Other animals that you are likely to encounter include hippos, lions and herds of zebras. Near Lugard's Falls is the black rhino sanctuary, created to conserve the population, which had dwindled to a mere 50 animals because of poaching.

Tsavo West is smaller and offers what can be a more approachable experience, although it is still packed with a wide range of wildlife, including more than 70 species of mammals.

The 70-m (230-ft) wide river, created by Mzima Springs, affords excellent views of Nile crocodiles, as well as hippos, plains zebras and gazelles as they drink at its banks, while both blue and vervet monkeys can be heard in the surrounding fever trees.

**JUST HOW BIG IS IT**
The park is just over 21,000 sq km (10 million acres) – larger than Jamaica!
**WHY SO POPULAR?**
It boasts more than 60 major species of mammals and 1,000 plant species.
**WHAT ELSE IS THERE**
Lugard Falls, where white water rages through spectacular rock formations and the natural volcanic Mzima springs that produce 50 million gallons of fresh sparkling water daily.

*Elephants gather round
a waterhole in
Tsavo National Park.*

*Aerial view of Mount Kenya.*

# Mount Kenya

Opened to visitors in 1949 and designated a UNESCO World Heritage Site in 1997, Mount Kenya National Park offers one of the most impressive landscapes in all of East Africa.

There are 12 remnant glaciers on the mountain, all of which are receding rapidly, and four secondary peaks that sit at the head of the U-shaped glacial valley that is littered with wild flowers. With its rugged glacier-clad summits and forested middle slopes, Mount Kenya is simply spectacular to behold for nature lovers.

The park has incredible lakes, tarns, glaciers, peaks and natural mineral springs. At the lower levels are dry upland forests that give way with height to montane forest with cedar and podo, then thick bamboo forest, upper forests of smaller trees and high-altitude moss and finally high-altitude heath and shrubs followed by open moorland, where animals like elephants, buffaloes, zebras and eland have been sighted as high as 4,000m (13,123 ft). Other animals of the forests include bushbuck, black and white Colobus monkeys and Sykes monkeys, while lower down the slopes the wide variety of wildlife includes black rhinos, leopards, hyenas, genet cats, olive baboons, waterbucks, black-fronted duikers, bush pigs and giant forest hogs. Endangered animals here include bongos (a shy forest antelope), Mount Kenya Mole Shrew, Sunni buck and skinks.

**WHY VISIT**
Offering rare and endangered wildlife, pristine wilderness and peaks of great beauty, Mount Kenya attracts a multitude of mountain climbers.

**WHEN TO GO**
Large animals are in the high elevations during dry seasons Jan–Mar and July–Oct. High elevation birds go to lower elevations during the rains of Mar–June and Oct–Dec.

**ALSO KNOWN AS**
'Kere Nyaga' or 'Mountain of Brightness' – it is believed to be the abode of the Supreme Being, Ngai.

**TRIVIA**
At 5,199 m (over 17,000 ft), it's the second highest mountain peak in Africa.

# Mount Elgon National Park

Giving new meaning to the term 'salt lick', the Elephant Caves at Mount Elgon National Park provide these gentle giants with the vital mineral, and offer a once in a lifetime opportunity for wildlife-watchers to witness a rare, natural phenomenon.

*The elephant caves at Mount Elgon.*

Many herbivores experience what is known as 'salt hunger' because their diet doesn't supply them with adequate nutrients and minerals, including sodium, so they are forced to seek out an alternative source. In many safari parks, the rangers provide salt licks for the animals and they make good spots to watch the vegetarian animals as they congregate around them. And as if this doesn't offer enough of a spectacle, sometimes their predators follow quickly behind to have a feast of their own!

In Mount Elgon National Park, the elephants have found their own source of salt and most people come to view the single large herd of more than 100 individuals who, every night, venture in convoy into the vast caves within the volcanic underground of this ancient caldera to lick the natural salt-rich deposits caused by Elgon's high rainfall leeching the soil from the rock. There are four caves: Kitum, Makingeni, Chepnyalil and Ngwarisha, all of which can be explored. Kitum is the largest, and extends 200 m (660 ft) into the depths of the mountain.

Spotted hyenas and other wildlife can be seen sheltering in the more remote caves, and leopards creep watchfully in the surrounding dense vegetation near their entrances, hoping to catch a meal.

Mount Elgon itself is best seen from the Endebess Bluff, where you can get a panoramic view of the many gorges, lakes, mesas, rivers and hot springs that lie in the shadow of the mountain peaks.

**WHERE IS IT**
470 km (292 mi) from Nairobi.
**TRIVIA**
Third highest mountain in East Africa.
**WHAT TO SEE**
Kitum Elephant Caves.
**WHAT ELSE IS NEARBY**
Kerio Valley National Reserve and the Saiwa Swamp National Park.
**ALSO KNOWN AS**
'Kitum' meaning 'Place of the Ceremonies'.

# Zuma Market

**WHAT TO SEE**
The Queen's Palace and Royal Village, or Rova, a national monument, and the Tsimbazaza Zoological and Botanical Garden are worth a visit.
**ALSO KNOWN AS**
The capital, Antananarivo is often referred to as 'Tana'.

Looking down on Analakely, you'll see an ocean of hundreds of huge white umbrellas, under which vendors sell their wares. Anything you can think of can be found here. Bustling with people and filled with exotic scents, Zuma Market is an assault on the senses. Widely claimed to be the second largest market in the world, there is a flower section bursting with vivid colours and amazing fragrance, a section for handicrafts including an abundance of leather, woodcarvings, straw hats as worn by the locals, batik and other fabrics, and even semi-precious stones and beads – all strewn across mats on the ground, on tables, or on any other available surface. There are areas filled with fruits and vegetables, clothes, paintings, plants, tyres and housewares. A cacophony of sounds and even more stimulation for your eyes, Zuma is part Indian Bazaar, part country fair and part circus.

Floating in the Indian Ocean off the coast of Mozambique, Madagascar is the fourth largest island in the world. The country, formerly a French colony, includes several smaller islands and has a central chain of high mountains, the Hauts Plateaux, that occupies more than half of the island.

Apart from Zuma Market, the Queen's Palace and Royal Village, or Rova, which was formerly the Merina Dynasty residence, the Tsimbazaza Zoological and Botanical Garden are worth a visit. In the spectacular natural surroundings of this otherwise noisy and somewhat polluted city, exist fantastic wildlife viewing opportunities. Perinet, 140 km (90 mi) from the capital, is a nature reserve where you can see a multitude of the famed indri, or tail-less lemurs made popular by the cartoon, *Madagascar*.

*Rice and beans for sale at Antananarivo's Zuma or Friday market.*

# Livingstonia

*Livingstonia beach.*

Livingstonia, a mission settlement established in 1894 by Robert Laws, a disciple of David Livingstone, is situated high above Lake Malawi, with stunning views across to Tanzania.

David Livingstone, the Scottish explorer, visited Lake Nyasa in 1859 and was shocked by the slave trade that he witnessed. He drew public attention to the situation when he returned to Europe and by 1873 two Presbyterian missionary society bases had been established in the region.

Missionary activity, the threat of Portuguese annexation and the influence of Cecil Rhodes led the UK to send a consul to the area in 1883 and to proclaim the Shire Highlands Protectorate in 1889. In 1891 the British Central African Protectorate (known from 1907 until 1964 as Nyasaland), which included most of present-day Malawi, was established.

During the 1890s, British forces ended the slave trade in the protectorate while other Europeans were busy exploiting African slave labour in their coffee-growing states. Following a minor revolt against British rule in 1915, other Africans became inspired to end foreign domination.

Stone House is where Robert Laws once lived and can now be rented overnight as a pleasant historical accommodation to enjoy. Also to see in Livingstonia, apart from the lovely scenery, is the church, built in 1894 in Scottish style. Here there are some lovely windows showing the arrival of David Livingstone at Lake Malawi. Also of interest is the large bell, erected in honour of Laws and his family as well as the stone cairn, in memory of where Dr Laws and his companions pitched their camp during their first night on the plateau. Nearby is the David Gordon Memorial Hospital, once the biggest hospitals in Central Africa.

**WHEN TO GO**
With the exception of the sultry lowlands in the south, the climate is relatively pleasant throughout the year. September to December is probably the best time to visit.
**WHAT TO SE**
The mission settlement and the Stone House, formerly the home of the Laws family, is now a guest house and museum.
**WHERE IS IT**
Above Lake Malawi at 900 m (3,000 ft)

25

*Intensive habitation around Money Bay.*

# Lake Malawi

Lake Malawi, in Lake Malawi National Park, is Africa's third largest lake and the ninth largest lake in the world. A designated World Heritage Site, Lake Malawi is second only in importance to the history of evolutionary study to that of the finches of the Galapagos Islands. Lake Malawi hosts the richest variety of tropical fish of any freshwater lake in the world. Nearly 500 species of cichlids are unique to its waters, encompassing 30 percent of the entire group. Of particular interest is the brightly coloured 'mbuna' rock fish. There is a total of 28 other species endemic to the lake.

Dr David Livingstone claimed the honour of 'discovering' Lake Malawi, although he was most certainly not the first European to see its splendour. Livingstone described it as a 'lake of stars' because of its glittering surface.

This area of spectacular scenery, forming the western part of the Rift Valley, encompasses several offshore islands, the Nankumba Peninsula and Cape Maclear. Its wooded hills and rocky outcrops, rising sharply from crystal blue waters, are mirrored in the lake's crystal clear azure waters.

There are no human settlements within the park's boundaries, however the lakeshore is heavily populated. The locals are dependent on the fishing industry for their livelihood as farming is not possible due to the poor soil conditions.

The area's various habitats include wooded hillsides, swamps, reed beds and lagoons, providing home to hippos, leopards, chacma baboons, vervet monkeys, bush pigs and the occasional elephant. The lake islands, especially Mumbo and Boadzulu, are important nesting areas for several thousand white-breasted cormorants. Reptiles include crocodiles and an abundance of water monitor lizards.

**WHAT IS IT KNOWN FOR**
The richest variety of tropical fish of any freshwater lake in the world.
**WHY IS IT IMPORTANT**
A scenic lake, noted for its importance in the study of evolution.
**HOW BIG IS IT**
It's 560 km (348 mi) long, 80 km (50 mi) wide and 700 m (2,297 ft) deep.
**CLIMATE**
Average annual temperature is 22.7 °C (73 °F). May–August is cool and dry and September–November is hot and dry. December–April is hot and humid.

# Zomba

The Zomba Plateau, forming the faulted edge of the Great Rift Valley and the Shire lowlands, is a magnificent massif largely forested with cypress, Mexican pine and Mulanje cedar. Its series of small waterfalls and rapids join to form the Mulunguzi.

This tranquil forest reserve, renowned for its temperate climate and natural splendour, is blanketed with wild flowers, ferns, thorn bushes and orchids. The summit is an impressive 1,800m (5,906ft) tower rising to over 2,080m (6,824ft) tall. The face of the southern edge, shadowing the colonial town of Zomba, is 750m (2,461ft) high.

Queen's View, named after Queen Elizabeth following her visit in 1957, is said to offer 'the best view in the whole of the British Empire'. Birds and butterflies hover above as you gaze towards the Mulanje Massif and the city of Blantyre. Emperor's View, named after Emperor Haile Selassie of Ethiopia, has equally awe-inspiring vistas.

Settled in the late 19th century as a temperate alternative to the hot and humid low-lying plains, the colonial town of Zomba also offers a rewarding experience. The market here is one of the most colourful in Malawi featuring an abundance of fresh fruits and vegetables set amidst tinsmiths, second-hand clothes stalls, witch doctors and everything you can imagine in between!

**WHAT IS IT**
A plateau forming an edge of the Great Rift Valley, overlooking the old colonial capital of Zomba. It is one of Malawi's prettiest forest reserves.
**WHAT IS THERE TO SEE**
Queen's View, named after Queen Elizabeth following her visit in 1957 is said to offer 'the best view in the whole of the British Empire'.
**WHEN TO VISIT**
The weather is temperate all year.
**YOU SHOULD KNOW**
The state of the roads on the plateau is not good – the best way to see Zomba is by trekking.

*A typical village on the Zomba Plateau, Malawi.*

# The Island of Mozambique

**WHAT IS IT**
An idyllic coral island paradise in the Indian Ocean.
**WHAT IS THERE TO SEE**
The oldest European building in the southern hemisphere.
**HOW DO I GET THERE**
Located 4 km (2.5 mi) off the coast of Mozambique, near Madagascar, daily flights leave from Maputo for Nampula. There is also regular boat service to the mainland – a great opportunity to ride on a traditional dhow!
**WHEN TO VISIT**
The island is temperate all year round. There are two rainy seasons (February–April, November–January). The weather in the mountains is mild with occasional frost and snow possible.
**YOU SHOULD KNOW**
Bikes can be rented from the tourist office.

*Makuti town at the south end of the island.*

First settled by Vasco da Gama in 1498, the idyllic coral paradise of the Island of Mozambique floats languorously in the Indian Ocean's crystalline waters near Madagascar. A study in architectural contrast, the island's port is resplendent in Arab, Indian and Portuguese influences, a reminder of its days as a major trading post on the sea route from Europe to the East Indies.

The town grew from the port outwards, with the land nearest the sea occupied by local business operations. Eventually, the town spread, and villagers built homogeneous limestone, wood-beamed homes on winding, tangled streets surrounding a central square. The façades of the structures include cornices, high rectangular framed windows and rows of pilasters for decoration, while their flat roofs served to collect the rainwater vital on an island with no fresh water springs.

The World Heritage Site, located in the north of Mozambique Island, includes a variety of attractions such as the Chapel of Nossa Senhora de Baluarte, considered the oldest European building in the southern hemisphere – dating back to 1522 – as well as the current Customs House, originally erected as a Portuguese fortress.

Enjoy a walk here as the languid breezes rustle your hair and the dappled sunshine caresses your shadow. In the 30 minutes or so it will take you to traverse this small island, you will be touched by the quaint, rustic feel of the place as well as the friendliness of the locals who will undoubtedly smile and tip their hat to you as you pass.

# Rwanda – Parc National des Volcans

Known everywhere as the place where Dian Fossey, the eminent primatologist, spent years studying the habits and habitats of the rare mountain gorillas, the Parc National des Volcans is truly a must-see.

In the heart of Central Africa, on the steep, lush slopes of north-west Rwanda, the diverse ecosystems of the Congo basin meet the great rift valleys of the west, creating a rich biodiversity not found anywhere else on the continent.

As you trek through evergreen and bamboo forest and open grassland, at the foothills of the scenic Virungas mountains – encompassing six volcanoes – traversing rivers and streams that flow into the Nile, you walk up, up, up towards where the rainforest converges with the rest of this green, tropical paradise. It is here you will find yourself cloaked in the heart of the Parc National des Volcans – or Volcano National Park.

Nearly 4,572 m (15,000 ft) from the forest bed, this is the home to the rare mountain gorilla. As your guide leads you towards the gorillas, you will be surrounded by the sounds of bird calls – more than 670 species are found here – and the squawking and haunting noises of monkeys climbing above you, while getting an occasional peek of a buffalo or elephant. You will find yourself holding your breath as you walk silently on fallen leaves, hoping to catch an up-close glimpse of a silverback gorilla.

At three times the weight of an average grown man, these gentle giants are surprisingly tolerant of their human guests, so long as the latter follow the rules about maintaining their distance and keeping quiet. Meeting these beautiful creatures is certainly an experience that will not be forgotten!

*Western Lowland gorilla.*

**WHAT IS IT**
The national park renowned for Dian Fossey's study of its gorilla population.
**WHAT IS THERE TO SEE**
The home of nearly 400 rare mountain gorillas.
**HOW DO I GET THERE**
Ruhengeri is a 90-minute drive from Rwanda's capital city, Kigali.
**YOU SHOULD KNOW**
If you intend to make a gorilla visit, you will need to organise transport from Ruhengeri town to the park boundaries, where you will continue your guided trip on foot. For the protection of the gorillas, access is limited to a handful of people a day, and strict rules about how to behave around them apply.
**ALSO KNOWN AS**
The 'Land of a Thousand Hills'.

*Tropical island beach on Silhouette Island.*

# Silhouette Island

Silhouette, the third largest granite island in the Seychelles, is an unspoilt oasis of calm and tranquility. The lush, circular island is covered in dense prehistoric rainforest. Accessible only by boat or helicopter and crossed only by unpaved tracks, this island remains virtually untouched by modern man.

The summit of Mount Dauban (740 m (2,428 ft)) looms above the idyllic, unexplored rainforest thick with rare hardwoods, incense trees and pitcher-plant orchids endemic to the shores of Silhouette.

The lack of development means that Silhouette has retained its expansive biodiversity and has become an important habitat for Indian Ocean conservationists to study. One of the amazing local draws is the giant tortoise, known to originate from only the Seychelles and the Galapagos Islands in the Pacific Ocean.

The Seychelles tortoise was almost completely eradicated by sailors who used to pillage the island's resources, using the giant tortoises for food as they were able to survive aboard ships for up to six months without food and water. This activity lasted until 1840 when the last of the, by then endangered, animals was put in captivity. A handful of them were found in captivity in the 1990s, as were a few Arnold's giant tortoise, which were also previously thought to be extinct. There are also currently 100,000 Aldabran giant tortoises on the island.

Today there is a large conservation drive to keep both Seychelles and Arnold's giant tortoises in from extinction – the Seychelles Giant Tortoise Conservation Project. You can view these massive animals at the breeding farm near the old Dauban Coconut Plantation.

The lack of commercialisation makes the Seychelles a paradise for honeymooners – complete with secluded coves and magical scenery. A designated National Marine Park, the island is surrounded by vast, colourful coral reefs that shelter exotic fish of all shapes and sizes, making it appealing to snorkelling and scuba fans.

Other than relaxing on pristine beaches, enjoying the sunshine and exploring the rainforest and reefs – there is not much to do on Silhouette Island…heaven.

**WHAT IS IT**
The third largest granite island in the Seychelles.
**WHAT IS THERE TO SEE**
Prehistoric vegetation and an idyllic island paradise with spectacular underwater delights and famous giant tortoises.
**HOW DO I GET THERE**
Only reachable by helicopter or sea, Silhouette Island is a 15-minute flight from the International Airport. Spectacular views of the Ste Anne Marine Park, Port Victoria and the west coast of Mahe can be enjoyed during your flight.
**YOU SHOULD KNOW**
They have a cast-iron neoclassical mausoleum here that is supposedly the most remarkable piece of eccentricity in all of the Seychelles islands!

# Bagamoyo

Designated a UNESCO World Heritage Site, Bagamoyo is the oldest town in Tanzania and one of the most attractive, combining natural beauty with a significant, although sometimes grim, historical heritage.

The palm-studded, white sandy beaches of the area, with the crystalline blue waters of the Indian Ocean lapping on the shore, make for a relaxed atmosphere in Bagamoyo. Looking out towards the clear blue sea, it is difficult to tell which century you are in as the traditional hand-built wooden dhows continue to ply the waters. The local fisherman sail in these Arabian-designed craft with their billowing triangular sails aloft, vying for space on the waves among the many dugout canoes. Women wade through the surf with impossibly large piles of laundry or fresh produce carried securely in baskets on their heads.

Once a busy port and the major slave trading post in East Africa, Bagamoyo, meaning 'lay down your heart' in Swahili, was the last place slaves stayed in Tanzania before being transported to other countries – largely heading on to Zanzibar or Arab nations. Although the slave trade officially ended here in 1873, slaves continued to be sold and traded through to the end of the nineteenth century. It was not uncommon to see multitudes of them, shackled at the neck, converged on the docks awaiting their fate. At the time, Livingstone calculated that for every slave who reached the coast, ten did not.

Relatively untouched by time, the town of Bagamoyo largely comprises stone architecture that has been influenced by its Arab and Indian traders, the German colonial government and Christian missionaries who settled here. One of the main features of the buildings is the elaborately carved wooden doors. Outside of the town, you will gradually encounter more traditionally African houses with fences made of palm fronds.

Historically significant sites include the nearby thirteenth-century Islamic Kaole Ruins, built of coral and comprising two mosques and several tombs.

In the 1800s, Christian missionaries established a 'Freedom Village' here to protect freed slaves and the Roman Catholic Mission is also worth a visit; it is the oldest Roman Catholic Church in East and Central Africa, built in 1868. In 1874, Dr Livingstone's body was kept here before its return to England for burial.

Bagamoyo is also home to the most famous art college in Tanzania, Chuo cha Sanaa. Students from all over the world come here to learn traditional Tanzanian drumming, sculpture, carving and painting. While you are here you can arrange to take a class or hear an African drumming performance at the college.

**WHEN TO GO**
During the dry season – June–October and January–February.
**WHERE IS IT**
50 km (31 mi) north of the capital, Dar es Salaam.
**ALSO KNOWN AS**
Bagamoyo means 'lay down your heart' in Swahili.
**WHAT IT'S KNOWN FOR**
The town itself has pristine beaches and a pleasant downtown area. The surrounding areas have ruins, a mission and it is worth your while to take a trip in a dhow down the Ruvu River Delta where you will hopefully spot some hippos and other wildlife.
**HISTORICAL SIGNIFICANCE**
Bagamoyo is the oldest town in Tanzania and it once served as a large port for the sale and trading of slaves.

*Local fisherman on Bagamoyo beach.*

# Mount Kilimanjaro

Located in Mount Kilamanjaro National Park in the north-east of Tanzania, the famed Mount Kilamanjaro, Africa's highest peak, is a dormant volcano. It contains three cones: Kibo, Mawensi and Shira. Kibo is the highest and youngest peak, linked to Mawensi by an 11-km (7-mi) expanse at roughly 4,600 m (15,000 feet). Mawensi, the oldest cone, believed to have been the core of a former summit, is 5,400 m (17,564 feet) high. Shira rises to 3,800 m (12,395 feet).

Although Mount Kilamanjaro is only three degrees south of the equator, its high altitude keeps the Kibo crater capped with snow throughout the year.

The strenuous climb up the mountain is a very rewarding experience, and is a must for those seeking adventure. Experienced guides, accompanied by porters, lead visitors to the top of the mountain via various routes, passing through a variety of vegetation – forests, alpine vegetation, semi-desert, and moorland – before reaching the icy top. Visitors can arrange such tours from Moshi or Arusha and the climbs can take anywhere from 5–8 days. The highlight is reaching the summit to view the vast expanse of Kenya and Tanzania below you at sunrise.

*Peak of Mount Kilimanjaro.*

# Zanzibar

A low-lying coral island, possibly part of the African continent at one time, Zanzibar is a jewel rising proudly out of the azure waters of the Indian Ocean. The island lures tourists with its coconut palms swaying in tropical breezes, its gently undulating hills still covered in some places with native forest and its stunning white sandy beaches. Another lure for visitors is the abundance of coral reefs surrounding the island. Dense with many types of marine life as well as different types of coral formations, Zanzibar is a scuba diver and snorkeller's dream.

The island also hosts abundant wildlife. Two kinds of turtles nest on Zanzibar, the green turtle and the hawksbill turtle can both be found dragging themselves ashore to lay their eggs, particularly near the lighthouse at Ras Ngunwi.

Humpback whales, migrating through the channel in spring and then again in September, can also sometimes be seen off the coast. Long-snouted spinner and bottlenose dolphins are also favourites in these waters. Monitored swimming with the dolphins is a major tourist attraction.

Red colobus and blue monkeys can be found in Jozani Park, the largest area of mature native forest remaining on the island following years of deforestation. The park offers a refuge for many types of other types of mammals as well including red-bellied and sun squirrels and about 200 species of birds.

*Zanzibar town waterfront at sunset.*

Fishing plays an important role in the local economy, in conjunction with tourism. Residents continue to grow coconuts and cacao for export, and together with the people of the nearby Pemba Island, produce most of the world's clove supply. Visiting the spice plantations or haggling for carvings in the Central Market is great fun.

The island's history is one of foreign occupation, intensive commerce, and slavery. The earliest known inhabitants on the island were Bantu-speaking Africans – the Hadimu and the Tumbatu. Local legend says that in the 10th century the yearly monsoon trade winds carried Persian sailors to Zanzibar along their Indian Ocean trading routes. Because they needed the monsoon winds to return home, they found themselves stranded on the island for months at a time and eventually decided to build permanent settlements.

Over the centuries different cultures have blended together to create the Zanzibar of today. Here, Africa meets Persia, Arabia, India and China with some Portuguese, Dutch and British thrown in just to confuse the outcome. Shirazi Persians and the Omani Arabs, settled and ruled the Sultanate which explains the Arab-dominated influences that endure today.

Indian influence can be seen in the ornamental fretwork balconies and coloured glasswork, and Gujerati traders selling anything from coriander to curios. The British left some solid imperial buildings that stand 'aloof' in the more select parts of town, and some ex-pats who couldn't bear to leave. It may not have a particularly romantic name, but Stone Town is the old city and cultural heart of Zanzibar, little changed in the last 200 years. It is a place of winding alleys, bustling bazaars, mosques and grand Arab houses whose original owners vied with each other over the extravagance of their dwellings. This one-upmanship is particularly reflected in the brass-studded, carved, wooden doors – there are more than 500 different examples of this handiwork.

**WHAT IS IT**
An island 35 km (22 mi) off the coast of Tanzania in the Indian Ocean.
**HISTORICAL SIGNIFICANCE**
It was once the commercial centre of East Africa and the last place to abolish the slave trade.
**ALSO KNOWN AS**
'the Spice Island'
**WHERE IS IT**
40 km (25 mi) north-east of Tanzania in the Indian Ocean.

*Prairies of the Serengeti National Park.*

# Serengeti National Park

Serengeti National Park, established in 1951 as a wildlife refuge, occupies a vast expanse of land in Northern Tanzania. Serengeti means 'endless plains' in the Masai language. It is an appropriate description, as the park, the largest in Tanzania, rests on a high plateau with elevations ranging from 914-1,829 m (3,000–6,000 ft).

Roughly the size of Northern Ireland, and considered to be the last great wildlife sanctuary, it comprises 14,763 sq km (5,700 sq mi) of rolling plains covered in savanna grasses. Home to more than 35 types of mammals including lion, cheetah, leopard, elephant, giraffe, hyena, hippopotamus, buffalo, rhino, baboon and antelope, as well as over 500 species of birds, the Serengeti is home to many plains animals that cannot be found anywhere else in the world. Its sparse vegetation allows for some of the best game viewing in Africa and it draws masses of visitors from across the globe.

The annual 800-km (497-mi) migration of wildebeest and zebras, driven by their search for food and water in the dry season around May, is one of the main attractions of the park. The unforgettable sight of a horde of one to two million of these animals stomping across the plains in organised chaos towards the western corridor is a spectacle not to be missed. The return pilgrimage generally takes place around December, depending on conditions.

**WHAT IS IT**
A National Park and wildlife refuge in Northern Tanzania.
**HOW BIG IS IT**
The park comprises 14,763 sq. km (5,700 sq mi) of rolling plains.
**ALSO KNOWN AS**
Serengeti means 'endless plains' in Masai.
**WHAT IS IT KNOWN FOR**
The annual migration of wildebeest and zebra.
**WORTH A SPLURGE**
This is the only park in Tanzania where you can take a hot air balloon ride over the plains – If you do not treat yourself to this, you'll always wish that you had.

# Ngorongoro Conservation Area

Nestled between Serengeti National Park and Lake Manyara National Park, lies the Ngorongoro Conservation Area, often called 'The Eighth Wonder of the World' for its stunning beauty and fabulous wildlife viewing.

It is believed that millions of years ago Ngorongoro was roughly the same size as Mount Kilimanjaro. However, when the volcanic activity subsided, it collapsed, forming the crater – the world's largest unbroken caldera. The crater is 610 m (2,001 ft) deep and covers an area of 260 sq km (162 sq mi).

The park's diverse ecosystem includes active volcanoes, mountains, rolling plains, forests, lake dunes and the Olduvai Gorge. The area supports more than 550 species of birds and 115 species of mammals including elephants, cape buffalo, zebra, wildebeest and hippo. It is the only place in Tanzania where you can more or less be guaranteed a sighting of the indigenous black rhino, but you will not find giraffes as the tree-level food is sparse.

Another highlight of the park is the abundance of flamingoes of Lake Magadi on the crater's floor. The spectacle of a bubble-gum coloured cloud of these magnificent birds against an emerald green backdrop is unforgettable!

The otherworldly scene is punctuated by the sight of Masai tribesmen in their traditional attire, herding cattle, sheep and goats.

In the northern, and more remote, part of the conservation area are the Olmoti and Empakaai craters, Lake Natron and Oldoinyo Lengai, or the Mountain of God as the Masai call it. East Africa's flamingoes breed at Lake Natron. On the eastern side of Empakaai are the Engakura ruins, which feature a terraced stone city and a complex irrigation system. The stone buildings are rare because the concept is unusual in this part of Africa.

**WHEN TO VISIT**
Ngorongoro is accessible all year round, though during the rainy seasons (April, May and November) the tracks can be muddy.

**ALSO KNOWN AS**
'The Eighth Wonder of the World'.

**WHAT IS IT KNOWN FOR**
The 16-km (10-mi) diameter volcanic caldera is the land of the Masai, their cattle, and wildlife and it is the only place in Tanzania where you can consistently view black rhinos.

**WHERE TO STAY**
A number of lodges and camps on the crater rim are well placed to provide fantastic views of the crater floor.

**HOW BEST TO VIEW IT**
Tourists can observe wildlife from their vehicles (4x4s recommended) or go on guided walking safaris.

*Lake in Ngorongoro Crater*

# Olduvai Gorge

**ALSO KNOWN AS**
Oldupai or 'The Cradle of Mankind'.
**WHERE IS IT**
Between the Ngorongoro Crater and
the Serengeti.
**HISTORICAL SIGNIFICANCE**
Where Dr Mary Leakey found the
fossil fragments of a distant human
relative dating back 1.8 million years
and the Laetoli footprints, proving that
our ancestors walked upright 3.8
million years ago.

The home of the famous discoveries by Mary and Louis Leakey, Olduvai, or Oldupai, is the site where the fossil fragments of 'Nutcracker Man' or *Australopithecus boisei*, a 1.8 million-year-old fossil hominid, was discovered and is a must see for archaeologist and anthropologist junkies.

In 1976 Dr Mary Leakey invited Peter Jones to work with her at Olduvai. He helped assess the possible uses of the various stone tools and eventually uncovered the famous Laetoli footprints, which proved that our ancestors walked upright as long as 3.8 million years ago.

The Olduvai Gorge contains a significant number of archaeological sites with fossils, settlement remains and stone artefacts. Many of these can be seen in the museum.

Olduvai Gorge is situated in the short grass plains, 20 km (12 mi), or an hour west of Ngorongoro Crater by car, in the Ngorongoro Conservation Area. In addition to the fossils, there are three species of birds that cannot be seen elsewhere in the surrounding areas: the red-cheeked cordon-bleu, the purple grenadier and the red-and-yellow barbet.

Olduvai is definitely worth adding to your itinerary for a day trip *en route* to either Serengeti National Park or the Ngorongoro Conservation Area.

*Olduvai Gorge is built of lava strata and is rich in fossils.*

# Lake Manyara

The lush, tropical oasis of Lake Manyara National Park, located at the foot of the Rift Valley, makes an excellent diversion on your visit to the Ngorongoro Crater and the Serengeti. Its shallow, alkaline waters are home to a variety of wildlife including the huge flocks of flamingoes, lured by the crustaceans and algae that thrive in the high salt content.

*Hippo with young in Lake Manyara.*

The park, rich in acacia trees, attracts a number of giraffes, baboons, vervet and blue monkeys and there is also a healthy elephant population, although poaching means that the numbers are far below those when Ian Douglas-Hamilton camped here in the 1970s, conducting extensive studies of these beasts which he subsequently published in his classic book *Among the Elephants*.

While you are here, you can watch the 350 species of birds that reside here, as well as a variety of mammals including gazelles, impalas, buffaloes, wildebeest, hyenas, hippos and the famous tree-climbing lions.

The best place for viewing lions and elephants, as well as many of the other larger mammals is the Ndala River area. There are two hot springs, Maji Moto Ndogo and Maji Moto, that have large numbers of flamingo if the river waters are low.

Nearby Mto-wa-Mbu is a colourful village where you can buy merchandise, such as kangas, the traditional sarongs worn by Swahili women, tribal brass bracelets and Masai jewellery, from the local townspeople, as well as a large selection of fresh fruit and vegetable.

**WHEN TO GO**
From June to October during the dry season is the most pleasant although wildlife congregates all year round.
**WHERE IS IT**
130 km (81 mi) from Arusha.
**HOW BIG IS IT**
40 km (25 mi) long and 13 km (8 mi) wide.
**WHAT IS THERE TO SEE**
Massive flocks of flamingoes and lions sleeping in trees.

# Rwenzori Mountains National Park

Lying in the forested slopes of the Mubuku Valley, The Rwenzori National Park is an exotic paradise. Home to the third largest mountain in Africa, Mount Stanley (5,109 m (16,762 ft)), which was named after the first foreign explorer to lay eyes on it during an 1887 expedition, Rwenzori is known for its lush Afro Alpine vegetation and the plants and animals that thrive within it.

Although as part of the East African Rift Valley system, unlike other high mountains such as Kilimanjaro and Mount Kenya, those here are not volcanic.

*A Senecio forest flourishes right up to the glaciers at 15,500 feet.*

**WHEN TO GO**
July and August, December to February for hiking in the dry season, although Alpine birds move to the lower elevations during the wetter months.
**WHAT TO SEE**
Luscious forest filled with a variety of trees, flowers, birds and small mammals.
**WHERE IS IT**
25 km (16 mi) from Kasese.
**ALSO KNOWN AS**
'Rain maker'
**WHAT IS THERE TO DO**
Mountaineers and trekkers of all abilities will enjoy a visit to the park.

The landscape here is a dense canopy of varying shades of green, and its textures make it resemble an enormous, leafy quilt. Symphonia trees, with their silver trunks and scarlet blooms, and podocarpus trees, with their fragrant evergreen scents, lend a soft, fresh, crispness to the air. Below these, adding to the tropical aromas, lie giant tree ferns, wild ginger, hisbiscus, begonias, balsams and aram lilies.

The giant lobelias and groundsels shade the pink and green giant earthworms, some of which can reach 45 cm (18 in) in length. The varied bird life, including the conspicuous regal, purple-breasted sunbirds, handsome francolins, olive pigeons and Rwenzori turacos creates a delicious cacophony from above.

Visitors can also view animals like chimpanzees, black and white colobus monkeys, blue monkeys, elephants, bushbuck, giant forest hogs, hyraxes and leopards. You will not regret taking a trip to this African paradise.

# Murchison Falls National Park

Murchison Falls National Park, Uganda's largest, is bisected by the River Nile. Animals such as buffaloes, antelopea, Rothschild's giraffes and elephants lurk by the rivers of the north-western savannas of the park, while the dense rainforests in the south-west host large groups of chimpanzees, vervet monkeys and olive baboons as well as red-tailed and patas monkeys.

The Buligi Circuit, the peninsula between the Victoria and Albert Niles, is stunningly beautiful and contains the highest concentration of wildlife including the tiny malachite kingfisher, carmine bee-eater, African fisheagle, saddlebill stork and the wahlheaded, or shoebill, Stork.

Take an afternoon and trek through the grassland, woodland and papyrus swamps, catching glimpses of the buffaloes, with their sentinel cattle egrets, grazing among Borassus palms north of the Victoria Nile.

Undoubtedly the highlight of the park is the roaring Murchison Falls, best enjoyed by boat. Here the Nile falls vertically 40 m (131 ft) through a 7-m (23-ft) gap crashing into the river below. From your river cruise you can watch, and listen to, hundreds of hippos wallowing along the shores, keeping the many Nile crocodiles company. If you perfer, the falls can be enjoyed from a path leading from above the falls to where the water crashes below.

Below the southern bank of the falls, thousands of bats can be seen roosting on the aptly named 'Bat Cliffs', swarming like large ravens at feeding time in the late evening. Giant kingfishers perch on low branches alongside Pel's fishing owls and pennant-winged nightjars fly among herds of Uganda kobs and Jackson's hartebeests.

Murchison Falls is certainly an adventure not to be missed.

**WHAT IS IT**
Uganda's largest National Park.
**HOW BIG IS IT**
The park is 3,840 sq km (2,386 sq mi).
**WHERE IS IT**
97 km (60 mi) north of Masindi, 354 km (220 mi) north of Kampala.
**WHAT IS THERE TO SEE**
The 40-m (131-ft) cascade of Murchison Falls is the highlight.
**WORTH A SPLURGE**
Take a boat trip at the base of the roaring falls among the massive hippo population.

*Murchison Falls.*

# Victoria Falls

**WHAT ARE THEY**
Victoria Falls are a spectacular natural phenomenon.
**WHERE ARE THEY**
On the Zambezi River, bordering Zambia and Zimbabwe, 18 km (11 mi) south of Livingstone.
**ALSO KNOWN AS**
'Mosi-oa-Tunya' – 'the Smoke that Thunders' or 'the greatest known curtain of falling water'
**WORTH A SPLURGE**
Take a flight above these magnificent, thundering waterfalls in a biplane or helicopter, or whitewater raft them if you dare!
**WHAT ELSE IS THERE TO DO**
The 'Adventure Centre' of South Africa: various adrenaline sports are offered in the area.

Described by the Kololo tribe living in the area in the 1800s as 'Mosi-oa-Tunya' – 'the Smoke that Thunders' or 'the greatest known curtain of falling water', the vast columns of spray emanating from the majestic Victoria Falls can be seen from over 64 km (40 mi) away as they plummet over a vertical drop of 100 m (330 ft) into a deep gorge below. In the height of the rainy season, over 546 million m$^2$ (2.5 million gallons) of water explodes through the nearly two km- (1.5 mi-) wide basalt fissure every minute, transforming the Zambezi from a tranquil, placid river into a tumultuous current of roaring water.

Dr David Livingstone, the first European known to witness Victoria Falls, named this natural phenomenon in honour of his queen. Facing the falls, a twin sheer wall of basalt, about the same height, is capped by mist-soaked rainforest that has a path along its edge providing unparalleled views to the brave visitor who is not afraid to get soaked to the bone by the tremendous smoke-like cloud of spray.

Another vantage point for viewing the Eastern Cataract, Main Falls and the Boiling Pot, where the river turns and heads down the Batoka Gorge, is across the Knife-Edge Bridge. The Victoria Falls Bridge, commissioned by Cecil Rhodes in 1900, and the Lookout Tree also command panoramic views across the Main Falls and down the gorge, allowing you to get a true appreciation of the scope of the falls' thundering magnificence. The combination of the sea-green river below, the shiny black rock face and the lush emerald green foliage, make the 360-degree perspective from here truly awe-inspiring.

To appreciate fully the incredible size of the falls, and the awesome power of the water as it carves into the deep gorges for 8 km (5 mi), one must see it from the air, or if you dare, from a whitewater raft. Pilots fly along the upper Zambezi and down into the gorge – making for an exhilarating and unforgettable experience.

*Lone hiker on cliff above Victoria Falls.*

# Luangwa

The Luangwa Valley, at the western end of the Great Rift Valley opposite Lake Malawi, encompasses one of Africa's prime wildlife sanctuaries. Offering high concentrations and varieties of wildlife, the Luangwa National Park is framed by the Muchinga Mountain range where the Valley floor lies 1,000 m (3,281 ft) beneath the surrounding plateau, bisected by the Luangwa River.

*African Cape Buffalo.*

The Luangwa River is fed by sandy rivers carving through the valley floor, their outer edges eroding when flood waters rise. The resulting silt deposits eventually cause the river to change course, forming 'ox bow' lagoons, an important ecological feaure of this area of Zambia.

Flanking the river's western banks are the North and South Luangwa National Parks, separated by the 30-km (19-mi) Munyamadzi corridor. To the east, between the two main parks, is another small and as yet undeveloped park called Luambe. Farther east, on the rocky uplands beyond the flood plain, the Lukusuzi National Park is soon to be developed.

The Luangwa National Parks encompass the scenery that Africa is famous for. Their rugged beauty is made up of grass plains and woodlands dotted with thorn trees, with the the vegetation growing more densely the closer it gets to the river banks. Because of the vast number of streams and tributaries, the many-hued green forest beckons animals year round.

Game watching here is impressive with animals like the rare black rhino, buffaloes, lions, leopards, spotted hyenas, roan antelopes and hartebeest. There is also a rich variety of birds.

The area has suffered from poaching and hunting with subsequent bans and the numbers of hippos and rhinos have been difficult to maintain. Today there is a swell in the population of hippos along the Luangwa River, which is great as a tourist spectacle, but hard on the environment. Elephant populations have also seen a resurgence. Unfortunately, the rhinos have not fared so well, and today they are absent from the area despite the efforts of the privately funded 'Save the Rhino Trust'. Regardless of this calamity, the park's spectacular scenery and abundant wildlife make it a required listing for this book of 'musts'.

**WHAT IS IT**
A national park at the western end of the Great Rift Valley in Zambia.
**WHEN TO GO**
The park is open all year round, but between January and February, the Luangwa River floods and turns the area into a rich, productive, beautiful ecosystem.
**HOW TO GET HERE**
Fly into Lusaka Airport then take a flight to the Mfuwe airfield on the outskirts of the park. Only 4x4 vehicles are recommended for travelling throughout the park.
**WHAT TO KNOW**
Malaria and the tsetse fly pose hazards to visitors here.

*The ruins of Great Zimbabwe.*

# Great Zimbabwe Ruins

Portuguese traders were the first to encounter the vast stone ruins of Great Zimbabwe in the sixteenth century. Because of the scope and beauty of the ruins, they thought they had discovered the fabled capital of the Queen of Sheba. This was just the beginning of the myths, legends and folk lore to surround these massive structures, the largest in sub-Saharan Africa. Because of their sophistication, their origin was at first thought to be the work of Egyptians or Phoenicians. Eventually it was confirmed that they were created by Africans, proving that ancient African civilisations were much more advanced than previously thought by scholars.

The ruins, a UNESCO World Heritage Site, are an architectural marvel covering nearly 730 ha (1,800 acres), in an area stretching from eastern Zimbabwe into Botswana, across Mozambique and into South Africa. At its height, the capital of this wealthy Shona society was an important trading and religious centre, with upwards of 15,000 residents.

The imposing structures, built by skilled masons on an open, wooded plain surrounded by hills, are made of regular, rectangular granite stones, carefully placed on one another in intricate patterns, without the use of mortar. The complex can be divided into three distinct architectural groupings known as the Hill Complex, the Valley Complex and the Great Enclosure. The most impressive identified structure is the immense, elliptical Great Enclosure, which is thought to have been the royal compound. At nearly 100 m (330 ft) across and 255 m (840 ft) wide, it creates a vivid image of what this city may have looked like in its prime. The walls rise 11 m (36 ft) in height and are 5 m (16 ft) thick. The 10 m (33 ft) solid Conical Tower, also of note, was probably significant in religious ceremonies and may have had phallic symbolism.

**WHAT IS IT**
The largest archeological ruins in Africa south of the Great Pyramids in Egypt.
**HOW TO GET HERE**
30 km (19 mi) beyond the south-eastern town of Masvingo
**YOU SHOULD KNOW**
The ruins, although extremely impressive in their own rights, mostly consist of crumbling rock and meandering pathways.

# Matobo National Park

The Matobo Hills, in Matobo National Park, are one of the world's most mythical places, their history dating back nearly four million years to when man first walked upright. The area, once flat and covered in sand and rock, has been formed into giant granite boulders in distinct shapes over time from the wind and rain. The granite outcrops have been associated with human occupation since the middle Stone Age, providing natural shelter against the elements for the hunters and gatherers of the area.

The granite boulders are home to hidden caves, sacred sites and one of the highest concentrations of rock art in Africa. The rock art is notable not only for its diversity, but also for its animation. The drawings depict men running, playing, hunting and dancing. Mammals are shown anatomically correctly and trees, birds, insects and reptiles are also accurately rendered, allowing ancient species to be identified.

Mzilikazi, founder of the Ndebele nation, named the area 'amaTobo', or 'the bald heads' as the smooth granite boulders reminded him of a gathering of his old ancestors. Mzilikazi's remains are interred in a hillside tomb here and his belongings, sealed in a nearby cave for more than a century, can be viewed through small openings in the rocks.

Cecil Rhodes is also buried here. His remains are located in a massive, dominating granite formation called World's View. In his will, Rhodes made the Matobo National Park a gift to the people of Bulawayo and his grave has become a place of pilgrimage for thousands since his death. People come here not only to pay their respects, but also to see the spectacle of the park rangers feeding the masses of rainbow-coloured lizards that race out from under every surrounding surface to snack on proffered sadza (cooked cornmeal).

There are 39 species of snakes flourishing in the hills here, the most well-known and feared being deadly black mamba. Fortunately, the high cliffs and craggy outcrops are a favourite haunt for the world's largest concentration of black eagles and other natural snake predators including Wahlberg's eagles, tawny eagles, secretary birds, snake eagles and peregrine falcons.

The wooded valleys and grassy marshlands surrounding the hills are also home to many species of wildlife including white rhinos, rare black rhinos, antelopes, baboons, monkeys, impalas, zebras and a large population of leopards.

With its quiet, tranquil air, spiritual and anthropological history and majestic scenery and wildlife, it is difficult not to feel at peace in the Matobo Hills. That is, if you can stop thinking about those black mambas long enough to relax and enjoy it!

**WHAT IS IT**
A UNESCO World Heritage Site boasting more than 300 rock paintings, precariously balanced boulders and stunning scenery.
**WHEN TO GO**
April–August is the cool, dry season, September–early November is the hot, dry season, and the end of November-March is the rainy and humid season.
**HOW TO GET HERE**
Take the A47 south-west from Bulawayo, Zimbabwe. The hills are reached after driving about 32 km (20 mi) along a well-tarred road.
**YOU SHOULD KNOW**
Some peaks, such as Shumba, Shaba and Shumba Sham, are considered sacred and locals believe that even to point at them will bring misfortune. Also, there are 39 species of snakes here, most notably, the deadly black mamba.

*The unusual rock formation in the Matobo National Park.*

# Grand Erg Occidental Desert

**WHEN TO GO**
In the north, summers are hot and humid and winters are mild and wet. Algeria is prone to the sirocco, a hot dust and sand wind storm especially in summer.
**GEOLOGICAL SIGNIFICANCE**
The Grand Erg Occidental is the second largest erg in Algeria.
**WHAT TO SEE**
An endless sea of sand dunes.

Algeria, nestled between Morocco and Tunisia, is the second largest country in Africa. The northern portion, an area of mountains, valleys and plateaux between the Mediterranean Sea and the Sahara Desert, forms an integral part of the section of North Africa known as the Maghrib.

Contrary to popular belief, the majority of the Sahara is not soft, rolling sand dunes broken by a lush, green oasis complete with a blue lake in the centre. In reality, it's a vast expanse of rocks roughly the size of the United States. There is however, an area where the Sahara turns into an endless sea of sand dunes that you may recognise from photographs – this landscape phenomenon is known as an erg.

The Grand Erg Occidental is the second largest of the two dominating ergs of Algeria. The harsh conditions are such that no human life can be sustained here, so no villages are found within it, and no roads cross through it. The endless dunes are experienced from the outside. You do not have to travel far into the erg before you experience the feeling of solitude and inferiority in this vast and majestic space.

*Sand dunes and palm trees at Taganet in the Grand Erg.*

# El Golea

El Golea is a beautiful, lush oasis town in central Algeria and the gateway to the Sahara in the south. Situated 300 km (186 mi) south of M'zab, and 400 km (249 mi) north of In Salah, El Golea offers the best water in the country as well as a wide range of first-class agricultural products. Unlike most oases, which produce only dates, El Golea also offers plums, peaches, apricots, cherries, oranges and figs.

The city of Ghardaia was founded in the 10th century when Berber tribes settled here and well-preserved ruins of their fortifications can still be found on the hills surrounding the oasis.

A devoutly Islamic city, the women can be seen wandering through the over 200,000 date palm trees, completely covered by their robes apart from a single eye peering out through a triangular opening.

Highlights of the city include the tomb of Marabont Moulay Hass, a gentleman who made three pilgrimages to Mecca – a triple hadj. A local custom in his honour is to drive around the tomb three times. Also interesting to see is the series of rock carvings in the Atlas Saharien created more than 5,000 years ago. Images include cape buffaloes, elephants, hippos, giraffes and other animals long since extinct in northern Africa. The animals represented prove that this area was once a much wetter place.

About 2 km (1.2 mi) south from the oasis is the first Catholic church to be built in the Sahara, which was consecrated in 1938. Charles de Foucauld, a priest who wanted to bring Christianity to this part of Africa, is buried here.

**WHAT IS IT**
A lush oasis town in Central Algeria.
**WHERE IS IT**
300 km (186 mi) south of M'zab and 400 km (249 mi) north of In Salah
**ALSO KNOWN AS**
'Little Eden'
**CUTURAL ETIQUETTE**
This is a devoutly Islamic city and women should remain covered.

*The Old Fort above El Golea.*

*Cave paintings at Tassili N'Ajjer.*

# Tassili N'Ajjer

Tassili N'Ajjer, a vast mountainous plateau to the north of the Hoggar Mountains, is protected as a national park, biosphere reserve and World Heritage Site.

Much of its wild landscape is characterised by deep chasms and dramatic cliffs. Composed largely of sandstone, erosion in the area has resulted in nearly 300 natural rock arches being formed, along with many other spectacular landforms.

Because of the altitude and the water-holding properties of the sandstone, the vegetation is somewhat richer than the surrounding desert; it includes a very scattered woodland of the endangered endemic Saharan cypress and Saharan myrtle in the higher eastern half of the range.

The range is also noted for its prehistoric rock paintings and other ancient archaeological sites, dating from the last Ice Age when the local climate was much wetter, with savannah rather than desert. The rock paintings, which are up to 8,000 years old, can be found in the central area of Tassili N'Ajjer and depict a life in the region very different from today's Sahara. This area can only be entered if you have an official guide with you, or you are travelling with an accredited tour group – most of which leave from Djanet.

**WHAT IS IT**
A national park, biosphere reserve and World Heritage Site.
**WHAT IS THERE TO SEE**
Dramatic sandstone cliffs and mountains.
**WHERE IS IT**
About 1,500 km (932 mi) south of the capital, Algiers and just west of Tamanghasset.
**HOW DO I GET THERE**
Flights are available from Illizi to Algiers, Djanet and Ghardaïa.
**WHERE CAN I STAY**
Very basic accommodation can be found in In Amenas, Illizi and Djanet. A guide is required as the rugged scenery is difficult for even SUVs.

# Djemila

Djemila is the modern name of ancient Cuicul and home to some of the greatest Roman ruins in Northern Africa. Although the site itself is not one of the largest, the area is well preserved and the adjoining museum is filled with excellent mosaics.

Djemila was a military garrison founded in the first century AD to exploit and control the surrounding rich agricultural areas. The city has two forums and a theatre with a capacity of 3,000 just outside the city walls. A baptistry and a basilica were added to Cuicul in the fourth century. Cuicul was abandoned in the fifth century. Excavations began in early 1909.

The entrance to the site passes through the museum which is bursting at the seams with its treasures. Its three rooms are loaded with mosaics, marble statues, oil lamps and traditional cookware.

Europe House, named after its most famous mosaic, is the best known area of the ruins. Consisting of 18 rooms, it surrounds a courtyard dotted with decorative Ionic columns. The baptistery is ornamented by its original mosaics and the dome has been restored to its original glory. The Great Baths are in exceptionally good condition, and the pipes and double panels, where hot water once circulated, are visible in many places. Behind the Great Baths is the door leading to what was once the Christian quarter.

**WHAT IS IT**
Home to some of the greatest Roman ruins in North Africa.
**WHAT IS THERE TO SEE**
The ruins, the museum, Europe House, the bapistry and the Great Baths.
**WHERE IS IT**
50 km (31 mi) southwest of Setif and 150 km (93 mi) east of Constantine.
**HOW DO I GET THERE**
Taking a taxi is your best option as the bus service is erratic at best.

*Columns in the North Forum of Djemila.*

# Hoggar

**WHEN SHOULD I GO**
The climate is very hot in the summer and temperatures fall to below 0°C (32 °F) in the winter.

**HOW DO I GET THERE**
There is no public transport to the Hoggar region, but it is easy to rent a 4x4 and a guide.

**WHAT IS THERE TO DO**
Take the Hoggar Circuit.

**WHAT IS THERE TO SEE**
The Ahaggar Mountains consist of volcanic rocks. The climate is less extreme than most other areas of the Sahara, and the Ahaggar Mountains are a major location for biodiversity and host a variety of species.

The Ahaggar massif is the home of the Imuhagh or Kel Ahaggar, a subdivision of the Tuareg people. The Tuareg, one of the most mythical peoples of Africa, are famous for their blue garments and for having veiled men in contrast to the women, who enjoy a great deal of freedom. The Tuareg count their family by matrilinear descent. The rest of the population are mainly descendants of slaves from other parts of Africa, as well as a good number of northern Algerians.

The Hoggar Mountains, one of the true highlights of the Sahara, are too enormous and too scarcely populated for easy exploration, but it is worth the effort. If you have three days to explore the area, you can enjoy the journey known as the Hoggar Circuit.

The first village of importance you will reach, after passing the Ermitage de Père Foucauld, is Hirafok, before Tazrouk. Tahifet, beyond the pass of Azrou, is a beautiful village set by a wide oued river. At Tamekrest, there are waterfalls even more impressive than those at Cascades de Imeleoulaouene.

In the oasis of Abalassa, near the town of Tamanghasset, lies the tomb of Tin Hinan, the famous matriach believed to be the ancestor of the Tuareg of Ahaggar. According to legend, Tin Hinan originated from the Tafilalt region in the Atlas Mountains. Today, the Ahaggar region is one of the prime tourist destinations in Algeria.

*Mount Ilamen and rock formations.*

# Aswan

Aswan is the southernmost frontier town in the Egypt, considered the 'gateway to Africa'. It lies at the first of seven cataracts, or Nile rapids, created by exposed granite that made the river impassable to boats, and thus created a thriving trade centre.

The relaxed atmosphere of this riverside town made it popular as a winter resort among wealthy Europeans enticed by the setting and the rumours that the dry heat provided a cure for various ailments. Because of the influx of foreigners, a Nile-side Corniche was created, providing moorings for the many steamers.

The Aswan Corniche is the most attractive waterfront boulevard in Egypt and, with its attractive walkways and gorgeous views of palm-covered islands with a backdrop of sandy white hills, has been compared to the French Riviera. It is worth the cost of hiring a felucca and floating amidst the scenery as if in a dream.

At the southern end of the Corniche is the Old Cataract Hotel – famous as one of the locations for the film *Death on the Nile*. Built in 1899 on a rocky outcrop in the river, its grand pink exterior and Moorish dining halls are a reminder of times past. Its large terrace has been enjoyed by such luminaries as Winston Churchill, Jimmy Carter and the late Princess of Wales.

Sharia el-Souq, a short way inland, is a bustling outdoor market full of vivid colours and the aromas of exotic spices. Traditional food, Nubian jewellery and textiles (as well as the usual tourist souvenirs) should not be missed.

*The Nile and city skyline.*

**WHAT TO SEE**
Sharia el-Souq market, Nubian dancers at the Cultural Centre, the Old Cataract Hotel, the Aswan Museum and Elephantine Island.
**WHERE TO FIND IT**
129 km (80 mi) south of Luxor, 899 km (559 mi) south of Cairo.
**HISTORICAL FACT**
Aswan is the location of the only granite quarry in Egypt.
**WORTH THE EFFORT**
Travel the short distance to the High Dam and visit Abu Simbel, the famous temple of Ramses II.

*Columns associated with the Valley of the Kings.*

# The Valley of the Kings at Luxor

**WHY TO GO**
King Tut's Tomb, just one of 62 in the Valley of the Kings

**WHAT TO KNOW**
Tickets cannot be bought at the site and must be purchased at the West Bank Ticket Office – individual tickets are required for each tomb, temple or group of tombs.

**WHEN TO GO**
Visit in winter – from October to March – is recommended, the desert is hot in summer. Tombs open at 6am so go early to beat the crowds.

**HOW TO GET THERE**
Take a taxi over the bridge 6 km (4 mi) upriver from Luxor to the west bank of the Nile or cross the river by public ferry or private motorboat.

**CULTURAL ETIQUETTE**
Women should cover their knees and shoulders in public. In mosques, shoes should be removed and women should be completely covered. If you're invited to a local's home take an expensive gift since they're sure to roll out the red carpet.

The Valley of the Kings lies in an unassuming, sun-scorched desert valley surrounded by steep rocky hills on the west bank of Thebes, the political and religious capital of the New Kingdom.

The last king known to have built a tomb in the Valley was Ramesses XI, the last king of the New Kingdom, although it is doubtful that he ever used it. A total of 62 tombs has been discovered to date, although not all of them belong to pharaohs, despite the name of their location.

Accessed through a single entrance, the tombs were created to preserve the pharoah's mummies for eternity. Each of these, located deep within the ground, was designed to resemble the underworld with an descending corridor leading to an antechamber, or hall, and connected to a burial chamber.

Mesmerising floor-to-ceiling images inspired by the *Book of the Dead*, the *amduat* and the *Litany of Re*, decorate the chambers to offer a guide to the afterlife. Lavish jewels, papyrus scrolls, furniture, ritual objects, statues of various gods and effigies of the king filled the spaces as offerings to the gods.

The most famous tomb in the Valley is that of Tutankhamun, discovered nearly intact in 1922 by British archaeologist, Howard Carter. This was a particularly noteworthy discovery as almost all of the other tombs in the valley had already been looted long ago.

# The Temple of Karnak at Luxor

Karnak, or Ipet-Isut as it was known to the Ancient Egyptians, was built as the heart of Thebes, the thriving capital of Egypt, over a period of 1,500 years beginning during the Middle Kingdom (*c*.1900 BC) with the erection of the Great Temple of Amun.

Surviving as the most stunning architectural example of the day, as well as the largest temple ever built, Karnak was known as 'the Most Perfect of Places'.

Its enormous stature and ominous presence dwarfs anything else you will encounter in Egypt, and most probably the rest of the world.

The dizzying size and breadth of the legendary Great Hypostyle Hall is difficult to comprehend. It comprises 134 massive columns, measuring from 15 m (50 ft) up to an awe-inspiring 21 m (69 ft) in height. The columns are so wide, it takes six adults to reach around one, and it is estimated that at least 50 adults could comfortably stand on top of one. At one point the hall was covered, allowing minimal light among these dense columns – between each of which would have been large statues of the pharaohs – creating an incredibly imposing sight.

The main place of worship for the Theban holy trinity (Amun-Re, Mut and Khonsu), the residence of the pharoahs, the centre of administration and the cornerstone of the economy employing tens of thousands of workers, the compound of Karnak served as the hub of the area, although only priests and the royal retinue were allowed to enter its hallowed walls.

**WHAT TO SEE**
The sound and light show in the evenings is one of the best in the world.
**LOCATION**
2.4 km (1.5 mi) from downtown Luxor.
**HOW TO GET THERE**
It is walkable, but travel by taxi or caleche is recommended.
**WHAT TO KNOW**
It opens at 6am, but less crowded in the afternoon because of the heat.
**HIGHLIGHTS**
Hypostyle Hall, Colossus of Ramses II and the Great Festival Hall of Thutmose III.

*Descending the Nile by the Temple of Karnak.*

# The Pyramids of Giza and the Sphinx

**WHAT TO KNOW**
Only 300 tickets are sold a day for each of the two entrances – it is first come, first served – and only two of the three pyramids are open at a time. Go early to get in line.

**WHAT TO SEE**
The Great Pyramid, The Egyptian Museum, Ahmad Ibn Tulun Mosque and The Khan el-Khalili market.

**WHAT TO MISS**
The evening pyramid light and sound show.

**WHAT TO TRY**
Treat yourself to dinner in one of the grand hotels such as the Nubian Village in the Grand Hyatt Hotel and/or take a dinner cruise down the Nile.

**KITSCH BUT WORTH IT**
Have your photo taken on camel-back with the pyramids in the distance!

The pyramids of Giza are the world's oldest tourist attraction and remain cloaked in mystery. The only one of the Seven Ancient Wonders of the World in existence, the pyramids continue to amaze and confound archaeologists, physicists and astrologists alike.

Created within almost pinpoint accuracy, the three structures – Khufu, the oldest and largest; Khafre, which seems taller because it is built on higher ground; and Menkaura, with a base area of less than a quarter of the others – inspire questions about their greater meaning.

The sides of The Pyramid of Khufu are oriented to within three degrees of true north. The base, with each of its sides measuring 230 m (756 ft), is level to within 1 in (2.6 cm), and the difference in length between each of the four sides is a mere 2 in (5.2 cm) – a minute margin of error. Until the 19th century, the pyramids remained, after nearly 5,000 years, the tallest structure in the world.

At first sight, the pyramids, not unlike the Mona Lisa at the Louvre, can be disappointing. After so many photographs of these hulking structures surrounded by nothing but desert, it is a bit disconcerting to see suburban Cairo virtually resting against the paws of the great Sphinx.

Still, the enchanting half lion (representing royalty), half human (with a traditional headdress symbolising power) figure casts an impressive image, particularly with the shadow of the Great Pyramid of Khufu looming in the near distance. Carved from a single outcrop of bedrock, it is the earliest example of colossal Egyptian sculpture.

Stone from the monuments has been used to erect many of Cairo's oldest buildings. This destruction continued until the late 19th century when conservation efforts and a resurgence in national pride put a stop to it. Had they not been vandalised, it is believed that the pyramids would remain today much as they were when they were built. As the saying goes, 'Many fear Time, but Time fears the Pyramids'.

*The Great Sphinx and the Pyramid of Khufu.*

# Mount Sinai

Mount Sinai, considered by many to be where Moses spent 40 days and received the Ten Commandments, continues to be one of the major pilgrimage sites in the world.

Whether you believe in the mountain's history or not, at a height of 2,285 m (7,500 ft), you certainly can't deny the spectacular desert views than can be seen from its top at sunrise. Ask any of the hordes of visitors that make the trek daily!

Mount Sinai can be reached by various routes – the most direct, and challenging one is via the 3,750 Steps of Repentance, named after the penitent monk who built them. The Camel Path – named after the Bedouin who wait here with their camels in case of an opportunity to help weary travellers - is slightly easier on the knees and takes on average three hours to reach the summit. The Camel Path joins up with the last 750 Steps of Repentance at Elijah's Basin, a hollow in the mountainside marked by a 500-year-old cypress tree where God is said to have spoken to Elijah as he hid from Jezebel. This is the spot where you're asked to sleep if you decide to spend the night here.

On the actual summit is the Chapel of the Holy Trinity, a Greek Orthodox church built in 1934 on the ruins of a fourth century church. The chapel once held beautiful paintings and ornaments, but usually remains locked now because of desecration by tourists.

*Chapel of the Holy Trinity on Mount Sinai*

**HISTORICAL IMPORTANCE**
Many believe Moses received the Ten Commandments here.
**WORTH THE EFFORT**
Take the Steps of Repentance if you're up to it.
**DON'T MISS**
Spend the night on the mountain and watch the sun rise over the desert.
**HOW TO GET THERE**
Mount Sinai is about three hours from Sharm El Sheik.

*White Desert sandstone formation.*

# White Desert

The White Desert is one of the most frequently visited places in western Egypt. Its surreal rock formations, and truly white sands offer a stunningly stark contrast to the yellow desert. The rocks take on tints of blue, pink and orange as the sun sets, and at night the sands resemble snow. Apart from the heat, it could easily be mistaken for an Arctic landscape.

The formations, composed of a combination of chalk and limestone, were created by wind erosion. They consist of various organic shapes, sometimes defying the laws of nature and gravity, with enormous rocks perched precariously on particularly thin bases.

The area is referred to by Bedouin as 'Wadi Gazar', or Valley of the Carrots, after the shape of some of the pinnacles found here. It has also been said that the rocks resemble white sphinxes, stone camels or mythological birds. One thing is for certain, the rock formations offer a stunning backdrop to an otherwordly desert experience.

Also worth exploring are the springs found in the surrounding area. Unlike the rest of the desert which lies in the 120 km (75 mi) Farafra Depression, the springs are marked by hillocks created when sand attaches itself to vegetation near water. The plants continue to grow despite their struggle against being suffocated by sand and eventually form hills that are often quite dramatic.

**HOW TO GET THERE**
Trips into the desert can be arranged from either Bahariyya or Farafra – Farafra is recommended.
**WHEN TO GO**
October to March is the most popular time to visit.
**WHAT NOT TO MISS**
While you are in the area, the local springs are worth a look.

# Siwa Oasis

Siwa is the most remote of all Egypt's oasis lying some 18.3m (60ft) below sea level on an old date caravan route. It's a small life-sustaining area marooned in the middle of the Western desert, isolated from Cairo by 550km (342mi) of nothing but desert.

Famous for its oracle that was once consulted by Alexander the Great, Siwa remains largely unspoilt and has retained much of its cultural heritage, despite its new status as a major tourist destination. It continues to be a largely Berber (Zenatiya) community seemingly lost in time. Alcohol is not drunk here and women remain nearly fully covered in their traditional milayah wraps. Siwi, a Berber language, is still spoken here rather than Arabic – a testament to the town's inaccessibility as well as historic roots as wandering Bedouin. Siwans have also retained their traditional tribal governing body consisting of 11 chiefs, the sheikhs, who act as local council. Until as recently as the 1980s there were no televisions and transport was by donkey cart.

A newly paved asphalt road leading to Marsa Matruh, however continues to bring changes including a spate of new restaurants, hotels, an internet café and a planned airport. However, visitors can still enjoy the dreamlike setting of dense green date palms, an abundance of olive trees, and more than 300 freshwater springs and streams.

The town of Siwa is built around Shali, the thirteenth-century mud-brick settlement, surrounded by high walls created to protect against attack. As Siwan society flourished, rather than building outside the wall, they decided to build upwards within it – their structures sometimes reaching five storeys. In 1926, a series of violent rain storms caused the buildings to disintegrate, creating a Dali-esque appearance. These surreal buildings are fun to explore and afford an excellent view of the oasis and distant desert bluffs.

Also within the oasis is a small market offering the highly valued and rare embroidered clothing and heavy silver jewellery local to the area. Siwa is also known for its basketware woven from date palm fronds, as well as its highly coveted pottery.

The Siwan House Museum, created by a former Canadian ambassador concerned that the traditional Siwan lifestyle and crafts would be lost to tourism, is worth a stop.

**NEED TO KNOW**
The museum is located in the town centre.
**HOW TO GET THERE**
Overland from Cairo on a tour through a travel agent or by rental car – check for special driving requirements. Busses and taxis are also available.
**WHAT TO BRING**
Your appetite for dates and something to wrap up in – women remain nearly fully covered here.
**WHAT NOT TO BRING**
Alcohol – this is a largely Berber community and they do not tolerate it.

*A donkey-drawn cart makes its way through palm groves of Siwa Oasis.*

# Temple of Edfu

The Temple of Edfu remains the best preserved ancient temple in Egypt, as well as the second largest temple after Karnak. It was built during the reigns of six Ptolemies in dedication to Horus, the falcon-headed god, with construction beginning in 237 BC and ending in 57 BC.

The temple was believed to be built on the historic site of the great battle between Horus and Seth, so the current temple is only the last of many erected in this location. Legend has it that the original structure, home to a statue of Horus, was a prehistoric grass hut. The current ruins are built of sandstone, on top of a smaller New Kingdom temple Pylon.

This masterpiece was found completely submerged underneath the desert sands, except the top of the entrance pylon. A small amount of stone had been removed from the exposed part, but upon excavation it was found to be in otherwise perfect condition.

On the undersurface of the main archway into the temple are six sets of winged images, each varying slightly from one another. Farther inside the entrance to the inner temple stands a 3-m (10-ft) magnificent black marble statue of the god Horus.

The main building, including the great Hypostyle Hall, is impressive for both its size and its condition. Nearly every surface is covered by carvings, hieroglyphs and numerous reliefs, including a depiction of the Feast of the Beautiful Meeting, the annual reunion between Horus and his wife Hathor. The reliefs are found largely inside the first pylon, spiritually connecting Horus' temple with that of Hathor at the Dendera complex.

Every summer, the priests at the Dendera complex would sail the statue of Hathor on her barque, or ceremonial barge, to the Edfu Temple, where it was believed that Horus and Hathor shared a conjugal visit. Each night, the god and goddess would retire to the mamissi, or birthing house. An entrance colonnade to this mamissi still exists, and reliefs portraying the birth ritual of Harsomtus, the son of Horus and Hathor, remain just outside the main temple.

Beyond the Hypostyle Hall is a second, smaller hall leading to a well called the Chamber of the Nile, where the priests obtained pure holy water. In a similar arrangement to Dendera, there are doors on the west side leading to a small laboratory with recipes for ointments and perfumes used to anoint the statue of Horus engraved into the walls, and then leading to a treasure room where offerings were stored.

Beyond the second, smaller Hypostyle Hall lies the offering hall, followed by the vestibule and finally the sanctuary. The granite naos is the oldest relic in the temple. Historians and archeologists surmise that a golden gilded wooden statue of Horus about 60 cm (23.6 in) in height would have rested on the naos. This statue would have been washed, dressed, anointed, fed and entertained by the priests.

The sanctuary is surrounded by chapels, chambers, tombs and rooms, some of which were dedicated to the god Osiris, or Mehit, the lioness who guards the soul's path on its journey towards eternal life.

*RIGHT: The Temple of Horus.*

*Temple of Zeus*

# Cyrene

Cyrene, an ancient Greek city, the oldest and most important of the five in the region, lying in the scenic lush valley of Libya's Jebel Akhdar uplands with unobscured views to the Mediterranean Sea, was once an important site for trade.

A thriving community from its very beginning, because of the fertility of the region, its flocks, herds and especially its horses were famous. It had an abundance of precious metals, from which it produced its coinage, featuring the medicinal herb for which it was known, *silphium*. The port of Apollonia, 16 km (10 mi) from Cyrene, was on an important trading route.

It is now an important archeological site near the village of Shahat. More than 76 Roman statues dating back to the 2nd century AD were found here in 2005. According to architects, so many of the statues remained undiscovered for such a long period because a supporting wall of the temple fell on its side during an earthquake in 365, burying them. The statues remained hidden under stone, rubble and earth for 1,600 years, protected from the elements.

One of Cyrene's more significant features is the Temple of Apollo, originally constructed in the seventh century BC, and rebuilt three centuries later. The Great Baths of the Temple of Apollo are in exceptional condition, with their pipes still visible. About 50 m (165 ft) from the temple, lies the Fountain of Apollo, whose waters were once considered to be curing. Inside, one can still see the seats of the treatment rooms.

At the extreme north-west is the Roman theatre, which stands on Greek foundations and is partly Greek in style. The theatre's setting is stunning, with hills behind the stage falling down to the landscape stretching out to the sea.

Other ancient ruins include a Temple of Demeter and a partially unexcavated Temple of Zeus. There is a large necropolis part-way from Cyrene on the road to Apollonia. There are still hundreds of tombs cut into the hills here, many in the shape of mausoleums or temples.

In the centre of Cyrene, in the Agora, or town square, is the Tomb of Battus, as well as the Forum of Proculus, which remains in relatively good condition.

Cyrene was originally a colony of the Greek people of Thera, modern-day Santorini, established in 630 BC by Aristotle (later called Battus). In a strategic location between Egypt and Carthage, the city promptly became the chief town of the Libyan region until its demise following the death of Alexander the Great in 323 BC.

The ruins, which are only partly excavated, are in incredible condition, the floor mosaics still clearly visible and the foundation structures largely intact. The earthquake of 365 destroyed the majority of the city, and its ruins were left to decay. If you're lucky you may be able to find your own undiscovered treasure!

# Leptis Magna

Leptis Magna is a UNESCO World Heritage site on the Mediterranean coast of North Africa, in the Tripolitania region of Libya. Originally founded by the Phoenicians in the tenth century BC as a trading port, it survived colonisation by Spartans, became a Punic city, and was eventually established as part of the new Roman province of Africa around 23 BC.

The spectacular city of Leptis Magna was built in traditional Roman architectural styles and was a hub for trade, culture and the arts.

Serving as the Mediterranean outlet of a trade route through the Sahara into the interior of Africa, its economy was based on agriculture, and some of its products, particularly olives, became profitable trade items. Olive cultivation added so much to the town's prosperity, in fact, that Julius Caesar imposed an annual tax of three million pounds of oil on the city in 46 BC!

The prosperous Roman city was sacked by Berbers in 523 AD and subsequently abandoned. Various materials from the site have been recycled by pillagers throughout history, but during a series of excavations in the 1920s, the magnificent ruins, one of the best preserved Roman cities in the world, were uncovered.

Archeologists have unearthed several layers of ruins including the remains of a large theatre built in the first century AD, beneath which is a cemetery probably dating from the fourth or third century BC. Particularly well-preserved are second- and early third-century Roman buildings, which include the elaborate Hadrianic Baths, the forum and the basilica, all of which were erected during the era of Emperor Septimius Severus (193–211 AD).

Despite the condition and range of the incredibly well-preserved ruins and its status as a World Heritage Site, Leptis Magna remains largely ignored, apart from some recent interest from a team of British archaeologists.

Thankfully, the arid desert climate has preserved the ruins of Leptis Magna, which were covered in sand for at least half a century. These amazing structures provide an incredible insight into the life and times of the early Romans in Africa and are well worth a visit of at least a few days.

*Roman amphitheatre at Leptis Magna.*

**WHAT IS IT**
The home to Hadrian's baths and other significant ancient ruins.
**WHERE IS IT**
On the Mediterranean coast of North Africa in the Tripolitana region of Libya.
**HISTORICAL SIGNIFICANCE**
Founded by the Phonecians in the tenth century BC, the tremendous ruins are in excellent shape.
**ALSO KNOWN AS**
Lepcis Magna
**WHEN TO VISIT**
Summers are oppressively hot here – visit in spring or autumn.

*Doors of the Royal Palace.*

# Fès – Fez el Bali

Fès is the 'symbolic heart' of Morocco – its intellectual, historical and spiritual capital. As you wander through its labyrinthine shady streets, exotic smells of mint and spices waft through the air, dappled light falls on the whitewashed, crumbling grandeur of the old city and you can feel the tangible mystery and intrigue of this, the oldest of the four imperial cities.

Unlike many walled cities, Old Fès hasn't burst its banks, and its gates and walls remain intact. The population has expanded out of the city, flowing towards the south-west and arching towards the hillsides that stretch north and south of the new city. The towering Medersa Bou Inania, a theological college built in 1350, dominates the old city in the Fez River's fertile basin.

The medina of Fès el-Bali (Old Fès) is one of the largest living and working medieval cities in the world. Consisting of the 'traditional seven elements', mosques, medersas (Koranic schools), souks (markets), fondouks (lodging and trading houses), fountains, a hammam (steam bath) and a bakery, it is a bustling combination of city, museum and workshop that has changed very little with the passing of time.

The streets are filled with artisans creating and selling their wares using traditional techniques. You can see baby-soft leathers being tanned, the sun glinting off copper pots as they are being soldered, brass plates being engraved, colourful ceramics and embroidery, cedar, woodwork and carpets being hawked in hoarse voices that echo in the many courtyards. One of the experiences that cannot be missed is a stop into a Morrocan carpet shop. There you will be plied with mint tea and shown hundreds of stunning, intricately woven rugs selling for a fraction of the price that you would pay in a department store for one of inferior quality. Some visitors may feel intimidated, but if you are looking for a quality carpet, and you enjoy bartering – this will be an unforgettable treat!

**WHAT TO TASTE**
Harira, a hearty bean-based soup with vegetables and meat as well as Tagines, stewed vegetables, meat or fish cooked in earthernware cones, and cous cous. For the adventurous Pastilla de pigeon – pigeon meat, topped with scrambled eggs, then filo pastry, sugar and cinnamon.

**WORTH A VISIT**
Meknes, the Moroccan Versailles, surrounded by 40 km (25 mi) lime and earth walls.

**WHAT TO BUY**
Leather goods, ceramics, spices and carpets.

**WHEN TO GO**
June to September on the Atlantic-Mediterranean coastline. March to June and September to December for the central plateau.

# Tangier

As you arrive in Tangier, sailing on the turquoise Mediterranean, you will see a vast, rustic yet developed coastline outlined by the Rif Mountains. As you disembark, you may be surrounded by swarms of touts trying to get you to stay at one resort or another. This can be disarming, as sometimes they are pushy, but they are harmless so just tell them no thank you and take it all in – it is all part of the charm of this traditional, international, diverse, colourful land.

Many visitors come to Tangier because of its easily accessible location – from Spanish day-trippers to those seeking sunshine on lovely beaches in modern resorts and those wanting to experience a piece of history. Tangier is a melting pot with something for everyone. It has led a varied cultural existence through the years and the city bears witness to Phonecian, Roman, Portugese, British and French influences.

As you wander through the busy streets you are likely to rub shoulders with rural Rifi Berbers in their traditional striped mehndis (bright woven blankets) expats, tourists, diplomats, princes, poets and artists. Morocco has always been a land of free spirits and Tangier is no exception.

Wander through the crumbling walls of the Kasbah, getting lost in the myriad streets of the medina, while taking in the exotic scents of cinnamon and tobacco floating on the coastal breeze. Stop in a local coffee shop and enjoy a cup of the traditional mint tea.

When you want a break from the crowds, head 4.8 km (3 mi) north-west to the rocky coast where the Mediterranean meets the Atlantic. Visit the Caves of Hercules, known for their window-like opening in the shape of Africa where surf crashes through the hole into the lagoon and caves. There is a small café where you can enjoy the views and eat a traditional tagine, watching the local fishermen haul in their nets after a rough day at sea. With the smell of salt in your nostrils, the sound of the crashing surf in your ears and the sun on your face, you are nearly guaranteed a feeling of peace in your soul.

**HOW TO GET THERE**
Accessible by ferry across the Straits of Gibraltar from Algeciras in Spain – 15 km (9 mi), or just under 2 hours.
**WHERE TO GO**
Quemado beach around Al Hoceima, a cove nestled between hills with fine sand and clear water perfect for snorkelling to see fish and coral.
**WORTH A VISIT**
Caves of Hercules.

*Tangier Harbour and city.*

# Marrakesh

**ALSO KNOWN AS**
'Assembly of the Dead' or 'meeting place at end of the world', which is believed to refer to the practice of executing criminals here.
**WHAT TO SEE**
Djemaa el-Fna will satisfy your appetite for the traditional and the strange – it is an assault on the senses.
**WORTH A SPLURGE**
Take a ride on a caleche – a green canopied horse-drawn carriage – to tour the city including the Menara and Agdal Gardens.
**WHAT YOU SHOULD KNOW**
The market is a thieve's dream so watch your bag or wallet.

Marrakesh is the lively former capital of Morocco, famed for its markets and festivals, hippies and criminals, devout and destitute, debauched and intellectual – it is a study in dichotomies.

Surrounded by 9.7 km (6 mi) of unbroken walls, Marrakesh is punctuated by towers and battlements, which cast shadows across the rich, red soil that reflects a peachy red in the sunlight, deepening to crimson as the day passes. As you wander down the crowded, maze-like, colourful broad avenues you will pass crumbling architectural treasures, donkeys and mules carrying produce, wood and weaving workshops, steam-billowing hammams, ancient mosques and shiny modern hotels.

The pulsating energy centre of Marrakesh is the Djemaa el-Fna. Follow the enticing aromas and deafening noise into the calamitous atmosphere of this enormous market in the midst of the medina. Part mystic zoo, part animalistic carnival, part Olympic village – this market has to be seen to be believed.

Housed in an enormous rectangular space, snake charmers, acrobats, monkey tamers, henna artists and veiled ladies selling bracelets or begging for money with outstretched hands, everyone vies for your attention.

Jugglers and storytellers jostle for position with magicians, dancing transvestites playing cymbals, fire-eaters and fortune tellers. Boxers, astrologers and men with scorpions crawling on their faces all contribute to the melée.

At one end of the market, where the gates lead into the souk, you can sit on a balcony or roof terrace to watch the madness unfold beneath you as you sip on a cup of tea and munch tagine. The tourists generally take advantage of this respite, while the locals prefer to sup at the food stalls, joining in a circle in the centre of the Djemma, with the majestic 70-m (230-ft) Koutoubia mosque holding court above it.

Stay for sunset when the surrounding buildings turn orange, blue and pink, after which the hundred of gas lamps are lit, creating haunting shadows. The carnival-like atmosphere continues and grows in ferocity through the wee hours and begins again at dawn.

*Dusk falls over Marrakesh.*

# Tafraoute

Tafraoute is a conglomeration of ochre-covered buildings set amid green trees, offering a spectacular contrast of colours against the surrounding pink rocks of the Anti-Atlas Mountains.

*Tafraoute, in the Anti-Atlas Mountains.*

The area is known for its dramatic geography, with its expanses of red desert, and is also the official almond capital of Morocco. If you are fortunate enough to be here in early spring, you may catch the annual Almond Blossom Festival. The delicate blooms offer another dimension to this already spectacular landscape, with their stark contrast to the rugged soil and dark, rich sand. During the festival, the otherwise sleepy town of Tafraoute is transformed by a carnival-like atmosphere when the souk (market), complete with dancers and musicians, springs up. This event is ideal if you want to escape the popular modern beach holiday area for something a little different.

While visiting Tafraoute, there are three attractions that should be on any traveller's list – the Les Pierres Bleues – Jean Veran's famous Blue Rock, the palm groves south-east of Tafraoute and the gazelle rock carving.

Over a period of three months in 1984, the Belgian artist and a team of Morroccan firemen collaborated in the creation of one of the most unusual art installation pieces on earth. They covered the small hills and granite boulders of the Anti-Atlas Mountains with 18 tonnes of blue, red, violet and white paint. Although now somewhat faded, the fusion of art and nature is still mesmerising and the contrast of bright blue against the brilliant reds of the desert is unforgettable.

Also worth a full day's trip are the palm groves. Past 'Napoleon's Cap' with its massive boulders on your right, there is a winding paved trail that leads you through the Anti-Atlas mountains where you can enjoy scenic views of the Ammeln Valley from Ait Mansour, to Afellan-Ighir and back to Tafraoute.

Just 2 km (1.2 mi), south of town is the prehistoric gazelle rock carving. The sparse etching has recently been retouched but offers an insight into the long history of inhabitation of the area.

**WHERE IS IT**
City is 152 km (94 mi) south-east of Agadir, 92 km (57 mi) south-east of Ait Baha

**WHAT TO SEE**
Trafraoute is known for its prehistoric rock carvings and the painted blue rocks of Belgian artist Jean Veran as well as its stunning palm groves.

**OTHER REASONS TO VISIT**
A heaven for rock climbers – stacks of massive boulders and dizzying mountains surround the city. The palm Groves south-east of the city take at least a full day to see properly.

**WHEN TO GO**
Winter, spring or autumn – summer is unbearably hot.

# Sidi Ifni

**WHAT IS IT**
A sleepy coastal town.
**HISTORICAL SIGNIFICANCE**
The last Spanish colonial outpost in Morocco.
**WHERE IS IT**
150 km (93 mi) south of Agadir.
**WHEN TO GO**
February–November.
**WHAT TO SEE**
Art Deco architecture surrounding Place Hassan II.

The charming, sleepy coastal town of Sidi Ifni, the last Spanish colonial outpost in Morocco, offers impressive Art Deco architecture and a hospitable Spanish atmosphere to its guests. Its cliff-top location with Andalusian-style gardens and tiled fountains are a testament to its Spanish roots – they left only in 1969. The buildings are painted in whimsical Easter-egg pastels – in contrast to the surrounding French-influenced towns with their rich palette of dark hues – which lend a peaceful and relaxed air.

In the main square, Place Hassan II, you can wander among some modest private homes, the now defunct Spanish Consulate, the law courts which were once a church, the town hall, the royal palace and the Hotel Bellevue which overlooks the beach and the port.

There is a Sunday souk, held at an abandoned airstrip near town, filled with storytellers and musicians. The beaches are pleasant, with camels wandering through the misty sea air, and quieter than the more established, but sometimes overrun areas around Agadir.

*Sidi Ifni.*

# Chefchaouen

A short drive from Tangier nestled in the Rif mountain region, the picturesque medieval town of Chefchaouen was settled at the end of the fifteenth century as a mountain retreat for the Moors and Jews who had been expelled from Spain by the Catholic Monarchs. Its striking medina is one of the most charming in Morocco, with signature blue-washed gabled houses and artisans on narrow streets selling traditional wares, including caftans and embroidered jellabahs, carpets, leather goods, pottery and copper.

The Plaza Uta El Hammam is dominated by a seventeenth-century mosque with a delicate six-sided brick and plaster minaret and is punctuated by mulberry trees shading welcoming cafés where you can sit and enjoy a refreshing mint tea. There is also a cluster of elegant buildings including the medersa (Koranic school) and the old castle with its palm and cypress-filled garden. It is said that until 1920 only three Christians had ever found their way into the town, and that slaves were openly traded in its market until 1937.

The surrounding area is particularly scenic with abundant natural springs, low-lying clouds and wildflower-strewn meadows dense with sheep.

Chefchaouen is also one of the main producers of cannabis, or kif, in Morocco. The growth of and trade in marijuana has become such an intrinsic part of the town – it is sold in the open markets alongside the traditional vegetables, herbs and spices – that after a while you do not even notice the oddity.

Unlike any other city in Morocco, Chefchaoen consistently ranks as a favourite among travellers from across the globe.

*The Old Medina at Chefchaouen.*

**WHAT YOU SHOULD DO**
Wander through the Plaza Uta El Hammam and stop to enjoy a mint tea.
**WHAT YOU SHOULDN'T DO**
Chefchaouen is one of the largest producers of marijuana in Morocco.
**WHAT TO SPLURGE ON**
A meal at the famous 350-year old family-run Hotel-Restaurant Tissemlal (Casa Hassan) where you can take in the views of the surrounding Rif mountains on their rooftop terrace.
**WHAT TO BUY**
Wool items and quality traditional crafts such as hand-made bronze bowls, trays and plates.
**ALSO KNOWN AS**
'The Blue City'.

# Taroudant

An ideal base for the exploration of the Souss Valley and western High Atlas, Taroudant is known for its bustling market and fresh produce. A mixture of Arabic and Tashelhit Berber languages can be heard as you stroll through the town's recently restored salmon-coloured walls.

As you head towards the market you'll weave through crowds of men on bicycles with fresh bundles of coriander in their baskets, fish mongers, men tanning leather, shining brass pans or carving wood. The enticing smells of lavender, thyme, saffron and mint waft through the hazy sunshine, as you stop to admire the Grand Mosque with its yellow minaret and teal-green houndstooth tiling.

On a clear day, the snowy peaks of the Djebel Toubkal can be seen hovering in the distance past the gates of the Kasbah. The native women, the Roudani, can be seen in the early evenings chatting in lines around the ramparts in their colourful clothes. They look, and often sound, like an exotic species of bird as they wander around gossiping and laughing.

Stop at one of the many reasonably priced cafés and enjoy a snack as you watch daily life unfold, take a calèche, (a horse-drawn carriage), around the city and watch the fading light of sunset highlight the olive trees surrounding the town.

*ABOVE: Spice stalls in the souk.*

*BELOW: The old town walls.*

# Ait-Ben-Haddou

Ait-Ben-Haddou, a UNESCO World Heritage site at the crossroads of the southern oasis routes, is a striking example of the architecture of southern Morocco with its earthen buildings surrounded by high walls on a hillside. The red pise (straw and mud) towers in this village fortress are said to resemble a melting sand castle. The surrounding almond trees lend a sumptuous air to the village, which has beautiful views over the river valley.

Among the dramatic terrain of the snowy Atlas mountains reaching to the Sahara desert, is a varied landscape encompassing large canyons, gorges and lunar steppes, making the province of Ouarzazate a preferred choice for filmmakers, and the Hollywood of Morocco. Films such as *Soddom and Gomorrah*, *Lawrence of Arabia*, *The Last Temptation of Christ* and *Gladiator* were all made here.

Ait-Ben-Haddou is notable for its kasbah, the Kasbah Taourirt, which is said to be the best preserved in the country. As you wander along the dusty streets, crowded with small cafés and tourist shops, the friendly vendors, who are much less aggressive than at other tourist spots, will come outside to greet you and engage you in conversation. The village is known for its fine crafts including its traditional carpets and ceramics.

**WALK OF FAME**
This is Morocco's version of Hollywood – many famous films have been shot here.
**KNOWN FOR**
Great 4x4 driving through stunning scenery.
**COMPARED TO**
Its towers are said to resemble a melting sand castle.
**HOW TO GET THERE**
Roughly 70 km (42 mi) north of Ouarzazate in the High Atlas.
**WORTH A SPLURGE**
Have dinner at Chez Dimitri, one of the best traditional restaurants in town.
**WORTH A TRY**
Mechoui – shoulder of lamb with fennel and peas.

*Mud brick homes of Ait-Ben-Haddou.*

*A Roman mosaic at Lixus.*

# Lixus

Perched on a hilltop overlooking the sea, surrounded by hills and forests, with views of the serpentine waters of the Wadi Loukkos River and down to the ocean, Lixus is a wonderfully scenic site with some impressive ruins of a Roman imperial outpost.

Settled by the Phoenicians in the seventh century BC and later an important Carthaginian site, Lixus remains a most impressive ruin, for its relics as well as its stunning location.

Largely unexplored and unexcavated, Lixus has the ruins of an ampitheatre dating back to the first century AD, which would have held a few hundred people. Behind it are the baths, with spectacular mosaics that remain largely intact, except for some damage caused by local children playing in the unguarded area. Unfortunately, one of the victims was the face of the sea god, Neptune, in the centre of one of the largest and most impressive mosaic panels.

Also here is the Christian basilica, located right in the centre of Lixus. Although not as architecturally striking as some of the other buildings, it is still in good condition considering age and is worth a look, particularly from its unadorned roof, offering sweeping views of the valleys below.

If you can imagine back 2,000 years, it would be easy to realise that Lixus could quite easily have been one of the most beautiful Roman cities in existence.

**WHAT IS IT**
A spectacularly gorgeous location on the Locus River, home to the site of the ancient city of Lixus.
**WHY IS IT IMPORTANT**
Largely unexcavated ruins of a former imperial Roman outpost.
**WHAT IS THERE TO SEE**
Remains of ancient baths, temples and other historical remnants.
**WHERE IS IT**
North of the modern seaport of Larache, Morocco, on the right bank of the wadi Loukkos, or Locus River.

# Volubilis

The Roman ruins of Volubilis, stretching out across 40 ha (100 acres), are the most well preserved ruins in Morocco and well worth a visit. Located between Rabat and Fez near the Moroccan town of Meknes, Volubilis served as a central Roman administrative city in the third century BC.

Built on top of a Carthaginian city, Volubilis, unlike most Roman outposts, was not abandoned after the Romans lost North Africa to the Arabs. The city remained inhabited until the eighteenth century when it was largely demolished to provide building materials for the palaces of Moulay Ismail in nearby Meknes. Although much of the Roman architecture, largely dating back to 217 AD, was lost, there are still some well-preserved columns, a basilica, a triumphal arch and *c*.30 high-quality mosaics.

The Victory Arch, built in honour of the emperor Caracalla, formerly had a bronze chariot on top of its ancient stones. Facing proudly outwards towards the main entry route to the city, it was restored in 1962.

The Capitol, located on a headland towering over the arid plain, faces the basilica. Nearby is also the house of Ephebe, providing shelter for one of the remarkable mosaics, this one in particular depicting Bacchus on his chariot. Also to be enjoyed is the mosaic showing the myth of Orpheus and Amphitrite's Chariot located in the home of a rich merchant.

It is truly a pleasure to witness such beautifully well preserved artwork, whether or not you're an art history buff.

*Ruins of the Roman forum.*

**KNOWN FOR**
The best-preserved Roman ruins in Morocco, especially the mosaics.
**BEST TIME TO VISIT**
Sunset, when the shadows on the monuments grow longer and you will have the place to yourself.
**WHERE IS IT**
Near Meknes, between Rabat and Fez.
**WHAT TO SEE**
Over 30 nearly perfect mosaics.

# The Sudd

Sudan is the largest country in the African continent occupying an impressive 2,505,813 sq km (1,557,040 sq mi). Covering much of central and north-east Africa, it consists of an enormous plain running from the northern Sudan to the Ugandan frontier and from the Central African Republic all the way to the Ethiopian highlands.

The White Nile bisects the plain, providing large areas of water including Lake Fajarial, Lake No and Lake Shambe. The Sudd, the world's largest swamp, provides an expanse of lakes, lagoons and aquatic plants, and its flood waters cover an area roughly as large as Belgium.

More than half of the water flowing down the White Nile, or the Bahr al Jabal as the river is referred to in this region for its sluggish rate, is held in The Sudd, creating a massive floodplain called the toic. The Sudd is roughly 320 km (200 mi) long and 240 km (150 mi) wide. The dense aquatic vegetation making up The Sudd disperses the river into various channels.

The Sudd has created such an obstacle that passage was not managed until Egyptians completed the first navigation in 1840. The first effort to create a channel took over four years and constant maintenance is required to keep the channel clear.

**WHAT IS IT**
The world's largest swamp: a region of thick aquatic vegetation in the Nile.
**HISTORICAL SIGNIFICANCE**
The Sudd has long hindered navigation of the Nile.
**HOW LARGE IS IT**
The Sudd is 320 x 240km (199 x 150 mi) wide, the plain itself is roughly half the size of Belgium.
**WHERE IS IT**
Southern Sudan.

*The White Nile meanders through the marshes near Bor.*

# Tunis

The old Arab town of the medina, the unofficial centre of Tunis, is easy to navigate and there is a lot to see – a perfect starting point for your journey through Tunisia. Built in the seventh century AD, the medina lost its status as the heart of Tunis when the French built the new town around the turn of the twentieth century. Recognized by UNESCO as a World Heritage Site in 1979, the medina remains the central artery to this diverse port city at the end of the Gulf of Tunis.

The lively, oval, walled city of the medina is made up of covered alleyways, hidden passages and tunnelled bazaars, all of which are active with traders and artisans hawking their wares and creating an enticing energy filled with exotic scents and vivid colours. There are 700 historical monuments to see including palaces, mosques, mausoleums, madrasas and fountains dating back to the Almohad and Hafsid periods. Particularly worth a visit are the Great Mosque, the Dar-al-Bey (Bey's Palace), the Ziadib-Allah II al Aghlab Palace, the Bardo Museum (the original Hasfid Palace) with the most impressive collection of Roman antiquities and mosaics from Ancient Greece and the nearby ruins of ancient Carthage. Be sure to stop into one of the many relaxed cafés where you'll have to navigate through the chicha pipe smoke to order yourself a refreshing mint tea or coffee.

The medina is characterised by its quirkiness, with various architectural and decorative styles including 400 Art Deco buildings. The picturesque Villa Boublil near Belvedere Park is a highlight with its intricate lines and metalwork. Even its semi-neglected state somehow seems to add to its charm.

The ruins of Carthage, on the northern gulf shore lie in the suburb by the same name. The original city, home to Hannibal and his elephants, was razed to the ground in 146 BC. About a century later Julius Caesar rebuilt it as a symbol of the resurrection of Africa and it became the second city of the Empire after Rome. Following a period of decadence and prosperity, Arab invaders levelled the city once again in the late fifteenth and early sixteenth centuries. Not much is known about the original appearance of Carthage, and excavations have proved difficult because of the utter demolition of the site and subsequent pillaging, but a UNESCO-inspired international dig has managed to uncover a smattering of ancient sites amid the beautiful countryside by the sea.

*Great mosque of Medina, Tunis.*

**WHEN TO GO**
Tunisia has a typical Mediterranean climate, with hot, dry summers and mild, wet winters. Spring and autumn are considered the best times to visit.
**HOW TO GET THERE**
Tunis-Carthage International Airport is located close to the city, 8 km (5 mi) from the lake shore.
**HISTORICAL IMPORTANCE**
In 1979 the medina was made a UNESCO World Heritage Site because of its 700 monuments.
**WHAT TO SEE**
The medina, the Great Mosque, Bey's Palace, Bardo Museum and the nearby ruins of Carthage.
**WORTH A DIVERSION**
The pretty cliff-top resort town of Sidi Bou Said with its whitewashed buildings and bright blue shutters.

# El Djem

El Djem was once a thriving agricultural region known for its production of olive oil and wheat, as well as its grand coliseum, second only in size to the one in Rome, and the most impressive remaining Roman monument in Africa. The sight of this monument rising in the distance surrounded by modest houses on the flat Sahel plain as you enter this small town is both wonderful and slightly incongruous, its present surroundings lending no hint of its former glory.

Built around 200 AD, it was the scene for often cruel and bloody gladiator circus 'games' modelled on those of ancient Rome. Today, the echoing cries of martyrs and large beasts have been replaced by classical Arabian music and haunting European concertos as the coliseum is now home to performances by the world-famous orchestras who come to play at its annual summer International Festival of Symphonic Music.

The craft of mosaic making has been rediscovered and El Djem has been reborn as a centre for the art. Examples of a spectacular selection of original mosaics can be seen at the impressive archeological museum, which, in conjunction with the looming structure of the coliseum, makes this site worth a visit.

*The magnificent Roman amphitheatre at El Djem.*

# Dougga

*Ruins of the Roman theatre.*

Dougga is an imposing site – some say the most dramatic in Tunisia. Once the seat of power for the Numidian King, Massinissa, it was a large and prosperous town and now stands as the best preserved Roman monument in Northern Africa.

A welcome addition to the UNESCO World Heritage Site roster since 1997, Dougga is scenically positioned high on the side of a valley overlooking wheat fields.

At one time more than 25,000 people lived here and the intact remains to be explored include 12 Roman temples (three of which were transformed into churches in the fourth century), three baths, numerous cisterns and fountains, two heavily restored theatres, a nymphaeum, an aqueduct, a market, a circus, several necropolises and a handful of mausoleums.

The site is so well preserved that even the scars of chariot wheels on cobbled streets continue to bear witness to its history. The sheer number of buildings in such remarkable condition allow one to imagine the thriving metropolis's grand infrastructure.

Numidian rulers lived here in the second century BC before the Romans invaded. Some of the highlights of this vast site that should not be missed include the remains of the Libyco (Carthaginian) tower dating back to the second century BC. This structure looms above the southern edge of the town at an impressive 21 m (69 ft) high. The mausoleum has three tiers; the top tier is marked by a pyramid-shaped roof which was formerly flanked by four harpies; the second tier is decorated with horsemen and the third tier with a bas-relief of quadrigas. Each tier is separated by steps and decorative Ionic columns. The tower was once also ornamented by a stele bearing the names of its builders.

The Capitol, with its impressive peristyle, or column-enclosed court, is also not to be missed. Built in 166–167 AD, the Capitol consists of a 13 x 14-m (43 x 46-ft) cella, or inner sanctuary, which housed an impressive 6-m (19.5-ft) marble statue of Jupiter as well as more modest statues of Juno and Minerva. The cella was approached via a monumental flight of steps with a right-angle turn and a four-bay Corinthian portico. In front of the Capitol lies an esplanade linking the 'Compass of the Winds' square to the forum.

The ruins of Dougga are a fantastic representation of a large Roman site, offering an interesting historical flashback for both the novice and the scholar.

**HOW TO GET THERE**
Access is easy from Nouvelle Dougga, and it is a day trip from Tunis or Le Kef.
**WHAT TO SEE**
UNESCO-recognized Roman ruins.
**WHERE IS IT**
110 km (68 mi) south-west of Tunis, 72km (45 mi) east of Kef and 8 km (5 mi) from Teboursouk.

*Fortress on Jerba Island.*

# Jerba Island

**WHERE IS IT**
A Tunisian resort island 120 km (75 mi) from the Libyan border.

**HISTORICAL SIGNIFICANCE**
Rumoured to be the fabled Land of the Lotus Eaters in Homer's *Odyssey*.

**HOW DO I GET THERE**
Mellita International Airport has daily services from Tunis and western Europe. It can also be reached by bus or taxi.

**WHAT TO DRINK**
Boukha, the noxious local brew said to mimic the fabled response to imbibing lotus juice.

**WHAT NOT TO DRINK**
The slightly saline tap water.

The island of Jerba, 120 km (75 mi) from the Libyan border, claims to be the Land of the Lotus Eaters, celebrated in Homer's *Odyssey* as the perfect respite for relaxation and surrender. In the legendary tale, Odysseus and his crew stayed here enjoying the soothingly narcotic fruits of the lotus as they recovered from battle. Today there is a modern example of this fabled elixir, the locally brewed boukha, a fermented beverage made from dates or figs.

This small, semi-arid, palm-fringed island of myth has pretty, but touristy, beaches on its shores and unique homes and mosques inland. The quaint interior of the island is divided into farms by date and olive groves. The whitewashed, fortified mosques, an anomaly in Tunisia, glow in the bright sunshine. A bicycle ride around the island is an excellent way to experience its charms.

Fishing is a large industry in Jerba, and is still done with traditional methods. On the dockside at Houmt Souk there are rows of stacked terracotta pots, each about 45 cm (18 in) high and in the shape of a turnip. Each pot has a rim at the top, around which a string is tied. These pots are attached together in a long line and then dropped into the sea a few miles offshore. For some unknown reason, octopuses are irresistibly drawn to the pots – and have been caught in this way since the Phoenicians discovered it more than 3,000 years ago.

The souk on Jerba is lively and well stocked, with wares that seem mostly aimed at the tourists. Rugs, tiles, lamps, leatherwork, hands of Fatima, sculptures made of crystallised desert gypsum and carved pipes are just a few of the things that can be purchased here.

# Kairouan

Tunisia's oldest city, and Islam's fourth holiest centre after Mecca, Medina and Jerusalem, Kairouan has been a religious pilgrimage site since 670 when it was chosen by Oqba Ibn Nafi because of divine inspiration.

A few omens led him to the pronunciation of Kairouan as a holy site and capital city. First, upon leading his army to a stop, he looked down and spied a golden cup that he had last seen on a trip he had taken to Mecca long ago. Second, he discovered a spring connected to the holy well of Zem Zem in Mecca. Finally, he witnessed the appearance of 'noxious beasts and reptiles' that he had previously banished for eternity.

The main attraction in Kairouan, a UNESCO World Heritage Site, is its Great Mosque, or the Mosque of Iqba, at the far north-eastern section of the Medina. The mosque is grand in its simplicity in comparison with the more delicate details seen in later examples of mosque architecture. The most recent iteration of this solid and commanding structure was built in 836, and most of its venerated outbuildings date back to the seventeenth century.

Inside the mosque, through a large asymmetrical courtyard once used as a rain catchment area, the off-centre minaret, the oldest in the world – dating back to 730 – can be seen. The windows in the minaret increase in size as the structure reaches skyward decreasing in size, giving an interesting and imaginative perspective. The prayer hall, with six aisles on either side, and eight aisles inside, is entered through elaborately carved wooden doors. The hall has been compared to a forest for the large number of columns holding up the ceiling and much speculation and myth surround them. Some say that anyone who tries to count all of the columns will go blind, others say that if you cannot squeeze between them you will never reach paradise.

Because of the Great Mosque's religious prominence, legend has it that seven trips here by the faithful equates to the one time pilgrimage to Mecca in Saudi Arabia. This religious significance of the area guarantees the Great Mosque is often a very busy place for pilgrimage.

**WHERE IS IT**
Centrally located, Kairouan can be reached by bus, or louage, from Tunis, Sousse, Maktar and Sbeitla.

**WHAT CAN I EXPECT**
An imposing and grand mosque, the pilgrimage spot for many from across the globe.

**WHAT I SHOULD KNOW**
The street names here change often, and usually have two names to begin with!

**HISTORICAL SIGNIFICANCE**
Tunisia's oldest city and Islam's fourth holiest centre in the world.

**WORTH A SPLURGE**
Kairouan is well known for its beautiful knotted and woven carpets.

*These prayer mats show why Kairouan is famous for its carpets.*

# Matmata

**WHERE IS IT**
40 km (25 mi) south of Gabes.
**HOLLYWOOD WALK OF FAME**
Part of the *Star Wars* trilogy was
filmed here in the 1970s.
**HOW DO I GET THERE**
Three roads lead to Matmata – from
Gabes, Toujane and Douz.
**WORTH A SPLURGE**
Enjoy the novelty of spending an
unforgettable night in a hotel room
that is a converted pit dwelling such
as the Les Berberes off the
Douz Road.

As you approach Matmata, it is difficult to discern any life in this isolated and seemingly deserted lunar-like outpost. Upon further examination, you'll discover the fascinating underground homes of the troglodytes. Made famous in the first *Star Wars* film, these traditional residences for the Berbers of the area have turned Matmata into one of the key tourist stops in Tunisia.

The sandstone pit dwellings of the troglodytes are carved from the soft sandstone hills of Matmata and boast a population of more than 5,000 Berbers. Before the majority of the tribe moved here, the small town of Matmata was in the distant hillside fortress, just visible today behind the new town which lies above ground.

The pit dwellings are made using a design that is more than 400 years old. Rooms are dug around a vertical-walled circular pit, which is 7 m (23 ft) deep and 10 m (33 ft) in diameter. Often, smaller rooms are created on a second floor, and are reached by stairs. Generally these are used as store rooms for grain, or as cisterns. A short, covered

*Rock-cut Berber dwellings.*

passageway leads from ground level down to the courtyard. The Berbers began living in the pit dwellings because of their natural temperature control, which is essential in this arid location, particularly in the baking summer months and the frigid winters.

While you are in the village, take advantage of viewing the traditional homes, but be sure to respect the privacy of the locals. Instead of peering through into their personal space, visit the museum, which was created by the local women, and stay overnight in one of the converted caves, watching the stars wheel overhead.

# The lagoon at Dakhla

*Ruins of earlier fortresses overlook Dakhla.*

The Dakhla Lagoon in the Western Sahara is an oasis of beauty between the desert and the sea. Located in north-western Africa, this part of the Sahara is one of the least populated areas on earth, and the 37 km (23 mi) lagoon, separated from the sea by a system of dunes, offers a surprisingly prolific variety of wildlife.

The natural habitat consisting of sea grass beds, plains of algae and salt pans, hosts over 120 species of mollusc, including an endemic crustacean, the *Cerapopsis takamado*, and 41 species of fish.

This is also the most northerly area to find Atlantic humpbacked dolphins, as well as the second most important wintering site for migratory birds in Morocco. Here you are most likely to see Caspian terns, lesser black-backed gulls and great ringed plovers.

The dilapidated and faded town of Dakhla itself is largely made up of military headquarters, with a few remaining archeological signs of its Spanish history. It may be worth wandering down the beach to see the traditional fisherman in their coloured boats, but otherwise head straight for the lagoon.

Fishing and tourism are both important activities, but the majority of thrill seekers come here for water sports. The constant warm temperature, combined with regular wind, creates the ideal atmosphere for wind surfing, kite surfing and wake boarding. The novelty of participating in water sports in the desert is reason enough to come and visit this fantastic Saharan outpost.

**WHAT IS IT**
A huge lagoon, open to the sea, at the edge of the Sahara desert.
**WHERE IS IT**
A two-hour flight from Marrakesh.
**WHAT IS THERE TO DO**
This is one of the best places on earth for windsurfing and kite surfing.
**WHAT SHOULD I KNOW**
The town of Dakhla is a military outpost with not a lot to see.
**WHEN SHOULD I GO**
There is a year round average temperature of 26 °Celcius (79 °F).

*The delta of the Okavango River.*

# The Okavango Delta

The Okavango River, originating in the uplands of Angola, flows into, and then spreads over, the sandy spaces of the Kalahari forming an immense and wonderful inland delta. The lagoon, with its labyrinthine channels, palm-fringed islands and fertile floodplain, is home to more than 450 bird and 1,000 plant species. This wilderness and the nearby game-rich Moremi Game Reserve and Chobe National Park appeal to game- and birdwatchers, hunters and sports fisherman, as well as those who simply like to explore hidden treasures in their loveliest and least spoilt state.

During the growth of the Rift Valley, the Okavango River, the seventh largest river in Africa, was created. Its banks overflow annually because of abundant rainfall in Angola, where its source lies, creating the largest inland delta in the world on its way to Botswana, the Okavango Delta.

This inland delta covers 15,000 sq km (932 sq mi), and its swamp waters are crystal clear and deliciously clean. One of the best ways to explore is by mokoro, the traditional dug-out canoe paddled by one of the skillful local guides who can weave through the passages showing you some of the best wilderness that the country has to offer. Crocodiles, hippos, elephants, buffaloes and several rare species of antelope, in addition to other large game can be found here, earning the Okavango its reputation as one of the world's premier wilderness areas.

Why not sit back and listen to the tranquil sounds of the wild, the splashing of water buffaloes on the shore and the flapping of wings or watch giraffes grazing in the distance, passing termite hills up to 4 m (13 ft) high while date palms sway in the breeze?

**WHAT IS IT**
An Eden-like swamp in the middle of the Kalahari desert, created from the overflowing Okavango River.
**WHERE IS IT**
Near the Moremi Game Reserve and Chobe National Park.
**WHY SHOULD I GO THERE**
To witness this wonderful delta filled with a multitude of plants and animals.
**WHEN SHOULD I VISIT**
Mid-May to mid-September, when the water levels are neither too high nor too low.

# The Skeleton Coast

The Skeleton Coast Park in Namibia stretches 500 km (310 mi) from the Kunene River south to the Ugab River and is one of the least visited and most inhospitable places on earth. The aptly named coast is famed for the numerous ghostly shipwrecks located on its remote and inaccessible shores.

This Skeleton Coast Park encompasses 2 million-ha (7,720 sq mi) of dramatic and surprising landscape including sand dunes, canyons and mountain ranges. The dunes come in a variety of guises, from hummock dunes to transverse dunes and crescent dunes, offering a loud whisper when a profusion of tiny multi-coloured pebble granules, consisting of agates, lava and granites, slide down their steep surface. The windswept dunes and flat plains give way to rugged canyons and extensive mountain ranges with richly coloured walls of volcanic rock.

The climate here, atypical of an arid desert, is also surprising. The dense fog and cold sea breezes of the Benguela Current flowing offshore, meeting with the extreme heat of the Namib Desert, cause the temperatures to vary widely. A surprising number of plants and animals thrive in the harsh conditions. The far-ranging sea mist creeps deep inland, giving life to a singular unique ecosystem and unusual plants. The 'Elephant's Foot' anchors itself in the crevices of rocks and desert succulents such as lithops resemble small rocks then blossom into tiny yellow flowers.

The desert elephant ekes out a living inland along parched riverbeds and feeds on grass and trees fed by underground springs. Strong and sturdy oryx are completely at home in the desert and can go for weeks without water. Giraffes, brown hyenas, springbok, ostriches, rare black rhinos and even lions might be seen farther inland in Damaraland and Kaokoland, where fresh water and better grazing can usually be found.

Nobody can exist on this inhospitable coast, but further inland on the edge of the desert, the nomadic Himba tribe ekes out an existence.

If you're fortunate enough to be one of the visitors to the Skeleton Coast, you will not quickly forget the feeling of walking back through time and into a forgotten world.

**WHERE IS IT**
The coast of Namibia, stretching from the Kunene River south to the Ugab River.

**WHAT IS IT**
A naturally fogged-in coastal area of natural beauty and surprisingly abundant wildlife.

**WHEN SHOULD I GO**
Because of the fog-belt, temperatures at the coast vary considerably from 6–36 °C (42–97 °F), but never drop below freezing point. In the interior, although it is warm in the mornings, it cools off as the day progresses. A general lack of moisture gives rise to chilly nights.

*One of the many shipwrecks on the Skeleton Coast.*

# Cape Cross Seal Reserve

**WHAT IS IT**
A breeding area for between 80,000 and 100,000 of Cape Fur Seals.
**WHERE IS IT**
On the Atlantic coast of Namibia, 53 km (33 mi) north of Henties Bay and 120 km (75 mi) north of Swakopmund.
**WHY SHOULD I GO THERE**
To witness these animals in their natural habitat.
**WHAT DO I NEED TO KNOW**
There is no accommodation in this area – stay at either Henties Bay or Swakopmund.
**WHEN SHOULD I GO**
The breeding season, including birth and the next rutting, takes place between November and December.

*Cape Seal breeding colony at Cape Cross.*

The Cape Fur Seal is the largest of the world's nine species of fur seals, and they are, in fact, a species of sea lion. Along the Namibian and South African coastline, there are as many as 650,000 fur seals in the 24 colonies. Cape Cross Seal Reserve in Namibia is the largest breeding area, with a population of between 80,000 and 100,000 seals.

The bulls, or males, arrive at the colony in October and, after marking their territories, will fiercely defend them. The pregnant cows, or females, usually arrive at the colony in November. Each will give birth to a single baby and become fertile again in a single week – this is when the 'rutting' season begins.

A bull, hosting between five and 25 cows in his territory during any one mating season, loses an incredible amount of his original 360 kg (794 lbs) weight defending his territory against his fellow bulls. The young fur seals are born pitch black, weighing 5–7 kg (11–15.5 lb) each. They suckle immediately after birth, and will continue to do so for nearly a year. They will supplement their mother's milk with fish when they reach about five months. The mothers continue to feed at sea while their pups are on shore and it is during this time, when their young are left alone on the shore in the colony, that they are sometimes eaten by black-backed jackals or brown hyenas. One out of four pups born at the colony will not survive infancy.

The warm-blooded fur seals are able to withstand the waters of the frigid Benguela current because of their many layers of blubber and special double-layered fur coats. Although the fish they subsist on are not commercially caught species, many fishermen still consider the seals to be a threat to the fishing industry.

Witnessing the spectacle of such an enormous number of these beautiful creatures in their natural habitat is certainly worth the day trip from Henties Bay or Swakopmund.

# Spitzkoppe

*The unusual rock formations typical of Spitzkoppe.*

**WHAT IS IT**
A 100-million year old
granite mountain.
**WHERE IS IT**
Near Swakopmund in Namibia.
**ALSO KNOWN AS**
'The Matterhorn of Africa'
**WHY SHOULD I GO**
To climb, to camp or just to watch the
spectacular sunrise and sunset.

Spitzkoppe, also known as the 'Matterhorn of Africa', is located between Usakos and Swakopmund in the Spitskop Nature Reserve. The 100-million year old granite mountain is one of the most photographed sites in Namibia, particularly during its stunning sunrise and sunset when the brown and grey granite turns stunning saffron and ochre colours.

Rising a majestic 1,829 m (6,000 ft) from the valley floor, the granite massif can often been seen dotted with experienced climbers of all nationalities. Although it is not the country's highest peak, it is commonly regarded as the most famous. First conquered in 1946, Spitzkoppe is a difficult mountain to climb, despite first appearances.

Part of the Erongo Mountains, Spitzkoppe, or Spitskop, was created by the collapse of a giant volcano, creating many interesting and sometimes bizarre rock formations. If you look carefully you may see Bushman paintings, particularly in the area called, appropriately enough, 'Bushman Paradise' underneath a large rock awning. Next to Spitzkoppe lies its smaller cousin, 'Little Spitzkoppe', at a height of 1,584 m (5,197 ft), and the nearby Pontok Mountains.

Trotting throughout the reserve are springbok, gemsbok, eland, Burchell's zebras and occasionally a camel. Also found in this area are the yellow butter trees and the poison tree, which leaks an extremely dangerous white juice that the Bushmen use to poison their arrows.

# Namib Desert

The Namib Desert, the oldest desert on earth, is located in the Namib Naukluft Park, the fourth largest conservation area in the world covering an astounding 49,768 sq km (19,215 sq mi). The desert occupies stretches along 1,600 km (1,000 mi) of this seemingly endless barren land with its enormous red and gray sand dunes, the highest in the world.

An unforgettable experience is to climb these dunes at sunrise or sunset, and look over the wind-sculpted rock formations, valleys and plains as the sun turns the dunes an array of yellows, pinks and purples.

Climbing the 300-m (762-ft)dunes is no small feat – you may have to stop to catch your breath a few times! From the summit of these dunes, you feel as though you are on the crest of one of thousands of waves in this sea of dunes, stretching as far as you can see.

From this vantage point you will also be able to witness countless birds and animals. In the rainy season there are a number of water birds, and in the dry season oryx, springbok and ostriches can be found. The mists from the Atlantic keep many species alive in this otherwise unforgiving terrain.

A night spent camping here under the dense blanket of stars on the darkest of nights will be one of the highlights to your African adventure.

*The stunning dunes of the Namib desert.*

# The Drakensberg Mountains

*Kwa Zulu, Royal Natal National Park.*

**WHAT IS IT**
The highest mountain range in South Africa.
**WHEN TO VISIT**
Spring and autumn.
**WHAT IS THERE TO SEE**
More than 40,000 ancient rock paintings from The San peoples.
**ALSO KNOWN AS**
'The Dragon Mountains' or 'Barrier of Spears'.
**HOLLYWOOD ATTRACTION**
The Drakensberg are said to have inspired JRR Tolkien's Middle Earth in his 'Lord of the Rings' trilogy.

The Drakensberg Mountains, or the Drankensberg as they are referred to by Afrikaaners, are a spiky wall of bluish rock rising menacingly from the floor of the mountain kingdom of Lesotho, providing a natural defensive barrier. The highest range in South Africa, the Drakensberg, a World Heritage Site, is a hikers' paradise offering spectacular scenery and a variety of cultural attractions.

The air surrounding the mountains is called 'champagne air' by the locals because its sparkling breezes blow around the pinnacles of this unusual topography – an escarpment separating a high interior plateau from the Natal coastal lowlands. Many of the peaks exceed 3,000 m (10,000 ft) and host streams and rivers that have carved out spectacular gorges.

More than 40,000 rock paintings exist within the caves and rock overhangs of the area, made by the San, the hunter-gatherers who roamed the area over 8,000 years ago. The paintings describe dances, hunts and battles as well as the almost mythical relationship that these people had with the animals found here.

# The Blyde River Canyon

The Blyde River Canyon Nature Reserve offers one of the most spectacular views in South Africa. Home to gigantic rocks, deep gorges and high grass-covered mountain peaks, the reserve stretches for 60 km (37 mi) and includes The Blyde River Canyon, which is nearly 30 km (19 mi) long.

The Blyde River Canyon is home to many unforgettable natural wonders. Pinnacle is a 33-m (108-ft) needle made of quartzite rising dramatically from a fern-blanketed ravine. The river drops 450 m (1,475 ft) down the escarpment, creating a series of stunning waterfalls.

At the Three Rondavels viewpoint you will discover an unforgettable view of three huge rock spirals rising out of the far wall of the Blyde River Canyon. Resembling the round, thatched African huts of the same name, these formations' red rocks create a magical contrast to the snaking blue river below. They are also known by the indigenous people as 'The Chief and his Three Wives' – the flat-topped peak, Mapjaneng, represents the Chief, named in honour of a great Mapulana chief, Moholoholo, while the 'three wives' are Maseroto, Mogoladikwe and Magabolle in descending order from left to right.

Where the Blyde River, 'the river of joy', and the Treur River, 'the river of sorrow', meet, water erosion has formed one of the most remarkable geological phenomena in the country, known as 'Bourke's Luck Potholes'. Named after a gold prospector, the surreal cylindrical rock sculptures created by whirlpools of emerald-green water, have formed a series of dark pools that make a very pleasant contrast to the white and yellow lichen-streaked rocks.

The wildlife in the Blyde River Canyon Reserve is as varied as the habitats. Mountain reedbuck can be found on the escarpment, hippos and crocodiles live in the Blyde Dam and impala, kudus, blue wildebeest, waterbuck and zebras subsist on the lush Lowveld plain near the canyon's mouth.

The descent from the nature reserve, down the escarpment to Abel Erasmus Pass is one of the most beautiful drives in the country and shouldn't be missed.

**WHAT IS IT**
One of the great natural wonders of the South African landscape.
**WHERE IS IT**
15 km (9 mi) north-east of Graskop.
**WHAT IS THERE TO SEE**
Some of the most spectacular mountain scenery in the country.
**WHAT DOES IT MEAN**
Blyde means 'joy'.

*Bouke's Luck potholes at Blyde Canyon.*

# Cape Point

**WHAT IS IT**
The edge of Table Mountain, where the lighthouse sits.
**WHERE IS IT**
The south-western tip of Africa.
**WHAT IS THERE TO SEE**
Historic shipwrecks, amazing views of the ocean.
**ALSO KNOWN AS**
'Cape of Storms' or 'Cape of Good Hope'.

Bartholomeu Dias, the Portuguese seafarer, was the first to sail around the Cape in 1488. On his particularly inclement return voyage, he stopped at the south-western tip of Africa and named it Cabo Tormentoso, or 'Cape of Storms'. Later renamed Cabo da Boa Esperanca, or 'Cape of Good Hope' by King John of Portugal, it was rounded by Vasco da Gama in 1497 on a trip to India. The daring journeys of these Portugese explorers led to the establishment of the Cape Sea Route, which led to more regular traffic around the Cape, also thus a great number of casualties here because of the treacherous landscape and vicious fogs obscuring the coastline.

To try to minimise the shocking number of shipwrecks, the lighthouse at Cape Point was erected. The first lighthouse was built in 1857 on Cape Point Peak, 238 m (781 ft) above sea level, but because of its elevated position, clouds and fog obscured it for an alarming average of 900 hours per year. After the Portuguese liner *Lusitania*

*The lighthouse at end of the Cape of Good Hope.*

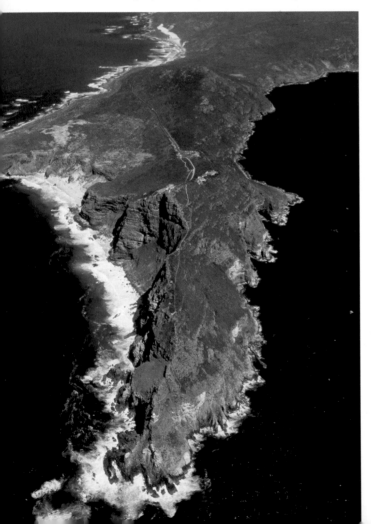

ran aground in 1911, the lighthouse was moved to its present location above Cape Point, only 87 m (285 ft) above sea level. Work on the site commenced in 1913 and was completed some six years later because of the difficulty in moving the building materials in adverse weather conditions. This lighthouse is the most powerful lighthouse on the South African Coast. With a range of 63 km (39 mi), the light beams out three flashes of 10 million candlepower, every 30 seconds.

Stark reminders of the 26 ships that did not make it around the Cape are dotted around Bellows or Albatross Rock, and on some of the nearby beaches. One of the most famous wrecks is that of the *Thomas T. Tucker*, one of hundreds of liberty ships built by the United States to enable the Allies to move supplies during World War II. The fog closed in during her maiden voyage and she ended up on Olifantsbos Point, never to sail again.

The lighthouse is within Table Mountain National Park, a UNESCO World Heritage Site. The surrounding area consists of green rolling hills laced with miles of trails leading to deserted beaches and serves as home to eland, baboons, ostriches and bontebok, a colourful antelope. From this side of the cape you would never know of the historical tragedies that took place just around the corner.

# Table Mountain

*A bird's-eye view of Table Mountain.*

Table Mountain is Cape Town's most famous landmark and one of the city's greatest attractions. There are many scenic routes that can be taken to climb the 1,086-m (3,500-ft) mountain, but most people take the revolving cable car, which whisks them to the top in just a few minutes. At the summit, the views from all directions are magnificent, especially on a clear day, although the fog can descend at any time from seemingly out of nowhere. Legend has it that an old Afrikaaner pirate, Jan van Hunks, who lived on Devil's Peak, challenged the devil to a pipe-smoking contest. The devil lost and the fabled 'tablecloth' cloud is said to serve as a reminder of his defeat.

Despite its location, virtually in the middle of the city of Cape Town, the mountain is home to a remarkably unspoiled wilderness and nature reserve. Wooden walkways and other designated paths allow you to wander around without damaging the 2,200 unique species of plants, while still affording you views of the grysboks, baboons and dassies, which resemble a cross between a giant guinea pig and a rabbit. Curiously, these funny little creatures are more closely related to elephants than any other species.

Table Mountain is truly a spectacular geological asset to Cape Town, the fabulously cosmopolitan city in south-western Afric.

**WHAT IS IT**
The landmark of Cape Town and one of the city's greatest attractions.
**WHAT IS THERE TO SEE**
Excellent views of the city and the sea, a large selection of rare flora and some fantastic wildlife.
**WHAT SHOULD I KNOW**
Bring a jacket, because when the fog descends the temperatures drop rapidly.
**IF YOU DARE**
If you are feeling adventurous, you can abseil down the mountain!

*Local women prepare the day's catch.*

# Juffureh

The small village of Juffureh, on the north bank of the River Gambia, was founded by the Taal Family in 1455. Adjacent to Fort James Island on the Mainland, Juffureh Village is the birthplace of Kunta Kinte, made famous by the 1976 best selling novel, *Roots*, written by his descendant, Alex Haley.

One of the oldest villages in the Upper Niumi District, Juffureh is a typical Mandinka settlement and has a long history of suffering prior to its rediscovery through the words of the 1979 television adaptation of the novel in which the family of Kunte Kinte was chronicled.

The story of *Roots* speaks of the days when Juffureh was a slaving centre and the Gambian population was at the mercy of the Portuguese, French, Spanish and English, who transported many of them from here to Europe, the West Indies, America and the rest of the world. The story of Kunta Kinte's 1767 capture and subsequent enslavement in America has created an interest in this chilling, undeveloped, and otherwise rural town, because of its importance in the awareness of the racial injustice that took place.

Inspired by the stories of his grandmother Cynthia, emancipated from slavery in 1865, Haley traced his roots back to his African ancestry. After research into village customs, historical texts and, most importantly, the oral traditions and stories passed down from the village griot, or oral historian, Haley put together his colourful novel – a combination of social commentary and family legends based on the lives of the Kinte family from the mid-eighteenth century to the mid-twentieth century.

A British building in the town, dating to 1840, holds a small museum detailing the slave trade in Senegambia.

**WHAT IS IT**
The birthplace of Kunta Kinte.
**WHERE IS IT**
Near Albreda and Banjul in The Gambia.
**WHAT IS THERE TO SEE**
'The factory' a fortified slave station built by the French in the late 17th century.
**WHAT IS THERE TO DO**
Visit the small historical museum.
**WHAT SHOULD I BUY**
The area is known for its beautiful batiks.

# Bandiagara Plateau

Amidst the stunning cliffs and sandy pleateaux of Mali in Western Africa, the Cliffs of Bandiagara on the Bandiagara Plateau are home to one of the few remaining communities still practising many age-old traditions and rituals. A UNESCO World Heritage Site, the cliffs have been recognised for their natural beauty as well as their historical significance in understanding these ancient cultures through their surviving traditions.

The Bandiagara Plateau, one of the main centres of Dogon culture, houses various small peripheral villages of the four Dogon tribes who migrated from the land of Mande centuries ago: the Dyon, Ono, Arou and Dommo. The village communities consist of desert-edge subsistence farmers divided into 'living men' and 'dead men', existing in symbiotic union with each other as well as having a symbolic attachment to their environment. Both of these relationships are represented in the ancient rock art that appears in and around the Bandiagara.

The village of Sangha, the most populated in the area, is celebrated for its continued practice of rock carving and its ancient circumcision ceremonies that have taken place here for more than a millennium, complete with the use of beautifully and elaborately carved masks. The rock art, continually updated, works as an ongoing historical and social dialogue for these ancient peoples.

Two main themes of rock art that have been identified are bammi, or ritual paintings, and tonu, or other, more mystical or practical paintings. The bemmi paintings show the various stages of the triannual circumcision ceremonies, as well as those of traditional rain dances, burial rituals and fertility dances. The tonu paintings were mostly created to release the potentially dangerous nyama, or life forces, of the dead.

Rock art sites are located near to, or inside, the places where the ritual masks are stored. Here, the participants in mask festivals, the largest of which is the Sigui mask festival, rest before they perform.

Some rock sites remain in use today, particularly the shelter at Kondi Pegue in Sanga, but these are not always open to visitors.

**WHAT IS IT**
A subtropical paradise with areas historical and archeological importance.
**WHERE IS IT:**
Mali, Western Africa.
**WHAT IS THERE TO SEE**
Ancient rock art sites, traditional masks and ritual ceremonies.
**ALSO KNOWN AS**
Land of the Dogons.

*A typical village of the Bandiagara Plateau.*

# Djenne

**WHAT IS IT**
The oldest existing city in sub-Saharan Africa.

**WHERE IS IT**
In the floodplain of the Niger and Bani rivers, 354 km (220 mi) south-west of Timbuktu.

**WHAT IS IT KNOWN FOR**
Its importance as a trade centre as well as its several beautiful examples of Muslim architecture.

**WHAT SHOULD I SEE**
The Great Mosque in the market square.

Djenne, the oldest known city in sub-Saharan Africa still in existence, has been recognized throughout history for its importance as a trade centre, as well as a centre of Islamic learning and pilgrimage. Established by merchants around 800 AD, Djenne served as a meeting place between the Sudan and the Guinean tropical forests. During the 16th century it thrived as the most important trading centre because of its direct river connection to Timbuktu and its location on routes leading to the gold and salt mines. Following control by Moroccan kings, Tukulor emperors and the French, commercial activity moved to Mopti, at the confluence of the Niger and Bani rivers.

The Great Mosque, built in 1240 by the sultan Koi Kunboro, is one of the most stunning examples of Muslim architecture in Mali, dominating the large market square of Djenne. The mosque, formerly a palace, was deemed too sumptuous by Sheeikh Amadou, an early nineteenth-century ruler, who allowed it to fall into disrepair, replacing it with a smaller, less flashy version in the 1830s. The current mosque, built between 1906 and 1907, was designed by Ismaila Traore, the head of Djenne's guild of masons.

Built on a raised rectangular platform of adobe-like bricks, the walls are between 41 and 61cm (16 and 24 in) thick, varying according to height. Not only do these thick walls bear the weight of the massive structure, but they also provide a natural heating and cooling system. The mosque also boasts roof vents covered by removable ceramic caps. Made by the local women, these caps can be removed to ventilate the mosque.

A UNESCO World Heritage Site, the Great Mosque of Djenne incorporates architectural elements found in mosques throughout the Islamic world. Using locally found mud and palm wood in the construction, senior masons coordinate and maintain the structure every spring. This event has turned into an annual festival, sometimes compared to a community fair. For weeks beforehand mud is cured with rice husks, periodically churned by boys in bare feet. On the eve of the event, drums and flutes are accompanied by chanting. On the day of the big event, women carry buckets of water perched precariously on their heads while men bring the mud through the square. Inevitably, throughout the day and into the evening, crowds in the hundreds become caked with mud from head to toe, creating a fun and festive atmosphere for the entire village.

*The Great Mosque at Djenne*

# Niger Delta

Mali's Niger Delta (or the Inland Niger Delta), between the Bani and Niger rivers in the south-west of the country, has provided the region with a fertile floodplain and a natural thoroughfare for trade, securing the area's position as a central economic, social and urban hub of the western Sudan. Comprising lakes and swamps channelled by the Erg Ouagadou sand dunes and located in the semi-arid Sahelian zone south of the Sarhara Desert, the delta expands to over 20,000 sq km (12,427 sq mi) during the rainy season and contracts to only 3,900 sq km (2,423 sq mi) during the dry season. The delta eventually tapers into a braided river near Timbuktu, where the Niger River curves east.

A diverse mix of vegetation excels here, including submerged and floating plants in shallow or stagnant water, partially submerged grasses and plants growing on seasonally-exposed sand. Algal blooms are also common on the lake, greatly reducing water visibility.

The southern half of the delta is low-lying floodplain, dense with grasses that are heavily grazed by large numbers of wetland birds including roughly 500,000 garganey and nearly 200,000 pintail. Also plentiful are ferruginous ducks, white-winged terns, the black-tailed godwits and purple swamp-hens.

The large wildfowl breeding colonies located here hold 80,000 breeding pairs of 15 species including cormorant, heron, ibis, spoonbill and the endangered West African black-crowned crane.

As well as the birdlife, the floodplains and delta are also home to Nile crocodiles and numerous mammal, such as the largest surviving population of West African manatees, hippos, antelope, reedbuck and waterbuck as well as a few types of gazelle, warthogs, otters and elephants.

Two endemic fish species found here are the *Syndodontis gobroni* and a cichlid, the *Gobiocichla wonderi*, which have been here since the Niger was linked to the Chad and Nile waterways.

**WHAT IS IT**
A large area of lakes and swamps in Mali.
**WHERE IS IT**
Between the Bani and Niger rivers in southwestern Mali.
**WHY IS IT IMPORTANT**
It is the earliest iron industrial trade route and urban centre as well as a home to great numbers of flora and fauna, including a large breeding ground for numerous species of waterfowl.
**ALSO KNOWN AS**
Niger Inland Delta so that it is not confused with the Niger Delta in Nigeria

*The floodplain of Mali's Niger Delta.*

*Painted houses line a street in Saint-Louis.*

# Saint-Louis

Saint-Louis, an island with a strategic position at the mouth of the Senegal River, was founded in 1659 by the French as a slave and gum arabic trading post. Located between the mainland of Senegal and the 'Langue of Barbarie' it is a narrow strip of land floating in the Atlantic Ocean, connected to the mainland by the 500-m (1,640-ft) Faidherbe steel bridge, which is a work of art in its own right. The district of Sor, a UNESCO World Heritage Site, is a lively fishing village that retains much of its charming French colonial architecture with wrought iron balconies and verandas, a reminder of its early occupation.

In 1790, Saint-Louis was a dynamic port town and an important commercial centre with a growing population in the tens of thousands. A starting point for the French colonisation of Africa, the city was alive with European, African and mixed-race peoples. Saint-Louis was the capital of Senegal from the beginning of the nineteenth century until 1958, when Dakar took its place.

**WHAT IS IT**
The Capital of the Saint-Louis region of Senegal.
**WHERE IS IT**
North-west of Senegal near the mouth of the Senegal River.
**WHY IS IT IMPORTANT**
The first French colonial city, it maintains much of its beautiful architecture.
**ALSO KNOWN AS**
'Ndar' in the local Wolof language.
**HOW DO I GET THERE**
Dakar-Bango airport.

Among the sites and monuments to see on the island are the Governor's Palace, a fortress built in the eighteenth century across from Place Faidherbe, a sandy square where a statue is erected in governor Louis Faidherbe's honour. Also of interest are the museum at the southern end of the island, the large Roman Catholic Cathedral and numerous mosques.

Although the centre of town is concentrated on the island of Saint-Louis itself, the urban sprawl continues in both directions on the mainland, the northern part occupying a long, sparse beach that stretches to the border of Mauritania as well as the nearby Parc des Oiseaux du Djoudj, famous for its bird life. Along with Gorée Island, Saint Louis remains the most characteristically French colonial destination in West Africa.

# Isle of Gorée

First discovered by the Portuguese explorer Dias in 1444, the Isle of Gorée off the coast of Senegal was colonised by the Dutch in 1817 and was later ruled by English and French powers. Gorée served as a way station for Dutch ships sailing the trade route between the Gold Coast of Ghana and the Indies.

Between the fifteenth and nineteenth centuries Gorée served as the largest centre of slave trade on the African coast. An estimated 40 million Africans were held here as they waited in anguish to be shipped to the Americas.

Built by the Dutch in 1776, and preserved in its original state, the UNESCO World Heritage Site of the Slave House, or Maison des Esclaves, featuring the 'Door of No Return' is an emotional shrine and pilgrimage site for those wishing to reflect upon the horrors of the period.

Some historians argue that Gorée was not the site of the transportation of such immense numbers of slaves, but no one can disagree with the awe and contemplation that the imposing, silent walls of the Slave House inspire.

Other points of interest include the French provincial architecture of the church of Saint-Charles on the Place de l'Eglise, the picturesque ruins of Fort Nassau, the Castle of Saint-Michel, which was originally built on the steep basalt hill by the Dutch in the seventeenth century, and the Historical Museum in the old Fort Estrees. Also worth a visit are the Botanical Gardens on the Rue du Port. If you want to take a dip, there is a small swimming beach near the ferry slipway.

**WHAT IS IT**
A former French colonial-occupied island.
**WHERE IS IT**
3 km (1.8 mi) from the capital of Dakar by ferry.
**WHY IS IT IMPORTANT**
It was once the home to the largest slave trade in Western Africa.
**WHAT IS THERE TO SEE**
Visit the Maison des Esclaves, or Slave House with its 'Door of No Return'.
**ALSO KNOWN AS**
The name Goree comes from the Dutch 'Goeree' meaning 'Island' or possibly 'Goode Reede' meaning 'good harbour' for its sheltered bay.

*Masion des Esclaves*

# AMERICAS
# AND THE
# CARIBBEAN

# Cat Island

Cat Island, home to Mount Alvernia, the highest point in the Bahamas at an astounding 63 m (206 ft) above sea level, is the sixth largest island in the Bahamain island chain. It is rumoured to have been named after Arthur Catt, the famous British sea captain, or from the hordes of wild cats that the English encountered here upon their arrival in the 1600s, depending on who you listen to. The cats were said to be descendants of those orphaned by the early Spanish colonists who left them behind in their rush to find the gold of South America. Cat Island stretches out into the Atlantic Ocean and is rumoured to be the original landing site of Columbus in the New World.

Cat Island is approximately 77 km (48 mi) long and averages between one and four miles in width. It is located south-east of Eleuthera and north-east of Long Island.

The first permanent settlement at Cat Island was made by prosperous Loyalists in 1783. The island gained its wealth from the many cotton plantations established during this time. Now, vine-covered, semi-ruined remnants of their mansions, as well as the crumbling remains of slave villages and artefacts in Arawak caves stand among the many tropical flowers, grasses and sand. One such plantation is located in Port Howe, a small picturesque village which was believed to have been built by the intrepid Colonel Andrew Deveaux who recaptured Nassau from the Spanish in 1783.

*Motor boats docked on the beach.*

This boot-shaped, untamed island is one of the most beautiful and fertile in The Bahamas. From its high cliffs there's an uninterrupted view of the densely forested foothills and the 97 km (60 mi) of deserted pink and white sand beaches.

Descendants of many early settlers remain in the same towns as their ancestors. One example is Sidney Poitier, the internationally acclaimed actor who spent his boyhood days at Arthur's Town, one of the many settlements on the island, and later returned to settle here.

# Anegada

Anegada is the northernmost of the British Virgin Islands (BVI), a group of islands forming part of the archipelago of the Virgin Islands. It is the only island in the chain formed from coral and limestone, rather than volcanic rock. While the other islands are mountainous, Anegada is flat and low – its highest point stretches up to a mere 8.5 m (28 ft) above sea level, earning it the name which translates as 'the drowned land'.

The primary business on the island is tourism, and on a typical day, tourists account for an additional 200 inhabitants. While charter boats sail freely among the majority of Virgin Islands, yacht-hire companies often forbid clients to sail to Anegada because in the past so many have run aground on its many surrounding shallow reefs. A record of past shipwrecks exists in the many vessels littering the island's underwater depths, including the HMS *Astrea*, which ran aground in 1808.

The 29-km (18-mi) long Horseshoe Reef, the largest barrier reef in the Caribbean and the third largest on earth, extends south-east from Anegada. In an effort to protect it, the BVI government has made anchoring here illegal, creating one of the most idyllic scuba spots in the world.

Anegada is also known for its postcard-perfect white sandy beaches and the large salt ponds that cover the west end of the island. In the 1830s, thousands of roseate flamingoes lived in these ponds. Hunted for food and their feathers throughout the nineteenth and early twentieth centuries, they had all but disappeared by 1950. The flamingoes are currently being reintroduced into the ponds, creating a draw for tourism that officials are trying meter to ensure the birds can flourish.

At about 38 sq km (15 sq mi), Anegada is one of the larger British Virgin Islands, but it is also the most sparsely populated of the main islands (with a population of roughly 200, including the tourists). Most of the inhabitants live in The Settlement, the main town on the island.

**WHAT IS IT**
The northernmost of the British Virgin Islands.
**HOW DO I GET THERE**
Access to the island is via the small Auguste George Airport, thrice-weekly ferries, and private boat.
**WHY IS IT IMPORTANT**
It is the only island formed from coral and limestone rather than volcanic rock and is home to the largest barrier reef in the Caribbean, the third largest on earth.
**ALSO KNOWN AS**
'The Drowned Land'.

*Anegada Island.*

*Arenal Volcano and the artificial lake.*

# Lake Arenal

Soaking in the bubbling thermal hot waters of the Tabacon Hot Springs, surrounded by lush, tropical greenery, the sound of thunder rumbles in the distance. To the uninitiated this may sound like the forewarning of an upcoming storm, but it is actually the eruption of the nearby Arenal Volcano, in the northern central area of Costa Rica, located next to the friendly town of La Fortuna.

Currently ranked as the world's fourth most active volcano, the awe-inspiring Arenal Volcano and its stunningly beautiful surroundings of pristine ancient rainforest will leave you enchanted. Located next to the large, gorgeous, man-made Lake Arenal, this experience is a highlight of any trip to Costa Rica.

Driving through the winding roads, the lush verdant hillsides and farmlands fading to low-lying, monkey-filled jungle, the landscape, flora and fauna of this incredible landscape are captivating.

Many visitors come here for the world-class windsurfing or to fish the abundant machaca and rainbow bass, but the most enjoyable spectacle of all is watching a live volcano erupt before you, as the lava creeps down the sides of the steep cone, and fire hisses from its mouth.

Charming La Fortuna, the small town next to Arenal Volcano National Park and Cano Negro Reserve, is the starting point for many of the varied outdoor activities available in the region. The nearby waterfall, 3.2 km (1.9 mi) east of La Fortuna is one of the most spectacular in Costa Rica, and it is a pretty walk through lush green countryside, forest and deep rocky canyons to get there.

An hour's drive south of La Fortuna are the Caves of Venado, which were created by water currents penetrating and passing through the surrounding limestone rocks over a period of more than 7 million years, forming an endless network of deep tunnels.

**WHAT IS IT**
The fourth most active volcano in the world set amidst the incredible beauty of Costa Rica.
**WHERE IS IT**
Between Panama and Nicaragua.
**WHAT IS THERE TO DO**
Swim, laze in hot springs, windsurf, raft, cycle, hike, fish, cave.
**WHAT IS THERE TO SEE**
A volcano erupting daily!
**WHEN SHOULD I GO**
November through March is the 'dry season'.

# Havana

There is nowhere in the world like the magical Caribbean island of Cuba or its capital, Havana. From the spectacular dilapidation of Havana Centro to the UNESCO World Heritage Site of Havana Vieja, with its Spanish colonial buildings, Cuba is a city of survivors, artists, masterful musicians and an endless stream of colourful characters.

Bereft of the consumer trappings of other cities, Havana is full of character and packed with interesting museums, history and beaches. One of the last bastions of Communism, its political isolation has prevented it from being overrun by tourists, although those who make it to the island will not be disappointed with the amenities or the welcoming locals.

The island, the largest in the Caribbean, boasts 1,207 km (750 mi) of beautiful mountain ranges and plains, dotted with more than 200 bays and 289 exquisite sun-drenched beaches. The mountain ranges include the Sierra Maestra to the East, the Cordillera de los Organos to the West and the Sierra del Escambray in the central region.

Cuba is rich in culture, music, food and art. There is nothing better than sitting at a café with a mojito in hand, watching the locals go about their day, as the beat of a Cuban samba floats through the air.

If you are fortunate, one of the locals, who by nature are incredibly generous and warm, will invite you into their homes. They will offer you anything and everything they have available to share and may cook you a wonderful homemade meal consisting of plantains, rice, beans, pork and freshly squeezed mango juice, followed by many cups of strong Cuban coffee. Even though the people are very poor here, there is a sense that they would give you the shirts off their backs to ensure you enjoy your stay in their homeland.

The grand colonial architecture, although largely faded by time and a lack of resources, would have rivalled that of many of the European cities of the world in its heyday. Regardless of its current state, there is a certain beauty in the peeling paint and crumbling walls. Cuba is a photographer's dream, a place where it is impossible to take a bad picture – the once-vibrant colours, dreamy light filtering through the cracked plaster and forlorn shutters, the smiling faces of the locals, and laughing children running through the dusty streets.

Cuba is many things: romantic, sad, rich, devastated, challenging, easy and, above all, beautiful.

**WHAT IS IT**
A jewel of an island in the Caribbean.
**WHY IS IT IMPORTANT**
It is one of the last remaining bastions of Communism.
**WHAT IS THERE TO SEE**
Spanish colonial architecture, stunning beaches.
**WHEN SHOULD I GO**
May–November is the rainy season/hurricane season, but otherwise there is no bad time to visit Cuba!

*American vehicles from the 1950s abound in Havana.*

# Carriacou

With a mix of Scottish and African ancestry, the Grenadine Island of Carriacou, located north-east of the mainland, offers a glimpse into the mixed ancestry of its population with its wealth of historical attractions and cultural festivals.

Known as the Land of Reefs, Carriacou is the largest of Grenada's sister islands, even through it is a mere 33 sq km (13 sq mi). Despite its size, Carriacou is filled with activities to satisfy your thirst for adventure, or to fill your day with the relaxing rhythms of local flavour.

Dive into the crystal clear waters and take advantage of the world-class snorkelling and diving on some of the Caribbean's most pristine reefs, or enjoy a day simply lounging on the stunning beaches of Anse La Roche, Paradise Beach or Sandy Island. With a restaurant or bar on every corner, you are sure to satisfy your appetite as well – be sure to sample the local Maroon food of rolled rice and corn with stewed meats and peas cooked over an open wood fire.

Stop in the town of Hillsborough, the bustling heart of the island and wander around the shops, or take a stroll through the botanical gardens. Visit the museum and see the internationally known works of the self-taught artist, Canute Calliste, or watch the traditional boat building passed down by the Scottish settlers in the village of Windward. There is something for everyone on Carriacou.

*A boat moored off Paradise Beach, Carriacou.*

**WHAT IS IT**
An island of natural beauty – on land and under the sea.
**WHERE IS IT**
North-east of Grenada in the Caribbean.
**GETTING AROUND**
There are a variety of options from island tours in air-conditioned taxis, vehicle or bicycle rentals, to water taxis or the island ferry.
**WHAT SHOULD I SEE**
Visit the historical museum or Kido Ecological Station.In the village of Windward, sailing boats are built using the traditional methods passed down from Scottish settlers. Recent initiatives are encouraging younger people to learn to art of boat building and to produce model boats.
**WHEN SHOULD I GO**
The annual Carriacou Regatta, held in July and August seeks to rekindle the art of traditional boat making – it is well worth the trip to witness this spectacular craft in action.
**ALSO KNOWN AS**
'The Land of the Reefs'.

# Port Antonio

Port Antonio was described by American poetess Ella Wheeler Wilcox as, 'The most exquisite port on earth'. The town's twin harbours, azure sea and verdant hillsides still ensnare visitors to this day.

The story of this old port town is the story of men who came, saw and were conquered by its beauty and character. All of them, from Captain Lorenzo Dow Baker to film star Errol Flynn and billionaire Garfield Weston, sought to develop the town and all of them failed. Like Montego Bay, Port Antonio claims to be the hub of the tourist trade, but unlike other resort areas on the island, its potential remains underdeveloped.

The town was originally settled by the Spanish and its name comes from an early governor who named the harbours Puerto de Anton and Puerto de Francisco after his two sons. Today they are referred to as East and West harbours.

Following the British conquest in 1655, the government tried to develop the area by offering land grants to British families. They laid out the town, and built a fort on the peninsula and a naval station on Navy Island. The British army and navy protected the settlers against the French, the Spanish and the pirates, but proved inefficient against the Windward Maroons. These runaway slaves fought the British troops until 1734 when the British granted them their own land.

Bananas, introduced by Canary Island Spaniards, flourished in the hot, damp climate of Port Antonio and the district of Portland thanks to its rich alluvial soil. Bananas grew prolifically alongside the native sugar cane plants. During the town's golden age, a Yankee skipper, Lorenzo Dow Baker, planted and harvested large banana plantations and subsequently sold his fruits through the United Fruit Company to North America. It was said that on Banana Day, whenever the cargo ships were being loaded at the port, the farmers would light their cigars with five dollar bills. This age of prosperity ended with the onset of Panama disease which crippled the industry. The banana trade and Port Antonio have never quite recovered.

Actor Errol Flynn was the next foreigner to fall for the charms of the port. Upon arriving on his yacht, the *Zacca*, he immediately bought land including Navy Island, the Titchfield Hotel and several cattle and coconut estates, including some of those once owned by

*Port Antonio Beach.*

**WHAT IS IT**
A twin harboured port on the Island of Jamaica.
**WHY IS IT IMPORTANT**
It was once the prosperous port town for the banana industry.
**WHAT IS THERE TO SEE**
There are many remains of the port's previous wealth including some resorts and mansions.
**WHAT IS THERE TO DO**
Swim in the beautiful blue seas, visit some of the ruins and relax.
**HOLLYWOOD CONNECTION**
*Cocktail*, *Club Paradise* and *Treasure Island* were all filmed nearby.

Captain Dow Baker. Flynn's plans to develop tourism through a series of upmarket resorts never materialized as he died suddenly early in the construction process.

During the 1960s, Port Antonio became a haven for the jet set. Billionaire Garfield Weston, whose empire included Fortnum and Mason in London, built a beautiful hotel, rumoured to be the most expensive in the world, at Frenchman's Cove. The discreet, luxurious bungalows, scattered over the headlands on both sides of the river, beach and bay were hidden by dense shrubbery and played host to, among others, the Duke of Edinburgh and Prince Sadruddin Khan. Today the hotel, owned by his son, has largely fallen into disrepair, but the sheltered bay with its golden sand, warm water and lush vegetation make it well worth a visit.

During the booming 1960s, many wealthy foreigners bought land on the island, building themselves opulent mansions. Millionaire Michael Rosenberg was one of the investors, building the hotel of his dreams, Dragon Bay, at Fairy Hill. The property, long since sold, is bordered by tropical rainforest and set in gorgeous gardens overlooking a private cove with a white sand beach. This highly photogenic setting has provided the backdrop for many films including *Cocktail*, *Club Paradise* and *Treasure Island*.

The island continues to slowly regain its prosperity, with the re-development of the harbours, and is sure to become the height of fashion once again!

# Blue Lagoon

**WHAT IS IT**
A large, deep, stunningly beautiful cove.
**WHERE IS IT**
Near Port Antonio, Jamaica.
**WHAT IS IT KNOWN FOR**
Its emerald-green and azure crystalline waters.
**HOLLYWOOD CONNECTION**
This is where Brooke Shields and Christopher Atkins swam together in the film of the same name, *The Blue Lagoon*.
**WHEN SHOULD I GO**
The weather is fairly consistent, with daily temperatures a sweet tropical 30 °C (86 °F) during the day and 20 °C (68°F) at night. Rain is moderate and occurs throughout the year.

Instantly recognizable as the paradise where Brooke Shields was ship wrecked with Christopher Atkins in the 1980s film, *The Blue Lagoon*, the swimming hole by the same name lies just outside Port Antonio, Jamaica.

This is an unspoiled oasis where you will feel as though you are the only remaining person on earth. Here the magnificent turquoise blue and emerald-green waters are an astonishing 56 m (185 ft) deep. Created by underground mineral springs fed from the Blue Mountains, it is one of the last remaining truly tropical paradises on the island. The spectacular cove is surrounded by lush, steep hills, which complete the dreamlike setting.

While swimming in the Blue Lagoon you will feel streams of warm water at times, and streams of cold water at others. There are parts where the water is shallow enough to walk right in, some with steep slopes and others with only slight slopes. You can even watch as the mineral water bubbles through the ground.

On the nearby banks there is a restaurant with a dive shop that rents out kayaks and scuba equipment.

A relatively unknown attraction, the Blue Lagoon is one of the definite 'must sees' of Jamaica and the world.

The Nearby Somerset Falls are also worth a swim. This peaceful retreat is off the beaten track, so it takes an adventurous spirit to find it, but if you go for a short stroll through the wooded surroundings, you can take a canoe trip down to the crystal clear falls and take a relaxing swim in this quiet haven.

*The Blue Lagoon.*

*The untouched reefs of Saba are a must for divers.*

# Saba

The Leeward Islands, lying in the northern area of the Lesser Antilles, are part of the greater West Indies. Just over 1,000 people populate this small 13 sq km (5 sq mi) Dutch island paradise.

The rugged island is the cone of an extinct volcano, rising skyward 850 m (2,800 ft) to Mount Scenery, the highest peak in the 'Kingdom of the Netherlands'. The peak can be climbed via a series of more than 1,000 steps. Alternatively, you can drive up the single spiral road that winds its way up the steep cliffs through lush greenery. The road connects the quaint villages of Hell's Gate, Windwardside, St John's and The Bottom.

These four small villages of this largely unspoiled island are as quaint and charming as the gentle, friendly Saban people. A trip to Saba is like wandering back in time. The emerald forests, punctuated by their crimson cottage roofs, offer a stunning contrast to the still, clear blue sea with all of its underwater delights.

Dive tourism began slowly here. In the early days, most of the visitors came for a one day visit from St Maarten, but as word of Saba's underwater riches spread, the number of tourists increased. Realizing the tourist potential, the local fishermen made a pact with the local dive shop to avoid fishing on the favoured diving reefs. This makes Saba an anomaly in that the reefs were protected before any damage could be done.

The developments did not go unnoticed by the Saban government, who worked with marine biologists and the World Wildlife Fund to create the now famous Saba National Marine Park, with 27 varied dive spots situated among its many pristine reefs.

Although Saba's underwater attractions include spectacular shallow reefs and walls, it is mostly known for its pinnacles. The pinnacles are actually the summits of underwater mountains beginning at around 26 m (85 ft) and extending in to the abyss. The pinnacles are incredibly impressive and host many large fish and pelagics.

Annual scientific surveys indicate that fish density, variety and size are increasing, as can be seen from the growing number of shark sightings. Because of the numbers of people diving in the area, the Saban government decided to invest in a hyperbaric chamber, to treat people suffering from decompression sickness (the bends).

There's nothing quite like sipping a Saba Spice after a day of diving in the sparkling waters of this underwater Eden.

**WHAT IS IT**
A small, scenic Dutch Island in the Leeward Islands.
**WHAT IS THERE TO DO**
Amazing scuba diving and snorkelling abounds here.
**WORTH A TRY**
The local Saba Island Rum, Saba Spice, is masterfully blended with Canadian rum to achieve a smooth, distinctive, complex taste – truly a national treasure!
**WORTH A SPLURGE**
Buy some of the famed local needlework – it is worth taking home.

# Barbuda

Barbuda is one part of a three-island state with Antigua and Redonda, located in the north-eastern Caribbean. An unspoiled paradise of seemingly endless stretches of white and pink sandy beaches, Barbuda is surrounded by the deep blue Atlantic Ocean on one side, with its driftwood and sea-shell strewn wild beaches, and the calm clear waters of the Caribbean Sea on the other. Undeveloped except for a small number of boutique resorts, Barbuda is perfect for swimming and snorkelling, with plenty of opportunities to see turtles and tropical fish as well as some interesting shipwrecks that lie undisturbed in the turquoise water.

A short trip from the nearby island of Antigua, Barbuda was first settled by British and French, unsuccessfully until 1680 when Christopher Codrington began cultivating sugar on the island after establishing a British colony large enough to survive the ravages of nature and the local Carib population.

For much of the eighteenth century his sugar plantations proved a successful industry, the island's prosperity rivalling that of its larger neighbours. The Codrington family influence can still be seen in the island's street names and architectural remains.

The ruins of the Codrington's Highland House lie at Barbuda's highest point (38 m (124 ft)) and on the island's south coast sits the 17 m (56 ft) high Martello tower and fort used both for defence and as a vantage from which to spot valuable shipwrecks on the outlying reefs.

The population seems to largely consist of the more than 5,000 graceful magnificent frigatebirds (*Fregata magnificens*) that gather on the north-western lagoon at the bird sanctuary. They cannot walk or swim and instead rely on flight for survival. They harass less agile flyers like pelicans, egrets and cormorants until they drop their catch.

Barbuda, just 24 km long and 13 km wide (15 mi by 8 mi), is largely rocky and flat, with much of the island covered in bush. It is home to a variety of wildlife including deer and boar, land turtles and guinea fowl as well as the occasional wild cat. Feral cattle, horses and donkeys wander about and sheep and goats roam freely in the village, returning to their pens at night. There are several salt ponds where it is possible to see a wide array of birdlife, and there are many caves to explore in the area surrounding Two Foot Bay. On one of these caves there are ancient cave drawings and in others it is possible to climb right through to the top of the Highlands from where you can see for miles. Other caves go underground and underwater requiring expert knowledge for exploration. Darby Cave, a 45-minute walk from Highland House, is an extraordinary example of a sink hole where, in very dry weather, the salt ponds sparkle with crystalline sea salt.

**WHAT IS IT**
An idyllic tropical island in
The Leeward Islands.
**WHERE IS IT**
A 20-minute flight or a 3-hour boat
trip from Antigua.
**WHAT IS THERE TO SEE**
Pristine white and pink sandy
beaches, coral reefs and shipwrecks.
**WHAT IS THERE TO DO**
Beachcombing, golf, tennis,
snorkelling, diving, sun-seeking
and relaxing.
**WHEN SHOULD I GO**
November to April is the best time
to visit.

*One of the many wonderful
beaches on Barbuda.*

# Perito Moreno

Patagonia encapsulates many things: vast wildflower-strewn valleys, daunting snow capped craggy Andean peaks, gorgeous lakes surrounded by lush pine-dotted emerald hillsides and dramatic glacial environments – most notably in the Los Glaciares National Park.

Declared a World Heritage Site by UNESCO in 1981, the park holds many glaciers that belong (or used to belong) to southern Patagonia's ice cap. Among them, the most impressive is the Perito Moreno glacier, one of the few in Argentina that is not retreating.

The small town of El Calafate, where the Santa Cruz plateau meets the Andes, is the gateway to the Perito Moreno glacier. The western end of the Lago Argentino gives access to the glacier, which periodically advances across the lake, blocking it until the weight of water upstream ruptures the ice in one of nature's most spectacular events.

Travelling down the Brazo Rico, you will pass more than 356 large glaciers in a graveyard of snow and ice, with icebergs of all sizes creaking and groaning around you.

At Curva de Los Suspiros you will get the first panoramic view of the daunting Perito Moreno glacier, its front stretching 5 km (3 mi) across and soaring to a height of more than 60 m (197 ft) above the frigid waters.

It is a humbling and awe-inspiring experience to watch the simultaneous creation and destruction of the continent through a completely natural process. In this never ending display of nature, visitors can watch and listen to the roar as ice calves from the enormous glacier, crashing into the waters below, renewed as brilliant turquoise and milky white icebergs.

A number of tourist ships of various types ply these icy waters and many offer the chance to take a heavy duty raft out to the glacier for a closer view. A highlight of the trip is collecting some of the pure waters to use later in a celebratory drink as you and your companions talk over your amazing adventures in this prehistoric Arctic landscape.

*Perito Moreno glacier.*

# Patagonia

Few places in the world have captivated the imagination of explorers and travellers like Patagonia. Since Ferdinand Magellan sailed here many have settled, and yet this vast, remote region is still, for the most part, unexplored and largely uninhabited.

Patagonia's beautiful, untamed landscape consists of narrow straits and steep-sided fjords rich in marine life, rugged mountains, harsh, windswept plateaux and glacial valleys. It is home to some of the most beautiful natural attractions in the world, from the granite towers of Torres del Paine and Los Glaciares national parks to the northern and southern ice fields with their enormous glaciers, the flat pampa broken only by bluffs of multi-coloured sedimentary rocks and stunning emerald lakes and rivers.

Considering its size and variety of terrain, Patagonia is surprisingly easy to navigate. One of the most spectacular areas of Patagonia is the Lake District in Argentina which is broken into two regions; the Northern Lakes and the Southern Lakes.

The Northern Lakes, strung along the foot of the Andes, are bordered by both Chile and Argentina. Trekking is the best way to explore the area as this enables you to reach the summit of many spectacular peaks in addition to seeing the wildflower-strewn valleys and everything in between.

Within the Northern Lakes area lie a number of national parks – the Parque Nacional Nahuel Huapi, situated on the Chilean border and the oldest national park in Argentina, the Parque Nacional Los Arrayanes, which surrounds the picturesque port of La Villa, and the Parque Nacional Los Alerces, one of the least spoiled and most beautiful stretches of the Andes, named after its impressive and rare ancient alerce trees.

The Southern Lakes, stretching down to Los Glaciares National Park, also offer spectacular scenery, with the mighty Moreno and Upsala glaciers, and challenging trekking around Mount Fitzroy.

From dense woods to petrified forests, from deserts to shoreline, Patagonia offers something for everyone, literally from the heights of the Andes, down to what many consider to be the southernmost city in the world, Ushuaia.

*El Chalten, Patagonia.*

**WHAT IS IT**
A vast stretch of largely unsettled terrain encompassing a variety of terrains of fantastic beauty.
**WHERE IS IT**
On the south-western border of South America.
**WHAT IS THERE TO DO**
Trek, raft, ski, drink wine, eat gourmet food and experience lovely hospitality and even lovelier scenery.
**WHAT IS THERE TO SEE**
A visit to the northern Lake District near the border between Chile and Argentina is unforgettable.
**WHEN SHOULD I GO**
October to April is the most popular time to visit.

*Marking the border between Argentina and Brazil, the Devil's Throat is the most spectacular part of the Iguazú Falls.*

# Iguazú Falls

The pounding impact of nearly 300 waterfalls, with heights averaging up to 70 m (230 ft), spanning a verdant, jungle-clad stretch of 2.7 km (1.7 mi) is not quickly forgotten. The Iguazú Falls of the Iguazú River on the border of the Southern Region of Brazil and the Argentine province of Misiones, is one of the great natural wonders of the world. Taller than Niagara Falls, and more than twice as wide, Iguazú Falls makes its smaller cousin appear to be a mere gentle overflow.

Part of the Iguazú National Park on the Argentine side and Iguaçu National Park on the Brazilian side, the Iguazú Falls have been recognized as a UNESCO World Heritage Site for their ferocious beauty.

One of the highlights of the falls is The Garganta del Diablo, or Devil's Throat, a u-shaped cliff marking the border between the two countries. At 150 m (492 ft) wide and 700 m (2,297 ft) long, the fall of water over the cliff is impressive for its staggering strength and vast power. The majority of the falls lie on the Argentine side, but panoramic views are also available from the Brazilian side. That being said, the view from a boat *en route* to Isla San Martin, on the Argentine side, is hard to beat.

Iguazu Falls derives its name from the Guarani words 'y', meaning water, and 'guasu', for big. Legend has it that a god pretended to marry a lovely aborigine named Naipu who then fled in a canoe with her mortal lover. Incensed at the betrayal, the god sliced the river in two, creating the waterfalls and condemning the lovers to an eternal fall.

The Brazilian National Park of Iguaçu is home to many rare and endangered birds and wildlife that live among the five types of forests and ecosystems. On the Argentine side visitors can explore various walkways and trails, some of which lead to the precarious edge of the precipice located beneath the falls.

**WHAT IS IT**
Nearly 300 waterfalls of unbelievable scope and width.
**WHERE IS IT**
Iguazú National Park (Argentina) and Iguaçu National Park (Brazil).
**NOMENCLATURE**
The name Iguazú comes from the Guarani words y (water) and guasu (big).
**HOW DO I GET THERE**
There are frequent flights to Foz do Iguaçu from Rio de Janeiro, and other Brazilian cities, and daily flights from Buenos Aires to Puerto Iguazú, or you can take the Friendship Bridge from Ciudad del Este on the Paraguayan side.
**NOTABLE QUOTE**
Upon her first sight of the Falls, Eleanor Roosevelt is said to have exclaimed, 'Poor Niagara!'

# Santa Cruz Carnival

Among the most famous carnivals in the world are those of Rio de Janeiro, New Orleans and Venice, but in different countries carnivals take on their own local character and the tropical fiesta that is carnival in Santa Cruz, Bolivia is one not to be missed!

Part religious procession, part dance party and part paint-ball game, the carnival in Santa Cruz is a riot of colour, sound and movement that is often compared to that of Rio for its sheer exuberance.

For the two weeks before Ash Wednesday, the streets come alive with troupes of jewellery- and costume-clad locals and foreigners dancing in wild abandon to the beats of salsa, samba or anything else that is being played. A feature almost unique to Bolivia is the way that revellers throw ink-filled 'globos' at each other or spray one another with foam and water. A modern innovation is to use water pistols filled with ink. This tradition may hark back to local customs from before Christianity was imposed by Spanish conquerors.

One theory for the origin of the word carnival is that it derives from the Latin words *carnem* (meat) and *levare* (raise), meaning to remove the meat, and so relates to the fact that people who observe Lent do not eat meat, fish or eggs.

Regardless of its origin, the Santa Cruz carnival is a fantastic experience – a heady mix of dancing, parades, floats and fun-loving crowds that will ensure you'll still be tapping your feet to the samba beat long after the celebrations are over.

**WHAT IS IT**
One of the most exciting places in the world to go wild before Easter.
**WHERE IS IT**
South-eastern Bolivia between Brazil and Paraguay
**WHAT IS THERE TO SEE**
Traditional and non-traditional dress, dancers, parades, floats and crowds!
**WHAT IS THERE TO DO**
Dance, dress up, sing and celebrate!
**WHEN IS IT**
Carnival season is in February/March for the two weeks before the traditional Christian fast of Lent.
**HOW DO I GET THERE**
Viru Viru International Airport, Bolivia's largest, or by train from the Brazilian border, close to the city of Curumba.

*Traditional dress at the Santa Cruz carnival.*

# Rio de Janeiro

*A dancer in one of Rio's samba schools.*

According to Brazilians, God made the world in six days and the seventh he devoted to Rio.

A large city on the South Atlantic coast, Rio is famous for its glorious backdrop of tumbling wooded mountains, stark rocky crags and a deep blue sea studded with islands. From the statue of Cristo Redentor (Christ the Redeemer) on the hunchbacked peak of Corcovado, or the conical Päo de Açúcar (Sugar Loaf Mountain), you can get an aerial view of this lush, dynamic beach playground sweeping 220 km (137 mi) along the south-western shore of the Baia de Guanabara.

From the stunning, curved Copacabana beach with its scantily clad beauties to Ipanema, land of the world's most striking sunsets, and the boisterous, Bacchanalian carnival, Rio is one of the world's most dynamic cities, bursting with charm, culture, art and colour.

Often mistaken for the capital of Brazil, Rio de Janeiro is largely divided into four regions: Zona Sul, the South Zone, including Copacabana and Ipanema, the location of some of the more up-market neighbourhoods and the majority of the city's tourist activity; Centro, including Santa Teresa, the financial and business centre of the city with many historical buildings; Zona Norte, the North Zone, home to the Maracana stadium; and the West Zone, with the Barra da Tijuca, popular for its beaches.

The inhabitants of Rio, called *cariocas*, are renowned for their easy-going attitude and friendly demeanour. It is no wonder when you consider the awesome array of gorgeous beaches that surround them. Rio is also known for its incredible art and architecture, with many historic buildings dotting the landscape. Mosteiro de Sao Bento, St Benedict's Monastery, dates back to 1663, Paco Imperial to 1743 and the Lapa Aqueduct to 1750.

One of the most thrilling sites in the city is Corcovado, a mountain with a sheer granite face topped by the Cristo Redentor statue rising more than 30.5 m (100 ft) from a 6 m (20 ft) pedestal. Reachable by an 1885 rack-and-pinion train, or via a winding road, this affords one of the city's most magnificent views.

The second famous peak, Sugar Loaf Mountain, is just as impressive, consisting of a huge granite slab at the entrance of the Guanabara Bay. From the top at 395 m (1,295 ft), you can see the whole city, plus the beaches and the Atlantic Ocean. To ascend, you catch a two-stage cable car with a length of 1,300 m (4,265 ft). The sunsets here are fabulous.

Still the greatest reason for visiting Rio seems to be the carnival. The most advertised party in the world lasts for nearly two weeks when the city is taken over by people adorned in feathers, beads, headdresses, thongs and little else. The streets teem with parades of samba groups gathering thousands of people at every corner, noisily revelling to the exotic beats. Carnival time in Rio is an experience not to be forgotten!

# Trancoso

Trancoso is a rustic fishing village situated on the wild, jungle-like shores of Bahia, the north-eastern part of the vast Brazilian coast, which has become a haven for those seeking solitude with a touch of glamour. Surrounded by untouched tropical forests, turquoise bays and white, sandy beaches, Trancoso was one of the earliest Portuguese settlements in Brazil.

The early Portugese influence is evident in the sixteenth-century church of São João Baptist perched on a cliff above the emerald sea. From here, there are panoramic views of the beaches running north and south of the town as well as the surrounding 'Quadrado', a large central grassy square that is the town's epicentre. Here, traditional fishermen's cottages painted in electric blue, bubble-gum pink and banana yellow are interspersed with fashionable boutiques and gourmet cafés whose tables spill out of doors underneath the leafy canopy of overhead palms.

During the day, laughing children play football in the town square, the elderly stroll beneath the vast rows of palm trees and sarong-clad visitors, loaded with sunscreen and cameras, head for some of the most beautiful beaches in Brazil.

At sunset, people ride horses and enjoy a glass of wine or a cocktail, gearing up for the magic to begin. At nightfall, the entire Quadrado is lit up by hundreds of candles, musicians play drums and guitars and the dancing begins, in a truly dreamlike setting underneath the starry skies.

Despite its status as an up-market resort, Trancoso has remained a charming village with strong threads linking it to its past – the weathered fishermen still haul in their fresh catch from their brightly coloured schooners in the shallow waters of the bay.

**WHAT IS IT**
A former rustic fishing village turned fashionable and fabulous beach resort.
**WHERE IS IT**
Bahia, on the north-eastern coast of Brazil, 700 km (435 mi) south of Salvador.
**WHAT IS THERE TO DO**
Surf, shop, dine, windsurf, laze on the beaches or enjoy entertainment in the lively town square.
**WHEN SHOULD I GO**
Any time is a great time to visit paradise.
**HOW DO I GET THERE**
By air from Porto Seguro.

*Ship in the Blue Lagoon, Ilha Grande.*

# Ilha Grande

Ilha Grande is a mountain ridge emerging from an emerald sea, blanketed in tropical forest and fringed with some of the world's most stunning and pristine beaches. The Bay of Ilha Grande is dotted with more than 360 idyllic, hardly developed islands. Much of Ilha Grande is designated as the Ilha Grande State Park and Praia do Sul is now a Biological Reserve.

Once infamous for the Penal Colony Cândido Mendes, which housed the country's most notorious criminals and political dissenters, the island is now solely used as an area of relaxation and regeneration within a setting of stunning natural beauty.

Abraão, the unofficial capital of Ilha Grande, is a peaceful, quaint village with whitewashed churches and low, colourful buildings in pretty hues of yellow, blue and pink with tiled roofs. The village of Abraão consists of inns, restaurants, bars and handicraft shops. Walking tracks through the forest lead to the beaches, waterfalls and historical monuments such as the aqueduct and the old lazaretto of the Black Beach.

Although the beach at Vila do Abraão may look picture-perfect at first sight, there are even more idyllic sands to explore in this tropical paradise. The spectacular Lopes Mendes is excellent for surfing, windsurfing and other water sports. The crescent sands of Abraaoozinho and Grande das Palmas are a short walk to the east of the town and other beaches, accessible only by boat, notable for their soft sands and clear waters are Lagoa Azul, Freguesia de Santana and Saco do Ceu.

On these virgin shores you will find a varied selection of flora ranging from hill vegetation dotted with exotic, vibrantly painted blooms, to coastal plains and mangroves.

The island also shelters many bird species including parrots and saracuras in addition to a variety of monkeys, iguanas and snakes.

**WHAT IS IT**
360 islands of impeccable, unspoiled beauty.
**WHERE IS IT**
South-east of Rio de Janeiro in the Agra dos Reis district of Brazil.
**WHAT IS THERE TO DO**
Sail among the pristine beaches.
**WHAT IS THERE TO SEE**
The biological reserve and its beautiful beaches.
**WHEN SHOULD I GO**
March to June.
**NOMENCLATURE**
Ilha Grande translates as 'Long Island'.

# Barra Grande

Located on the south coast of Bahia, in north-east Brazil, the Maraú Peninsula is an area of pristine beaches, tropical forest, rivers and waterfalls. Barra Grande, the main village on Camamu Bay, the third largest bay in Brazil, is a great base from which to explore this paradise.

With the atmosphere of a traditional fishermen's village and an unspoiled landscape, Barra Grande is a charming and peaceful haven for those who want to get away from it all. There are virtually no cars and the streets are unpaved, as the locals prefer to live to the rhythms of the lapping tide. The simple architecture is punctuated by lush gardens with the vivid hues of purple, orange, yellow and red exotic flowers.

This quaint village, surrounded by coconut palms and mango trees, has a surprisingly vast cultural diversity, apparent through its range of bars and restaurants, which treat the visitor to a multitude of tastes. The real lure of the area, however, is its beaches. Mangueiras Beach, the main beach of the village, boasts fine, white sand and calm, azure waters. It is an excellent spot to relax over a caipirinha and take in the brilliant sunsets.

The snorkelling and diving here are both rewarding, with a diversity of underwater life including an abundance of fish species and rich, colourful corals.

A short walk from Barra Grande takes you to Ponta do Mutá, the north-easternmost point of the peninsula and the site of Três Coqueiros beach. Here, you will find beautiful rock formations jutting from the water and a lighthouse serving as a beacon at the site of an ancient Portuguese fort.

**WHAT IS IT**
An idyllic bastion of pristine beaches, tropical forest, rivers and waterfalls.
**WHERE IS IT**
The southern coast of Bahia in north-east Brazil.
**WHAT IS THERE TO DO**
Hike, swim, sunbathe, snorkel, dive, sail and relax.
**HOW DO I GET THERE**
The closest international airport is in Salvador and the nearest domestic airport is Ilheus.

# Fernando de Noronha

*Sunset over the beach at Cachorro, on Fernando de Noronha.*

Calling the archipelago of 21 islands that includes Fernando de Noronha an idyllic paradise is an understatement. This area is one of the most important ecological sanctuaries in the world and in 2001, together with Rocas Atoll, it became a UNESCO World Heritage Site.

Seemingly abandoned amidst the clear blue waters of the Atlantic Ocean, the verdant mountains and sheer cliffs of Fernando de Noronha, a National Marine Reserve, jut out from the sea in all their lush, tropical glory. A beacon to divers from around the world, the waters surrounding the islands are home to a multitude of fish, manta rays, lemon sharks and spinner dolphins.

Every morning in the aptly named Baia dos Golfinhos (Bay of Dolphins), more than 1,000 spinner dolphins gather to frolic and dance in the early sunshine. Sea turtles are also prolific here, using many of the wide, secluded beaches as ground on which to lay their eggs.

The main island, Ilha de Fernando de Noronha, is the only one that is inhabited. To ensure the area's natural landscape is not damaged, only 420 guests can visit the island at any given time. The untouched land, 70 per cent of which is national parkland, is dotted by a limited number of sustainable tourist inns that are nearly always at full capacity, particularly in December and January.

The island has two distinct sides, a gentle coast facing Brazil and a rockier, rough coastline facing the Atlantic. The island is bisected by a single road running from Baia do Sueste to the eastern port of Baia Santo Antonio, close to Vila dos Remedios where the majority of the population resides. Here you will find the town hall, a church, the post office, a dive shop and a bar. Vila do Trinta, up a small hill, has a few restaurants, a chemists and a grocer's.

The most impressive structure in town is the Forte dos Remedios, a crumbling reminder of the Portuguese occupation. Dating back to 1737, its ancient cannons are half buried, its ramparts on the edge of collapse. Down some cobbled streets you will also find a quaint yellow-and-white baroque church, the Igreja Nossa Senhora dos Remedios, built in 1772, as well as the bright red colonial Palacio São Miguel.

The surrounding islands are largely characterised by their various formations. Meio Island, eroded to form a sort of inverted pyramid, is a well known landmark for sailors, its neighbour, Sela Gineta Cliff, is also recognizable for its similarity in shape to a cowboy's saddle. Likewise, Chapéu do Sueste Island has been compared to a small mushroom and Ilha do Frade Cliff has been said to resemble a bell, not only for its shape, but also for the sound of the waves striking against its rocky base. Morro do Leão Cliff resembles a reclined sea lion, and the two imposing dark volcanic islands of Dois Irmãos Cliff are said to resemble a woman's breasts.

Whatever you see in the cliffs, the image of a tropical paradise is the one that will remain with you forever.

# Búzios

Compared by many to St Tropez for its glorious beaches, picturesque setting and tropical sophistication, the town of Búzios on the peninsula of the same name, is where those seeking year-round elegance and amenities, combined with a charming, traditional fishing atmosphere come to play.

Only a two-hour drive from Rio de Janeiro, this is the perfect place to recover from the excesses of that famed party town. Or not. Búzio offers a vast array of dining, shopping, golf, watersports and nightlife options for the visitor wanting a respite, but not a total break from the Brazilian joie de vivre!

Considered to be Rio's premier beach resort, Búzios is home to many local and international celebrities – a trend that started after Brigitte Bardot's visited in 1964. Despite this influx, the town has managed to retain a certain degree of the charm of its fishing-village past.

Búzios boasts more than 20 magnificent beaches leading down to crystal clear waters, forming a striking contrast to the sculpted landscape inland with its lush, exotic vegetation.

Búzios, or Armação de Búzios, lies on a long, beach-rimmed peninsula that juts out into the clear Atlantic. Every activity imaginable is available on the stunning beaches – Geriba Beach is the place for surfing, Ferruda, or Horseshoe, Beach with its rocky headlands providing shelter for its calm, deep waters is an idyllic snorkelling spot and Ossos Beach is the place to sit at a café and watch the world go by.

In addition to its fabulous watersports and stretches of white, sandy coastline, Búzios offers the best of Brazilian nightlife, including fine restaurants and a lively bar scene, particularly on the Rua das Pedras, which is the place to strut your stuff or watch others doing so.

**WHAT IS IT**
An idyllic island rated as one of the ten most beautiful areas of the world.
**WHERE IS IT**
169 km (105 mi) or two hours from Rio de Janeiro.
**HOLLYWOOD ATTRACTION**
Home to many celebrities – Brigette Bardot helped to make this area popular when she visited in 1964.
**WHEN SHOULD I GO**
Búzios offers tropical weather year round although spring and autumn are less crowded.
**ALSO KNOWN AS**
Armação de Búzios.

*Fishing boats in the harbour at Búzios.*

*Surf boards dry in the sun on the pristine sands of Florianopolis.*

# Florianopolis

Brazilians love their beaches and the Ilha de Santa Catarina, also known as Florianopolis, or Floripa for short, is known throughout the country for its endless stretches of sand, excellent seafood and traditional Azorean fishing villages. Tropical weather, beautiful coastline, exotic landscapes, attractive inhabitants and a laid-back lifestyle are characteristic of this hot spot, which is particularly favoured by Brazilians.

The island itself can be divided into five areas – north, east, central, south and west. The beaches of Canasvieiras, Jururê and Praia dos Ingleses on the northern part of the island are largely urbanised and packed with tourists, particularly in the high summer months of December to February. Jururê is popular with Brazilian celebrities, many of whom own homes in the area's exclusive neighbourhoods.

Just to the east are the beautiful, wide, sandy beaches of Galheta, Mole and Joaquina. Surrounded by lush green hills and big, surfable waves, this area is a magnet to many of those looking for that perfect ride. In the centre of the island, near Lagoa da Conceição, a large lagoon partially surrounded by large sand dunes, is where some of the best restaurants and nightlife in the region can be found.

The southern end of the island is divided into two areas – on the east side towards the rugged, deserted beaches of Campeche, Armaçao, Lagoinha do Leste and Naufragados, which look out towards the clear Atlantic waters; and on the west side, Ribeirão da Ilha, opposite the mainland. Ribeirão da Ilha features beautifully preserved Acorean and Portuguese fishing villages with colourful architecture and friendly inhabitants. It is accessible only via a narrow, winding and picturesque seaside road affording scenic views of Baia Sul and the lush hills of the mainland across the bay. Similar quaint port towns are dotted throughout the south-western tip of Florianopolis, boasting sea-front cafés and oyster farms as well as some fantastic diving opportunities.

**WHAT IS IT**
An area of spectacular beaches.
**WHAT IS THERE TO DO**
Enjoy diving, snorkelling, sailing, surfing, fishing or just relaxing by the sea.
**WHEN SHOULD I GO**
From June to November you have a fairly good chance of seeing small pods of Right Whales migrating along the coast, often accompanied by young calves.
**HOW DO I GET THERE**
Florianopolis International Airport is 19 km (12 mi) from the city centre.

# Jericoacoara

Jericoacoara, a former fishing village in the north-east of Brazil, in the state of Ceará and close to the equator, was until recently an isolated area with little contact with modern civilization and no modern amenities like electricity, telephones, roads, television or even newspapers, and with an economy based on bartering fish for goods. The government declared this extraordinarily beautiful place an Environmental Protection Area in 1994, and it has finally been reached by tourism, but its peaceful and unhurried atmosphere and its pristine natural environment are carefully maintained. To this end, hunting and building paved roads are forbidden, as is anything that might cause pollution. No buildings may be constructed outside the village, and all new homes must conform to the traditional architectural style. The number of tourists is limited by the number of amenities here and, despite the numbers of visitors who would like to travel to this paradise, no new hotels can be built.

A variety of different types of scenery and activities are available to entertain you at Jericoacoara, and the beach here has been voted as one of the ten most beautiful in the world. One of the best known attractions is the Arched Rock, a huge natural gate of stone sculpted by the waves over thousands of years. It is situated in the Rocky Region, an area which stretches along more than 2 km (1.2 mi) of coastline from Malhada Beach. It is just one of a seemingly endless sea of weirdly shaped rocks, caves that can be explored if accompanied by a guide. Make sure that you keep an eye on the tides, as this unique landscape is only accessible when the tide is out.

What makes Jericoacoara almost uniquely beautiful is that it is almost surrounded by sea, so it is possible to watch sunrise, sunset, moonrise and moonset over the blue waters. A tradition has sprung up for visitors to watch sunset from Sunset Dune to the west of the village. The lighthouse is the best place to observe sunrise and moonrise.

After sunset, locals demonstrate the ancient art of Capoeira by torchlight, a combination of fighting and dancing that was brought to South America by African slaves.

A walk to the west of Sunset Dune brings you to an area called the Moving Sand Dunes, which are gradually encroaching on farmland. Another 5 km (3 mi) stroll takes you first to the isolated village of Mangue Seco, which stands by a freshwater lake, and then on to Guriu, a traditional fishing community which is so far virtually untouched by tourism.

**WHAT IS IT**
An EPA protected area of natural beauty.
**WHERE IS IT**
North-east Brazil.
**WHAT IS THERE TO DO**
Hike across the sand dunes.
**WHAT IS THERE TO SEE**
Watch sunrise, moonrise sunset and moonset over water.
**HOW DO I GET THERE**
By air to Fortaleza airport.
**WHEN TO GO**
Between 15 June and 30 July do not miss the sunset at Arched Rock. This is the only time of the year that the sun sets in the right place.
**NOMENCLATURE**
From the tupi-guarani language: *yuruco* (hole) + *cuara* (turtle), meaning 'hole of the turtles', as Jericoacoara is a beach where turtles come to make holes in which to lay their eggs.

*Fisherman launching their boats at Jericoacoara.*

# Monte Verde

**WHAT IS IT**
A small, peaceful mountain village
outside of São Paulo.
**WHERE IS IT**
South-eastern Brazil on top of the
Mantiqueira Ridge in the Brazilian
Highlands.
**WHAT IS THERE TO DO**
Hike around the hills and mountains
or just enjoy a beer at the local
watering hole.
**WHAT IS THERE TO SEE**
Gorgeous alpine scenery and
European-style architecture.
**WHEN SHOULD I GO**
April to August and December to
January are the high seasons.

The charming mountain village of Monte Verde is situated on top of Mantiqueira Ridge, in the Brazilian Highlands of south-east Brazil. The quaint and scenic town is surrounded by gorgeous peaks of up to 2,000 m (6,562 ft) and dotted with European-style architecture, which has gained the area a comparison to the Swiss Alps.

Monte Verde has green grassland and tall, strong trees as far as the eye can see. The bushy woodland belongs to the remains of the Mata Atlântica, the relic of what was once an extensive Atlantic rainforest. With the scent of fresh pine and eucalyptus in the air, the dense trees, some of which date back 500 years, provide a haven for many animal species, including a large variety of tropical birds. Locals lure hummingbirds into their gardens through a sweet concoction of sugar water in their flower-shaped bird feeders.

Outdoor activities abound in the Monte Verde region. In particular, there are hiking opportunities for all levels, a great excuse to get outside into the fresh air amid stunning scenery. Beginners opt for the Pinheiro Velho Trail, a narrow road leading up to the airport, for a short and easy stroll. For a more challenging hike, visitors can scale the Mantiqueira Ridge on the border of the Minas Gerais and São Paulo states. The highest peaks, Chapéu do Bispo, Pedra Redonda and Pedra Partida can be seen from the centre of the village. The views from the top are spectacular, taking in the nearby city of Campos do Jordão situated amid the luscious green landscape. Pico do Selado is another peak, rising 2,083 m (6,834 ft) from the forest floor. If you are not quite ready to attack this, perhaps you should consider discussing your options over a pint with the friendly locals first.

# Salvador

Salvador de Bahia, or Salvador, is the third largest city in Brazil and capital of the state of Bahia. Dubbed 'Africa in exile' for its cultural mix of African and Brazilian population and influences, Salvador, sometimes referred to simply as Bahia, is home to colonial architecture and stunning beaches. Perched on the magnificent Bahia de Todos os Santos, the biggest bay on the Brazilian coast, its emerald waters are punctuated by 38 lush islands.

A dominating cliff rises 71 m (233 ft) above the eastern side of the bay, where the older city districts, with buildings dating back to the seventeenth and eighteenth centuries, can be found. In the upper city lies the historic centre, a UNESCO World Heritage Site and national monument. Here, the Portuguese erected their fortified city, including some of the most important examples of colonial

*Church of Nosso Senhor do Rosario Dos Pretos.*

architecture in the Americas. The pastel colours are a striking contrast to the azure skies.

The Praça Municipal, Praça da Sé and Terreiro de Jesus are punctuated by mimosa trees and home to a variety of important buildings and churches, including the Palácio Rio Branco, once the governor's palace, and the Santa Casa Misericórdia with its high altar and painted tiles.

The Largo do Pelourinho, off the pretty cobbled Rua de Alfredo Brito, is considered the finest complex of colonial architecture in Latin America. Once the site of a public pillory where dishonest tradesmen were punished and ridiculed, the area has been gentrified and now hosts galleries, boutiques and cafés, as well as a lively nightlife scene.

South of the Praça Municipal you will find a number of interesting museums and churches, including the Museu de Arte Sacra, São Bento Church, Museu de Arte Moderna, Museu Costa Pinto and Museu de Arte da Bahia.

Barra is home to the city's best beaches, restaurants and nightlife. Crowded and lively, the area is where the Bahia de Todos Os Santos and the South Atlantic Ocean meet, affording brilliant sunsets over the water. It is also home to a lighthouse, built in 1580, on the site where Amerigo Vespucci landed in 1501.

**WHAT IS IT**
Brazil's third largest city, the capital of the state of Bahia.
**WHERE IS IT**
The central coast of Brazil between Recife to the north and Rio de Janeiro to the south.
**WHAT IS THERE TO SEE**
The Upper City is home to some of the most important examples of colonial architecture in the Americas.
**ALSO KNOWN AS**
'Africa in Exile' for its mixture of African and Brazilian cultures.
**WHEN SHOULD I GO**
October to April.
**WORTH A TRY**
One local delicacy is acaraje, or black-bean cakes, deep-fried and slathered with a spicy vatapa, or shrimp paste.

# Easter Island

**WHAT IS IT**
One of the most isolated islands on earth, famous for its giant stone statues.

**WHERE IS IT**
Roughly half-way between the coast of Chile and Tahiti in the Pacific Ocean.

**WHAT IS THERE TO DO**
View the giant moai figures, explore the caves, body surf.

**HOW DO I GET THERE**
There are regular flights from Chile en route to Tahiti.

**ALSO KNOWN AS**
Known as Rapa Nui, or Te Pito O Te Henua, 'the navel of the world'.

**IF YOU DARE**
Pisco, originally from Peru, a hard alcohol made from fermented grapes is the unofficial drink of the island. Try a pisco sour, which is pisco mixed with lemon juice. Another common cocktail is the piscola – pisco and coke. Drinking pisco straight is possible, but not advisable.

Easter Island, or Rapa Nui, is a remote, roughly triangular island with an extinct volcano at each corner. The chief reason to visit is to see the 600 or so giant carved stone statues (moai) gazing out to sea from the shoreline. The origin of the statues, and the islanders who created them, has provoked controversy ever since the first Europeans set foot on its shores.

The early settlers called the island 'Te Pito O Te Henua', or 'The Navel of The World'. It was rediscovered by the Dutch Admiral Jacob Roggeveen, and its name was unofficially changed to Easter Island as it was on this day in 1722 that he landed here.

Located more than 3,219 km (2,000 mi) from the nearest area of any significant population, roughly half-way between Tahiti and coastal Chile in the South Pacific, Rapa Nui is one of the most isolated places on Earth.

Archaeological evidence suggests that Rapa Nui was originally discovered and subsequently settled by Polynesians around 400 AD. As well as the legendary statues, these people have left evidence in the Rongorongo script – the only written language in Oceania. A UNESCO World Heritage Site, it is a unique and starkly beautiful landscape with volcanic craters, lava formations, brilliant blue water, beaches, low rolling hills, cattle farms and a vast array of archeological sites, most notably, the hulking moai figures. These are an imposing 9 m (30 ft) in height and very broad. One of them, on Anakena beach, was restored to its near original state along with a plaque commemorating the visit of Thor Heyerdahl in 1955.

The remaining figures are scattered about the island. Poike, a statue with a gaping mouth, is one of the locals' favourites. Ahu Tahai is another notable statue for its eyes and its topknot. From here, two of the island's many caves can be reached – one of them appears to be a ceremonial centre, while the other has two 'windows'. Beyond here you can join a path that will take you to Te Pahu cave and the seven moai at Akhivi, which face into the setting sun.

Rano Kau, where the birdman cult flourished, south of Hanga Roa is another important site, with the interesting Orongo ruins and ancient petroglyphs. Hanga Roa, the capital of the island, is home to the majority of the population. Here you will find a variety of quaint guest houses and restaurants, and extremely friendly locals intent on making your stay memorable.

*The statues of Easter Island.*

# Tayrona National Park

*The coastline of the Tayrona National Park is dotted with white sandy beaches and massive boulders.*

North from Taganga, the Parque Nacional Tayrona (Tayrona National Park) stretches for 85 km (53 mi), a largely unspoiled and beautiful coastline where you can see monkeys, iguanas and snakes in their natural habitat. It covers 300 sq km (115 sq mi) of the Caribbean Sea and 1,200 sq km (460 sq mi) of coastline that rises to an altitude of 975 km (3,200 ft) above sea level, affording gorgeous views of the surrounding hillsides and pristine beaches. Here the main objective is relaxation and swimming in these azure protected waters. If you are feeling inspired, you can always visit the archeological site of Pueblito and its indigenous peoples.

Visitors to the park hike the scenic trails to the mouth of the Piedras River, to the beautiful beaches of Cabo San Juan de Guia, Arrecifes, Shell Bay or the Cove of Chengue.

The park is ideal for exploring and consists of a tropical dry forest, marine grass prairies and an exciting array of coral reefs with an abundance of undersea life. More than 100 species of land mammals and birds, from the common deer to the elusive white eagle, also call the park home.

Camping and ecotourism are the only options for overnight accommodation because here the importance of the conservation of the environment is taken very seriously. The ecohabs, or ecologically-friendly structures, are characteristic of the local Tayrona architecture, adding another element of charm to this already special place. If you prefer staying out of doors, El Cabo where you can hang your hammock and sway to the sea breezes, is one of the most popular campsites.

**WHAT IS IT**
A gorgeous stretch of unspoiled coastline.
**WHERE IS IT**
34 km (21 mi) from Santa Marta, serviced by air from Bogota.
**WHAT IS THERE TO SEE**
Crystalline waters and lush, tropical landscape.
**WHAT IS THERE TO DO**
Snorkel, dive or just relax in a hammock.

# San Augustín Archaeological Park

St Augustín Archaeological Park (Parque Arqueológico de San Agustín) is a UNESCO World Heritage Site known for its large number of ancient carved statues, the relics of a civilisation that flourished and died between the sixth century BC and twelfth century AD. Thought to be a cultural centre for various indigenous groups before the Incas arrived, the site at San Agustín, hosts a variety of pre-Colombian artefacts.

The park sprawls across an area of 800 sq km (300 sq mi) and is considered the largest pre-Colombian site in South America. The archaeological remains represent an amalgam of cultural influences from peoples of the Andes, Amazonia and the Caribbean groups.

Although little is known of the peoples who created the statues, megalithic monuments and carvings, the relics speak of a time of former prosperity. There are about 500 statues and tombs scattered here in groups across both sides of the Rio Magdalena Gorge, sporting images of mythical and real creatures, gods and men, serving as guards to the ancient tombs and burial chambers, protecting offerings of gold and pottery to the gods.

Some of the statues feature jaguar mouths and fierce expressions, others resemble birds of prey, snakes or other animals such as monkeys, frogs or eagles. The jaguar figure is thought to be associated with a religious leader or shaman, who could transform himself into a jaguar to keep balance in the world. It is thought that the concept of reincarnation is a large part of the rationale behind these monoliths.

Archaeological excavation began in the 1930s and unearthed figures where the paint or dye, mainly red, blue and yellow, was still visible. The vivid colours began to fade as soon as the air touched them, but traces of colour remain. Adorned with various modes of clothing, hairstyles and accessories, the statues share a common feature of blank eyes staring into the distance.

**WHAT IS IT**
A World Heritage Site notable for its pre-Colombian statues.
**WHERE IS IT**
Parque Arqueológico de San Agustín is 3 km (1.8 mi) west of San Agustín.
**WHAT IS THERE TO SEE**
More than 500 pre-Colombian statues, monuments, tombs and carvings.
**WHAT IS THERE TO DO**
Wander through the idyllic scenery and gaze at these ancient antiquities.
**HOW DO I GET THERE**
By bus from Bogota or Popayan.

*Stone sculptures stand among the trees.*

# Galapagos Islands

The Galapagos Islands, a small archipelago of islands belonging to Ecuador in the remote waters of the eastern Pacific Ocean, are remarkable for their untouched variety of unique and fearless wildlife, providing the inspiration for Charles Darwin's theory of evolution though natural selection.

Lying roughly 1,000 km (620 mi) west of the South American continent, the Galapagos archipelago consists of 13 main islands and 6 smaller isles, together covering more than 50,000 sq km (19,500 sq mi).

The largely barren and volcanic islands are home to some of the best wildlife in the world including giant tortoises, the indigenous Galapagos sea lions, penguins, marine iguanas, Galapagos flamingos, magnificent frigatebirds, otters, Darwin's famous finches and blue and red-footed boobies to name just a few. Through a quirk of evolution, large predators failed to evolve here, so the animals have no fear, not even of human visitors.

Strict controls on tourist access are maintained in an effort to protect the natural habitats of this UNESCO World Heritage Site and all visitors must be accompanied by a national park-certified naturalist tour guide.

*A giant Galapagos Tortoise.*

In addition to wildlife, the Galapagos Islands provide some of the best snorkelling and diving sites in the world, and their colourful reefs and abundance of fish varieties are simply awe-inspiring.

Some of the islands deserve a special mention – Bartolomé is famous for its dramatic vistas and barren volcanic landscape where you can climb more than 200 steps to reach the top of an extinct volcano, Genovesa is home to the stunning magnificent frigatebirds as well as the largest colony of red-footed boobies, Cerro Dragon (Dragon Hill) has iguanas that do not exist anywhere else in the world and Fernandina is home to the flightless cormorant and the largest colony of marine iguanas. Espanola is an enchanting island where albatrosses mate and care for their young and the famed blue-footed boobies perform the mating dance known as the 'sky point', where the male extends his wings and lifts his beak as he howls at his prospective mate. She does the same if suitably impressed. Isabella, the largest island in the chain, is home to Darwin's Volcano, Tagus Cove and the highest peak of the islands, the Wolf Volcano, which rises 1,707 m (5,600ft) above sea level.

There are far too many glorious things to see in one trip to these idyllic islands, but visiting the Galapagos Islands is an experience that you will never forget.

# Machu Picchu

As it appears dramatically from the verdant, jungle-clad peaks and steep, terraced slopes that fall to the valley below, with the Urubamba River snaking through its emerald floor, Macchu Picchu takes your breath away when you first catch sight of it.

If you decide to trek to these monumental ruins, you will take the arduous but awe-inspiring Inca Trail, a pilgrimage route for centuries, winding from the Sacred Valley near Ollantaytambo through exotic vegetation and magnificent mountains that afford unforgettable views. The exceptional towering Huayna Picchu and its surrounding ruins are well worth the effort, although the train is a quicker alternative.

A complete Incan city, Macchu Picchu, a UNESCO World Heritage Site, was uncovered in 1911 by American archaeologist Hiram Bingham. Perched dramatically 305 m (1,000 ft) above the valley, the site comprises staircases, terraces, temples, palaces, towers and fountains.

From the top of Funerary Rock you will be able to take in the picture-postcard view – this is the ideal spot to watch the sunrise if you do not mind the crowds, including the herds of llamas grazing nearby. From here, the layout of the ancient city, with its clearly defined

**WHAT IS IT**
A complete Incan City in the Sacred Valley of the Incas.
**WHERE IS IT**
Near Cuzco, Peru.
**WHAT IS THERE TO SEE**
The most impressive Incan ruins in the world.
**WHEN SHOULD I GO**
April–May and October–November.

*The mountain city of Machu Picchu.*

agricultural and urban zones separated by a long dry moat, is clearly laid out in front of you.

One of the most famous edifices is the Temple of the Sun, or Torreon, with its extraordinary masonry and rounded, tapering tower with windows that are perfectly aligned for the sun to illuminate the central temple during the June winter solstice. Below the temple is the Royal Tomb, carved inside the rocks, complete with an altar, and the Royal Sector, a series of dwellings around a still-functioning water canal and interconnecting fountains.

North of the quarry is the main ceremonial area of the Temple of the Three Windows with the Sacred Plaza, the Principle Temple, Sacristy and the House of the Priest.

Up a short flight of stairs is the famed Intihuatana, the remarkable 'Hitching Post of the Sun', an astronomical and agricultural calendar. Intrinsically connected to the surrounding mountains, its shape echoes that of the sacred peak Huayna Picchu looming in the distance. Huayna Picchu, the craggy outcrop punctuating the Machu Picchu landscape, has a viewing platform, accessible by a steep climb, directly overlooking the ruins, with the most astounding 360-degree panoramic views available.

The Temple of the Moon is a less visited ruin encompassing mysterious caverns, niches and portals as well as carved thrones and an altar – its purpose has not been determined. Situated off the Central Plaza, the Temple of the Condor is notable for its dark rock symbolising the great bird's wings and the pale rock below representing its head.

However much of this stunning landscape you chose to explore, a trip to Machu Picchu is an unforgettable one.

# Coro

**WHAT IS IT**
A charming colonial city, the oldest in western Venezuela.
**WHERE IS IT**
177 km (110 mi) from Tucacas.
**WHAT IS THERE TO SEE**
Enchanting architecture and excellent museums.
**WHAT IS THERE TO DO**
Visit the nearby park with its gorgeous sand dunes.
**WHAT I SHOULD KNOW**
The traditional adobe architecture has been damaged in recent years, putting the city on UNESCO's 'at risk' list.

Founded in 1527 by Juan de Ampies, the lovely and relaxed city of Coro is home to many beautiful colonial buildings including Los Arcaya, one of the best examples of eighteenth-century architecture. Founded by Spanish colonists, Coro is the capital of the Falcon State and the oldest city in western Venezuela.

Recognized as a UNESCO World Heritage Site, the port, with its cobbled streets and hundreds of historic buildings, reflects a variety of cultures including the Spanish Islamic style and the Dutch influence with its colony of Curaçao.

Coro's traditional buildings are constructed of adobe, earth reinforced by a technique known as 'bahareque'. Vulnerable to rain damage, the heavy storms in recent years have damaged some of the city's buildings, one factor in its current UNESCO 'at risk' status.

Punctuated by lush gardens and shady plazas, Coro is home to the

*Rippled sand dunes at Coro.*

continent's oldest Jewish cemetery as well as the country's oldest wooden cross, located in the plaza in front of the San Clemente Church, a national monument and site of the first mass given in Venezuela.

The city has a tropical atmosphere, its colourful homes are painted in deep indigoes, intense burgundies and ochre yellows, while the tree-fringed promenades entrance visitors with their charm.

Coro is also home to a number of notable museums including the Diocesan Museum, The House of the Iron Windows, Arcaya's Balcony Museum, the Contemporary Art Museum and the Coro Art Museum.

Surrounded by the massive sand dunes of Los Médanos de Coro National Park, the only desert in Venezuela, and the lush gardens of the Jardin Botanico, Coro has something for every visitor to enjoy.

127

# Vancouver

**WHAT IS IT**
Canada's fastest growing metropolis, a magical city filled with exotic cultures, cosmopolitan theatre and dining, surrounded by fantastic wilderness and awe-inspiring scenic beauty.
**WHERE IS IT**
The south-western coast of British Columbia.
**HOW TO GET THERE**
Vancouver is 15 km (9 mi) north of Vancouver Intl airport.
**TRIVIA**
Vancouver is the third largest film production centre in North America outside of Hollywood and New York. It will be Hosting the 2010 Winter Olympics.
**ALSO KNOWN AS**
'Lotus Land'.

Vancouver is a magical city, full of contradictions. The gateway to the Pacific, it is a multi-cultural city with an easy-going air, filled with cosmopolitan restaurants and boutiques, and offering visitors the opportunity to sail and ski in the same day.

The first European to discover the area was Captain George Vancouver, who wrote of a deep, sheltered harbour with 'innumerable pleasing landscapes'. Before his arrival by sea, the area had largely been a seasonal outpost for the indigenous peoples of the Burrard inlet – the Musqueams on the northern arm of the Fraser River and the Squamish in the Squamish and Cheakamus Valleys.

White settlement began in 1862 with the discovery of coal in the aptly named Coal Harbour and by the 1880s, major development was underway. However, the true pioneer of Vancouver was 'Gassy' Jack Deighton, who became the first saloon proprietor in 1867, in the area now known as 'Gastown'.

Located near the cruise ship terminal, Gastown is a charming Victorian cobbled area, complete with mews, antique shops, boutiques and art galleries housed in historic buildings. The sound of the unique Steam Clock sounding the Westminster chimes every quarter of an hour echoes through the quaint courtyards and passages. At the entrance to Gastown, you can enjoy the sweeping 360-degree views from the Lookout Tower, a 33-floor observation deck above Harbour Centre. From here, awe-inspiring vistas greet you at every turn.

Vancouver's centrepiece is the 1,000 acre Stanley Park. One of the largest urban parks in North America, it is the city's most famous landmark and has woodland trails, secluded lakes, vast gardens and the largest aquarium in Canada. The meandering path around the park's perimeter offers views of the stunning skyline, the glistening harbour and the pristine beaches, as well as the spectacular North Shore Mountains looming in the distance.

Another reminder of the city's cultural heritage is its Chinatown, the second largest in North America after San Francisco. The area is alive 24 hours a day and filled with red pagoda-roofed phone boxes and the aroma of exotic spices, while traditional herbal medicines and exotic foods are stacked precariously high on tilting, over-stuffed shelves. By contrast, this area is also home to the tranquil Dr Sun Yat-Sen Classical Chinese Garden, the only Ming Dynasty Classic Chinese Garden outside China.

Other multi-cultural landmarks include the Punjabi Market, Little Italy, Greektown, Japantown, Commercial Town and a handful of Koreatowns, all of which are marked by their bilingual street signs.

Granville Island is another area of the city not to be missed. Home to theatres, studios, galleries, restaurants and the famous public market, which offers a truly dizzying array of fresh produce, this once industrial island now hosts outdoor entertainment and a boisterous nightlife.

From trendy Robson Street to timeworn Hastings Street, Vancouver is a paradise for those seeking thrills in the wilderness, on their palate, on the stage or in their wardrobe. This is certainly a must-see destination.

*Downtown Vancouver along False Creek.*

# Vancouver Island

Vancouver Island, known for its laid-back artistic culture, stunning coastal scenery and year-round blanket of flowers, is separated from the western mainland of British Columbia by the Strait of Georgia.

This region is a paradise of pristine beaches and lush emerald rainforests, pounded by the Pacific Ocean. It is home to various plants and animals, the majestic snow-capped Olympic mountains and glistening bays, rivers and lakes. The varied ecosystem includes farmland, vineyards and wildflower-strewn meadows – allowing its visitors the luxury, variety and adventure of having the opportunity to ski and play golf in the same day.

The picturesque capital, Victoria, at the southern tip of the island, offers a snapshot of Britain with its historic parliament, narrow streets dotted with cafés, pubs and colourful gardens and boats floating lazily in the sparkling harbour. There is an abundance of sights to experience here, including the internationally acclaimed Butchart botanical gardens, which hold more than one million plants. Each garden area has a designated theme such as roses, Japanese gardens or Italian gardens, and all are artistically planted. They are particularly spectacular when viewed during an outdoor concert on summer evenings, illuminated by coloured lights.

The fishing village of Tolfino, located on Clayoquot Sound, is a centre for ecotourism. The sandy beaches south of the town are the main attraction of the area, along with whale watching and surfing.

Vancouver Island is truly a remarkable place with plenty to keep you occupied, and entranced, during your entire visit.

**WHERE IS IT**
90 minutes from Vancouver by ferry across the Strait of Georgia.
**WHAT IS THERE TO DO**
Enjoy spectacular scenery and take advantage of the wealth of outdoor activities.
**WHAT TO KNOW**
'The island' is considered paradise for the opportunity to ski and play golf in the same day!
**ALSO KNOWN AS**
'The Island'.

*Seaplane over an island in Clayoquot Sound.*

# Raft Cove

On the north-west coast of Vancouver Island is Cape Scott Park. At the southern end of the park you will discover Raft Cove, a provincial park consisting of an isolated, forested coastline at the mouth of the meandering Macjack River.

Cutting through an unpaved, twisting trail, among ancient towering hemlock, western red cedar and Sitka spruce, you will come upon the rugged shoreline, notable for its unobstructed majestic views of the pounding Pacific. From here you might be lucky enough to see migrating whales.

At the end of the beach is a wild sandy bay, accessible at low tide, which is home to the dilapidated trapper's cabin of Willie Hecht, an early Cape Scott settler. Abandoned and crumbling, the remnants of Hecht's home lie on the southern bank, opposite the tip of the wooded peninsula. The best fresh water is available from the nearby stream.

Camping on the beach, or in wilderness campsites amongst the canopy of trees, is popular as are surfing, swimming, fishing and hiking. Black bears, cougars and wolves live in the park so caution should be exercised when staying overnight.

This is the land of pioneers, virtually untouched by man. Hiking here, you will feel as though you are discovering your own secret wilderness.

*Hiking across Raft Cove.*

# Whistler Mountain

Located in the Mountains of British Columbia, Whistler and Blackcomb, the spectacularly scenic mountains, are home to the internationally-known ski and snowboard resort of Whistler Blackcomb. Nestled in a cosy scenic river valley, it is reached by a spectacular two-hour drive from Vancouver along the 'Sea to Sky Highway', one of Canada's most breathtaking corridors.

The scenic splendour of the glorious mountain tops soaring high above are reflected in Alta Lake as you enter the resort. Whistler, (highest lift – 2,182m (7,160 ft)), and Blackcomb ( 2,284 m (7,494 ft)) have the largest vertical drop and the largest area – more than 28,000 ha (7,000 acres) – of ski and snowboard terrain on the continent. There are over 200 marked trails, 12 massive Alpine bowls, three glaciers and 33 lifts that service the mountain.

Often referred to as a 'toy town' or as 'Disneyesque' for its modern, rustic architecture, casual-chic atmosphere and clean and inviting village, the resort is very well maintained, with a unique customer focus. Guests are treated to complimentary live entertainment as they wait in the efficient queues for the lift, free orientation to the village is offered to new guests and accommodation, transport and restaurants are available for all budget levels.

Although this is a big mountain, offering big thrills for the adventure-seeking outdoor enthusiast, there is also a lot for those less inclined to take advantage of the array of year-round sports activities. This village is packed with shops, restaurants and spas, so there is something for everyone here.

Whistler has all the conveniences of a city in a village, but just a few steps away is untamed wilderness. One of the most desirable summertime experiences is to watch a black bear in its natural habitat. Your best chance of doing so is to join a bear-watching trip or ecology tour, during which you will have the opportunity to learn about the species as well as their ecological surroundings. The lush wilderness is also home to cougars, deer, rabbits and various species of birds.

If you tire of the breathtaking scenery and never-ending activities, you can always visit the Whistler Museum and Archives to re-live the town's history, or visit Fernie, the friendly nearby mining town.

*Misty peak of Whistler Mountain.*

**WHERE IS IT**
120 km, (75 m) north of Vancouver.
**WHAT IS IT**
The largest ski area in North America with over 28,000 ha (7,000 acres) of ski and snowboard terrain.
**DID YOU KNOW**
Whistler will be hosting the 2010 Winter Olympics and ParaOlympics in conjunction with Vancouver.
**HISTORICAL TRIVIA**
Named Whistler by early settlers after the shrill sound made by the local western hoary marmots living among the rocks.

# Okanagan Valley

*A farm in Okanagan valley.*

The Okanagan Valley, stretching from the arid Osoyoos at the United States' border north to lush Vernon in British Columbia, interspersed with blankets of orchards and vineyards, makes an excellent place to stop and experience the various fruits of the earth.

The warmest region in Canada, the Okanagan Valley offers a veritable feast of flavours. The vast Osoyoos and Oliver regions of the Okanagan Valley are nearly arid enough to warrant being called a desert, but farther north cherries, peaches, pears, apricots, plums, apples and grapes all grow in abundance. The fruit trees blossom in spring, making this a particularly pleasant time to visit.

Autumn is also beautiful, as this is when the grapes are plump on the vines. Winemaking is serious business in Okanagan. British Columbians have long taken pride in their wines, and Kelowna in the Okanagan Valley is the centre of this burgeoning industry. Home to large producers as well as estate and boutique wineries, there is a taste of France in this beautiful valley. No visit is complete without a vineyard tour and a winetasting session. In Kelowna if you happen to visit from mid-September to mid-October you might catch the astonishing sight of wild salmon spawning in Lion's Park.

In summer, there are countless sandy beaches where you can loll in the sunshine, swim, fish and dive in the scenic Okanagan Lake. You could also take in a round on one of the many high-quality golf courses in the area, or visit some of the many surrounding parks.

For a special wildlife-watching experience, take a day to visit Vaseux Lake Provincial Park, 25 km (15 mi) south of Penticton, where the surrounding cliffs are home to California bighorn sheep, and the stands of willow and shrubs along the shoreline offer spectacular birdwatching opportunities. Wildfowl, including trumpeter swans, widgeons, Canada geese, wood ducks and blue-winged teal are also common. In spring, the beautiful lazuli bunting has been seen. Other bird species present include chukar partridge, wrens, swifts, sage thrashers, woodpeckers, curlews and dippers.

**WHAT IS IT**
An area of abundant fruit and wineries.
**WHERE IS IT**
Southern British Columbia.
**HOW DO I GET THERE**
The airline service to the Okanagan is via Kelowna and road access is easy.
**ALSO KNOWN AS**
The Shushwap natives called the area Naitaka or 'long fish'.
**LOCAL FOLKLORE**
People around Lake Okanagan have reported sightings of a serpent-like creature in its waters – unlike the Loch Ness Monster, sightings have been made at least once a year.

# Queen Charlotte Islands

Arguably one of the most beautiful and diverse landscapes in the world, the Queen Charlotte Islands have such thriving and abundant flora and fauna that they are sometimes called the 'Galapagos of the North'.

The scenery of the 1,884 islands of the archipelago is stunning. The seven largest islands, peaks of a submerged mountain chain, are Langara, Graham, Moresby, Louise, Lyell, Burnaby and Kunghit islands. Just 2 or 3 km (1.2–2 mi) offshore, the continental shelf falls away dramatically to the immense depths of the Pacific Ocean, making this the most active earthquake area in Canada and landslides are common.

Haida Gwaii has been home to the Haida people for at least 7,000 years. In 1774, Juan Perez was the first European to reach this isolated paradise. Fur traders followed, creating a major impact on the Haida as Europeans arrived *en masse* to exploit the abundant resources. In 1787, the islands were renamed after Lord Howe's flagship, HMS *Queen Charlotte*, in honour of Queen Charlotte, wife of King George III.

The islands retain their wild peace and have a rich cultural history. The Haida earn their living traditionally, the main industries being mining, logging and commercial fishing. Tourist activities include sport fishing, hiking, camping, kayaking and whalewatching.

Graham Island is the most accessible and populated of the islands, and is where the majority of the Haida communities reside. The adjacent islands great for exploring the Haida culture include: Skidegate, on the shores of Rooney Bay, the cultural centre of the area where you can see artefacts and local art; Tlell, home to an artistic collective, the heart of the art community and the Haida's administrative seat; Old Masset, home to native carvers; and the remote and rugged Langara Island, at the north-west tip of the archipelago, with its ancient rainforest, an impressive seabird colony and a restored 1913 lighthouse.

Other places to explore are the logging and fishing village of Port Clements, where you can see the giant trees of the temperate rainforest and North Beach in Naikoon Provincial Park where, the Haida believe, the raven first brought people into the world by coaxing them out of a clam shell.

The vast rugged coastline of Rennell Sound, bordered by the snow-capped Queen Charlotte Mountains, offers scenic beaches, great hiking, fishing and kayaking and Louise Island, where you can view one of the largest displays of ancient totem poles in these spiritual islands.

**WHAT ARE THEY**
An archipelago of 1,884 islands, with snow-topped mountains and fiords that plunge into the sea, mist-enshrouded forests and windswept sandy beaches. They are sometimes referred to as the Galapagos Islands of the north.

**WHERE ARE THEY**
The Queen Charlottes are located in British Columbia, Canada, west of the northern BC town of Prince Rupert. Two islands, Graham Island in the north and Moresby Island in the south, make up the majority of the land mass.

**HOW DO I GET THERE**
The main airport for the islands is at Sandspit.

**ALSO KNOWN AS**
The Haida people refer to the islands as *Haida Gwaii* – islands of the people or *Xhaaidlagha Gwaayaai* – Islands at the Boundary of the World.

**WHAT IS THERE TO DO**
There are countless beaches, streams, fishing holes, coves and abandoned Indian villages to explore. Many unique subspecies of flora and fauna share these islands with the residents.

**HISTORICAL SIGNIFICANCE**
According to Haida legend, Haida Gwaii is the place where time began.

*Skidegate Channel at sunset.*

# God's Pocket

God's Pocket, on the north side of the Goletas Channel, is a provincial marine park set on group of small islands at the entrance to the Queen Charlotte Strait. The largest islands are Hurst, Bell, Boyle and Crane islands. Bald eagles and whales are common in the area, and there is a seabird breeding colony as well as various archaeological sites.

Locals say that a Sasquatch- (Yeti-) like creature also lives here, and that the islands are haunted by spirits.

Above all, God's Pocket is known for the quality of scuba diving on offer. The clean, clear waters here are alive with marine life. Most diving takes place in nearby Browning Pass, an area that Jacques Cousteau, the great underwater explorer considered one of the best dive sites in the world.

Experienced divers can witness orcas, harbour seals, Pacific white-sided dolphins, Steller sea lions and somewhat less often humpback and grey whales.

The commercial lodge next to the park on Hurst Island arranges kayaking and diving trips to the area. There are no designated camping sites within the park, but random wilderness camping is allowed.

# The Calgary Stampede

The territory of Alberta, Canada is a modern take on the old wild west. Its cities, Calgary and Edmonton, are hospitable and friendly, surrounded by vast stretches of lush, unspoiled prairies and grassy cattle-rich ranges from Montana to the south, the Rocky Mountains to the west and Saskatchewan in the east. Calgary is home to a quarter of the population, but it remains a friendly, convivial town, known largely for some of the finest mountainous scenery in Canada. This is where the breathtaking vistas from the film *Brokeback Mountain* were filmed.

Calgary has the largest, rowdiest and most prestigious annual rodeo in North America, The Calgary Stampede. Every year, at Stampede Park, locals and fans from around the globe don their best cowboy gear and whoop it up at this outrageously riotous occasion. Not just a rodeo, this event has everything you can imagine to keep your boots moving and your spurs jingling. There are petting zoos, handicrafts, a casino, a food fair, dancers, clowns, live bands and other organized activities.

Aspiring cowboys try their hand at the top attraction, the rodeo events. Here there are competitions for riding bucking broncos and bulls, calf roping and steer wrestling. The Chuckwagon race, one of the event's highlights, is where old western cook wagons thunder around the track, covered in dust, as the wagons tilt precariously as they round the corners.

Come on up to Calgary and step back in time to the wild, wild west!

*Horse and rider compete in a barrel race at the Calgary Stampede.*

**WHAT IS IT:**
The world's largest western rodeo in Calgary.
**HOLLYWOOD ATTRACTION**
The home of true cowboys and extraordinary scenery, this is where *Brokeback Mountain* was filmed.
**DRESS CODE**
Do not forget your jeans, cowboy boots and your Stetson – this is the real thing!
**WHAT SHOULD I KNOW**
This event is so popular that hotels get booked up a year in advance so plan ahead if you want to get rowdy with these cowboys!

# Algonquin Provincial Park

**WHAT IS IT**
One of Canada's largest provincial parks.
**WHERE IS IT**
Immediately east of Muskoka in Ontario.
**HOW DO I GET THERE**
The main access points are via Highway 60, east of Huntsville.
**WHY IS IT IMPORTANT**
It inspired the famous Group of Seven Artists.
**WHAT IS THERE TO DO**
You can canoe in the 1,610 km (1,000 mi) or so of canoe routes, hike among the 6–88 km (4–55 mi) of backpacking trails, ride a mountain bike, cross-country ski, fish or birdwatch.

Algonquin's Provincial Park in Ontario encompasses 7,725 sq km (4,800 sq mi) of forests, lakes and rivers, reminiscent of wilderness from a vanishing past. The park is set in a transition zone amid both deciduous and coniferous forests, with a lush landscape of maples, spruce bogs, beaver ponds, lakes and wildflower-strewn cliffs, each of which provides ample opportunities to see a wide array of plants and wildlife not commonly found together.

Within the park's boundaries you will find 53 species of mammals, 272 species of birds, 31 species of reptiles and amphibians, 54 species of fish and roughly 7,000 species of insects! More than 1,000 species of plants, as well as more than 1,000 species of fungi are also found here.

Originally inhabited by aboriginals who came here to fish, hunt and pick berries, the rugged Algonquin highlands were not settled by pioneers until the nineteenth century when loggers arrived from the Ottawa Valley in search of white pines whose wood was increasingly in demand by a growing British economy.

Algonquin Provincial Park was established in 1893 as a wildlife sanctuary to protect the headwaters of the five major rivers that flow from the park. Eventually this area of majestic beauty was 'discovered' by adventurous fishermen, then by Tom Thomson and the famous Canadian landscape painters, the Group of Seven, and a host of other visitors. People travel from around the world to hear the howls of wolves echoing in the beautiful area, as well as to catch sight of the moose that inhabit the park in large numbers.

*McIntosh Lake, Algonquin Provincial Park.*

# The Gaspe Penninsula

The Gaspe Peninsula, or Gaspesie, on the eastern tip of Quebec, north of New Brunswick, is a largely coastal region surrounded by the St Lawrence estuary and gulf as well as by the Bay of Chaleur. First claimed for the king of France by Jacques Cartier in 1534, today Gaspe is known for its deep-water port and the three salmon rivers that empty into it.

Far from the crowds, Gaspe offers an abundance of attractions worth seeing. Heaped with woodland-covered hills whose slopes drop into the sea and low rolling pastures with sleepy cattle grazing, Gaspe is dotted with small fishing villages populated with friendly locals, offering guests an intimate and relaxing experience. Camping, hiking, biking and fishing attract people, far away from the bright lights of the big city.

One of the highlights of the north shore near Grand Métis is the Jardins de Métis, a horticultural spectacle offering more than 2,500 varieties of plants in a British-style garden. The 100,000 plants attract an array of colourful butterflies with their fragrant aromas and singing birds flit from branch to branch.

The Parc de la Gaspesie, encompassing the Chic-Choc mountains of the northern Appalachians, affords views of rivers brimming with baby salmon and speckled trout. The woody, meadowed landscape is host to herds of moose, caribou and deer. The Parc National Forillon is also worth visiting as its rugged coastline, with steep, craggy rock cliffs and dense forests is very representative of the native eastern Canadian landscape.

Perce, the Pic de l'Aurore, or Peak of the Dawn, has stunning views of Perce Rock, the famous Quebec landmark, and Bonaventure Island. Perce Rock, also known as Rocher-Percé, is a narrow butte jutting out into the Pacific. On the rock, which you can visit by catamaran, are large numbers of nesting birds including gannets, cormorants, puffins and razorbills. If you are lucky you may even spot a whale in these frigid waters.

South of Perce are many scenic beaches including Cap-aux-Os, Penouille, Haldimand, Coin-du-Banc, Cap-d'Espoir, Petit-Pabos, Pabos Mills and Newport, where you can beachcomb, collecting shells and sea glass, and enjoy the lulling sound of the crashing waves.

Also of interest is the UNESCO World Heritage Site of the Listuguj Indian Reserve, Miguasha Park near the Bay of Chaleur, the most temperate area on the peninsula.

**WHAT IS IT**
Five different regions –
The Coast, Upper Gaspe, Land's End, Bay of Chaleur and The Valley, each with its own charms and activities to experience.

**WHERE IS IT**
On the eastern tip of the province of Quebec, north of New Brunswick, surrounded by the St Lawrence estuary and gulf.

**HOW DO I GET THERE**
The Gaspe Peninsula is 560 km (348 mi) from Montreal and 340 km (211 mi) from Quebec City. Road and rail services are available from both.

**ALSO KNOWN AS**
'Gaspesie', in its native French.

*Forillon national Park in Quebec.*

*Snow Palace during the Winter Carnival.*

# Quebec City Winter Carnival

In the winter wonderland that is the annual Quebec City Winter Carnival, everyone in the city flocks into the streets to celebrate the bitter cold while the rest of the population, if they are not skiing, are wishing it to end.

This is the most celebrated global winter event, and the largest carnival in the world after Rio de Janeiro, and New Orleans' Mardi Gras. Although the French settlers had long got together with family and friends at this time of year to cheer themselves up before Lent, the first organized winter carnival here was in 1894. Further carnivals took place intermittently until 1955 when they were made an annual institution, taking place every year from late January to mid-February.

Old Quebec is the only North American urban site on UNESCO's World Heritage List, recognized for its cultural and historical significance.

The symbol of the carnival is Bonhomme, a talking, dancing snowman, who entertains the crowds at many of the events. His shining Ice Palace is the backdrop to the firework spectaculars that mark the opening and closing ceremonies of the carnival, as well as laser shows.

Sporting competitions include the International Canoe Race, in which teams have paddle, drag and push their canoes over the St Lawrence River from Quebec City to Levis. In this battle between man and nature, the teams struggle against ice floes, treacherous currents and freezing water. Another must-see spectactor-sport is the Provincial Dogsled Racing Championship, in which the dog teams race around the cobbled, icy streets, sliding into snow banks to the roar of the jubilant crowds. There are also several other races on the ice, dog agility competitions on the snow and a soapbox derby.

A variety of activities is available for every age range, from the snow board park, snow 'rafting', a multitude of fabulous parades and horse-drawn sleigh rides and Bonhomme's Ball. You can visit a traditional Aboriginal igloo village, and stay in one overnight if you wish. In the International Snow Sculpture Event artisans from around the world create dazzling examples of enormous ice art.

The Quebec Winter Carnival is a bright, delicious treat for the senses in an otherwise cold and dark season.

**WHAT IS IT**
The largest winter carnival in the World.
**WHERE IS IT**
The stunning city of Quebec.
**WHAT IS THERE TO DO**
Revel in the cobbled streets enjoying live music, parades, fire works, jugglers, dog sled races and other delights.
**DON'T MISS**
Guaranteed to warm your chilly bones, 'caribou' is a potent but tasty concoction of red wine, white rum and maple syrup.
**WORTH A SPLURGE**
Get into the spirit and rent an igloo, instead of a hotel room for a night.

# The Laurentians

The village of Mont-Tremblant, now merged with the village of Saint-Jovite, is a spectacular, all-season paradise in the heart of the Laurentian Mountains, is a famous scenic European-style resort just north of Montreal.

The area was colonized in the late nineteenth century by Father Antoine Labelle, in reaction to the threat of Protestant expansion. He chose the Laurentian Mountains for their rich, fertile soil, access to waterways, and their potential contact with Quebec. These initial pioneers of the area fought poverty and struggled in the undeveloped landscape. Eventually, through the father's generosity and vision, they thrived in this lush, majestic scenery.

Father Labelle sensed that tourism would provide a key resource for the region and arduously petitioned for the installation of the Montreal – Saint-Jérôme railway line, which was completed in 1892, enabling the development and growth of the settlement.

In 1938, Joseph Bondurant Ryan, a wealthy American from Philadelphia came north to prospect for gold. He was immediately taken with the pristine beauty of the 'mountain of the spirits'. He scaled it, and upon seeing the breathtaking view of the snow-blanketed landscape, vowed to transform the wilderness into a world-class alpine village. In February 1939, his dream was realized, when the Mont-Tremblant Lodge, its architecture reminiscent of Old Quebec, was opened for business and in 1991, the Swiss-style pedestrian village was created.

The beauty of the landscape has been luring visitors since the Amerindians, although rather than hunting and gathering food, the hordes now come to ski, hike, fish, bike, golf, raft or simply enjoy a respite from the nearby urban chaos. Maintaining the beauty of the area remains a priority with the people who live here.

In the autumn, the Laurentians put on a brilliant display of colourful autumn foliage. The annual Tremblant 'Symphony of Colours' festival allows visitors to enjoy the spectacular natural canvas from a gondola. This sight is enough to make you understand why Jo Ryan risked everything to live his dream in this majestic enclave.

**WHAT ARE THEY**
Mountains of awe-inspiring beauty dotted with the charming European-style villages of Mont-Tremblant and Saint-Jovite.
**WHERE ARE THEY**
145 km (90 mi) north of Montreal.
**ALSO KNOWN AS**
Little Switzerland.
**WHAT IS THERE TO DO THERE**
Every imaginable outdoor activity throughout the year is available here, or you can just sit back and enjoy the spectacular scenery.

*Autumn colours at Lac Monroe.*

# Montreal

**WHAT IS IT**
Quebec province's largest city.
**WHEN TO GO**
Montreal's climate varies a great deal throughout the year, from a chilly 13 to –5 °C (10–25 °F) in January to a pleasant if humid 18–27 °C (65–80 °F) in July.
**HOW DO I GET THERE**
Pierre Elliot Trudeau International Airport is 16 km (10 mi) west of the city.
**WHAT IS THERE TO DO**
A veritable feast for the senses, whether enjoying the urban sights and sounds above ground, or in the underground city.
**CULTURAL ATTRACTION**
The Summer International Jazz Festival is a must for jazz lovers.

*Altar of the basilica of Notre-Dame, Montreal.*

Montreal, Quebec's largest city, offers an exciting mix of French and English history and culture dating back to European settlement in 1642. More than half of the population is French and all residents are bilingual, adding a European charm to this vibrant, cosmopolitan hub.

Whether sipping a cappuccino at an outdoor café in Little Italy, gambling at the massive Casino de Montreal complex or exploring historic Old Montreal, you will find the energy of this urban playground contagious. The international flavour of the city pervades all aspects of daily life, from the award-winning cuisine to the jazz festival and music scene, large gay community, fashionable shops and edgy arts scene.

Montreal is divided into neighbourhoods, each representing a unique and lively part of this fabulous, tourist-friendly city. A wide range of museums, including the fantastic Museum of Fine Arts in the downtown area. This area was formerly known as 'the Golden Square Mile', because of the large, luxurious houses built by the wealthy Scottish and English industrialists who helped shape the city's political and social life. It is now also home to some spectacular modern architecture.

Veux-Montreal is the oldest part of the city, filled with Parisian-style outdoor cafés, artists, street performers and florist stands. St Denis is a convivial area dense with cafés, bistros, quirky boutiques and art

galleries. It has been compared to St Germain des Pres in Paris, for this is the heart of French Montreal.

Parc du Mont-Royal, Royal Mountain, is named after the single giant peak, more a large hill than a mountain, which affords stunning 360-degree views of the city, surrounded by the vast St Lawrence River. Frederick Law Olmsted, the famed American landscape artist who also created Central Park in New York, designed the stunning park which contains skating ponds, hiking trails, cross-country skiing paths and many spots for the locals to just sit and enjoy the flora and fauna of what they affectionately call 'the mountain'.

The Underground City, or la ville souterraine, is a climate-controlled city, built below street level, beneath the major downtown building developments. Although some buildings in this area are partially above ground, the majority of structures remain underground, including more than 1,600 shops, 40 banks, 200 restaurants, 30 cinemas and 10 Metro stations connecting the vast area, which is a welcome respite against the freezing Montreal winters.

# Historic Quebec

The first significant settlement in Canada, the French-inspired historic district of Quebec is a UNESCO World Heritage Site. Slate-roofed granite houses surround the fabulous, romantic Château Frontenac, with sweeping views of the scenic St Lawrence River below.

Vieux-Quebec, the old walled city, comprises two areas, Basse-Ville and Haute-Ville. Both are almost entirely French-speaking, and very proud of their French culture. Basse-Ville, the original colony, located at the foot of Cap Diamant, is a burgeoning area of cafés and boutiques, once the home to merchants, traders and boatmen. Haute-Ville, fortified by walls and connected to Basse-Ville by funicular, is particularly European in architecture and style. Pavement cafés, horse-drawn carriages and cobbled streets prevail here.

*Chateau Frontenac Hotel towers over Quebec's Old Town.*

As you wander through the gas-lit lanes of compact Haute-Ville, you may come across an ancient convent and museum, and the nearly hidden, partially star-shaped Citadelle – the largest group of fortified buildings in North America, despite no shot having been fired here. Dufferin promenade at the height of the city affords majestic river and mountain views.

The Basilique Notre-Dame is also worth a visit. Its interior, rebuilt after a fire in 1922, is neo-Baroque in style and features paintings and treasures from the French regime, its original exterior, built in 1647, was largely reconstructed in 1771.

The majestic Château Frontenac, on Cap Diamant, is the city's iconic landmark. A large-scale model of a Loire valley château, it can be seen from nearly every quarter of the city.

If you visit this beautiful city in summer, take advantage of the free concerts given at the stunning Parc des Champs-de-Bataille. This 108 ha (270 acre) park has more than 5,000 trees, grassy mounds, monuments and fountains, as well as the fantastic art museum, the Musée du Quebec. The park is also home to the Plains of Abraham, where in 1759, General Wolfe and the Marquis de Montcalm fought in the battle that ended French rule in North America.

A short walk down the Breakneck Stairs is Basse-Ville's Rue Sous-le-Fort. From here you can head to the picturesque Place Royale, the heart of seventeenth-century industry and commerce. While you are here, a visit to the Musée de la Civilisation is a must.

**WHAT IS IT**
Canada's first settlement, it is a lively, scenic metropolis.
**WHY SHOULD I GO THERE**
Art, culture, history, fine dining.
**ALSO KNOWN AS**
'Vieux-Quebec'.
**WORTH A SPLURGE**
Treat yourself to a night in the magical Château Frontenac, or at the very least to drink at one of its bars overlooking Terrasse Dufferin.

# Niagara Falls

Niagara Falls was formed when melting glaciers created the five Great Lakes, one of which, Lake Erie, ran downhill towards another, Lake Ontario. The rushing waters carved out a river during their descent, passing the Niagara escarpment, causing the water to back up into the river. The path left from this phenomenon, created roughly 12,000 years ago, is known as the Niagara Gorge. Its current rate of wear is roughly 30 cm (12 in) a year.

The falls at Niagara consist of the cataract of Niagara Falls on the New York side of the bridge, and the Horseshoe, or Canadian Falls across the border. The crescent-shaped Canadian Falls are 54 m (177 ft) high and carry nine times more water than their American counterpart, flowing at roughly 56.3 kph (35 mph). The combination of height and water flow is what makes the falls so incredibly beautiful and dramatic. Every minute the Canadian Falls spew 168,000 cubic m (6,000,000 cubic ft) of water over their lip.

Niagara Falls, also known as the 'Honeymoon Capital of the World' or 'onguiaahra' meaning 'a thundering noise', has long been a source of wonder and entertainment for large crowds of tourists. It is a natural landmark that has inspired breathtaking feats of courage, created legends and myths and taken numerous lives.

Blondin, a tightrope walker performed numerous crossings of the gorge in Niagara Falls during the mid-19th century, including while blindfolded, while carrying a cooking stove as he prepared an omelette on the high wire and, amazingly, while carrying his 67-kg (10½-stone) manager Harry Colcord on his back!

For the more sane among us, the best way to experience the spectacular grandeur of the falls is by boat. The *Maid of the Mist* takes intrepid tourists right to the base of Horseshoe falls for a simply breathtaking (and wet!) view of the crashing waters.

**LITERARY TRIVIA**
*Uncle Tom's Cabin,* a famous novel by Harriet Beecher Stowe was partly inspired by the writer's trip to Niagara Falls and her subsequent interest in Reverend Josiah Henson who smuggled runaway slaves across the Niagara River into Canada.

*A tourist boat edges closer for a wetter view.*

# Banff National Park

Designated Canada's first national park in 1885, Banff's jagged majestic outlines set against vast blue skies epitomise the Canadian Rocky Mountains. Declared a UNESCO World Heritage Site for its world renowned rugged, scenic splendour, the park attracts more than four million guests from around the world every year.

Banff National Park encompasses 6,641 sq km (2,564 sq mi) of grassy meadows, lush fir, pine, aspen and spruce forests as well as craggy, lichen-covered limestone and shale mountains dating as far back as 45–120 million years.

Apart from its scenery, Banff is famous for its wildlife. The 54 mammal species here include moose, elk, mountain goats, bighorn sheep, white-tailed and mule deer, cougars, black and grizzly bears and Alberta's southernmost herd of the endangered woodland caribou.

There is so much to see and do here – hiking, fantastic birdwatching, trout-fishing, boating, exploring Castleguard (Canada's longest cave system) and driving on the scenic Icefields Parkway. The park is also home to seven national historic sites – Skoki Lodge, Abbot Pass Hut, Howse Pass, Cave and Basin, Banff Park Museum, Fairmont Banff Springs Hotel and the Cosmic Ray Observatory on Sanson Peak.

Particularly wonderful is the sensation of being surrounded by 10 snow-clad peaks towering more than 3,030 m (10,000 ft) above you, as you paddle a canoe through the turquoise waters of Moraine Lake.

*Moraine Lake.*

# Churchill

The area around Churchill, Manitoba has many sights to offer, but it is best known for its status as the 'Polar Bear Capital of the World'. Polar bears have been here since 1771 when the town was founded. From October to early December, these magnificent creatures gather where the Churchill River runs into Hudson's Bay, waiting until the bay freezes over to resume seal-hunting.

*Mother and cub venture out in the 'Polar Bear Capital of the World'.*

At this time, the population of Churchill swells from 900 permanent residents to more than 10,000 visitors, and upwards of 1,200 polar bears. It is not unusual to see 20 polar bears in one day, particularly since some of the more curious ones actually wander into town!

Polar bears are the largest land carnivores in the world, an average adult male weighing between 350 kg (775 lb) and over 680kg (1,500 lb), reaching maximum size by the age of 10. An average adult female is roughly half the size of a male, weighing anywhere from 200–300 kg (450–650 lb) and reaching maximum size by the age of five. Female bears give birth to their cubs about two months after they enter their dens. Newborns are 30–35 cm (12–14 in) long and weigh little over 0.5 kg (1 lb). The Wapusk National Park was established to protect one of the largest polar bear maternity denning sites in the world.

Found throughout the Arctic tundra, the bears are largely marine animals, preferring to remain on the sea ice where they hunt their main prey of seals. In most of the Arctic, polar bears are able to hunt on the ice year-round, but in areas where the ice melts in the summer, such as the south-western Hudson Bay, they are forced ashore until the autumn when temperatures drop enough for the ice to freeze. If you cannot make it during this time, or you do not want to watch polar bears outside of their natural setting, you can always take a 'bear buggie' trip out onto the tundra where you can safely watch and photograph the polar bears at one of the denning sites.

The town of Churchill itself is known for its exportation of grain. While you are there, you can watch some of the 25 million bushels of wheat and barley produced here being loaded onto ships, the grain elevators looming in the distance.

The Prince of Wales Fort, originally constructed in 1730 by the Hudson Bay Company but surrendered to the French in 1782 before it could be completed, is worth a visit. There are excellent opportunities to view Beluga whales from June to November. If you do not have any luck here, try Cape Merry, at the mouth of the Churchill River, which is also a prime vantage point to witness these awesome creatures.

**WHAT IS IT**
The world's polar bear capital.
**WHERE IS IT**
Churchill's remote Wapusk National Park is in Manitoba, 1,000 km (620 mi) north of Winnipeg.
**WHEN SHOULD I VISIT**
The Northern Manitoba Trappers' Festival in February hosts the world championship dog sled races, a moose-calling contest, ice fishing and beer fests, but October to early December is when you will see polar bears.

*A northern right whale comes up for air.*

# Bay of Fundy

The Bay of Fundy lies to the south-east of Canada, off New Brunswick and Nova Scotia, and touches on the US state of Maine. It is best known for its huge tidal range. Twice a day, 100 billion tonnes of water ebb and flow, creating the highest tides in the world. At the outer end of the bay, along the south-west shoreline of Novia Scotia, the tides are fairly normal at 3.5 m (11ft) or so, but they steadily increase in height as the waters travel the 280 km (174 mi) to the head of the bay, where, in the narrow Minas Basin, the height of the tide can reach over 16 m (53 ft). They achieve such heights because of the bay's unique geology, which gets progressively narrow and shallow. Not only are the tides high, in some places, such as the Western Passage of Passamaquoddy Bay, there are very fast-flowing currents, while underwater mountains and trenches create additional turbulence.

The strength of the tides has differentially eroded the red sandstone and volcanic rock surrounding the water, resulting in the creation of dramatic cliffs, caves and sandstone sea stacks, the most famous of which are the Flower Pot Rocks on Hopewell Cape. The erosion has not only formed breathtaking shapes, it has also revealed fossils from when the sandstones were created some 300 million years or more ago as well as others from about 200 million years ago when the volcanic rocks were formed. There is also a vast saltmarsh and extensive mudflats are exposed at low tide.

The tide's effects are also felt in the rivers that flow into the bay. For example, at low tide, the waters of the St John River produce wild rapids in St John Harbour when they drop into the bay, but at high tide the ocean waters overwhelm the river current, creating a tidal bore, which makes for an amazing experience in a boat. Similar tidal surges also occur in narrow parts of the bay proper.

Another result of the tides that sweep here is 'Old Sow', the second largest whirlpool in the world after Norway's maelstrom, and the largest in the western hemisphere. It lies in the Western Passage of Passamaquoddy Bay, towards the mouth of the Bay of Fundy and can be seen from the New Brunswick shore. It gets its name because of the sounds that the churning waters produce. About three hours before high tide, the incoming current swirling around islands in the bay and over, round and into underwater geological formations forms a wide area of churning, turbulent water anything up to 76 m (250 ft) wide. Most often the turbulence consists of small troughs, spouts and gyres but if a spring tide (strong tides just after a full or new moon) coincides with a tidal surge or high winds, the currents may be as fast as 11 kph (6.9 mph) and a single large funnel or many intense ones, may form.

The bay is also famous for its wildlife, ranging from the small to the extremely large, yet again the result of the tidal currents, which stir up nutrients from the sea bed and provide the basis for a healthy food chain, from the lobsters and scallops that are important for the bay's economy, to puffins, common terns and millions of migrating waders to the krill and fish on which the area's most famous visitors, the whales and dolphins, feed. Whales sighted regularly include finback, minke, sei and northern right, while orcas, humpback and blue whales visit occasionally. Seals, porpoises and bottlenose, saddle-back, striped and atlantic white-sided dolphins are known to be here, as are basking and mako sharks. Even a great white shark has been caught!

The most important of the cetaceans are the northern right whales because they are the most endangered whale in the world, with perhaps only 300 remaining. Each summer, many of them come to the Bay of Fundy to mate and feed before returning to their wintering grounds off of the south-eastern coast of the US. This slow, blubber-rich giant, named by hunters who considered it the 'right whale to hunt', was once plentiful in the Atlantic Ocean, but its numbers are so low that it has been internationally protected since 1935. They are spectacularly graceful creatures, and seeing them swimming effortlessly at the surface will make any whalewatching trip here worthwhile.

**WHERE IS IT**
Located between New Brunswick and Nova Scotia

**NATURAL PHENOMENA**
It is home to spectacular whirlpools, the largest in the western hemisphere and second largest in the world, and the famous 16-m (53-ft) tides, the largest in the world.

**WHAT IS THERE TO DO**
Look at the amazing natural phenomena of the tides and the whirlpools in a breathtaking landscape of cliffs, sandstone statues, mud flats and saltmarsh, while you see a variety of mammal species.

**ECOLOGICAL IMPORTANCE**
The Bay of Fundy serves as the summer home to many northern right whales – the most endangered whale in the world.

**MAMMAL TRIVIA**
The right whale gets its name because, according to hunters, it was the 'right whale to hunt'.

**NATURAL TRIVIA**
The famous whirlpool, 'Old Sow', is called after the sounds that emanate from the churning waters.

# The Great Lakes

**WHAT ARE THEY**
The largest group of freshwater lakes on earth.
**ALSO KNOWN AS**
'Inland Seas' because there are parts where no land is visible because of the curvature of the Earth and the immense size of the lakes.
**WHERE ARE THEY**
On the United States/Canadian border.
**WHY ARE THEY IMPORTANT**
They account for 20 per cent of the world's freshwater resources, and the scenery is stunning.
**HISTORICAL IMPORTANCE**
The Great Lakes allowed the transport of people and resources, opening up the entire continent for commerce.
**WHAT SHOULD I KNOW**
The mosquitoes are fierce, so bring repellent.

The five Great Lakes of North America make up the largest group of freshwater lakes on the Earth and they are also known for their contribution to the Earth's ecology and their diversity and beauty. Lying on or near the Canadian/US border, the Great Lakes consist of Lake Superior, Lake Michigan, Lake Huron, Lake Erie and Lake Ontario.

They formed at the end of the last ice age, roughly 10,000 years ago when the Laurentide ice sheet retreated and the meltwater filled the valley that had been gouged out by glaciers. As the glaciers melted and began receding, their leading edges left behind high ridges, some of which can be seen today in the cliffs of Door County, Wisconsin, and the Bruce Peninsula in Ontario, as well as at Niagara Falls.

The five lakes contain more than 20 per cent of the world's entire freshwater supply – 22, 812 cu km (5,473 cu mi). All five of the lakes are among the world's 18 largest lakes by area and volume. The combined surface area of the lakes is 151,681 sq km (94,250 sq mi) – larger than England, Scotland and Wales together.

Lake Superior is the largest and deepest of the Great Lakes – larger in fact, than the entire Czech Republic. Lake Michigan is the second largest lake in volume, while the shallower Lake Huron is the second largest in area. Lake Erie, the shallowest, is the smallest in volume while Lake Ontario is the smallest in area. It is also at a much lower altitude than the other lakes.

The primary outlet of the five interconnected lakes is the Saint Lawrence River, eventually flowing through Quebec, past the Gaspé Peninsula and into the northern Atlantic Ocean. In the days before mass rail freight this link allowed the development of the large industrial cities on and near the lakes' shores. Now, tourism is important to the economy on both sides of the border, as is commercial fishing.

Because of their size, the lakes actually have an effect on the region's climate, which is known as the lake effect. In summer, their waters absorb heat and keep the surrounding areas cool, then during autumn as they slowly lose heat, they stave off the cold of winter. However, it is during winter that their most spectacular effect is seen – lake effect snow. Dry continental air masses, which usually come from the west, absorb moisture from the lakes. As soon as they reach colder air over the land to the east, they dump the snow, sometimes to depths of several feet. This can produce the strange effect of snow falling from an apparently clear sky.

There are several national parks on the shores of the lakes and a wide range of activities is available. As well as water-based activities such as yachting, canoeing and kayaking, fishing and scuba diving, the surrounding land is great for biking, birding, hiking and camping. The birdlife that may be found in the unpopulated areas includes bald eagles and peregrines, while the remote wilderness areas contain black bears, grey wolves, elk and the highly endangered Canada lynx.

More than 33 million people inhabit this drainage basin, that is over one-tenth of the population of the United States and a quarter of the population of Canada. Strenuous efforts are being made to clean up the effects of their waste, as well as that of pollution from industries around the lakes, in order to prevent any further damage to this beautiful wilderness.

*The Great Lakes as seen from space.*

# Los Cabos

The two towns at the tip of the rugged Baja Peninsula are commonly referred to together as Los Cabos, although they could not be more different. San José del Cabo and Cabo San Lucas are separated not just by 30 km (20 mi), but also by their attitudes and personalities. Cabo San Lucas focuses mostly on sports and fiestas, whereas San José del Cabo remains a tranquil small Mexican town.

This serene colonial town was the only one here for many decades and supported Indian communities before Spanish colonization in 1730 when a Jesuit mission was established.

San José del Cabo offers the best of traditional Mexico: graceful, tree-lined pavements, small cafés, smiling locals and an unhurried pace of life. It has a beautiful, fairytale town hall in its centre with murals of old Baja decorating its inner corridors and its two-storey courtyard shaded by a large Mexican laurel. As you stroll through the streets you can enjoy art exhibitions and live concerts by traditional Mexican bands in the tiled plaza. There are plastered and columned old colonial buildings with their paseos, or inner courtyards, full of shops.

Since its regentrification in the past decade, Cabo San Lucas has become host to some of the best resorts in the world. The beaches here are magnificent, coloured a variety of pinks, yellows and oranges as the sun sets. It is also a place where nature lovers can watch turtles lay their eggs, hike in the estuary, birdwatch or just collect shells on the seafront. This gorgeous landscape, a mix of unspoiled desert, white sandy beaches and dramatic rock outcroppings, including the distinctive 'El Arco' at the tip of Land's End – the most famous geographic landmark of the area where the Pacific Ocean meets the Sea of Cortez – will blow you away.

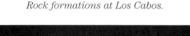

*Rock formations at Los Cabos.*

Between San José del Cabo and Cabo San Lucas there are more than 20 beaches to explore including Playa Palmilla; Santa Maria Bay, with its protected cove and marine sanctuary; Playa Chileno, known for its fine swimming and snorkelling; and Playa del Amor, accessible only from the sea near 'El Arco'. Whether you are looking for seclusion or nightlife, the two towns of Los Cabos have something to appeal to every visitor.

# Puerto Angel

Puerto Angel, a rural fishing village on the Pacific coast of Oaxaca, lies in a picturesque bay surrounded by craggy peaks and sandy beaches between Puerto Escondido and Bahias de Huatulco.

In the ninteenth century this port town experienced a boom, shipping coffee and wood from its harbour. The boom ended with the construction of the railway between Oaxaca and Salina Cruz and these days the pier is solely used by local fishermen, bringing in their catches of fresh tuna, ocean perch, shark, swordfish, lobsters, oysters and octopus.

The two beaches in the area, Playa Principal and Play del Panteon, are in the centre of the village. The main beach, Playa Principal, is largely used by fishing boats and has strong waves, whereas Playa del Panteon is surrounded by rocks that host some interesting marine life.

This sleepy town with its dusty, largely unpaved roads is not for the adventurous, rather one seeking solitude in a peaceful environment. A good starting point for day trips to various ruins, Puerto Angel is a wonderful place to put up your feet and breathe in the salty air and listen to the sounds of the waves lapping on the shoreline. Nearby sights include the lagoon of Ventanilla where birds and crocodiles are in abundance, the Los Reyes waterfall and the tropical spring-fed El Paraiso. The surrounding caves can be accessed for diving and snorkelling trips as well.

The town of Playa Zipolite, 6.4 km (4 mi) west of Puerto Angel, is a popular surfing destination with a long beach and excellent waves. This makes a nice day trip or a pretty area to enjoy a sunset cocktail. West of Zipolite is Playa Mazunte where turtles come to lay their eggs.

The other beach worth mentioning is known as Playa La Tijera, or the Scissors, after its scissor-like rock formations that jut out into the water. This small bay is a nice spot for swimming, snorkelling and scuba diving.

This beautiful area is ideal for a relaxing holiday taking in the best that this part of Mexico has to offer.

*The idyllic fishing village of Puerto Angel.*

**WHAT IS IT**
An idyllic rural Mexican fishing village.
**WHERE IS IT**
The Pacific Coast of Oaxaca
**WHAT IS THERE TO DO**
Visit ancient ruins, look at the wildlife, dive, snorkel and laze on the beach.
**WHEN SHOULD I GO:**
Autumn and winter are the best times to visit.

# Oaxaca

*The church of Santo Domingo.*

Most people visit Oaxaca for its white sandy beaches with clear aquamarine waters that form an area of spectacular natural beauty. Some of the most attractive beaches are Zicatela, which is ideal for surfing; Escobilla, a turtle beach; Zipolite, a nudist beach; and Puerto Angel and Puerto Escondido, two bays with a truly Oaxacan environment.

Oaxaca and Chiapas have larger Indian populations than other states in Mexico and throughout the centuries, their practices, beliefs, traditions, folklore and customs have shaped the local culture, making these two states fascinating places to visit. The central highlands of Oaxaca, a stunning mountainous area dotted with lush valleys and checquered cornfields, has a large population of Zapotec and Mixtec Indians. Famous for handicrafts and corn, the area is at its prettiest during the rainy season when the corn is green on the stalks.

The city of Oaxaca itself is a lovely place with colonial architecture and numerous plazas, courtyards and narrow streets. High above the city on a mountaintop lies the magnificent ceremonial centre of Monte Alban. An impressive collection of buildings, ball courts and plazas, its design varies from the Mayan ruins most commonly visited in the eastern part of the country.

A day trip to Hierve el Agua, two hours from the city, is highly recommended. Here you can relax in the warm waters of the mineral springs at the base of a 50-m (160-ft) waterfall.

**WHAT IS IT**
A stunning region of beaches and traditional Mexican villages.
**WHERE IS IT**
Along the Mexican Pacific between the districts of Jamiltepec, Pochutla and Juchitan.
**WHAT IS THERE TO DO**
Visit during one of the spectacular festivals such as Dia de los Muertos (Day of the Dead) in early November or the Guelaguetza festival in July.
**WHEN SHOULD I GO**
June to March is when the city is considered the most enjoyable, but the tourist season runs from late July to spring.
**WHAT SHOULD I BUY**
Chocolate and Mezcal.

# Pyramid of Kukulcán

The famed pyramids and temples of Chichén Itzá are the Yucatán Peninsula's best-known ancient monuments. Walking among these stone platforms, pyramids and ball courts helps you to better understand and appreciate this ancient advanced civilization.

Led by Quetzalcoatl (who the Mayans called Kukulcán), the Toltec came here from their capital, Tula, in north-central Mexico in roughly 987 AD. Along with Putún Maya coastal traders, they built a magnificent metropolis, Chichén Itzá, constructing it using Puuc Maya methods and embellishing it with Toltec motifs including the feathered serpent, warriors, eagles and jaguars.

Chichén Itzá became the most powerful place in the Yucatán peninsula, a centre of pilgrimage and worship of the Mesoamerican Feathered Serpent deity, who had the same name as their leader, Quetzalcoatl.

Overgrown with jungle and slowly decaying, the massive structures of Chichén Itzá were first seriously explored by archaeologists in the 1920s. Many of the ancient structures have been restored, including the temple known as El Castillo, or the Pyramid of Kukulcán.

**WHAT IS IT**
The most impressive ruin of Chichén Itzá, the best known of Yucatan's ancient monuments.

**WHERE IS IT**
179km (112 mi) west of Cancún; 120km (75 mi) east of Mérida

**WHAT IS THERE TO SEE**
King Kukulkan's jaguar throne inside the interior temple of the Pyramid of Kukulcán.

**WHY IS IT IMPORTANT**
They are some of the largest, most grand and best restored monuments of this age.

# Monasteries of Popocatepetl

**WHAT IS IT**
An active volcano and the second highest peak in Mexico.
**WHERE IS IT**
70 km (43.5 mi) south-east of Mexico City.
**WHAT IS THERE TO SEE**
The 14 monasteries on the slopes of the volcano.
**ALSO KNOWN AS**
El Popo or Don Goyo.

Popocatepetl, an active volcano and the second highest peak in Mexico, is host to 14 monasteries, standing on its slopes. The monasteries are well-preserved examples of the architectural style adopted by the first missionaries – Franciscans, Dominicans and Augustinians – who converted the indigenous populations to Christianity in the early sixteenth century after the Spanish conquest of Mexico.

The first monastery, at Huejotzingo at the foot of the volcano, was dedicated to the Archangel Michael. Perched on an ancient mound in the bustling town centre, its walled courtyard is secluded from the noise of the outside streets. It is chiefly famous for its extraordinary sixteenth-century art and architecture including the elaborately carved corner chapels of the churchyard, medieval Moorish arches emblazoned with Franciscan escutcheons and stunning murals lining the walls of the church and cloister.

The north doorway, the most complex of the many entries to the church, reflects the Franciscan style. In addition to commemorating St Francis, the doorway served as the main processional entry to the church, also known as the 'Door of Jublilee', as it signified the friars' entrance to the New Jerusalem.

The late sixteenth-century altarpiece, known as the Pereyns

*The altarpiece in the church of St. Francis Xavier in Tepotzotlan.*

Retablo after its creator, the Flemish artist Simon Pereyns, rises in four tiers to the high vault of the sanctuary. Its seven gilded bays frame a series of paintings expressing scenes from the life of Christ, while its niches house expertly carved statues of saints, apostles and other church luminaries, which are undoubtedly the finest and best-preserved work uncovered here.

The other 13 churches host a great number of treasured antiquities and religious artefacts, and all are recognized by UNESCO as World Heritage Sites.

# Teotihuacán

*Temple of the Moon.*

The ruins of Teotihuacán are among the most important in the world. The fate of its civilization remains unclear, but we do know that this was once the centre of an advanced society with a population of more than 200,000. Occupation began about.500 BC, but it was only after 100 BC that building of the Pyramid of the Sun began. The magnificent pyramids and palaces once covered 31 sq km (12 sq mi) but were abandoned in about 700 AD and little is known about the people.

Archaeologists discovered that the Teotihuacán followed a cult of the planet Venus, determining wars and sacrifices based on rituals timed with its appearance as the morning or evening star. Numerous tombs with human remains, jewellery, pottery and items from daily life have been uncovered near the foundations of the buildings.

Today, the rough stone structures of three pyramids, sacrificial altars and some grand houses, all of which were once covered in stucco and painted with brilliant crimson frescoes, remain.

The front wall of the Pyramid of the Sun is exactly perpendicular to the point on the horizon where the sun sets at the equinoxes and the rest of the buildings were built at right angles to it. The main axis, Calzada de los Muertos (Avenue of the Dead) runs north–south with the Pyramid of the Moon to the north and the Ciudadela (Citadel) at the south. Only 1 km (0.6 mi) has been uncovered and restored.

Archaeologists tunnelling inside the Pyramid of Quetzalcoatl found evidence of ceremonial burials. Drawings of how the building once looked show that every level was covered with feathered serpents.

As you stroll north along the Avenue of the Dead to the Pyramid of the Moon, look on the right for a crumbling wall sheltered by a modern corrugated roof. The wall still bears a painting of a jaguar from which you may be able to imagine how amazing this site once was.

The Pyramid of the Sun, east of the Avenue of the Dead, is the third-largest pyramid in the world, an imposing 221 m (730 ft) per side at its base and 64 m (210 ft) high. Built on top of an already existing structure, it was completed around 300 AD, and the views from its apex are among the most extraordinary in Mexico.

The Pyramid of the Moon is surrounded by small temples and the Palace of Quetzalpapalotl, with its striking butterfly paintings, and its straight perspective down the Avenue of the Dead is breathtaking.

**WHAT IS IT**
The largest known pre-Columbian city in the Americas.
**WHERE IS IT**
40 km (25 mi) north-east of Mexico City.
**WHAT IS THERE TO SEE**
Three ancient pyramids.
**WHAT IS THERE TO DO**
Explore the ancient ruins
**WHAT SHOULD I KNOW**
There will be a lot of walking, especially if you choose to climb the pyramids, at an alititude over 2,120 m (7,000 ft) so take it slowly, bring sunscreen and water.
**ALSO KNOWN AS**
'The place where gods were born' or 'The place of the precious sacrifice'

157

*Mount Rushmore Memorial.*

# Mount Rushmore

Carved into the south-east face of a mountain in South Dakota, at a height of 1,737 m (5,700 ft) above sea level, are the faces of presidents George Washington, Thomas Jefferson, Theodore Roosevelt and Abraham Lincoln. Looking down from its position high above the Black Hills, this majestic memorial to American history is spectacular to behold.

It was conceived by Doane Robinson in 1923 as a way to attract more people to the Black Hills of South Dakota and lies in the former Harney National Forest Preserve.

A sculptor, Gutzon Borglum, was contracted to undertake the job of carving the Needles area into a tall granite figure, but instead chose Mount Rushmore for the work because it was the highest peak in the area and its south-eastern facing site meant it would receive sunlight for most of the day. He then selected the subjects of national focus that would be highlighted in his work – the four presidents mentioned above.

Borglum began work in 1927 by creating a plaster model from which measurements were taken. Dynamite was used to blast the rock until there was only a thin, 7.6–15-cm (3–6-in) layer of granite remaining. This final layer of granite was removed by a process called 'honeycombing', and then the final surface was smoothed.

George Washington's face, the first to be carved, was dedicated on 4 July 1934. President Franklin D. Roosevelt attended the dedication of Thomas Jefferson's in 1936. Abraham Lincoln's was dedicated on 17 September 1937, on the one hundred and fiftieth anniversary of the signing of the US Constitution. In 1939, Theodore Roosevelt's was dedicated. That year modern plumbing and night lighting were installed at the memorial.

Borglum continued working on the final details of the sculptures for a further two years. In 1941 he died suddenly and his son Lincoln took over on the project until funding ran out a few months later. The studio on Mount Rushmore was shut and the presidential faces were left as they were.

Mount Rushmore continues to be a reminder of these four important figures in American history, and the original goal of increasing traffic to the Black Hills has been met with resounding success.

**WHAT IS IT**
An enormous sculpture on the side of Mount Rushmore
**WHAT IS THERE TO SEE**
The faces of former presidents George Washington, Abraham Lincoln, Theodore Roosevelt and Thomas Jefferson.
**WHERE IS IT**
The Black Hills of South Dakota
**WHEN SHOULD I VISIT**
Visitor numbers peak at Mount Rushmore between June and August. The best times to visit are September–October or April–May.

# Custer State Park

Custer State Park in the Black Hills of South Dakota is home to a selection of historical monuments, spectacular parkland and abundant wildlife. Covering an area of roughly 29,000 ha (72,000 acres), the park boasts gently undulating meadows, rolling foothills, pine forests, large lakes and the giant, finger-like granite spires of the Needles.

The scenic drive on the Needles Highway (SD 87) highlights the towering rock formations, including the awe-inspiring 'Needles Eye', an impressive granite spire jutting 9–12 m (30–40 ft) into the air, with an 'eye' just 90–120 cm (3–4 ft) in width.

Do not be surprised if you encounter bison on your drive. A 1,500-strong herd – one of the largest in the world – roams freely throughout the park, and often stops traffic along the 29-km (18-mi) Wildlife Loop Road. Other wildlife here includes pronghorn antelope, mountain goats, bighorn sheep, deer, elk, wild turkeys and friendly donkeys (burros).

French Creek is where Custer's expedition first discovered gold in 1874. A major attractions is the Crazy Horse Memorial, known by locals as the 'Fifth Face' in the Black Hills. The carving of the legendary Lakota Chief Crazy Horse was dedicated in 1948, and work continues on what will be the world's largest sculpture 172 m (563 ft) high. The chief's face is complete and the carving of the horse's head is underway. When the sculpture is complete, Crazy Horse will sit pointing over his stallion's head to the sacred Black Hills.

Begun by the late sculptor Korczak Ziolkowski, and carried on by his family, the memorial is dedicated to all American Indians, 'as a symbol to the white man that the red man has great heroes too', according to Sioux Chief Henry Standing Bear.

Visitors driving past the site, 8 km (5 mi) north of Custer, often hear dynamite blasts, a signal that work on the mountain carving is progressing. At night, blasts are impressive events.

As well as watching the carving in progress and an audiovisual display about the work, visitors may stop at the Indian Museum of North America at Crazy Horse, which is home to one of the most extensive collections of American Indian artefacts in the country.

Favourite outdoor activities in the park include hiking the 2,207 m (7,242 ft) Harney Peak, mountain biking, horseback riding, rock climbing, fishing, enjoying chuckwagon suppers and taking jeep rides to see the bison.

**WHAT IS IT**
A National Park that is home to spectacular landscapes and historical monuments.
**WHERE IS IT**
Between Mount Rushmore and Wind Cave National Park.
**HOW DO I GET THERE**
The closest airport is in Rapid City, providing direct access to the Black Hills and Mount Rushmore. By road Interstate 90 is the most direct route.
**WHAT SHOULD I KNOW**
Do not feed the bison as they can be dangerous.
**WHEN SHOULD I GO**
May-October are the best months to visit, but beware, temperatures can drop drastically when the sun goes down.

*The Needles in South Dakota.*

# Badlands – South Dakota

**WHAT IS IT**
A desolate moonscape of saw-toothed spires, eroded buttes and ragged ridges.

**WHEN SHOULD I GO**
Spring and autumn are the best times to visit. Summers are extremely hot and winters extremely cold.

**WHERE IS IT**
South-west South Dakota.

**WHAT I SHOULD KNOW**
The park is open 365 days a year.

**HOW DO I GET THERE**
There are airports in Rapid City and Sioux Falls. There are various routes to drive into the park, including Hwy 240, 'Badlands Loop Road', which is a scenic drive.

**ALSO KNOWN AS**
'Mako sica' or 'land bad' or 'les mauvaises terres a traverser' or 'bad lands to cross'.

*Layered hoodoos of the Badlands.*

The Badlands National Park in south-west South Dakota is an eerie place of startlingly beautiful desolation. From the ragged ridges and saw-toothed spires, to the sharply eroded buttes and pinnacles and the wind-ravaged moonscape of the Sage Creek Wilderness Area, Badlands National Park is an unsettling yet awe-inspiring experience.

The Sioux Indians named this land '*mako sica*' or 'land bad' and early French-Canadian trappers labelled it '*les mauvaises terres a traverser*' or 'bad lands to cross' because of its inhospitable terrain, the result of deposition and partial erosion of sedimentary rocks.

The serrated ridges and deep canyons of the Badlands were formed about 500,000 years ago, when water began to cut through the rock layers, carving fantastic shapes in the flat floodplain. Ancient rocks, buried for millions of years, became exposed. Erosion averages around 2.5 cm (1 in) a year, so the buttes will be gone in 500,000 years.

The Badlands are one of the richest Oligocene fossil beds known. Fossils of 25–35 million-year-old three-toed horses, dog-sized camels, sabretooth tigers, giant pigs and other species have been found. Some 11,000 years of human history are here, too, including the sites of Sioux Ghost Dances (protests at government land-grabs) of 1890.

A walk through the Badlands visualising its human history and the geological processes that have taken place here is truly a must.

# Wounded Knee

Wounded Knee, South Dakota represents the last major clash between American Indians and white U.S. troops in North America.

On the morning of 29 December 1890, the Sioux chief Big Foot and 350 of his followers camped on the banks of Wounded Knee Creek, surrounded by US troops with orders to arrest him and disarm his warriors.

This tense moment had been building for years, as the once proud Sioux, a nomadic people, had found their way of life destroyed, as they were confined to reservations and dependent on Indian Agents for their existence, especially after the government reneged on a treaty in order to grab more of their land.

In a desperate attempt to return to the days of their glory, many sought salvation in a new mysticism called 'the Ghost Dance', or a version of it, preached by a Paiute shaman called Wovoka. Emissaries from the Sioux in South Dakota travelled to Nevada to listen to this self-proclaimed Messiah, who prophesied that the dead would soon join the living in a world where the Indians could return to their old way of living with plentiful game, fertile soil, no white men and a restored prairie.

The Sioux were encouraged to dance the Ghost Dance, wearing brightly coloured shirts emblazoned with images of eagles and bison. These 'Ghost Shirts' were believed to protect the Indians from the white men's bullets. During the autumn of 1890, the Ghost Dance spread through the Sioux villages of the Dakota reservations, revitalizing the Indians and bringing fear to the whites. A desperate Indian Agent at Pine Ridge contacted his superiors in Washington to warn that an uprising was on the horizon. The order went out to arrest Chief Sitting Bull at the Standing Rock Reservation. Sitting Bull was killed on 15 December and Chief Big Foot was next on the list.

When he heard of Sitting Bull's death, Big Foot led his people to the Pine Ridge Reservation to seek protection. The US army intercepted them on 28 December and brought them to the edge of the Wounded Knee to camp. The next morning the dying chief met the army officers, but a shot sounded nearby and within seconds the scene erupted as Indians and US troops exchanged fire.

Approximately 200 Sioux were killed that day, including Big Foot, as well as 25 US soldiers. Many others on both sides were wounded. The massacre at Wounded Knee effectively ended the Ghost Dance movement as well as the Indian Wars.

The site of the Wounded Knee Battleground includes the cemetery with the graves of those Indians who died that day.

*Wounded Knee massacre gravestone.*

**WHAT IS IT**
A battlefield in Wounded Knee, South Dakota.
**WHERE IS IT**
Pine Ridge Indian Reservation.
**WHY IS IT IMPORTANT**
This is the site of the last major clash between American Indians and US troops in North America.
**WHAT IS THERE TO SEE**
The battleground and cemetery for those killed in the fight.

*Autumn trees reflect their colours in a lake.*

# Autumn colours of New England

Every October, the leaves in New England burst into a spectacular symphony of vibrant colours before they fall to the ground as the trees become dormant for winter, and 'tree peeping' is a common pastime here during the autumn. Once you see the joyous explosion of colours bursting over the picturesque landscape, you will understand why this is the most popular season for visiting the area.

So why do leaves change colour in autumn? At this time of year the production of chlorophyll in leaves stops and so they lose their vibrant green colours revealing the underlying tones caused by the presence of other pigments, such as carotenoids which provide yellow, orange and brown colours and anthocyanins which give red and purple colours.

Autumn leaf colour is specific to the species of tree because of the different chemicals in the leaves. Oaks turn red, brown, or russet; hickories become golden bronze; dogwoods go purplish red; beech fade to light tan; red maple turn a brilliant scarlet; sugar maple go orange-red; black maple become glowing yellow; sourwood and black tupelo change to crimson and aspen, birch, and yellow poplar turn a golden yellow.

The range and intensity of autumn colours are greatly influenced by the weather and the brightest autumn colours are produced when dry, sunny days are followed by cool, dry nights.

Regardless of timing, if you are fortunate enough to see the stunning autumn colours that cover vast swathes of New England you will understand why there is even a foliage hot line offering hourly reports on the best places to go.

**WHAT IS IT**
Autumns in the north-eastern seaboard of America are known for their vibrant autumn leaf changes.
**WHERE IS IT**
From Maryland northwards up the east coast to Vermont.
**WHY SHOULD I VISIT**
It is the equivalent of nature showing off.
**WHEN SHOULD I VISIT**
Early October.
**WHAT SHOULD I KNOW**
The timing for the changing of the leaves is dependent on the weather.

# Museum of Modern Art

Founded in 1929 as an educational institution, the Museum of Modern Art, or MoMA, in New York City is dedicated to being the foremost museum of modern art in the world.

From an initial endowment of eight prints and a single drawing, the Museum of Modern Art's collection has grown to include more than 150,000 paintings, sculptures, drawings, prints, photographs, architectural models and drawings as well as design objects. In addition, MoMA owns some 22,000 films, videos and media works, as well as film stills, scripts, posters and historical documents. The museum's library contains 300,000 books, artists' sketchbooks and periodicals, and the archives hold approximately 762 m (2,500 ft) of historical documents and a photographic archive of tens of thousands of photographs, including views of exhibitions and images of the museum's building and grounds.

Considered by many to have the best collection of modern masterpieces in the world, MoMA's holdings include such notable works as Vincent van Gogh's *Starry Night*, Pablo Picasso's *Les Demoiselles d'Avignon*, Salvador Dali's *The Persistence of Memory*, Piet Mondrian's *Broadway Boogie Woogie*, a triptych of *Water Lilies* by Claude Monet, Henri Matisse's *Dance*, Paul Cezanne's *The Bather* and Frida Kahlo's *Self Portrait with Cropped Hair*.

MoMA also holds works by leading American artists such as Jackson Pollock, Jasper Johns, Edward Hopper, Andy Warhol, Chuck Close and Ralph Bakshi. The museum's design collection includes works from Paul Laszlo, the Eameses, Isamu Noguchi and George Nelson as well as many industrial pieces ranging from a self-aligning ball bearing to an entire Bell 47D1 helicopter.

The Museum of Modern Art seeks to create a dialogue between the established and the experimental and the past and the present, in an environment that is responsive to the issues of modern and contemporary art, while being accessible to all visitors to this beautiful space.

**WHAT IS IT**
One of the world's premier collections of modern art and design.
**WHERE IS IT**
New York City.
**WHAT IS THERE TO SEE**
Works from masters ranging from Dali, Monet, Picasso, Eames and Noguchi to Mondrian and Kahlo.
**ALSO KNOWN AS**
MoMA

*Recently refurbished, MoMA features a huge exhibition space.*

# The Statue of Liberty and Ellis Island

**WHAT ARE THEY**
National monuments serving as the gateway to America, they define the country's culture and history.
**WHERE ARE THEY**
New York harbor.
**WHY ARE THEY IMPORTANT**
They are symbols of the American ideal of freedom, liberty and democratic justice for all.

Two famous New York City landmarks are the Statue of Liberty and Ellis Island, making up the Statue of Liberty National Monument. With their historical and symbolic significance, these two icons of America stand as a reminder of the American ideals of freedom, liberty and justice for all.

The people of France gave the Statue of Liberty to the people of the United States more than a century ago in recognition of the friendship established during the American Revolution. Since then, the Statue of Liberty's symbolism has grown to include freedom and democracy as well as international friendship.

Commissioned by the French government to design a sculpture by 1876 to commemorate the hundredth anniversary of the American Declaration of Independence, Sculptor Frederic Auguste Bartholdi, with the help of Eiffel Tower designer, Alexandre Gustave Eiffel, began to create the colossal copper monument. The statue was completed in 1884 and shipped to New York Harbor, arriving in 1885 in 350 pieces, packed in 214 crates. The pedestal was completed in 1886 and the statue rebuilt in time for the final dedication in October of that year.

Declared a UNESCO World Heritage Site after its refurbishment in 1986, the Statue of Liberty stands for the pillars on which the American constitution was established, including life, liberty and the pursuit of happiness. It serves as a beacon to all visitors to this busy port.

Ellis Island has played an integral role in the shaping of America. Between 1892 and 1954, more than 12 million immigrants entered the United States through this portal, a small island in the shadow of the Statue of Liberty. Before 1890, individual states, rather than the Federal government, had regulated immigration into the United States. Between 1855 and 1890, Castle Garden, or Castle Clinton, in the Battery, had served as the New York State immigration station allowing about eight million immigrants, mostly from northern and western Europe, to pass through its doors. These early immigrants came from countries such as Britain, Ireland, Germany and Scandinavia and constituted the first large wave of immigrants who settled and populated the United States. Throughout the nineteenth century, political instability, famine and deteriorating economic conditions in Europe caused the largest mass migration in human history. In 1890 President Benjamin Harrison designated Ellis Island the first federal immigration station in order to handle the growing numbers of immigrants.

It opened on 1 January 1892 and the following day Annie Moore, a 15 year-old Irish girl, was the first immigrant to be processed here. Over the next 62 years, more than 12 million people followed her.

While most immigrants entered the United States through New York Harbor, others sailed into Boston, Philadelphia, Baltimore, San Francisco, Savannah, Miami and New Orleans.

During the early twentieth century, immigration officials mistakenly thought the peak of immigration had already passed, but it was actually on the rise and in 1907 around 1.25 million were processed at Ellis Island.

As the United States entered World War I, emigration to the United States slowed. Between 1918 and 1919 numerous suspected enemy aliens from across the United States were detained on Ellis Island, then transferred to other locations to allow the US Navy and the Army Medical Department to take over the complex. During this time, regular inspection of arriving immigrants was conducted on board ship or at the docks. At the end of the war, a big 'Red Scare' spread across America and thousands of suspected alien radicals were interred at Ellis Island. Hundreds were later deported simply because they were associated, however loosely, with any organizations advocating revolt against the federal government. In 1920, Ellis Island reopened as an immigration receiving station processing a further 225,206 immigrants.

Because of concerns about increased immigration in the years up to 1924, increased restrictions on immigration were brought in.

Ellis Island remained open for many years and in 1965, President Johnson declared it part of the Statue of Liberty National Monument. Following a thorough restoration, Ellis Island opened to the public in partnership with the National Park Service. Today the Ellis Island Immigration Museum receives almost 2 million visitors annually.

*The Statue of Liberty stands on Liberty Island with Ellis Island in the background.*

# Fallingwater

**WHAT IS IT**
A famous architectural masterpiece
by Frank Lloyd Wright
**WHERE IS IT**
Bear Run on Rural Route 1 in Fayette
County, Pennsylvania outside
Pittsburgh.
**WHY SHOULD I GO**
Fallingwater is the most acclaimed
American architectural work
promoting harmony between man
and nature.
**WHAT DO I NEED TO KNOW**
Since its opening as a museum in
1964, there have been more than 2
million visitors – book in advance.

Frank Lloyd Wright, internationally recognized as one of the leading modern architects of his day, is best known for creating a new form of American housing, the prairie house, as well as the award-winning single family home, Fallingwater.

Frank Lloyd Wright was commissioned by the wealthy Pittsburgh businessman Edgar Kaufman Sr to build a weekend home in the rural Bear Run area near Pittsburgh, Pennsylania. Kaufman requested a simple structure overlooking the waterfall and its attendant cabins.

Instead Wright asked for a survey of the area surrounding the waterfall, including all of the boulders and trees. He then proceeded to build one of his most acclaimed works, which was voted 'the best all time work of American Architecture' by the American Institute of Architects, despite some structural issues and problems with damp. A spectacular example of organic architecture, a harmonious blend of man and nature through design, Wright used every modern construction tool available in 1935 to create this naturally integrated home, seemingly part of the underlying rock bed and waterfall.

Mimicking the natural pattern of the existing rock ledges, Wright built the house over the falls in a series of cantilevered concrete 'trays', using the same material as the boulders, Pittsville sandstone, for the walls. Rising more than 9 m (30 ft) above the falls, Wright's strong horizontal lines and low ceilings maintain a sheltering effect, which is seamless with the exterior. He built as much floor space on outdoor terraces as he did indoors, effectively bringing the outdoors inside.

Completed in 1939, Fallingwater is the only Wright house with its original Wright-designed furnishings and artwork intact open to the public. The Kaufman family's collection of fine art, textiles, objets d'art, books and furnishings, which they collected from the 1930s to the 1960s, is on view, representing the eclectic tastes of a sophisticated, well-travelled family. Works by Audubon, Tiffany, Diego Rivera, Picasso, Jacques Lipchitz, Richmond Barthe and by Japanese artists Hiroshige and Hokusai can be seen in this magnificent modern architectural wonder, a reminder that only our imaginations have limitations.

*Falling Water blends in with the rocky cliffs.*

# Washington DC

Washington DC (District of Columbia) is the capital of the United States. Nestled between Maryland and Virginia on the eastern seaboard, the district covers an area of 108 sq km (67 sq mi) centring on the US Capitol.

As one of the most historically significant and charming areas in the United States, Washington is well worth a visit. Tourist highlights include the US Capitol, the many monuments and museums of 'the mall', the White House, Georgetown and Adams Morgan.

Tours of the Capitol, where senators and representatives meet to shape legislative policy, are available. These include the stunning Rotunda, the Statuary Hall, the original Supreme Court chamber and the Crypt, intended burial place of George and Martha Washington.

The Washington Monument, a 169-m (555 ft 5⅛-in) granite spire with 893 steps (or a lift ride) to the top, affords amazing 360-degree views of Washington's metropolitan area.

The Smithsonian Institution, the world's largest museum complex and research organisation, is composed of 17 museums and the National Zoo. The museums cover diverse aspects such as American History, Natural History, Air and Space, African Art, American Indian art and culture and Asian art among others. The Hirshhorn Museum and Sculpture Garden and the Portrait Gallery feature incredible art works and the Holocaust Museum is also not to be missed.

Charming areas worth exploring are the cobbled streets of old Georgetown, on the Potomac River with its brick town houses and luxury boutiques and many charming gourmet restaurants. Adams Morgan, another area of note, is a more culturally diverse section of Washington with every kind of cuisine and shopping available. Here you will find Ethiopian, Indian, Chinese and Greek restaurants amid local markets, lively cafés and bars and colourful shop fronts.

The nearby Arlington National Cemetery, a serenely beautiful spot marked by tens of thousands of white headstones surrounded by lush green countryside, is home to national heroes, presidents, law makers, astronauts, veterans, explorers and other historical figures.

Washington DC is a rich cultural and friendly city filled with historical and political stories in its beautiful waterfront landscape.

*The Washington Monument and the Lincoln Memorial.*

**WHAT IS IT**
The capital of the United States
**WHERE IS IT**
On the eastern seaboard bordered by Maryland and Virginia.
**WHEN SHOULD I GO**
The city is alive with activity throughout the year but highlights include the Cherry Blossom Festival in early spring, the Fourth of July celebrations and the lighting of the national Christmas tree. Winters are cold and summers are hot and humid.
**WHAT IS THERE TO DO**
An historical city, Washington DC is home to some of the nation's best museums, art galleries, restaurants and scenery.

*Visitors and the Washington Memorial are reflected in the Memorial.*

# The Vietnam Veterans Memorial

The Vietnam Veterans Memorial in Washington DC recognizes and honours the men and women who served and sacrificed their lives in one of America's most divisive wars. Sometimes referred to simply as 'the wall', the memorial was born from a need to heal the nation's wounds. Conceived and designed to make no political statement, it is a place where people can come together and honour their loved ones. It is made of three elements: the Wall of Names, the Three Servicemen Statue and Flagpole and the Vietnam Women's Memorial.

Set in Constitution Gardens, the long, black granite wall is not prominent, grand or imposing, but is simple, thoughtful, powerful and profound. Etched into the granite are the names of the 58,249 men and women who died and 1,200 who went missing in the Vietnam War. The two panels of the wall extend from a central point at a wide angle, with one side pointing towards the Washington Monument, the other towards the Lincoln Memorial. The descent to the centre of the wall reveals a towering 3 m (10 ft) looming shape surrounded by grassy slopes, which is oddly ominous in its serenity. The names appear in a seemingly endless stream, in chronological order from 1959 to 1975. Many family and friends leave mementos or flowers.

The Three Servicemen Statue symbolizes the spirit of compromise and reconciliation. Many veterans did not believe that the stark granite memorial spoke of the patriotism and sacrifice made by the servicemen and that its placement below ground hid it from view, hinting at shame. The Three Servicemen Statue was created to appease these thoughts, showing the valiant efforts of the armed forces rather than simply focusing on the country's loss of life.

The third element was created after a campaign by Diane Carlson Evans, a former army nurse, who fought to highlight the service of women in the war. In 1993 her efforts were rewarded with the Vietnam Women's Memorial. The sculpture depicts three uniformed women with a wounded soldier. One nurse comforts the soldier, another kneels in thought or prayer and the third looks to the skies for help from either a medevac helicopter or a higher power.

This memorial is impressive and powerful in every way and it is worth visiting to share a moment of silence for those who fought in the Vietnam War.

**WHAT IS IT**
A memorial to those who were killed in the Vietnam War.
**WHERE IS IT**
In the Constitution Gardens, Washington DC.
**WHY IS IT IMPORTANT**
It is an aid to healing the conflicted emotions felt by Americans about this war and an ode to those who lost their lives or went missing.
**WHO BUILT IT**
The granite wall was designed by Yale undergraduate, Maya Ying Lee, the Three Soldiers was built by Fredrick Hart and the Women's Memorial sculpture was designed by Glenna Goodacre.

# The National Air and Space Museum

The Smithsonian Institution's National Air and Space Museum maintains the largest collection of historic air- and spacecraft in the world. A vital centre for research into the history, science and technology of aviation and spaceflight, as well as planetary science, terrestrial geology and geophysics, its treasures are kept in two buildings, one on the National Mall and the other in the Steven F. Udvar-Hazy Center located near Dulles Airport. A shuttle bus service runs between the two sites.

The mall building in Washington, DC has hundreds of artefacts on display including the original Wright 1903 *Flyer*, the *Spirit of St Louis*, the Apollo 11 command module and a touchable lunar rock sample.

The Steven F Udvar-Hazy Center near Dulles Airport has artefacts including a Lockheed SR-71 Blackbird, a Concorde, a Boeing B-29 Superfortress *Enola Gay* and the Space Shuttle *Enterprise*. The centre's ten-storey trusses suspend the Monocoupe 110 Special *Little Butch* and the deHavilland Chipmunk aerobatic airplane.

Other memorabilia includes the spacesuits worn to the Moon by Buzz Aldrin and Neil Armstrong. The exhibition, Exploring the Planets, highlights both earth-based and spacecraft history and achievements of planetary explorations. There is a full-scale replica of the Voyager spacecraft which travelled to Jupiter, Saturn, Uranus and Neptune.

The centre has an IMAX theatre, flight simulators and a fantastic shop where you can buy impractical but fun gifts such as freeze-dried ice cream and other astronaut food items. This museum offers a thrilling ride through the history of this important and fascinating topic.

**WHAT IS IT**
The largest collection of historic air- and spacecraft in the world.

**WHERE IS IT**
There are two facilities, one on the National Mall in Washington DC and the other at the Stephen F. Udvar-Hazy Center just outside the city on Route 270.

**WHAT CAN I SEE**
Orville and Wilbur Wright's original 1903 Wright Flyer, the *Enola Gay*, which dropped the atomic bomb on Hiroshima, the Space Shuttle *Enterprise*, the *Spirit of St Louis*, in which Charles Lindbergh made the first solo, non-stop flight across the Atlantic, and the Apollo 11 command module.

**WORTH A SPLURGE**
Stop in the gift shop and pick up some freeze-dried ice cream, just like the astronauts enjoy in space!

*Entrance hall of the museum.*

# The Smoky Mountains

**WHAT ARE THEY**
The most visited national park in the Eastern United States.
**WHERE ARE THEY**
On the border of Tennessee and North Carolina.
**WHAT IS THERE TO DO**
Hike the Appalachian Trail.
**ALSO KNOWN AS**
The Smokies.
**NOMENCLATURE**
The name of the area comes from the natural haze that often hangs over it. As in the neighbouring Blue Ridge Mountains just to the east, hydrocarbons produced by trees and other vegetation, together with higher humidity, give the sky a bluish cast, even over short distances.

A major mountain range in the southern part of the Appalachians, the Smoky Mountains straddle the border between Tennessee and North Carolina. The name comes from the natural haze that often hovers above it. As in the neighbouring Blue Ridge Mountains just to the east, hydrocarbons produced by trees and other vegetation, together with higher humidity, give the sky a bluish cast, even over short distances.

The most visited national park in the Eastern United States, Great Smoky Mountains National Park is home to Clingmans Dome, the highest point on the Appalacian Trail at an elevation of 2,030 m (6,643 ft). A paved road leads to within 91 m (300 ft) of the summit from where visitors can walk to the top for a view over Tennessee, North Carolina, South Carolina and Georgia. It also holds significant numbers of the Smokies' symbol, the black bear, and other important wildlife.

The Appalachian National Scenic Trail, generally known as the Appalachian Trail or simply The AT, is the main attraction here. A 3,500-km (2,174-mi) marked hiking trail, The AT extends between Springer Mountain in Georgia and Mount Katahdin in Maine. Along the way, the trail passes through North Carolina, Tennessee, Virginia, West Virginia, Maryland, Pennsylvania, New Jersey, New York, Connecticut, Massachusetts, Vermont and New Hampshire.

Many wildflowers grow here, including bee balm, fire pink, Solomon's seal, Dutchman's breeches, various trilliums and even hardy orchids like showy orchids, as well as purple-flowered Catawba rhododendron, light pink rosebay rhododendron, orange-flowered flame azalea and mountain laurel. In autumn, nearly-bare mountaintops covered in rime ice, or frozen fog, are separated from green valleys by bright and varied leaf colours.

Several rivers rise from streams in the Smokies, including the Little Pigeon River, Oconaluftee River and the Nantahala River. The French Broad River crosses the north-eastern end of the Smokies. Pigeon Forge and Gatlinburg in Tennessee, and Cherokee, North Carolina are famous for both leisurely tubing and full whitewater rafting in summer, while the short winter skiing season is centred on places like Cataloochee and Ober. Gatlinburg.

*Evening in the Great Smoky Mountains National Park from Morton Overlook.*

# Charleston

Charleston is located on a narrow peninsula between the Ashley and Cooper Rivers where they flow into the Atlantic Ocean. Originally known as 'Charles Town' after King Charles II of England, the town was established in 1670 and settled a decade later. Downtown Charleston serves as the central business district of Greater Charleston and is home to many historic and cultural sites and buildings of architectural interest.

The scenic community of Charlestown, strategically located halfway down the South Carolina coast, became the centre of the Carolina colony, the eighth state to join the Union, and the cultural centre of the pre-Civil War South. Until 1800, Charleston was the fifth largest city in North America, behind Philadelphia, New York City, Boston and Quebec City.

Originally a walled city of the British colony, the town played a key role in the events leading up to the Civil War, and subsequently experienced a resurgence during the late nineteenth century, eventually becoming one of the most complete and intact historic districts in the country. It is the location of Fort Moultrie, which withstood the British in the American Revolution, and Fort Sumpter, the reputed site of the 'first shot' of the American Civil War. The city is still home to many naval acadamies and training camps.

Made prosperous by shipping and many local plantations, the city is home to Boone Hall and Magnolia plantations and Middleton Place.

The majority of Charleston's public and community buildings reflect a time when it was one of the wealthiest and most important port cities of the colonies. Architectural remnants of this time include the Old Exchange and Customs House, the Market Hall and Sheds, St Michael's Episcopal Church, the Post Office, the County Court House and City Hall.

'Old Charleston' – with its homes with wrought-iron gates, courtyard gardens and oak and palm-lined streets – is a fine example of southern colonial charm. It is like stepping back in time as you sniff the clean salty air and listen to the horse-drawn carriages clop past the grand homes of this beautiful historic city, one of the most elegant places in America.

**WHAT IS IT**
A lovely historic town in South Carolina.

**WHAT IS THERE TO SEE**
Charming 'Old Charleston'.

**LITERARY CONNECTION**
Charleston has inspired many novels including Pat Conroy's *Prince of Tides*.

**WHEN SHOULD I VISIT**
The best time to visit is March to November.

**HOW DO I GET THERE**
The area is served by Charleston International Airport.

*The evening sun sets on the historic mansions of Charleston.*

*Spanish moss hangs from the trees.*

# Savannah

In 1733, General James Edward Oglethorpe and 120 travellers landed on a bluff high along the Savannah River, naming the thirteenth and final American colony, Georgia, after England's King George II. Savannah became its first city.

Oglethorpe was befriended by the native Yamacraw Indian chief, Tomochichi, who granted the new arrivals permission to settle on the bluff, thus allowing the town to flourish without the warfare and hardship that stifled the beginnings of many of America's early colonies.

Oglethorpe laid the city out in grid form, with wide open streets intertwined with shady public squares and parks to serve as meeting places and business centres. Of 24 original squares, 21 still exist.

As farmers discovered, Savannah's soil was rich, and the climate favourable for the cultivation of cotton and rice. Plantations and slavery became highly profitable for whites in the neighbouring South Carolina areas, causing Georgia, the last free colony, to legalize slavery. The transatlantic slave trade brought millions of Africans to the Americas, and many of them passed through Savannah, forming the Gullah culture of the Atlantic coastal communities in Georgia and South Carolina.

The economic boom from exporting cotton allowed residents to build lavish homes and churches. With the growth in trade, especially after the invention of the cotton gin, the city rivalled Charleston as a commercial port. Many of the world's cotton prices were set on the steps of the Savannah Cotton Exchange, which still stands today.

From 1819, Savannah was the home port of the S.S. *Savannah*, the first steam-powered vessel to cross the Atlantic. After more than half a century of growth and prosperity, Savannah suffered two devastating fires in 1796 and 1820, each leaving half of Savannah in ashes. In 1818 a tenth of the population was lost to an outbreak of the yellow fever epidemic.

**WHAT IS IT**
A stunning historically significant southern town, the first planned city in America.
**WHERE IS IT**
On the coast of Georgia.
**WHEN SHOULD I GO**
Savannah enjoys a subtropical climate that makes outdoor activities possible year-round, the summers are hot and the winters are mild.
**HOLLYWOOD CONNECTION**
*Midnight in the Garden of Good and Evil*, based on a true story, was filmed here.
**WHAT IS THERE TO SEE**
Exceptionally preserved and restored architecture dating back to the early 1800s.

The glorious city managed to bounce back and pre-Civil War Savannah, with its grand oak trees dripping with Spanish moss, was hailed as the most picturesque and serene city in America.

During the Civil War, in 1864, when General William Sherman entered the city, having burned every southern city north of Atlanta to the ground, he was so taken by its beauty that he sent a telegram to Abraham Lincoln, presenting the city of Savannah to him as a Christmas present. The war was over for Savannah and reconstruction began. After the war many freed slaves remained in Savannah, founding their own churches, schools and communities. Savannah, Georgia's oldest black community, went on to become one of the most historically significant African-American cities in the nation.

As the economy grew and cotton regained its importance, Savannah entered the new century re-establishing herself as the 'Belle of Georgia'. The Historic District was designated a National Historic Landmark, and remains one of the largest historic landmarks in the country.

Many restored old buildings survive, including: the Pirates' House, built in 1754; the Herb House, dating back to 1734 and the oldest existing building in Georgia, and the Pink House, built in 1789 as the site of Georgia's first bank. There are also several restored churches.

The fourth largest city in Georgia, Savannah is known not only for its historical architecture and famed cemeteries, but also for its jazz and blues, tranquil and pristine beaches, excellent golf courses, deep-sea fishing and exceptional museums.

*Lush tropical foilage grows in the garden of this fine Savannah mansion with two levels of verandahs.*

# St Augustine

**WHAT IS IT**
The oldest city in the United States.
**WHERE IS IT**
Central north-east Florida.
**WHY IS IT IMPORTANT**
The longest continually occupied
European settlement in the
continental US.
**WHAT IS THERE TO SEE**
Castillo de San Marcos Monument, a
cobbled historic district with many
cafés and inns, as well as a lovely
coastline with pretty beaches.
**ALSO KNOWN AS**
the 'Ancient City'.

St Augustine, Florida, also known as the 'Ancient City', is the oldest city in the United States as well as the longest continually occupied European settlement in the continental United States. First discovered by the Spanish admiral Pedro Menendez de Aviles in 1565, it was founded as San Agustín.

The Castillo de San Marcos, built from 1672 to 1695, served as an outpost of the Spanish Empire, guarding the town and protecting the sea route for treasure ships returning to Spain. Although the castillo has served a number of nations throughout its history, it has never been taken by military force. During the eighteenth century, the castillo went from Spanish control to British and back to the Spanish, as a result of a series of treaties.

The Spanish remained in power in Florida until the area was bought by the United States in 1821. The castillo was renamed Fort Marion and was used by the US army until 1899. Designated a national monument in 1924, the elaborate fort with its double drawbridge became part of the national park system in 1933. In 1942, Congress restored its original name of the Castillo de San Marcos.

Built of coquina, a durable limestone construction of broken sea shells and corals, the walls of the fortress remained impenetrable through 300 years of enemy mortar attacks and violent storms. Castillo de San Marcos is built alongside picturesque Mantazas Bay with its well-preserved Spanish style watchtower, Fort Matanzas, which provided a platform for overseeing any potential enemy advance from the Matanzas River.

The town of St Augustine retains some of its original European charms. Strategically located among the intercoastal waterway, the Matanzas river and the Atlantic, the area's historic district has quaint cobbled streets lined with charming cafés, bars, boutiques and guest houses.

The area is home to 69 km (43 mi) of lovely beaches offering the visitor the opportunity to take advantage of the fishing, diving, surfing, parasailing and many other water sports that are on offer. In addition to its historical importance, St Augustine is simply a pleasant town to visit.

*The impressive fotification of the Castillo de San Marcos.*

# Miami South Beach

South Beach, or 'SOBE', the lower section of Miami Beach, Florida, originally developed in the early 1900s, has stunning Art Deco architecture. Although many of the art deco buildings are either crumbling or have been demolished, South Beach retains the world's largest collection of Streamline Moderne Art Deco architecture, and a recent resurgence in the popularity of the area has caused a lot of regeneration and restoration of this lovely area.

A long-standing spring break favourite, the long stretches of white sand and crystalline waters of South Beach are separated from 'the strip' by Ocean Drive. The pastel cityscape of boutique hotels, mixed with expensive high-rise blocks of modern flats, nightclubs, cafés, restaurants and bars shows evidence of the rampant tourism, but if you sit back and enjoy the show, you are guaranteed to get into the swing of things – there's something for everyone in South Beach.

Whether you want to sip a mojito and enjoy some Cuban fried plaintains and black beans while you watch tanned locals flex their muscles in strong-man competitions, dine on fresh seafood at one of America's gourmet hot spots, dance the night away at a world famous club where you are likely to bump into rock stars and supermodels or spend a few hours among the many scantily clad sun worshipers on the often crowded beach as the sounds of Spanish music waft through the air, you will never be at a loss for something to do here.

According to magazines like *The New Times* and *GQ*, South Beach has replaced Los Angeles and New York City as the United States' most popular nightlife spot. There are more than 150 clubs, lounges and bars, most of which stay open until 5 am, so here you can truly dance the night away. Entry can be expensive, and access is often difficult, but if you can wangle your way in, it is worth the investment.

A major location for photoshoots and high fashion, South Beach's palm-studded promenade is a well recognized backdrop for events ranging from the *Sports Illustrated* Swim Suit Issue to the National Women's Volleyball Championship. Here, people pride themselves on their physique and fashionable appearance, whatever it may be, and they are not afraid to show it off. Viva South Beach!

*Homes, hotels and cafés jostle for space on South Beach.*

**WHAT IS IT**
An art-deco inspired, Cuban-influenced strip of hotels and cafés along the waterfront of Miami Beach.
**ALSO KNOWN AS**
South Beach or 'SOBE'.
**WHAT IS THERE TO SEE**
Scantily clad women, beach bums, bon viveurs, clubby teens, supermodels. South Beach is full of exotic sights, sounds and scents.
**WHAT IS THERE TO DO**
Go to the beach and watch the toned men tan, try some authentic Cuban cuisine, stay at one of the ritzy hotels on the waterfront, sip a Cubra Libre or mojito as you watch the colourful crowds walk by and take advantage of fashionable shopping.
**WORTH A SPLURGE**
Stay overnight in one of the fashionable art deco hotels, sip an expertly prepared mojito surrounded by supermodels by the stunning poolside at the Delano Hotel.
**WHEN TO GO**
Every season is party season in South Beach, but summers are humid and prone to tropical storms.
**HOLLYWOOD CONNECTION**
*The Bird Cage* starring Robin Williams was filmed in South Beach.

*Airboat cruising the swampy Everglades.*

# Florida Everglades

Everglades National Park, a World Heritage Site, encompasses the largest designated wilderness east of the Rocky Mountains. This sub-tropical preserve, comprised of both temperate and tropical plants, includes sawgrass prairies, mangrove and cypress swamps, pinelands and hardwood stands. It is also known for its marine and estuary environments, with its rich bird life, numerous manatees and noteworthy existence of alligators and crocodiles living side by side, the only place in the world where this takes place.

As you approach the park via 'Alligator Alley', you immediately begin to get the sense of history here. It is easy to visualize the indigenous Indians plying the waterways in their hand-hewn canoes, the early morning sun beating on their bare backs. Here there are no peaks, no mountains and no hills to shelter you – it is just swampland and grasses as far as the eye can see.

Driving through the lush, flat countryside you will notice the alligators – penned off by high fences – sunning themselves along the banks of the river and lurking in the waters, their eyes peering out at you from their otherwise submerged world, the only hint of their existence being the slight ripple caused by the blink of their eyes or the swish of their tails. What strikes you most about these massive prehistoric beasts, covered in brackish mud, is not only their age and size, but also their numbers – they seem to be everywhere!

Dotted along this emerald-green wonderland of backwater swamps and mangrove forests is the evidence of the rich bird life, particularly the large wading birds such as the roseate spoonbill, wood stork, great blue heron and many types of egrets – their white, delicate frames a startling burst of colour among the otherwise brown and green backdrop surrounded by seemingly endless vibrant blue skies.

**WHAT IS IT**
The third largest National Park in the United States.
**WHERE IS IT**
Southern Florida.
**WHEN SHOULD I VISIT**
November to March is the best time to visit.
**WHAT WILL I SEE**
This is the only place on earth where alligators and crocodiles cohabit.

# The Florida Keys

The Florida Keys are a subtropical archipelago consisting of 1,700 islands off the south-eastern tip of the Florida peninsula, the farthest of which is Key West, its southern tip is only 145km (90 mi) from Cuba. They are accessed via the scenic Overseas Highway, an extension of Route 1, the largely two-lane road consisting mostly of bridges that connects the islands, each of which has its own laid-back character.

The subtropical keys are closer in nature to the Caribbean than the rest of Florida, though unlike the Caribbean's volcanic islands, the Upper Keys are remnants of large coral reefs, fossilized and exposed as sea levels declined, and the Lower Keys are composed of sandy limestone grain produced by plants and marine organisms.

The keys have many endemic plant and animal species as well as some that seem at home, but are not native. The key lime is a naturalized species introduced from Mexico but has become a local delight in the form of key lime pie. The Key deer and the American crocodile live here, as well as many types of dolphins and porpoises as well as the endangered manatee (sea cow).

Key West is the best known of the islands, and serves as a seaport for cruise ships. Sunsets from the pier are stunning, and many people enjoy them from the large promenade or Mallory Square. Explore the history and architecture of Old Town Key West where you can take in scenic Duval Street with its charming colonial architecture, bars, cafés, restaurants and shops in wide, clean, palm-fringed streets. For culture, head for the Tennessee Williams Theater and Performing Arts Center or take a tour of Ernest Hemmingway's home, where five-toed cats lounge on the stairs of the large white porch.

Nancy Forrester's Secret Garden is like a lush, green rainforest, and is an excellent example of nature's wilderness tamed in an artistic woodland garden. The Key West Botanical Forest and Garden is also worth a stroll to see its large number of 'champion tree' specimens.

Two events that take place here are spring break, when students from across the world come to drink to excess, and PrideFest, a week-long series of events presented by the large gay and lesbian population in early June. Key West has adopted the unofficial motto of 'One Human Family' reflecting the freedom and individuality that is celebrated in this lively American outpost.

**WHAT IS IT**
An archipelago of 1,700 islands off the coast of Florida.

**WHAT IS THERE TO DO**
Relax on one of the fabulous beaches, go sport fishing, have a romantic seaside meal, swim with dolphins, look for manatees or relive Hemmingway's lifestyle at one of his favourite watering holes after a visit to his home.

**HOW DO I GET THERE**
Fly into one of the small airports, particularly in Key West or take the scenic Overseas Highway.

**WHEN SHOULD I GO**
November to May has the nicest weather, as summers are hot and humid.

**WORTH A SPLURGE**
Stay in one of the lovely guest houses with their wrap-around porches in Key West and enjoy the tropical hospitality of Jimmy Buffet's famed 'Margaritaville'.

**MUST HAVE**
You cannot leave without a taste of conch fritters followed by key lime pie.

*Bridges connecting the keys.*

# San Antonio

San Antonio, the only major city in Texas founded before it won independence from Mexico, was once populated by Spanish missionaries and militiamen, German merchants, Southern plantation owners, Western cattle ranchers and Eastern architects. Their existence is still felt in the city's downtown area and is evident in the current culture and cuisine. San Antonio is largely known for three things: its parties, its eclectic architecture and the Alamo.

San Antonio hosts many celebrations, some comparable to Mardi Gras. Here they might break confetti eggs called cascarones, listen to oompah bands, and cheer rodeo bull riders in festivals that mingle all the area's cultural backgrounds. It is also America's capital for Tejano music, a unique blend of Mexican and German sounds. The city's architecture also reflects its multi-ethnic history in an eclectic mixture of different styles.

Most fiestas take place just a few steps below the streets of downtown San Antonio. The River Walk (*Paseo del Rio*) is alternately relaxing and exhilarating, depending on where you choose to explore. The 4 km (2.5 mi) cobbled area of winding riverbank, shaded by cypresses, oaks and willows, exudes an exotic and sultry tropical aura. The River Square and South Bank sections, crowded with pavement cafés, gourmet restaurants, lively bars, modern hotels and a large shopping complex, have a festive, sometimes frenetic feel. Tour boats, water taxis and floating picnic barges regularly ply the river, while local festivals and parades fill the river's banks with revellers.

The Alamo, the most visited site in Texas, is San Antonio's most famous landmark. The small, graceful mission church is where 188 Texas volunteers repelled Mexican dictator Santa Anna's much larger force for 13 days in February and March 1836. All the men, including Jim Bowie and Davy Crockett died, their deaths inspired Sam Houston's cry, 'Remember the Alamo!' which rallied his troops to beat the Mexican army at San Jacinto a month later. The Alamo has largely deteriorated and currently the mission displays the Long Barrack, formerly the missionaries' living quarters and the mission church. The Wall of History offers a helpful timeline explaining the events that took place here.

*Illuminated Presa Street bridge and a section of River Walk.*

# Santa Fe

Nestled in the picturesque Sangre de Cristo Mountains, Santa Fe was planned around a central plaza, according to Philip II of Spain's 'Laws of the Indies' in 1573. The north side of the plaza is home to the Governor's Palace, to the east is the church, now the Cathedral Basilica of Saint Francis of Assisi.

In 1912, in an effort to establish tourism, it was decreed that a single style of architecture should be used across the city to promote a unification of the varied styles that had been built through the town's history. Local officials decided on the Spanish Pueblo Revival look, inspired by the defining features of local architecture: vigas and canales from the old adobe homes, the churches found in the pueblos and the earth-toned, adobe-coloured exteriors. By 1930 this was broadened to include the 'Territorial' style and white-painted window and door pediments.

The city is a well-known centre for the arts, reflecting its multicultural character. Outdoor sculptures ranging from Baroque to postmodern include many of Saint Francis and Kateri Tekakwitha.

Canyon Road, east of the Plaza, has many art galleries, exhibiting an array of contemporary south-western, indigenous American and experimental pieces. The city's art market is the third largest in the United States, after New York and Los Angeles.

Artists have long flocked here, capturing the natural beauty of the landscape, the flora and the fauna. Georgia O'Keeffe's museum is devoted to her work and associated artists or related themes.

Santa Fe's major museums include the Museum of New Mexico, the Museum of Fine Arts, the Museum of International Folk Art, the Wheelwright Museum of the American Indians, the Museum of Indian Arts and Culture Laboratory of Anthropology, the Institute of American Indian Arts Museum and the Museum of Spanish Colonial Art.

One highlight is the Loretto Chapel. Commissioned in 1872 by Bishop Lamy, it was designed by French architect Antoine Mouly in the Gothic Revival style, with spires, buttresses and stained glass windows imported from France, but he died before completing the stair to the choir loft. The Sisters of Loretto did not wish to use a ladder and prayed for nine days for St Joseph to intercede. A shabby stranger appeared, offering to build the staircase if they gave him total privacy. After three months, using only a square, a saw and some warm water, he constructed a spiral staircase of non-native wood. Not only was this work impressive, the 6-m (20-ft) staircase was constructed without nails. Before the stranger could be questioned, he had disappeared. The mystery of his identity, as well as his construction techniques, has never been solved.

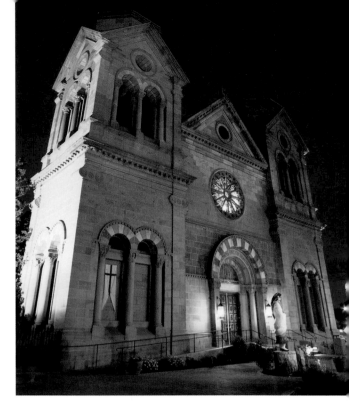

*Cathedral Basilica of Saint Francis of Assisi.*

**WHAT IS IT**
The capital of New Mexico.
**WHERE IS IT**
112 km (70 mi) South of Taos.
**WHAT IS THERE TO DO**
The city is a mecca for artists, it is not far from scenic Taos and there's also a local ski area.
**WHEN SHOULD I GO**
Santa Fe enjoys 300 days of sunshine a year, but temperatures are most hospitable in spring and autumn. Mid-September when the aspens in the surrounding mountains turn yellow and the skies are clear and blue is beautiful.
**LOCAL CULTURE**
A fun time to visit is during the annual autumn Fiesta to celebrate the 'reconquering' of New Mexico by Don Diego De Vargas, a highlight is when Santa Feans burn Zozobra, a 15 m (50 ft) puppet also called 'Old Man Gloom'.

# Taos

Taos, a scenic New Mexican community, is famous for many things, including skiing, art and architecture and historical sites. A mix of Native American, Spanish and Anglo-American cultures is represented in art and architecture, music, dance, food and festivals. Historic Taos Plaza and its side streets have old adobe buildings, once the homes of some of Taos' leading citizens such as Kit Carson. Renovated into galleries, stores and boutiques it offers a pleasant stroll with many hidden treasures.

Taos Pueblo (or Pueblo de Taos), is the ancient town of the northern Tiwa-speaking tribe of the Pueblo American Indians. Lying 1.6 km (1 mi) north of modern Taos on the Rio Pueblo, it has been home to this tribe for more than 1,000 years. The Pueblo's reddish-brown adobe housing, built between 1000 and 1450 AD, is a National Historic Landmark and a World Heritage Site and it remains occupied to this day.

Just 32 km (20 mi) to the north-west is the ranch DH Lawrence lived in during the 1920s, while just outside Taos in Ranchitos is the Martinez Hacienda, the residence turned museum of the late Father Martinez, one of the first Spanish settlers of Taos. Artists began settling in Taos in 1898, creating the 'Taos Society of Artists'. Many painted local scenes, especially of Taos Pueblo. Some of the artists' studios, including the Blumenschein House, have been preserved and make a worthwhile visit.

Once home to miners, trappers, cattlemen and shepherds, Wheeler Peak, the highest peak in New Mexico at an elevation of 4,011 m (13,161 ft) is now home to The Enchanted Circle, a winter playground where snowshoe and cross-country ski enthusiasts enjoy the many back country trails and meadows in Carson National Forest and the trails at the Enchanted Forest Cross Country Ski Area.

Home to the ski resorts of Taos, Red River, Sipapu and Angel Fire, Taos offers uncrowded skiing on wonderfully diverse terrain, feather-light powder and an intimate alpine village for skiers of all levels.

Taos is a natural wonderland. Whether you want skiing, horse riding, biking, hiking, rafting or kayaking, the stunning mountains and the Rio Grande Gorge offer a number of fantastic outdoor pursuits.

*The historic Taos Pueblo is still inhabited by the Tiwa Indians.*

# Kauai

*The spectacular Na Pali coast.*

Hawaii, an archipelago of more than 19 volcanic islands near a geological 'hot spot' in the Pacific plate, is a tropical paradise and home to some of the most spectacular scenery.

Six of the eight big islands are open to tourism: Big Island (also called Hawaii), Oahu, Maui, Molokai, Lanai and Kauai.

Formed over six million years ago, Kauai, the oldest and most northerly of the main Hawaiian islands, is roughly 550 sq mi (1,430 sq km) in area.

Hanalei Bay is on the wet north shore, the wettest shore and is known for its spectacular, picture-postcard beauty. It is a long half-moon of sandy beach carved into the base of a sheer cliff on one side and a rocky point on the other. The westernmost curve of the bay is a calm shoreline. The quaint town has gourmet bistros, pretty boutiques and a yoga studio and is a haven for the beachgoer seeking peace.

The Na Pali coast has spectacular scenery. Emerald valleys, jagged 1,219 m (4,000 ft) cliffs towering above the blue Pacific, caves, lava tubes and pristine beaches, make this one of the most stunning and unspoilt areas on the entire island. Helicopter above or hike or kayak along this beautiful coastline for guaranteed lasting memories.

West Kauai is full of spectacular natural wonders and Hawaiian cultural landmarks. Awe-inspiring Waimea Canyon is the main draw. A vast 16 km (10 mi) long and 1,098 m (3,600 ft) deep, its scale and scope, and the rainbow colours streaking it are incredible. The view into Kalalau Valley is one of the most beautiful sights on the island: at sunset the walls reflect pink, orange, red and grey. From Kokee State Park, at the top of Waimea Canyon Road, drive to Kalalau Lookout for an amazing view of the canyon's jagged cliffs and overgrown gorges dropping dramatically into the sea 1,219 m (4,000 ft) below.

Kauai's south shore, on the sunny side of the island, is home to the National Tropical Botanical Garden, the only garden of its kind to be chartered by Congress, and to Spouting Horn, a series of natural lava tube formations, where water rushes in, creating a howling geyser effect. The beaches around Poipu, near the southern tip of the island are favourites for snorkelling and scuba diving.

Kauai is best explored by 4x4 (fantastic scenery is round every turn), while exceptional views can also be seen from the air.

**WHAT IS IT**
One of the most stunning islands in the Hawaiian archipelago.
**ALSO KNOWN AS**
'The Garden Isle'.
**WHAT IS THERE TO DO**
Tour the Grand Canyon of the West, kayak along the beautiful Na Pali coast or just lounge on any of the pristine beaches.
**HOLLYWOOD CONNECTION**
Large parts of *Jurrassic Park, Fantasy Island, Raider's of the Lost Ark,* the original *King Kong* and *6 Days and 7 Nights* were filmed here.
**WHEN SHOULD I GO**
Kauai is beautiful throughout the year. Poipu on the south-eastern side of the island is generally warm and sunny even when the tropical northern part of the island is overcast and rainy.
**WORTH A SPLURGE**
Take a helicopter ride over the island; this is an incredible way to experience the amazing variety of vegetation and geology on this small island.

*Red Rock State Park and lake.*

# Sedona

Founded in 1902, Sedona has become a gathering place for mystics who believe that the earth's energy flows around the area's famed red rocks, concentrating into power spots, called vortices. Believers in Vortex Healing cite the Sedona area as home to several of these vortices, which allows them to access a 'healing realm' of divine consciousness, empowering them to cure both physical and emotional conditions.

In addition to the spas that have arisen from this belief, Sedona is also home to many yoga, art and literary societies, as well as a number of luxury resorts catering for visitors who want to visit the stunning array of red sandstone, mudstone and limestone formations that glow brilliant orange and red when lit by the rising or setting sun.

Named after Sedona Schnebly, the wife of the city's first postmaster, Sedona is a popular stopover for visitors. Its location at the base of the Mogollon Rim, surrounded by fascinating natural crimson sandstone monoliths, inspired *Weekend Travel Report* to name Sedona, Arizona as The Most Beautiful Place in America.

The natural monoliths, such as Cathedral Rock, Coffee Pot and Bell are named after objects that they resemble.

Here you can bike, fish, go birdwatching, take a pottery or art class, go on a narrated star gazing trip or a Native American-led hike or play golf on any of the first-class resort courses. There's even a natural water slide at Slide Rock State Park.

Boynton Canyon is another area of beauty in Sedona, where cliff dwellings from centuries ago can still be seen on the canyon walls. To view some ancient petroglyph sites, visit the V Bar V Ranch in Coconino National Forest.

Whether you are a mystic or just interested in majestic surroundings, there is something for everyone in magical Sedona.

**WHAT IS IT**
A stunning city made of red sandstone formations, the red rocks of Sedona.
**WHERE IS IT**
Between Coconino and Yavapai Counties in the Verde Valley north of Phoenix.
**TRIVIA**
Sedona is home to the world's only McDonald's with turquoise arches.
**WHAT IS THERE TO DO**
Hike, bike, fish, spa, play golf or just soak up the mystic energy in this beautiful part of Arizona.

# Painted Desert

The Painted Desert is an area of breathtaking beauty, stretching along the Little Colorado River from the Grand Canyon to the Petrified Forest National Park in Northern Arizona. The desert, named 'el Desierto Pintura' by the Spaniards, because of its brightly coloured land forms, consists of badland hills and Chinle Formation rocks as well as spectacular mesas and buttes rising from the desert floor.

The Painted Desert's rocks and soils have various combinations of minerals and decayed plant and animal matter that contribute to the many colours, particularly the red rocks, throughout the formations. At sunrise and sunset, the crimson formations are especially beautiful when they turn shades of violet, blue and burnt orange.

The park changes continually and winds shift the sediments, causing lower layers of fossil and petrified wood to surface, most notably the 220-million-year-old remains of a conifer forest from the Triassic Period Petrified Forest.

Geologically similar to many other parks of the Colorado Plateau, this was once a vast floodplain, crossed by many streams and filled with an abundance of stately pines. Covered by silt, mud and volcanic ash, the trees' oxygen supply was cut off, slowing the logs' decay. Gradually, silica-bearing ground waters seeped through the logs and slowly encased the original tissues with silica deposits. Over time, the silica crystallized into quartz, and the logs were preserved as petrified wood. The Petrified Forest National Park is home to the largest example of this phenomenon in the world.

Short hikes will take you through this spectacular scenery. One outlook offers views of Newspaper Rock, a huge sandstone block covered with petroglyphs. In the Blue Mesa area, you will find pedestal logs acting as capstones to the soft clays beneath.

The Flattops, massive remnants of a once continuous layer of sandstone capping parts of this area, protect the layered deposits long eroded from other parts of the park. From here you can also access the Long Logs trail, part of Rainbow Forest. Iron, carbon, manganese and other minerals colour the petrified wood.

**WHAT IS IT**
A spectacular area of natural beauty.
**WHERE IS IT**
Stretching south-east from the Grand Canyon to the Petrified Forest National Park.
**WHAT IS THERE TO SEE**
A stunning ever-changing landscape offering spectacular views.
**ALSO KNOWN AS**
The desert got its name from the Spaniards, who named it 'el Desierto Pintura' because of its brightly coloured landforms.
**WHAT SHOULD I KNOW**
Stick to marked trails in the Petrified Forest as the plants are very fragile. It is illegal to remove the petrified wood.

*Colourful banded hills showing sediment deposits.*

# Monument Valley

Monument Valley is an area of sandstone rock formations rising majestically up to 300 m (1,000 ft) from the desert floor, providing one of the most enduring images of the American West. These isolated red mesas and buttes, surrounded by vast, empty desert, have been filmed and photographed countless times, giving the visitor a sense of familiarity, but once in the valley you cannot fail to be amazed at the true vivid, deep, rich colour palette of this otherworldly landscape.

Lying entirely within the Navajo Indian Reservation near the south-eastern corner of Utah, the most famous landmarks are concentrated around the small town of Goulding. This isolated settlement, 250 km (175 mi) from the nearest city – Flagstaff, Arizona – was established in 1923 as an Indian trading post, and is now home to a comprehensive range of visitor services.

The view from the visitor centre is spectacular enough, but the majority of the park can only be seen from the Valley Drive, a 27-km (17-mi) road. Winding among the magical towering cliffs and mesas including The Totem Pole, a stunning 91-m (300-ft) rock spire only a few metres wide. As well as eroded rocks, this area is also home to a series of ancient cave and cliff dwellings, natural arches and petroglyphs.

Not a valley in the conventional sense, Monument Valley is actually a wide flat, desolate landscape, interrupted by the crumbling formations, the final remnants of the sandstone layers that once covered the entire region. Monument Valley is the quintessential, spectacular, breathtaking Wild West.

*Cars head up to Monument Valley from Kayenta.*

# Grand Canyon

**WHAT IS IT**
One of the seven natural wonders of
the world.
**WHERE IS IT**
The desert highlands of Arizona.
**WHAT IS THERE TO SEE**
322 km (200 mi) of stunning
landscape
**HOW DO I GET THERE**
Flagstaff and Page in Arizona, and
Kanab in Utah, are the closest cities
to the park.

The Grand Canyon, cut by the Colorado River, is one of the United State's most famous landmarks and stretches an incredible 322 km (200 mi) across the desert highlands of northern Arizona. Named as one of the seven natural wonders of the world, the Grand Canyon was designated a National Park in 1919.

Here you will find a breathtaking chasm of unimaginable scope in a palette of crimson, gold and orange cliffs, purple abysses and clear rushing waters, making it one of the most astonishing landscapes on Earth. Upon seeing the drama of a Grand Canyon sunset, the poet Carl Sandburg remarked, 'There goes God with an army of banners'.

The southern rim of the Grand Canyon is the most popular area because it allows easy access from the main road that parallels the canyon edge for a substantial distance and has many scenic overlooks as well as a selection of hiking trails.

The north rim, higher in elevation, is less densely populated with tourists because it is more remote. On this side of the canyon, the remote Tuweep area can be reached by several dirt tracks with some spectacular viewpoints, but much of this area is inaccessible by road.

The Grand Canyon contains a large variety of spectacular but largely hidden and hard-to-reach places including waterfalls, pools, narrow ravines and oases. Many of the vast side canyons require more than a day's travel on foot from the canyon rim, or complicated journeys involving boat trips down the Colorado River, to reach them.

After one trip here, pondering the vastness of this special place, you will quickly understand its popularity and status as a natural wonder of the world.

*South rim of the Grand Canyon.*

# Mesa Verde

Mesa Verde is a large archaeological area in the United States, with more than 4,000 sites dating from 600 to 1300 AD, including the most impressive cliff dwellings in the south-west.

The inhabitants of the Four Corners region of Mesa Verde were the Anasazi (Ancestral Puebloans), who in the thirteenth century built houses in the shallow caves but abandoned them less than 100 years later.

The caves were discovered in 1888 by ranchers Charles Mason and his brother-in-law Richard Wetherill, but many artefacts were looted before a Denver newspaper aroused national interest in the site's protection and it was declared a national park in 1906. The Chapin Mesa Archaeological Museum provides information about the Anasazi civilization and displays findings and artwork from the dwellings. Spruce Tree House, Balcony House and Cliff Palace are open to the public and mesa-top ruins include the Far View Complex, Cedar Tree Tower, and the Sun Temple. Badger House Community is on Wetherill Mesa.

Ute Mountain Tribal Park, set aside by the Ute Mountain tribe to preserve its heritage, adjoins Mesa Verde National Park and includes wall paintings and petroglyphs as well as hundreds of surface sites and cliff dwellings that are similar in size and complexity to those in Mesa Verde.

Among the country's newest national monuments, Canyons of the Ancients created in June 2000, is a 660 sq-km (256 sq-mi) national monument in the area that contains thousands of archaeological sites, in what some claim may be the highest density of archaeological sites in the United States, including the remains of villages, cliff dwellings, sweat lodges, and petroglyphs ranging in age from 700 to as much as 10,000 years old.

Canyons of the Ancients includes Lowry Pueblo, an excavated twelfth-century village, which was probably abandoned by 1200 AD and is believed to have housed up to 100 people. It has standing walls from 40 rooms plus 9 kivas (circular underground ceremonial chambers). A short, self-guided interpretive trail leads past a kiva decorated with geometric designs and continues to the remains of a great kiva, which, at 16.4 m (54 ft) in diameter, is among the largest ever found.

*Cliff Palace at Mesa Verde National Park.*

**WHAT IS IT**
The largest archaeological site in the United States
**WHERE IS IT**
The park entrance is located on US 160, 16 km (10 mi) east of Cortez in Colorado.
**WHY IS IT IMPORTANT**
It is the only national park devoted entirely to the works of humans.
**NOMENCLATURE**
Mesa Verde is Spanish for 'green table', named after the tree-covered flat geological formations.

# Las Vegas

**WHAT IS IT**
The gambling centre of the United States.
**WHEN SHOULD I GO**
Summers are hot here, but everything is air conditioned, making this a year round centre of entertainment of all kinds.
**WHAT IS THERE TO DO**
Gamble, watch live entertainment, eat at gourmet restaurants, play golf, shop, stay in luxurious resorts or just hang out by the pool. Day trips to the Grand Canyon are also possible.
**HOLLYWOOD CONNECTION**
*Honeymoon in Vegas* and both versions of *Ocean's Eleven* were filmed here as well as *CSI Las Vegas*.
**ALSO KNOWN AS**
Sin City or the entertainment capital of the world.

Las Vegas is known for many things: glitz, glamour, ostentation, gambling, entertainment, debauchery, shopping and excess. The most populous city in the state of Nevada, it is the largest founded in the twentieth century, and is the centre of gambling in the United States.

Beginning as a stopover *en route* to the pioneer trails to the west, Las Vegas became a popular railway town in the early twentieth century, serving as a staging point for the mines in the surrounding area, that shipped their goods out to the country from its station. With the growth of the railway, Las Vegas became less important, but the construction of the Hoover Dam injected a new vitality into Las Vegas and the city has never looked back. The increase in tourism caused by the dam and the legalization of gambling led to the advent of the casino-hotels for which Las Vegas is famous.

In the mid- to late 1940s a small building boom included several hotel-casinos by the two-lane main road leading into Las Vegas from Los Angeles, and this is now home to today's 'Strip'. Among the most notable buildings was Bugsy Siegel's Flamingo Hotel, with its neon signs and pink flamingo lawn ornaments that opened in 1946..

In the 1950s, resort building continued to accelerate. Wilbur Clark, once a hotel bellman in San Diego, opened the Desert Inn in 1950. Two years later, Milton Prell opened the Sahara Hotel on the site of the old Club Bingo. The Sands Hotel opened that same year. In 1955, the Riviera Hotel became the first Strip highrise at nine stories. Other resorts that opened during the building boom begun in the 1950s included the Royal Nevada, Dunes, Tropicana and Stardust hotels.

During this time the entertainment industry in Las Vegas took off. In the 1950s Las Vegas became synonymous with the Rat Pack. Entertainment, not just gambling, became the reason to visit the city. For 43 years Frank Sinatra played to sold-out shows in resorts from The Desert Inn to the Sands to the MGM Grand. Sinatra's Rat Pack image of all-night singing, dancing, drinking and womanizing brought a new demographic to the Strip. As the Rat Pack charmed Eisenhower-era America, the Strip continued to expand.

The 1970s saw a decline in Las Vegas tourism. Las Vegas had become a run-down town with little to bring in the crowds. The local government and hoteliers decided it was time to clean up their act. In the late 1980s the Strip was reborn with the construction of the 3,049-room Mirage at a cost of $630 million. Featuring a white tiger habitat, a dolphin pool, an elaborate swimming pool and waterfall and a man-made volcano belching fire, the days of glamour were officially back. Treasure Island, with its full scale pirate ship that engages in combat with a British frigate in its nightly shows, sinking its enemy as a grand finale, is another example of the more recent excesses available here.

The Excalibur, a 4,000 room colossus was the next to open in1990. The imaginative medieval 'castle' has some floors devoted solely to non-gambling entertainment for children and the young at heart including court jesters who perform in public areas. The showroom features jousting on horseback by knights of King Arthur's court.

The Luxor, a black glass pyramid boasts the world's most powerful beam of light shining from its top, as well as a full-scale reproduction of Tutankhamun's tomb. The atrium in the middle of the pyramid could hold nine Boeing 747s stacked on top of one another.

As the luxury resorts appeared so did the retailers. Here you can find nearly every brand on earth from Tiffany to Gucci to Prada and Valentino. Entertainment has also made a resurgence with performers such as Cirque de Soleil, Elton John and Celine Dion.

Other spectacular hotels and resorts have continued to spring up including the MGM Grand, New York New York, the Palms, the Hard Rock Hotel, the Bellagio and the Venetian.

Inspired by the Lake Como resort of Bellagio in Italy, the Bellagio is famed for its its 3.2 ha (8-acre) artificial lake between the hotel and the Strip. The lake encompasses thousands of fountains, their high streams of water lit by a rainbow of coloured lights, flowing to the accompanying music. Vegas is definitely back!

*The Strip sparkles brightly after nightfall.*

# San Diego

Set around a graceful curving bay, free from the smog and the crowded sprawling freeways of Los Angeles, sits the beautiful city of San Diego. The site of the first mission in California, it was not until the arrival of the Santa Fe Railroad in the 1880s that the city became a significant trading port. The second largest city in California, it has farms, state parks and forests, desert areas and mountains rising above the snow line, as well as kilometres of stunning Pacific coast beaches. It has an eclectic mix of architectural styles from Spanish Colonial Renaissance to neo-Gothic and Moorish and offers a wide array of art and culture.

Balboa Park is home to San Diego Zoo and its 4,000 or so animals. The city is also home to Sea World, where Shamu the Orca performs and there are sea lion and dolphin shows.

Mission Beach Boardwalk is another highlight, with roller coasters, an arcade, restaurants and surf shops. You can hire bikes, surfboards, roller skates and roller blades or just enjoy the white sandy coastline.

Another lovely beach is Pacific Beach. Known as the 'PB' by local residents, it is also home to one of San Diego's larger nightlife areas, with dozens of bars and cafés lining Garnet, the main street. A golden beach stretches for miles from the Mission Bay jetty up to the stunning cliffs of ritzy La Jolla. For a different atmosphere, try the historic Gaslamp Quarter, where many of the buildings are Victorian-inspired.

San Diego also has many naval bases, including Miramar, where *Top Gun* was made. Silver Strand Beach National Park and Mt Soledad are other highlights. San Diego is a city with something for everyone.

*The Marina with the city in the background.*

# Hollywood

Hollywood is a region west of downtown Los Angeles, known around the world as the home to the American film industry.

Hollywood is all about celebrity. You can visit your favourite Celebrity Grave, take a tour of Celebrity Homes, walk down Sunset Strip, Hollywood Boulevard and Sunset Boulevard, shop along the celebrity-studded Rodeo Drive and Wilshire Boulevard in Beverly Hills or take a stroll down the Walk of Fame. No trip is complete without a visit to the Hollywood Entertainment Museum or a tour of the Hollywood Studios.

Grauman's Chinese Theatre, on Hollywood Boulevard, was opened in 1927 and received historic-cultural landmark status in 1968. He needed government permission to import the pagodas, stone Heaven Dogs and temple bells from China.

Nearby is the Hollywood Entertainment Museum where you can see how movies and TV shows are made, or sit in Captain Kirk's chair or Norm's seat on the set of *Cheers*.

The Hollywood Forever Cemetery is the 'resting place of Hollywood's immortals', LA's answer to Père Lachaise in Paris, where pilgrims can visit the tombstones of everyone from Rudolph Valentino to Johnny Ramone. Among the palm trees and mausoleums, there are even video screens that show Life Stories. Occasionally in the summer, the public is invited to charity screenings when you can take a picnic dinner and watch a film in the graveyard.

Los Angeles is an outdoor enthusiast's heaven. Nobody walks in LA, but they do hike. There are great trails along the Santa Monica Mountain bluffs overlooking the Pacific Ocean, and the forested Angeles Crest. Or you can just walk uphill into Hollywood's Runyon Canyon, where somewhat disheveled celebrities can be glimpsed walking their dogs off-leash.

Venice Beach is still quintessential California, with street performers, outdoor cafés and lots of life. Hire a bike and ride the cycle path south to Redondo Beach. Take a trip to Santa Monica's pier or stop by Zuma Beach up the Pacific Coast Highway from Malibu.

Catalina Island in Anaheim is where the Angelenos go to scuba dive. Skip the tourist-ridden Avalon and explore the wild side of the island with its excellent hiking, camping, fishing and kayaking.

There are many other excellent ways to pass the time in Los Angeles, such as the LA County Museum of Art and the Museum of Contemporary Art. This relatively small museum is devoted to postwar art and has a permanent collection of 5,000 works. If you like great art, stunning architecture, peaceful gardens and wonderful views (smog permitting) then the Getty Center is not to be missed.

And of course, no trip to LA is complete without spending a day at Disneyland, just a 45-minute drive from downtown Los Angeles.

*The famous sign dominates from Hollywood hills.*

**WHAT IS IT**
The quintessential tinsel town known for its cinematic glamour.
**WHAT IS THERE TO SEE**
Film studios, the Walk of Fame, Grauman's Chinese Theatre
**WHERE IS IT**
Los Angeles, California
**WHEN SHOULD I GO**
Los Angeles enjoys year-round sunshine, but the most beautiful weather is in early spring when the wildflowers are in bloom.

*Morning fog on the Big Sur Coast.*

# Big Sur

'Big Sur' is derived from the Spanish '*el sur grande*', meaning 'the big south'. Named by early Monterey settlers, the southern coastal area is imposing but treacherous to ships.

Although the region includes many state parks, the Big Sur region covers a much larger area of central California, occupying roughly 143 km (89 mi) of the Pacific coastline.

The magnificent coastal scenery of jagged cliffs, pristine beaches, precarious bridges, lofty emerald hills, forests and hot springs has been a beloved landmark for Californians since it was discovered in 1872.

In addition to the many stunning hikes, cycle trails and other abundant outdoor facilities available here, there are also beautiful cliffside hotels and restaurants. Famous actors have found solace here, as have hippies, naturalists, authors, artists and .com millionaires.

One of the interesting sites in Big Sur is Hearst Castle. Built from the amassed fortunes of George Hearst, a wealthy miner, the ranch originally known as 'Camp Hill' was used for relaxing getaways for the billionaire and his friends. Hearst commissioned famed San Francisco architect Julia Morgan in 1919 to 'build a little something'. Hearst and Morgan's collaboration, destined to become one of the world's greatest showpieces constructed on a rocky perch was renamed '*La Cuesta Encantada*', or The Enchanted Hill. By 1947, Hearst and Morgan had created an estate of 165 rooms with more than 50 ha (127 acres) of gardens, terraces, pools and walkways.

The estate's magnificent main house, the 38 bedroom 'Casa Grande', and three neighbouring guest houses, are built in Mediterranean Revival style, with the imposing towers inspired by a Spanish cathedral. This eclectic blend of architectural styles combined with the surrounding land, and Hearst's superb European and Mediterranean art collection created what world-renowned architectural historian, John Julius Norwich called 'a palace in every sense of the word'. Now open to visitors it is a treat strolling through these luscious grounds and living vicariously through the Hearst family, imagining that this is a palace that you could call your own.

**WHAT IS IT**
A stunning area of natural beauty along the Pacific Coast.
**WHERE IS IT**
143 km (89 mi) along California's coastal Highway 1, between San Francisco Bay and Los Angeles.
**WHAT IS THERE TO SEE**
Stretches of scenic beauty along the winding Route 1.
**WHAT IS THERE TO DO**
Hike, kayak, dine, camp or just enjoy the view.
**LITERARY CONNECTION**
*Big Sur and the Oranges of Hieronymus Bosch*, by Henry Miller, and the novel *Big Sur*, by Beat Generation author Jack Kerouac, were both inspired by this lovely coastline.

# Carmel-by-the-Sea

Carmel-by-the-Sea, more commonly called Carmel, is a charming small town on the Pacific Coast of the Monterey Peninsula in central California. Predominantly a residential community, it is also celebrated as having one of the best, and certainly most scenic, golf courses in the United States at Pebble Beach, as well as a lively arts scene.

Built as a seaside artists' colony, attracting such people as Robinson Jeffers, Sinclair Lewis, Robert Louis Stevenson and Ansel Adams, Carmel was created as a peaceful and intellectually inspiring enclave.

Carmel was built of largely cottage-style homes with a fairytale twist including rambling gables, shutters, trellises and large front and rear gardens. These homes were planned to retain the town's character as a 'village in a forest', and some of the homes look as though Little Red Riding Hood or the Big Bad Wolf should be peeking out through the curtains of this picture-postcard landscape. Situated between lush woodland and stunning Pacific Coastline dotted with majestic Cypress trees, Carmel affords spectacular views at every turn.

It is home to many artistic and sports events including the Bach Festival, a series of outdoor concerts and plays, the Concours d'Elegance for car fans, polo and equestrian competitions, and the annual Pebble Beach Pro Am, known after it's founder, Bing Crosby.

The Mission San Carlos Borroméo de Carmelo was founded in 1770 by Father Juniperro Serra, Gaspar de Portola and Father Juan Crespi. Originally located at the Presidio in the centre of the settlement, the National Historic Landmark was subsequently moved to its present site at the southern edge of town overlooking the Carmel River. The stone church, with its curving walls and Moorish bell tower, was erected in 1793. Its walls are covered with a lime plaster made of burnt seashells, and it is home to the first library in California.

The '17-Mile Drive', a meandering road from Pacific Grove to Carmel has awe-inspiring cliff top vistas, multi-million dollar homes to stare at and the occasional spot of wildlife to enjoy.

At Point Lobos, just south of Carmel, you can picnic above the crashing waves and large coves dotted with wildlife and spring flowers. The white sandy beaches surrounded by cypress trees at the Carmel Beach City Park are lovely, as is the Carmel River State Beach and bird sanctuary, just south around the promontory.

**WHAT IS THERE TO SEE**
Gorgeous coastline dotted with pretty beaches, world-class golf at Pebble Beach and the magical '17 mile drive'.

**WHAT IS THERE TO DO**
Walk on the beach, play golf, swim, shop in the many boutiques, surf, dine and sightsee.

**WHAT IS IT KNOWN FOR**
Stunning scenery, extraordinary golf, beautiful homes and artistic history.

**HOLLYWOOD CONNECTION**
Clint Eastwood was once mayor of this beautiful seaside town.

**WHERE IS IT**
8 km (5 mi) south of Monterey, 195 km (121 mi) south of San Francisco and 53 km (33 mi) north of Big Sur.

*The Mission at Carmel.*

# San Francisco

San Francisco is consistently rated one of the top tourist destinations in the United States and is also one of the most recognizable. One visit and you will understand the famed lyrics, 'I left my heart in San Francisco'.

A relatively compact city, the fourth largest in California, San Francisco is only 18 sq km (7 sq mi) in area – making it the second most densely populated American city after New York. However, its largely waterfront location, its rolling hills and its many parks, ensure that it never seems more than a large town.

Whether you are searching for the best in sightseeing, dining, culture, history, sports, outdoor activities or splendid scenery, San Francisco has something to offer everyone.

China Town, the largest Chinese community outside China itself, is entered through the ornate and colourful gates on Bush and Stockton Streets. Here you will see every kind of tea shop, grocer's, knick-knack shop, pharmacy, restaurant, bakery, florist and market filled with live animals for sale and swarming with people, a sea of activity and a cacophony of exotic sounds and aromas.

Next to China Town is North Beach, also known as 'Little Italy', once home to the beat poets like Alan Ginsberg and Jack Kerouac who used to drink here and give readings at the City Lights bookstore. Here is Washington Square Park with its gorgeous church and many street fairs, fabulous Italian cuisine and authentic and charming coffee shops, where you can fortify yourself for the walk up to Coit Tower.

Nearby is Fisherman's Wharf, home to the famous Dungeness Crabs, sourdough chowder bowls and hordes of sea lions basking on the docks. From here you can pick up the ferry to Alcatraz, the maximum security prison once home to the toughest criminals in the world, and Angel Island, the other island and national park floating in the San Francisco Bay, as well as to nearby Sausalito and Tiburon, two upmarket waterfront suburbs.

The Embarcadero, a palm-fringed promenade, hosts the newly refurbished Ferry Building, home to organic farmers markets, fantastic restaurants, bars and shops in a charming building reminiscent of European railway stations. Stop off any morning to get the best in local cheese, fruit and bread for a picnic in Golden Gate Park. Often fogged in, Golden Gate Park is home to the de Young Museum, the fabulous botanical gardens, many large ponds and lakes, fields of bison and picnic spots.

On one edge of the park is Haight-Ashbury, another colourful area, where the hippies of the 1960s and 1970s practised free love. It is still home to tie-dyed teenagers and organic cafés, so a stroll through 'the Haight' is like a step back in time.

*The Golden Gate Bridge – the anti-rust paint makes it red.*

Another well known neighbourhood is the Castro, home to the largest percentage of the city's gay population. The Castro has many lively bistros, cafés, galleries and restaurants among the well kept lovely Victorian homes and well groomed gardens.

In front of the Letterman Digital Arts Center is the Marina Green, a grassy expanse of playing fields, running tracks and pretty beach with the most dramatic views of the landmark red Golden Gate Bridge. While you are here try the scenic Palace of Fine Arts.

Other neighbourhoods of note are the Nob Hill/Russian Hill area, the upmarket playground of many of the wealthiest homeowners. Atop the hill are the luxurious Fairmont, Huntington and Mark Hopkins Hotels as well the impressive Grace Cathedral. The Marina/Cow Hollow is filled with charming boutiques and cafés along Chestnut and Union Streets. Wander up Fillmore Street, up, up, up the hill past the mansions of the rich and famous.

The best way to get a full view of the city is to take the scenic '49 mile drive', which will lead you through the parks and beaches as well as the various historical and scenic spots of interest. Also a must is a trip on one of the cable cars, the two routes will take you from Fisherman's Wharf through Russian and Nob Hills – down to Union Square – do not forget your camera!

*Sausalito nestles in Richardson Bay beneath the hills of Marin County.*

# Sausalito

At the north end of the Golden Gate Bridge in Marin County, Sausalito receives a steady stream of visitors crossing the bridge or using the ferry service from San Francisco.

Named for the 'little willow' trees, or saucelito, found in abundance growing along its streams by eighteenth-century Spanish explorers, Sausalito is the gateway to beautiful coastal Highway 1 that twists and winds among the rugged and spectacular Pacific Ocean cliffs. With only 7,500 residents, and best known for its waterfront views, peaceful Sausalito is said to resemble the Mediterranean. With a slower pace than its bigger neighbour and friendly atmosphere, Sausalito has a scenic waterfront with galleries, boutiques, cafés and restaurants, bars and souvenir shops. Tourists flock here for the seafood and sometimes spend the night in one of the lovely hotels overlooking the bay.

Home to outdoor concerts such as Jazz/Blues by the Bay and Arias in the Afternoon, there are also autumn festivities such as Floating Homes Showcase Tour and Doggy Day and the winter celebration known as Winterland Festival.

**WHAT IS IT**
A scenic coastal town on the San Francisco Bay.
**WHERE IS IT**
On the north side of the Golden Gate Bridge.
**WHAT IS THERE TO SEE**
Stunning bay views and an attractive waterfront promenade with boutiques, cafés and galleries.

*Waterfall above Emerald Bay at Lake Tahoe.*

# Lake Tahoe

One of the United State's most beautiful landmarks, Lake Tahoe's shimmering waters span 19 x 35 km (12 x 22 mi). With nearly 300 days of sunshine a year, and the surrounding majestic Sierra Nevada Mountains, Lake Tahoe offers stunning scenery and a multitude of year-round activities.

The second deepest lake in the US and the tenth in the world, it has a maximum depth of 501 m (1,645 ft) and an average depth of 305 m (1,000 ft).

Lake Tahoe is host to year-round activities. North and South Lake Tahoe are where you will find the majority of the world-class ski resorts. North Lake Tahoe is home to some of the ritzier and more upmarket neighbourhoods and resorts including Alpine Meadows and Squaw Valley USA, home to the 1960 Winter Olympics; South Lake Tahoe is the most populated area, with larger high rise resorts, some excellent skiing areas such as Heavenly, and many casinos.

East Lake Tahoe is virtually undeveloped, but West Lake Tahoe is focused on residential areas, smaller hotels and inns and a variety of dining options featuring gorgeous views as their backdrop.

One of the most scenic areas to explore in the south-west is Emerald Bay, one of the most photographed natural locations in the United States. With its amazing views of the mountains, the lake, and Tahoe's only island, Fannette Island, Emerald Bay State Park serves as a stunning backdrop to Vikingsholm, a striking reproduction of a Norse Fortress commissioned by a wealthy Chicago widow. Accessible only by boat, this folly is considered to be a fine example of Scandanavian architecture. Turrets, towers, intricate carvings and hand-hewn timbers were used to recreate the fortress. The turf roof, with its living grass and wildflowers, is like those used in Scandinavia to feed livestock in winter. Many of the furnishings that Mrs Knight desired for Vikingsholm were of such historical significance the Norwegian and Swedish governments would not grant export licences, so she had them copied down to every detail.

Whether you are interested in hiking or camping, skiing or snowmobiling, being pampered at a spa, eating gourmet cuisine, or picnicking while watching live Shakespeare – there is something to fulfill everyone in this area of incredible beauty.

**WHAT IS IT**
A spectacular lake surrounded by the High Sierra Mountains.
**WHERE IS IT**
In northern California on the Nevada border.
**WHAT IS THERE TO DO**
An alpine resort area, it is home to casinos, skiing, hiking, sailing one of the world's most stunning lakes.
**WHEN SHOULD I GO**
Lake Tahoe offers year round fun – January through March has world-class skiing and June through September has the best watersports and hiking trails available.
**HOLLYWOOD CONNECTION**
*Indian Love Call*, *The Godfather* and *The Bodyguard* were all filmed here.

# Mount St Helens

Mount St Helens, once known as 'the Fuji of America' for its symmetrical beauty similar to that of the famous Japanese volcano, with its graceful cone top capped by snow is now largely gone.

Today, visitors come to Mt St Helens to marvel at the destruction and devastation caused by this natural disaster as well as to gaze in awe at nature's remarkable ability to recover.

On 18 May, 1980 at 8:32 am, the north face of Mount St Helens collapsed in the largest debris avalanche ever recorded, caused by an underlying earthquake that measured 5.1 on the Richter scale. The volcano's height was reduced from 9677 ft (2950 m) to 8364 ft (2550m).

Within seconds of the earthquake, the volcano's bulging northern side slid away, triggering a destructive, lethal lateral blast of hot gas, steam and rock debris that swept across the landscape. Blasted with temperatures as high as 300 °C (572 °F), snow and ice on the volcano rapidly melted, forming violent torrents of water and rock that rushed from the volcano. Within moments, a massive cloud of ash thrust 19 km (11.8 mi) into the sky, and the strong winds carried more than 540 million tons of ash across 57,000 sq km (35,418 sq mi) of the western United States.

Shortly afterward, a cloud of ash rose skyward, while a pyroclastic flow sent even more ash down the Toutle and Cowlitz rivers, dragging

# Yellowstone National Park

Yellowstone National Park, designated as the world's first national park by Ulysses S Grant in 1872, is also a biosphere reserve and World Heritage Site for its spectacular topography. Lying mostly in Wyoming, its 8,987 sq km (3,472 sq mi) extend into Montana and Idaho. Elevations range from a maximum height of 3,462 m (11,358 ft) at Eagle Peak to 1,610 m (5,282 ft) at Reese Creek. Most of the park is covered by forest interspersed with grassland and water.

The park is home to the planet's most diverse collection of geysers, hot springs, mudpots and fumaroles. Two-thirds of the earth's geysers – more than 300 – are here – and combined with over 10,000 other thermal features, you have a place like no other.

The park is also home to an active volcano, roughly 2,000 earthquakes a year, one of the world's largest petrified forests, one of the world's largest calderas – measuring 72 by 48 km (45 by 30 mi), and some 290 sizeable waterfalls, the highest of which are the 94-m (308-ft) Lower Falls of the Yellowstone River.

The Upper Geyser Basin is home to the largest numbers of geysers. Within 2.5 sq km (1 sq mi) there are at least 150, of which five  can be accurately predicted – Castle, Grand, Daisy, Riverside and the most famous, Old Faithful.  Driving down Firehole Lake Drive you will find the sixth predictable geyser – Great Fountain – whose twice-daily eruptions send water bursting 30–61 m (100–200 ft) into the air.

The Midway Geyser Basin, although smaller than its surrounding blow holes, offers the incredible gaping crater of the Excelsior Geyser, 61 x 91 m (200 x 300 ft) with a constant discharge of more than 4,000 gallons of water per minute into the Firehole River, which was named because early trappers thought it appeared to be smoke from wild fires. Also found here is Yellowstone's largest hot spring, Grand Prismatic Spring, over 113 m (370 ft) in diameter and more than 37 m (121 ft) in depth.

The most popular attraction of Yellowstone National Park, located in the Upper Geyser Basin, is Old Faithful. Named for its punctuality, Old Faithful, although not the largest or most spectacular of the geysers, erupts more frequently than any of the others, on average every 80 minutes, spraying waters up to 57 m (184 ft) into the air.

Not only host to incredible natural features and awe-inspiring scenery, Yellowstone also hosts a number of large mammals including both black and grizzly bears, coyotes, grey wolves, red foxes, bobcats, mountain lions, lynx, otters, a number of deer species, bison, bighorn sheep and mountain goats among others.

*At the Lower Geyser Basin, a geyser erupts. Old Faithful can be seen in the background.*

**WHAT IS IT**
The world's first national park
**WHERE IS IT**
Largely in Wyoming, but extending into Montana and Idaho.
**WHAT IS IT KNOWN FOR**
Fantastically diverse geological features, particularly Old Faithful geyser, and stunning scenery.
**WHEN SHOULD I VISIT**
Yellowstone has four distinct seasons, cold in winter, pleasant in spring, hot in summer, and cool in autumn.

# Yosemite National Park

*Bridalveil Falls in the Yosemite National Park.*

Yosemite National Park, famously known as the focus of the American photographer Ansel Adams, is a spectacular combination of awe-inspiring mountain-and-valley scenery in the Sierra Nevada Mountians, named a national park in 1890. The park encompasses a grand collection of waterfalls, meadows and forest land including massive groves of giant sequoias, the world's largest living trees.

If there is one remarkable landmark that stands out here, it is probably Half Dome. Rising 1,219 m (4,000 ft) from the Valley floor, it is the most photographed mountain in the park with its shaved surface offering a stunning contrast to the surrounding jagged peaks. Those who dare can choose to either hike it or climb it, but be prepared for sore muscles the next day!

Another favourite of experienced rock climbers is El Capitan, the largest granite monolith in the world at 914 m (3,000 ft) high. Opposite Bridalveil Fall, it is best seen from the far west of Yosemite Valley.

Another of the park's natural highlights is Yosemite Falls with its roaring runoff from a height of 740 m (2,425 ft). One of the world's tallest, Yosemite Falls is actually made up of three separate falls: Upper Yosemite Falls measuring 436 m (1,430 ft), the middle cascades at 206 m (675 ft), and Lower Yosemite Falls at 98 m (320 ft). It is a very short walk to Lower Yosemite Falls, but it is a strenuous, all day trip to reach the towering Upper Yosemite Falls.

Glacier Point's views of Yosemite Valley, with its high cliffs and waterfalls, are what dreams are made of. The Mariposa Grove, containing hundreds of ancient giant sequoias, is something not to be missed and Tuolumne Meadows, a large subalpine meadow surrounded by mountain peaks, will leave you breathless.

And if that is not enough to tempt you to visit this wilderness wonderland, Yosemite is also home to a variety of animals, although they are sometimes difficult to spot. Bears and deer are plentiful but shy, as are the coyotes whose howls you will hear in the night, adding to the atmosphere of this oasis of natural beauty.

# Giant Redwoods

There are three species of giant redwood trees in the world, two of which can be seen in California; the coastal redwood and the giant sequoia. Standing near them is a humbling and surreal experience.

Tourists come every year to drive along the Avenue of the Giants, a 50-km (31-mi) stretch of the scenic old Highway 101 in Humboldt Redwood State Park.

Here you will be surrounded by a dense 20,730 (51,222 acre) forest of the largest remaining stand of virgin redwood groves in the world. Stretching through the mist, over 91 m (300 ft) into the air, these 3,000-year-old trees, protected as part of an international biosphere reserve and noted as a UNESCO World Heritage Site, are known to weigh up to 2000 tonnes: this is truly an experience not to be missed.

Just to put these numbers into perspective, stop by One Log House, built completely from one 40-tonne log from a fallen Redwood tree in Phillipsville. Also on show there is the famed Giant Sequoia Chimney Tree. Standing at a relatively dwarfish 24 m (78 ft), it may not be impressive in size, but its tenacity will amaze you considering it continues to grow even after it was nearly destroyed in a wildfire in 1914.

Another legendary Sequoia is the Shrine Drive-through tree, which can accommodate smaller vehicles. The Immortal Tree, another feat of nature, stands near Redcrest; it has endured flooding, fires, numerous lightning strikes and more than a few loggers' axe cuts.

The California redwood forests have been referred to as nature's cathedrals; when you feel the peacefulness and reverence passing between the lofty red-brown pillars, sunlight filtering through the dense canopy high above like a stained glass window, you will understand this completely.

*The giant redwoods are great in both height and girth.*

**WHAT ARE THEY**
The tallest trees in existence.
**WHERE ARE THEY**
Humbolt County, California
**HOW DO I GET THERE**
The Avenue of the Giants parallels Highway 101 and the Eel River for 50 km (31 mi), and can be accessed from a number of signposted exits. The Avenue can be reached from Eureka in just over 30 minutes.
**WHAT IS THERE TO SEE**
Two of the world's three giant redwood species.

anything and everything in its path downstream, destroying roads, bridges, homes and businesses and blanketing much of the Pacific north-west with a grey, dusty powder.

Even before its eruption, Mount St Helens was not one of the highest peaks in the Cascade Range, it was only the fifth highest peak in Washington. What was impressive was its handsome outline against the neighbouring craggy peaks.

Today, over a quarter of a century later, the signs of healing are evident. The pre-eruption landscape, once dominated by dense coniferous forests and clear streams and lakes has begun to re-establish itself. The lower forests once dominated by Douglas fir and western hemlock have started to regrow and tourism has returned to this area of scenic beauty.

*Mount St Helens from Rock Lookout.*

ASIA

# Guilin

Guilin's scenic splendour is difficult to comprehend. Large emerald green limestone karsts seemingly float on the Li River, whose natural beauty and historic treasures combine to create a magical landscape.

Situated majestically south-east of Guilin city and on the west bank of the Li River, Elephant Trunk Hill is regarded as the main symbol of Guilin's landscape. Originally named 'Li Hill', 'Yi Hill' or 'Chenshui Hill', it has a history of 360,000,000 years. The large karst formation resembles a mammoth elephant leisurely sipping water from the river with its long trunk.

Towering 55m (180ft) above the water, 108m (354ft) long and 100m (328ft) wide, the the elephant has between its trunk and legs a cave in the shape of a full Moon, which penetrates through the hill. Locals refer to this as 'Moon-over-Water Cave'. When the waves lap and the moonlight gleams, the scene is particularly enchanting. On the walls in and around the cave, there are more than 70 inscriptions from the Tang and Song dynasties (618–907 and 960–1279 respectively) praising the beauty of hills and waters nearby. Half-way up the hill lies another cave, which goes through the hill and serves as the eyes of the elephant, through which visitors can look at the beauty of Guilin city.

On top of the hill stands Puxian Pagoda. Built in the Ming dynasty (1368–1644), it looks like the handle of a sword. The pagoda has many carvings and inscriptions, the most famous of them being a poem by Lu You, one of the four great poets of the Southern Song dynasty.

The Li River cruise from Guilin to Yangshuo is the highlight of any trip to north-eastern Guangxi Province. Water buffalo patrol fields, peasants wade through rice paddies, schoolchildren smile at you from the lush banks and fisherman float by on bamboo rafts with their flocks of cormorants. With its breathtaking scenery and taste of a life far removed from the metropolis, the landscape along the Li River is dreamlike and unforgettable.

*Fishermen using cormarants to fish on the Li River.*

# Old Town Lijiang and Dali

The Old Town of Lijiang, built on a plateau 2,400 m (7,874 ft) above sea level is surrounded by mountains to the north and west, and vast fertile fields to the south-east. Crystal-clear water runs through it and it has been described as resembling a large jade ink slab and has also been called the Venice of the Orient.

This UNESCO World Heritage Site was first built during the late Song and early Yuan dynasties (960–1279 and 1271–1368). Under Kublai Khan (1271–1294), Lijiang was an important political, cultural and educational centre and played a large role in trade between Yunnan, Tibet, India and the rest of Asia. Walking through the blue slate streets, one can feel the historic prosperity of this charming town.

The only old city built without a city wall, Lijiang became a multicultural city, with architecture incorporating styles from Han, Bai and Tibet into a unique Naxi form. It has narrow, meandering lanes, timber and tile homes with engraved figures on their windows and doors and vibrant gardens decorating their fronts.

Water is the soul and blood of Old Lijiang, and Black Dragon Pool (Heilongtan) is the main artery. The water is fed into streams so every family and every street has access. The aqueducts feed the abundant willow trees that shade the nearly 350 pretty bridges, some of which were built during the Ming Dynasty (1368–1644).

Jade Dragon Snow Mountain, (Yulong Mountain) has 13 peaks, of which Shanzidou, at 5,600 m (18,360 ft), when viewed from Lijiang Old Town 35 km (9 mi) away, resembles a jade dragon lying in the clouds.

Erhai Lake in Dali is one of the seven biggest freshwater lakes in China. Its name means, 'sea shaped like an ear'. On a sunny day, its crystal waters reflect the snow-capped Cangshan Mountain in the distance.

The Three Pagodas, c.1 km (0.6 mi) north-west of ancient Dali, at the foot of Mt Cangshan, have a history of over 1,800 years. Their triangular placement is unique in China.

**WHAT IS IT**
A beautiful ancient town with meandering slate lanes threaded by rivers.
**WHERE IS IT**
North-west of Yunnan province.
**WHY SHOULD I GO**
In addition to the charming town, there are a variety of fascinating nearby attractions.
**ALSO KNOWN AS**
'Town of Big Ink Slab' or 'Venice of the Orient'

*Black Dragon Pool in Lijiang.*

# Huang Long Valley

*Waterfalls in Huang Long Valley.*

Bordered by the Tibetan Plateau, the Three Gorges and the Yangtze River, and lofty mountains, Sichuan is known as the 'Land of Abundance' boasting three places on the World Cultural and Natural Heritage List: Jiuzhaigou Scenic and Historic Interest Area, Huanglong Valley and Mt Emei Scenic area including Leshan Giant Buddha Scenic Area.

A UNESCO World Heritage Site, the Huang Long Valley is one of the most stunning areas of the province, covering an area of roughly 700 sq km (270 sq mi) and consisting of Huanglong and Muni Gorge.

Huanglong has unique scenery, rich natural resources and a primeval forest. The majestic and unrivalled emerald lakes, layered waterfalls, colourful forests, snow-capped peaks and Tibetan folk villages blend harmoniously into the mountains sparkling like jewels, giving it the nickname of 'mountain fairyland'.

Huanglong Valley translates to 'Yellow Dragon Valley'. This incredible valley undulates through the southern part of the Minshan mountain range in Songpan County about 250 km (155 mi) away from Chengdu, the capital of Sichuan.

Legend has it, that about 4,000 years ago, a yellow dragon helped Xiayu, the king of Xia Kingdom, channel floodwater into the sea, making the Minjiang River. Because of the calcium carbonate deposits and the golden hue of the water, the river resembles the tail of a yellow dragon. The valley was named and a temple built in honour of the yellow dragon.

Huanglong's magical landscape of lime formations carved by the river, also consists of 3,400 multicoloured ponds paved with golden calcium carbonate deposits, as well as five waterfalls, four stalactite caves and three ancient temples.

**WHAT IS IT**
A stunning valley that resembles a yellow dragon surging down from the snowcapped peaks of Mt. Minshan.
**WHERE IS IT**
In the Minshan mountain range about 250 km (155 mi) away from Chengdu, the capital of Sichuan.
**ALSO KNOWN AS**
'Yellow Dragon Valley' or 'Mountain Fairyland'.
**WHAT IS THERE TO SEE**
Huanglong and Muni Gorge.

# Shanghai

Shanghai, on the estuary of the Yangtze River, is the largest industrial city in China. Originally a seaside fishing village it is now a multicultural metropolis combining the best of modern and traditional China.

An important seaport and China's largest commercial, industrial and financial centre, Shanghai is also great for tourists. Sightseeing, business and shopping are centred around People's Square and along the Huangpu River. The cultural centre, with public activities, community facilities and the main entertainment and tourist sites are at Mt Sheshan, Chongming Island, Dingshan Lake and Shenshuigang.

Shanghai is a shopper's paradise. Nanjing Road and Huaihai Road are perfect for those seeking the lastest fashions, while Xujiahui Shopping Centre, Yuyuan Shopping City, and the Jiali Sleepless City are popular destinations for those looking for a memento of their visit.

Huaihai Road is also known for its cafés, antique shops and the marvellous old French Concession. Once designated for the French, the area still has a number of mansions with colourful flower boxes on tree-lined avenues. There are also remnants of Japanese occupation, and buildings from the now defunct Jewish and Russian quarters.

The Bund, a stretch of Zhong Shan Dong Yi Road by the Huangpu, was once home to British, French, American, Russian and Japanese banks and trading houses, and remains a major financial hub. Locals gather on the promenade at dawn to practise kung fu, qi gong, tai chi and ballroom dancing. For the rest of the day tourists queue up on the docks for scenic riverboat tours.

Shanghai offers culinary delights focusing on the traditions of Beijing, Yangzhou, Sichuan and Guangzhou as well as its own local dishes. Its restaurants are among the finest in China and cutting-edge international cuisine can be enjoyed in stylish surroundings.

Additional sights that shouldn't be missed include a trip to see the Shanghai Acrobatics Troupe, the Shanghai Museum and the spectacular Yu Yuan Garden. This garden and temple were commissioned in 1559, but later destroyed in the Opium Wars. Their current incarnation includes pathways winding through scenic rock gardens and bamboo stands and stone bridges casting shadows over giant carp ponds. 'Yu' translates to 'peace and health'.

**WHAT IS IT**
The largest industrial city in China, the hipper cousin of Hong Kong and the more alluring sister of Beijing.
**WHERE IS IT**
On the estuary of China's Yangtze River.
**WHAT IS THERE TO DO**
Dine at fantastic restaurants, visit cultural museums, look at stunning modern architecture and shop among one of the top fashion hot spots in the world.
**ALSO KNOWN AS**
'Hu' or 'The Oriental Paris'
**WHEN SHOULD I GO**
Shanghai is a year-round destination, but summer is its peak travel season. To avoid the tourist rush, visit in late spring or early autumn and avoid Chinese national holidays.

*Traditional dance at the Bund.*

# Imperial Palaces in Beijing

Beijing, China's capital city, is the nation's political, economic, cultural and educational centre as well as being the country's most important international trade and communications centre. Rich in history, Beijing has been inhabited for more than 3,000 years, serving as the capital for the last 800 years through the Yuan, Ming and Qing Dynasties. It is a stunning combination of ancient splendours and modern delights. Thirty-four emperors lived and ruled here and their Imperial Palaces stand as a reminder of the strength of this vibrant country's past.

The Forbidden City (Gu Gong) is the most grand and best-preserved imperial palace complex in the world. Lying at the centre of Beijing, it served as the imperial palace during both the Ming and Qing dynasties. Now called the Palace Museum, it covers the northern half of Tiananmen Square. The world's largest palace complex, the Palace Museum is a rectangular structure with 9,999 buildings covering 74 ha (183 acres) and is surrounded by a 6-m (20-ft) deep moat and a 10-m (33-ft) high wall with a gate on each side. Opposite the Tiananmen Gate is the Gate of Divine Might (Shenwumen), facing Jingshan Park. They are 960 m (3,150 ft) apart, while the gates in the east and west walls are 750 m (2,461 ft) apart. Delicate towers dot the four corners of the curtain wall, giving views over both the palace and the city outside.

The Forbidden City is divided into two parts: the southern section, or the Outer Court where the emperor exercised his supreme power over the nation, and the northern section, or the Inner Court where the royal family lived. Until 1924 when the last emperor, Puyi, was driven from the Inner Court, 14 Ming and 10 Qing emperors lived here.

A UNESCO World Heritage Site, the Palace Museum is one of the most popular tourist attractions in the world. Because yellow was the symbol of the royal family, it was the main colour used in the Forbidden City. Roofs have yellow glazed tiles, palace decorations are painted yellow and even the brick paths are yellow. The exception is the royal library, Wenyuange, whose black roof represents water, and so was believed to be able to extinguish fire.

In the western outskirts of the Haidian District, 15 km (9.3 mi) from central Beijing, is another UNESCO World Heritage Site, the Summer Palace. The largest and best preserved royal park, the Summer Palace is an archetypal Chinese garden, encompassing graceful landscapes, magnificent architecture and ancient art. Originally called 'Qingyi Garden' (Garden of Clear Ripples), its construction was begun during the Jin Dynasty (265–420) and continued to the Qing Dynasty (1644–1912). The luxurious garden provided the royal families with rest and entertainment. It was destroyed by fire and rebuilt in 1886 by the Empress Dowager Cixi.

Composed mainly of Longevity Hill and Kunming Lake, the Summer Palace covers 294 ha (726.5 acres), three quarters of which is water. Guided by nature, landscape artists designed the gardens to maximize

*The Forbidden City, Beijing.*

viewpoints from every angle. Centred on the Tower of Buddhist Incense (Foxiangge), the Summer Palace consists of over 3,000 structures including pavilions, towers, bridges and corridors.

The Summer Palace can be divided into four parts, each with its own character. Front-hill is considered the most magnificent, with the most impressive architecture. Rear-Hill and Back-Lake Area have tranquil landscapes, with dense green trees and winding paths. Front-Lake covers a large part of the Summer Palace, with stunning views of the lake and many exquisite bridges.

The Temple of Heaven is larger than the Forbidden City, but smaller than the Summer Palace with an area of *c*.270 ha (670 acres). It was built in 1420 to offer sacrifice to Heaven. The northern part of the temple within the enclosing wall is semicircular symbolising the heavens, and the southern part is square, symbolising the earth.

Not only are the magnificent temples architecturally and artistically breathtaking, there is also a fascinating structure famous for its acoustics. Enclosing the Imperial Vault of Heaven, Echo Wall has a perimeter of 193 m (633 ft). If you whisper facing the vault while standing on one side of the wall, you will be heard on the opposite side!

# The Great Wall

**WHAT IS IT**
One of the greatest man-made wonders of the world.
**HOW BIG IS IT**
The wall covers more than 6,700 km (4,163 mi) from east to west China.
**HOW LONG DID IT TAKE TO BUILD**
More than 1,800 years.
**WHERE SHOULD I GO**
Head 60 km (37 mi) north of Beijing to the Huanghua (Yellow Flower Fortress) section of the wall where there are fewer tourists.

The Great Wall of China, a UNESCO World Heritage Site and one of the great man-made wonders of the world, lies like a gigantic dragon, stretching up and down across deserts, grasslands, mountains and plateaus covering an area of approximately 6,700 km (4,163 mi) from east to west. At more than 2,000 years old, some sections of the Great Wall are understandably in ruins or have disappeared, but it remains one of the most incredible feats of man and its architectural grandeur and historical significance are breathtaking.

The construction of the Great Wall was started by the Qin dynasty between the seventh and eighth centuries BC and took more than 1,800 years to complete. It is believed that it was originally intended as military fortification against intrusion from the north, but over time grew to become not only a symbol of defence, but also of the great power of the emperor.

The architecture of the Great Wall is a marvel of ancient building work. Weaponry of the time consisted only of swords, spears, lances and bows and arrows, so walls with walkways, watchtowers and signal towers, together with moats, became an important part of defensive strategy. After the work done by the Qin dynasty (221–206 BC), the later sections of the wall include an even more sophisticated defensive system with garrison towns, garrison posts, walkways, blockhouses, additional wall structures, watchtowers and beacon towers enabling the imperial court to stay in touch with the military and gave the frontier troops the facilities to carry out defence effectively.

*The Great Wall disappears across the hills.*

To the uninformed tourist, the wall is just a majestic crumbling feat of man. When taking the strenuous hike through the various sections, it is difficult to comprehend how many men it must have taken to build this massive structure nearly 8 m (26 ft) across and how the enormous quantities of stones must have been transported here. Looking out over the spectacular emerald hills and valleys you can sense the history and understand what effort and sacrifice must have taken place to enable the construction of such a massive undertaking. It is truly one of the most memorable experiences that you will ever have.

# Pingyao

Ancient Pingyao, a UNESCO World Heritage Site, is a small city about 90 km (56 mi) away from Taiyuan, the capital city of Shanxi Province, and is known for its well-preserved city wall as well as the nearby Wang and Qiao family compounds. At the southern edge of the Taiyuan Basin and next to the Loess Plateau in the south, its location on the banks of the Yellow River enabled it to serve as an important communications and commercial hub.

The ancient walls surrounding Pingyao are one of the best examples of Ming Dynasty building, being an unbroken rectangle that features a rammed-earth and brick structure 6.2 km (3.85 mi) around. The wall rises to 12 m (40 ft) with a bottom width of 8–12 m (26-40 ft) tapering to 2.5–6 m (8–20 ft) at the top. The wall is said to resemble a tortoise, the sacred symbol of longevity in Chinese. The south and north gates count as the head and tail with the pairs of east and west gates as the four feet. Two wells, resembling the eyes of the tortoise, stand just outside the south gate, and the criss-crossing streets inside the city are taken to be the markings on the shell.

A moat, 4 m (13 ft) deep and wide also surrounds the city, serving both as the first line of the city's defences and a reservoir to in case of fire. When the wall was first built, a drawbridge served as the single entry and exit point for the city.

Each corner of the wall has a watch tower and, in addition, there are 72 watch towers built into the wall at intervals of 40–60 m (131–197 ft), giving the guards excellent sight of any enemies attempting to climb the walls.

There are some 4,000 old buildings and family compounds in the city and in the surrounding region. Two particularly grand family compounds outside the city are the Wang and the Qiao mansions. The Qiao compound, built from the proceeds of a vast banking and trading empire, has 313 rooms and covers an area of 3,528 sq m (37,980 sq ft). The Wang family acquired their wealth from farming and commerce during the Ming and Qing Dynasties and their compound includes a massive mansion built as a monument to the glory of the family. Building work lasted for more than half a century, and the mansion covers an area of 3.2 ha (8 acres). Consisting of 54 courtyards and 1,052 rooms, the Wang compound is the epitome of Oriental domestic architecture.

*The ancient city of Pingyao.*

**WHAT IS IT**
A fantastic example of Ming Dynasty walls surrounding a quaint and historic city, as well as the famed compounds of the Wang and Qiao families.
**WHERE IS IT**
90 km (56 mi) away from Taiyuan, the capital city of Shanxi Province.
**WHEN SHOULD I GO**
Spring and summer are the best times to visit.
**ALSO KNOWN AS**
The 'Tortoise City'.
**HOLLYWOOD CONNECTION**
*Raise the Red Lanterns* was filmed in the Qiao mansion.

# Mogao Caves

Listed as a UNESCO World Heritage Site in 1987 the Mogao Caves in Gansu Province contain more than 1,000 years of Buddhist art. According to legend, in 366 AD a monk called Lo-tsun had a vision of 1,000 Buddhas, and began to carve out the first cave. The site is strategically placed on the Silk Road – one of the most important east-west trade routes – and he sought funding from passing merchants. As Buddhism spread, the caves became a pilgrimage site. The caves were carved out of the soft sandstone, and 492 of them survive: the largest is 40 m (130 ft) high and the smallest under 1 m (39 in) and the total length is some 1.6 km (1 mi). Known as the 'Caves of 1,000 Buddhas', they contain 2,415 painted clay statues of the Buddha, holy men, Bodhisattvas (beings who help humans on the path to enlightenment) and the Buddhist faithful, ranging in size from 10 cm (4 in) to 33 m (108 ft). Some 50,000 sq m (484,000 sq ft) of wall paintings survive, with subjects as diverse as floral patterns, Buddha's teachings, fairy tales and legends and episodes from the Sutras, all of which were designed to teach and inspire illiterate worshippers in much the same way as stained-glass windows in medieval cathedrals. Five of the wooden buildings within the caves also surive.

After the fourteenth century, the caves were abandoned and all-but forgotten until they were 'rediscovered' at the turn of the twentieth century by Wang Yuan-lu. He found a large cache of 40,000 scrolls, bronze statues and silk paintings in cave 16, and embarked on a refurbisment programme, funded partly by donations from neighbouring towns and partly by selling the treasures found in cave 16 to western archaeologists until the Chinese government stopped him doing so. They set up a research unit in 1949 and archaeological work continues to this day. It is a major tourist attraction and can be very busy at times, but the scale of the open parts of the complex and the beauty of the paintings are inspirational.

*Steep stairs lead to several entry structures to the caves.*

**WHAT ARE THEY**
492 caves famous for their statues and wall paintings.
**WHERE ARE THEY**
Near Dunhuang Gansu province.
**WHY ARE THEY IMPORTANT**
They are a fine example of Buddhist art, spanning more than 1,000 years.
**ALSO KNOWN AS**
'Caves of the Thousand Buddhas' or 'Qianfodong'.
**WHAT SHOULD I KNOW**
Photography is forbidden anywhere in the complex.

# Lushan National Park

Lushan National Park, is a UNESCO World Heritage Site and Geopark in the north of Jiangxi Province, centred around Mt Lushan. Covering 302 sq km (117 sq mi) set within a larger protected area, this 2.5-million-year-old landscape contains 100 scenic peaks, the highest of which, Dahanyang Peak, soars to 1,474 m (4,836 ft). Mt Lushan's spectacular landscape of mist-shrouded peaks and roaring waterfalls is also home to many Pure Land Buddist, Taoist and Confucian sites.

The White Deer Cave Academy is one of the oldest known institutions of higher learning in China. First built by Li Bo, a Tang Dynasty official, in the early seventh century, it was later expanded during the Song Dynasty. One of four major academies in the country, it hosted scholars and philosophers such as Zhu Xi and Lu Xiangshan.

At the base of Mt Lushan the Five Elderly Men Peaks (Wulaofeng) can be seen reflected in the clear waters of Poyang Lake, a well-known summer resort for locals and tourists alike. Other scenic lakes in the area that have inspired Chinese poets for centuries include Small Heavenly Lake (Xiaotianchi) a spring-fed lake 1,200 m (3,900 ft) above sea level and Big Heavenly Lake (Daitianchi), which is said to have been hand dug from the rocks by an immortal. Both of these are good spots for watching sunrise and sunset.

The Flower Path (Huajing) is renowned for its beauty. This is where stunning peach blossoms combine with the foliage of other trees to create an area of stunning beauty.

Other highlights of the area include Immortal's Cavern (Xianrendong) a 10 sq m (108 sq ft) cave where an immortal is said to have lived and where an eternal spring trickles year round. A stone statue carved into the side of the cave is a perennial attraction.

The Dragon Head Cliff, the Lushan Botanical Garden and the Three Precious Trees are also sites not to be missed here. Most important however, is the Three-stage Spring, or Sandiequan, formed by spring water flowing down a series of large rocks, creating a thunderous waterfall. The spring is often referred to as 'the first wonder of Lushan' and legend has it that 'a visit to Lushan does not count if you do not see the Three-stage Spring!'

**WHAT IS IT**
A mountainous region of spectacular beauty including Great Hang Yang Peak, 1,474 m (4,836 ft) above sea level.

**WHERE IS IT**
In the north of Jiangxi Province.

**WHAT IS IT KNOWN FOR**
Stunning landscapes, important sites of early Taoist and Confucian thought, Lushan Village and the international villa complex, and as the birthpace of Pure Land Buddhism.

**WHEN SHOULD I GO**
Summer is the best time to visit.

*Lushan National Park has 22 major waterfalls.*

# Wolong Nature Reserve

The Wolong Nature Reserve is best known for its tremendous efforts in the protection and reintroduction of the endangered giant panda. Located in Wenchuan County, Sichuan Province, 136 km (85 mi) from Chengdu, the reserve covers nearly 200,000 ha (494,000 acres) at the eastern foot of the Qionglai Mountains. The Sichuan Giant Panda Sanctuary, of which it forms a part, gained UNESCO World Heritage Site status in 2006. The reserve lies on the transition zone between Qinghai, the Tibetan Plateau and the Sichuan Basin, hosting over 4,000 species of plants, 50 mammal varieties, 300 bird species and 29 rare and endangered species including the giant panda and the lesser panda, which is also called the red panda or small panda, and snow leopards.

The snow-capped peaks of the reserve have been home to the Panda Breeding Centre since it was established by the Chinese government in the early 1980s. Only about 1,600 of these precious bears remain in the wild and this breeding centre is key to the hopes of keeping the species alive. The goal of the group is to breed the animals and release them from captivity, but they also rescue those found in the wild who are injured and release some to zoos.

The Wolong Nature Reserve is a teaching academy where students come from all over the world to learn about the breeding practices. While they are here, they may also track for wild panda footprints, or enjoy the many flowers that can be found in the area. Fifteen types of azalea have been discovered in the park and in autumn, brilliant blossoms and leaves of various colours decorate the mountains and forests. Birdwatchers are also drawn to the area as the many species of plants and flowers attract some of the most attractive and rare birds found on the continent.

*A giant panda enjoying his bamboo.*

# Hong Kong

Hong Kong is a dynamic city, a kaleidoscope of cultures, a sophisticated fusion of East and West. Standing at the railing of the Star Ferry as it glides across the harbour past junks, with a vast skyline of towering buildings in the distance, it is hard not to marvel at this city of striking contrasts, with its eclectic mixture of the exotic and technically advanced, the modern and the ancient, the past and the present.

Modern sky scrapers and five-star hotels are covered with bamboo scaffolding, Cantonese and Mandarin food stalls are surrounded by gourmet French bistros, Rolls Royces pass old men pushing wheelbarrows, hawkers selling chicken feet and dried squid talk on mobile phones and the largest shopping centres in the world jostle for your attention with lively street markets selling traditional wares.

Much of Hong Kong's Western fabric comes from its legacy as a former British colony. British influence remains evident, from the school system to the free market-economy, from rugby teams to double-decker buses and from English pubs and afternoon tea to orderly queues.

Although moulded by the British, Hong Kong has always been rooted in Chinese traditions, with Chinese medicine shops, street vendors, lively dim-sum restaurants, old men taking their caged birds for walks in the park and colourful festivals.

An easy city to navigate, Hong Kong is surprisingly compact, with most streets clearly marked in English. Not only is public transport well organized and punctual, but the Star Ferry and the trams are sightseeing attractions in themselves. In general, however, walking is the best way to get around the city, particularly in the narrow, fascinating pedestrian-only lanes and alleyways.

**WHAT IS IT**
A fascinating and dynamic city blending the best of east and west.
**WHERE IS IT**
Off of mainland China.
**WHAT IS THERE TO SEE**
Ancient buildings, beautiful parkland and gorgeous scenery.
**WHAT IS THERE TO DO**
Wander the streets and secret alleys, enjoy the modern and ancient combined with the exotic and the traditional.

*The spectacular night skyline of Hong Kong Island, looking across to Kowloon.*

*Tarboche pole at Sagadawa Festival.*

# Kailasa and Lake Mansarovar

According to Hindu belief, Shiva, the God of destruction and regeneration, resides at the summit of the legendary mountain Kailasa, regarded by many religions as the centre and spiritual birthplace of the entire world. Located between six mountain ranges, symbolising a lotus flower, there are four rivers that flow down Kailasa's slopes into the four quarters of the world, dividing it into four regions.

Dating back to before the great Hindu epics, the *Ramayana* and the *Mahabharata*, were written, Kailasa is considered sacred by various religions. The Jains refer to the mountain as Astapada, believed to be where Rishaba, the first of their 24 Tirthankaras (spiritual leaders) attained enlightenment. According to the followers of Bon, Tibet's pre-Buddhist, shamanistic religion, the mountain, Tise, is the site of the legendary twelfth-century magical battle between the Buddhist sage Milarepa and the Bon shaman Naro Bon-chung where, upon Bon's defeat, Buddhism became the primary religion of Tibet.

Tibetan Buddhists refer to the mountain as Khang Ripoche, 'the Precious One of Glacial Snow', the home of Demchog (Chakrasamvara) and his consort, Dorje Phagmo. The three hills in the distance are believed to be the residence of the Bodhisattvas: Manjushri, Vajrapani and Avalokiteshvara, who help humans achieve enlightenment.

The ultimate destination of souls, the sacred peak of Kailasa is an ancient pilgrimage site, difficult to get to and even more difficult to walk around. Pilgrims must take the 52 km (32 mi) route around the mountain – clockwise for Buddhists, anticlockwise for Bons, in the ritual known as a Kora, or Parikrama. The journey takes from one day to three weeks, depending upon the devotee's stamina. It is believed that a pilgrim who completes 108 circuits of the mountain is assured enlightenment.

Most pilgrims to Kailasa also take a plunge in the sacred waters of the nearby Lake Mansoravar, which at 4,585 m (15,043 ft), considered to be the highest freshwater lake in the world, is also known as the Lake of Consciousness and Enlightenment and lies next to Rakas Tal, or Rakshas, the Lake of Demons.

**WHAT IS IT**
According to Buddhists, it's the birthplace of the world.
**WHERE IS IT**
The remote Tibetan Himalayas.
**WHAT IS THERE TO SEE**
The mythical mountain, Kailasa, and Lake Mansarovar, the highest freshwater lake in the world.
**WHAT IS THERE TO DO**
Take the 52km (32 mi) arduous pilgrimage around the mountain.
**ALSO KNOWN AS**
Kailasa means 'crystal' in Sanskrit. The Tibetan name for the mountain is Ghang Rimpoche or Khang Ripoche, meaning 'precious jewel of snows'. Tise is another local name for the mountain. In the Jain tradition, the mountain is referred to as Astapada.
**TABOO**
According to all religions that revere the mountain, setting foot on its slopes is a dire sin. It is claimed that many people who ventured to defy the taboo have died in the process.

# Lhasa

Lhasa, the traditional capital of Tibet and now capital of the Tibet Autonomous Region of the People's Republic of China, as well as the traditional seat of the Dalai Lama, literally means 'place of the gods'. One of the highest cities in the world at an elevation of 3,650 m (12,000 ft), the city rose to prominence more than 1,300 years ago when the original Jokhang Temple and the first Potala Palace were built in the seventh century. Three large Gelugpa monasteries – Ganden, Sera and Drepung – were built by Je Tsongkhapa and his disciples in the fifteenth century.

Lhasa is a mystical, mysterious and remote city with an impressive heritage and spiritual history that defines Tibetan culture. Surrounded by the majestic Himalayas, Lhasa is punctuated by the snaking Kyi Chu River, a tributary of the Brahmaputra, which runs through the city.

The massive Jokhang Temple, within which is Tibetan Buddism's most sacred statue, the Jowo Shakyamuni, consists of three floors filled with chapels. There are three concentric paths, one within the complex and two outside it, around which pilgrims walk, although the outermost is now difficult because of the construction of a busy road.

Forming a UNESCO World Heritage Site with the temple and Norbulinkga (the Summer Palace) about 3 km (2 mi away) is the vast Potala Palace, once the spiritual and political hub of Tibet, but now a museum. The 1,000-room fortress is gracefully perched above Mount Marpo Ri and was built in the seventeenth century under the fifth Dalai Llama. The inner section, the Red Palace, contains the temples and reliquary tombs of the Dalai Llamas. The White Palace served as the seat of government and the winter residence of the Dalai Llama until he was forced to flee after an unsuccessful revolt against Chinese rule in 1959.

**WHAT IS IT**
The traditional capital of Tibet and the capital of the Tibet Autonomous Region of the People's Republic of China as well as the traditional seat of the Dalai Llama, it's the highest city in the world.
**WHERE IS IT**
In the south of the Tibet Autonomous Region of the People's Republic of China, high in the Himalayas.
**WHAT IS THERE TO SEE**
Stunning landscape and architecture including the breathtaking Potala Palace.
**WHEN SHOULD I GO**
March to October
**ALSO KNOWN AS**
'The place of the gods'

*Jokhang Temple roof structure with Makara head and the Potala Palace in the background.*

*Early morning view of Rishiri Island from Rebun Island.*

# Rebun and Rishiri Islands

These two beautiful and isolated islands lie off the north-west coast of Hokkaido, about as far north as it is possible to go in Japan. They form the main area of a national park, together with Sarobetsu and other areas on Hokkaido itself.

Rebun is a narrow, low-lying island that is rightly famous for its wildflowers. More than 300 different species of alpine plants grow here, and the island is perfect for hiking. The most popular route is the Hachi-jikan, which runs down the whole of the west coast from Sukoton Misaki (cape) in the north through woods and across green slopes covered with flowers to Motochi in the south. There are several other, less lengthy and arduous hikes to be enjoyed, including the Momoiwa route, a cliff-top trail that takes you to the lighthouse (Motochi Todai) at the southern tip of the island.

Rishiri Island could not be more different. It is formed by the almost circular dome of Rishirifuji, a 1,721-m (4,170-ft) dormant volcano. The climb can take up to 12 hours, starting out from the Rishiri Hokuroku campsite – there are several other routes, but this one is the nearest to the port of Oshidomari. There is a small shrine at the summit, and the views are spectacular. If you cannot face such a long hike, there is a lovely three-hour trail from the lake at Himenuma to the campsite, crossing the lower slopes of two smaller peaks.

**WHAT IS THERE TO SEE**
Wildflower meadows and Rishirifuji volcano.
**WHAT IS THERE TO DO**
Climb Rishirifuji (or drive part-way up to the observation decks), hire a bike and take a trip on the island's cycle road, visit Rishirifuji Onsen's spa.
**HOW DO I GET THERE**
Travel by air or ferry from Wakkanai to Rebun and Rishiri.
**WHEN SHOULD I GO**
The best time is between May and September.

# Shiretoko National Park

*The mountains of Shiretoko National Park covered in snow.*

Shiretoko National Park lies on the peninsula of the same name on the island of Hokkaido. The landscape here is wild and dramatic, and the active volcanoes that march up the centre of the island have thrown out vast black rocks that litter the coastline.

The main port in the area is Uturo, which is 10 km (6 mi) from the wonderful Shiretoko Go-ko. Here you will find five perfectly beautiful lakes all joined by paths and wooden walkways. The complete circuit takes over an hour to walk, although it is no more that 2.5 km (1.5 mi). The landscape is glorious and you can spend longer than you would imagine admiring the reflections of the mountains in the water.

A little further along the peninsula and you come to Kamuiwakka-no-taki, a strong reminder that this is volcano country. Iozan volcano produces hot water for this river and its waterfalls and there are natural hot pools at three different levels. To reach the pools, which become warmer the closer they are to the top, you have first to climb up the river, which is quite tricky, but the water is warm.

Iozan volcano can be climbed, but the most popular hike is up Rausu-dake, the highest peak on the peninsula. Even if you stick to the lower trails, the scenery is splendid and you will probably spot deer, foxes and other wildlife. During summer you can take a boat from Uturo to the lighthouse that stands on the end of the peninsula.

**WHAT IS THERE TO SEE**
The spectacular landscape and varied wildlife.
**WHAT IS THERE TO DO**
Climb up the river to see the natural hot pools.
**HOW DO I GET THERE**
By air from Tokyo to Kushiro, train from Kushiro to Shari, then by bus.
**WHEN SHOULD I GO**
Between June and September for the best weather.
**WHAT SHOULD I KNOW**
If hiking, avoid the brown bears!

*Mt Fuji overlooks Hakone National Park with Lake Ashi in the foreground.*

# Mt Fuji

Japan's most recognizable landmark must surely be Mount Fuji. Situated about100 km (60 mi) west of Tokyo, this almost perfect volcano is venerated by the Japanese, who know it as Fuji-san, their most sacred mountain. The last eruption was in 1707, but the volcano is dormant rather than extinct. In summer people like to be at the summit to see the dawn, and at night the light from their torches can look like a thin trail of lava on the mountainside.

The small town of Fuji-Yoshido is the traditional departure point for making the ascent of Mount Fuji. Walking from here can take 11 or 12 hours before reaching the summit and the ascent is divided into recognized sections or 'stations'. Usually people take the bus to Lake Kawaguchi fifth station, where the road comes to an end, and set off from there.

The main climbing season is during July and August. At this time all the seventeen resting huts are operational, although if you want to stay the night you will have to make an advance booking. At other times of year it is still possible to make the ascent, but there are no guarantees that any of the huts will be open, let alone the post office at the summit from which it is traditional to send a card or two. The crater itself takes about an hour to walk around, and it is often extremely cold up there – Mount Fuji is 3,776 m (12,340 ft) high, and the summit is snow covered between October and May.

**ALSO KNOWN AS**
Fuji-san.
**WHAT IS THERE TO SEE**
The Sengen shrine of Fuji Sengen-jinja, Fuji Five Lakes, Mt Tenjo.
**DO NOT MISS**
Climb to the summit of Mt Fuji and watch the sunrise.
**HOW DO I GET THERE**
By bus or train from Tokyo.

# Hakone

Hakone is a lovely, mountainous national park that lies south of Mount Fuji. It is dotted with lakes and hot springs, shrines and art museums, and its easy access from Tokyo makes it a perfect place to visit if you want some time out relaxing away from city life. It is possible to visit in a day, but it is much more fun to spend at least one night in a traditional, wooden Japanese ryokan (inn) or a smart hotel, and enjoy unwinding in one of the many hot-spring baths.

Railways, funiculars, cable cars and buses enable you to get about the area. There are even brightly coloured 'pirate ships' on which you can travel the length of Lake Ashi, to the west of the park. The lake, with its view of Mount Fuji in the background, was formed 3,000 years ago, in the caldera of Mt Hakone. People have been coming for centuries to take restorative baths in the hot springs, the best-known of which is the spring at Yumoto, at the entrance to the park.

The Hakone Open-Air Museum consists of 7 ha (17 acres) of beautifully landscaped gardens with views across the mountains to the sea. It is full of sculptures – Rodin and Giacometti feature as do 26 pieces by Henry Moore. There is a Picasso pavilion and galleries displaying works by Joan Miró and Marc Chagall as well as modern Japanese artists such as Takeshi Hayashi. From Sounzan a cable-car will take you to Owakudani, where you can trek up the valley to bubbling hot pools where Japanese tourists boil eggs until they are black and eat them with evident relish.

At Hatajuku craftsmen have been honing the art of marquetry for more than 1,200 years, and you can visit their workshops and find a perfect little box or puzzle to remind you of this lovely place.

**WHAT IS IT**
A national park south of Mt Fuji.
**WHAT IS THERE TO SEE**
The Hakone Motomiya shrine, the Tokkaido Barrier and highway, Hakone Tozan Railway.
**DO NOT MISS**
Take a restorative bath in one of the hot springs.
**YOU SHOULD KNOW**
Entrance fees are payable.
**HOW DO I GET THERE**
By train or bus from Tokyo.

# Nikko

**WHAT IS THERE TO SEE**
The Toshogu Shrine, Rinnoji Temple, Yomeimon, Taiyuinbyo, Futarasan Shrine, Lake Chuzenji and the Kegon Falls.
**WHAT IS THERE TO DO**
Spend an afternoon admiring the works in the Nikko Toshogu Shrine Museum of Art.
**YOU SHOULD KNOW**
Entrance fees are payable at the Toshogu complex.
**HOW DO I GET THERE**
Take a train from Tokyo.

The pilgrimage town of Nikko is the site of an outstanding Shinto and Buddhist shrine complex, surrounded by wonderful mountainous landscapes, and less than two hours' journey from Tokyo.

In 1616 the powerful shogun, Tokugawa Ieyasu, left a will requesting that a shrine be built here in his honour. The site already had religious significance – the Buddhist temple of Rinnoji had been standing there since the middle of the eighth century. Ieyasu's shrine was completed within a year, but his grandson, Tokugawa Iemitsu, decided to erect a far more grandiose affair for him, the Toshogu Shrine. Iemitsu's own mausoleum is only slightly less elaborate. Every year, in May, a grand festival is held here to re-create Ieyasu's burial rites, featuring 1,000 or more costumed monks and warriors. The spectators are left in no doubt as to the absolute power wielded by this dynasty.

Rinnoji is a large red hall containing three huge golden statues. You walk under a huge stone gate towards the main entrance to Toshogu, passing a five-storey pagoda painted in green and red. Toshogu means 'sunlight', and the shrine and its surrounding sacred buildings are alive with riotous colour and fantastic carving and decoration. Steps lead up to the impressive Yomeimon gate, and 200 more lead uphill to Ieyasu's tomb. The Hall of Worship, directly in front of the gate, is notable for the extraordinary original paintwork of its interior.

*Winter snow does not deter visitors to the Toshogu Shrine.*

# Ogasawara Islands

The Ogasawara Islands (Bonin Islands) are a remote group of 30 islands in the Pacific Ocean. They were formed by an ancient submarine volcano, and are home to more than 140 species of indigenous plants as well as insects such as the Ogasawara damsel fly. Of the 97 species of tree on the islands, 73 are endemic.

In 1827 a British warship found and declared possession of the islands and they were not returned to Japan until 1876. During World War II the inhabitants all moved to the Japanese mainland and by the end of the war the islands were ruled by the United States. Finally handed back in 1968 they are now part of the Tokyo prefecture, despite being about 1,000 km (600 mi) away.

Only Chichijima (father island) and Hahajima (mother island) are inhabited, and their total population is about 2,300. Their main products are timber and fruit such as pineapples and bananas. Ogasawara is unspoiled and unpolluted, and the crystal-clear waters are full of coral reefs and tropical fish.

This is a great place for watching whales and dolphins and there are several trips on offer. Humpback whales and their calves can be seen between February and April, while sperm whales are about all year round, although the best time to see them is from August to October. Many different types of dolphin can be seen here too, and it is sometimes possible to swim with bottlenose and spinner dolphins. The small, flat island visible from Hahajima has a sweeping, white beach which is ideal for swimming, where highly endangered green turtles come to lay their eggs.

*Anijima and Chichijima islands.*

**ALSO KNOWN AS:**
In English they are called the Bonin Islands.
**WHAT ARE THEY**
A remote group of islands in the Pacific.
**DO NOT MISS**
Take a day trip out to the open sea for an amazing day whale and dolphin watching.
**HOW DO I GET THERE**
Travel by ship from Tokyo to Chichijima. The ship leaves once a week and the journey takes 25 hours.

*Shrine at Kenrokuen Gardens.*

# Kanazawa

The charming and ancient castle town of Kanazawa lies mid-way along Honshu's western coast. The name means 'marsh of gold' and comes from a story of a peasant who made his living digging potatoes, washed gold dust from the potatoes and stored it in his well. The Japanese Alps surround the city and two rivers run through it, the Saigawa, said to be a lively masculine river and the Asano, a sweet feminine river.

Kanazawa Castle seems like an enormous bird set for flight with its white lead roof tiles and massive American cypress beams. It is encircled by a maze of intricately winding paths designed to protect the castle from enemies. There are still some samurai houses surrounded by mud walls and in the Teramachi area there are 70 temples in less than 1 sq km (0.5 sq mi). One of them, the Moyoryuji Temple, has hidden staircases and trap doors.

Bicycle to the Omicho market and delight in the huge array of vegetables, fish and, especially, crabs. Cool your hands on the huge blocks of ice standing in the market. You will also find many crafts practised here. Buddhist altars, brightly painted Kutani pottery, elegant Kanazawa lacquerware, glittering Kanazawa gold leaf, hand-painted Kaga-Yuzen silk, Kaga embroidery and fishing flies are all made in this city.

Kanazawa's crowning glory is its Gardens of Kenrokuen covering 10 ha (25 acres) and arguably the most beautiful in Japan. They were designed and laid out originally in the seventeenth century. In spring listen to the grasshoppers as you wander amongst the apricot and cherry blossoms, past cascades and over little bridges with stone lanterns. In the winter the gardens glisten with a thick carpet of snow and ropes called 'yukitsuri' support the branches of the delicate pine trees.

**WHAT IS THERE TO SEE**
The samurai houses in the Nagamachi District and Seisonkaku villa in Kenrokuen gardens
**DO NOT MISS**
Nearby are the temple at Eihei-ji, the market at Wajima and the splendid rugged coastline of Noto-kongo.
**WHEN SHOULD I VISIT**
The best time to visit is from July to September.
**HOW DO I GET THERE**
By train or air – the nearest airport is Komatsu which is 50 minutes by road.

# Matsumoto

Matsumoto is a delightful city in the area of central Honshu known as Chubu. It is the gateway to the Japanese Alps, with all their trekking and mountaineering opportunities, but is famous in its own right for its remarkable castle.

The city is divided by the Metoba River, on the south bank of which is an area of traditional old buildings known as Nakamachi. Many of these attractive, white-walled houses have been turned into inns and shops and there is a wonderfully restored Sake brewery that you can visit. To the west is the Japan Ukiyoe Museum, a rather ugly, modern concrete and glass building which houses a superb collection of 100,000 woodblock prints, including works by Hiroshige Utagawa and Hokusai Katsushika.

The castle, standing in lovely grounds, is approached across a moat. Originally built in 1504, it was rebuilt almost a century later by Lord Ishikawa. He commissioned the five-tiered donjon, or castle keep, which is now the oldest in the country. Most Japanese castles traditionally had a hidden, extra floor, and Matsumoto Castle is no exception. The view from the sixth storey over the town and mountains is superb. The castle's black, forbidding façade makes a strong impression on visitors, who can visit the Matsumoto City Museum inside the grounds for an insight into the castle's feudal history before entering the main building.

**WHAT IS IT KNOWN FOR**
Matsumoto castle, the oldest of its kind in Japan.
**WHAT IS THERE TO SEE:**
Mt Hotaka, Kamikochi mountain resort for access to the climbing areas and Norikura Kogen (Heights).
**HOW DO I GET THERE**
Domestic flights from Sapporo, Osaka or Fukuoka, train from Nagano, train or (cheaper) bus from Tokyo. The nearest international airport is near Nagoya.
**WHEN SHOULD I VISIT**
April and October are the best times to go.

*A footbridge leads to the castle at Matsumoto.*

# Isejingu, Shima Hanto

**WHAT IS IT**
A national park and home to a sacred Shinto shrine.
**WHAT IS THERE TO SEE**
Other sights within the national park include the waterfalls of the Takigawa valley, Toba – the home of cultured pearls – and the beautiful coastline of the Shima-hanto Peninsula.
**WHEN SHOULD I GO**
The park is open from sunrise to sunset and entry is free.
**HOW DO I GET THERE**
Travel by train from Nagoya, Kyoto or Osaka.

South-east of Osaka is the Shimo Hanto National Park, an area of great natural beauty and home to Japan's most sacred Shinto shrine, Isejingu (Ise Shrine), which was established during the fourth century and dedicated to Amaterasu Omikami, the sun goddess from whom, it was claimed, all of Japan's emperors are descended.

Legend has it that the shrine houses a mirror Amaterasu gave to her grandson when he was sent to Earth to rule Japan. His great-grandson, Jimmu, became the first Emperor of Japan and the mirror has been protected here ever since, wrapped in layers of fabric. Only the Imperial family and certain priests can enter the inner sanctum, but no-one has looked into the mirror itself for more than 1,000 years.

The Naiku, or inner shrine, is approached over a bridge that arches over the river, and through a formal garden to the first gate. The path leads towards several buildings including a theatre, where the faithful dedicate performances to the gods, and halls containing sacred foods. The inner sanctum is protected within four enclosures, each more sacred than the last. The architecture is simple, severe and typically Japanese. The shrine is rebuilt every 20 years for religious reasons, and each one is a perfect reproduction of its predecessor.

*The Isejingu (over 200 buildings) is rebuilt every 20 years.*

Closer to the town the outer shrine, Geku, is a simple, thatched building standing on pristine white gravel and surrounded by a high, wooden fence. Geku is dedicated to the goddess Toyouke Omikami, protector of the rice harvest. Although both the shrines are simple to look at, and hidden in woodland, they exude an aura of sanctity.

226

# Kyoto

For most people who have not visited Japan, Kyoto represents the epitome of traditional Japanese culture. Images of ancient temples and imperial palaces, wooden houses, geishas elegantly performing the tea ceremony and cherry blossom drifting in the wind come to mind. In fact, although Kyoto contains all these and more, it is also a sprawling modern city with a population of 1.5 million.

For over 1,000 years, from the late eighth century, Kyoto was Japan's capital city. It lies in a wide valley surrounded on three sides by hills, and was designed with the entrance to the south and the Imperial Palace to the north. During the fourteenth century many great monuments and Zen temples were built but its golden age was during the sixteenth and seventeenth centuries when it became the centre of Japanese artistic achievement. In all, Kyoto is home to about 1,700 Buddhist temples, 300 Shinto shrines, and 200 important gardens as well as imperial villas.

The Higashiyama district in Kyoto is the place to aim for if you have limited time – it has an amazing concentration of sights within a reasonably compact area. The Kiyomitzudera is a temple built on a steep hill with a wooden platform overhanging the valley, giving spectacular views over the gorge. Walk through the old, cobbled lanes of Sannenzaka and Ninenzaka, with their traditional two-storey wooden townhouses known as machiya, and round to the temple of Kodaiji. Continue past more temples, pavilions, gardens and teahouses until you reach Ginkakuji, the Silver Pavilion. This simple, elegant two-storey pavilion is set in a spectacular garden of soft greens and a 'sea of silver sand' designed to reflect the moonlight.

*Cherry blossom at the Kiyomizu-dera.*

**WHAT IS IT KNOWN FOR**
Being the epitome of traditional Japanese culture.
**WHAT IS THERE TO SEE**
The Imperial Palace, Gion quarter, Toji and Sanjusangendo Buddhist temples, and Shugakuin imperial villa.
**DO NOT MISS**
The Higashiyama district if you're short on time.

# Himeji

*Perched on a rock wall, the sixteenth-century castle was significantly enlarged in the seventeenth century.*

**WHERE IS IT**
North-west of Osaka.
**WHAT IS IT KNOWN FOR**
The finest castle in Japan.
**WHAT IS THERE TO SEE**
Hyogo Prefectural Museum of History, Otokoyama Senhime Shrine (Princess Sen's Shrine), the city museums of literature and art, Engyoji temple complex and the Inland Sea.
**DO NOT MISS**
Climb to the top of the daitenshu donjon for a spectacular view.
**TRVIA**
The city featured in the James Bond film *You Only Live Twice*.

Himeji lies north-west of Osaka, and contains the most impressive fortress in Japan. There has been a fortress here since the early fourteenth century, but the existing complex was built by Ikeda Terumasa in the early seventeenth century. It is designed to look like the shape of a bird in flight, and is often known as Shirasagijo, the white egret castle.

This fantastic place, a UNESCO World Heritage Site, is surrounded by moats and thick, defensive walls enclosing four donjons, the central one of which is five stories high. The outer corridor and the so-called 'cosmetic tower' are all that remain of the original palace. The feudal lord (daimyo) lived with his family in the western citadal, using the central donjon, daitenshu, only in times of trouble. You follow a path that winds past turrets and walls, and through gates that eventually lead to the inner citadel. To the east of the daitenshu is a small courtyard where the daimyo's Samurai committed seppuku, ritual suicide, and there is a haunted well to the south. Daitenshu itself is spectacular, with five stories framed by vast wooden pillars. The view from the top is superb – all the way to the Inland Sea on a good day.

Beyond the moat to the west of the fortress are nine linked gardens. They are designed in the Edo-era style and separated by mud walls surmounted by roof tiles. Today the gardens shelter tea houses, rock gardens and, of course, beautifully landscaped pools filled with Koi carp.

# Asuka

Asuka is a small village in the heart of the Yamato area, the plains east of Osaka, where Japanese imperial culture first flourished. It was one of the ancient imperial capitals, and archaeological finds such as burial mounds and sophisticated artefacts dating back to 350 AD have been found. Asuka was first mentioned as being the seat of Emperor Kenzo in 485 AD, and during the following 250 years 43 imperial palaces were built in this area, although, being wooden structures, virtually nothing of them remains. It was customary for each new emperor to found a palace as the existing one was believed to be tainted by the death of the previous incumbent.

Takumatsu's Tomb is a burial mound set on a hillside. It was excavated in 1972. The mound is fairly small, just 18 m (60 ft) in diameter and 5 m (16.5 ft) high, but it contains some superb paintings on the rock walls that date back to the sixth century. These depict the Four Gods and the constellations as well as some gorgeous ladies of the imperial court.

South of the Oka-dera temple is a bizarre collection of huge rocks known as the Ishi-butai or stone stage. The stone stage itself is formed from a block weighing 72 tonnes, by far the largest of its kind in the country, and it is surrounded by others, all stacked up and carefully arranged. It is believed to be the tomb of Sogano Umako, a powerful sixth-century lord. Umako was responsible for commissioning the Asuka-dera Temple, the first true temple in Japan. It contains a large bronze Buddha, which was cast in 606 AD, making it the oldest image of Buddha in Japan.

**WHAT IS IT**
A small village east of Osaka.
**WHAT IS IT KNOWN FOR**
Being an ancient imperial capital and the birth place of Japanese culture.
**WHAT IS THERE TO SEE**
The region's many burial mounds and mysterious stone objects.
**WHY IS IT IMPORTANT**
The Asuka-dera was the first temple built in Japan and contains the oldest Buddha image in Japan.

*Beautiful ceiling paintings at the Asuka-dera Temple.*

# Shimanami Kaido

The Shimani Kaido (the highway above the sea) is a road connecting the prefectures of Hiroshima and Ehime, from Onomichi City to Imabari City, at either end of the Inland Sea. This has been achieved by the use of a series of seven bridges linking each of the six smaller islands that lie between Honshu and Shikoku. The route was opened in 1999, and the total length of the road is about 60 km (40 mi).

The Inland Sea is tranquil and beautiful and dotted with more than 600 islands. The viewing platforms on Omishima Island and Mt Hoko-san on Hakatajima Island afford probably the best views of sparkling blue water and picturesque islands.

Many of the islands are well worth a visit, but Ikuchijima and Omishima are two of the most popular. Ikuchijima is an island of palm-fringed beaches and citrus groves and home to Kosanji, a brilliantly coloured temple complex modelled on famous temple buildings and is a big tourist draw. The island also houses the Hirayama Ikuo Museum of Art, with the works of one of Japan's greatest contemporary artists. Conversely, Omishima's main attraction is one of the oldest shrines in the country. Dedicated to the older brother of the Shinto goddess, Amaterasu, it was founded in the thirteenth century.

Each of the bridges along the route is unique. The Tatara Grand bridge is the longest cable stayed bridge in the world, and Kurushima Bridge was the first of the three linked suspension bridges spanning the 4 km (2.5 mi) wide Kurushima Strait. Spend a few days cycling along the road and stop off at a few of the islands to enjoy the good beaches and lovely scenery.

*One of the bridges along the Shimanami Kaido that cross the Kurushima Strait.*

# Izumo Taisha

The shrine of Izumo Taisha lies in the town of Taishamachi, at the foot of the sacred hills of Yakumo and Kamiyama. It is the oldest and most sacred Shinto shrine in Japan and is of major cultural significance.

According to legend, the shrine was built by Amaterasu, the sun goddess. It is dedicated to Okuninushi-no-Mikoto, the deity of medicine, agriculture and good relationships. Couples come here to ask for happiness in their marriage, summoning the deity by clapping their hands four times.

*The Oracle Hall of Izumo Taisha shrine.*

According to ancient Japanese chronicles, the main shrine was 96 m (315 ft) high, and the biggest wooden structure in the country until 1200 AD. Since then it has been rebuilt 25 times – the present structure dates from 1744. Today it is 25 m (82 ft) high, but recently the remains of enormous pillars have been discovered, which lend credence to the early references.

Once through the bronze gateway, the first building you reach is the Oracle Hall, a simple, elegant building with an enormous 'shimenawa'. This ceremonial rope, made from plaited straw, is 13 m (42 ft) long and weighs some 1.5 tonnes. The inner shrine, designated a national treasure, is built in the unique Taisha architectural style, with an elevated floor and roof rafters that project from the roof. You cannot enter here, but you can stand by the entrance, a gate that is beautifully decorated with wooden carvings, and look in. Round about the shrine the trees are covered with the fortune-telling papers that pilgrims tie to the branches for good luck.

Many ceremonies take place at Izumo Taisha every year, but November is a particularly special month when, supposedly, all the Shinto gods and goddesses come together here for an annual get-together.

**WHAT IS THERE TO SEE**
The Homostuden (Treasure Hall) the Shokokan exhibition hall and the Kagura Den sacred music hall.
**YOU SHOULD KNOW**
Entrance fees are payable.
**HOW TO GET THERE**
By train from Matsue.
**WHEN SHOULD I GO**
November is a good, if busy, time if you want to see a ceremony.

# Aso National Park

*Cinder cones and lava flows create a forbidding but fascinating landscape at Aso National Park.*

Almost in the centre of the island of Kyushu stands Mt Aso, not only the world's largest caldera, but possibly the most beautiful as well. The mountain is a typical active, composite volcano, the circumference of its outer caldera being 128 km. It encloses seven towns and villages and five mountains, and some 75,000 people live here, their lives completely dominated by volcanic activity.

Apart from the peaks, the scenery within the caldera is of fertile fields and gently rolling, green meadows, grazed by cows and horses. The landscape of the foothills of Eboshi is particularly lovely, with shallow crater lakes peppering the plain. High in the crater wall to the north a huge outcrop, completely covered with greenery and known locally as the 'Green Niagara', can be seen.

Most visitors to the area come to see the active volcano within the caldera, Mt Nakadake, which last erupted during the 1990s. It frequently emits such strong sulphuric and other noxious gases that it has to be closed to visitors for a day or two, and those with respiratory problems are advised not to approach the rim of the crater. The top can be reached by cable-car, by road or on foot, and looking down through the belching, turbulent, sulphur-ridden smoke to the green-blue lake beneath is an awe-inspiring experience. Kusasenri is a round ash-covered plain, the result of an earlier eruption, next to Mt Nakadake.

For those who prefer not to get so close, the Aso Volcano Museum is the place to visit. You can see satellite pictures of Japan's fault lines and film of recent eruptions worldwide and continuous images from within the crater, thanks to cameras placed in its walls.

**WHAT IS IT**
One of the world's most beautiful mountains.
**WHAT IS THERE TO SEE**
The dormant volcano of Komezuka, Yamaga Toro museum, Kusasenri, Aso Uchinomaki-onsen (spa).
**YOU SHOULD KNOW**
Those with respiratory problems are advised not to go near the rim of the crater.
**HOW DO I GET THERE**
By air to Kumamoto Airport then by train from Kumamoto.

# Yaku Island

Yaku Island (Yakushima) is situated about 70 km (45 mi) south of Kyushu's southern tip. It is a relatively small and mountainous island that boasts more than 30 peaks of over 1,000 m (3,280 ft), and one, Mt Miyianoura, that is almost 2,000 m (6,560 ft) high.

The vegetation here ranges from subtropical at sea level, to subarctic on the mountain-tops, and the extraordinarily heavy rainfall ranges from 4–10 m (13–32 ft) per year. The combination of heavy rainfall and remote location has allowed lush, primeval forest to flourish without interference.

The subtropical zone consists mainly of various ficus trees, and the temperate zone is predominantly evergreen oak, tabu and chinquapin. From 800-1,600 m (2,625-5,250 ft) is a band of coniferous forest containing some of the world's oldest trees, the Yaku cedars. The most ancient of these are about 3,500 years old, and the biggest of them, known as Jomon Sugi, has a circumference of 16.4 m (54 ft), which would make it about 7,000 years old. It takes eight adults with their arms outstretched to encircle its trunk. These cedars are considered sacred, and they all have names – Meoto-Sugi, or Married Couple, used to be two separate trees, which over time have joined together and begun to coexist. Wilson Stump is a huge stump that you can walk into. A small stream runs through it and a shrine has been made in the interior.

The island is full of beautiful rivers and waterfalls, and along the shore are wonderful tropical gardens. There are deer here, and macaques, as well as several endangered bird species. It has the nesting sites of both green and loggerhead turtles, both of which are also endangered.

*A Yaku cedar can be up to 7,000 years old.*

**WHERE IS IT**
The island is situated 70 km (45 mi) south of Kyushu's southern tip.
**WHAT IS THERE TO SEE**
Yakushima Environmental and Cultural Centre, the Sea Turtle Museum, Yakushima Fruit Garden, Shakunage Rhododendron Park.
**WHAT IS IT KNOWN FOR**
The Yaku cedars, some of the world's oldest trees.
**HOW DO I GET THERE**
By air, jet-foil or ferry from Kagoshima.

# Hateruma Island

Hateruma (Haterumajima) is Japan's southernmost inhabited island and part of the Yaeyama Island group. Its name comes from the Okinawan for coral. Out on a limb in the Pacific Ocean, Hateruma is not far from Taiwan, and the Tropic of Cancer. Of the 88 constellations, 84 can be seen from here and it is a well-known observation point for the Southern Cross.

Life here is simple and rustic – empty roads lead to the endless reaches of the sea and sky. There are no tour groups or large hotels, just one village in the centre of the island. Some of the wooden houses are plain and weathered, while others are painted lime-green or blue, with traditional orange tiled roofs.

In 1972, when Okinawa reverted to Japan, a monument was built at Takanazaki, home to Japan's southernmost police station and lighthouse. It was made of stones gathered from all across Japan. Here too is an observatory, built for the clear skies above the island, which is sometimes open to visitors.

The beach at Nishi, edged with pandanus trees, is thought by many to be the most beautiful beach in Japan. Diving and snorkelling here are a joy. Beneath the clear blue water is a world of coral reefs, rock arches and wonderful tropical fish. In the spring migratory fish, such as the dogtooth tuna and hammerhead sharks, can be seen.

This is a lovely place to cycle around – there are banyan trees, Indian almonds, bamboo orchids, hibiscus and frangipani. You feel that you are at the world's edge, with virtually no man-made noise, just the sound of the breeze rustling the sugarcane and the occasional scratchy notes of the three-stringed sanshin.

*A monba tree drapes across a beach on Hateruma.*

# Band-e Amir

*Amir Dam on Band-e Zulfiqar Lake.*

Visitors to Afghanistan have always marvelled at the country's raw, natural beauty. The highlights of this landscape, in the middle of the Hazarajat in the central Hindu Kush Mountains, are the legendary lakes of Band-e Amir. Here you will find six stunningly blue lakes, nestled among 3,000 m (9,850 ft) magenta and grey rock walls, making a stunningly beautiful and unforgettable contrast. The deep blue of the lakes is due to the combination of water purity and the high lime content.

Just 75 km (46 mi) from Bamiyan, the lakes of the Band-e Amir Valley are considered one of the country's natural wonders. The lakes are created by the flow of water of a succession of natural travertine terraces created through the deposition of calcium carbonate, running from the highest lake down to the ones below. The strikingly clear cobalt waters come as a shock to the senses amid this barren and rocky desert landscape.

Although there is no lush foliage here, there is a variety of animal species. Wolves, foxes, hares, wild sheep and Markhor goats as well as large yellow fish, known locally as Chush, are found in and around the lakes. Mules and donkeys, commonly used by locals for transport, can also been seen in the area.

Band-e Amir was declared a national park, the first in Afghanistan in 1973, although it has no legal status.

**WHAT IS IT**
Six breathtakingly blue lakes amidst the Hindu Kush mountains.
**WHERE IS IT**
75 km (46.6 mi) from Bamiyan
**WHEN SHOULD I GO**
Spring and autumn are the best times to visit.
**WHAT SHOULD I KNOW**
Check with the Foreign Office or your local embassy to ensure safe travel is sanctioned in this often war-torn area.
**HOW DO I GET THERE**
4x4 from Bamiyan.

*Bathing in the Ganges. The sacred river of Hinduism is believed to have special soul-cleansing powers.*

# Varanasi

The colourful holy city of Varanasi (Benares), a famous Hindu pilgrimage site perched on the banks of the River Ganges (Ganga), has been an important cultural, historic and religious centre of India for more than 5,000 years. Presided over by Shiva, Varanasi is to Hindus what Mecca is to Muslims or the Holy Sepulchre in Jerusalem is to Christians.

Here pilgrims come to sit on the many ghats (riverbank steps leading to the sacred Ganges), and to have a ritual bath and perform puja to the rising sun, in accordance with centuries of tradition. It is believed that bathing in the sacred waters results in the remission of sins and that dying here circumvents rebirth.

The Dasashvamedh Ghat, believed to be where Shiva sacrificed ten horses, offers a splendid view of the river front. Legend has it that the sacrifice was performed by Brahma to pave the way for Shiva's return to Varanasi after a period of banishment. Other special ghats are the Asi, Barnasangam, Panchganga and Manikarnika.

Home to the shrine of Lord Kashi Vishwanath, one of the 12 revered Jyotirlingas of Shiva (shrines where he is worshipped in the form of a phallus of light), the current version of Kashi Vishwanath Temple was built in 1780 by Maharani Ahilyabai Holkar of Indore on the banks of the sacred Ganges, and is the place of pilgrimage for millions of Hindus every year. This temple is the most sacred shrine in Varanasi. Its original structure was destroyed by the Mughal Emperor, Aurangzeb. The gold plating of the dome was done during the nineteenth century by Maharaja Ranjit Singh of Punjab.

The holy Buddhist site, Sarnath, where Buddha preached his first sermon, lies 12 km (7.4 mi) from Varanasi. Here Buddha revealed the eight-fold path that leads to the attainment of inner peace, enlightenment and the ultimate, nirvana. Later, Ashoka, the great Mauryan emperor, erected magnificent stupas and other buildings along with his 33.5-m (110-ft.) stone pillar, Dharmarajika Stupa, to honour Buddha's presence. Sarnath has a rich collection of ancient Buddhist relics and antiques including numerous images of Buddha and Bodhisatva, which are on display at the Archaeological Museum.

**WHAT IS IT**
One of the ancient seats of religious learning in India, a sacred pilgrimage site for Hindus.

**WHERE IS IT**
The left bank of the River Ganges in Uttar Pradesh, 700 km (435 mi) south east of Delhi.

**HOW DO I GET THERE**
There is an airport at Babatpur, 20 km (12 mi) from the city centre.

**ALSO KNOWN AS**
Benares, Banaras, Benaras, Kashi, Kasi and, at one time, 'the cultural capital of India'.

**NOMENCLATURE**
The name Varanasi is derived from two tributaries of the Ganges, one in the north end of the city, called Varuna and Assi, at the southern end.

**LITERARY QUIP**
Mark Twain said of the 5,000-year-old Varanasi, 'Benaras is older than history, older than tradition, older even than legend and looks twice as old as all of them put together!'

# Srinagar

Srinagar, a romantic city situated in the valley of Kashmir surrounded by glistening lakes and forested, snow-capped mountain peaks, is a lively, vibrant city with a number of stunning parks. Perched on the banks of both sides of the river Jhelum (Vyath), the city is well known for the nine ancient bridges that connect the two parts of the city as well as the houseboats floating listlessly on the city's many lakes, particularly Dal Lake.

A summer retreat for many of the great rulers of antiquity, Srinagar lays claim to one of the most pleasant climates in India and has been a tourist destination for centuries, attracting rulers from the plains of India travelling to avoid the oppressive heat of the plains. The city was popular with the Mughal emperors who left their mark in the form of beautiful mosques and stunning gardens.

The Mughal Gardens include Chasma Shahi, the royal fountains; Pari Mahal, the palace of the fairies; Nishat Bagh, the garden of spring; Sahlimar Bagh and the Nashim Bagh.

Like the state of Jammu and Kashmir, Srinagar has a distinctive blend of cultural heritage and religious diversity, depicted through its holy places in and around the city.

The Shankaracharya Temple, dedicated to Shiva, was constructed in 371 BC by Gopadatya on the top of a 335-m (1,100-ft) hill. There is a great view of the city from the Temple.

The Hazrathbal shrine is one of the most revered pilgrimage sites of the Muslims. Located on the left bank of Dal Lake, it is here that the sacred hair of Muhammad (Moi-e-Muqqadas) is preserved.

The Jama Masjid mosque, in the old city and big enough for 30,000 worshippers, was built in 1398 by Sultan Sikandar and is also worth a look.

**WHAT IS IT**
A beautiful city surrounded by lakes and mountains.
**WHERE IS IT**
In the valley of Kashmir on both sides of the Jhelum River, 876 km (544 mi) north of Delhi.
**WHAT IS THERE TO SEE**
Spectacular scenery and pretty houseboats.
**WHAT IS IN A NAME**
Srinagar is composed of two Sanskrit words: Sri, meaning abundance and wealth; and Nagar, meaning city. Sri is also the name of a Hindu goddess.
**WORTH A SPLURGE**
The area is known for its traditional handicrafts and dried fruits as well as its cricket bats. *Tsot* and *tsochvoru*, small round breads topped with poppy and sesame seeds washed down with salt tea, and kulcha, a sweet or savoury melt-in-the-mouth variety of shortbread topped with poppy seeds are also worth a try.
**WHEN SHOULD I VISIT**
The alpine climate is temperate throughout the spring, summer and autumn months, December to February gets heavy snowfall.

*Typical houseboats of the region's lakes.*

# Himachal Pradesh region

**WHAT IS IT**
An important pilgrimage site for Buddhists, Sikhs and Christians.
**WHERE IS IT**
Surrounded by Tibet to the east, Jammu and Kashmir to the north and north-west, Punjab to the south-west, Haryana and Uttar Pradesh to the south and Uttaranchal to the south-east.
**WHAT IS THERE TO SEE**
Thousands of temples and shrines in a variety of architectural styles.
**ALSO KNOWN AS**
'Devabhoomi' or 'the abode of the Gods' or 'Little Lhasa in India'.
**WHY IS IT IMPORTANT**
Dharamsala is home to the Dalai Llama and more than 80,000 Tibetan refugees.

*Mountains of the Himachal Pradesh.*

Known for centuries as 'Devabhoomi', the abode of the Gods, the splendid heights of the Himachal Pradesh region of the Himalayan ranges, with their great scenic beauty and aura of spiritual calm, are dotted with thousands of temples serving as pilgrimage sites for a variety of pilgrims including Christians, Sikhs and Buddhists.

Full of isolated valleys and high ranges, the area is home to various styles of temple architecture such as carved stone shikharas, pagoda shrines, temples resembling Buddhist Gompas and Sikh Gurudwaras among others.

The area is divided into a series of 12 districts where Hinduism, Buddhism and Sikhism are the main religions. Dharamsala, in the western area of the state, is home to the Dalai Lama and other Tibetan refugees.

Also known as 'Little Lhasa in India', Dharamsala lies on a spur of the Dhauladhar range in the Pir Panjal region of the Outer Himalayas, commanding majestic views of the impressive snow-capped mountains rising 5,200 m (17,000 ft) from the scenic, fertile Kangra Valley below.

The area is divided into Lower Dharamsala, with the Kotwali Bazaar, at an average height of 1,250 m (4,101 ft), and Upper Dharamsala, dominated by McLeod Ganj at the height of nearly 1,800 m (5,906 ft), and surrounded by pine, Himalayan oaks, rhododendron and deodar forests.

The area surrounding McLeod Ganj has served as the home to the Dalai Llama and nearly 80,000 Tibetan refugees since the failed rebellion in Tibet in 1959. The residence of the Dalai Lama is opposite the Tsuglag Khang (Central Cathedral) in Dharamsala.

*LEFT: Jaisalmer Fort overlooks more recently constructed parts of the town.*

*BELOW: Traditional dancers in Rajasthan.*

**WHAT IS IT**
A stunning city with an impressive fort and several ornate Jain temples.
**WHERE IS IT**
The Thar Desert on the border of India and Pakistan in western Rajasthan.
**NOMENCLATURE**
Jaisalmer was named after its founder, Rawal Jaisal. The name means 'the Hill Fort of Jaisal'.
**ALSO KNOWN AS**
'The Golden City'.
**WHEN SHOULD I GO**
September to June.

# Jaisalmer

Jaisalmer, in Rajasthan in north-western India, is also known as 'The Golden City'. It stands near the border with Pakistan, isolated on a ridge of yellow sandstone on the western edge of the Thar Desert and crowned by a fort containing the finely sculptured palace and several ornate Jain temples.

Founded in 1156, by the Rajput ruler Rawal Jaisal after his people fled here from their homeland, the Jaisalmer Fort is situated on Trikuta (three-peaked) Hill. Its massive sandstone walls, with 99 sturdy turrets loom 300 m (1,000 ft) above the town and are a tawny brown during the day, but turn a magical golden honey every night as the sun sets. The majority of the population are descendents of the original settlers.

Located at an important crossroads of camel caravan routes between India and Central Asia, Persia, Arabia, Egypt and Africa, Jaisalmer gained its prosperity through taxing merchants, but the advent of shipping routes led to its becoming a backwater once more and, fortuitously, led to the preservation of much of its architecture. The fort itself contains five interlinked palaces, including the Raj Mahal (royal palace) and the Badal Mahal (cloud palace), as well as three Jain temples built from the twelfth to fifteenth centuries, the Hindu Laxminath Temple and many exquisite havelis (mansions).

The landscape outside the city is desolate, but beautiful. The Desert National Park has a varied landscape and is home to wolves, desert and Indian foxes, desert cats, blackbuck and a range of birds including the highly endangered Indian Bustard. The Akai wood Fossil Park has the fossilised remains of a 180-million-year-old forest.

# Gwalior

An ancient site of Jain worship, the city of Gwalior occupies a strategic location in the Gird region of North India and has served as the centre of several of northern India's historic kingdoms. Historically and architecturally fascinating, the city of Gwalior is most notable for its fortress and its palaces.

Gwalior fortress is one of the most formidable in India. On an isolated sandstone outcrop, and surrounded by high walls, it encloses a variety of buildings dating back several periods. A rampart, cut from the steep rock face, surrounds the fort, flanked by statues of the Jain tirthankaras (people who have gained enlightenment). The Man Singh Palace stands at the north-eastern corner of the enclosure, decorated with interesting tile work with symbolic images.

Within the fort are some marvels of medieval architecture including the fifteenth-century Gujari Mahal, a perfectly preserved monument to the love of Raja Man Singh Tomar. Converted into the Archaeological Museum, Gujari Mahal is home to the statue of Shalbhanjika from Gyraspur, the tree goddess, said to be perfection in miniature.

*Jain statues sculpted in rock.*

Man Mandir Palace, also built by Raja Man Singh Tomar in 1486–1516, forms the most interesting example of early Hindu architecture in India.

Although many of the decorative tiles that once adorned the exterior of the palace have not survived, a few traces remain around the entrance. The vast rooms, many with fine stone screens, although empty, exude an elegance of times past. Below, circular dungeons housed the state prisoners of the Mughals.

The impressive palace chamber, the Baradari, now in ruins, was once supported on 12 columns. The 15 m (45 ft) square stone-roofed structure was one of the most beautiful halls in the world, with vaults imitating Islamic architecture.

Near the heart of the fortress lies the splendid Jai Vilas Palace. It is still the residence of the Maharajah and his family, but a number of its rooms have been turned into the Jivaji Rao Scindia Museum. The palace's architecture is a proud and striking combination of Tuscan and Corinthian styles, and its interiors are evocative of a privileged regal lifestyle. The two main chandeliers in the Darbar Hall weighs 2 tonnes and were only installed after the strength of the ceiling had been tested by standing ten elephants on it.

The palace's rooms are decorated with gilding, heavy draperies and tapestries, fine Persian carpets and antique furniture, including four-poster beds from France and Italy. Among the more extravagant treasures that show how royalty in India lived are a silver train with cut-glass wagons which went around the dining table on miniature rails, an Italian glass cradle used for the baby Krishna, silver dinner services and swords once worn by Aurangzeb and Shah Jahan.

There are several remarkable Hindu temples within the fort. One pair, completed in 1093, known as the Sasbahu Ka Mandir, is beautifully adorned with bas-reliefs.

Teli Ka Mandir is a ninth-century temple dedicated to Vishnu. It is built in an intriguing mixture of Dravidian and Indo-Aryan architectural styles with its walls smothered in statues and decoration. It is probably the first temple to have been built in the fort and is the highest structure within the complex.

*The Man Singh Palace.*

# Taj Mahal

*The magnificent Taj Mahal is more a work of art than a mausoleum.*

Located outside the city of Agra in the north Indian state of Uttar Pradesh, the Taj Mahal is one of the most beautiful architectural masterpieces in the world. Shah Jahan, a Mughal ruler, ordered the construction of the Taj Mahal in honour of his wife, Arjumand Banu, to commemorate their 18 years of marriage and her death in childbirth with their fourteenth child. As a testament to his love for his wife he commissioned the most beautiful mausoleum on Earth.

The architect of the Taj Mahal is not known for certain, but Ustad Ahmad Lahori, an Indian architect of Persian descent, has been widely credited. Construction began in 1630 when the best masons, craftsmen, sculptors and calligraphers were summoned from Persia, the Ottoman Empire and throughout Europe.

The site, on the south-west bank of the River Yamuna outside Agra, has five main structures: the Darwaza, or main gateway; the Bageecha, or garden; the Masjid or mosque; the Naqqar Khana, or rest house and the Rauza, the mausoleum, where the tomb is located.

The unique Mughal style combines elements of Persian, Central Asian and Islamic architecture. Highlights include the black-and-white marble checked floor, the four 40-m (656-ft) minarets at the corners of the mausoleum's plinth and its majestic middle dome.

The lettering of the Qur'anic verses around the archways appears to be uniform in height no matter how far it is from the ground, an optical effect caused by increasing the size and spacing of the letters higher up. Other optical effects can be spotted throughout the Taj. The

impressive *pietra dura* artwork includes geometric elements as well as plants and flowers, mostly common in Islamic architecture. The level of sophistication and intricacy of the monument becomes apparent when you take the time to examine the small details – for instance, in some places, one 3-cm (1.2-in) decorative element contains more than 50 inlaid gemstones.

The Taj Mahal truly is a great work of art.

# Orchha

Orchha is a medieval town in the Tikamgarh district of Madhya Pradesh in north-central India and is notable for its well-preserved temples and palaces on the Betwa River. Built by Bundela rulers in the sixteenth and seventeenth centuries, Orchha's stone façades continue to exude the grandeur of centuries past.

Orchha's fort complex, approached by a multi-arched bridge, has three palaces set in an open quadrangle, as well as a number of impressive temples and memorials. The most spectacular palaces are Raj Mahal, Rai Parveen Mahal and Jahangir Mahal.

Situated to the right of the quadrangle, Raj Mahal was built in the seventeenth century by Madhukar Shah, the deeply religious predecessor of Bir Singh Ju Deo. The plain exteriors, crowned by chhatris (memorials), give way to interiors decorated with exquisitely detailed and colourful murals depicting a variety of religious themes.

Poetess and musician, Rai Parveen, one of Raja Indramani's concubines, was sent to Delhi on the orders of the Emperor Akbar, who was captivated by her beauty. Upon meeting the Great Mughal, Rai Parveen managed to convince him of the purity of her love for Indramani. Upon her return to Orchha, the Rai Parveen Mahal was built for her. The low, two-storey brick structure was designed to match the height of the trees in the surrounding, beautifully landscaped gardens of Anand Mahal.

Jahangir Mahal, built by Raja Bir Singh Ju Deo in the seventeenth century to commemorate the visit of Emperor Jahangir to Orchha, is notable for its strong lines counterbalanced by its delicate chhatris and trellis work, in what makes a striking mix of architectural elements.

In addition to its palaces, Orchha is well known for its fascinating collection of impressive temples, not least of which includes the soaring spires and palatial architecture of the Ram Raja Temple, one of the most unusual in India. It is also the only place in the country where Ram was worshipped as a king.

Erected upon a massive stone platform and reached by a steep flight of steps, the Chaturbhuj Temple was built to enshrine the image of Rama that remained in the Ram Raja Temple. Lotus emblems and

**WHAT IS IT**
A well-preserved medieval town with various royal temples of architectural note
**WHERE IS IT**
The Tikamgarh district of Madhya Pradesh on the Betwa River near Jhansi.
**WHAT IS THERE TO SEE**
Exquisite palaces dating back to the sixteenth century
**WHEN SHOULD I GO**
October to March.
**HOW DO I GET THERE**
By train to Jhansi from Delhi, Mumbai, Chennai or Gwalior airport, then by bus or taxi from Jhansi.

243

*Sundar Mahal and chhatris along the Betwa River in Orchha.*

other symbols of religious significance provide the delicate exterior ornamentation. Within, the sanctum is chastely plain with high, vaulted walls emphasising its deep sanctity.

Linked to the Ram Raja Temple via a flagged path, the Lakshmi Narayan Temple is an interesting synthesis of fort and temple styles and the interiors contain the most exquisite of Orchha's wall paintings. Covering the walls and ceiling of three halls, these murals are vibrant compositions and cover a variety of spiritual and secular subjects. They are in an excellent state of preservation, with the colours retaining their vivid quality.

Laid out as a formal garden, the Phool Bagh complex testifies to the refined aesthetic qualities of the bundelas. A central row of fountains culminates in an eight-pillared palace-pavilion. A subterranean structure below was the cool summer retreat of the Orchha kings. An ingenious system of water ventilation connects the underground palace with Chandan Katora, a bowl-like structure from whose fountains droplets of water filtered through to the roof, simulating rainfall.

The small palace of Sunder Mahal, although nearly in ruins, remains a place of pilgrimage for Muslims. Dhurjban, son of Jhujhar, converted to Islam when he married a Muslim girl in Delhi, spent the latter part of his life in prayer and meditation and came to be revered as a saint.

There are 14 chhatris (memorials) to the rulers of Orchha, grouped along the Kanchana Ghat of the Betwa River.

# Jain Temples

The Jain temples and innumerable Jain shrines dotting the Indian landscape, are a testament to the Jain Tirthankars (enlightened ones), who spread their message of peace, non-violence, love and enlightenment as a way to salvation, freeing themselves from the continual cycle of birth and rebirth and, in the process, managed to build some of the most stunning architectural landmarks in the country. There are important cave temples, as well as carved stones and numerous illustrated manuscripts scattered across Uttar Pradesh.

Some of the most notable Jain Temples include the five legendary Dilwara Temples in Rajasthan, 2.5 km (1.5 mi) from Mount Abu, Rajasthan's only hill station. Dating back from the eleventh to the thirteenth centuries AD, these marble temples, shaded by groves of mango trees and wooded hills and shrouded by a high wall, have a simple beauty and exquisite elegance, a reminder of the honesty and frugality encouraged in the Jain religion.

The Palitana Temples, located on the Shetrunjaya hills in Gujerat, are considered to be the most sacred of all the Jain temples. The complex consists of 863 temples, all exquisitely carved in marble, built as an abode for the gods. Construction began in the eleventh century and lasted more than 900 years. The temples' complex architectural details and intricate decorative embellishments are stunning.

Ranakpur, in Rajasthan, is one of the five most important pilgrimage sites for Jainists. Nestled in the Aravalli Hills, it is home to an extraordinarily gorgeous complex of temples, the first to have been built by the Jain community. The town of Falna donated more than 90 kg (200 lb) of gold for use in the decoration of the dome and internal statues. Located on the curved, boulder-strewn River Maghai, deep in the forested hills of Aravalli, the temple exploits shadow and light masterfully with its delicate lacy marble carvings and 1,500 pillars, each of which is different in design to its neighbours. Watching the sun shift through the pillars, as their colours change from gold to pale blue, is a remarkable experience.

**WHAT ARE THEY**
Stunning temples.
**WHERE ARE THEY**
Northern and north-western India.
**WHEN SHOULD I GO**
October to March.

*Columns in interior courtyard of a Jain temple.*

# Kochi

**WHAT IS IT**
A lovely seaside city that is the ideal starting point to tour Kerala.
**WHERE IS IT**
Flanked by the Arabian Sea and the western ghats on the south-western coast of the Indian subcontinent.
**WHAT IS THERE TO SEE**
There are a variety of interesting architectural gems and many religious pilgrimage sites.
**WHEN SHOULD I GO**
March to October.
**ALSO KNOWN AS**
Cochin or 'the gateway to Kerala'.

Kochi (Cochin), a vibrant Indian city nestled between the western ghats in the east and the Arabian Sea in the west, is considered the gateway to breathtakingly scenic and prosperous Kerala. The history and development of this lovely seaside city has been shaped by the cultures of its various occupiers including the Arabs, British, Chinese, Dutch and Portuguese. Over the years, Kochi has emerged as the commercial and industrial capital of Kerala, and despite its size, it is considered the second city in western India after Mumbai.

It became significant on the world trade routes after the port at Kodungallur (Cranganore) was destroyed by flooding in 1341 and a natural harbour formed at Kochi. The latter quickly developed into a centre dealing in pepper, cardamom, cinnamon, cloves and other products native to the area's lush soils. Kochi is a unique and charming amalgam of its varied cultural influences. It is the only place outside China where you will see fisherman plying the coastal waters with massive Chinese fishing nets (cheenavala) as you stroll down Fort Kochi beach against a backdrop of European-style residences.

Kochi is home to many architecturally and historically significant buildings and pilgrimage sites. St Francis' Church – where Vasco da Gama was buried – is the oldest European church in India, and Vasco House, on Rose Street, with its glass paned windows and sweeping verandahs, is one of the oldest Portuguese homes in the country. Santa Cruz Basilica, built by the Portuguese in 1505, was named a cathedral in 1558, then destroyed by the British. Rebuilt in 1905, it was made a basilica by Pope John Paul II in 1984.

Mattancherry Palace was built by the Portuguese, then modified by the Dutch in the seventeenth century and presented to the Raja of Cochin. It has fine murals depicting scenes from the *Mahabharatha* and *Ramayana*, and has served as the location for many coronations throughout history. The raja gave the area known as 'Jew Town' to the Jewish community to protect them from persecution. The Paradisi Synagogue, built in 1568, is magnificently decorated with Chinese tiles and Belgian chandeliers.

*Kochi is the only place these fishing nets are found outside China. It is thought that they were introduced by traders from the court of the Chinese ruler Kublai Khan.*

There are far too many stunning and significant religious sites to mention, but a few to note include Kalady, on the banks of the river Periyar, the birthplace of Sri Adi Sankaracharya, the Hindu philosopher. The Adi Sankara shrine and eight-storey painted Adi Sankara Keerthi Sthambam are a must-see for any visitor.

The elephant sanctuary, 3 km (1.9 mi) north of Guruvayur at Punnathur Kotta, a former rajas' palace, is home to 50 elephants.

# Lake Pichola

Lake Pichola lies in the foothills of the Aravalli Hills in southern Rajasthan. It is most famous for the beautiful royal palaces that lie on its islands and around its shoreline. The chief town in the area is Udaipur, which is also known as the city of lakes, which was founded as a residence by Maharana Udai Singh on the advice of a hermit in 1559. After his stronghold at Chittorgarh had been sacked by Mughal invaders he moved his capital here in 1568. Among its highlights are the City Palace and Museum, the Sajjangarh Palace – which overlooks the lake from the top of a hill and was the summer palace where the royal family spent the monsoon season. There are also many smaller palaces and temples, as well as picturesque streets, fountains and gardens.

The most famous sights on the lake are the island palaces, in particular Jag Niwas, now the Lake Palace Hotel, which was built in the 1740s and is made entirely of marble. This beautiful shining white building appears to float on the lake's clear blue waters. The Jag Mandir is a red sandstone complex on the island of the same name, with cool courtyards and a small museum. It was a refuge for Shah Jahan and is said to have provided inspiration for the Taj Mahal. The massive Jagdish Temple lies within its walls.

North-west of Udaipur is the craft village – Shilpgram – a centre dedicated to preserving and enhancing the craft and folk heritage of western India.

*The Lake Palace Hotel in the centre of Lake Pichola.*

**WHAT IS IT**
A beautiful lake surrounded by stunning scenery.
**WHERE IS IT**
Southern Rajasthan.
**WHAT IS THERE TO SEE**
Palaces and temples.

*Monks walk around the stupas at the birthplace of the Buddha in Lumbini.*

# Lumbini

Lumbini, in the Terai plains of southern Nepal, is where Siddhartha Gautama – the Lord Buddha – was born in 623 BC. The sacred place, marked by a stone pillar erected by Emperor Ashoka in 249 BC, is a UNESCO World Heritage Site.

Lumbini is 25 km (15.5 mi) east of Kapilavastu, the place where Buddha grew up and lived until the age of 29, and is one of the four holy places of Buddhism. According to the Parinibbana Sutta, Buddha himself identified four places of future pilgrimage: the sites of his birth, enlightenment, first discourse and death, so each year thousands of pilgrims visit Lumbini.

In Buddha's time, Lumbini (Sanskrit for lovely) was a beautiful garden full of green and shady sal trees, or Shorea. The tranquil gardens were owned by both the Kolias and Shakyas clans, to the second of which King Suddhodana, Gautama Buddha's father, belonged. Maya Devi, his mother, gave birth to the child on her way to her parent's home in Devadaha while taking rest in Lumbini under a sal tree. She is said to have been so spellbound by the natural grandeur of Lumbini, that as she was enjoying the view, she felt labour pains and catching hold of a drooping branch of the tree gave birth to her son.

The main attraction in Lumbini is the Sacred Garden. Spread over 8 sq.km (5 sq mi), it possesses all of the significant treasures of this historic area. As part of the global initiative to promote Lumbini, many countries have built or are building temples, monastries and stupas near the Sacred Garden in the International Monastery Zone. Currently there are religious representations such as the Myanmar Temple, the International Gautami Nuns Temple, China Temple and the Nepal Buddha Temple.

The Ashoka pillar, bearing an inscription identifying the holy site as the birthplace of Buddha, is situated near the Sacred Garden. To one side of the pillar is the Mayadevi Temple, housing a bas relief depicting the birth. Recent excavations have uncovered a stone bearing a 'foot imprint' indicating the exact place of birth.

The Puskarni pond, where Buddha's mother, Queen Mayadevi, bathed before giving birth lies south of the pillar.

The Lumbini Museum, located in the Cultural Zone, holds collections of coins, stamps, religious manuscripts, terracotta fragments as well as pottery and metal sculptures.

**WHAT IS IT**
The site where Siddharta Gautama – Buddha – was born.
**WHERE IS IT**
The Rupandehi District in the Terrai plains of Nepal by the Indian border
**NOMENCLATURE**
Lumbini is Sanskrit for 'lovely'
**WHAT IS THERE TO SEE**
The Sacred Garden
**HISTORIC IMPORTANCE**
This is one of the four holiest places of Buddhism

# Makalu

Makalu is the fifth highest mountain in the world and lies 22 km (14 mi) east of Mt Everest. An isolated peak soaring 8,463 m (27,766 ft) into the sky, it resembles a four-sided pyramid. Chomo Lonzo, at an elevation of 7,818 m (25,650 ft) is a subsidiary peak separated by a narrow saddle rising just north of the higher summit.

These stunning peaks provide the backdrop for the Makalu region, an amazingly pristine area in the north-western corner of the Sankhuwasabha district. To the west, it is bordered by the Everest region, to the north by China, to the east by the Arun river and to the south by the Sabha river. Designated a national park and conservation area, the Makalu Barun Conservation Project (MBCP) was established to ensure the preservation of the region through its development with the least amount of impact on the natural beauty of the area, with tourism secondary on its agenda.

The region is very close to the Everest region, but drastically different in many ways. Most of the people live in the lower hills with the highest concentrations in the southernmost third of the district, close to the Arun River, including the ethnic groups of Rai, Limbu and Sherpa.

Makulu is one of the hardest summits to reach because of its narrow, exposed ridges and steep sides.

Americans made the first attempt on the summit in the spring of 1954, but their attempt on the south-east ridge failed at 7,100 m (23,294 ft ) because of a series of severe storms. The first successful attempt, via the north face and north-east ridge, was achieved on 15 May the following year by Lionel Terray and Jean Couzy from Jean Franco's expedition. Eventually, the south-east ridge was conquered when two climbers from a Japanese expedition completed this most difficult route on 23 May 1970.

The Makalu trek is one of the most difficult in the Himalayas – witnessing the spectacle from the Arun Valley, one can only imagine the views from the ice-capped top.

**WHAT IS IT**
The fifth highest mountain in the world and a conservation area of natural beauty.
**WHERE IS IT**
22 km (14 mi) east of Mt Everest on the China-Nepal border in the Himalayan mountain range.
**HOW DO I GET THERE**
Hike from Tumlingtar airport.
**WHEN SHOULD I GO**
The best times to visit are spring and autumn.
**HOW HIGH IS IT**
8,463 m (27,766 ft).

*Base camp below Makalu peak.*

# Kandy

Kandy, originally named Senkadagala after the hermit Senkada, and also known as Maha Nuwara meaning the 'Great City', is a sacred Buddhist site and the cultural centre of Sri Lanka. The royal palace in Senkadagala was built by King Vikramabahu III of Gampola, on the advice of a Brahmin who selected the site as lucky ground for a capital city. In the centre of the island and surrounded by lush mountains, a large lake, and the longest river in Sri Lanka, it was the royal capital from 1592 until 1815 when it came under British rule.

Although much of Sri Lanka's royalty suffered under the hands of the British, the city of Kandy, the last stronghold of local kings, managed to retain a rich heritage of living monuments. The best known of these is the sacred pilgrimage site of the Temple of the Tooth, which is said to house one of Buddha's teeth.

Legend has it that the tooth was smuggled here in the hair of a princess after being taken from the flames of his funeral pyre. Pirated to India by an invading army, the tooth was eventually restored to its rightful place in the monument in Kandy, constructed during the seventeenth and eighteenth centuries.

Sri Lanka's grandest celebration, the Kandy Esala Perahera, takes place each year in the month of Esala (July or August). A ten-day festival ending on the night of the full Moon, its highlight is a procession of drummers, dancers and elephants led by the Maligawa Tusker, a bull elephant carrying a canopy sheltering a duplicate of the Buddha's sacred tooth.

This beautiful city is certainly a stunning place to learn about the history and culture of Sri Lanka.

*The Temple of the Tooth, a famous destination for pilgrims is said to house one of the Lord Buddha's teeth.*

# Ambalangoda

Ambalangoda, a quiet, unspoiled beach town on Sri Lanka's south-west coast, serves as the home of devil dancing and mask- and puppet-making traditions that have been kept alive for generations.

Devil dances are performed on a variety of occasions to exorcise evil spirits and diseases, and to seek blessings from good spirits. The colourful masks worn during the many festivals and ceremonies are carved from the local soft kadura wood and stained with vegetable dyes. The masks, which are associated with local legends and folklore, depict humans, demons and animals. The main types of masks included the kolam, naga and sninii or sanni, each of which is used for a different kind of ceremony, festival, opera or drama.

A sanni mask, for instance, is worn to combat illness. Grotesque representations of 18 different devils associated with various afflictions are used to drive out the evil spirits responsible for the ailment in ceremonies that sometimes last all night. Common representations include combinations of snakes and demons or a bird and a demon.

The tradition of hanging a masked dummy on a new home to prevent evil spirits entering during building work continues in the village. Masks and other local handicrafts can be bought in the village. It is worth a visit to the Mask Museum to see the stunning variety and craftsmanship of this local art form.

Several Buddhist temples in the area surrounding Madampe Lake are worth visiting, including the Thalwatta Totagamuwa, which dates back to the ninth century.

The virtually undiscovered beach resort of Hikkaduwa is worth a trip for its surf and its Coral Sanctuary – a haven for both snorkellers and divers with its abundance of colourful reef fish and turtles.

*Castle of King Fasil and his descendants.*

**WHAT IS IT**
A traditional beach village on the southern coast road.
**WHERE IS IT**
Near the resort of Bentota, 86 km (53 mi) from Colombo and 24 km (15 mi) from Beruwela.
**WHAT IS THERE TO SEE**
Devil dancing and hand-carved masks.
**WHAT SHOULD I BUY**
The area is known for its masks, hand-loomed batiks and hand-woven cottons.
**WHAT IS THERE TO DO THERE**
Go to the Mask Museum or visit nearby Hikkaduwa and its coral garden.

251

*Head and upper torso of painted reclining Buddha sculpture.*

# Cave temples at Dambulla

Dambulla is a small town known for its high concentration of cave temples, some of which have been used by local monks as meditation locations since the first century BC. With more than 80 caves within its reach, Dambulla's major attraction is the aptly named Dambulla Rock Temple, or as it is more commonly known, the Golden Temple of Dambulla, which is the largest and best preserved temple in Sri Lanka. Consisting of five cave temples, each of which contains an impressive variety of Buddhist and Hindu statues and paintings that date back to between the twelfth and eighteenth centuries.

A UNESCO World Heritage Site, the Golden Temple of Dambulla has ceilings painted with intricate patterns of images depicting the life of Buddha. Statues here include Buddha, bodhisattvas (beings who help humans to achieve enlightenment), kings and gods (including two Hindu gods).

The first cave is called Temple of the King of the Gods and its well preserved statue depicts the passing away of the Buddha. Typical of Anuradhapura sculpture, it is roughly 14 m (47 ft) high with a shapeless, expressionless face and a textured robe covering the body nearly to the floor. The cave also holds an additional five statues, including those of Buddha's attendant weeping at his death, Vishnu and one of the four guardian deities of the island.

The second cave is the largest and most impressive at 22 m (72 ft) in length, with a lofty archway 6 m (21 ft) high guarded by stone Makara figures on either side. This cave now has 56 seated and standing statues of Buddha, as well as statues of bodhissatvas, Vishnu, Saman, King Vattagamini Abhaya (who founded the cave) and King Nissanka Malla (who paid for 50 of the Buddha statues to be gilded).

Cave three is separated by a masonry wall and is the second largest cave. It is painted in rich colours, particularly yellow, that are respresentative of depictions of Buddhist history during the 18th century. The highlight in the cave is the figure of the recumbent Buddha, his head resting on his right hand, his head on a pillow. The lifelike serenity of expression is an exceptional feat considering it was carved from granite.

The fourth cave, the Western Temple, has ten figures of Buddha with clearly delineated features, all hewn out of rock and painted vibrant colours. The final cave is the smallest of the five shrine rooms, made by a local chieftain in the beginning of the twentieth century. There are 11 statues in the cave, the chief of which is a large recumbent Buddha showing an excellent degree of workmanship.

Whether you are religious or into the arts, or neither, you cannot fail to be impressed by the Golden Temple of Dambulla.

**WHAT IS IT**
A small town known especially for its Buddhist Golden Temple.
**WHAT IS THERE TO SEE**
Ancient caves, temples and forests.
**WHERE IS IT**
19 km (12 mi) from Sigiriya on the Sigiriya–Kandy road.
**WHAT ELSE IS THERE TO SEE**
The Iron Wood forest and Rose Quartz Mountain.

# Galle

Sri Lanka's fourth biggest town, the port of Galle, was founded by the Portuguese in the sixteenth century. The Dutch took over in 1598, demolishing all signs of the Portuguese presence, building their own 36-ha (90-acre) fort, which is now a UNESCO World Heritage Site. Galle is the best remaining example of a European fortified city in south Asia, and is particularly impressive for its mix of Western architecture and south Asian traditions.

Until the British decided to use Colombo as their main port, Galle had been a major port, the largest city in Sri Lanka and the European administrative centre for more than four centuries. The Portuguese built the original fort to withstand attack from the Sri Lankan kingdoms to the north. The Dutch, who captured the coastal cities from the Portuguese, rebuilt and enhanced the defence system of the fort, widening the moat and improving the ramparts and the bastions. The architecture of the fort is significant in that the weight of the roof is supported solely by the walls as there are no pillars inside. The British who captured the city from the Dutch did not make many changes since they eventually shifted the capital north to Colombo, thereby preserving the atmosphere of the days of Dutch occupation.

The Dutch Reformed Church, built by a Dutch Army officer on the site of a previous Portuguese church, was completed in 1754. Close to the entrance of the fort, the church contains records of marriages from 1748 and baptism records from 1678.

Unique to this area is stilt fishing, a traditional method in which fishermen stand in the water on tall stilts. It is an amazing feat of dexterity, and a fascinating activity to watch.

**WHAT IS IT**
The best remaining example of a European fortified city in south Asia.
**WHERE IS IT**
The southern coast of Sri Lanka, 6 km (4 mi) north-west of Unawatuna and 116 km (72 mi) south of Colombo.
**WHAT IS THERE TO SEE**
The Dutch Fort and nearby Unawatuna beach.
**WHEN SHOULD I GO**
October to April is the most popular time to visit.

*A Spanish-style church at the top of the hill.*

# Sigiriya Fortress

**WHAT IT IT**
A garden city with a monastery and palace as well as incredible murals.
**WHERE IS IT**
A 3½-hour drive from the airport in Colombo.
**WHAT IS THERE TO SEE**
A fascinating and stunning example of early architecture, engineering and hydraulics inside a massive rock fortress.
**ALSO KNOWN AS**
'The eighth wonder of the ancient world'.

Sigiriya, once the capital of Sri Lanka, was built during King Kassyapa's reign (477–495 AD). Lying on a steep granite peak and jutting 370 m (1,214 ft) into the sky, Sigiriya, A UNESCO World Heritage Site, offers the best example of an ancient Asian city centre and an excellent example of advanced Sri Lankan urban planning.

The fortress was built in the form of a crouching lion, and entrance to the enormous rock structure was once through the lion's mouth. The gigantic paws are the only remaining feature of the lion today, but its outline still dominates the surrounding jungle-covered plains. Halfway up the rock are giant, beautifully painted maidens.

Sigiriya is home to a magnificent complex of geometric gardens, pools, fountains and buildings. From the summit of the rock, you can see the once magnificent royal pool, the throne, and remains of the majestic palace, walkways and gardens.

The water garden, an astounding example of early hydraulics, provided surface drainage, erosion control, cooling systems and ornamental and recreational water features. There was a man-made lake featuring a 12 km (7.5 mi) dam and the water gardens held pools, cisterns and islands surrounding a large pavilion. The water supply for the fountains operated through gravity and pressure and they still work today.

To the north is the Pidurangala Rock, where there is a Buddhist monastery and cave temples. Near the summit is one of the largest reclining Buddha statues ever made out of bricks and mortar.

*Huge, stone-sculpted claws flank the walled temple stairway.*

# Anuradhapura

Rediscovered in the nineteenth century and declared a UNESCO World Heritage Site, Anuradhapura is said to be the greatest monastic city of the ancient world. The royal capital of 113 kings and a Buddhist pilgrimage site, Anuradhapura is the home to some of Sri Lanka's grandest monuments, palaces and monasteries.

The city was founded by Anuradha, a king's minister, in 500 BC and Sanghamitta planted Buddha's fig tree, the 'tree of enlightenment' here in the third century BC. The city flourished until 993 AD when the capital was moved to Polonnaruwa.

Highlights of this city, which was hidden away in dense jungle for many years, include the Aukana Buddha and the guard stone at Thuparama. The 13-m (43-ft) granite Buddha, which dates back to the fifth-century reign of King Dathusena, is said to be of such sculptural accuracy that droplets of rainwater falling off the tip of the nose hit the ground exactly between the toes. The guard stone at Thuparama is considered to be the oldest dagoba in Sri Lanka and is said to enshrine one of Buddha's collarbones.

Also notable in Anuradhapura are the site where Thero Mahinda, the son of the Indian Emperor Asoka introduced Buddhism to Sri Lanka, which is marked by a Bo tree, and Ruwanweli Seya, which is regarded as the greatest stupa in the world. Erected in the second century BC, this dagoba is said to have the most perfect water bubble shape.

The religious site of nearby Mihintale is also spectacular, with the remains of a monastery and hospital, dagobas, sacred caves and pools, a modern statue of Buddha and an outcrop called meditation rock, all of which are reached via a granite stairway with 1,840 steps leading to the summit, from where there are amazing views.

*Thuparama Dagoba.*

**WHAT IS IT**
The greatest monastic city of the ancient world, the royal capital of 113 kings.
**WHERE IS IT**
North central Sri Lanka.
**WHAT IS THERE TO SEE**
Many of Sri Lanka's most grand palaces, monuments and monasteries.

*Colossi of standing and reclining Buddhas outside Gal Vihara Temple.*

# Polonnaruwa

Polonnaruwa became the capital of Sri Lanka after the destruction of Anuradhapura in 993 BC. Strategically located at the crossing of the Mahaveli River, the city, a UNESCO World Heritage Site, was used as a country residence before becoming the capital. In addition to the Brahmanic monuments built by the Cholas, Polonnaruwa is also home to the monumental ruins of the fabulous garden city created by Parakramabahu I in the twelfth century.

The city is known for its unique irrigation system, Lake Parakrama (Parakrama Samudra), a man-made irrigation tank spread over an area of 2,400 ha (5,940 acres). Built by Parakramabahu I, it is one of the most striking features of Polonnurawa.

Also of note here is the Royal Citadel, which houses Parkramabahu's palace and administrative buildings. An impressive building with elaborate stone carvings, it is enclosed by a 1-m (3.2-ft) thick rampart. Outside the walls lies the Royal Bath, or Lotus Bath. Made of stone and reached by stairs, it has a small pavilion once used as a changing room.

Gal Vihara, a Buddhist shrine, contains intricately carved and well-preserved standing and reclining statues of Buddha. Hatadage, another important shrine, was built by Parakramabahu I to house the Sacred Tooth.

**WHAT IS IT**
The second capital of Sri Lanka.
**WHERE IS IT**
216 km (134 mi) north-east of Colombo.
**WHAT IS THERE TO SEE**
Brahmanic monuments and a fabulous garden city.

# Adam's Peak

Adam's Peak, surrounded by a group of mountains known as 'the Wilderness of the Peak', is best known for containing Buddha's left footprint. A pilgrimage site for the faithful since ancient times, the peak, although not the highest on the island, is the most impressive because it dominates the others around it, seemingly rising out of the ground on its own.

Soaring to 2,243 m (7,360 ft), the conical mountain has been compared by some to a drop of water or teardrop, its pendant shape lying on the southern forested plains of the country.

According to a legend, when Buddha visited Sri Lanka he planted one foot north of the royal city and the other on Sumana-kuta, Adam's Peak, 160 km (100 mi) away. According to another legend the Buddha is believed to have left his left footprint on Adam's Peak, then his right footprint at Phra Sat in Thailand, as the two impressions are very similar in size and appearance.

The sacred footprint on the mountain is a giant shallow hollow 156 cm (61 in) long, and 76 cm (30 in) across the toes and 71 cm (28 in) across the heel. It is believed that the actual footprint lies on a giant blue sapphire beneath the boulder that lies on the top of the summit, and that what people see is just an enlarged representation.

The pilgrimage season to Sri Pada, the holy mountain, begins at 'Unduvap', the December full Moon, and ends on 'Vesak', full Moon in the following May. During this time a statue of the Saman god of the mountain, an insignia of a white elephant and other sacred offerings are taken up the mountain to be placed by the footprint. From June to November, when no pilgrimage is taking place, the objects are kept in safety in Pelmadulla.

King Vijayabahu (1058–1114) built rest camps along the route of the pilgrimage and provided them with food and water, but pilgrimages did not begin until the reign of Sri Nissankamalla (1187–1196).

The steep and often difficult climb is usually made at night so that pilgrims can see the spectacular sunrise from the peak. There are various points along the way where visitors can stop, rest, cook and sleep.

Before entering the sacred site, pilgrims take a ceremonial bath in the nearby river and change into clean clothes. From the river there is a footbridge leading to the sacred mountain, where the path merges into a series of steps leading up to the famous site.

**WHAT IS IT**
The second highest peak in Sri Lanka.
**WHERE IS IT**
In the Ratnapura district of south-western Sri Lanka.
**WHAT IS THERE TO SEE**
Buddha's left footprint.
**ALSO KNOWN AS**
*Sri Pada, Pico de Adam* or 'Peak of Adam'.

*A long line of lights illuminates the path to the summit of Adam's Peak during the Vesak Full Moon Poya Festival.*

# Sinharaja Forest Reserve

**WHAT IS IT**
Sri Lanka's last tropical rainforest.
**WHERE IS IT**
South-western Sri Lanka, north-east of Galle.
**WHY IS IT IMPORTANT**
It is home to many rare and endemic species of birds and other mammals, reptiles, amphibians and butterflies.
**ALSO KNOWN AS**
'Kingdom of the Lion'
**WHEN SHOULD I VISIT**
August–September and January–April.

Sinharaja Forest Reserve, a UNESCO World Heritage Site, is Sri Lanka's last remaining tropical rainforest. Located in south-western Sri Lanka, it is home to many endemic and rare trees and wildlife, including a variety of mammals, butterflies, reptiles and amphibians.

At a mere 21 km (13 mi) across, and an average of 5 km (3 mi) long, the reserve is a national treasure. Highlights of the park include leopards, although these are rarely seen, and the purple-faced langur – a species of monkey.

The large bird population tends to fly in mixed feeding flocks, some of which have been known to contain up to 48 species. Rare birds seen in Sinharaja are the red-faced malkoha, the Sri Lanka blue magpie, the ashy-headed babbler and the white-headed starling as well as the green–billed coucal, which is the rarest of Sri Lankan birds.

Reptiles found in Sinharaja include both green pit and hump-nosed vipers and many amphibian groups, especially tree frogs.

The vegetation of Sinharaja is a combination of tropical lowland rainforest and tropical wet evergreen forest, with many trees averaging a height of nearly 47 m (154 ft). Out of the 211 woody trees and lianas so far identified within the reserve 139 are endemic. Many of the plants at lower levels, such as epiphytes, occur only here. Similarly, out of the 25 of these that are indigenous to Sri Lanka, 13 can be found in Sinharaja.

# Samarkand

**WHAT IS IT**
One of the oldest and most important cities of Asia.
**WHERE IS IT**
In the Zarafshan Valley in Uzbekistan.
**ALSO KNOWN AS**
'The Rome of the East' or 'the pearl of the Muslim world'
**WHAT IS THERE TO SEE**
Incredible architecture, an enduring history and a dazzling mixture of cultures.

A UNESCO World Heritage Site, Samarkand is the third largest city in Uzbekistan and is home to a dazzling array of architecture and culture representing its long and sometimes violent history. Majestic and beautiful, it has been called 'the Rome of the East', 'the pearl of the Muslim world', and 'the land of scientists'.

Strategically located in the Zarafshan Valley, Samarkand lies on the ancient Silk Road and has historically been a key entry point on any visit to Central Asia, which helps to explain its turbulent past and mixture of cultures. Samarkand has experienced rule by the Persians, Alexander the Great, Arabs, Genghis Khan, Timur Gurkani (Tamerlane or Tamburlaine the Great), Turks and Russians, leading it to develop a culture consisting of Persian, Indian and Mongolian influences with a splash of both Western and Eastern cultures.

At the centre of the city lies the Registan ('sandy place'), which is surrounded on three sides by the medieval Ulugh Beg, Sherdar and Tilla-Kari madrasahs – universities – which sparkle with turquoise mosaic patterns. Decorated inside and out with glazed bricks, mosaics and carved marble, they are considered to be the finest representations of Islamic art and architecture in existence.

The blue, ribbed dome of the Gur Emir Mausoleum, which houses the remains of Timur and his family, dominates the skyline of central Samarkand. Inside, the broken, gigantic slab of dark green jade commemorating this once mighty ruler is said to be the largest jade stone in the world.

Another architectural treasure, albeit much restored after earthquake damage in the nineteenth century, is the Bibi Khanum Mosque, named in honour of Timur's senior wife. Its dome is considered to be the largest in the Muslim world and the multi-coloured decorated roof is one of the largest and most grand in Samarkand. The main gate, an impressive 35 m (115 ft) high, looms above a noisy, crowded market brimming with colourful fruits, vegetables and locally grown spices. The main bazaar, which lies around the mosque appears to have changed little in centuries.

Shah-i-Zinda – the tomb of the living king – houses the shrine of Prophet Muhammad's cousin, Qusam ibn Abbas, who brought Islam to this region. The beautiful shrine is one of the oldest structures in Samarkand and is a popular pilgrimage site.

*Ulugh Beg and Sherdar madrasahs in the Registan.*

259

# Angkor

*The temple of Angkor Wat.*

The vast, majestic temples at Angkor, the Lost City, were discovered in 1860 spread across a 64-km (40-mi) site surrounding the modern village of Siem Reap.

Originally built between the eighth and thirteenth centuries, the temples range from a single, brick tower to vast, stone complexes such as Angkor Wat, the largest single religious monument in the world, which was built for King Suryavarman II in the early twelfth century.

The Khmer temples are located at two main sites. The first, at Roluos, 16 km (10 mi) south-east of modern day Siem Reap, is where a select few of the earlier temples were constructed. This was home to the first Khmer capital in the Angkor area, but in the late ninth century Yasovarman I created his new capital at Angkor, itself and it is at this much larger site that the majority of the bigger Khmer temples are located.

Some of the most impressive temples of the City of Angkor include Bakong, Banteai Srei, the Baphuon, the Bayon, and Ta Prohm. Bakong, the central temple, a large pyramid built in the ninth century measures 55 m (180 ft) along each side at the base. Banteai Srei, a small, delicate temple is a particularly fine example of a multi-building temple complex and has intricate, well-preserved pink sandstone carvings. The Baphuon, a large pyramid temple built by Udayadityavarman II between 1050 and 1066, features beautiful carvings including a 40-m (130-ft) reclining Buddha. The Bayon is a massive complex with incredible 1,200 m (3,936 ft) bas-relief carvings including a series of mysterious Buddha faces on the third level. Ta Prohm, one of the larger complexes, enclosed by a moat, is also one of the most beautiful. Built by Jayavarman VII in the late twelfth century, Ta Prohm has not been restored and its location in the lush jungle gives it a romantic and mysterious aura.

**WHAT IS IT**
The largest temple in the world.
**WHERE IS IT**
Siem Reap, 309 km (192 mi) from Phnom Penh.
**HOW DO I GET THERE**
Flights are available to Phnom Penh's Pochentong Airport from Bangkok, Hanoi, Saigon, Vientiane and Moscow.
**ALSO KNOWN AS**
'The Lost City'.

# Borobudur Temple

Dating from the eighth century, Borobudur Temple in the Kedu plain of Central Java is one of the greatest architectural monuments in Asia. The Buddhist temple, a UNESCO World Heritage Site, is a stepped pyramid made up of six rectangular stories, three circular terraces and a central stupa forming the summit, the structure forms a lotus, the sacred flower of Buddha.

The walls and balustrades are decorated with low reliefs, covering a total surface area of 2,500 sq m (8,202 sq ft). Around the circular platforms are 72 openwork stupas, each of which contains a statue of Buddha.

Surrounded by an idyllic landscape of emerald rice-terraced hills and overlooked by four volcanoes, Borobudur Temple was built over a period of 80 years for the Sailendra dynasty, to resemble a microcosm of the universe, to provide a visual image of the teachings of Buddha and show, in a practical manner, the steps through life that each person must follow to achieve enlightenment.

Visitors to this pilgrimage site would first have been led around the successive levels from the base with its friezes illustrating the consequences of living in the world of desire, then up through five levels showing how to conquer desire and attachment.

The square section of the temple's right-angled then gives way to a round unadorned summit where meditating Buddhas and saints sit in supreme peace contemplating a view of exquisite beauty. In the centre, a bell shaped tower, or stupa, points to heaven, a realm beyond form and concept, known as Nirvana.

**WHAT IS IT**
One of the greatest monuments in the world.
**WHERE IS IT**
The Kedu Plain in Central Java.
**WHAT IS THERE TO SEE**
An eighth-century Buddhist temple in the shape of a lotus flower.
**WHY IS IT IMPORTANT**
It is an almost unique survival of a substantially intact Buddhist temple from this era.

*Borobudur Temple*

# Mt Bromo

**WHAT IS IT**
The most famous attraction in Eastern Java.

**WHERE IS IT**
145 km (90 mi) south of Surabaya in the Bromo-Tengger-Semeru National Park.

**WHAT IS THERE TO SEE**
The sun rising at the crater rim of this spectacular mountain.

**WHEN SHOULD I GO**
The fourteenth day of the month of Kasada in the Tenggerese calender for the festival.

Mt Bromo is the most famous attraction in Eastern Java and many people from all over the world come here to make the pre-dawn trek to view the stunning sunrise over its spectacular active crater.

Located in the Bromo-Tengger-Semeru National Park in the centre of East Java, the largest volcanic region in the province is the Tengger Caldera. Bromo is only one of many peaks inside the massive caldera, but it is easily recognized as the entire top has been blown off and the crater inside constantly belches white smoke. The inside of the caldera, aptly dubbed the Laut Pasir (Sea of Sand) is an area of 10 sq km (4 sq mi) coated with fine volcanic ash. Compared to the surrounding lush emerald valleys, this vast ashy desert lends an eerie and unsettling effect.

The Buddhist Tenggerese, an ethnic group inhabiting the highlands of East Java's Tengger range, live almost entirely from agriculture. On the fourteenth day of the month Kasada, they gather at the rim of Mt Bromo's active crater to present annual offerings of rice, fruit, vegetables, flowers, livestock and other local products and ask for blessing from the Supreme God, Hyang Widi Wasa.

According to legend, the ceremony dates back to the time of the Majapahit kingdom, during the reign of King Brawijaya. The queen gave birth to a daughter, Rara Anteng, who married Jaka Seger, a young Brahmin. They fled east from Majapahit as Islam expanded in Java during the fifteenth century. Despite the new kingdom's prosperity the king and queen were unhappy because they had no children so they decided to climb up to the top of Mt Bromo and pray for help. Moved by their prayers, the god of the mountain assured them that they would have children but demanded that their youngest child be sacrificed to him in return. When their twenty-fifth child,

*Members of the Tengger tribe throw their offerings into the Mount Bromo crater during the annual Yadnya Kasada festival in East Java.*

Kesuma, was born, the mountain's god became angry that they had not fulfilled their side of the bargain. They were forced to comply and the child was thrown into the crater. As he fell he told his family to perform an annual ceremony of offering.

The trek across the sand sea to watch the sun rise from the rim of the crater is popular with both local and foreign tourists. The largely undeveloped national park has interesting wildlife and its peaks offer challenging climbs.

# Yogyakarta

The provincial capital and cultural centre, Yogyakarta, lies amid lush emerald rice paddies under the shadow of Mt Merapi. Once the centre of the ancient Mataram Palace, its environs are home to many important monuments and temples, including the Gebang and Mendut temples, as well as a variety of nearby scenic beaches.

The Gebang Temple, to the north-east was rediscovered after a statue of Ganesha was uncovered in 1936. Built at about the same time as the nearby Borobudur temple in the eighth century, the ruins of the roof, part of the body and much of the base appeared intact upon further archaeological research. This unadorned square building measures roughly 5.25 m (17 sq ft) across and 7.75 m (25.4 ft) high.

The Mendut Temple, 3 km (1.8 mi) east of Borobodur was built in 824 AD by King Indera of the Cailendra dynasty. Inside the square terraced temple decorated by stupas are three large, colourful statues. Each year, on Waisak Day (the May full Moon), pilgrims come to this ceremony from around Indonesia and the rest of the world.

The Pramaban Temple, which is known locally as the Loro Johggrang Temple or the Temple of the Slender Virgin, is the largest in Indonesia and one of the most beautiful. It was built in the ninth century. The main shrines are dedicated to Shiva, Brahma and Vishnu and Shiva's holds a richly decorated statue of his consort, Durga.

The most important building within Yogyakarta is Ngayogyakarta Hadiningrat Palace, also known as the Kraton, the Sultan's Palace, an elegant building that is partly open to the public.

There are a variety of stunning beaches to choose from near Yogyakarta. There is Baron Beach with its mouth to an underground river, the coral island of Drini Beach, Kukup Beach with its rich sea life, Siung Beach nestled underneath two spectacular cliffs and Wediombo Beach with its white sandy bay and idyllic sunsets to name just a few.

*Yogyakarta and its surrounding areas are rich in cultural and religious history.*

**WHAT IS IT**
An area of natural and historic beauty and the cultural capital of the region.
**WHERE IS IT**
Central Java.
**WHAT IS THERE TO DO**
Visit the many Candi, or religious sites or go to the many beaches.
**ALSO KNOWN AS**
Jogjakarta, Yogya, Jogia or Jogya.

263

# Lake Toba and Samosir Island

**WHAT IS IT**
The largest and deepest caldera lake in the world.
**WHERE IS IT**
In the middle of Danau Toba in northern Sumatra.
**WHAT IS THERE TO SEE**
The Toba Bakat sarcophagi.
**WHEN SHOULD I VISIT**
June to September.
**ALSO KNOWN AS**
Island of the Dead.

*Traditional Batak house.*

The island of Samosir, in the middle of Lake Toba, the original home of the fierce Toba Bataks, has many stone tombs and traditional villages. Believed to be the largest and deepest caldera lake in the world, Lake Toba spans over 1,707 sq km (436 sq mi) and reaches a depth of 529 m (1,735 ft). Created by an enormous volcanic eruption more than 74,000 years ago, it is a giant caldera high in the treeless mountains of northern Sumatra.

Samosir, the giant arid 'Island of the Dead' in the middle of Danau Toba, or Lake Toba, measures 45 x 20 km (28 x 12 mi). The eastern coast of the island rises steeply from a small bank towards a central plateau with an altitude of 780 m (2,559 ft), and the land gradually descends towards the southern and western coasts of the island, which is scattered with small villages.

The Samosir plateau consists mainly of rock, some scattered forests and swamps and a small lake. From Pangururan on the western side, a bridge connects the island with mainland Sumatra.

The island is best known for its Toba Bakat sarcophagi, which were first discovered in the 1930s. These 'adat houses', or stone graves with coffins have been found in 26 villages.

In Tomok, under the sacred Hariara tree, lies the 200-year-old stone sarcophagus of King Sidabutar's clan. Although they resemble coffins, the sarcophagi normally contain the collected skulls of an entire family or clan.

The island's traditional wooden houses are interesting and may be decorated with clan symbols and beautiful examples of batak handicrafts and musical instruments are on sale in several villages. The museum in Simanindo has fine examples of these and of traditional puppets used in ceremonies and dances.

# Ubud

*Palm trees on terraced rice fields.*

Ubud, in the middle of the island of Bali, has been the island's pre-eminent centre for fine arts, crafts, dance and music for more than a century. Once a hang-out for bohemians and backpackers, Ubud has developed into a town better known for its elegant resorts, galleries and mansions for discerning art collectors and travellers.

Because of its location, it also makes a good base for visiting other Balinese attractions, but there is plenty to see and do here. Ubud is surrounded by the traditional stunning landscape that Bali is known for including rice paddies, scenic villages, art and craft communities, ancient temples, palaces, rivers, unique character and friendly locals.

Ubud has been a 'royal town' for well over a hundred years and its princes, who bear the title 'Tjokorda' or 'Agung' still live in traditional palaces, called 'Puris', that dot the countryside.

In the south of the town is a small reserve called Monkey Forest, housing an abundance of long-tailed macaques that clamber over the temple. Bananas are on sale so that tourists can feed them. Just beyond the Monkey Forest is one of the many craft villages in the area, which specialises in wood carvings. The Museum Puri Lukisan (Museum of Fine Arts) has a wide collection of traditional and modern Balinese arts and the wood carvings are particularly good.

Ubud is bursting with colour and light, perhaps it is this profusion of plants, flowers, palms and rice paddies that inspire the creative minds of the population.

**WHAT IS IT**
Bali's pre-eminent centre for fine arts, dance and music.
**WHERE IS IT**
In the centre of the island of Bali
**WHAT IS THERE TO DO**
Visit the many temples, explore the galleries and boutiques, look around the luxury resorts or just take in this paradise.

# Kelimutu

Indonesia is one of the world's most geologically active countries, and among its volcanoes is Kelimutu on the island of Flores with its brightly coloured exotic lakes. Considered a national treasure by the people of Indonesia, each of the three lakes on the eastern summit of the volcano has distinctive features.

Tiwu Ata Polo, the 'enchanted lake', lies on the south-east flank of the volcano. A thermal plume in the north-west of the lake creates a white froth on its surface, indicating that gas or hot water is being vented into the lake from the volcano.

Tiwu Nua Muri Koohi Fah, the 'lake of young men and maidens', the deepest lake, is adjacent to Tiwu Ata Polo. A sizable tear in the western wall is apparent and a large thermal plume in the centre of the lake causes a yellow sulphurous froth to appear, particularly at the base of the north wall.

**WHAT IS IT**
A volcano with three brightly coloured lakes
**WHERE IS IT**
On the island of Flores in Indonesia.
**INTERESTING TRIVIA**
The lakes, considered a national treasure, are featured on the local currency.

Tiwu Ata Mbupu, the 'lake of elders', is the westernmost lake. It is structurally different to the other two in that the pit crater is itself located in the centre of a larger crater. Small landslides constantly add to the steep slopes of scree along the lake's shore, and large boulders periodically drop into the lake. Tiwu Ata Mbupu's shoreline is coated with a film in various shades of red, orange and yellow depending on its density.

Many Indonesian guide books describe the vibrant colours of the Kelimutu lakes as resulting from the minerals in the lakes. Although partly correct, the most important determinant of colour in the lakes is oxygen. When the lake waters lack oxygen they appear green, conversely, when they are rich in oxygen, they become a shade of deep red verging on black. The lakes are a stunning natural phenomenon not to be missed!

*The brightly coloured lakes of Kelimutu.*

*Coral reef along Manado Bay.*

# Manado Bay

Manado Bay, surrounded by lush tropical peaks, serves as the gateway to North Sulawesi, particularly for those diving the volcanic islands of Bunaken, the Lembeh Strait and Bangka.

The deep waters of the Bunaken Island National Marine Park in Manado exhibit some of the highest levels of biodiversity in the world, with outstanding fish variety and world-class wall diving. The clear, warm waters contain an astonishingly high number of different species, whether corals, sponges or fish. When you are scuba diving in Bunaken you can see seven times more genera of coral than in Hawaii, 33 species of butterfly fish and more than 70 per cent of all fish species known to live in Indonesian waters.

Ocean currents sweeping into Bunaken bring a steady stream of nutrients that provide sustenance for the area's rich marine life, which includes huge schools of black triggerfish, barracuda, moray eels and sea snakes. Napoleon wrasse, angelfish, turtles, blue ribbon eels, sting rays, eagle rays, snappers, groupers and sharks can also be seen.

The various superb diving and snorkelling sites put the marine park in the top ten dive sites in the world, making it a must for seasoned and beginner divers alike.

**WHAT IS IT**
A series of small islands offering world-class underwater activities.
**WHERE IS IT**
The capital of North Sulawesi province.
**WHAT IS THERE TO DO**
Snorkel and dive on some of the world's most pristine reefs.
**WHAT IS THERE TO SEE**
The Bunaken National Marine Park.
**WHEN SHOULD I GO**
April to October.

# Komodo National Park

Komodo National Park, home to the world's largest lizards, includes three major islands – Komodo, Rinca and Padar – and is located in the centre of the Indonesian archipelago. Established in 1980, the main purpose of the park was to conserve the unique Komodo dragon and its habitat. However, over the years, the goals for the park have expanded to protecting its entire biodiversity, both terrestrial and marine.

Declared a World Heritage Site and a Man and Biosphere Reserve by UNESCO, the park boasts one of the world's richest marine environments including coral reefs, mangroves, seagrass beds, seamounts and semi-enclosed bays. These habitats harbour more than 1,000 species of fish, 260 species of reef-building coral and 70 species of sponges. Dugong, sharks, manta rays, dolphins, sea turtles and at least 14 species of whales also make Komodo National Park their home.

The islands of the Komodo National Park are hot, arid and relatively barren compared to their lush, jungle-filled neighbours. The most popular reason to visit is to take a guided tour to the famous dragons, monitor lizards that can reach a length of 3 m (10 ft). Large, ferocious predators, the dragons are capable of consuming a fully grown human. As they languidly sashay past, their leery eyes staring menacingly and their forked tongues flickering, it is easy to imagine the strength of their massive jaws and powerful claws.

What is difficult to comprehend is that these lumbering creatures, with their stumpy legs, can run as fast as a dog. The dragons are also excellent swimmers and it is common for them to travel between the islands. Although the stunning pink and grey beaches of these islands are open for visitors, you should watch out for the dragons' foot and tail prints in the sand.

Once the sun gets high and temperatures soar, the Komodo dragons head down the riverbank to the dry stream bed below, where they dig deep burrows to cool themselves and lay their eggs. These ancient creatures are truly a spectacle to behold.

**WHAT IS IT**
A UNESCO World Heritage Site and Biosphere Reserve.
**WHERE IS IT**
In the centre of the Indonesian archipelago.
**WHAT IS IT KNOWN FOR**
The world's largest lizard, the Komodo dragon
**WHAT IS THERE TO DO**
Watch the impressive Komodo dragons and enjoy some of the world's best marine life.
**WHEN SHOULD I VISIT**
April to October

*A male Komodo dragon patrols the beach.*

# Bukit Lawang

The rainforests of Gunung Leuser National Park in Northern Sumatra are a beautiful area for trekking and river tubing and also, most notably, home to the Bukit Lawang Orangutan Rehabilitation Centre. Located on the banks of the Bohorok River, the centre was founded in 1973 by two Swiss zoologists, Monica Borner and Regina Frey, to study and protect these fascinating creatures and to return them to their natural habitat.

They gained support from the World Wildlife Fund, and made huge progress in the rehabilitation of Orangutans rescued from captivity, or from the forests that are quickly being destroyed through deforestation.

*Orangutans eating bananas at the rehabilitation centre.*

**WHAT IS IT**
Home to the Bukit Lawang Orangutan Rehabilitation Centre.
**WHERE IS IT**
86 km (53 mi) by road to the north-west of Medan on the banks of the Bohorok River.
**WHAT IS THERE TO DO**
Tubing, trekking or watching the gorgeous orangutans
**NOMENCLATURE**
Orang-utan is Indonesian for 'Man of the Forest'.

The Bohorok Orangutan Rehabilitation Centre is now run by the Indonesian government and visitors can come to see the orangutans that have been released back into the wild. To assist in this transition, there are two open feedings a day, during which the orangutans may come swinging through the jungle for a free meal. The hope is that, within time, each orangutan will learn to find enough fruit in the jungle on its own, so that it no longer needs a free meal.

Other attractions in the area include a cave full of bats that fly out at dusk, watersports, the Accoustic Cave and trekking in the jungle to see orangutans in the wild.

# Luang Prabang

Luang Prabang must surely be one of the most beautiful cities in the world, and in 1995 it was added to UNESCO's World Heritage list, recognised as the best preserved city in south-east Asia.

Set on a peninsula where the Mekong and the Khan rivers meet, and surrounded by misty green mountains, Luang Prabang was a kingdom from the fourteenth century until the Lao monarchy was dissolved in 1975. It is the only city in Laos where the ethnic Lao population outnumbers Vietnamese and Chinese.

The old city is rightly famous for its historic temples and monasteries (there are more than 30 of them) and for its splendid Royal Palace, which now serves as a fascinating museum. There are lovely old French-Indochinese colonial houses, and two-storey shop houses featuring both French and Lao architectural influences. Two parallel streets run the length of the peninsula and one runs all the way around it on the river's edge. These are criss-crossed by many fascinating little lanes and back streets.

Walking in Luang Prabang is a joy – several of the streets are shaded with palms and flowering trees, sweeping, gilded temple roofs can be glimpsed every few yards, colourful prayer flags flutter in the breeze and temple gongs echo around the town. You can watch the sunset from the top of Phou Si Hill or enjoy a cool drink by the river's edge. Explore the markets or visit one of the monasteries, such as Wat Xiang Thong, and soak up the serene and spiritual atmosphere that still pervades the town despite its influx of visitors.

**WHAT IS IT**
One of the most beautiful cities in the world and the best preserved city in south-east Asia.
**WHAT IS THERE TO SEE**
The Royal Palace, Phou Si Hill, Wat Xiang Thong, Pak Ou Buddha caves and the Kouang Si waterfalls.
**WHAT IS THERE TO DO**
Visit one of the 30 temples in the city or the Royal Palace.
**DO NOT MISS**
Watching the sunset from from the top of Phou Si Hill.

*Wat Xiang Thong, a temple in Luang Prabang.*

271

# Vientiane

**WHAT IS THERE TO SEE**
Mekong River, Wat Sisaket and That Luang.
**WHAT IS THERE TO DO:**
Visit the colourful morning market (talat sao).
**WHAT SHOULD I BUY**
Textiles and silks at the morning market.
**HOW DO I GET THERE**
By air, or across the Friendship Bridge from Thailand.

Vientiane is the capital city of the Lao People's Democratic Republic. Set on a broad curve in the Mekong river valley, it is a sleepy backwater of a city, full of charm.

The city's architecture is largely low-rise, and there are old French colonial buildings to be seen as well as two-storey Indochinese shop houses, which are often painted yellow, and lovely ramshackle wooden homes by the side of the river. The city centre is marked by a fountain in a square named Nam Phou Place. Almost all of Vientiane's important sights are located within walking distance from here, including a few socialist-style buildings such as the Lao Revolutionary Museum. That Luang, the old royal stupa is 3 km (2 mi) north of the city and Wat Sisaket is the city's oldest temple.

Strolling along the shady, tree-lined streets you will find it hard to believe you are in a capital city. Small groups of Buddhist monks in orange or rust-coloured robes, sporting umbrellas against the sun invite you to visit their temples and want to practise their English on you. On the banks of the Mekong, farmers grow vegetables and water buffalo graze peacefully, barely looking up as you pass. At the morning market (talat sao) you can find the best of Lao weaving – glorious silks, cottons and ethnic textiles, old and new.

Vientiane is changing. Where there were once hundreds of bicycles, there are now motor bikes and cars. However, the overwhelming impression you receive is of a city in a time warp, enjoying a gentle pace of life and in no particular hurry to become just like everywhere else.

*The gate of That Luang and its stupa at sunset.*

# Tad Lo Falls

The Tad Lo falls are not particularly high, in fact they are only about 10 m (33 ft) high, but they are broad and long and beautifully situated in the forested hills on the north-western edge of the Bolaven plateau in southern Laos. High above the steamy Mekong River valley, the plateau is cool and fertile, and here Laven, Alak and Katu tribal farmers grow top-quality coffee, which fetches some of the highest prices in the world. Rivers plunge off the plateau in all directions, and Tad Lo is one of the most accessible and delightful.

A striking feature of the lower falls are the large granite boulders that make perfect places upon which to lie and enjoy the sun, allowing you to drop down into the cool, clear water of a swimming hole, or to wade back to the shore quite safely and easily. Make sure you are out of the water by 8.00 pm in the hot season, however, as this is when the floodgates of a dam upstream are opened, and a huge torrent of water comes pounding down with a tremendous roar.

There are several places in which to stay nearby, but the Tad Lo Resort has a few lovely rooms with balconies overlooking the falls. If you are not up to exploring and climbing the falls by foot, take an elephant ride instead. These last for a couple of hours, and an elephant can carry two people, sitting in a securely attached wooden seat. You go through a couple of interesting tribal villages in the forest where the houses are built on stilts and domestic animals are kept below. You will marvel at the way your elephant negotiates the steep riverbanks and pick its way delicately through the water avoiding invisible rocks. It is a wonderful experience.

*Tad Lo Falls, Bolaven Plateau.*

**WHAT IS THERE TO DO**
Spend a lazy day lying on a rock with the waterfall behind you.
**WHAT IS IT KNOWN FOR**
The elephant rides that will take you through tribal villages.
**WHAT IS THERE TO SEE**
The Bolaven Plateau.
**HOW DO I GET THERE**
By road from Pakxe

273

*Ruins at Wat Phou.*

# Wat Phou

The temple of Wat Phou is one of the finest Khmer temple sites outside Cambodia, and is really a series of ruined temples and shrines that date from the sixth to the thirteenth centuries. Although it has been earmarked for restoration, (UNESCO has already undertaken archaeological surveys), there has been very little work as yet, and you can wander around the site soaking up the atmosphere in the company of pilgrims, but uninterrupted by coachloads of tourists.

Wat Phou means 'Mountain monastery' in Lao, and indeed it is situated at the foot of Lingaparvata Mountain. Although it is a Theravada Buddhist site, several Hindu gods are depicted in some of the sandstone reliefs. The site itself is arranged in three main levels ascending the hill and linked by a long stone causeway leading from a dilapidated royal residence at the bottom to stone steps that become steeper the farther up you get. On either side there are the remains of stone pillars and pedestals, and mythical creatures such as nagas, (water serpents). There are ruined pavilions, Khmer statues lying half buried in the grass, and fantastic carved lintels depicting Vishnu, Shiva and Kali, as well as images of Buddha.

The stairway up to the main temple sanctuary is lined with plumeria, the national tree of Laos, and the sanctuary itself is surrounded by magnificent mango trees. The view from here is extraordinary. There is an annual festival at Wat Phou, which usually takes place during February, when thousands of pilgrims from Thailand and Cambodia, as well as Laos itself, converge here for almost a week.

**WHERE IS IT**
In southern Laos, near Champasak
**WHAT ELSE IS THERE TO SEE**
Don Khong and Don Det islands
**YOU SHOULD KNOW**
There is an entrance fee.
**WHEN SHOULD I GO**
The annual festival of Wat Phou usually takes place during February and is a must-see event.

# The Plain of Jars

The Plain of Jars is a large, rolling plateau in north-east Laos, named after the mysterious groupings of stone jars to be found there in over a dozen sites. Others lie strewn across the plain and the surrounding hills. At Thong Hai Hin, or Site 1, there are 250 jars that range from about 600 kg (1,300 lb) to 1 tonne, and the largest jar on the plain weighs 6 tonnes. Some have stone lids lying nearby.

Many different theories have been advanced regarding their purpose, but as no other material has been discovered, they remain a mystery. They may have been storage vessels, or possibly funerary urns. Even dating them reliably is difficult, although archaeologists seem to agree that they are about 2,000 years old.

Although this is a site of intense interest to archaeologists, and has been for decades, the Indochinese wars have prevented much work being done here. As the flattest area in northern Laos, the plain has been extensively fought over for centuries, and during the Vietnam War it was heavily bombed by the US. Local legend has it that the jars were made to ferment the rice wine needed to celebrate victory over a cruel chieftain – even this story reflects the war-torn history of the area.

The plain itself is often forgotten, as visitors concentrate on the jar sites, but it is beautiful in its own right, with its grassy meadows and rolling brown and purple hills. Villages have been rebuilt, and rice and fruit trees planted. Sadly the area is still not free of unexploded ordnance, and only the main three jar sites are considered reasonably clear, so stay on the footpaths or take a guide.

**WHERE IS IT**
Near Phonsavan in Laos's Xieng Khouang Province.
**YOU SHOULD KNOW**
Only three of the main jar sites are safe, and the others still have unexploded ordnance, so make sure you stick to the paths.

*Large stone jars thought to be about 2,000 years old, cover the Plain of Jars in Xieng Khuoang Province.*

# Tioman Island

**WHAT IS IT**
The largest island in the Malaysian archipelago of 60 volcanic islands.
**WHAT IS THERE TO DO**
Spend the day snorkelling or diving around the beautiful coral reefs or relaxing in a hammock by the beach.
**WHAT IS THERE TO SEE**
Monkey Bay, Tulai Island and Renggis Island.
**TRAVEL**
By boat from nearby islands.

Tioman Island is the largest in an archipelago of about 60 volcanic islands, some inhabited, that are situated off the southern shores of the Malaysian east coast. The island is about 20 x 12 km (12.5 x 7.5 mi), and boasts fabulous tropical beaches set around the mountainous interior.

Tioman Island was first recorded in the journals of Arabian merchants in the tenth century. Traders from India, Persia and China also came this way because Tioman had betelnut, sandalwood and camphor to trade and was a safe haven from monsoon storms. The island also marked the navigational point at which to head north-east towards Cambodia.

In 1830 the islanders deserted their homes for 15 years, after pirates landed and took 70 people for the slave trade. In the 1920s the island was again deserted after a devastating outbreak of malaria swept through the population. After World War II, when a Japanese

*Beachside on Tioman island.*

detachment used the island as a base, it sank into oblivion until, in the late 1950s, it was chosen as the setting for the Rogers and Hammerstein musical *South Pacific* because of its unspoiled beauty.

Many coral reefs surround Tioman Island and there are several good dive sites. It is possible to walk across the island in a couple of hours and explore the forest that is home to many species of flora and fauna.

*View from Penang Hill.*

# Penang Hill

The island of Penang is the site of the oldest British settlement in Malaysia, founded in 1786 by Captain Francis Light. Captain Light was searching for a base where ships of the East India Company could set anchor and make repairs. He made a treaty with the Sultan of Kedah, and in exchange for military protection, received permission to colonize the jungle-covered and virtually uninhabited island.

In the middle of today's busy, modern city of Georgetown rises Penang Hill (Bukit Bendera). Almost 900 m (1,000 ft) high, it dominates the island and from its summit there are amazing views not only of the town and the whole island but also, on a clear day, of the mountains on the mainland.

The hike up Penang Hill takes about two hours, but the best way to see it is to take the funicular railway. Built by Swiss engineers, this trundles up an incredibly steep angle at a leisurely pace through the tropical forest, allowing you a close look at palms and creepers and cascading tropical flowering trees. At the top is a plateau, with a few shops, a café, a small Hindu temple and a mosque. Here you will also find a tatty 1930s hotel, set in pretty gardens that house a bird sanctuary. Other attractions on the hill include the botanic gardens and the rope walk.

**WHERE IS IT**
In the centre of Penang, overlooking Georgetown.
**WHAT ELSE IS THERE TO SEE**
Khoo Kongsi, Kek Lok Si Temple, Fort Cornwallis and Penang's beaches.
**WHAT IS THERE TO DO**
Trek up the hill or take the funicular railway to experience amazing views of the whole island and beyond.

# Taman Negara National Park

Taman Negara means 'national park', and indeed this is not only the world's oldest rainforest, but also the oldest national park in Malaysia. Almost 4,500 sq km (1550 sq mi) are protected here, and the park spreads across the west Malaysian states of Pahang, Trengganu and Kelantan. The rainforest has a wealth of biodiversity, dominated by hardwood forest in the lower areas and cloud forest at the higher elevations. There are no roads, and the only way to see it is by trekking the forest trails or by boat on the rivers.

This rainforest is about 130 million years old, which means that while other parts of the planet were undergoing ice ages, this area's climate is much as it was during the age of the dinosaurs. The flora and fauna are superb – Sumatran rhinoceros, tigers, Asian elephants, sun bears, leopards and tapirs roam, and monkeys and birds chatter and call from the trees. South-east Asia's tallest tree, the tualung, grows here and there are hides on the jungle paths, from where you may be lucky enough to see some of the wildlife.

In the north-west of the park is the formidable Gunung Tahan. Standing at 2,187 m (7,175 ft) it is the highest mountain in west Malaysia. The most amazing experience in this forest is the canopy walkway – the longest in the world at 430 m (1,475 ft), leading from tree to tree as high as 50 m (165 ft) above ground. The view of plants and wildlife living at this height is extraordinary.

*The forest canopy is home to a rich variety of animals.*

# Schwedagon Pawa

The Shwedagon Pawa, a great bell-shaped brick stupa, is the most impressive building in Yangon (Rangoon) and among the most splendid in Myanmar. The Buddhist monument is completely covered in gold, shining from the Thein Gottara Hill hillside, the highest point in Yangon, rising 51 m (168 ft) above the city.

Four entrances lead onto the stupa, parts of which only monks and other men may visit. The contents of the base are are unknown, but according to legend, eternally flying and spinning swords protect it from intruders. It is rumoured that underground tunnels lead from here to Bagan and Thailand.

*Schwedagon Pawa in Yangon.*

Believed to have been built single-handedly by King Okkalapa, the Shwedagon Pawa is home to many treasures including, most significantly, eight of Buddha's hairs.

The Shwedagon Pawa is decorated with nearly nine tonnes of pure gold and the upper reaches are encrusted with precious stones. Last renovated during the reign of King Mindon in the 1871, the temple's gold plating has, not surprisingly, been gradually deteriorating over time.

The stupa looms 99 m (326 ft) above the platform, which has a perimeter of 433 m (1,420 ft). Each side has a smaller stupa at its centre and 64 even smaller ones surround the structure. The corners are guarded by a sphinx, flanked on either side by three leogryphs (mythical half-lion-half-griffons). Projecting beyond the base of the stupa, one on the centre of each side, are tazaungs (pavilions) that house images of the Buddha to which the faithful make offerings, as they also do in the shrines by the stupa's base. There are also crouching elephants, and representations of spirits and a variety of animals.

The foundation of the stupa is commemorated by a group of figures embossed on the wall below the first terrace, including King Okkalapa and his mother.

**WHAT IS IT**
An impressive golden Buddhist monument on top of a hill
**WHERE IS IT**
In Yangon, Myanmar.
**WHAT IS THERE TO DO**
Imagine what lies beneath the mysterious underground tunnels.
**WHAT IS THERE TO SEE**
The amazing gold structure, carvings and shrines.

*Mandalay Palace.*

# Mandalay

Mandalay is the second largest city in Myanmar (Burma) after Yangon and the former capital. It has a rich cultural tradition and a stunning landscape dotted with the carved wooden roof of temples and pagodas.

The city, residence to the last two kings of Myanmar – Mindon and Thibaw – is centred around the Royal Palace, and is known for its millionaires, its religious sites and its monks.

Established by King Mindon and named Yadanabon meaning 'where all the prosperity accumulates', Mandalay, bordered on the east by the blue-ridged Shan mountains and the lifeblood of Myanmar, the Ayeyarwady, or Irrawaddy, River on the west, continues to be the country's hub of culture, faith and communications.

The Royal Palace is a walled city within Mandalay at the base of the scenic 230-m (754-ft) Mandalay Hill. Built in 1861 by King Mindon, the palace, although destroyed in World War II, has been restored to its original glory. The palace contains many moats as well as several pavilions and chambers with highly ornamental decorative features.

Mandalay is a stunning city with too many important religious sites to detail. Maha Myat Muni Paya is Myanmar's second holiest pilgrimage site. Here lies a 4-m (13-ft) high statue of Buddha, made of gold and decorated with precious jewels. Kuthodaw Paya, at the foot of Mandalay Hill, is the site of the world's largest book. Built by King Mingdon in the 1800s, 729 white stupas within the complex contain the complete text of the Tripitaka, Theravada Buddhism's most sacred text.

**WHAT IS IT**
The second largest city in, and former capital of, Myanmar.
**WHAT IS THERE TO SEE**
Monks, millionaires and a host of religious sites.
**WHAT SHOULD I BUY**
Zegyo Market is a collection of bazaar street markets located near the city centre where you can pick up some interesting curios.
**ALSO KNOWN AS**
The 'City of Gems'.

# Bagan

Bagan is a rich archaeological site 145 km (90 mi) south-west of Mandalay. Between the eleventh and thirteenth centuries, the kings of the Bagan dynasty built thousands of pagodas and temples here.

Many of the most important temples are located in and around the old walled city. The Ananda temple was begun in 1091 by King Anawrahta and inspired many of the later temples. The sides of the central square block are 53 m (174 ft) long and 10.7 m (35 ft) high with a large gabled portico on each. The six receding terraces are crowned with a pine-cone shaped sikhara topped by a tapering stupa, echoed by four smaller ones at the roof's corners. On misty mornings, the gold-clad stupas seem to float in the air.

The Gawdawpalin Temple was begun by King Narapatisithu (1174–1211) and completed by his son, King Htilominio. Despite earthquake damage, it is a good example of the later style of temple construction on the site. The main shrine is situated on the upper level, its curved spire crowned by a slender stupa. Good views over the Ayeyarwady River can be obtained from the upper terraces.

Seeming out of place among all the typically bell-shaped temples, the Indian-looking Maha Bodhi Temple is a copy of the one located at Bodhgaya in Bihar in India. It is the only one of its kind here and was built during the reign of King Htilominlo (1211–1234).

Among the Bagan Archaeological Museum's chief treasures is the Myazedi Pillar, which could be described as the Burmese version of the Rosetta Stone. It is inscribed in Pyu, Mon, Pali and Burmese, and its discovery in 1917 led to the Pyu script being decoded for the first time. It was found at the pagoda of the same name, next to the Gubyaukgyi temple. The museum also holds thousands of inscriptions and artefacts found during excavations here, including a bronze sculpture of a lotus bud that opens to reveal a minute stupa with delicately carved Buddhas at its base. There are also several tenth- and eleventh-century Buddhas located in the Statue Gallery.

**WHAT IS THERE TO SEE**
Stunning temples that inspired future architecture of Myanmar.
**WHAT IS THERE TO DO**
Visit the museum to see the Myazedi Pillar.
**WHAT IS IT**
One of the richest architectural sites in the world.
**ALSO KNOWN AS**
Pagan

*Buddhist temples in morning mist*

# Banaue Rice Terraces

**WHAT ARE THEY**
Gigantic rice terraces carved from the mountainside.

**WHERE ARE THEY**
The Luzon Province of the northern Philippines.

**WHAT ELSE IS THERE TO DO**
Visit the quaint market village of Ifugao.

**HOW DO I GET THERE**
It is a nine-hour bus ride from Manila.

**TRADITION**
Ancestral spirits are still worshiped here and it is not unusual to see the sacrificing of three chickens or a pig to appease an angry spirit. Another tradition is that when a person dies, their body is hung from the thatched roof of their hut for three days as a sign to the villagers that the deceased has moved on to a better place. Afterwards, the bones are collected and placed inside the roof of the family's dwelling, to give comfort and protection to the living.

*The terraced rice fields on the hillsides of Cambulo.*

Considered by many to be the eighth wonder of the world, the Banaue rice terraces, a UNESCO World Heritage Site, are a feat of incredible engineering, created over the past 2,000 years by the people of Batad. This area is in the scenic Luzon Province of the Northern Philippines and contains jagged, forested mountains rising to more than 1,500 m (4,292 ft) above sea level. The jaw-dropping terraces, carved from the mountainside, stretch as far as the eye can see.

The terraces, a seemingly endless stairway of cultivated rice and vegetable paddies were largely built by hand, one stone at a time, and cover an area of more than 10,500 sq km (4,000 sq mi) of mountainside. Fed by a natural irrigation system from the rainforests high in the mountains above, the local population continues to survive on the traditional farming methods employed throughout their existence.

There are no roads or electricity because the Batad prefer to live as they have for centuries, retaining a spiritual connection with the Earth and their surroundings.

Home to a number of popular hiking trails, the region has a healthy tourist population that come to gaze at these majestic creations. Four similar, albeit smaller, terraces nearby include the ampitheatre-shaped Batad terraces, the Mayoyao terraces, where organic red and white Ifugao rice is grown, the stone-enclosed Hapao terraces, which date back to 650 AD, and the well-known Kiangan terraces, made up of the Nagacadan and Julungan terraces.

# Palawan Island

Palawan Island lies between the South China Sea and the Sulu Sea. Its 2,000-km (1,243-mi) coastline is renowned for having one of the most beautiful seascapes in the world, with thousands of square kilometres of protected coral reefs. Palawan Island has a stunning array of flora, fauna, ecology, biology and marine life, including highly endangered dugongs.

The island's variety of exotic terrain includes rainforests, lush green hills and plains by pristine beaches. It is home to many species of African and endangered Palawan animals including Palawan monkeys and parrots, bear cats and peacocks, as well as mongoose, scaly anteaters, porcupine and mouse deer, which are protected in the Calauit Game Reserve and Wildlife Sanctuary.

Puerto Princesa Subterranean River National Park, a UNESCO World Heritage Site, with ancient cave and river networks, is an amazing place. It is thought to be the longest navigable subterranean river and its cavern contains an incredible array stalactites and stalagmites in all shapes and sizes.

Considered by many to be the Philippine's 'last frontier', the province is also home to the UNESCO World Heritage site of Tubbataha Reef National Marine Park. The Coron Reefs, in Coron Bay, Busuanga, consist of seven enchanting lakes surrounded by impressive craggy limestone cliffs.

Palawan is rated as one of the top dive sites in the world and divers come from around the world to see the 12 World War II Japanese shipwrecks here ranging in depth from surface level down to 40 m (131 ft). Along with the undisturbed reefs and multitude of aquatic life, this is an underwater paradise!

*Palawan Island in the Bacuit Archipelago.*

**WHAT IS IT**
A pristine area with gorgeous beaches, fantastic diving and tropical rainforest.
**WHERE IS IT**
The northern Philippines.
**WHAT IS THERE TO SEE**
The nearby Calauit Wildlife Sanctuary and the Subterranean National Park as well as the many Japanese shipwrecks from WWII.
**WHAT IS THERE TO DO**
Snorkel, swim, dive.

*Selling traditional Thai textiles at the Chatuchak weekend market.*

# Chatuchak Market

Chatuchak Market, in northern Bangkok, is one of the largest and most spectacular markets in the world. Open on Saturdays and Sundays, it has about 10,000 stalls selling just about everything you can imagine to the 25,000 visitors who come here each day. You could spend every weekend here for a year and still not have seen everything!

Just at the edge of Chatuchak market are two more markets, which are also open during the weeks. One is a food market, selling fresh fish and shellfish, meat, fruit and vegetables, as well as dried goods such as rice and flour. The other is Bangkok's largest plant and flower market, which also sells seeds, tools, pots and urns, statues and everything else a gardener could wish for.

The main market is like an Aladdin's cave, packed with treasures. The market is vaguely divided into sections such as clothing and textiles – where you will find everything from fake designer clothes to fabulous hand-woven tribal wear, and antiques – which includes everything from opium weights to ornately carved teak screens. If you were setting up home in Bangkok you could buy everything you needed right here – furniture, bedding, kitchenware, paintings, lamps, rugs, sound systems, CDs and DVDs, musical instruments, images of Buddha and even pets.

If you are hungry, there are all sorts of food stalls selling delicious meals and if you are thirsty you can buy fresh fruit juice, delicious coffee or alcohol from one of the bars. Even if you do not buy anything, the browsing is a fabulous, fascinating experience.

**WHAT IS IT**
A visit to Chatuchak Market is a sensory experience. Take in the sights, sounds and smells.
**HOW BIG IS IT**
The market is vast and sprawling, with about 10,000 stalls.
**WHAT IS THERE TO SEE**
Colourful food, flower, furniture and clothing markets.
**WHAT SHOULD I BUY**
Tribal crafts and clothing.

284

# Wat Tham Pha

**WHAT ELSE IS THERE TO SEE**
The Dao Caves, the Elephant Training
Centre at Taeng-Dao and Chiang Mai.
**YOU SHOULD KNOW**
There is an entrance fee.
**HOW DO I GET THERE**
You can only travel here by road.

Situated in the mountains above Chiang Dao stands one of the most beautiful temples in Thailand. Virtually unknown to tourists, it is sufficiently remote as to be visited hardly at all, and yet it is a working monastery with a serene and spiritual atmosphere. Made from stone, with a gilded stupa, the temple sits easily with its surroundings, and its simplicity comes as a relief after the scores of painted and glittering temples you will have already seen.

To reach the temple you must climb a pathway that meanders up and through the forest. Surrounded by tall trees and with bougainvillea and frangipani tumbling down the rocky outcrops, it is some time before you catch a glimpse of the lovely mountain wat perched way above you. The only sound to break the silence is bird song, and the only people to be seen are monks sweeping the leaves from the path and steps. At about the half-way point is a look-out spot with excellent views, but it is not until you have reached the temple itself, with its shrine dug out of the rock face, that you realise how high you are, and find that the view from the top is not just beautiful, it is absolutely spectacular.

*Stupa and hills of
Wat Tham Pha.*

# Ayutthaya

*Wat Ratchaburana.*

For 400 years, from 1350, Ayutthaya was the capital of Siam, and the home of 33 kings. Wealthy and powerful, merchants from all over Europe and the Far East came here. During a brief Burmese invasion in 1767, the city was all-but destroyed and the new capital was established at Bangkok. Today the ancient city is a UNESCO World Heritage Site and a canal has been built to connect the three rivers that join where it stands, thus creating an island.

Ruined temples are scattered across the site, and there are others on the rivers' edges too. The main temples can be visited on foot, but if you hire a bike you will be able to see much more of this extensive site. Wat Phra Si Sanphet was the largest temple in Ayutthaya, and also served as the palace. Built in the fourteenth century, it has three magnificent stupas. The adjoining Wat Mongkhon Bophit contains one of Thailand's largest Buddha figures, which was cast in bronze in the fifteenth century.

Some of the temples are built in the Khmer style. Many are ruined but still magnificent, and there are a great many Buddha figures, including one in Wat Phra Meru from Sri Lanka that is said to be 1,300 years old. Sadly, many figures were damaged by the Burmese invaders, and more recently art thieves have stolen some of the heads. Nevertheless, this is a sacred site for Thais, who dress many of the Buddha figures in yellow robes, scatter flower petals and burn incense sticks reverently at their feet.

**WHAT IS THERE TO DO**
Hire a bike to see the scattered ruined temples.
**WHAT IS THERE TO SEE**
Wat Ratchaburana, Bang Pa-In and Lopburi.
**YOU SHOULD KNOW**
Do not pose behind the Buddhas for 'comic' photos as it causes offence.
**HOW DO I GET THERE**
By boat or train from Bangkok.

287

# Chao Phraya River, Bangkok

**WHAT IS THERE TO DO**
Take a river ferry to experience a more peaceful side to Bangkok.
**WHAT IS THERE TO SEE**
Royal Barge Museum, floating markets, temples, Bangkok's skyline, the Grand Palace, Ko Kret island.

Bangkok is a huge, sprawling city on the Chao Phraya River and is home to about 6 million people. Locally known as Krung Thep, the City of Angels, it is everything and more than you would imagine a great south-east Asian city to be. One of the best ways to escape the bustle and explore the heart of the old city on the east bank, the river and the network of canals (khlongs) is by river ferry, tour or chartered boat. From here you can see the many beautiful temples, the Grand Palace, ramshackle old houses on stilts, 19th-century architecture, the naval dockyard and customs house and the famous floating markets.

The Royal Barge National Museum houses the kings' ceremonial barges, which were used on such state occasions as the procession at the end of the annual rainy season. Among the temples are the ancient Wat Kaeo Fa, Wat Amphawan and Wat Suwannaram. At Wat Sai floating market tourists can buy souvenirs, while at Taling Chan a food market is held at weekends.

Ko Kret, a small island in the Chao Phraya River is worth a visit. It houses the Wat Paramai Yikawat and Wat Phal Lom, as well as a village where visitors can watch potters at work and see the Ancient Mon Pottery Centre. The journey along the river is also the best way to travel from the city centre to the former capital, Ayutthaya.

There are numerous boat tours during the day as well as dinner cruises in the evenings, which give visitors an opportunity to dine in luxury while watching the lit-up old buildings and beautiful skyline of the city glide past.

*Traditional barges cruise past the Grand Palace in Bangkok.*

# Ang Thong Archipelago

The Ang Thong archipelago is a national marine park made up of around 50 islands lying about 30 km (20 mi) from Ko Samui. Most are uninhabited and were fortunately saved from the developers because the area was used by the Thai navy before it was given national park status. The islands themselves are a photographer's dream, with limestone cliffs, tropical vegetation, caves and secret lagoons, pristine white sand beaches, coral reefs and aquamarine waters. The headquarters of the national park are situated on Ko Wua Ta Lap, where bungalow-style accommodation is available. Popular island activities include sea-kayaking tours from Ko Samui, a great way to see the islands and discover the best spots for snorkelling. It is also possible to charter boats from here, which will give you greater freedom to explore this stunning area at your own pace.

Several of the islands have paths that lead up through beautiful, untouched forest to their peaks, affording a panoramic view of the whole archipelago, with its steep-sided islands and striking rock formations. Not to be missed is the saltwater lake known as the 'inner sea' on Ko Mae Koh. Enclosed by vertical cliffs, it's a strenuous climb to view the lake but well worth the effort as you gaze down on the stunningly beautiful emerald green water.

**WHAT TO SEE**
Ko Samui, Ko Pha-Ngan and Ko Tao are three of the most beautiful islands.
**WHAT IS THERE TO DO**
Take a sea-kayaking trip or snorkel around the coral reefs.
**DO NOT MISS**
The saltwater lake on Ko Mae Koh.

*View from trail on Ko Wua Ta Lap Ang Thong National Marine Park.*

# Phang-Nga Bay

Phang-Nga province is in south-western Thailand, on the Andaman Sea, and it contains a number of spectacular places to visit, including the Surin Islands National Marine Park and the Similan Islands National Marine Park, both renowned for diving, snorkelling and sport fishing. Khao Lak – Lamru National Park – boasts cliffs and forests, hills and beaches, all of which are teeming with wildlife. Trips to the islands are only viable during the winter months – during the summer the sea is too rough

The scenery in Phang-Nga Bay is spectacular – karst (limestone) formations and islands burst from the sea. This is where the James Bond film, *The Man with the Golden Gun* was made. Take a tour by boat and explore the bay for the day, or, even better, go on a two- or three-day camping trip. If you take a kayak trip, you can explore the interior of some of the marvellous semi-submerged caves – such as the Drawing Cave, full of murals – which are inaccessible to the larger boats. Another beautiful site is the Ko Panyi Muslim fishing village, built on stilts in a mangrove swamp.

Stay on an island or in Phang-Nga, a small town surrounded by forested limestone cliffs, and use this as a base from which to explore other places such as the inland cave at Wat Tham Suwankhuha, a shrine that is full of images of Buddha. In October, the annual Vegetarian Festival – a time of purification for the locals – occurs and for nine days there are processions and performances ending in a wild frenzy, with mediums in a trance walking on burning coals and piercing their cheeks and tongues with daggers and spears.

**WHEN SHOULD I VISIT**
The winter months are best as this is when the sea is calmer.
**WHAT IS THERE TO DO**
Take a kayak trip to explore the interior of Drawing Cave.
**WHAT IS THERE TO SEE**
Similan Islands and Surin Islands.

*Phang-Nga Bay*

# The Grand Palace

**WHERE IS IT**
Bangkok.
**WHAT IS THERE TO SEE**
Teak Mansion, Abhisek Dusit Throne
Hall, Wat Pho, Wat Arun.
**YOU SHOULD KNOW**
There is an entrance fee.
**HOW TO GET THERE**
Take the Chao Praya River express,
metro, Skytrain or bus from
Bangkok bus station.

The best way to approach the Grand Palace complex is from the Chao Praya River. The palace complex and Wat Pra Kaew (Temple of the Emerald Buddha) are set within almost 10 ha (25 acres) of flat ground that was consecrated in the eighteenth century. It is surrounded by a white wall that belies the unbelievably colourful wat within.

The Grand Palace itself is not lived in by the king, but used by on ceremonial occasions. The four buildings that make up the complex are not open to the public, but you can admire their exterior architecture. The largest building, the Grand Palace Hall was built by British architects in the late 1880s.

Nothing could prepare you for your first sight of Wat Pra Kaew. The colours of Theravada Buddhism are red, green, orange and yellow and along with masses of gilding and gold leaf, lotus bud patterns and columns encrusted with gleaming mosaics, these colours are everywhere – so bright they almost hurt the eye. The stupas are gilded and the swooping layers of the roofs are tiled in shining orange and green tiles. The Thai version of the *Ramayana* story is illustrated in its entirety around the interior walls.

The Emerald Buddha is tiny in comparison to many of the famous Buddha statues in Thailand, but it is of immense significance. Its origins are surrounded in mystery, but it was first recorded in Chiang Rai, in the fifteenth century. Laotian invaders removed it to Luang Prabang and then Vientiane, but it was recovered and returned to Thailand in the eighteenth century by Rama I, the founder of the current Chakri dynasty. It sits high up in a glass case in a huge shrine that was built specially to house it.

*The Temple of the Emerald Buddha is the most important temple in Thailand. In the foreground is Lak Muang, the City Pillar.*

# Mekong Delta

The Mekong River, at over 4,000 km (2,485 mi), is the twelfth longest river in the world. It rises high up on the Tibetan plateau, flows down through south-western China, around Myanmar, down through Thailand and Laos, where it forms a border, through Cambodia and finally into Vietnam where its fertile delta forms the country's agricultural heartland. The rich nutrients provided by the alluvial sediment enable about 40 per cent of Vietnam's food to be produced from an area that covers only 10 per cent of the country.

Known to the Vietnamese as Cuu Long (Nine Dragons) because of the nine tributaries that spread out across the floodplain, the area has been criss-crossed with canals to channel the excess flood water in the most practical fashion. It was not until the French colonized Vietnam in the nineteenth century that the agricultural potential of the area was understood. Ironically the boggy marshlands and rice fields subsequently provided excellent cover for Vietnamese resistance fighters against the French and later the Americans.

The river, with its network of tributaries and canals, is what makes the region so beautiful. It is essential for travel and transport and thousands of boats ply up and down these waterways, from tiny rowing boats to cargo boats carrying rice, fruit and sugarcane. All life is there to be seen on the water: colourful floating markets, river villages and Khmer pagodas can all be seen, and the areas not given over to farmland are rich with wildlife. Thousands of birds nest in colonies, and there are five species of dolphin to be found, including the rare Irrawaddy dolphin.

*In the Mekong Delta town of Phung Hiep, seven canals intersect to form one of south-east Asia's most colourful floating markets.*

**WHY IS IT IMPORTANT**
It is the twelfth longest river in the world.
**WHAT IS THERE TO DO**
Take a trip out to An Binh Island and discover some of the wildlife that inhabits the area.
**WHAT IS THERE TO SEE**
An Binh Island, Sa Dec, Sam Mountain, Hon Chong Peninsula.
**ALSO KNOWN AS**
Cuu Long or the Nine Dragons.

*A street hawker walks past a Chinese temple in Hoi An.*

# Hoi An

At the heart of Hoi An, a small coastal town, is an extraordinary architectural wealth that combines Japanese, Chinese, European and Vietnamese influences that go back to its heyday in the sixteenth century. At that time the Thu Bon River was crowded with merchant ships from many nations, and the port of Fai Fo played an important part in maritime trade. Ships from Europe brought weapons, sulphur and lead, and left with silks, porcelain and exotic oils and spices from the Far East.

Many Chinese and Japanese settled here and each community had its own laws and its own governor. By the mid-eighteenth century the Shoguns in Japan forbade foreign travel, and as the Japanese presence dwindled, the Chinese community swelled with more and more immigrants. Prosperous Chinese merchants built elegant wooden houses, interspersed with assembly halls and temples for the different ethnic Chinese communities. Today the houses are often still lived in by the descendants of those original merchants, and are furnished with astonishing antiques and memorabilia. The Assembly Halls, in contrast to the houses, are a riot of colour with glazed roof tiles shining green, red and gold and vividly painted and decorated exteriors sporting dragons and other mythical creatures.

The Japanese covered bridge is Hoi An's emblem and best-known monument. A small Taoist temple hangs over the water and nearby is a mysterious shrine placed within the roots of an ancient banyan tree. There are also fascinating Chinese family chapels to visit where you can learn the history of individual families from 300 years ago to the present day.

**WHY IS IT IMPORTANT**
The area is steeped in history and rich with different cultures.
**WHAT IS THERE TO SEE**
Cham islands, the ruins of the sanctuary at My Son.
**HOW DO I GET THERE**
By air to Da Nang.
**WHEN SHOULD I VISIT**
March to September is the best time to visit.

292

# Hue

Hue is a city with a long and distinguished history and despite the bitter battles that have taken place here in recent times, during the Vietnam War, it has kept its air of romance, refinement, scholarship and spirituality. The founder of the Nguyen dynasty, Emperor Gia Long, made Hue his capital in 1802, and it soon became known for its cultural activity. On the north bank of the Perfume River, the Emperor built a huge citadel in the Chinese style, with a Forbidden City at its heart, reserved for the sovereign's use. The Imperial City which surrounds it was the hub of the administration, and the whole complex is enclosed by a wall 7 m (23 ft) high and 20 m (66 ft) thick, surrounded both inside and out by a moat and a canal.

The Imperial City was devastated first by fire in 1947, and later by some of the most terrible battles of the Vietnam War. However, some of the buildings remain and have been perfectly restored. Rebuilding has been continuous since 1975 and received a boost when Hue became a UNESCO World Heritage Site in 1993. The Ngo Mon Gate and the Thai Hoa Palace are two of the highlights, but there are ancestral altars, Chinese assembly halls, pagodas, temples, royal mausolea and fascinating museums to be explored, too.

Hue is not simply a city of glorious historic relics, it is a lively, thriving place, home to five universities. In 1995 it was given independent city status by the government to mark its growing economic importance.

**WHAT IS IT**
The former capital of Vietnam, on the east coast
**WHAT IS THERE TO DO**
A visit to Ngo Mon Gate and Thai Hoa Palace are essentials on any intinerary.
**WHY IS IT IMPORTANT**
This is not only a place steeped in history, but also a thriving economic city.
**WHEN SHOULD I VISIT**
The best weather is from March to September.

*Concrete statues line a courtyard at the tomb of Khai Dinh, built to the south of Hue in the 1920s.*

# Tay Ninh

Tay Ninh is the site of the extraordinary Cao Dai Cathedral. In fact it is not just a temple, a cathedral or a pagoda it is the Cao Dai Holy See, built in 1927 by Ngo Van Chieu, who founded Cao Daism a few years earlier. Ngo Van Chieu was a spiritualist, and he was given the basic tenets of his new religion by a superior spirit called Cao Dai during a seance. It is a blend of religions: Buddhism, Taoism, Confucianism with additions from Christianity, Islam and spirituality. Cao Daists believe in a universal god represented by the Divine Eye, with surprising intermediaries from the spirit world such as Winston Churchill, Napoleon Bonaparte and Shakespeare. They have five commandments, and believe in reincarnation.

The cathedral is painted in a riotous confusion of gaudy colours, and the Divine Eye, the symbol of Cao Dai, tops the balcony overlooking the central portico. Square pagodas stand at either side of the building's façade. The interior is where you can really see the mix of religions that are at work here. The vaulted ceiling of the nave is sky blue and decorated with stars and clouds as well as mouldings of lions and turtles. Pink pillars with green dragons twining up them mark the nave, which is dominated by a huge blue sphere representing the heavens and dusted with stars through which the Divine Eye takes a good look at his congregation.

*Worshippers gather at the Cao Dai cathedral in Tay Ninh.*

# The Tunnels of Cu Chi

The tunnels of Cu Chi are a relatively modern, man-made phenomenon, but their fame, deservedly, is worldwide. They are the outstanding symbol of the dogged determination of the Vietnamese desire to be free of Western colonists.

The tunnels were first thought of in the late 1940s, when the Viet Minh (the League for the Independence of Vietnam) were trying to remove the French from their country. Originally thought of as hiding places for arms and ammunition, they soon became hiding places for the Viet Minh fighters. By the mid 1960s, 250 km (155 mi) of tunnels threaded their way under Cu Chi and the areas around it. One even ran under the American army base situated there. These tunnels allowed the many groups of Viet Cong fighters in the area to liaise with one another at will and even to infiltrate Saigon itself.

The tunnels were dug to as many as four levels. The building work was incredibly hard – not only were there poisonous snakes, scorpions and insects, but these tunnels had to be made sufficiently solid not to collapse. People lived below ground for weeks on end, and there were not only living quarters but also functioning hospitals, kitchens, classrooms and even operating theatres and a small cinema.

More than 12,000 people died here during the Vietnam War, but the Tet offensive, which was dreamed up in these tunnels, probably turned the tide of opinion and made the Americans begin to realize that this was a war they would not win.

**WHY IS IT IMPORTANT**
These tunnels were an essential tool to the Viet Cong in the winning of the Vietnam War.
**WHAT IS THERE TO DO**
Visit Ho Chi Minh City to gain a perspective of the importance of these tunnels.
**HOW DO I GET THERE**
Take an organized bus tour.

*A Vietnamese soldier holds an earth-cover hatch to one of thousands of secret tunnels at Cu Chi, where the US 25th Infantry Division had its base camp during the Vietnam War.*

# AUSTRALASIA
# & OCEANIA

# Uluru (Ayers Rock)

Uluru, otherwise known as Ayers Rock, is an enormous monolithic rock that rises majestically from the plain around it. It is part of the Uluru-Kata Tjuta National Park, which also includes the Olgas, a fantastic group of 36 huge red rocks that stand about half an hour's drive away. Uluru is formed from almost vertical layers of extremely hard sandstone, the surface layer of which has become red as the result of oxidation. On the north-west and south-east sides, erosion has cut into the rock forming channels down which water pours after storms, forming spectacular but short-lived waterfalls.

Uluru and Kata-Tjuta belong to the Anangu Aboriginal people, who manage it in tandem with Parks Australia. It is deeply significant to the Anangu, firstly as a constant source of water and food in this inhospitable desert region, and secondly as a landmark along the Songlines of Anangu culture and mythology.

Most people who visit Uluru try to climb up to the summit, although the Anangu would prefer it if they did not. Every year someone dies making the attempt, and many others have to be rescued. The plateau at the summit affords vast views, and is interesting to explore, but it is a tough climb, and is often windy, sometimes so much so that the climb has to be closed for safety reasons. The 9-km (6 mi) walk around the rock is probably a better option and affords you a good look at various Anangu sites.

*Ayers Rock, Uluru National Park, Northern Territories.*

# Kakadu National Park

*Aboriginal paintings depicting X-ray figures on Nourlangie Rock in Arnhem Land.*

Kakadu National Park is an area of 20,000 sq km (7,720 sq mi) lying about 150 km (90 mi) east of Darwin, and is the largest national park in Australia. It includes the whole of the South Alligator River, which is actually home to a large crocodile population, and various other habitats including heathland, eucalyptus woods and rainforest.

Two different species of crocodile live here – Johnston crocodiles, which live in fresh water and mainly eat fish, and estuarine crocodiles, which are a very different thing. These creatures are the largest reptiles in the world, and can live in both fresh and salt water. They can grow up to 6 m (20 ft) in length, can be extremely dangerous and occasionally kill careless tourists.

The park is home to a huge range of flora and fauna – more than 10,000 species of insects, 25 per cent of Australia's freshwater fish, kangaroos, wallabies, dingoes, water buffalo and many more. There are also about 5,000 sites of Aboriginal art, from many different eras. The town of Jabiru, on the eastern side, is near the Ranger Uranium Mine, and has a small airport from where it is possible to arrange scenic flights across the park in helicopters or light aircraft. The area is far too large to see in one day, but there are camping sites and resorts where you can base yourself for longer stays, and the Park Headquarters and Visitors Centre is full of useful information.

**WHAT IT IS IT**
The largest national park in Australia.
**HOW BIG IS IT**
The park covers an area of 20,000 sq km (7,720 sq mi).
**WHAT IS THERE TO SEE**
Nourlangie Rock, Ubirr rock galleries and lookout, Jim Jim Falls and Barramundie Gorge.
**YOU SHOULD KNOW**
The park is home to two different species of crocodile, and they have been known to kill the occasional, careless tourist.
**HOW DO I GET THERE**
Drive or take a tour from Darwin.

*The vast Great Barrier Reef is the world's most extensive coral reef system.*

# The Great Barrier Reef

The Great Barrier Reef on Australia's north-eastern continental shelf is a site of exceptional natural beauty stretching for 2,000 km (1,250 mi) and covering an area of about 350,000 sq km (135,100 sq mi), making it larger than the whole of Italy. It is not only the largest UNESCO World Heritage Site on earth but also contains the world's most extensive coral reef system.

The reef runs mainly north to south, passing through a number of different climates, accounting for the thousands of different species of marine life that inhabit it. It is made up of 3,400 individual reefs, including nearly 800 fringing reefs, coral islands, continental islands covered in forest, sandbars, and mangrove systems linked by huge turquoise lagoons.

The whole reef is under threat from global warming, with increasing damage to the coral itself, but it is of vital importance to the world's ecosystem, containing as it does a third of the planet's soft coral species, the largest existing green turtle breeding site, 30 different species of mammal, including breeding humpback whales and a large dugong population, as well as sponges, molluscs, 1,500 types of reef fish and 200 species of birds. It also contains fascinating Aboriginal archeological sites and is probably the most spectacular marine wilderness on earth.

**WHAT IS IT**
The world's most extensive coral reef system.
**DON'T MISS**
Learning to scuba dive.
**WHAT IS THERE TO DO**
Visit Lady Elliot and Lady Musgrave islands; the loggerhead turtle nesting site near Bundaberg.
**YOU SHOULD KNOW**
There is a reef tax payable.
**HOW DO I GET THERE**
Travel by road from Brisbane.

*BELOW: The beach at Noosa.*

# Noosa

Noosa is situated at the most exclusive end of the Sunshine Coast, about 140 km (90 mi) north of Brisbane, and is an area where many celebrities have a home. It sits within a beautiful headland with the mouth of the Noosa River west of the town, a stretch of beach to the east, and the small but charming Noosa National Park covering the headland itself, an area of 23 sq km (9 sq mi).

Noosa has been popular with the surfing fraternity for about 40 years, since the big waves that crash into the headland first came to their notice. Today all kinds of water sports are pursued upon the river and its creeks as well, such as windsurfing, kayaking and jet skiing. It is an ideal place for boating, or you can just take it easy and go fishing at the river mouth.

The headland and cliffs in the national park rise to 200 m (660 ft) and overlook sheltered bays and splendid ocean views. The park contains high dunes and coastal heath as well as different types of grasslands and scrub, forest and rainforest. In all, 13 separate plant communities have been defined in this small area, and various walking trails have been formed, such as the palm grove route and the coastal route. You may see koalas clinging to the eucalyptus but the main focus of the park's diverse habitats is the 121 different species of bird that make their homes here.

**WHERE IS IT**
In the most exclusive part of Queensland's Sunshine Coast, *c.*140 km (90 mi) north of Brisbane.
**WHAT IS THERE TO DO**
Spend a day hiking in the Noosa National Park.
**WHAT IS THERE TO SEE**
The Glasshouse Mountains and Eumundi's Saturday market.
**IF YOU DARE**
Learn to kite surf or sea kayak.
**HOW DO I GET THERE**
By road from Brisbane.

# The Whitsunday Islands

*The Whitsunday Islands, named for the day on which Captain Cook discovered them in the 1770s.*

The Whitsundays are the holiday destination of your dreams. Their great and simple attraction is their generally unspoiled tropical beauty – to visit them is to be greeted by an island paradise set in crystal-clear waters and fringed by magnificent reef formations.

The islands – there are 74 in all – lie just off Queensland's coast and are perfectly situated for exploring one of the truly great marvels of nature, the Great Barrier Reef. There are plenty of day cruises from different places on the islands that take you to the best places on the reef for scuba diving and snorkelling.

A few of the islands have in recent years been quite heavily developed to cater for tourism – the expensive resort on Hayman Island is reputed to have cost A\$300 million (\$110 million) to build and there are tall apartment blocks and gift shops on Hamilton Island. However, most of them are still completely unspoiled, essentially little changed from the 1770s when Captain Cook sailed through and named the islands for the day he arrived there. Whitsunday Island itself, the largest in the group, is a national park, as are many of the other islands either in whole or part. Here all you will find are great white sandy beaches, secluded bays, often spectacular marine life in the warm tropical waters, dense green pine forests and perhaps the occasional basic camp site.

Several of the islands are completely uninhabited and some are still privately owned. Such is the popularity of sailing and cruising around the Whitsundays that you can often get the impression that there are more people about at sea than there are on land.

# Great Ocean Road

Victoria's Great Ocean Road was built between 1919 and 1932 as a memorial to the Australian soldiers who died during World War I. It also gave employment to those who returned and some of those people who needed employment during the Great Depression. It stretches for 285 km (177 mi) between Warrnambool and Torquay, excavated manually along the mountainous and heavily forested coastline. The road is often very narrow, with steep cliffs to one side, and constant switchback bends to negotiate. Fortunately there are plenty of spots where you can pull over to admire the fabulous views.

The road passes through some stunning scenery, running along the shore for the whole length of the Port Campbell National Park, a stretch otherwise known as the Shipwreck Coast, the forests of the Otway National Park and along the coastal edge of Angahook-Lorne State park, which is characterized by its immense blue eucalyptus.

The Shipwreck Coast is a spectacular stretch of rugged coastline upon which at least 80 ships have come to grief. The weather is often violently stormy here and the combination of huge ocean waves and high winds have formed dramatic rock formations such as the famous Twelve Apostles. These are vast limestone stacks that were once part of the shoreline cliffs but that, over millennia, have been eroded and now stand alone looming upwards from the wild southern ocean floor.

**WHAT IS IT**
A road built as a memorial to the Australian soldiers who died in World War I.
**WHAT IS IT KNOWN FOR**
The road passes along the coastline giving stunning views.
**WHAT IS THERE TO SEE**
The Twelve Apostles, Lake Corangamite and the Princess Margaret Rose Caves.
**HOW DO I GET THERE**
Drive from Torquay to Warrnambool.

*Some of the Twelve Apostles sea stacks that rise from the sea near Port Campbell.*

*The vineyards at Coldstream Hills Winery.*

# Yarra Valley

The Yarra Valley, a mere half an hour's drive north-east of Melbourne, is famous for its 30 or so small wineries, which are probably the best in Victoria. With the Dandenong Range to the east, the valley rolls out ahead, towards the Great Dividing Range. This is charming countryside dotted with eucalyptus forests and tree ferns, splendid old farms, little villages and lovely gardens. This is peaceful, pretty countryside, with ranks of vines loaded with fruit on every suitable hillside.

Many visitors come here to tour the valley and visit the wineries. The area has a growing reputation for its excellent restaurants, some of which are attached to the wineries themselves. Yering Station is on the site of the first vineyard in the area, which was planted as long ago as 1838. The restaurant here has glass walls that afford lovely views of the valley beyond. All of the wineries can be visited and tastings can be arranged, whether you have come independently or as part of a tour group.

Warburton, a pretty town on the Upper Yarra River, is at the start of the 80-km (53-mi) Upper Yarra Track. This follows an old vehicle trail all the way to the Baw Baw National Park, and can be walked either in sections or continuously as a five- or six day trek.

**WHAT IS IT KNOWN FOR**
Some of the best wineries in Victoria and excellent restaurants.
**WHAT ELSE IS THERE TO SEE**
Maroondah Reservoir Lookout, Steavensons Falls and Cathedral Mountain.
**YOU SHOULD KNOW**
Tastings can be arranged at some of the wineries by prior arrangement.
**WHAT IS THERE TO DO**
Walk the Upper Yarra Track.
**HOW DO I GET THERE**
By road from Melbourne.

# Mornington Peninsula

Melbourne is situated on Port Phillip Bay, which is almost completely enclosed within two peninsulas. Mornington Peninsula, to the east, has three distinct shorelines - each side of the peninsula faces a different bay, and at the end, the Mornington Peninsula National Park faces the open sea.

Point Nepean, at the tip of the peninsula, is one of several parks that together are known as Mornington Peninsula National Park. It contains Fort Nepean and its defences, an old army base and a quarantine station. The environment here is fragile and visitor numbers limited, so you must book. There are beautiful walks around the park and Cape Schanck has a historic lighthouse and fantastic views. There are beaches on all sides, and one of the peninsula's most popular attractions is swimming with seals and dolphins. Inland from Cape Schanck is Arthur's Seat, a huge granite outcrop that rises 300 m (1,000 ft) and offers superb views over Port Phillip Bay.

Inland, the landscape is a gently rolling vista of bush, grazing land, orchards and more than 170 vineyards where very good red and white wines are produced. Touring the wineries and enjoying very good food at their attached restaurants is a popular occupation for the citizens of Melbourne. Here also is the Pearcedale Conservation Park which specializes in rare nocturnal animals and offers an unusual evening tour.

**WHAT IS IT KNOWN FOR**
You can swim with seals and dolphins from many of the beaches.
**WHAT IS THERE TO SEE**
Sullivan Bay, French Island, Phillip Island and the penguin parade.
**WHAT IS THERE TO DO**
Spend an evening at the Pearcedale Conservation Park.
**YOU SHOULD KNOW**
You must book in advance to visit the national park.
**HOW DO I GET THERE**
By road from Melbourne.

*Mornington Peninsula National Park.*

# Byron Bay

Byron Bay is a gorgeous 30-km (18.5-mi) stretch of sandy beaches with a small town of the same name at one end. Originally the town was best known for its abbatoir, and was, until the late 1960s, an ordinary working class town. Then the area became popular with surfers because Lennox Head, which is just a short distance away, is one of the top ten surfing beaches in the world. From May to July hundreds of professional surfers gather here to ride the big waves.

By the 1970s the hippies had arrived, and as time went on, their community grew and prospered. It is a perfect spot in which to live an alternative lifestyle, although these days Byron Bay has become very popular with both backpackers and more wealthy holiday-makers. The wide choice of accommodation reflects this, varying from camp sites and hostels to the most luxurious up-market resorts favoured by the rich and famous.

The alternative lifestyle is still very visible here, with endless New Age therapies to try, from straightforward yoga to esoteric flotation tanks. New Age bookshops abound, as do little places offering crystals, Tarot readings, Indian head massage and much more. The area has also attracted many artists and craftspeople, writers and musicians. An arts and music and a writers' festival are held annually. This is a lovely, laid-back place in which to spend time relaxing.

*Cape Byron Headland.*

# Sydney Harbour

Sydney Harbour is probably best seen first from the water. When those who have never visited Australia think of that country, the picture in their mind's eye is, more often than not, that iconic image of Sydney harbour and its stunning opera house. Sydney is a beautiful city anyway, but its fabulous location lifts it to a position where it is a genuine contender for the title of the world's most beautiful city.

Sydney is divided by Port Jackson, with the south and north shores linked by both the bridge and a tunnel. The busy waterfront of Circular Quay is packed with boats: harbour and river ferries, water taxis and cruisers all ply their trade from here, and many of Sydney's classic views can be seen from this spot. The Rocks, as the rocky spur beneath the bridge is known, is the historic heart of the city and it was here that Captain Arthur Phillip formally established the colony of New South Wales in 1788, making it the first permanent European settlement in Australia. In the 1970s this historic area was rescued from imminent demolition and the workers' cottages, delapidated warehouses, winding alleys and rock-hewn steps were gradually renovated to become what is now a major tourist destination.

The Harbour Bridge can be reached from The Rocks and pedestrians can walk its length, enjoying marvellous views across the sparkling waters of the harbour itself. The Opera House, designed by the Danish architect Jorn Utzon, stands on Bennelong Point. With water lapping at its base, and its high white roofs billowing like sails in the wind, the building took 16 years to complete, and came in at ten times its original estimated cost, but has proved to be a landmark known throughout the world.

*The two icons of Sydney – the Opera House and the Harbour Bridge.*

**WHAT IS IT KNOWN FOR**
The Sydney Opera House is one of the most iconic images of Australia.
**WHAT IS THERE TO DO**
See the harbour from the water with a boat tour.
**WHAT IS THERE TO SEE**
Darling Harbour, the Royal Botanic Gardens, the Museum of Contemporary Art, Sydney Sculpture Walk and Manley.
**DON'T MISS**
A day at Bondi Beach, Australia's most famous resort.

*Sunlight on the Three Sisters.*

# Blue Mountains

The Great Dividing Range stretches right up the east of Australia, from Melbourne in the south to Cairns in the north. The area nearest to Sydney is known as the Blue Mountains because of the blue vapour that rises from the millions of eucalyptus trees growing there that colours the whole range and even the sky above.

When Sydney was first colonized, it was thought that the Blue Mountains were impassable after several unsuccessful expeditions. In 1813 Wentworth, Blaxland and Lawson, who followed the ridges rather than the valleys, found their way across, thus enabling the western plains to be opened for settlement.

At the top of the range, at an altitude of over 1,000 m (3,300 ft) is an extraordinary plateau into which over the millennia rivers have carved deep valleys. The scenery is spectacular, cut by ravines and walled canyons, and by the early twentieth century three mountain resorts had been established here. Today the villages and towns lie on a mountain ridge surrounded by the Blue Mountain National Park, a wonderful place for walking, climbing and abseiling. In 1994 a group of canyoners discovered a stand of 30-m (100-ft) high Wollemi pines, previously only known from fossil material. Designated a World Heritage site in 2000, the Blue Mountains are now protected, and abseiling on the Three Sisters – the mountains' most famous peaks – which had suffered marked erosion, has been banned.

**WHERE ARE THEY**
The Blue Mountains are part of the Great Dividing Range which stretches from Melbourne to Cairns.
**WHAT IS THERE TO SEE**
Wentworth Falls and Everglades Gardens.
**DON'T MISS**
Make sure you go up to Sublime Point Lookout for spectacular panoramic views.
**IF YOU DARE**
Abseil down the cliff faces in the Blue Mountain National Park.
**HOW DO I GET THERE**
Travel by road from Sydney.

# Rottnest Island

Rottnest Island is situated in the Indian Ocean, 19 km (12 mi) west of Fremantle, on the south-west coast of Australia, close to Perth. It is renowned for its superb diving and snorkelling, and is a perfect spot for a relaxing break.

The island was discovered in 1696 by a Dutch explorer named Willem de Vlamingh. He believed the quokkas (indigenous small marsupials) he saw here to be rats, and named the island accordingly. During the nineteenth century the island became a barbarous penal colony for native Australians, but today its old colonial architecture, fabulous beaches and Mediterranean climate have made it a popular destination for western Australians.

The island is 11 km (7 mi) long and 4.5 km (2.8 mi) across at its widest, with one settlement at Thompson's Bay on the east side. Private cars are not allowed on Rottnest, and the best way of exploring the island is by bicycle – you can ride right round it in less than three hours. There are beautiful coves with small, sandy beaches and pristine, sparkling water with offshore reefs altogether superior to anything found on the nearby mainland coast. Activities based on or around the water such as sea kayaking or self-piloted glass-bottomed boats attract up to 500,000 visitors a year. On the island itself you can visit the Rottnest Museum or take a train ride on the historic Oliver Hill train. There are plenty of places in which to eat and drink, and a variety of places in which to stay – just make sure you book somewhere in advance if you are visiting during school summer holidays.

**WHAT IS IT KNOWN FOR**
Amazing diving and snorkelling.
**WHERE IS IT**
In the Indian Ocean off the south-west coast of Australia.
**INTERESTING TRIVIA**
The island was named after its discoverer, Willem de Vlamingh, who saw a quokka and believed it to be a rat.
**YOU SHOULD KNOW**
There are no private cars allowed on the island. It is best to get around on bicycle.
**HOW DO I GET THERE**
Take a high-speed ferry or fly from Perth.

*Gentle waves lap the shores of Rottnest Island, near Perth.*

# Wineglass Bay

**WHAT IS IT**
Some of the most beautiful coastline in Tasmania.
**WHAT ELSE IS THERE TO SEE**
Schouten Island, Great Oyster Bay, Governor Island and Grosvenor Island Marine Nature Reserve.
**WHAT IS THERE TO DO**
Explore the national park and many walking tracks.
**HOW DO I GET THERE**
Travel by road from Hobart.

Wineglass Bay is situated on the rugged Freycinet Peninsula, part of the Freycinet National Park, on the east coast of Tasmania. The peninsula is made up of granite mountains that sweep down to sparkling vivid blue coves, the most beautiful of which is Wineglass Bay, so called because of its perfect shape. A stunning white sandy beach fringes the bay, set off by strange rocks which appear orange thanks to the lichen that has colonized them.

The peninsula enjoys some of the most beautiful coastline in Tasmania and a pleasantly mild climate. Coles Bay, at the north of the park, is a deep inlet with an imposing backdrop of three pink granite rocks, known as The Hazards, that rise straight from the sea to 300 m (1,000 ft) high. Coles Bay makes a good base for visiting the national park, although it is possible to stay within the park itself.

There are many walking trails to be explored but very little water, so you will need to carry plenty with you, and take advice as to the safety of drinking the water from streams. Walks start from the car park, and from there up to the lookout point over Wineglass Bay, and down to the beach and back could take as long as five hours. Another, lovely, way of seeing the bay is to take an organized cruise or hire a boat from Coles Bay, and approach it from the sea.

*The strikingly blue cove of Wineglass Bay.*

# Cradle Mountain

Cradle Mountain stands brooding over the northern end of the Cradle Mountain-Lake St Clare National Park, which itself is part of the enormous wilderness that forms Tasmania's World Heritage Area. It is a craggy peak that was formed by glaciers and forms a stunning backdrop to the lovely Dove Lake that lies below it.

There are many great walking opportunites in this area, ranging from easy ten-minute strolls through rainforest, or a three-hour walk around the shores of Lake Dove to a hard, full day's hike to the summit of the mountain and back. The most famous hike, the Overland Track, runs from Cradle Mountain to Lake St Clare, Australia's deepest freshwater lake, which lies at the southern end of the park. This is one of Australia's best known bush trails, and it draws walkers from around the world.

It takes 5–6 days to walk the 80 km (50 mi) of the Overland Trail, and there are nine basic huts placed along the route which takes walkers through some astonishing scenery. There are fields of wildflowers, ancient forests of pine, pandanus and deciduous beech, Alpine streams, lakes and waterfalls. About 8,000 walkers pass this way each year, mainly between November and April, but even though this is summer, it may rain and could even snow.

**WHAT IS IT**
Lake St Clare is Australia's deepest freshwater lake.
**WHAT IS THERE TO SEE**
Lake St Clare, Mount Ossa.
**WHAT IS THERE TO DO**
Spend a day rafting on the Franklin River.
**HOW DO I GET THERE**
Travel by road from Devonport, Launceston or Derwent Bridge.

*Cradle Mountain overlooks the shores of Lake St Clare.*

*Lichen on the rocks at the Bay of Fires, Mt William National Park.*

# Bay of Fires

Mt William National Park is in the north-east corner of Tasmania, and the Bay of Fires is the local name for the unparalleled coastline that is found here. The best way to experience the coastline and surrounding wilderness is with a guided walking tour.

Mt William National Park was set aside as a wildlife refuge in order to protect the bountiful wildlife within – the birdlife is particularly rich with raptors such as sea eagles, wedge-tailed eagles and peregrine falcons, all of which are able to find plentiful food in the area. Wallabies, wombats, echidnas, brush-tailed possums and Tasmanian devils are also to be seen, and this is the only area of Tasmania where forester kangaroos maintain a strong community. In the spring the park is a mass of wildflowers that attract butterflies and other insects as well as numerous smaller birds – more than 100 different species of which occur in the park.

The shoreline is empty and beautiful. Secluded white sandy beaches are tucked between sand dunes and granite outcrops and from the ridgeline magnificent views of heathland, woods and coastline stretch out around you. Flocks of yellow-tailed black cockatoos can sometimes be seen flying overhead. Coastal waters here offer great fishing – Anson's Bay is one of the few places in Tasmania where the Australian bass may be caught, and there are also great opportunities for snorkelling and scuba diving. The park contains many significant Aboriginal sites, and has been recommended for return to Aboriginal ownership.

**WHAT IS THERE TO DO**
If you are a keen fisherman, spend a day fishing for the Australian bass.
**DON'T MISS**
Take a guided walking tour around the coastline to really experience the scenery.
**WHEN SHOULD I GO**
Spring is beautiful as the park becomes a mass of wild flowers.
**HOW DO I GET THERE**
By road from Launceston or Hobart.

# Spirits Bay, Cape Reinga

Cape Reinga is at the northern tip of New Zealand's North Island, on the Aupuri Peninsula. A mere 500 m (5,640 ft) offshore the seas are wild and dangerous where the warm South Pacific meets the Tasman Sea. A lighthouse stands at the point, painted white it flashes its warning light every 26 seconds. Staff at the small post office will stamp your cards with its own unique postmark, but other than that you are alone with Mother Nature.

Spirits Bay, east of the Cape, is windswept and remote, with amazing pale pink sand. In the Maori language reinga means 'place of leaping' and Maoris believe that at the moment of death, the soul journeys to Cape Reinga, where it climbs down the roots of an ancient Pohutakawa tree to plunge into Spirits Bay, the final leg of its journey to the spirit world. This is a sacred place and visitors are politely requested not to eat and to behave with respect during their visit to the site.

The best way of travelling to Cape Reinga is by specially designed bus. You can drive yourself in a 4x4 or even on a quad bike, but it is a really tricky journey and you sometimes see the rusting hulk of a vehicle that has come to grief. The problem is Ninety Mile Beach, south of the Cape. Although it is in fact only 88 km (55 mi) long, you do actually drive along the beach, with the surf on one side and vast sand dunes on the other, negotiating the occasional patch of quicksand along the way. If you go by bus, you will probably get the opportunity to surf a sand dune as part of your excursion.

**WHAT IS IT**
A sacred place within the Maori tradition.
**ALSO KNOWN AS**
Reinga means 'place of leaping' in Maori, and relates to the journey of the soul after death.
**WHAT IS THERE TO SEE**
The Subritsky/Wagener Homestead and Museum and Ninety Mile Beach.
**HOW DO I GET THERE**
By road and on the beach from Kaitaia.

*The lighthouse at Cape Reigna.*

# Rotorua

Rotorua is at the south-west end of Rotorua Lake, on a volcanic plateau. The extraordinary amount of thermal activity in the area, with more than 1,200 geothermal features, has made it North Island's top tourist attraction, and the countryside around it is a mass of lakes, volcanos, dense pine and redwood forests, hot springs and geysers.

The area is extremely important within the Maori tradition, indeed it is home to about a third of New Zealand's Maoris. Mokoia Island, in the middle of the lake, is the site of the best-known Maori love story, in which Hinemoa braved the wrath of her family and swam naked from the mainland to the island to await her lover in a hot pool. Unlike the great European romances such as Romeo and Juliet, or Abelard and Heloise, Hinemoa and Tutanekai overcame their problems and lived happily ever after. You can still soak yourself in Hinemoa's Pool and make a wish at the Arawa Wishing Rock .

The most dramatic thermal scenery is found at the Whakarewarewa Thermal Reserve, a weird and wonderful nature park that looks as though it belongs on another planet altogether. Huge pools of mud bubble and gurgle, steam rises from cracks in the rocks and geysers erupt without warning. The most spectacular of these is the Pohutu geyser, which can blow as high as 30 m (100 ft). You can visit a restored Maori village dating from the early twentieth century, and there are still Maoris living nearby, cooking their food in natural steam ovens. The whole area smells of sulphur, and the town is heated by steam piped up from below the surface.

*Steaming, bubbling mud pools in Rotorua's thermal area.*

# Bay of Islands

*Some of the 150 islands located in the Bay of Islands.*

The Bay of Islands is a maritime park that lies off the north-east coast of New Zealand's North Island, in a region known as Northland. Altogether there are some 150 islands of varying size dotted about the clear blue waters of the bay.

The bay is one of the world's most popular areas for big-game fishing, and from December until June fishermen do their best to catch striped and blue marlin, yellowfin tuna, broadbill and sharks. In 1926, the best selling American writer Zane Grey set up camp on the largest of the islands, Urupukupuku, and made his name by catching a 50-kg (110-lb) yellowtail, which took the world record.

For those who prefer to look at wildlife but not hunt it, there are wonderful opportunities to go dolphin- and whalewatching. One of the best-known companies offering trips is so confident that it volunteers an extra trip free if you have the bad luck not to see a dolphin or whale the first time round. You can even swim with the dolphins, which is the experience of a lifetime. If you like scuba diving, there are several good dive sites, and you can even go to look at the wreck of the *Rainbow Warrior*, sunk by the French secret service in 1985.

The best way to see the islands is, of course, by boat. You can charter your own, or sail on the romantic tall ship, the *R Tucker Thompson*. Visit uninhabited islands and swim from lonely beaches, or take the Cream Trip cruise which delivers post and supplies to farmers in remote locations, taking you up and down little inlets and hidden bays for five hours of peaceful relaxation and gorgeous views everywhere you look.

**WHAT IS IT**
A maritime park containing 150 islands.
**WHAT IS THERE TO SEE**
Paihia, Waitangi National Trust Reserve, Poor Knights Marine Reserve.
**WHEN SHOULD I VISIT**
Big-game fishing is the sport here, so arrive between December and June to take part.
**WHAT IS THERE TO DO**
Spend a day dolphin- and whalewatching.
**HOW DO I GET THERE**
Travel by air from Auckland or Rotorua to Kerikeri, then bus or ferry.

# Milford Sound

Milford Sound is in Fiordland, on the isolated west coast of lower South Island. It is the best known of the fiords and sounds that were gouged out of the coast by glaciers some 15,000–20,000 years ago, and it is the only one that is accessible by road. This vast and glorious wilderness of forests and mountains, lakes and waterfalls contains some of the best of New Zealand's hiking trails.

The far end of the sound is dominated by the 1,412-m (4,633-ft) Mitre Peak, but it is the combination of the constantly changing light, clouds, sunshine, pouring rain and rainbows that make it such a dramatically beautiful place. Captain Cook famously passed the entrance to Milford Sound twice, in 1770 and 1773, without discovering the entrance, which was hidden in mist on both occasions. The sound got its name from John Grono, a sealing captain who discovered it in 1822 and named it after his birthplace, Milford Haven in Wales.

*Mountains surround Milford Sound, an inlet of the Tasman Sea.*

The Milford Track is a four-day hike from Te Anau Lake, across the Mackinnon Pass to Milford Sound. It is renowned amongst hikers as one of the most beautiful walks in the world, taking in rapids, mountain passes, alpine fields, rainforest and the Sutherland Falls, one of the world's highest. Fiordland has a huge amount of rain – 7,600 mm (300 in) per year and the forest reflects this – giant trees wreathed in moss and vines, lichen and ferns, and all dripping with water. If walking doesn't appeal, take a cruise to the mouth of the sound – you will see Sinbad Gully, a classic glacial valley that is the last refuge of the endangered kakapo, as well as seals and dolphins, even penguins if you are there in the autumn.

# Blenheim

Nelson and Blenheim are towns in the north of the South Island of New Zealand in what is known as the Marlborough area. Nelson lies in a fertile area, on the coast of the Tasman Bay, and it is a really attractive town with old-fashioned, colonial-style wooden buildings and a laid-back, arty atmosphere. Blenheim is the largest town in the region, and is almost entirely devoted to the wine industry.

The climate in this region is almost Mediterranean in summer, and not only does Nelson have great beaches nearby, but it is surrounded by orchard-filled valleys and vineyards. This area of the South Island is the sunniest place in New Zealand and it not only has the perfect climate but also just the right soil for growing grapes. Altogether there are more than 4,000 ha (10,000 acres) given over to vines, and over 40 wineries, many of which welcome visitors.

Montana Wines of Aukland expanded here in the 1970s and many other companies followed suit. Merlot, Cabernet Sauvignon, Chardonnay, Pinot Noir and Riesling are among the varieties that thrive here, and the best way to try them out is to organize your own wine tour if you can. Organized tours are easy to find but tend to take you to too many places to really be able to enjoy any of them.

Other leisure activities in the area include swimming with dolphins in the Marlborough sounds, fishing, water-skiing and kayaking. The coastline is popular with hikers and Kaikoura Bay for whalewatching.

**WHAT IS IT**
Blenheim is one of the largest towns in the Marlborough area of South Island.
**WHAT IS IT KNOWN FOR**
Most of the area is dedicated to the wine industry.
**INTERESTING FACT**
This part of the island is the sunniest place in New Zealand.
**WHAT IS THERE TO SEE**
Marlborough Wine and Food Festival, Golden Bay, Marlborough Sounds and Maritime Park.

*Sheep graze around hop fields on a farm in the Upper Moutree region.*

# Queenstown

Queenstown is a beautifully situated resort town on the shores of Lake Wakatipu. A backdrop of mountains, the Southern Alps and the Remarkables, stretch away into the distance, with their snow-covered peaks reflected in the calm, blue waters of the lake.

The town is perfectly positioned for all sorts of outdoor activities, at all times of year. In winter, many people come to ski here – there are slopes within half an hour's drive for skiers of every level of ability, as well as cross-country skiing and, in good weather, guided tours by helicopter or ski plane can be arranged to take you to remote peaks that are otherwise inaccessible.

In summer you can try white-water rafting, trekking or horse riding, fishing, scenic helicopter rides, and cruises around the lake. Jet-boat riding is a New Zealand invention, and is not for the fainthearted. The specially-built boats are powered by gas turbine – water is pumped out through a nozzle at high speed and the boat, which can reach 70 kph (44 mph), skims over the surface of the water as it whizzes through mountain canyons, spinning round in a terrifying fashion. Queenstown is also the home of bungee jumping. The first commercial bungee operation was set up here by A.J. Hackett in 1988. Kawarau Suspension Bridge was the original site, but today there are four others to choose from.

If energetic sporting activities pall, there are plenty of gentler alternatives, such as the Kingston Flyer, a lovely old steam train that potters along between Kingston and Fairlight, the old goldrush settlement of Arrowtown and New Zealand's rare and endangered birds at the Kiwi and Birdlife Park.

*Queenstown sits on the shores of Lake Wakatipu.*

# Aitutaki

In terms of its population of around 2,500, the beautiful island of Aitutaki is the second largest of the Cook Islands. This group of 15 islands, named after Captain Cook who landed there in the 1770s, are scattered over 1,830,000 sq km (706,380 sq mi) of the South Pacific, yet have a total land area of only 240 sq km (93 sq mi). Aitutaki was probably first settled by Polynesians in about around 900 AD and its first known European contact was with Captain Bligh and the crew of *HMS Bounty* in 1789, two weeks before the mutiny.

It is a coral atoll with low rolling hills, banana plantations and coconut groves. Along with the small uninhabited islets to the south and east, Aitutaki is surrounded by a barrier reef, thus creating the spectacular turquoise lagoon that makes it such a perfect place for swimming, snorkelling and scuba diving.

Although it is the second most visited of the Cook Islands and tourism has now become the main source of income, Aitutaki is still very unspoiled. The palm-fringed white sandy beaches, the magnificent clear sea, coupled with the wonderfully relaxed pace of life on Aitutaki contribute to making this remote island the stuff of which dreams are made.

*One of the many secluded beaches of the Cook Islands.*

**HOW DO I GET THERE**
Fly from Auckland via Rarotonga.
**WHAT IS THERE TO SEE**
The old church in Arutanga; the gigantic Banyan trees.
**DON'T MISS**
A lagoon cruise to the islets of Akaiami and Tapuatae (One Foot Island), flyfishing for the fighting bonefish, ika mata – marinated raw fish with coconut sauce or Aitutaki's dancers, who are famous throughout the Cook Islands.
**STRANGE FACT**
Captain Bligh (who returned in 1792) is credited with introducing the paw paw to Aitutaki.

*The beach at Nuku Hiva.*

# The Marquesa Islands

The 7,500 inhabitants of the Marquesa Islands could reasonably lay claim to living in the remotest place in the world. Farther from a continental landfall than any other group of islands on earth, the Marquesas poke out of the open Pacific just south of the equator and about 1,400 km (870 mi) north-east of Tahiti. Unlike many of the islands in the South Pacific, the Marquesas are, because of their remoteness, almost entirely unspoiled. They are wild and rugged islands with steep cliffs and valleys leading up to high central ridges. Brooding volcanic pinnacles pierce the landscape, while the lush vegetation is overflowing with bougainvillea, orchids, spider lilies, ginger and jasmine, as well as all manner of fruit from grapefruit and banana to mango and papaya.

Of the 12 Marquesa islands, known in the local Polynesian language as 'Land of the Men', only six are inhabited, with most of the population living in the narrow fertile valleys, leaving the interiors to the hundreds of wild horses, cattle and goats. The birdlife is extraordinarily rich and varied and the waters around the islands are teeming with fish and lobsters. The size and quality of the ocean waves as they reach many of the beaches of the Marquesas make the islands a hot spot for surfers.

The town of Atuona on Hiva Oa, the second largest island, is famous as the final resting place of Paul Gauguin, the French impressionist painter who came to live here in 1901 and, more recently, of the Belgian singer, Jacques Brel, who died there in 1978 having run Atuona's open-air cinema for several years.

**HOW DO I GET THERE**
Either fly from Papeete or Rangiroa to Nuku Hiva, the largest island or take one of cruise ships or freighters that sail monthly from Papeete, calling at all six of the inhabited Marquesas.
**WHAT IS THERE TO DO**
Join the dedicated surfers who come for the waves.
**LITERARY CONNECTIONS**
Hermann Melville's *Typee* is a classic narrative of nineteenth-century Marquesan life and Thor Heyerdahl's *Fatu Hiva* is an account of his attempt to 'get back to nature'.

# Rangiroa

About 200 km (120 mi) north of Tahiti, Rangiroa is the most populous of the Tuamotu Islands, an archipelago of 78 low islands or coral atolls spread over several hundred kilometres of the eastern Pacific. It is the largest atoll in Polynesia and the second largest in the world. With some 220 motus, or islets, none more than a metre in elevation, separated by over 100 small channels, Rangiroa's lagoon is *c*.80 x 25 km (50 x 16 mi), giving an area of more than 1,000 sq km (nearly 400 sq mi) of magnificently clear water. The incomparable brilliance and colours of the lagoon from jade-green to purple, completely overwhelm the first time visitor to Rangi, as everyone calls it.

The marine life in the lagoon is truly astonishing – there are thousands of colourful fish of all shapes and sizes, together with several varieties of mostly harmless reef sharks. Rangiroa lagoon is world famous for its unsurpassed snorkelling and scuba diving. Outside the reefs is a breathtaking array of large species along the walls of the drop-offs, including squadrons of eagle rays and schools of sharks, barracuda and tuna.

Surrounded by two legendary bodies of water, Moana-tea (Peaceful Ocean) and Moana-uri (Wild Ocean), the main villages of Avatoru and Tiputa offer the visitor a unique look at the South Pacific lifestyle of the residents. Along the few roads, coral churches, craft centres, local restaurants and tiny shops provide enjoyable land-based experiences to complement the many activities awaiting the visitor in the lagoon.

Rangiroa offers the visitor sunshine, white coral beaches and an immense playground for water sports and activities.

*The largest coral atoll in the Tuamotu Archipelago, Rangiroa boasts a huge, brilliant blue lagoon.*

**WHAT IS THERE TO DO**
Explore some of the world's best diving sites.
**WHAT IS THERE TO SEE**
The bird sanctuary on Motu Paio or one of the many working pearl farms.
**DON'T MISS**
Take a lagoon cruise in a glass-bottomed boat.
**HOW DO I GET THERE**
Fly from Tahiti or Bora Bora.

EUROPE &
THE MIDDLE
EAST

# The Spanish Riding School

The Spanish Riding School (the Spanische Hofreitschule), is a unique institution, in central Vienna. It is the oldest riding school in the world and the last to train the horses and their riders in classic dressage routines.

In 1562 Emperor Maximilian II began importing Lipizzaner horses from Spain. They are a crossbreed of Arab, Berber and Spanish horses that are born black and become white as they mature. The horses are reared at the Piber Stud Farm (Bundesgestüt Piber) near Graz, and about 40 foals are born there every year. Of these, perhaps only five stallions will be the right height and temperament to be sent to Vienna for training – the rest are sold to wealthy horse lovers or kept as breeding stock.

Originally the school was based at the Imperial Palace, but Emperor Charles VI commissioned a Baroque Riding Hall to teach aristocratic youths riding skills. Completed in 1735, the hall looks more like a ballroom, complete with balconies and chandeliers. Performances here are booked out well in advance, but if you cannot get tickets, you could instead see the morning training session, also set to music or take a tour of the stables.

The riders all wear the traditional two-cornered hats and brown frock coats, and the horses all have gold-and-red saddlecloths. The performances include individual and two-horse displays, as well as the Grand Quadrille which consists of 16 horses in formation, performing something approaching a ballet, set to classical music.

*The Spanish Riding School in Vienna.*

# Salzburg

The old city of Salzburg is in a beautiful location between the Salzach River and the Mönchsberg, overlooked by the Hohensalzburg Fortress (Festung Hohensalzburg). The river divides the old and new towns.

Salzburg was the site of a Roman town, but the first Christian kingdom was established by St Rupert, in the late seventh century. Over the centuries the Archbishops of Salzburg became ever-more powerful and were given the title of Prince of the Holy Roman Empire.

Salzburg is famous as the birthplace of Mozart and although the city was not generous towards him during his lifetime it does its level best to make the most of him now. Everywhere you go Mozart's music is being played, and there are two Mozart museums and even chocolate balls called Mozart Kugeln.

The Hohensalzburg Fortress was built for the prince-archbishops and although it is interesting to see the lavish lifestyle that they led, one of the main reasons to come here is for truly astonishing views over the Alps and the city. The Schloss Mirabell, on the other side of the river, stands in large formal gardens. The palace was built in 1606 by Prince-Archbishop Wolf Dietrich for his mistress and their children. The marble hall is covered with Baroque reliefs and lit by magnificent, sparkling chandeliers. The fifteenth-century cathedral (Salzburger Dom) is just one of several wonderful churches to be seen as you stroll or take a horse-drawn carriage through the narrow streets, past ritzy shops and cafés full of elegant, well-heeled locals.

**WHERE IS IT**
Between the Salzach River and the Mönchsberg.
**WHAT IS IT KNOWN FOR**
Salzburg is the birthplace of Mozart.
**WHAT IS THERE TO DO**
Take a horse-drawn carriage around the city and enjoy the sites.
**WHAT IS THERE TO SEE**
The Mozart museums; the Residenz; Schloss Hellbrunn; St Peter's Abbey Church (Stiftkirche St Peter).

*The city covered in snow.*

*The old section of Graz.*

# Graz

Graz is a delightfully relaxed city situated in south-eastern Austria. It is set around the banks of the Mur River and the old town centre with its red roofs is dominated by the Schlossberg, the hill that rises above it. This UNESCO World Heritage Site is a picturesque place, full of cultural interest and wonderful architecture from Baroque palaces to innovative modern constructions such as the Kunsthaus, a British-designed art gallery on the river bank.

By the late fourteenth century, Graz became the seat of the Hapsburgs, and Friedrich III, King of Germany, Emperor of Austria and Holy Roman Emperor left his mark on the town in the form of his motto 'Austria Est Imperare Orbi Universo' or AEIOU. In the early nineteenth century Archduke Johann founded the first museum in Austria, and set the cultural tone for the future.

The Landesmuseum Joanneum is a vast natural history museum, but perhaps a more obviously Austrian museum is the Landeszeughaus with its amazing collection of more than 30,000 items of armour and weapons largely from the seventeenth century. Graz is full of museums but it is far from being a museum piece of a city – it has three universities, and a vibrant atmosphere.

The architecture is the main attraction for visitors. Among the highlights is the Landhaus's fabulous Italian Renaissance courtyard, with triple-tiered arcades. The Schloss Eggenberg, a Baroque palace built in the seventeenth century, has an extraordinary interior dedicated to astronomical and mythological themes, as in the memorable Planet Hall. There is a fine cathedral, the Domkirche, with an unusual exterior fresco dating back to the 1480s, next to which stands the Baroque mausoleum of Ferdinand II.

# Vienna

The magical city of Vienna (Wien) stands on the River Danube, with wooded hills to the north and west. The Danube runs through two man-made channels, built to prevent flooding, which have created a narrow island in the middle. The city is elegant and cultured, and is famous for its art and music. The old city centre is a UNESCO World Heritage Site.

The city has had a chequered past. From its Roman inception in 15 BC, it has changed hands many times. The glory days of the eighteenth century were when Baroque architecture began to appear, and classical music was nurtured by the Hapsburgs, bringing Mozart and Beethoven to the city, followed by Schubert and the Strausses in the nineteenth century. The musicians were joined by artists and writers, making Vienna one of the most culturally important cities in Europe.

The most recognizable landmark in Vienna is the slim, graceful spire of St Stephen's Cathedral (Stephansdom). Built on the site of an earlier church, some of which is incorporated into the present one, it is a fourteenth-century Gothic masterpiece with a gleaming tiled roof sporting the symbolic Austrian eagle. Inside and out are wonderful sculptures, and the pulpit and the altar are particularly fine.

The Imperial Palace (Hofburg) is also in the inner city, along with most of the important sites, and this is an area best explored on foot. The Schloss Schonbrunn, commissioned by Leopold I, is even more spectacular. The Imperial Treasury contains such a wealth of gold and gems, both secular and religious, that it is hard to know where to look first. You would need days to really see all the marvels this great city has to offer.

*Column at Kariskirche.*

**WHAT IS IT KNOWN FOR**
Being a nurturing place for classical music in the eighteenth century.
**WHAT IS IT**
One of the most culturally important cities in Europe.
**WHAT IS THERE TO SEE**
Kunsthistorisches Museum, Schloss Belvedere, Palais Liechtenstein, Kariskirche.

# Alpbach

**HOW DO I GET THERE**
Fly to Munich or Innsbruck then travel by rail and/or road.
**WHAT IS THERE TO SEE**
The stunning floral displays in spring and summer.
**DO NOT MISS**
Hiking around the Galtenberg mountain and in the area of Inneralpbach; climbing the Gratlspitz ridge; the Golden Roof in the Old Town in Innsbruck.
**WHAT IS THERE TO DO**
In summer there is hiking and in winter, skiing and snowboarding.

Alpbach is a perfect example of a gorgeous Tyrolean village. In the summer it is a splendid place for hiking and in winter, for skiing and snow boarding. The earliest written record of the name Alpbach is from 1150, but it was doubtless settled years before that, the region having already been inhabited for well over 1,000 years. High up in a valley, the village was isolated and little visited until the road was built in 1926. Because of this relative lack of contact with the outside world, the locals retained their traditional, distinctive style of building wooden chalets with sloping roofs and balconies that in summer are a mass of colourful floral displays. Although tourism has meant that the village has grown, all new buildings must, by law, be built in the traditional style of architecture so the village retains its charm.

The village is small enough to have a relaxed, intimate atmosphere, and although the pubs and bars stay open late, it all feels very laid back.

Now just 45 minutes from Innsbruck, Alpbach is popular with visitors both for its scenery and the first-class recreation it affords. It offers skiing for people at every level, from complete beginners to the black runs on the Wiedersbergerhorn.

The nearby Vorder-Unterberg Farm, which was built in the seventeenth century and lived in until 1952, is now a museum giving a fascinating glimpse into the traditional way of life of the region's mountain farmers.

*The typical Tyrolean village of Alpbach.*

# Bruges

*Pleasure boats cruising the canals.*

Bruges (Brugge) is one of the most beautiful medieval cities in Europe. Often referred to as the 'Venice of the North', it is criss-crossed by canals, the main ring of which encloses the historic centre. It is a wonderful city with cobbled streets and lovely gabled houses that cast their reflections onto the water.

In the eleventh century Bruges was a major commercial centre for the wool industry, and by the late thirteenth century it was the main link to Mediterranean trade. It soon became a major financial centre too, and in 1309 the Bourse opened, making the city the most sophisticated money market in the entire region. By the sixteenth century, however, Bruges had split from the Netherlands, and the port of Antwerp had taken over much of its trade, leaving Bruges to decline into a provincial backwater.

There is much fine art and architecture to see in Bruges. The Church of Our Lady (Onze Lieve Vrouwekerk) boasts the highest brick spire in Europe and contains a sculpture of the Madonna by Michelangelo. The Basilica of the Holy Blood (Heilig Bloed Basiliek) is another famous church that displays a phial said to contain the blood of Christ. The Groeninge museum contains paintings from six centuries, including works by Hans Memling and Jan Van Eyck, who lived and worked here.

If you tire of cultural sightseeing, take a trip on a canal or just sit in a pretty, peaceful spot and try one of the 350 or more beers.

**ALSO KNOWN AS**
The Venice of the North.
**WHAT IS THERE TO SEE**
The Groeninge museum, the Memling Museum, the Church of Our Lady, the Beguinage (the Market Place).
**YOU SHOULD KNOW**
This has been a UNESCO World Heritage Site since 2000.
**WHAT IS IT KNOWN FOR**
*Moules* and chocolate are specialities of the area.
**HOW DO I GET THERE**
By train or car from Brussels.

# Karen Blixen Museum

Karen Blixen was a Danish writer who became known throughout the world as Isak Dinesen, the author of the best-selling novel *Out of Africa*. Her family home, situated less than half an hour's drive north of Copenhagen, became a museum after her death here in 1962. She is buried in the grounds. (M'Bogani House, the Blixens' farm near Nairobi, is part of the National Museums of Kenya.)

Karen Blixen was born in 1885, in this house, to a family of landed gentry. Rungstedlund was one of four properties the family owned here, and indeed it still owns one. Blixen was brought up here, and returned here in 1931 after having spent 17 years coffee-farming in Kenya. *Out of Africa* is a marvellous book depicting some of the stories and characters that she came across during her life there and it was an instant success. In 1985 an Oscar-winning film was made of the book.

The living rooms are almost exactly as they were while the author was still alive. Some of the furniture was brought back from Kenya, including the favourite chair of her lover, Dennis Finch Hatton. One room is now a gallery displaying some of her art (she studied at Copenhagen's Academy of Art in her youth), including portraits that she painted while in Africa. Two others are devoted to Blixen's personal library. Poems, drawings, letters and manuscripts are on display.

In 2004, two more rooms were opened, one of which is dedicated to the birds she loved so much. Behind the house are 5.7 ha (14 acres) of garden, meadow and a grove of beech trees, which she made a bird sanctuary in the 1950s. Some 40 different species of bird breed here, in an area supervized by the Danish Ornithological Society.

**WHAT IS IT**
The musuem and former home of Denmark's first lady of literature.
**WHERE IS IT**
Half an hour's drive north of Copenhagen.
**HOW LONG SHOULD I SPEND THERE**
You will need a whole day as the house and grounds are extensive.
**OPENING HOURS**
Tuesday–Sunday May–September, Wednesday–Sunday October–April.

*Karen Blixen Museum, Rungstedlund.*

# Tivoli Gardens

The Tivoli Gardens, in Copenhagen, is one of the city's best known and loved attractions. It is situated on what was once part of the fortifications that surrounded Copenhagen. In 1841 King Christian VIII was persuaded to allow the establishment of an amusement park here in order to 'provide the masses with suitable entertainment and fun', and Tivoli has been doing just that ever since.

The gardens receive some 5,000,000 visitors a year, more than any other tourist attraction in the country. They are popular with young and old alike and open until midnight all week and 1am at weekends. The gardens are planted with thousands of brightly flowering summer bedding plants, and people stroll along paths beneath old, shady trees, before heading to one of the many cafés or restaurants in the park, some of which are among the most stylish in the city. There is an open-air stage with daily shows and an internationally renowned concert hall. At night, the park is lit with thousands of coloured lights that reflect off every surface. The lake in particular looks wonderful, especially when there are firework displays. These take place every weekend in summer.

The gardens are very popular with children, for whom there are all sorts of traditional fairground amusements such as roller coasters and merry-go-rounds. During winter, the lake is frozen and scores of skaters in brightly coloured winter hats and coats take to the ice. At Christmas the amusement park reopens and there are plenty of stalls to keep the adults happy while their children enjoy the fun.

**WHAT IS IT**
The most popular tourist attraction in the country.
**WHAT IS THERE TO SEE**
The statue of the Little Mermaid in the harbour, the Tycho Brahe Planetarium, Christiansborg, Christiania free city, the Nyhavn quaysides.
**WHAT IS THERE TO DO**
This is a perfect place for the whole family, where children can play and adults can enjoy the beautiful setting.

*The Tivoli Gardens, Copenhagen.*

*A view of the Old Town of Tallinn.*

# Tallinn's Historic Centre

Estonia has been invaded time and again in its long history, most recently by Soviet Russia, but fortunately the medieval centre retains its charm. Declared a UNESCO World Heritage Site in 1997, today the historic centre of Tallinn is a popular tourist destination.

The city lies on the Gulf of Finland and the Old Town tumbling down a rocky hill, is known as Toompea. By the mid-fourteenth century, the bishops and noblemen at the top of the hill were separated from the merchants and craftsmen in the lower town by a wall, much of which still remains.

The best way to enter Toompea is through the Pikk Jalg gate tower, built in 1380. You will soon reach Castle Square (Lossi plats), which is dominated by Alexander Nevsky Cathedral, its distinctive onion domes denoting its Russian Orthodoxy. Its beautiful icons and mosaics were imported from St Petersburg. Parliament meets in a pink Baroque addition to the second castle on the site. Three of the corner towers of that castle remain, including Tall Hermann (Pikk Hermann), Tallin's most impressive fortification. The fourteenth-century Lutheran cathedral (Toomkirik), Estonia's oldest church, contains some magnificently carved tombs.

The lower town is a mass of winding, cobbled streets and arches, and story-book, pastel-coloured houses. Town Hall Square (Raekoja plats) contains merchants' houses dating from the fifteenth century, and some splendid guildhalls such as the Great Guild, now housing part of the State History Museum (Eesti Ajaloomuuseum). To the east are Kadriorg Palace, which houses the national collection of foreign art, and the Kunsti Muuseum. Throughout you will discover numerous bars and restaurants that have all sprung up during the last few years, serving tourists and newly prosperous locals alike.

**WHERE IS IT**
The city is on a bay in the Gulf of Finland.
**ALSO KNOWN AS**
The historic centre of Tallin is also known as Toompea.
**WHAT IS THERE TO SEE**
The Town Hall, St Olaf's Church (Oleviste kirik), Kiek in de Kok tower, Kadriorg and the National Art Museum (Kunsti Muuseum, known as KUMU), the Estonian islands of Saaremaa, Muhu, and Hiiuma.
**YOU SHOULD KNOW**
This is a UNESCO World Heritage Site.

# The Finnish Archipelago from Helsinki to Turku

The greatest treasure of the Finnish landscape is its archipelagos, particularly the south western archipelago with more than 20,000 islands and skerries – small rocky islets. It is a unique maritime landscape that captures the imagination of everyone who sees it.

Many of the islands were inhabited as long ago as the late Stone Age and the remains of many Iron-Age settlements have been found here. Half of the villages in this national park have been inhabited since the Middle Ages.

Some of the oldest churches and relics in Finland, as well as traces of ancient agriculture, dating back to the twelfth century, can be found on the Åland Islands. A substantial number of ships have foundered here, the most famous of them being the *Vrouw Maria*, a Dutch vessel laden with treasures that had been acquired by Catherine the Great. In 1999 the ship's wreckage was finally located, and examination of it continues.

Turku is Finland's oldest city, largest port, and its former capital. This is a good base for visiting the islands, particularly by bicycle, as there is a fantastic system of free ferry services that cross back and forth all the time between islands. The biodiversity here is exceptional, and you can see wonderful seabirds, elks and seals as you soak up the tranquil, rural charm of the inner islands, the huge lighthouses of Bengtskar, Isokari and Uto and the astounding beauty of the seascapes.

**WHAT IS IT**
A collection of over 20,000 islands and skerries.
**WHAT IS THERE TO SEE**
The Blue Mussel Visitor Centre at Kasnas, the harbour village of Naantali, the town of Kotka, Helsinki.
**WHEN SHOULD I VISIT**
The best time is from May to September.
**YOU SHOULD KNOW**
The area is a UNESCO Sea Biosphere Reserve.

*Nauvo Island in the Turku Archipelego.*

# Mont-St-Michel

The view of Mont-St-Michel rising from the rippling sands that surround it is one of the iconic images of France, but no matter how often you have seen pictures of it, your first sight of the real thing is quite spectacular. The 80-m (260-ft) high granite rock rising from the bay has a long religious history. Legend has it that the Archangel Michael appeared to the Bishop of Avranches (later St Aubert) and told him to build a chapel here. A settlement grew up around the base of the mount and it became a place of pilgrimage.

In 966 the Duke of Normandy replaced the chapel with a Benedictine Abbey but in 1203 it was burned down by Philippe-Auguste's troops. He made reparation for this by building the great Gothic abbey that we see today, although the fortifications were added by Charles VI. After a period of decline, Napoleon made the abbey a prison. In 1874, it was declared a national monument and restoration work began. Mont-St-Michel is separated from the mainland by 1 km (0.6 mi) of water that becomes a floor of shifting sand and mud at low tide. The causeway was built in 1879 – before that pilgrims had to brave the tides that could sweep in and drown them. In 1966 Benedictine monks made the abbey their home once more. The abbey is reached up steep, narrow streets lined with souvenir shops and packed with visitors. The buildings are easier to see in winter, when there are fewer people.

*You can walk across the causeway at low tide.*

# Étretat

Étretat is a large village situated on what is known as the 'Alabaster Coast', west of Dieppe and north of Le Havre, in Normandy. Its high, white cliffs, the Falaises d'Étretat, are as well known to the French as the White Cliffs of Dover are to the British.

Étretat has been a draw for artists and writers since the nineteenth century. Victor Hugo loved it here and Guy de Maupassant lived here. Courbet, Degas and Matisse all came here to paint, but it was Alphonse Carr, the editor of *Le Figaro*, who made it fashionable with Parisians. Today, it is still a popular little resort in summer, but in winter it reverts to being the quiet and beautiful place it has always been, with the sweeping promenade and shingle beach empty but for the odd solitary walker.

*The cliffs of Étretat*

The western cliff, the Falaise d'Aval, has been formed into a huge arch by the action of the sea on these soft, chalk cliffs. You can climb a path to the top for a fantastic view of the rock formations here, including l'aiguille (the 'needle'), a 700-m (2,300-ft) rock that rises from the water. At the top of the eastern cliff, the Falaise d'Amont, is a tiny chapel, and behind it is a little museum and a monument in the shape of a wishbone dedicated to the two French aviators, Coli and Nungesser, who made the first attempt to cross the north Atlantic and were lost off the coast here in 1927. At low tide you can see eighteenth-century oysterbeds and walk through natural arches from one beach to another.

**WHERE IS IT**
In Normandy, west of Dieppe and north of Le Havre.
**WHAT IS THERE TO DO**
Climb to the top of the Falaise d'Aval for a view of the rock formations.
**WHAT IS THERE TO SEE**
Palais Benedictine in Fécamp; Honfleur; Trouville-sur-Mer and Deauville.
**HOW DO I GET THERE**
By bus or car from Le Havre.

# Monet's Garden at Giverny

**YOU SHOULD KNOW**
The garden is open from April to November.
**WHEN SHOULD I VISIT**
The lily pond is at it's best in late July and early August.
**WHAT IS THERE TO SEE**
Musée d'Art Américain; Rouen.
**HOW DO I GET THERE**
By train from Paris or Rouen to Vernon.

The Impressionist painter, Claude Monet, lived at Giverny for 43 years, from 1883. He first saw it from the window of a train, and fell in love. Though the world may consider Monet to be the grand master of Impressionism, he thought these beautifully crafted gardens that run down to the River Epte were his true masterpiece.

The house itself is long and low, painted pink with green shutters and steps. Inside it is decorated exactly as it was when Monet lived here, along with his mistress, whom he later married, and eight children. Although none of his originals are here, his wonderful collection of Japanese prints still hangs on the walls.

Gravel paths lead from one part of the garden to the next. At every turn a slightly different view is offered, and the light changes, too, not only because of the weather and the passage of the sun but also according to the position of the weeping willows and rhododendrons. This changing light was what entranced Monet, who painted his gardens over and over again.

May and June are the months when the wisteria is in flower above the Japanese bridge, but the garden is magical whenever you go. The lily pond looks its best in late July and early August when the lilies are in bloom, but the gardens contain more than 100,000 perennials and almost as many annuals are planted every year, providing a profusion of flowers, scents and butterflies.

*Monet's bridge in his garden at Giverny.*

# Chartres Cathedral

The market town of Chartres lies about 96 km (60 mi) south-west of Paris and it has been famous throughout the Christian world for centuries, thanks to its magnificent cathedral.

In 875, Charles II presented the 'Sancta Camisia' to Chartres. This was the garment supposedly worn by the Virgin Mary when she gave birth to Christ, and its presence led to an immediate influx of pilgrims. In 1194 the existing church burnt down, but the relic, seemingly miraculously, was untouched. Funds flooded in to enable a new church to be built, and by 1260, the new, glorious Chartres Cathedral (Cathédrale Notre-Dame de Chartres) had risen from the ashes. It was recognized as a UNESCO World Heritage Site in 1979.

Some of the original, Romanesque building can still be seen – in the smaller, octagonal tower, the Royal Portal and the rounded arches – but most of the rest of the building, including the superlative stained glass, dates from the twelfth and thirteenth centuries. The floor of the nave is inlaid with a black and white 'labyrinth'. This device served as a substitute for the pilgrimage to the Holy Land, and the faithful were expected to follow its path on their hands and knees.

There are wonderful carvings and statues to be seen, but it is the stained glass that really makes the cathedral special. During both world wars, the thousands of panes from the 172 windows were carefully taken apart and hidden in the Dordogne for safekeeping. The stained glass windows tell stories from the Bible that can be 'read' from the bottom (Earth) to the top (Heaven), and from left to right. The glass is gradually being restored and cleaned and glows with rich reds, greens and, in particular, the renowned Chartres blue.

*The rose window in the north transept.*

**WHERE IS IT**
96 km (60 mi) south-west of Paris.
**WHAT IS IT KNOWN FOR**
The exquisite stained glass has made the cathedral famous.
**WHAT IS THERE TO SEE**
The view from the tower; Jehan-de-Beauce; the Musée des Beaux-Arts.
**YOU SHOULD KNOW**
There are entrance fees payable for the crypt and treasury, and climbing the tower.
**HOW DO I GET THERE**
By train from Paris.

*The King's Pavilion with its Louis XIII mansard roof.*

# Place des Vosges

The place des Vosges is a beautifully proportioned, elegant square, situated in the Marais area of Paris. It is the oldest square in Paris, and the first example of planned development in the city. In 1559 Henri II was killed during a jousting tournament near the Hotel des Tournelles, which stood on what is now the north side of the square. His widow, Catherine de Medici had the palace demolished, and the huge space became a horse market. In 1605, Henri IV commissioned the square to be built in honour of Louis XIII's marriage and 36 rose-pink brick and stone arcaded mansions were built, all surrounding a central square. The houses were built to a specific design – the height and width of the façades are the same, and the roofs are half the height of the façades.

Henri IV named it the Place Royal, and it soon became the home of many aristocratic families. In 1800 it was renamed the Place des Vosges, when the administrative department of the same name became the first in the country to pay its taxes to Napoleon. The Marais went into decline for a long period during the nineteenth and early twentieth centuries, but today it is as fashionable as ever, and the Place des Vosges is full of chic shops and interesting restaurants. Many famous people have lived here: Cardinal Richlieu, Blaise Pascal and Madame de Sevigné to name but a few. One of its best-known inhabitants, however, was Victor Hugo, who lived on the second floor of number 6, and wrote much of Les Misérables there. His home is now a museum, and is the only one of these lovely houses that is open to the public.

**WHAT IS IT**
Place des Vosges is the oldest square in Paris.
**WHAT IS THERE TO SEE**
Musée Carnavalet, Musée Picasso.
**WHAT IS THERE TO DO**
Visit the Maison de Victor Hugo and gain an insight into one of the most famous inhabitants of the Place des Vosges.
**HOW DO I GET THERE**
Travel on the Metro to Bastille.

338

# The Cathedral of Notre-Dame

Notre-Dame is a Gothic masterpiece on the Île de la Cité in the Seine. The site on which it stands has been a place of worship since Roman times, when a temple to Jupiter was built here. Later the Merovingians, who ruled Gaul from about 500–751 AD, built the cathedral of St-Etienne on the same site. Notre-Dame itself was founded in 1160 by Maurice de Sully, the Bishop of Paris, and its foundation stone was laid by Pope Alexander III. The building took almost 200 years to complete.

The glory of the cathedral is its façade, with its lovely rose window and gallery above, and the flying buttresses to the side, holding up the choir. There are three magnificent entrances: to the left is the Portal of the Virgin, with signs of the zodiac and the coronation of the Virgin Mary; to the right is the Portal of St Anne, which features the Virgin and Child – possibly the cathedral's finest piece of sculpture; and the central Portal depicts the Last Judgement.

Inside the cathedral the end walls of the transepts are a mass of glass, including two more fabulous rose windows in imperial purple. The light that falls on the sanctuary is in great contrast to the darkness of the soaring nave. In the 1820s the cathedral went through some major restoration, partly through the popularity of Victor Hugo's *Notre-Dame de Paris* (*The Hunchback of Notre-Dame*) and partly through a nineteenth-century revival of interest in Gothic architecture. The architect, Viollet-le-Duc, added the steeple and the gargoyles, which you can get a good look at if you can face walking up the 387 steps of the tower.

**WHERE IS IT**
On the Île de la Cité in Paris.
**WHAT IS IT KNOWN FOR**
Victor Hugo's *The Hunchback of Notre-Dame* made this one of the most famous cathedrals in the world.
**WHAT IS THERE TO SEE**
Crypte Archaeologique; Kilometre zero.

*Notre-Dame sits on a misty Seine.*

# The Louvre

The Louvre is the world's largest museum, a classically grand building that stretches for about 1 km (0.6 mi) between the Seine and the rue de Rivoli. At one time, it was the world's largest palace. Its life as a museum began less than a month after the execution of Marie Antoinette, when the leaders of the Revolution decided that the public should be able to enjoy the royal art collection.

During the late eighteenth century the Louvre suffered a drastic decline. It became home to many families of squatters, who even kept livestock in the corridors. Napoleon ended this situation when he decided to restore the palace to its former glory. He chose to marry there and within the next few years he brought a mass of art and sculpture – his booty from his expeditions abroad – here.

In the 1980s, President Francois Mitterand decided to give the Louvre a controversial facelift by installing a futuristic steel and glass pyramid by IM Pei in the middle of the courtyard as the main entrance. Although the pyramid caused a furore at the time, Parisians are generally quite proud of it now.

The museum houses some 400,000 items, of which 35,000 are on display. The collections are divided into eight: Oriental antiquities, Egyptian antiquities, Greek, Etruscan and Roman antiquities, Islamic art, sculpture, paintings, objets d'art and graphic arts. The Denon wing is the most visited area of the museum, housing a wonderful collection of Italian masterpieces and the *Mona Lisa* (*La Joconde*).

*Fountains outside the Louvre's glass pyramid.*

# Sainte-Chapelle

The Sainte-Chapelle is a tiny, exquisite chapel situated on the Île de la Cité, east of the Pont Neuf. Originally it was part of the old royal palace, which was used by French kings until 1358, when they moved into the Louvre for safety. It is the only part of the palace that remains, but its graceful 74-m (243-ft) spire soars above the massive façade of the neighbouring Palais de Justice, which might otherwise render it almost invisible.

The chapel was built by Louis IX in 1248, in order to house the Crown of Thorns and pieces of the True Cross, which he had bought from the Emperor of Constantinople for an enormous amount of money – more than it cost to build the Sainte-Chapelle. Unlikely though it is that the relics are genuine, they are now housed at Notre-Dame, and are put on public display each Good Friday.

The chapel is built on two levels, the lower level was for the palace servants, whilst the courtiers and royalty used the upper level, which is reached by a spiral staircase. This upper chapel is one of the finest examples of High Gothic architecture in existence, and it is renowned for the dazzling stained glass windows that make up virtually all of the walls. The windows tell the story of the Bible from Genesis to the Apocalypse. They are supported by clusters of delicate columns, whose fragile appearance belies their great strength. When the sun streams through the gorgeous red and blue glass you see precisely why the Sainte-Chapelle is described as a 'jewel box'.

**WHAT IS IT**
A fine example of High Gothic architecture.
**YOU SHOULD KNOW**
The Sainte-Chapelle is open daily and entry is free.
**ALSO KNOWN AS**
A jewel box.
**WHAT IS THERE TO SEE**
Arrive in summertime and enjoy the concerts in the chapel.
**HOW DO I GET THERE**
Take the Metro to Cité, St-Michel or Chatelet.

*A large rose window located in the upper chapel in the Sainte-Chapelle.*

# Fontainebleau

The Château de Fontainebleau stands in the midst of a forest, about 55 km (35 mi) south of Paris. It began life as a hunting lodge during the twelfth century, but it was not until the sixteenth century that Francois I was inspired to turn it into a palace, and commissioned several well-known Italian artists, including Francesco Primaticcio, Benvenuto Cellini and Rosso Fiorentino, to adorn the interior.

Fontainebleau remained a popular getaway for royal hunting trips until Louis IV became obsessed with the palace at Versailles and it was in fact Napoleon Bonaparte who brought it back to its former glory.

Both his 'Petits Appartements' and the Musée Napoleon can be visited and provide a fascinating glimpse of his life here. It was here too, on the seventeenth-century exterior horseshoe-shaped staircase that Napoleon, having abdicated, said farewell to his army, and was then removed to Elba.

The ornately decorated Francois I Gallery (Galerie Francois I) boasts stucco framed panels along its entire 63-m (207-ft) length, painted with classical scenes celebrating wise rulership, and the ballroom is equally sumptuous, with a mass of frescoes. The palace itself is a mixture of styles, having been added to over the centuries – nevertheless, it is an extremely handsome building.

The gardens of Fontainebleau are superbly landscaped and include a large carp pond. This is a popular spot for visitors who throw baguettes into the water in order to see the resulting feeding frenzy. The Forêt de Fontainebleau is criss-crossed with hunting trails first trodden by the kings of France and, less romantically, bike trails.

*A dramatic, sweeping staircase leads from the Cour du Cheval up to the entrance.*

# The Loire and its Châteaux

*Château de Chenonceaux in the Loire Valley.*

The term Loire Valley is usually used to refer to the area between Orléans and Angers. The valley effectively divides France – to the north the climate is mild and wet but to the south it abruptly changes to the drier, hotter climate of the Mediterranean. There is a wealth of history, art and architecture to be found here and it is also famous for its food and wines – Sancerre and Muscadet, Chinon and Bourgeuil to mention but a few. This is a wonderful place to explore and enjoy.

It is an immensely fertile area, which – along with the easy transport provided by the river – made it highly desirable to wealthy lords and royalty, so the string of fabulous châteaux that can be seen today were built. There are so many of these gems that you could spend weeks trying to visit them all. This is no doubt why UNESCO designated the whole area a World Heritage Site instead of attempting to pick out individual châteaux for that distinction.

Chenonceaux, built in 1520 by a tax collector for his wife, is often thought to be the most romantic of castles. Its design was always controlled by the women who lived here, including Diane de Poitiers and Catherine de Medici. Azay-le-Rideau is a classic fairy-tale palace with its white walls and early Renaissance style. It stands in lovely gardens on its own little island in the Indre River. The château at Villandry is renowned for its ornamental 'garden of love' and its wonderful kitchen garden. Fontevraud Abbey, which contains the tombs of the Plantagenets, is a superb complex of Romanesque buildings and the largest abbey in France.

**ALSO KNOWN AS**
The Loire Valley is often referred to as 'the Garden of France'.
**WHAT IS IT KNOWN FOR**
Vineyards producing famous wines such as Sancerre and Muscadet.
**WHAT IS THERE TO SEE**
The Angers Tapestry, the Châteaux de Chambord, Chinon and Blois.
**WHEN SHOULD I VISIT**
Spring and autumn are the best times.

*Wildflowers grow on the hill above Paluden Beach.*

# Belle-Ile-en-Mer

Belle-Ile-en-Mer lies in the Atlantic Ocean, off the tip of the narrow Quiberon peninsula in south-western Brittany. It is the largest of Brittany's islands at 18 km (11 mi) long, and true to its name, it is indeed beautiful. The sheltered, eastern coast of the island is carved with deep estuaries, and there are a number of small fishing villages surrounded by fertile, cultivated land. The island is hilly, and the north-western coast, the Côte Sauvage, is a place of high cliffs, lashed by fierce seas.

The ferry drops its passengers at Le Palais, a town dominated by the Citadelle Vauban, built in the sixteenth century by Henri II to protect the monks of Redon from pirates. A prison until the 1960s, it now houses the island's museum. Later, the island belonged to Nicolas Fouquet and from 1761–63 to the British, but was returned as part of the Treaty of Paris.

The island is a lovely, peaceful place on which to spend a holiday. There are 90 beaches to explore – Donnant beach on the western

**WHAT IS IT**
The largest of Brittany's islands.
**WHAT IS THERE TO SEE**
La Grotte de l'Apothicairerie, the Great Lighthouse at Port Goulphar and Quiberon.
**HOW DO I GET THERE**
Travel by ferry from Quiberon.
**WHEN SHOULD I VISIT**
The weather is best between May and September.

shore is probably the most popular, and south east of Le Palais you will find the white sands of Grands Sables, which is the longest on the island. Sauzon is a picturesque fishing village running down one side of an estuary to the west of Le Palais, with picture-postcard houses looking at the rocky cliffs opposite. There are several major rock formations in the north of the island – Monet even painted one.

*Boats moored in the harbour near the lighthouse in Sauzon.*

# Niort and the Marais Poitevin

Between La Rochelle and Poitiers, in the Poitou-Charentes region, is an area known as the Marais Poitevin. This is a strange and beautiful region of natural marshland, criss-crossed by lazy rivers, streams, canals and dykes. Designated a regional park, it is often called 'La Venise Verte' – the Green Venice. This is an apt name as many of the farmers here have to travel by *pigouille*, a narrow, flat-bottomed boat, as they have no access to their fields by road.

This is a lovely, timeless and tranquil place to visit. You can walk along the footpaths or take bikes, but probably the best way to see it is by boat. Weeping willows overhang the water forming green tunnels over the canals, which are themselves at times so covered in weed that they look like solid paths. Water-loving plants – irises, marsh marigolds and rushes – abound and everywhere you hear the sound of birdsong and very little else to disturb the peace.

Niort is a small city about 50 km (30 mi) south-west of Poitiers and is a good base from which to explore the Marais Poitevin. It has several medieval buildings including the old town hall, a castle keep built by Henry II of England, and a fine fifteenth-century church, the Église Notre-Dame. At Maillaizes, some 35 km (22 mi) away, is the fascinating twelfth-century ruined abbey of St Pierre de Maillaizes.

**ALSO KNOWN AS**
'La Venise Verte' – the Green Venice.
**WHEN SHOULD I ARRIVE**
Arrive in August and take in the The Festival du Marais Poitevin.
**WHAT IS THERE TO SEE**
La Maison du Marais Mouilles, Coulon, Poitiers and La Rochelle.
**WHAT IS THERE TO DO**
The best way to see the region is by boat. Hire one for a day and enjoy the scenery.

# The Aven-Armand Cave

**WHAT IS IT**
A vast cavern which houses the world's tallest stalagmite.
**ALSO KNOWN AS**
The stalagmite formations are known as 'The Virgin Forest'.
**WHAT IS THERE TO SEE**
The Dargilan grotto; Montpellier-le-Vieux.
**YOU SHOULD KNOW**
The cave is closed in December.

The entrance to the amazing cavern of Aven-Armand was discovered by Louis Armand in December 1897. Situated on the Causse Méjean, a limestone plateau close to the small village of Lozère, it is possibly the most beautiful cave in the country.

Louis Armand was a blacksmith from Rozier who persuaded the caver Edouard Alfred Martel and his colleague, Armand Vire, to join him in an exploratory expedition. What they discovered was a 40-m (130-ft) limestone chimney reaching down to the ceiling of an enormous cavern, with a second chimney plunging another 90 m (300 ft) into the cave itself. For the next 30 years the only way to see the cave was by climbing down a rope ladder or by being winched down in a bucket, but by 1927 visitors could brave the steps down a 208-m (680-ft) tunnel to a viewing platform and a pathway through the cave. In 1963 a funicular railway was installed, making access even easier.

The cave is vast, 110 m (360 ft) long by 60 m (200 ft) wide and 45 m (150 ft) high – large enough to house Paris's Notre-Dame comfortably. The Virgin Forest, as it is known, is a forest of stalagmites, more than 400 of which are more than 1 m (39 in) high. Many reach 15 to 20 m (66 ft), and the most famous of them all, the world's tallest stalagmite, tops 30 m (100 ft) in height. Walking through the Aven-Armand makes you feel you have been transported to some Tolkienesque wonderland. Thanks to the clever lighting that changes all the time, some of the stalagmites sparkle like diamonds whilst others, formed into weird shapes, suddenly loom up from the darkness.

*Giant stalagmites in the cave.*

# Les Gorges du Verdon

Les Gorges du Verdon is found high up in the Haut-Var region of Provence. This natural wonder is a vast chasm cut by the Verdon River over the course of time. Roads run around both sides of the gorge, which is up to 800 m (2,625 ft) deep at some points. The entire circuit is 130 km (80 mi) long, and the narrow ribbon of the river far below winds its way through the full 21 km (13 mi) of the gorge into the man-made Lac de Sainte-Croix.

This is the largest gorge in Europe and is sometimes referred to as Europe's 'Grand Canyon'. It has been formed by water eroding the soft limestone rock over some 25 million years. The water gradually worked its way through the limestone plateau, gouging out caves and tunnels as it flowed. These caverns grew larger until finally the roof of the plateau caved in, forming this dramatic V-shaped gorge. In some places at the top the walls of the gorge are as much as 1,500 m (4,920 ft apart), but at the valley floor the gorge can be as little as 6 m (20 ft) across. In 1997, the Parc Natural Régional du Verdon was set up to protect this unique, beautiful landscape.

In 1905 the caver, Edouard Alfred Martel, led a team to explore the area, which had until then been unknown to anyone except the locals. The gorge quickly became a tourist attraction and today drivers can stop at the lookout point of the Balcons de la Mescla, which affords an amazing view right down to the valley floor. West of this point the road has been designed to give the best possible views but drivers need to keep their eyes on the road!

*The gorge is the largest in Europe and runs mid-way between Avignon and Nice.*

**WHAT IS IT**
A gorge cut deep into the surrounding rock by the Verdon River.
**ALSO KNOWN AS**
As it is the largest chasm in Europe, it is sometimes called Europe's 'Grand Canyon'.
**WHAT IS THERE TO SEE**
Pont de l'Artuby; Lac de Sainte-Croix; Moustiers-Ste-Marie.
**YOU SHOULD KNOW**
The best way to see the gorge is by car, but the road is treacherous.

*The village of Castelbouc lies on the shore of the Tarn River, at the foot of the limestone Gorges du Tarn.*

# Gorges du Tarn

The River Tarn is 375 km (233 mi) long and flows from Mt Lozère to Moissac, where it enters the Garonne at the southern end of the Massif Central. The precipitous gorge, carved out of the limestone rocks of the Grands Causses is one of the most beautiful in France. Its steep sides are swathed in pine forest and extraordinary karst formations can be found here.

At Le Rozier, a pretty little village, the Tarn is joined by another river, the Jonte, and this is the beginning of probably the most appealing section of the gorge, a 60-km (37-mi) stretch that ends at Florac. Follow the road from here to the cliff-top at Point Sublime for some of the best views of stark rock faces and dramatic cliffs. The imposing fifteenth-century Château de la Caze stands close to the Cirque du Pougnadoires, a large, natural amphitheatre which, during the summer months, is the site of a fabulous *son-et-lumière* spectacle. From the nearby village of La Malène you can take a trip downriver in a glass-bottomed boat.

Perhaps the best way to see the gorge, however, is to walk along the riverside footpath or rent a canoe and paddle your way downriver. From this perspective the walls of the canyon seem to rise up endlessly and the constantly changing light dapples the rocks. This is good birdwatching country – eagle owls and peregrine falcons nest here, and you might even see huge golden eagles circling high above, looking for prey.

**WHAT IS IT**
One of France's most beautiful gorges.
**WHAT IS THERE TO SEE**
Ste-Enimie; Florac and Viaduc de Millau.
**WHAT IS THERE TO DO**
Take a trip in a glass-bottomed boat from La Malène.
**DON'T MISS**
One of the best ways to see the gorge is by canoe.

# Toulouse-Lautrec Museum

Albi is situated on the banks of the River Tarn about 75 km (50 mi) north-east of Toulouse. The painter Henri de Toulouse-Lautrec is Albi's most famous son and one of France's most famous artists. He died in 1901 at the age of 37. Henri de Toulouse-Lautrec was the son of the Count of Toulouse.

As soon as he was 18, he made his way to Paris, where he quickly became both fascinated by and obsessed with the seedy and Bohemian lifestyle that he found in the areas of Montmartre and Pigalle. He sketched and painted prolifically, perfectly capturing the atmosphere of the bars, music halls and brothels he frequented and the low-life characters he found within.

The Toulouse-Lautrec Museum is housed in the Palais de la Berbie, a red-brick fortress the oldest sections of which date back to the 13th century. Originally the home of the bishops of the Midi region the gardens were designed in the reign of Louis XIV in the French style, with terraces and knot gardens which offer great views of the Tarn. The museum's collection is extensive and holds more than 1,000 works, including all the posters he made for the nightclubs in Montmartre, including the Moulin-Rouge.

Albi is also home to the wonderful Gothic cathedral of Ste-Cécile, which is visible for miles around. Constructed between the thirteenth and fifteenth centuries the exterior is austere, but the interior is a mass of carvings and religious scenes by sixteenth-century Italian artists. The west wall has a huge fresco of the Last Judgement and above it is a splendid eighteenth century-organ.

*The Toulouse-Lautrec Museum is in the Palais de la Berbie.*

**WHERE IS IT**
Albi is on the banks of the River Tarn approximately 75 km (50 mi) north-east of Toulouse.
**WHAT ELSE IS THERE TO SEE**
Toulouse and Cordes-sur-Ciel.
**YOU SHOULD KNOW**
There is an entry fee payable for the museum.
**HOW DO I GET THERE**
By train from Toulouse.

# Mercantour National Park

**WHERE IS IT**
About 20 km (12.5 mi) north of
Monte-Carlo.
**WHAT IS IT KNOWN FOR**
Containing the largest high-altitude
lake in Europe.
**WHAT IS THERE TO SEE**
Barcelonette, the Vallée des
Merveilles,, the Bronze-Age rock
carvings near Mt Bégo.
**HOW DO I GET THERE**
By bus from Menton.
**WHEN SHOULD I VISIT**
The best time is from June
to October.

This national park stretches for about 75 km (47 mi) in a narrow, mountainous ribbon between Barcelonette in the Alpes Maritimes to Sospel, about 20 km (12.5 mi) north of Monte-Carlo. Although it is almost completely uninhabited it is criss-crossed with trails and refuge huts for hikers.

The park contains several peaks, the highest being La Cime du Gélas at 3,143 m (10,312 ft), as well as the largest high-altitude lake in Europe, the Lac d'Allos. It is a beautiful, completely unspoiled area, with stunning waterfalls and gorges, but it is best known for its flora and fauna. Inland there are unusual Alpine plants such as the multi-flowering saxifrage as well as unique types of orchid and lily. Closer to the coast more typical maquis plant life can be found, the tough, aromatic species for which the Provencal hinterland is famous. The park is home to a host of Alpine mammals such as ibex, chamoix marmots, ermine, mouflon and reintroduced wolves. There are superb birds here too – golden eagles, peregrine falcons, hoopoes and ptarmigans.

Sospel, at the southern boundary, is a lovely, peaceful town on the River Bevera. The place St-Michel is a classic Provencal dream of peach-coloured facades interspersed with two chapels and a church, all overlooked by a ruined castle. This is a splendid place in which to rest after hiking in the high mountains.

*The Mercantour National Park, north-east of the Côte d'Azur.*

# Orange

*Spectators watch a performance of* Aida *at the Théâtre Antique d'Orange.*

Orange is situated in north-west Provence, in a fertile region that is famous for its wines – in fact it is only 10 km (6 mi) north of Châteauneuf-du-Pape. Its name is thought to derive from its original Roman name of Arausio, and it was the home of the counts of Orange, a title created by Charlemagne in the eighth century.

Orange is best known for its superb Roman theatre. Built in the first century AD, the Théâtre Antique is built at the base of the hill at the south end of the old town, and it is the best-preserved Roman theatre in Europe. Its vast stone stage wall is one of only three left in the world, and it rises to 36 m (118 ft), so sounds bounce back off it towards the seating that is built into the hill itself. In an alcove in the centre of the wall stands a large statue of Augustus Caesar, the man responsible for its foundation. The acoustics here are virtually perfect and today the theatre is still used for theatrical and operatic productions, for which it still draws large audiences.

You can follow a footpath up the hill behind the theatre to the scattered ruins of the seventeenth-century castle of the Princes of Orange where Queen Juliana of Holland planted an oak tree in tribute to her ancestors. This gives you the best view of the theatre and the city. The other major Roman monument here is the Triumphal Arch – it stands on what used to be the Via Agrippa, the road linking Arles to Lyon. Its façades celebrate the Second Legion's victories over the Gauls.

**WHAT IS IT KNOWN FOR**
Its superbly preserved Roman theatre.
**WHAT IS THERE TO SEE**
The Musée Municipal,
the village of Châteauneuf-du-Pape.
**WHAT IS THERE TO DO**
Attend one of the performances in
the Théâtre Antique.
**HOW DO I GET THERE**
By train from Paris, Lyon, Avignon
or Marseilles.

*The Palais des Papes overlooks the Rhône as it flows under the Pont d'Avignon.*

# Avignon

Avignon stands on a bend in the River Rhône, some 95 km (60 mi) north-west of Marseille. Despite its superb medieval monuments and its bridge made famous by the nursery rhyme, it is a thriving, energetic city rather than a museum piece.

Known as 'the city of the Popes', Avignon was a major papal city. In 1309 Clement V, a French pope, fled here from political turmoil in Rome. The third pope of Avignon, Benedict XII, began building the vast, fortified Palais des Papes in 1335 and it was finished by his successor, Clement VI a couple of decades later. It is divided by the Great Court – to one side of this the building is austere while to the other it retains visible evidence of the lavish, secular lifestyle of Clement VI. The palace was desecrated during the French Revolution, and its treasures looted, but the scale of the rooms with their frescoes and tiles shows how luxurious life was here.

Next to the palace stands the cathedral of Notre-Dame-des-Doms, a Romanesque building that was partially rebuilt in the fifteenth century. A short distance away is the Petit Palais, where the Pope and his entourage lived before the palace was built. This now contains an amazing collection of early Renaissance Italian art, including Botticelli's *Virgin and Child*.

From the town's low ramparts you can reach what is left of the Pont St-Bénézet. It was built in the early fourteenth century, but collapsed and was mostly swept away by the river in the eighteenth century, but you can still walk, talk, dance and sing on what is left.

**WHERE IS IT**
Avignon is on the banks of the River Rhône, 95 km (60 mi) north-west of Marseille.
**ALSO KNOWN AS**
The City of the Popes.
**WHAT IS THERE TO SEE**
Palais du Roure Museum, Rocher des Doms, Musée Calvet.
**WHAT IS THERE TO DO**
Visit the Petit Palais to see Botticelli's *Virgin and Child*.

# Les Calanques

Les Calanques are a series of long, narrow inlets, like mini fjords, cut into the limestone cliffs around Cassis, on the Mediterranean coast.

Cassis is a pretty coastal town tucked in between tall white cliffs and the sea. Its picturesque fishing port is overlooked by the Château de Cassis, a medieval castle now owned by the Michelin family. Although it is a stylish resort town, Cassis still retains the atmosphere of a genuine Provençal port. It is full of narrow alleys and steps that lead farther up the hillside to pretty white houses that seem to cling to the slope, and the harbour has cafés galore at which you can sit and admire the view. There are at least 14 vineyards, which are known for their rosé wines, surrounding Cassis, and an enjoyable day can be spent visiting a few of these and sampling their wares.

It is easy enough to hike up the well-signed footpath that runs along the cliffs to the Calanque de Port Pin, but it is worth making the extra effort to reach Calanque en Vau, the most beautiful of the lot. From the top of the cliff here you can look over the white rocks to the sparkling turquoise sea and the tiny, but perfectly formed, beach. An easier way to get here is by boat from Cassis – tours leave from the harbour at regular intervals – or you could rent a kayak and make your own way. The swimming and diving here are fabulous.

*The Calanques provide safe harbour and some even have small beaches or tiny harbours.*

**WHAT ELSE IS THERE TO SEE**
Cap Canaille, Marseilles and the Château d'If.
**WHAT IS THERE TO DO**
Hike up to Calanque en Vau for the best view over the cliffs.
**HOW DO I GET THERE**
By bus or train to Cassis from Marseille.
**WHEN SHOULD I VISIT**
The summer has the best weather.

# Arles

**WHAT IS THERE TO SEE**
Musée de l'Arles Antique, Cryptoportiques du Forum, Les Alyscamps and the International Photography exhibition.
**WHEN SHOULD I VISIT**
Arrive in the summer and see the races and bull fights put on in Les Arenes, the Roman arena.
**HOW DO I GET THERE**
Travel by train from Avignon, Marseille, Montpellier and Nimes.
**YOU SHOULD KNOW**
This is a UNESCO World Heritage Site.

Arles is situated on the banks of the River Rhône, just north of the Camargue and the Mediterranean. Its medieval buildings, Roman arena and treasure trove of other antiquities have drawn visitors here for centuries.

In the first century BC, Julius Caesar conquered Marseille and designated Arles a Roman colony. It quickly became a wealthy commercial centre and one of the main cities in the region. Arles continued to profit from its position on the river, which was a main trade route through France. However, once the empire had disintegrated, the city gradually became less important, which is perhaps one reason why its monuments remain so well preserved.

The ancient theatre was once able to hold 20,000 spectators, and nowadays is used as a concert venue. The Venus of Arles, now housed in the Louvre, was found here. The real splendour is the Roman arena, Les Arènes, which can still hold about 12,000 people, and dates from the end of the first century. In the eighth century it was turned into a fortified village, but its towers are virtually all that remain from that period. Today it is used for the bullfights and races that are put on in summer.

The Romanesque church of St-Trophime is a marvellous example of twelfth-century sculpture. The Last Judgement frieze around the doorway is internationally renowned, and beautiful Gobelins tapestries hang in the chapter house. The cloisters should not be missed – each carved column is a gem.

*The Roman arena.*

# The Camargue

The Camargue is a vast area of marshlands formed by the delta of the Grand Rhône and the Petit Rhône rivers as they near the Mediterranean Sea. It is a protected area, full of wildlife and rich with beauty. It is thought that the name derives from Caius Marius, a Roman general who owned large tracts of land here.

The grasslands and lagoons (étangs) are the home of the famous black bulls, which roam at will and are tended by *gardians*, the French equivalent of cowboys, who ride the unique Camargue horses, thought to be the descendants of an ancient breed. These are brown or black at birth but become white in their fourth year and, like the bulls, they also run free.

The whole area is rich in wildlife, with beavers, badgers, wild boar and, above all, birds. In all, 337 bird species can be found here, and the best known are the flamingoes, the symbol of the region. The Étang Fangassier is the only area in Europe where flamingoes breed in any number, and here up to 13,000 pairs breed annually.

The northern marshes were drained some 60 years ago, and re-filled with fresh water in order to grow rice. By the 1960s the Camargue produced 75 per cent of all the rice eaten in France. Other crops are also grown – wheat, vines and fruit, and to the east, where the Grand Rhône meets the sea, there is one of the largest salt works in the world. There are walking trails along some of the dykes, or you can rent a canoe or a horse for exploring.

*The famous wild horses of the Camargue.*

**WHAT IS THERE TO SEE**
Les Stes-Maries-de-la-Mer; the Romany festival in May; the Parc Ornithologique.
**WHAT IS IT KNOWN FOR**
The area is famous for the flamingos that breed here in large numbers.
**HOW DO I GET THERE**
By bus or car from Arles.
**WHEN SHOULD I VISIT**
The best times to go are from March to October.

# Old Marseille

Marseille, France's second city, has a difficult reputation, and is often avoided by travellers, but it is an exciting, colourful place, with a long history. It is thoroughly cosmopolitan in its mix of peoples and cultures and finally, after decades of decay, it is undergoing something of a revival – old buildings are being restored and the TGV train link with Paris has made the city much more accessible to weekenders.

The area around the old port of Marseille is the true heart of the place, and Le Panier, the old town, lies to its north. The boulevard La Canebière runs north-east from the port and around it is the colourful Maghrebi quarter, full of markets selling exotic vegetables, colourful African fabrics and pungent eastern spices.

Two fortresses stand guard over the harbour entrance, but the basilica of Notre-Dame de la Garde standing high above the city to the south of the port, is probably its best known landmark. The vast statue of the Madonna and Child, covered with gold leaf, that stands on top of the basilica tower can be seen far out to sea.

Le Panier is the oldest part of town, a rabbit warren of narrow streets and stone stairways but it suffered some serious damage during World War II when the Nazis used dynamite to clear the area of undesirables such as Jews and resistance fighters. Luckily, after the war, archaeologists discovered a Roman warehouse here, which has now been turned into a museum. At the top of Le Panier is the beautifully restored Hospice de la Vieille Charité, a seventeenth-century workhouse with a stunning Baroque chapel and pink stone arcades. The hospice is now home to two museums, and art exhibitions and concerts are held in the chapel.

*Boats in the old harbour.*

# St-Tropez

No visit to the Côte d'Azur would be complete without at least popping into St-Tropez for an hour or so, even at the height of summer when the traffic is dreadful and the port thronged with expensive looking sun-bronzed people and the harbour is choc-a-bloc with floating palaces.

In reality, St-Tropez was a charming little fishing village built around a port originally founded in 68 AD, when a Roman named Tropes was beheaded by the Emperor Nero for publicly proclaiming his Christianity. A boat carrying his body was sent out to sea and was washed up at what is now known as St-Tropez, which became a place of pilgrimage. Centuries later the Impressionist painter Paul Signac made his home here, and many of his contemporaries moved to Provence after having come to visit him. However, 1956, when Brigitte Bardot arrived to make a film and decided to stay, marked the beginning of its current fashionable status. Now dozens of celebrities have villas in the region, while the mega-rich live on board their ships anchored nearby.

St-Tropez is lucky enough to be near a good many sandy beaches, unlike much of the rest of the Côte d'Azur, and it also has lovely pastel-coloured houses and winding streets, squares surrounded by plane trees and old men playing *pétanque* in the shade. There are, of course, endless chic boutiques, restaurants and ice-cream parlours too, and you could do worse than people-watch from a harbour-side café. If you want to see the town when it is less crowded, come out of season, buy a picnic and a bottle of wine and enjoy it on the beach.

**WHAT IS IT KNOWN FOR**
Being the beach holiday destination of the rich and famous.

**WHAT IS THERE TO SEE**
Musée de l'Annonciade, the baie de Pampelonne and Ste-Maxime.

**YOU SHOULD KNOW**
The museum and some of the beaches charge entrance fees.

**WHEN SHOULD I VISIT**
The least crowded time is between October and May, but the summer months can be fun as floating palaces descend on the harbour and the rich and sun-bronzed flock to the beaches. This is the best time for people-watching!

*Night time in the harbour.*

*The period houses of Lübeck are reflected in the canal.*

# Lübeck

Lübeck, the second largest city in Schleswig-Holstein, in northern Germany, served as the capital of the Hanseatic League. Sited on the Trave River, it is the largest German port city on the Baltic Sea. Its old town is a well-preserved ensemble of churches, merchants' homes, narrow alleyways and warehouses that have been recognized by UNESCO as a World Heritage Site.

The old town of Lübeck, the heart of the city, is dominated by church steeples, showing how wealthy it once was and including the Cathedral (Dom), St Mary's (Marienkirche); St Peter's (Petrikirche); St Aegidien's (Aegidienkirche) in the craftsmen's district and St Jacob's (Jakobikirche), the seafarers' church. The oldest, the Dom and the Marienkirche date back to the thirteenth and fourteenth centuries.

Also in this area are the Stiftshöfe (almshouses), founded by rich merchants, as well as all of the major museums, including the St-Annenmuseum, Behnhaus, Günter Grass Haus, Museumkirche St Katherinen, Buddenbrookhaus, the Völkerkundesammlyng (ethnology), Museum für Natur und Umwelt (nature and the enviroment), Lübecker Theaterfigurenmuseum (theatrical puppets) and the Holstentor (the history of the city).

The old town's many narrow lanes and alleys are lined by Gothic, Renaissance, Baroque and Classical town houses with red-brick, gabled façades. The impressive Town Hall (Rathaus), still in use, and the Art Nouveau Stadttheater, the Heiligen-Geist-Hospital and the Schiffergesellschaft can also be found here. The sounds of Brahms and Mozart sometimes float through the windows of the Hochschule für Musik (college of music), lending another layer to the city's already heady European charms.

Boat trips round the beautiful harbour – the origin of the city's wealth and power – leave from the Holsten bridge (Holstenbrücke), opposite the old Salzspeicher (salt warehouses).

**WHAT IS IT**
The second largest city in Schleswig-Holstein in northern Germany.
**WHERE IS IT**
On the Trave River by the Baltic Sea.
**WHAT IS THERE TO SEE**
Home to the UNESCO-recognized old town.
**WHY IS IT IMPORTANT**
For its historical buildings and cultural importance.
**ALSO KNOWN AS**
In 1375, Emperor Charles IV named Lübeck one of the five 'Glories of the Empire', a title it shared with Venice, Rome, Pisa and Florence.
**WHAT SHOULD I BUY**
Lübeck is known for its marzipan.

# Bremen Market Place

Bremen, Germany's oldest coastal city, once a small fishing settlement, is now second only to Hamburg among the country's ports. Recognized as a UNESCO World Heritage Site, its Marktplatz (market place) is home to significant buildings dating back to the thirteenth century.

Bremen, the 'ancient town by the grey river,' was once known as the 'Rome of the north'. During the Middle Ages, it was one of the strongest members of the Hanseatic League, and in 1646 it became a free imperial city.

The town centre is protected by a 9-m (30-ft) statue known as Roland, bearing the 'sword of justice' and a shield decorated with an imperial eagle. It is believed that as long as the statue stands in the market place, Bremen will survive as a free city. To this end, when the area was under attack during World War II, great measures were taken to preserve the statue.

The Town Hall (Rathaus), looming above the market place, was developed during the Holy Roman Empire in the early fifteenth century. Built in the Gothic style, the building was renovated in the local 'Weser Renaissance' style in the early seventeenth century.

Across the square from the Rathaus stands the Schötting, a sixteenth-century guildhall, a mixture of Gothic and Renaissance architectural styles. In contrast to, but also complementing, this ancient masterpiece is the home to Bremen's parliament, the Haus der Bürgerschaft, a 1966 modern structure of glass, concrete and steel.

The Böttcherstrasse, running from Marktplatz to the Weser River, is a brick reproduction of a medieval alley, which has boutiques, cafés, a museum and art galleries. Designed to present a picture of life in Bremen life from the past and present, it was dedicated in 1926 and rebuilt after World War II. Kunstsammlungen Böttcherstrasse consists of two adjoining buildings: the Roselius-Haus, a sixteenth-century merchant's home with a collection of medieval objets d'art and furniture; and the Paula Modersohn-Becker Museum, dedicated to Bremen's outstanding artist and containing many of her best paintings, drawings and prints. The two upper floors also contain the works of the sculptor, painter, and architect Bernhard Hoetger.

**WHAT IS IT**
A port town once considered the 'Rome of the North' for its architectural treasures.
**WHERE IS IT**
119 km (74 mi) south-west of Hamburg, 122 km (76 mi) north-west of Hannover.
**WHAT IS THERE TO DO**
Wander along the river banks and through the brick-paved streets, visit the ancient market place with its magnificent buildings.
**ALSO KNOWN AS**
'The ancient town by the grey river'.

*Christmas fair in Bremen.*

# Berlin

*The Brandenburg Gate shows signs of Germany's past.*

Since the reuinification of Germany in 1990, Berlin has emerged from its sometimes dark past and reinvented itself as a vibrant, forward-looking, modern centre of culture and Europe's capital of cool. The city has more than 170 museums and galleries that cover subjects as diverse as old-master paintings, twentieth-century and contemporary art, ancient Egypt, the city's past, Bauhaus design and architecture, its Jewish residents, erotica, the ancient Greek architecture in the Pergamon Museum, technology, natural history, ethnology, Indian art and European culture, as well as its more recent history in the Haus am Checkpoint Charlie and the Berlin Wall Memorial. This is a memorial to those who died attempting the crossing from east to west and preserves areas from both inside and outside sections, where you can peer through from the east side to see the remains of the electric fence and anti-tank devices in the death strip.

Berlin is also a magnet for the young and its vibrant nightlife and club scene are second to none. Among its many annual festivals are PopKomm, Myfest and Christopher Street Day, the last of which is among Europe's largest gay pride festivals.

Berlin has a wealth of architecture of various periods and among other attractions are the rebuilt Schloss Charlottenburg, the Reichstag building – whose debating chamber has been covered with a glass dome so that visitors can look down over the debates, the Brandenburg Gate, and the Bundeskanzleramt – the seat of the German Chancellor and just one stunning example of the modern architecture with which Berliners are rebuilding their city.

The Kurfürstendamm is home to expensive boutiques and there are hundreds of stylish restaurants and cafés to choose from. For quieter relaxation, try the Tiergarten Park or take a stroll along Unter den Linden from the Brandenburg Gate to the river.

Berlin, both old and new, historical and modern, is a fascinating city well worth the trip.

# Cologne Cathedral

Cologne Cathedral (Hohe Domkirche St Peter und Maria) is one of Germany's most famous landmarks; its towers have been a friendly outline on the city's skyline since 1880. It is the third church on the site. The first was commissioned in the fourth century by Maternus, the first Christian bishop of Cologne and a second cathedral was completed in 818, but burned down in 1248.

In 1164, the Holy Roman Emperor, Frederick Barbarossa had presented the relics of the Magi to the Archbishop of Cologne, Rainald von Dassel and it was decided that these should become the focal point of the new building because of their importance to pilgrims. The foundation of the new building was laid by Archbishop Konrad von Hochstaden on 15 August 1248 and work continued on and off for another 632 years. Unusually, subsequent builders kept more or less to the original design style.

The cathedral is 144 m (472 ft) long, 86 m (282 ft) wide and the twin towers at the west end of the building reach a height of 157 m (515 ft), making it the largest church in Germany.

The reliquary in which the bones of the Magi are held is a large, gilded sarcophagus, made in the thirteenth century in the form of an aisled basilica. Its gold and silver decoration includes reliefs of episodes from the life of Christ as well as figures of apostles and prophets.

Among the cathedral's other treasures is the Gero Cross, the oldest monumental cross north of the Alps, which is well over 1,000 years old. The choir stalls and choir screen date to the fourteenth century. The figures on the latter were painted by Stephan Lochner. Despite the severe damage the cathedral sustained during World War II, there is a substantial amount of beautiful medieval stained glass, and the carvings both inside and out are magnificent.

The cathedral's scale is stunning, but its importance also lies in its long existence as a pilgrimage church and monument to the enduring faith of its builders.

*Cologne Cathedral looms over the Gross St Martinkirche and the Rhine.*

**WHAT IS IT**
One of Germany's most famous landmarks, the largest cathedral in the country.
**WHERE IS IT**
Central Cologne, Germany.
**WHAT IS THERE TO DO**
Wander through this historic cathedral and look at the stunning religious relics.
**WHAT IS THERE TO SEE**
The world's largest church façade and the Sarcophagus of the Magi.
**ALSO KNOWN AS**
Hohe Domkirche St Peter und Maria.
**YOU SHOULD KNOW**
Pre-booking a ticket for the guided tours is necessary – few are available on the day, especially for tours of the tower, roof or crypt.

*Walter Gropius's Bauhaus school building in Dessau.*

# Bauhaus

In the social and political turmoil after the end of World War I, Walter Gropius and a group of like-minded designers and artists, merged Weimar's art school with Henry van der Velde's College of Arts and Crafts to create a new design school, the Staatliche Bauhaus. The aim was to start a new style of design and architecture to suit the needs of what he saw as a new age, in which aesthetics, function and technology worked together to produce objects that were at once aesthetically pleasing, efficient and capable of being mass-produced cheaply. Products from the school included pottery, furniture and wallpaper.

The most important surviving Bauhaus buildings are in Dessau, where the school moved in 1925, and include the Bauhaus school complex itself, which is once again functioning as a design school, the Master Houses (Meisterhäuse), the Moses-Mendelssohn-Centre, the Steel House (Stahlhaus), the Kornhaus and a reconstruction of one flat in Hannes Meyer's 'housing with balcony access' complex. In Weimar, the original school building is home to the Bauhaus-Universität-Weimer and the Bauhaus museum has notable examples of Bauhaus furniture. Together these sites have been listed as a UNESCO World Heritage Site.

In Berlin, the Bauhaus archives and museum are located in a Walter Gropius-designed building. As well as a wealth of documents for researchers, the collection holds numerous pieces made in the workshops by students, as well as books, paintings, drawings, examples of finished products, architectural plans and a photographic archive. Other Bauhaus buildings in the city include the Sommerfeld and Otte houses.

One of the most important contributions of the Bauhaus is in the field of furniture design including the ubiquitous Cantilever chair by Dutch designer Mart Stam with its utilization of the tensile properties of steel, and the Wassily Chair designed by Marcel Breuer.

**WHAT IS IT**
A collection of important modern buildings, furniture and art.
**WHERE IS IT**
The most important surviving Bauhaus buildings are in Dessau and Berlin.
**WHY IS IT IMPORTANT**
These buildings are examples of the school of thought that revolutionized twentieth-century architecture and design.
**WHAT IS THERE TO SEE**
Sommerfeld house in Berlin, the Otte house in Berlin, the Auerbach house in Jena and the definitive 1926 Bauhaus building in Dessau.

# The Black Forest

The Black Forest, synonymous with cuckoo clocks, folklore and primeval woodland punctuated by charming, gabled fairy-tale cottages, is one of the most popular tourist centres of the German countryside.

The northern region, crossed by broad, densely wooded ridges, thickly forested slopes and small picturesque lakes, such as the Mummelsee and the Wildsee, includes the 270-km (167-mi) Black Forest Spa Route, linking many of the spas in the region, from Baden-Baden to Bad Wildbad. A trip to the area would not be complete without a soak in their warm waters! The lovely Nagold River is also here, as well as the ancient towns of Bad Herrenalb and Hirsau and the magnificent abbey at Maulbronn, near Pforzheim.

The Central Black Forest is home to the Simonswald, Elz and Glotter valleys as well as Triberg and Furtwangen, which have interesting cuckoo-clock shops and museums. The area around the Triberg Falls, the highest in Germany, is renowned for its traditional pom-pom hats, thatched farmhouses and mountain railways. The Schwarzwaldbahn (Black Forest Railway), which passes through Triberg, is one of the most scenic in all of Europe.

In the south you will find the most spectacular and dramatic mountain scenery in the area, culminating in the Feldberg, at 1,493 m (4,899 ft) the highest mountain in the Black Forest. The region also has two large glacial lakes, the Titisee and the Schluchsee. Freiburg, a romantic university city with vineyards producing dry Baden wines and a superb Gothic cathedral with its perfect spires, is also located here.

**WHAT IS IT**
A magical, fairy tale resort area amidst dense forests in Baden-Württemberg south-west Germany.

**WHAT IS THERE TO SEE**
Charming architecture in a dreamlike alpine setting.

**WHAT IS THERE TO DO**
Drink wine, hike, paddle in the rivers, visit a spa.

**WHAT SHOULD I BUY**
A cuckoo clock.

**WHEN SHOULD I GO**
Spring to autumn is the best time to visit.

**ALSO KNOWN AS**
Schwarzwald.

*Cows graze in a pasture near Titisee in the Baden-Württemberg region of Germany.*

# The Berchtesgaden National Park

Berchtesgaden National Park, the only alpine national park in Germany, is located in south-east Germany in Bavaria bordering on the Austrian state of Salzburg. Its high mountain landscapes are characterized by dense forests, steep rock faces, rugged cliffs, deep gorges and glaciers, complemented by idyllic pasture and gentle valleys.

The alpine regions of the south have been Bavarian territory since the early Middle Ages, when in the eleventh and twelfth centuries, numerous mountain villages were settled, including Berchtesgaden.

The Berchtesgaden National Park covers an area of 210 sq km (81 sq mi), including the Watzmann massif, which rises to an impressive 2,713 m (8,901 ft), and the Königssee, a gorgeous 5.2-sq-km (2-sq-mi) glacial lake surrounded by majestic mountains and favoured by the Bavarian royal family.

Another notable peak in the area is the 1,835-m (6,020-ft) Kehlstein with the Kehlsteinhaus, the Eagle's Nest, which was built as a present for Hitler's fiftieth birthday and provides incredible views across the valley. The nearby remnants of Hitler's complex at Obersalzburg are a popular destination.

The town of Berchtesgaden lies just north of the national park. Famed for its rich salt deposits, the town dates back to 1102 and at varioius times in its history has been under Austrian, French and Bavarian rule. Its salt mine attracts up to 40,000 visitors a year.

The national park, which was declared a UNESCO biosphere reserve in 1990, has populations of chamois, roe deer, red fox and griffon vultures. Bearded vultures, golden eagles and snow finches are more rarely spotted.

*The town of Berchtesgaden is in a valley below some of the most spectacular peaks in the Alps.*

**WHAT IS IT**
An area of stunning natural beauty from its craggy peaks to its luscious valleys.
**WHERE IS IT**
The German Bavarian Alps, a few kilometres from the Austrian border.
**WHAT IS THERE TO SEE**
Scenery, wildlife, the Eagle's Nest, Marktschellenberg ice cave.
**WHAT IS THERE TO DO**
Hike, swim, wander and enjoy the natural spoils around you
**WHEN SHOULD I GO**
Spring to autumn is the best time to visit.

# Neuschwanstein

Built on a 92-m (300-ft) hill, Neuschwanstein, the royal palace in the Bavarian Alps of Germany, is the most famous of the three royal palaces built for Louis II of Bavaria, sometimes referred to as 'Mad King Ludwig'.

Named after the Swan Knight of Wagner's opera *Lohengrin*, the castle was exquisitely designed by Christian Jank. Located near the Hohenschwangau, where Ludwig was brought up in south-western Bavaria near the Austrian border, the enormous and whimsical castle is so spectacular that it inspired Walt Disney to use it as a model for Cinderella's castle, used on the Disney logo.

Ludwig was removed from power before the completion of the castle, which was opened to the public after his mysterious death in 1886. An embodiment of nineteenth-century Romanticism, the castle is reached by a meandering road that leads from the valley to the front gate. The castle is a mixture of medieval detail, such as narrow spiral staircases and a plethora of turrets and towers, and advanced engineering features such as forced air heating, running water on all floors and toilets with an automatic flush.

After 17 years' work, only 14 of the 360 rooms were finished before Ludwig's death, but these alone are worth the trip.

The Throne Room was designed in elaborate Byzantine style as the Grail-Hall of Parsifal. Inspired by the Aya Sophia in Istanbul, the two-storey throne room has a series of pillars made of imitation porphyry and lapis lazuli.

Ludwig's obsession with the legends on which Wagner based his operas continues in the other rooms on this floor: *Tannhauser* in the study, grotto and conservatory, *Lohengrin* in the salon and study, the *Nibelungenlied* in the dining room and lower hall and the *Meistersinger von Nürnberg* in the dressing room. The bedroom, which is neo-Gothic in style, features paintings of scenes from *Tristan and Isolde*. The Singers Hall on the fourth floor, above the grotto, is also decorated with episodes from *Parsifal*.

But Neuschwanstein is about more than one man's obsession with his medieval ancestors, it is a beautiful, visionary place, which sits perfectly within the stunning landscape of the Bavarian Alps.

**WHAT IS IT**
A nineteenth-century castle in the Bavarian Alps and one of Germany's most popular tourist destinations.
**WHERE IS IT**
South-west Bavaria near the Austrian border.
**WHAT IS THERE TO SEE**
The whimsical castle that inspired the Disney Castle.
**FILM CONNECTION**
The 1968 film *Chitty Chitty Bang Bang* was partly filmed here.

*Neuschwanstein.*

# Aachen Cathedral

*Aachen Cathedral.*

The first part of Aachen Cathedral, frequently referred to as the 'Imperial Cathedral,' is the diminutive Palatine Chapel, which was begun in 786 by Charlemagne, then King of the Franks and later the first Western Roman Emperor for some 400 years. It is in the form of an octagon with a cupola, surrounded by a 16-sided ambulatory, and is based on the design of the Byzantine church of San Vitale in Ravenna, in Italy and includes some material looted from other buildings there. The oldest cathedral in northern Europe, it is recognized as a UNESCO World Heritage Site and combines architectural elements from Classical, Byzantine and Germanic-Franconian styles. When he died in 814, Charlemagne was buried here in a shrine.

According to legend, in 1100, Otto III had the vault opened and found his predecessor seated on his marble thrown, his crown on his head and with the gospels in his hand. In 1165, Emperor Frederick Barbarossa persuaded the antipope Paschal III to declare him a saint (although this was never ratified by Rome) and the chapel became a site of pilgrimage. That year, Barbarossa reinterred the remains in a Parian marble sarcophagus, and in 1215 Frederick II reburied them in a gold and silver casket.

The popularity of the shrine as a site of pilgrimage made it imperative for the building to be extended, and it is the Gothic 'glass chapel' or choir hall for which the cathedral is best known today. It was consecrated in 1414, on the six hundredth anniversary of Charlemagne's death. Where the original part of the building is dark and intimate, the expanses of stained glass in the new part mean that Charlemagne's golden shrine, which stands behind the high altar, is flooded with light. This spectacular setting was the site of the coronations of Holy Roman Emperors until 1531.

The Cathedral's Treasury holds what is regarded as some of the most important ecclesiastical treasures in northern Europe, including masterpieces of the late Classical, Carolingian, Ottonian and Romanesque periods – among them there are some unique exhibits such as the Cross of Lothair the Bust of Charlemagne and the Persephone sarcophagus.

# Monastic Island of Reichenau

For more than 1,000 years, the Benedictine complex on Reichenau Island in Lake Constance (the Bodensee) in southern Germany was an important religious site on the main trade route between Italy and Germany. It has been listed by UNESCO as a World Heritage Site because of its importance both as the best preserved ancient monastery north of the Alps and its role in the development of Christian art.

The monastery was founded by St Pirmin in 724 and the oldest remaining part of the church was consecrated in 816. In the tenth and eleventh centuries, it was home to an extensive library and a scriptorium where some of the best illuminated manuscripts of the period were created. It was an important educational centre for the empire's élite, received royal patronage – Emperor Charles III is buried here – and was gifted many important relics, some of which are still held in the monastic treasury. As well as the abbey church (St Maria und Markus), there are two other important churches on the island. St Georg, in Oberzell, dates back to the late ninth century and has the oldest and most complete Ottonian murals north of the Alps, showing the miracles of Christ. St Peter und St Pau, in Niederzell was built in the eleventh and twelfth centuries and is noted for the painting in the apse.

The island's museum is housed in a twelfth–fifteenth-century building, which is one of the oldest half-timbered buildings in southern Germany. In the past it has served as the monastery bailiff's court and the town hall. As well as telling the story of the monastery, it has exhibits about life on this tranquil island and the surrounding area.

**WHAT IS IT**
A UNESCO-listed abbey of historical and archaeological importance.
**WHERE IS IT**
Lake Constance in Baden-Württemberg in southern Germany, between the Gnadensee and the Untersee, west of the city of Konstanz.
**WHAT IS THERE TO SEE**
The Benedictine Abbey of Reichenau and other religious buildings.
**WHAT IS THERE TO DO**
Wander through the pastoral landscape and breathe in the history of this charming island.

*Part of the cloister of the Benedictine abbey.*

*The small town of Bacharach on the Rhine, with Stahleck Castle overseeing the area.*

# The Rhine Valley

The Middle Rhine Valley in western Germany, with its castles, historic towns and vineyards, has a dramatic and varied natural landscape, a natural timeline of the area's historical and cultural past and its sheer, majestic beauty.

A UNESCO World Heritage Site since 2002, the Upper Middle Rhine Valley (Oberes Mittelrheintal) is both beautiful and an outstanding example of how its role as one of the most important transport routes in Europe for thousands of years facilitated cultural exchange between the Mediterranean and the north.

The steep slopes of the river have been terraced for agriculture for hundreds of years, and the warm south-facing slopes make ideal areas for the cultivation of grapes for the region's famous wines and add to the beauty of the river valley.

The captivating views of the narrow valley, dotted with pretty towns and ruined castles and surrounded by towering mountains have made this one of Germany's most important areas for tourism. Its waters are plied by both commercial and pleasure craft, especially cruisers, and the banks are home to more than 20 castles and historic ruins. Only two of the many fortresses, Pfalzgrafenstein near Kaub-in-the-Rhine, and the Marksburg by Braubach, are well preserved, most of the rest of the historic buildings, such as the Werner Kapelle and the Chapel in Bacharach, were ruined long ago, while others have been converted into hotels.

One of the best-known attractions in the river, which is seen to advantage from a boat cruise, is the Lorelei rock near St Goarshausen. It rises 120 m (390 ft) above the water, and there are many legends about the water spirit who is said to lure men to their doom here.

Since the Age of Enlightenment, the remarkable beauty of the Middle Rhine has captured the imagination of musicians, artists and writers. The romantic visions of the crumbling feudal castles, the lush emerald valleys and the dramatic mountains have inspired poets, authors and composers such as Lord Byron, Alexandre Dumas, Victor Hugo and Richard Wagner.

**WHAT IS IT**
The scenic area surrounding the River Rhine in Germany, made famous by musicians, artists and writers.
**WHAT IS THERE TO SEE**
Ancient crumbling castles perched above the river banks, pretty medieval towns, beautiful romantic landscapes.
**WHAT IS THERE TO DO**
Wander through cobbled alleys, sip delicious wines at one of the many vineyards or take a boat cruise down the river.
**WORTH A SPLURGE**
Stay overnight in one of the restored castles.

# Keukenhof Gardens

Every spring, more than seven million blooms open at the famous Keukenhof Gardens, including 1,000 varieties of tulips alone. A showcase for the Dutch flower industry, the gardens draw nearly a million visitors a year anxious to glimpse this phenomenal show of vivid colours bursting throughout the 28-ha (70-acre) area. Daffodils, croci, narcissi, tulips and hyacinths in every combination of yellow, gold, purple, red, orange, and with heavenly scents, offer an unmatched spectacle.

The Keukenhof Gardens were established in Lisse in 1949, in the bulb-growing region between Amsterdam and The Hague, in the grounds of a long-ruined castle, where a countess with an enthusiasm for Dutch flowers had lived during the fifteenth century.

Interestingly the tulip, which everyone associates with the Netherlands, does not originate here. In fact, they were not brought to this country until 1593 at the request of the Flemish ambassador to Constantinople who was captivated by their beauty.

Stories of the special flower spread rapidly and wealthy Dutchmen began to invest in importing bulbs, creating a prosperous trade that lasted until the market crashed in 1637 when the tulip was no longer a rarity. The over-supply problem brought the prices down and many fortunes were lost.

Their production continued however and the tulip, together with lilies, gladioli, daffodils and many other decorative flowers, is once again one of the Netherlands most important export products.

**WHAT IS IT**
The showcase for the Dutch flower industry.
**WHERE ARE THEY**
The bulb-growing area between Amsterdam and The Hague.
**WHAT IS THERE TO SEE**
Flowers, flowers and more flowers.
**WHEN SHOULD I GO**
Late March to mid-May
**NOMENCLATURE**
Keukenhof means Kitchen Garden – in the 15th century the land belonged to the Countess of Holland, Jacoba van Beieren, who once used this estate to grow herbs and vegatables.

*Swathes of multicoloured tulips in the Keukenhof Gardens.*

# The Rijksmuseum

Home to nearly one million objects, Amsterdam's Rijksmuseum is the largest museum of art and history in the Netherlands. Designed by Pierre Cuypers and opened in 1885, the museum has become a city landmark with its combination of Gothic and Renaissance styles. Perhaps best known for its unrivalled collection of seventeenth-century Dutch Old Masters, the Rijksmuseum counts 20 Rembrandts and many other highlights of the period as part of its treasures, including works by Johannes Vermeer, Frans Hals and Jan Steen.

The Rijksmuseum draws more than one million visitors a year, and ranks as one of the major museums of Western European painting and decorative arts. More than 400 highlights from the Golden Age are on display, and the landscapes, seascapes, individual portraits, domestic scenes and Dutch still lifes offer a good overview of the Dutch Golden Age, the period in Dutch history roughly spanning the seventeenth century, when the country's trade, science and art were some of the best regarded in the world.

Originally founded in The Hague as the National Art Gallery in 1800, as a place to exhibit the collections of the Dutch heads of state, the museum was moved to Amsterdam in 1808 by order of King Louis Napoleon, brother of Napoleon Bonaparte. It was renamed the Rijksmuseum and the paintings then owned by the city, such as the revered Rembrandt masterpiece, *The Night Watch*, became a permanent part of the museum's collection.

Located on the scenic Museumplein, near the Van Gogh Museum and the Stedelijk Museum, the building houses a stunning array of art and artefacts including paintings from the fifteenth to the nineteenth centuries, photography, sculpture and decorative arts such as furniture, jewellery, earthenware, glassware, porcelain, costumes, textiles, silver and Delft Blue pottery.

**WHAT IS IT**
The largest museum of art and history in the Netherlands.
**WHERE IS IT**
The Museumplein in Amsterdam.
**WHAT IS THERE TO SEE**
An impressive collection of seventeenth-century Dutch masters, 20 Rembrandts and works by Johannes Vermeer, Frans Hals and Jan Steen.
**WHAT IS THE HIGHLIGHT**
Rembrandt's *The Night Watch*.

*The Rijksmuseum.*

*The new wing of the Van Gogh Museum.*

# The Van Gogh Museum

Van Gogh was a highly prolific artist, creating 864 paintings and nearly 1,200 drawings and prints during his ten-year career. Home to the largest collection of Van Gogh's work in the world, the Van Gogh Museum in Amsterdam exhibits more than 200 paintings, 437 drawings and 31 prints including the highly prized *Sunflowers*, *The White Orchard* and *The Yellow House*, as well as many of the artist's self-portraits. Other works by various renowned nineteenth-century artists can also be found here, among them Paul Gauguin, Henri de Toulouse-Lautrec, Léon Lhermitte and Jean-François Millet. New acquisitions by the museum include Kees van Dongen's *Portrait of Guus Preitinger* and two paintings by Monet that date from his Dutch period.

A visit to the Van Gogh Museum is a unique experience. The museum consists of two buildings: the original main structure, designed by Gerrit Rietveld, opened in 1973, and the Exhibition Wing by Kisho Kurokawa, completed in 1999. The different wings contrast with and complement one another, Kurokawa's modern elliptical building aside Rietveld's functionalist design.

The Van Gogh Museum faces Paulus Potterstraat and backs onto Museumplein. Until a few years ago this square was bisected by a busy road running from the Concertgebouw to the Rijksmuseum, and was otherwise featureless. Following a major facelift, the area is now a large, open expanse in the city where people can meet, stroll and discuss the works of art that they have just had the privilege to enjoy.

**WHAT IS IT**
The largest collection of Van Gogh's artwork in the world.
**WHERE IS IT**
On Museumplein in Amsterdam, between the Rijksmuseum and the Stedelijk Museum.
**WHAT IS THERE TO SEE**
*Sunflowers, The White Orchard, The Yellow House,* and many of his self portraits, as well as many other works by various artists.
**WHAT IS THERE TO DO**
Enjoy one of the greatest selections of nineteenth-century art in a beautiful setting.

372

# Amsterdam

Amsterdam, the largest city in the Netherlands, is known for its liberalism, stunning architecture, friendly locals, culture and history. It has winding canals, cobbled streets, some of the world's greatest art collections, fascinating old buildings and even cannabis and sex museums.

Amsterdam was founded as a fishing village near a dam in the Amstel River in the thirteenth century and developed rapidly. Few of its medieval buildings survive, except the Oude Kerk (the charming Old Church with small houses clinging to its sides and its octagonal bell tower), Neuwe Kerk (New Church) and the Houten Huis (Wooden House).

The Golden Age (1585–1672) was the high point of Amsterdam's commercial success and some of the most important buildings from this period are the classical Royal Palace on Damplein, the Westerkerk, Zuiderkerk, and many canal houses including De Dolfijn (Dolphin), De Gecroonde Raep (the Crowned Turnip), the Huis met de Hoofden (the House with the Heads) and the Poppenhuis. Most of the houses in the city centre date from the eighteenth century.

The most famous museums in Amsterdam, including the Van Gogh Museum, the Stedelijk Museum and the Rijksmuseum, are located around Museumplein.

The nightlife in Amsterdam is notorious, its throbbing centres include: the Leidseplein, home to many vibrant restaurants, clubs, traditional 'brown' bars, coffee shops, cinemas and theatres; the Jordaan which oozes atmosphere with its narrow streets, picturesque canals, coffee shops, galleries and boutiques; Rembrandtplein, lined with pubs, restaurants, cafés and hotels as well as traditional Dutch pubs playing real Dutch music; and the infamous Red Light District, with its legalized prostitution and raunchy clubs, strip joints and sex shops.

Nearly 1,300 bridges criss-cross the canals of this beautiful city, known as 'the Venice of the North'. The four main city centre canals are Prinsengracht, Herengracht, Keizersgracht and Singel, which are best enjoyed by taking a boat tour or exploring the surrounding streets by bicycle. There are also numerous smaller canals, of which the Brouwersgracht, the Bloemgracht and the Leliegracht are especially pleasant.There are also a number of beautiful parks, a highlight is the Vondelpark.

*The canals and houses of Amsterdam in the evening light.*

**WHAT IS IT**
The largest city in the Netherlands.
**WHAT IS THERE TO DO**
The city offers an incredible and dynamic diversity of attractions – cultural, historical or just plain fun.
**WHEN SHOULD I GO**
Between May and September.
**ALSO KNOWN AS**
The Venice of the North.

# Riga

**WHAT IS IT**
The Baltic's most cosmopolitan city.
**WHAT IS IT KNOWN FOR**
It has more Art Noveau buildings
than any other city in the world.
**WHAT IS THERE TO SEE**
Riga Castle, St. Peter's Church, Three
Brothers, Cat House,
St. John's Church.
**YOU SHOULD KNOW**
This is a Unesco World Heritage Site.

Latvia's capital, Riga, was founded in 1201, and over the following 800 years was occupied by Germans, Poles, Swedes and Russians. Latvia finally became an independent country in 1991 after long years of Soviet domination, since when Riga has become the Baltic's most cosmopolitan city. Its cultural claim to fame is that it has more Art Nouveau buildings than any other city in the world.

Riga is full of architectural gems, both ancient and relatively modern. Possibly the best examples of medieval residential buildings are the Three Brothers, a picturesque row of houses, the oldest of which was built in the fifteenth century. The Doma Cathedral dominates the old town. It was founded in 1211 and has been partially destroyed and then restored several times since then. The old town is full of streets and squares of sixteenth- and seventeenth-century German buildings, decorated with carvings and statues, and it is a joy to wander here. The House of Blackheads, *Melngalvju nams* (a guild of unmarried, foreign merchants), is a fabulous reconstructed Gothic building, now used for state meetings.

The Art Nouveau buildings stand just outside the old city. Whole streets here are lined with flamboyant architectural beauties. The gorgeous group of buildings on Alberta Street (Alberta iela) was designed by Mikhail Eisenstein, father of the celebrated Russian film-maker Sergei Eisenstein, and the blue-and-white façade of the School of Economics is another highlight.

Apart from its historic centre, which is a UNESCO World Heritage Site, Riga is home to numerous academic institutions and is of major commercial and industrial importance in the Baltic region. Since the advent of cheap European airfares it has become a popular holiday destination, offering something for everyone.

*The Daugava River flows through the centre of Riga.*

# Oktoberfest

The Oktoberfest is the largest beer festival in the world, attracting up to six million visitors annually to the beer gardens of Munich, Germany every September–October. A truly riotous festival with crowds that rival those of Carnival in Rio, this event has inspired many celebrations around the world, but there is only one true Oktoberfest!

The first Oktoberfest took place on 12 October 1810, in celebration of the marriage of Prince Ludwig of Bavaria to Princess Therese of Sachsen-Hildburghausen. All of the citizens of Munich were invited to a meadow in front of the city tower, to raise a glass or two in honour of the union, and this became an annual tradition.

In the early years horse races were held in the local fields, but as the festival grew, the focus began to change. In 1896, businessmen working with the Munich breweries built the first giant beer tents for the Oktoberfest and drinking has been the primary objective of the festivities ever since.

Nowadays, enormous tents are filled with teeming throngs of locals and visitors from all around the world, and traditional musicians lead the crowds in well-known drinking chants.

The extra-strong Oktoberfest beer (or wiesn) is brewed by a handful of local breweries, and is served in traditional one-litre (2.1-pint) mugs called *mass*. As well as drinking roughly six million glasses of wiesn, the crowd gets through some 91 oxen, 383,000 sausages and 630,000 chickens as well as tonnes of local favourites such as cheese noodles and sauerkraut.

There is no better city to host this alcohol-filled extravaganza than fun-loving Munich.

**WHAT IS IT**
The largest beer festival in the world.
**WHERE IS IT**
Munich, in Bavaria, southern Germany.
**WHAT IS THERE TO DO**
Drink beer, listen to the traditional Bavarian music, watch the parades, go for a ride on a big wheel.
**WHAT IS THERE TO SEE**
Beer maidens hoisting large, heavy glasses to the heaving crowds.
**WHY IS IT IMPORTANT**
It is not actually important, except for its tradition, but it is fun!
**IRONY**
Oktoberfest actually starts in late September.

*Beer drinkers raise their glasses for the annual beer festival. Roughly six million people attend the festivities.*

# West Norwegian fjords

Two of Norway's most spectacular fjords, Geirangerfjord and Naeroyfjord lie 120 km (75 mi) apart in south-west Norway, north-east of Bergen. They are among the world's longest and deepest fjords, and are of exceptional natural beauty.

Geirangerfjord and Naeroyfjord are possibly the best known of Norway's natural wonders. They were formed about 1,000,000 years ago by glaciers that carved their way down through the mountains, forming deep chasms. The ice was at its thickest inland, which is why fjords are deeper inland than they are nearer the sea.

Geirangerfjord is a large fjord, about 16 km (10 mi) long. The water is saline, so it does not freeze during the long winter months. There is virtually no tide, so the waters are still and beautiful, reflecting the sky, the 2,000-m (6,600-ft) mountain walls on either side, and the famous rock formation that stands at the head of the fjord. Cruise ships visit, and as they wind their way up they pass magnificent waterfalls as well as abandoned farms perched precariously on the mountainsides.

Naeroyfjord is said to be the narrowest in the world. It is an arm of the Sognefjord, Norway's longest, which extends 200 km (125 mi) inland. At one point it is less than 250 m (820 ft) wide, with the steep-sided crystalline rock walls of the mountains towering some 1,500 m (4,900 ft) above the water. During the winter months the sun never reaches the bottom of the fjord. You may see seals lying on the rocks or goats – which belong to one of the small, traditional farms here – grazing along the steep slopes.

*Naeroyfjord is one of the longest and deepest in the world.*

**WHERE ARE THEY**
The fjords lie 120 km (75 mi) apart in south-west Norway, north-east of Bergen.
**WHAT ARE THEY**
Two of the worlds most beautiful fjords.
**WHAT IS THERE TO SEE**
The Sogne fjord, Flam Railway, Stalheimskleiva.
**DO NOT MISS**
Taking a trip down the fjords and looking out for seals lying on the rocks.

*Aurora borealis.*

# Norway's Midnight Sun and Aurora Borealis

The Arctic Circle is an imaginary line drawn at 66.5 degrees north, which denotes the southernmost limit of the area where the Midnight Sun is visible in summer. This line, however, includes the relatively mild, forested lands of Norway while excluding the seemingly Arctic regions of Hudson's Bay in Canada and southern Greenland.

The city of Tromsø is some 350 km (220 mi) north of the Arctic Circle, and here you can experience both Midnight Sun and Polar Night. From 21 May to 21 July the Sun never sets, but there is no real darkness between late April and mid-August, merely an extended twilight. Conversely, between 21 November and 21 January the sun never rises above the horizon, although there is always an hour or two of marvellous blueish twilight.

Svalbard is a group of islands lying just 1,000 km (620 mi) south of the North Pole. More than 40,000 people come here every year to experience life in the Arctic. At its largest settlement, Longyearbyen, the Midnight Sun can be seen from April to August.

The aurora borealis is easily seen during the winter from both Tromsø and Svalbard, though this can never be guaranteed. The phenomenon occurs when plasma particles from the sun are trapped in the ionosphere above the earth's surface, resulting in surreal light shows that ripple in curtains overhead. Ranging from light green to dark red depending on their height and varying in intensity and shape, these shifting, otherworldly lights dance and crackle their way across the night sky in one of nature's most stunning spectacles.

**WHEN SHOULD I VISIT**
For aurora borealis go during autumn, winter or spring. Polar Night occurs from November to February and the Midnight Sun occurs between 21 May and 21 July.
**WHAT IS THERE TO SEE**
Saltfjellet-Svartisen National Park.
**HOW DO I GET THERE**
By air from Oslo or Bergen.
**WHAT SHOULD I KNOW**
The aurora borealis can sometimes be seen farther south, especially in North America.

# The Lofoten Islands

The Lofoten Islands are an archipelago situated off the north Norwegian coast, high above the Arctic Circle. They rise from the green water like a wall, to a height of about 1,000 m (3,300 ft), and are fringed with white sandy beaches. The scenery here is magnificent but the population of the five main islands is only about 25,000.

The main source of income for the islanders comes from fishing, in particular, cod. Known as 'sprei', mature Norwegian Arctic cod that are ready to spawn arrive at Lofoten towards the end of January, migrating here from the Barents Sea. Some of the large females can be as long as 2 m (6 ft) and their roes will contain about 5 million eggs. Some 4,000 fishermen are there to catch as many as they can, and so are pods of orca, looking for an easy meal.

Back on the shore, the cod are hung on poles to dry, and it is an amazing sight to see. While cod stocks have been destroyed in other parts of the world's oceans, this region, which has been a substantial fish trading area for more than 1,000 years, is not badly affected.

Off the coast of Moskenesoy, the farthest island, is another natural phenomenon. This is a whirlpool known as the Maelstrom, caused by the meeting of several fast currents. This whirlpool was first mentioned 2,000 years ago by the Greek explorer Pytheas, and subsequently noted on sea charts with terrifying illustrations.

Tourism is another source of income here, and visitors can take adventure tours to see the Maelstrom and other sights such as the awe-inspiring Refsvikhula Cave with its stone age wall paintings. There are seal colonies and sea eagles, puffins and otters to be seen here and the mountains are wonderful for hiking and climbing, with superb views over the jagged peaks.

**WHAT IS THERE TO SEE**
The villages of Flakstad and Moskenes, Kabelvag Cathedral, the Lofoten Museum.
**WHAT IS THERE TO DO**
Take an adventure tour out to Maelstrom.
**HOW DO I GET THERE**
By air or sea from Oslo or Bergen.
**WHEN SHOULD I VISIT**
The best conditions are from March to October.

*A small harbour on the Lofoten islands.*

# Urnes Stave Church

The Urnes Stave Church is in Sogn county, north of Bergen. It was built in about 1130 and is believed to be the oldest of its kind. Architecturally it provides a link between the Vikings, with their animal-motif decoration, and Christian religious design. Archaeological evidence suggests that this is the third church on the site and that the two previous ones were simple post churches, created by ramming posts into the ground, walling between them and roofing them. Beneath the remnants of the first church are the remnants of Christian graves, evidence of the conversion of the Vikings to Christianity.

The survival of this wooden church for nearly 900 years is unusual enough, but its highlights are even older and include a fantastically carved wooden doorway, some planking, two gables and a corner post, which are thought to be from one of the earlier churches dating to the eleventh century. The wood is fantastically carved. The doorway portrays a four-legged animal (often known as a biting beast, and possibly meant to represent a lion) biting a snake that curls sinuously upwards among intertwining foliage. It is presumed to symbolize the fight between Christ and Satan, although no-one knows. This style of decoration became known farther south as the Vikings travelled and was influential in the development of Romanesque sculpture. Inside, as well as a twelfth-century altarpiece that depicts the Crucifixion are the remains of a later decorative scheme.

The church has been altered to over the centuries: the original roof would have been open, like an upturned boat but a roof was added towards the end of the seventeenth century.

*LEFT: The twelfth-century Urnes Stave Church.*

*ABOVE: Details of the carvings on the doorway.*

# Rock Carvings in Tanum

Northern Bohuslan is about two hours' drive north of Gothenburg, along Sweden's west coast and here you will find the amazing Bronze-Age petroglyphs, or rock carvings, of Tanum. This is an area where rock carvings are being discovered all the time, but the 350 separate and very varied groups carved in the flat rock here make it unique.

The site was not discovered until 1972, when Age Nilsen, a construction worker, found the first site, exactly where he had been planning to place an explosive charge. The carvings are thought to have been made between 1800-600 BC. They are in four distinct groups along a 25-km (15.5-mi) stretch of what was once a fjord, but which today is about 25 m (80 ft) above sea level. Archaeologists have found 13 types of motifs and figures, including ships, sleighs, people, weapons, animals and trees. They are thought to be single images for the most part, but there are several which have obviously been composed. One, the Fossum carving, has 130 closely ranged figures, none of which overlaps, and there are hunting scenes with beautifully carved animals, boats carrying passengers and people farming. They give an intimate look at the daily life and beliefs of Bronze-Age people.

Sadly these carvings are in danger because the action of frost, heat, sea salt and air pollution is beginning to crack the rocks and damage is occurring despite efforts being made to preserve and protect them. Additionally, a planned new road through the area would irreparably damage this UNESCO World Heritage site.

**WHAT IS THERE TO SEE**
Vitlycke Museum (May–September), Vitlycke Rock, Aspeberget, Torsbo and Greby Gravfalt.
**WHAT IS THERE TO DO**
Explore the rocks and discover rock carvings dating back to the Bronze Age.
**HOW BIG IS IT**
The carvings are along a 25-km (15.5-mi) stretch.
**HOW DO I GET THERE**
By road from Gothenburg.

*Rock carvings of long ships and hunters, Fossum.*

*Gamla Stan and
Riddarholm Church.*

# Stockholm

Swedish people say that Stockholm is made up of one-third water, one-third parkland and one-third buildings, and their lovely capital is in an amazing location, on a series of islands on the edge of the Baltic Sea.

In 1252, the Swedish statesman Birger Jarl erected a fortress on the small island of Gamla Stan, where the Royal Palace stands today. He chose this site because it would help in the defence of the narrow passage leading from the Baltic to Lake Mälaren, and the settlement that grew up around the fortress eventually became the Stockholm that we see today. By 1436 it was the capital city and Sweden, Norway and Denmark, together with Finland, Iceland and Greenland formed one huge Scandinavian kingdom. It was not until 1523 that the first independent King of Sweden, Gustav Vasa, was crowned. Today Sweden still has a royal family but one without any political power.

The old town (Gamla Stan) retains its medieval street plan, while the city has buildings in almost every western European style. An interesting feature is that the city fathers have tried to ensure that houses are painted in their original colour, so many seventeenth-century buildings are red, and eighteenth century buildings are yellow. Off white and grey buildings tend to be much more recent and are in the outer boroughs. All of this makes the city really visually attractive. There are several royal palaces, including the Baroque Drottningholm and Kungliga Slottet. Museums include the National Museet, which has a wide range of fine art, the Modern Museet, which has works by, among others, Picasso and Dalí, the Vasamuseet, which has the famous reconstruction of an ancient ship and the Nordiska Museet, dedicated to the culture and ethnography of Sweden.

**WHAT IS IT**
The capital of Sweden.
**WHAT IS THERE TO SEE**
Kungliga Slottet and Gamla Stan,
Stadshuset, Vasamuseet.
**WHAT IS IT KNOWN FOR**
Colourful buildings painted in their
original colours.

# Bern

Wandering through the UNESCO World Heritage Site of Bern's Old Town can be a magical and surreal experience, because its architecture and street plan are essentially unchanged since the late Middle Ages. Founded in the twelfth century on a hillside by the River Aare, Bern (or Berne) has a variety of architectural styles and characteristics representative of its long history including thirteenth-century arcades and sixteenth-century fountains. Largely restored in the eighteenth century, Bern has managed to retain its original charm and character.

According to legend, in 1191, Duke Berchtold V of Zähringen commanded nobleman Cuno von Bubenberg to build a city on the narrow, oak-covered peninsula, Von Bubenberg felled the forest and used the wood to build his town. After a disastrous fire in 1405, new buildings were built in sandstone and by the sixteenth and seventeenth centuries most houses had been updated in the new material.

The bear featured on the city coat of arms first appeared in 1224. Legend has it that the city was named after the first animal killed by the duke while he was out hunting. Along with the clock tower, the bear has continued to be the symbol of Bern to this day.

An imposing presence at the centre of the old town, the Zytglogge, or Clock Tower, is both the benchmark of official Bern time as well as the point from which all distances in the canton are measured.

Below the main east face of the clock is an intricate astronomical and astrological device, which displays a 24-hour clock, the 12 hours of daylight, the position of the sun in the zodiac, the day of the week, the date and the month, the phases of the moon and the elevation of the sun above the horizon throughout the year.

A few moments before the hour, mechanical figures appears from inside the clock, including a crowing cock, a parade of bears, Chronos with his hourglass and a dancing jester. The interior workings of the clock are impressive and guided tours allow you to explore the spire and enjoy the rooftop view.

Other beautiful buildings include the fifteenth-century Gothic cathedral – the Berner Münster – and town hall. The Rosengarten, on a hill overlooking the old town, offers panoramic views of this beautiful, atmospheric city.

**WHAT IS IT**
A city centre that dates back to the twelfth century, and is largely unchanged since then.
**WHERE IS IT**
In north-west Switzerland.
**WHAT IS THERE TO SEE**
The beautiful old city, the bear pits, the astronomical clock.
**WHAT IS THERE TO DO**
Go shopping in the vast covered markets.

*The historic clock tower and fountain.*

# Geneva

Geneva (or Genève) is known for many things: lakeside scenery, watches, knives and cutlery, chocolate, fondue and for being the site of several UN agencies. A stunning city in the shadows of the Alps, Geneva is a historical town filled with many interesting attractions.

In the lake the monumental Jet d'Eau is one of the symbols of Geneva, its waters spurting an impressive 140 m (459 ft) into the air. Once an overflow valve for hydroelectricity generated on the Rhône River, it was turned into a fountain in 1891.

Originally built to house the League of Nations, the Palais des Nations is worth visiting to see its magnificent Assembly Hall, large art collection, library and landscaped grounds.

St-Pierre, the medieval cathedral on the highest point in the Old Town once served as the guiding centre for the Reformation. Excavations have revealed remains dating back to the fourth century.

The city's museums include the thought-provoking Museum of the International Committee of the Red Cross and the Musée d'Art Moderne et Comtemporain, which has modern and post-modern works.

Geneva is renowned for its open spaces, and the Parc des Eaux Vives offers promenades and spectacular views over the lake to the UN campus and the Palais des Nations. Geneva beach is at the end farthest from the city, on the lakefront. Most of the wooded bluff of Bois de la Batie has been left in its natural state, although walking trails have been added around the edges. There is a small zoo at the western edge of the woods.

Lake Geneva (Lac Léman) is hard to ignore anywhere in the city. One of the largest lakes in Western Europe, it lies on the course of the Rhône River on the frontier between France and Switzerland, between the Jura mountains in the north, a hilly plain in the centre and the Alps in the south-west.

The clear azure lake covers 582 sq km (225 sq mi). The easiest way to travel around the lake is to cross it by boat, and the popular steam ships have been here since 1823. Nearly all the cities, hamlets and towns along the lake have landing quays with service usually running from Easter through October.

For decades, visitors have sought the scenic wonders of Lake Geneva including native son Jean-Jacques Rousseau who popularized the lake among the Romantics, and Lord Byron and Shelley both made pilgrimages here.

*Springtime in Geneva.*

# The Jungfrau

The Jungfrau is the highest peak of the Jungfrau massif in the Bernese Oberland region of the Swiss Alps overlooking Grindelwald. At an elevation of 4,158 m (13,642 ft), it is surrounded by two other notable peaks, the Eiger and the Mönch.

*View across the Swiss Alps towards the Eiger, Mönch and Jungfrau mountains.*

The summit was first reached by the Meyer brothers from Aarau in 1811, but now it is much easier as the Jungfraubahn cog railway runs inside the mountain up to the Jungfraujoch railway station, which, at a height of 3,454 m (11,333 ft), is the highest in Europe.

The first step in the journey up to the peak is the Wengernalp railway (WAB), a rack-and-pinion railway that opened in 1893 that takes you to Lauterbrunnen at 784 m (2,612 ft), where you change to a train heading for the Kleine Scheidegg station at an elevation of 2,029m (6,762 ft). From here you can view the Mönch, the Eigerwand and the Jungfrau and change to the highest rack railway in Europe, the Jungfraubahn. Some 6.4 km (4 mi) of its 9.6-km (6-mi) journey is through a tunnel carved into the mountain. There are two brief stops – at Eigerwand 2,830 m (9,400 ft) and Eismeer 3,110 m (10,368 ft) – where you can view the sea of ice from windows in the rock. As you emerge into the dazzling sunlight, you reach the Jungfraujoch terminus.

There are a lot of activities in this high alpine wonderland, but be warned, the altitude means that the air is thin and you may need to take things slowly. Fortunately, there is a lift to the famous Ice Palace (Eispalast), a series of caverns hewn from the slowest moving section of glacier on the mountain. Built 19 m (65 ft) below the glacier's surface in 1934 by a Swiss guide and subsequently enlarged and added to by other artists, this is an icy-blue fairytale museum filled with life-sized replicas of everything you can imagine from vintage automobiles to local chaplains!

Back at the station, you can take another lift via the Sphinx Tunnel to the observation deck of the Sphinx Terraces at an elevation of 3,550 m (11,647 ft). Nestled between the Mönch and Jungfrau peaks, here you can see the Aletsch Glacier, a 23-km (14-mile) river of ice, the longest in Europe, as the ice slowly melts into the high Rhône River before flowing into Lake Geneva and eventually making its way to the Mediterranean.

**WHAT IS IT**
The highest peak in the Jungfrau massif.
**WHERE IS IT**
In the Bernese Alps of western Switzerland.
**WHAT IS THERE TO DO**
Look at the views and visit the Ice Palace.
**WHAT SHOULD I KNOW**
Not for the faint of heart, Jungfrau's railway station is at an elevation of 3,454 m (11,333 ft)!

# Wengen

The Swiss holiday resort of Wengen, nestling at the foot of the imposing peaks of the Eiger, Mönch and Jungfrau is a stunning area of natural beauty.

A completely car-free area, this pretty village in the Bernese Oberland is part of the Jungfrau region as well as the UNESCO World Heritage Site of Jungfrau.

Tourists first came to Wengen by rail during the nineteenth century *en route* from Lauterbrunnen to the Wengernalp, Kleine Scheidegg and Grindelwald. The first guest house appeared in the 1890s and proved to be so popular following the development of the Wengernalp Mountain Railway, that a further 30 resorts were built over the next two decades.

This era of prosperity, albeit interrupted by the war, continued, encouraging further growth of transport facilities including cable-cars, chairlifts and more railway construction. Once a sleepy farming village, Wengen has become a stunning chalet-style resort town that has managed to retain its quaint charms and character including its beautiful reformed church.

Wengen, the ideal place to relax, walk and mountain climb, is also home to the most difficult marathon in the world, the International Jungfrau Marathon. Every September thousands of runners from many countries scramble around the high elevations attempting to make the best time over this difficult terrain.

Ideally located in the ski centre of Kleine Scheidegg-Männlichen with its famed Lauberhorn and Eigergletscher runs, Wengen is not just a summer destination, it is one of the most attractive and popular winter sports villages in Switzerland. The most challenging and exciting downhill races in the World Cup circuit take place every January in the Lauberhorn Downhill Ski Race.

Whether you're a skier, an après skier, a hiker or someone who just enjoys taking in scenic landscapes for a breath of fresh mountain air, Wengen is a beautiful place to visit at any time of year.

**WHAT IS IT**
A Swiss holiday resort at the foot of the Eiger-Mönch-Jungfrau range.
**WHERE IS IT**
The heart of the Bernese Oberland in western Switzerland.
**WHAT IS THERE TO DO**
Every outdoor activity imaginable.
**WHEN SHOULD I VISIT**
The scenery is fabulous throughout the year here.

*The Jungfraujoch and Lauterbrunnen Valley seen from Wengen.*

# The Old Man of Hoy

**WHAT IS THERE TO SEE**
Spectacular scenery and amazing wildlife.
**WHAT IS THERE TO DO**
Take a trip around the shore and be amazed at the sheer volumes of sea birds and seal colonies.
**IF YOU DARE**
Climb the Old Man of Hoy.
**HOW DO I GET THERE**
Travel by air to Kirkwall, then take a ferry. There is also a car ferry service that runs from Aberdeen and Lerwick.

Orkney is made up of about 70 islands off the north coast of Scotland, of which fewer than 20 are inhabited. Hoy is the second largest of the islands after Mainland. It is the only island that is not flat, and the views from its hills are of moorland, vivid green turf and vertical cliffs reaching down to white sand beaches and turquoise bays. The Old Man of Hoy is a rock stack 137 m (450 ft) tall on a promontory in the sea, and it is a favourite of rock climbers from around the world. The first successful recorded climb was made in 1966 by Chris Bonnington's team. If you walk from the pier along the road through the lovely Rackwick Glen you will pass the Dwarfie Stone, an unusual rock cut tomb, and thought to be 5,000 years old.

The remoteness of the Orkneys and their untamed landscape make them a haven for wildlife. The northern part of Hoy has been a Royal Society for the Preservation of Birds reserve for more than 20 years. At the right time of year, visitors can see seal colonies, porpoises and even otters, if they are fortunate, but they will surely see some of the millions of seabirds including puffins that thrive on the cliffs and shores. Botanists will find rare and beautiful wildflowers, and fishermen can fish for free – the brown trout are supposedly the best in Britain.

*The Old Man of Hoy, Orkney Islands.*

# The Scottish Highlands

The Highlands were created millions of years ago, when Europe and North America, having been one huge landmass, began to move apart and the distinct regions reflect their different underlying geology: sandstone, limestone, granite and basalt.

Ben Nevis, which lies within the Lochaber region of Scotland, is the highest mountain in the British Isles, reaching 1,344 m (4,410 ft), and overlooks the beautiful valley of Glen Nevis. This is an area as popular with serious climbers and hikers as it is with amateurs, but hiking up Ben Nevis is certainly a serious undertaking, and the barren summit of the mountain is often shrouded with thick, cold mist. The lower slopes are covered in native pine, oak and beech and home to many different kinds of wildlife. Farther up, the trees give way to moorland hosting wild thyme and bilberries. Near the summit only the toughest lichens and mosses can survive the near arctic conditions that prevail in winter.

In winter, the areas round Aviemore and Glencoe are popular for skiing and snowboarding.

Soaring peaks, broken boulders tumbling down sheer rock faces, dark glens and forbidding castles, sparkling streams and purple heather, golden eagles and deer – all this and more makes up this majestic part of the world.

*Ben Nevis, the highest mountain in Britain at 1,343 m (4,406 ft), is at the north end of Loch Linnhe.*

**WHAT IS IT**
A region of mountains running across Scotland, of which Ben Nevis is the highest.
**WHAT IS THERE TO SEE**
Magnificent lochs, beautiful castles, Inverness, Fort William, Glencoe.
**IF YOU DARE**
Hike up Ben Nevis, the highest mountain in Britain.
**HOW DO I GET THERE**
It is best to travel by car.

*Eilean Donan Castle,*
*Loch Duich.*

# The Scottish Lochs

There are hundreds of stunning lochs splashed like raindrops all over Scotland and exploring them all could take a lifetime – this is some of the most beautiful landscape in the British Isles. The lochs were formed during the last Ice Age, which sculpted this dramatic landscape in combination with ancient volcanic activity. Loch Lomond is the largest and contains the greatest area of fresh water in the British Isles. Its shores are lined with native oakwoods and its waters are home to 17 native species of fish. Loch Lomond is the centrepiece of the Loch Lomond and Trossachs National Park. It is 39 km (24 mi) long and incredibly beautiful. However, as it is so easily accessible from Glasgow, it is often very busy.

To the west of Loch Lomond, on the far side of the Cowal Peninsula, lies the sea loch Loch Fyne, which is renowned for its oysters and its sea fishing. A short distance north of the head of the loch is the Bentmore Botanic Garden. Affiliated with Edinburgh's Royal Botanic Garden it is particularly famous for its wonderful show of rhododendrons in the late spring.

The most famous loch, located in the Scottish Highlands, is, of course, Loch Ness, thanks to the Loch Ness monster, which was first mentioned by Saint Adomnán of Iona (627/8–704). Although the deep waters have been explored many times during the last 70 or so years, with up-to-the-minute technology, the monster has not been found.

**WHAT IS IT**
The lochs of Scotland provide some of the most beautiful scenery in the country and are scattered around the Highlands of Scotland.
**WHAT IS THERE TO DO**
Whether you like fishing, sailing or enjoying freshly caught, local food there is something for everyone in this beautiful setting.
**WHAT IS THERE TO SEE**
Urquhart, Loch Leven and Eilean Donan castles, Culloden Moor.
**HOW DO I GET THERE**
It is best to travel by car so you can see as many lochs as possible and enjoy the surrounding scenery.

# Edinburgh Castle

Edinburgh Castle is situated on the crags of Castle Rock, perfectly positioned to defend itself against incursions from countless numbers of invaders from Roman times right up to the middle of the eighteenth century. Not only has the castle served a military purpose but it was also a royal residence, beginning in the eleventh century with King Malcolm Canmore and Queen Margaret. St Margaret's Chapel, one of the oldest roofed buildings in Scotland, is said to have been built by her when she moved to the castle, although it could have been built by one of her sons in memory of their mother.

The castle has a dramatic and bloody history – before you even reach the Portcullis Gate, near the entrance to the Esplanade beneath, you pass the Witches' Well where over 300 witches were burned some 250 years ago. Just before the gate itself is a memorial to Sir William Kirkaldy who was implicated in the murders of Cardinal Beaton and David Rizzio, Mary Queen of Scots' secretary, and who was later hanged. Above the gate is Constable's or Argyll's Tower where the Marquess of Argyll was imprisoned before his execution in 1661.

The Scottish Crown Jewels are held in the Crown Room. These are the oldest surviving crown jewels in the British Isles. The jewelled crown is made of Scottish gold and last used by Charles II in 1651. In 1707 they were packed away after the Act of Union and were rediscovered by Sir Walter Scott, the novelist, just over 100 years later. The Stone of Destiny (the Stone of Scone) is also to be seen here since its return in 1996, having spent 700 years beneath the Coronation Chair in Westminster Abbey.

**WHAT IS IT**
Edinburgh's most iconic image dating back to the eleventh century.
**WHAT IS THERE TO SEE**
The Royal Mile, Arthur's Seat, Camera Obscura, Kirk of the Greyfriars, the Scottish Parliament, the Palace of Holyroodhouse.
**YOU SHOULD KNOW**
There are entrance fees.

*The castle sits on an extinct volcano and was probably the site of the city's first settlement.*

# Durham Castle and Cathedral

**DON'T MISS**
No visit to Durham would be complete without a visit to the stunning cathedral.
**WHAT IS THERE TO SEE**
Bishop Auckland, Raby Castle, Barnard Castle, Alnwick.
**WHAT IS THERE DO**
Make sure you have a walk around the city and take in cobbled streets and interesting architecture.
**WHERE IS IT**
24 km (15 mi) south of Newcastle in northern England.

Durham is a small and exquisite city set on a hilltop peninsula on a bend of the River Wear in north-east England. A lively university town since the early nineteenth century, its main attractions are its glorious Romanesque cathedral, founded in 1903, and its castle, originally built in 1072. Surrounding both these buildings is a maze of little cobbled streets and lovely walks down to the river.

Durham Castle was the home of the prince bishops of Durham, (so called by William the Conqueror in order to pacify both the locals and the Scots), right up until 1837 when it became the original college of the just-founded university, and it remains a university hall to this day. Each prince bishop added and changed the castle in the centuries that followed its inception, but as it was built of soft stone onto soft ground it needed constant restoration and renovation. The Norman chapel, which was built in 1080, is wonderfully preserved, and is only one of a number of highlights to be seen within this enormous castle.

The cathedral is also vast, and the interior is spectacular – it was the first cathedral in Europe to be roofed with stone-ribbed vaulting, and the transverse arches were the first of their kind to be built in Britain. The central and western towers were built in the thirteenth century, but the central tower had to be completely rebuilt in the fifteenth century after it was struck by lightning. The Galilee chapel, which was built in 1175, contains the tomb of the Venerable Bede and also some rare examples of twelfth-century religious murals.

*The town of Durham and its castle with the cathedral in the foreground.*

# The Lake District

The Lake District of Cumbria lies between the Scottish borders and Northumberland, Durham, North Yorkshire and Lancashire. The beautiful landscapes of mountains, valleys, fells and lakes have appealed to visitors for centuries. In the Victorian era it became very popular as a holiday spot, and it remains so today. Its status as a national park ensures the careful management of its varied environment.

The high ground of the central area is wonderful hiking territory, with valleys, lakes and ridges radiating from it in all directions. Lake Windermere is the largest lake in England, and Bowness-on-Windermere caters for the huge number of visitors it receives. If the town is too busy for your taste, you can always take a boat out onto the lake and enjoy the views. The least visited and also the deepest lake is Wast Water. Surrounded by high peaks such as Scafell Pike and wild mountain scenery, it is harder to reach than any of the others.

Keswick is situated in the north of the Lake District, beside Derwentwater, and is an important centre for walking and climbing. The Cumbria Way, a trail of almost 113 km (70 mi), is accessible from here. Keswick was particularly popular with the Victorians, and the museum holds original manuscripts by Wordsworth, Ruskin and others, while the art gallery displays works by Turner and Wilson Steer. Wordsworth lived at Rydal Mount, near Ambleside, for 37 years, and just below the house is Dora's Field, named after his daughter and planted with daffodils in her memory.

**WHAT IS IT KNOWN FOR**
The biggest lake in England and a literary heritage.
**WHAT IS THERE TO SEE**
Lake District National Park Visitor Centre at Brockhole, Kendal, Elterwater, Penrith, Hadrian's Wall.
**WHAT IS THERE TO DO**
There are many hiking trails and the Cumbria Way for those looking for a challenging walk.
**DO NOT MISS**
Take a boat out onto Lake Windermere for a better look at the area.

*Lake Windermere and Waterhead Bay in Ambleside, Lake District National Park.*

*The village of Thwaite and its surrounding fields in the North Yorkshire Dales. The Pennine Way, a popular trail, passes through the village.*

# The Yorkshire Dales

The Yorkshire Dales National Park covers an area of 1,770 sq km (683 sq mi) of countryside between the Lake District and the North Yorkshire Moors. Made up of hills, moors and valleys, it is a marvellous place for cycling and walking trips. The Yorkshire Dales Cycle Way, a route of 209 km (130 mi), shows the park's best scenery, or you could try one of the walks such as the Dales Way or the Pennine Way.

Wensleydale and Swaledale are the two main east/west valleys in the northern half of the park, and in the south Ribblesdale and Wharfedale are the main north/south valleys. Hawes is probably the best base for exploring the northern dales, and whilst there you can visit the Wensleydale Creamery and learn about the production of that world famous cheese. Hardraw Force, the highest waterfall in the country is also close by. Grassington is the place from which to explore beautiful Wharfedale, a classic landscape of rich, lush meadows, drystone walls and glorious views every where you look.

If you prefer, you can explore the dales by car, or take a trip on the Settle-to-Carlisle railway line. This is a fabulous journey and special passes are available so that you can see a bit at a time if you wish. Jump out at Dent station, one of the highest in the country, and walk down to the picturesque village in the valley below.

**WHAT IS IT KNOWN FOR**
Exquisite, rugged beauty that has inspired many authors and painters.
**HOW BIG IS IT**
The Dales cover an area of 1,770 sq km (683 sq mi).
**WHAT IS THERE TO SEE**
Skipton, Grassington, Malham, Bolton Priory.
**IF YOU DARE**
Try cycling the Yorkshire Dales Cycle Way.

# Saltaire

Salt's Mill was built by the wealthy textile magnate, Sir Titus Salt, and when it opened in 1853, it was the largest and most modern factory in the world. Sir Titus Salt was a philanthropist who decided to surround the mill with a complete village of 850 houses, almshouses, wash houses, public baths, schools, hospitals, parks and a railway station.

At this time, Bradford was the world's largest producer of worsted cloth, and both working and living conditions in the town were horrific. Life expectancy in Bradford was 18 years, and only 30 per cent of textile workers' children survived beyond the age of 15. The workers here must have thought themselves incredibly fortunate to have escaped the pollution and poverty of Bradford, although they were not permitted to drink or to join a trades union.

Saltaire was designed in Italianate style, with the mill resembling an enormous palazzo, and it is all well preserved. The mill is still the heart of the place, and is now home to shops and a restaurant. One floor, called the 1853 Gallery, now has a permanent retrospective of the work of David Hockney. Hockney was born in Bradford and was a friend of Jonathan Silver, who had the idea for the gallery. The transformation of the mill has been sympathetically designed and it is easy to spend a day here. Saltaire is now a UNESCO World Heritage Site.

*Saltaire in West Yorkshire was a purpose-built, model Victorian industrial village.*

**WHAT IS IT**
A beautiful village in West Yorkshire built around a textile mill that dates back to the nineteenth century.
**WHAT ELSE IS THERE TO SEE**
The National Museum of Photography, Film and Television, Kirkstall Abbey, the Brontë Parsonage Museum, Harewood House.
**HOW LONG SHOULD I SPEND THERE**
Saltaire can fill a lazy day spent taking in the Hockney gallery and enjoying the grounds surrounding the mill.
**HOW DO I GET THERE**
By train or bus from Bradford.

# The Giant's Causeway

**WHAT IS IT**
The only World Heritage Site in Northern Ireland.
**WHAT IS THERE TO DO**
Explore the caves by foot or by boat.
**DON'T MISS**
Bruce's Cave on Rathlin Island.
**WHAT IS THERE TO SEE**
Causeway Visitor Centre, Portcoon Cave, Runkerry Cave, Old Bushmill's Whiskey Distillery.
**HOW DO I GET THERE**
By car from Derry or Belfast.

It is thought that the Giant's Causeway was formed some 60 million years ago. As a result of a series of underground volcanic eruptions a vast amount of molten basalt was pushed through the surface. As it cooled, the basalt shrank and cracked into the 37,000 largely hexagonal columns that are found today, extending from the cliffs right into the sea. It is such a weird and wonderful place that it is the stuff of many legends, the most common of which tells of the giant warrior, Finn MacCool, who laid the causeway across the sea to the Isle of Staffa in Scotland, where his lover lived. Today it is the only UNESCO World Heritage site in Northern Ireland and attracts a great many visitors.

The Causeway coast is a fascinating area in its own right, with spectacular caves to be visited, some on foot and some by boat, ruined castles, and lovely sandy bays. The thirteenth-century Dunluce Castle is perched on a rock that is connected to the mainland by a bridge that spans the yawning chasm down to the sea. Dunseverick Castle is an even earlier fortification lying to the east of the Giant's Causeway, and further east still you can find the sixteenth-century Kinbane Castle. Rathlin Island lies five miles off Ballycastle and can be reached daily by boat in the summer. Its main interest lies in Bruce's Cave, where, in 1306, Robert Bruce, King of Scotland, was inspired by a spider to win back his kingdom.

*Part of the Giant's Causeway, a coastal formation of basalt columns.*

# Snowdon and Snowdonia

Snowdon is the highest mountain in Wales, standing at 1,085 m (3,560 ft) and is surrounded by a horseshoe of other peaks. Snowdonia National Park came into being in 1951 to ensure the area's protection. Hundreds of thousands of visitors every year come to scale Snowdon, either on foot or by taking the Snowdon Mountain Railway which runs from Llanberis to the summit. The views are magnificent, although the clouds may close in around the peaks here at all times of year, so check weather information before you start out. There are six main routes, of varying difficulty, to the top, most of which take about five hours.

This is a glorious part of the world with fantastic mountain scenery in all directions, and although Snowdon is the centrepiece, the park stretches 56 km (35 mi) from east to west, and 80 km (50 mi) from north to south, with mountain walks on the lower ranges, and beautiful forest and river walks lower still. If scaling mountains does not appeal to you, there are other activities in the area too – white-water rafting and pony trekking for example. Mountain biking is another favourite, with dedicated cycle trails that are graded for difficulty. If you simply want to explore the area by car, you can still enjoy its beauty, and as there are plenty of interesting small towns and villages in the area, it is not hard to find places in which to eat and sleep.

**WHAT IS IT**
The highest mountain in Wales, second in Britain only to Ben Nevis.

**WHAT IS THERE TO DO**
As well as climbing and hiking in the area, you can also go mountain biking or pony trekking.

**DON'T MISS**
You do not have to climb to reach the summit; you can take the Snowdon Mountain Railway.

**WHAT IS THERE TO SEE**
Llandudno, Conwy, the Lleyn Peninsula.

**YOU SHOULD KNOW**
The summit is often shrouded in cloud, so check the weather before you start.

*Snowdon in the Snowdonia National Park.*

# Portmeirion

**WHAT IS THERE TO SEE**
The village of Tremadog,
Harlech Castle.
**WHAT IS THERE TO DO**
Spend a day at the seaside resort
of Criccieth.
**DON'T MISS**
Venture over to Porthmadog and
enjoy the views of Mount Snowdon.
**HOW DO I GET THERE**
By car or the Ffestiniog Railway.

Portmeirion is the brain-child of Sir Clough Williams-Ellis – a unique and bewitching fantasy village, set in a beautiful position by the sea. For 40 years, from 1926, this Welsh architect perfected his vision – a village of about 50 Italianate buildings, said to be modelled on Portofino, painted in pastel colours and built on sweet little streets around a piazza. The village has a hotel, a restaurant, a town hall, gift shops and several self-catering lets. The whole place overlooks a tidal estuary and a sweeping beach of pale sand.

The magic of Portmeirion has been the inspiration for many artists and writers although it may still be best known for the cult television series, *The Prisoner*. Made in the late 1960s and starring Patrick McGoohan, *The Prisoner* was a bizarre and enigmatic story that kept audiences enthralled for weeks. Each spring, fans of the programme gather together in the village for a celebratory convention.

Portmeirion is only a couple of miles from Porthmadog, with its splendid views of Snowdon, and where visitors can experience the Ffestiniog Railway – a narrow gauge, vintage railway built in the 1830s to transport slate from the nearby mountain mines down to the port. You do not need to be a railway enthusiast to enjoy the trip by steam or diesel train. This scenic railway runs through the village of Minffordd, from where you can walk to Portmeirion in about 20 minutes.

*The central square of the Italianate village of Portmeirion.*

# Dylan Thomas's Boathouse

*Dylan Thomas's boathouse on the Taf Estuary.*

Half an hour's bus ride from Carmarthen, in south Wales, lies the pretty town of Laugharne, where Wales' favourite son, Dylan Thomas (1914–1953), spent the last few years of his life, and produced some of his most famous works. Laugharne is set on the 'heron priested' Taff estuary which broadens out into Carmarthen Bay, and boasts the remains of a twelfth-century castle.

From the castle, which can be visited all year round, Thomas's home, The Boathouse, can be reached by a short walk down a path by the water's edge, or alternatively, down a shady lane. The house, nestled in the cliffs over the estuary, is just as it was, perfectly preserved in honour of the poet and full of fascinating manuscripts, letters, photographs, and even recordings of Thomas's voice reading his own works. The only additions are a bookshop, a tearoom and a viewing platform. Peek through the windows of 'the shack', as he called it – a wooden garage above the house where, amongst other things, he wrote *Under Milk Wood*, his best-known play.

'It is spring, moonless night in the small town, starless and bible-black', thus was Laugharne described in that poem. Dylan Thomas's roots were in Carmarthenshire, which he loved, particularly Laugharne, which he first visited in 1934. His patron, Margaret Taylor, bought the house for him in 1949 and he described it lyrically as being 'sea shaken on a breakneck of rocks'. Windows on three sides of 'the shack' afford wonderful views of both the sea and the countryside of his beloved Wales.

**WHAT IS IT**
The home of the celebrated Welsh author, Dylan Thomas.
**WHAT IS THERE TO SEE**
Carmarthen and Tenby.
**WHAT IS THERE TO DO**
Visit the National Botanic Garden of Wales.
**HOW DO I GET THERE**
Travel by car or bus from Carmarthen.

# Pembrokeshire Coast

The Pembrokeshire Coast National Park occupies almost all the coastline of south-west Wales. It includes the offshore islands of Skomer, Skokholm and Grassholm off the southern headland, and Ramsey Island off the northern headland of St. Bride's Bay as well as Caldey Island, which is further south, off Tenby. It also includes the inland Daugleddau estuary and some of the moorland in the Preselli Hills. The Pembrokeshire coastal path stretches for 300 km (186 mi), which takes at least two weeks to walk and is a real test of endurance – most people opt for walking a section at a time.

The rugged coastline and spectacular cliffs, probably the most spectacular in the country, are dotted with little fishing villages and vast sandy beaches. It is an austere and remote landscape filled with castles – more than 50 of them – and also St David's Cathedral, which is the most significant religious site in Wales and was built in the late twelfth century on land where a church had already stood for 600 years. Generally speaking, tourists come for three reasons – to walk the coastal path, to look for wildlife (the islands are all marine nature reserves) and to practise outdoor pursuits such as surfing and windsurfing, sailing, canoeing, scuba diving, fishing, riding, sea kayaking and coasteering, which is a kind of rock climbing in the sea.

Several companies offer boat trips to the islands, and in spring and summer you can see colonies of thousands of seabirds including puffins and guillemots. Skomer and Skokholm jointly have the largest colony of Manx shearwaters in the world. You can also see seals, porpoises, dolphins and even, if you are lucky enough, minke whales.

*Headland cliffs in
Pembrokeshire.*

# Tintern Abbey

Tintern Abbey is situated between the southern end of the village of Tintern and the River Wye. It in is a lovely location and not only the woods that surround the hills around the abbey change with the seasons, but so does the river, which is tidal. In winter the river is high and surges down into the mouth of the Severn, but in summer it is low and meanders along peacefully.

Tintern Abbey was founded in 1131, by Cistercian monks. It was the first Cistercian monastery to be founded in Wales, and only the second in Britain. Rebuilt in the thirteenth century, it was home to about 400 monks, and despite the inroads made by the Black Death on the community, it survived until 1536, when Henry VIII brought about the dissolution of the monasteries and the Abbey began to decay. Nowadays the ruins are well cared for by Cadw, Welsh Historic Monuments, and maintenance and restoration work is carried out to ensure their preservation.

The imposing Gothic abbey church is the heart of the ruins (the other buildings on the site are in worse condition and little more than their foundations remain, but they are still worth seeing) and although it is roofless, it still looks fairly complete. The nave is 69 m (226 ft) long and most of the nave columns are still standing, as well as a complete southern arcade and part of the cloister. The columns support fabulously moulded arches, and the decorative work throughout is superb. At times the church is used for services that, even for a non-believer, have a particularly poignant and spiritual quality.

**WHERE IS IT**
In south Wales, about 8 km (5 mi) north of Chepstow, between southern Tintern and the River Wye.
**WHAT IS IT**
The first Cistercian monastery to be founded in Wales.
**YOU SHOULD KNOW**
There is an entrance fee.

*The picturesque Tintern Abbey.*

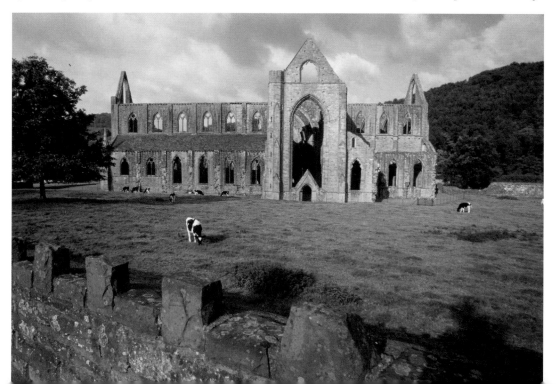

# Ely Cathedral

Ely Cathedral is possibly England's most awe-inspiring cathedral. Visible from miles around across the flat fen country, it towers over the landscape and its nickname, The Ship of the Fens, is very apt. St Etheldreda founded a Benedictine monastery here in 673, on a clay island surrounded by boggy marshland, which was sacked by the Danes 200 years later. The new monastery became the centre of resistance by Hereward the Wake against the Normans. In 1081, after the conquest, Abbot Simeon began the masterpiece of Romanesque architecture that is the cathedral we see today.

As you enter the cathedral, you look down the very long nave with its austere Romanesque arches and Victorian painted ceiling towards the centrepiece of the building, the unique octagonal Lantern Tower built by Alan de Walsingham in 1322 to replace the collapsed central tower. The tallest oaks in England were used to support the 400 tons of glass and lead that form the starburst lantern, surrounded by stunning fan vaulting. The Lady Chapel, built at about the same time, also has an astonishing fan-vaulted and carved ceiling, although much of the carving and statuary within easier reach on the walls was defaced during the Reformation and Commonwealth. The choir bays are also of interest – when the central tower collapsed it fell on the choir and three of the bays were rebuilt at the same time as the octagon, in contrast with the much plainer early English style of the remainder. Both the Prior's Doorway and the Monks' Doorway boast lovely Romanesque sculptures. There is so much to be seen in this marvellous building that it is worth going out of your way to see it.

*The magnificent ceilings of Ely Cathedral.*

**WHAT IS IT KNOWN FOR**
Ely Cathedral is known as England's most awe-inspiring cathedral.
**WHAT IS THERE TO SEE**
The Lantern Tower, the Stained Glass Museum and Wicken Fen.
**WHAT IS THERE TO DO**
A visit to Oliver Cromwell's house is worth the trip.
**HOW DO I GET THERE**
By train or car from London, Cambridge or Norwich.

# Lavenham

*Half-timbered buildings
in Lavenham.*

Lavenham is possibly the prettiest village in Suffolk. Situated in the Stour valley, it is a marvellously preserved medieval wool town, with more than 300 listed buildings. Lavenham has existed since Roman times, and was mentioned in the Domesday Book.

The Spring family were persuaded by John de Vere, the Earl of Oxford, to build a church tower in thanksgiving for the victory at the Battle of Bosworth (1485). He donated the porch where two boars are to be found carved in stone. They are actually a pun on his family name, *verres* being Latin for boar. The church was completed in 1525 and is a perfect example of Late Perpendicular architecture and has suffered little change since then.

The early sixteenth-century Guildhall is one of the finest half-timbered buildings in the country. After the decline in Lavenham's importance, it became a prison, and later a workhouse and an almshouse. Beautifully restored, it is now a local history museum.

Walking around this lovely village you can see marvellous buildings of all descriptions, some of the oldest of which are weavers' cottages in Water Street. There are ancient inns, crooked houses, thatched cottages painted the traditional Suffolk pink, thought to have been whitewash tinted with pig's blood, and higgledy-piggledy roofs. In the late seventeenth century the wool trade moved away from here, but it left behind a wonderful legacy for us to see today.

**WHAT IS IT**
A medieval wool town with more
than 300 listed buildings.
**WHAT IS THERE TO DO**
Visit the Guildhall and discover local
history at its best.
**YOU SHOULD KNOW**
Entrance fees are payable at most of
the local museums.

# The Suffolk Heritage Coast

**WHAT IS IT KNOWN FOR**
Churches, which are scattered throughout the area.
**WHAT IS THERE TO SEE**
Woodbridge, Orford and its castle, Thorpeness, Shingle Street.
**WHAT IS THERE TO DO**
Enjoy the walks and trails along the coast which will reveal much wildlife.
**WHEN SHOULD I VISIT**
The beaches are very popular in the summer so spring and autumn if you want to avoid the crowds.

Suffolk's Heritage Coast was designated as an Area of Outstanding Natural Beauty in 1970. Stretching from the Stour estuary in the south to Kessingland in the north, it encompasses a world of marshland, heaths, forests and shingle beaches as well as villages and historic buildings. The Royal Society for the Protection of Birds' flagship bird reserve at Minsmere is a microcosm of the landscape. Unlike much of Britain's coastline, the Heritage Coast is largely undeveloped and this contributes to its charm.

The coastal landscape with its huge skies and beautiful light has inspired artists and musicians down the years including the composer, Benjamin Britten, whose vision has resulted in the world famous annual music festival at Snape and Turner who painted Dunwich beach. The area is full of painters, musicians, writers and actors and visitors flock to seaside villages such as Southwold and Walberswick in the summer to enjoy the unspoiled old-fashioned atmosphere.

Suffolk is famous for its churches – one of the most spectacular of these is at Blythburgh, known locally as 'the Cathedral in the Marshes'. Built in the fourteenth century, it is beautifully situated on the Blyth Estuary. Sailing on the estuaries is a popular pursuit and birdwatchers are able to see many rare species of birds including bittern, avocet, marsh harrier and Montagu's harrier. As cliffs erode in some areas, beaches are building up in others, and the profiles of the beaches change from year to year. This is a subtle and beautiful coastline that constantly reminds you of the power of nature.

*A line of beach huts at Southwold.*

# Ironbridge Gorge

The UNESCO World Heritage Site of Ironbridge Gorge in Shropshire was designated in recognition of its importance as the birthplace of the Industrial Revolution, and there are ten museums in the area testifying to the transformation of industry that took place.

Three generations of the extraordinary Darby family helped shape history here. In 1709, Abraham Darby pioneered the smelting of iron ore with coke, thus enabling local factories to mass-produce locomotives, rails and iron wheels, and the beginnings of Britain's railway system. Abraham Darby II invented a new forging process that allowed single beams of iron to be produced, and enabled his son, Abraham Darby III, in 1779, to construct the first iron bridge in the world, here in Ironbridge Gorge.

The gorge itself is made up of a group of pretty little villages and there is even a completely reconstructed Victorian village theme park, with a working foundry and craftsmen demonstrating various skills, all in authentic Victorian dress. There is even a Victorian pub if you need some time out. You can visit a splendid tile museum, a clay-pipe-making museum in the largely unchanged factory which only closed down in 1957, and many others charting the history of industrialization and engineering. These are all set within lovely countryside and presided over by the semicircular bridge that gave the area its name.

**WHERE IS IT**
In the Midlands, 22 km (15 mi) east of Shrewsbury.
**WHAT IS IT**
The birthplace of the Industrial Revolution.
**WHAT IS THERE TO DO**
Wander through the gorge and take in pretty villages and the Victorian village theme park.
**WHAT IS THERE TO SEE**
Bridgnorth, Ludlow, Stokesay Castle.
**YOU SHOULD KNOW**
There is an entrance fee.

*The bridge and houses at Ironbridge.*

*A typical Cotswold stone cottage with a thatched roof at Great Tew.*

# The Cotswolds

The limestone hills of the Cotswolds are one of England's main tourist attractions. They encompass some of England's prettiest countryside and are peppered with picturesque villages all built in the local stone, which varies from honey coloured to silvery-grey.

Cirencester was a busy town in Roman times, when it was second in importance only to London. Today it remains a bustling town and is the *de facto* capital of the south Cotswolds, dominated by a splendid fifteenth-century church. Bourton-on-the-Water is possibly the prettiest of the Cotswold villages with its many low, stone bridges crossing the little River Windrush. Farther north, Stow-on-the-Wold, the highest town in the Cotswolds, boasts a large square surrounded by imposing honey-coloured houses. The 'tunes' or narrow alleyways leading into the square were originally used to run sheep into the market. Nearby Chastleton House is one of the most complete Jacobean manor houses in England.

Chipping Camden is another lovely town with its famous High Street and gabled Jacobean Market Hall. The Church of St. James is the most impressive in the area. In 1902, the Arts and Crafts movement, lead by the designer William Morris, set up their Guild in the Silk Mill, which now houses an exhibition and craft workshops.

Apart from towns and villages, the Cotswolds has marvellous gardens to see, such as those at Hidcote Manor and Batsford Arboretum, as well as castles such as Berkeley Castle and Sudeley Castle, Roman remains and even prehistoric sites.

**WHAT IS IT**
The Cotswolds are limestone hills in the south-west of England.
**WHAT IS IT KNOWN FOR**
The Cotswolds contain some of the most picturesque villages in England.
**WHAT SHOULD I BUY**
Locally made arts and crafts.
**WHAT IS THERE TO SEE**
Prinknash Abbey, Chedworth Roman Villa, Sezincote.
**WHEN SHOULD I VISIT**
The gardens of the local area are at their prettiest in late spring and early summer.

# Stratford-upon-Avon

Stratford-upon-Avon is renowned as the birthplace of William Shakespeare. The Shakespeare Birthplace Trust manages five properties relating to Shakespeare, all of which are worth looking at.

Shakespeare's Birthplace Museum has a modern visitor centre situated next door to the half-timbered building in which the bard is thought to have been born. Nash's House was the home of Shakespeare's granddaughter and from there you enter New Place, a memorial garden that marks the site of Shakespeare's own house, which he inhabited from 1610 until his death. Hall's Croft is another pretty house in which Shakespeare's daughter Susanna and her husband lived. Two other properties, Mary Arden's House and Anne Hathaway's Cottage, can be found at Wilmcote, and Shottery. The latter was the family home of Shakespeare's wife and is the prettiest of the Shakespeare buildings. It is a thatched farmhouse full of seventeenth-century furniture belonging to the Hathaway family.

Harvard House is a splendid sixteenth-century building with fabulously carved exterior beams. This was the family home of the mother of John Harvard, one of the founders of Harvard University. The thirteenth-century Holy Trinity Church is where Shakespeare and many of his family are buried.

The Royal Shakespeare Company has three theatres here, where some of Britain's finest actors perform the Bard's works.

**WHAT IS IT KNOWN FOR**
Being the birth place of William Shakespeare.
**WHAT IS THERE TO SEE**
Anne Hathaway's Cottage, the Swan Theatre, Gerard Johnson's alabaster bust of Shakespeare in Holy Trinity Church and Charlecote Park.
**WHAT IS THERE TO DO**
Venture away from Stratford and spend a day at the beautiful Warwick Castle.
**HOW DO I GET THERE**
Travel by train, coach or car from Oxford or Birmingham.

*Shakespeare's birthplace in Stratford-upon-Avon.*

# Oxford

Oxford stands at the confluence of two rivers: the Cherwell and the Isis, as the Thames is known at this point. Originally a Saxon town, it was not until the twelfth century that its Augustinian abbey began to attract students. The first colleges were built in the thirteenth century, and others followed, right up to the twentieth century, in order to keep pace with the growing student population.

The city's industrial side took off after the canal system was built, linking Oxford with the Midlands, and car manufacturing at Cowley began in earnest in 1912. The divide between 'town and gown' has always been in existence and to this day students rarely mix with locals. Tourism is always evident in Oxford because its wealth of historic buildings and world-famous museums draws visitors from around the world. Do not forget to visit the famous covered market – at Christmas the traditional butchers there have fantastic displays of game such as wild boar and venison for sale.

Colleges have visiting hours and entrance fees, but when they are off-limits there are plenty of other things to do and see: beautiful walks by the canal and rivers, and punting during the summer, museums such as the Ashmolean and Pitt Rivers, art galleries and of course hundreds of restaurants, pubs, bars and night clubs. Stroll around this historic city and soak up the atmosphere by day, and in the evening listen to a classical music concert.

*Radcliffe Camera and All Souls College.*

# The Houses of Parliament

*The Palace of Westminster with 'Big Ben' – St Stephen's Tower – on the right.*

In the eleventh century the original Palace of Westminster was built by Edward the Confessor, on the banks of the River Thames. It remained one of the palaces of every monarch until Henry VIII moved out after a fire, and has been the seat of government more or less ever since. In 1834, the old palace was almost completely devastated by another fire, leaving only Westminster Hall and the Jewel Tower intact, and Sir Charles Barry and AWN Pugin were charged with the rebuilding. They designed the fabulous Gothic Revival complex that we see today, which is better known as The Houses of Parliament.

Anyone can go to watch the business of the House of Commons and the House of Lords, which are open to the public throughout the week, at different times of day. Just join the queue outside St Stephen's Gate and, after passing through strict security measures, you will be able to find a seat in one of the Strangers' Galleries.

In August and September, when parliament is not sitting, guided tours of the complex are available.

St Stephen's Tower was built in 1858. It is commonly known as Big Ben, although this is actually the name of the 13-tonne bell that chimes within it. The sound of Big Ben's chimes is known throughout the world, and the tower is an instantly recognizable London landmark. Perhaps the best views of the Houses of Parliament are from the south side of the river and, at night, the floodlit towers and spires look particularly romantic.

**WHAT IS IT**
An instantly recognizable landmark of London and the seat of government.
**WHAT IS THERE TO SEE**
The Lord Chancellor's Residence, Westminster Abbey, Downing Street.
**WHAT IS THERE TO DO**
In the summer you can take a guided tour through both houses.
**YOU SHOULD KNOW**
Entry is free.
**HOW DO I GET THERE**
The nearest tube station is Westminster, which is across the road from the Houses of Parliament.

*Tate Modern by night with the Millennium Bridge in the foreground.*

# Tate Modern

Tate Modern is housed in a wonderful conversion of what was the looming and unprepossessing Bankside Power Station, on the south bank of the river Thames. Completely renovated and redesigned by Jacques Herzog and Pierre de Meuron, it is the largest modern art gallery in the world. This section of the south bank has gone through an extraordinary regeneration during the past ten years, with the Thames Path allowing you to walk west or east via many other attractions.

The best way to reach it is by crossing the Millenium Bridge, the first pedestrian only bridge in London and the first new bridge across the river for more than 100 years. Enter Tate Modern down the western ramp and into the vast Turbine Hall and the view will take your breath away. This superb space is used for specially designed shows that are changed every six months or so. It allows the display of monumental pieces of art, such as Louise Bourgeois' giant female spider, entitled 'Maman' and her three towers, all of which made up the opening show.

The galleries are large and light with levels 3 and 5 housing the permanent collection, and level 4 housing temporary exhibitions. You will be able to see examples of the work of Cubists, Surrealists, Impressionists, Pointillists, abstract artists and pop artists as well as multimedia installations. Some artists, such as Francis Bacon, have been given a whole room to themselves. Unusually, the art is arranged by theme rather than by timeline but this is very effective.

**WHAT IS IT**
The largest modern art gallery in the world.
**WHAT IS THERE TO SEE**
Millennium Bridge, the Globe Theatre, the Design Museum, the London Eye and the South Bank Centre.
**YOU SHOULD KNOW**
The permanent exhibitions are free but the temporary exhibitions require an entrance fee.
**HOW DO I GET THERE**
Via Blackfriars or Southwark tube stations.

# The British Museum

The British Museum is one of the greatest museums in the world, not only because of the volume of treasures that it holds but also because of the quality of the collections.

Situated in Bloomsbury, the present building dates from 1823, and is a most imposing example of nineteenth-century Neoclassical architecture. The collection began in 1753 when Hans Sloane offered his extensive collections of art and antiquities to Parliament for considerably less than their true value. Further collections were added, including the Royal Library, which was given by George II. The collection was soon too large to be housed in the existing house, and Robert Smirke began work on the building that we see today.

In the 1880s the natural history collection was moved to a new building in South Kensington and the British Museum was able to concentrate on collecting, housing and protecting treasures from around the world. In recent years more changes have been made – the British Library was moved out and the space it occupied was redeveloped into the Great Court, with its vast glass and steel roof, designed by Norman Foster, and opened in 2000. At its centre is the famous domed Reading Room, which now has a multi-media guide to the museum, and acts as a public study area.

The museum holds many priceless artefacts, including the Elgin Marbles from the Parthenon, the Rosetta Stone, the spectacular Egyptian collection, a giant head from Easter Island and the treasures of Sutton Hoo amongst the 70,000 exhibits on display in the extensive galleries. Altogether, including prints and drawings, the collection numbers over seven million items.

**WHAT IS IT**
One of the greatest museums in the world with superb collections.
**WHAT IS THERE TO SEE**
The Sainsbury African Galleries, Lindow Man, the Portland Vase, the Mildenhall Treasure.
**WHAT IS THERE TO DO**
Visit the world famous Reading Room.
**YOU SHOULD KNOW**
Entry is free.
**HOW DO I GET THERE**
Russell Square, Holborn or Tottenham Court Road tube stations.

*The Great Court of the British Museum.*

# The Tower of London

**WHAT IS IT**
A royal palace dating back almost one thousand years.
**WHAT IS IT KNOWN FOR**
It is most famous for being a prison and place of torture.
**WHAT IS THERE TO SEE**
The Royal Armouries, the Chapel of St John the Evangelist, Traitor's Gate, Beauchamp Tower.
**WHAT IS THERE TO DO**
Visit the world famous Crown Jewels.
**HOW DO I GET THERE**
The nearest tube station is Tower Hill.

The Tower of London was begun in 1078 by William the Conqueror, with the building of the White Tower – the first stone keep in England. In the early thirteenth century Henry III founded a palace here, and although no monarch has lived in it since Henry VII, the Tower remains a Royal Palace.

At various times it has been home to the Astronomer Royal, the Public Records Office, the Royal Menagerie and the Royal Armoury. It also, famously, houses the Crown Jewels. The tower's main claim to fame, however, is its bloody history, gained through having been a prison and a place of torture and execution.

In the thirteenth century Edward I built Beauchamp Tower, and it became a prison for high-ranking convicts and it is moving to see the many inscriptions that are carved into the walls. Prisoners entering the Tower through Traitors' Gate, arriving by boat along the Thames, would immediately have seen the Bloody Tower, so called because in 1483, after the death of Edward IV, his two young sons were incarcerated here by their uncle, Richard of Gloucester. They were never seen again, and Richard of Gloucester was crowned Richard III. It has always been assumed, but never proven, that he had them murdered. Most executions took place in front of a screaming mob at Tower Hill, but Tower Green saw the deaths of seven major historical figures, including two of Henry VIII's wives.

Yeoman Warders in Tudor costume, known as Beefeaters, guard the tower, as they have done since 1485. One, the Ravenmaster, is responsible for the Tower ravens. Legend has it that if the ravens leave the Tower, the kingdom will fall – so their wings are clipped!

*The White Tower, the main tower of the Tower of London.*

*The Roman Baths.*

# City of Bath

The City of Bath is a jewel of Georgian architecture but as long ago as 44 AD it was known for its medicinal hot springs – the only hot springs in the country. The Romans built a temple and a complex of baths over one of the three hot springs and called the town that grew up around it Aquae Sulis. In the tenth century a monastery was founded at Bath, but Bath Abbey as we know it today was not built until the sixteenth century. Medieval Bath was a prosperous wool trading town as well as a religious centre, but it was not until the eighteenth century that, in part thanks to 'Beau' Nash, it became a fashionable resort.

The Royal Crescent is a magnificent crescent of Georgian houses built between 1767 and 1775. This is only a short walk from the Circus, a circle of 30 wonderfully preserved town houses. Plaques proclaim the many famous people who lived here – David Livingstone and Clive of India to name but two.

The Roman Baths Museum gives a fascinating insight into the Roman complex that was here – you can even see the ruins of the 2,000 year old temple or try to drink the waters in the Pump Room. Part of the complex has recently been refurbished to provide a modern spa.

**WHAT IS IT**
A Roman site and the only hot springs in England.
**WHAT IS THERE TO SEE**
Museum of Costume and the Assembly Rooms, Jane Austen Centre, Castle Combe, Lacock Abbey.
**WHERE IS IT**
21 km (13 mi) south-east of Bristol.
**YOU SHOULD KNOW**
The city is a UNESCO World Heritage Site.

# Stonehenge

*The standing stones and
trilithons of Stonehenge with
the surrounding grassland of
Salisbury Plain.*

The instantly recognizable 5,000-year-old stone circle at Stonehenge is
the most famous prehistoric site in Europe. The outer, circular bank and
ditch were constructed around 3,000 BC, and the inner circle of vast
bluestones (granite that was originally blue) was added 1,000 years
later. It is now believed that these granite stones, some of which weigh
as much as 4 tonnes, were dragged all the way from the Preseli Hills of
south Wales – some 400 km (250 mi). Erected in pairs, each pair is
topped by an equally huge stone lintel. Within the inner circle stand two
horseshoe-shaped arrangements, one within the other, and at the centre
lies what is known as the Altar Stone. Further stones are to be found
here and there within the site, which is surrounded by barrow mounds.

Archaeologically fascinating, the site remains a mystery, although
many different theories have been advanced as to its original purpose.
The two inner horseshoes are aligned along the rising and setting of the
sun at the midsummer and midwinter solstices. Whilst this is evidently
extremely significant, so far its meaning eludes the experts.

Stonehenge is situated in an area that is littered with prehistoric
sites, some on private land, and none of which attract the same amount
of visitors. It is not surprising therefore that it is considered both
mysterious and magical, and is the focus of various sects such as the
druids, who perform ceremonies to mark the progress of the year. Since
it has been accorded World Heritage status it is hoped that this
relatively small site can be protected from the inevitable environmental
damage caused by the 800,000 people who visit it annually, while
enabling them to admire the remains of this magnificent structure.

# Salisbury Cathedral

The city of Salisbury is dominated by the soaring spire of the cathedral, which stands in a beautiful walled close with verdant water meadows stretching away into the distance. It is a quintessentially English scene that looks much the same now as it did in Constable's famous painting of 1823.

Salisbury Cathedral was designed and built in the almost miraculously short time of 38 years, between 1220 and 1258. It was made of Chilmark stone, quarried some 19 km (12 mi) away and transported to the site. The octagonal Chapter House, started in the 1260s, took 40 years to complete. The spire was added in the 1320s and, at 123 m (404 ft), it is the highest in the country.

In the late seventeenth century, Sir Christopher Wren was called in to work on the spire, which had some structural problems because of its height and weight, and in the mid-nineteenth century Sir George Gilbert Scott began another bout of restoration work to the spire. In fact the building is an extraordinary feat of engineering – the spire leans less than 1 m (3 ft) out of true, and the foundations were only sunk a couple of metres deep in boggy ground, so the fact that it still stands at all is testament to those medieval craftsmen.

The cathedral's interior is austere, the nave is lined with pillars of grey Purbeck marble, and carved tombs line the walls, adding to the sombre atmosphere. There is, however, an undeniable grandeur about the building. In the north aisle you can see what is probably the oldest working clock mechanism in Europe dating from 1386. The Chapter House contains a medieval frieze showing scenes from Genesis and the finest of the four original copies of the Magna Carta.

**WHAT IS THERE TO SEE**
The Magna Carta, the cloisters, Mompesson House, Malmsbury House, St. Thomas of Canterbury church.
**WHAT IS THERE TO DO**
Explore the water meadows in the surrounding area.
**INTERESTING FACT**
The spire stands the highest in the country at 123 m (404 ft) tall.

*Salisbury Cathedral and School.*

# Chesil Beach

Chesil Beach is the most extraordinary part of the Dorset coastline and one of the strangest features of the whole of the English coast. Stretching for 29 km (18 mi) it is a bank of pebbles about 170 m (555 ft) wide and 14 m (45 ft) high stretching from Portland to Burton Bradstock. The pebbles decrease in size from east to west – at Portland they are roughly the size of a fist, but at Burton Bradstock they have become 'pea shingle'.

This pebble bank was formed by longshore drift: the powerful currents off the coast mean that the waves hit the shore obliquely, which has the effect of sorting the millions of pebbles deposited here over thousands of years. These powerful onshore currents makes this one of the most dangerous beaches in Europe, and gravestones in many local churchyards testify to the many drownings and shipwrecks that have occurred here.

Chesil Beach is, however, extremely popular with anglers, who enjoy the wild, unspoiled and atmospheric environment. At the eastern end, the beach links the Isle of Portland to the mainland enclosing a lagoon known as the Fleet, which is home to thousands of seabirds and waders. The Chesil Beach Centre has an exhibition on the area which includes several interactive displays, and visitors can take a tour of the Fleet in a glass-bottomed boat.

*Chesil Beach and the Fleet Estuary.*

# Tresco

The Isles of Scilly lie 47 km (29 mi) off the south-west coast of
Cornwall and are made up of 140 islands, only five of which are
inhabited. St Mary's is the largest and the most populated island,
probably because it is the arrival point for ferries coming from the
mainland, and it has the airport as well. Tresco is the second largest
island, and is much visited largely because it is the home of the
Abbey Gardens, which are laid out on the site of a tenth-century
Benedictine abbey. Myth and legend are part of the island's heritage
– it is said that Tresco was part of Lyonnesse, the legendary 'land
across the sea', and was King Arthur's final resting place.

The strategic position of the Scilly Isles meant that England's
wars brought them misery and poverty, but in 1834 Augustus Smith
bought the islands and was appointed Lord Proprietor of the Scillies.
He came to live on Tresco and introduced many new ideas. A keen
botanist, he recognized the special weather conditions existing on
the islands and designed the now world famous Abbey Gardens with
their walled enclosures around the abbey ruins and terraces carved
from the rocky hillside.

Nowadays the gardens contain 20,000 exotic plants from
Australia, Asia, South Africa, New Zealand and South America. The
diversity is extraordinary, and recently a new Mediterranean garden
has been added.

There are only 150 residents here, and the island is still owned
by the Smith family. Tresco draws loyal holidaymakers who return
year after year to take a break from the real world and enjoy the
wonderful scenery, sandy beaches, sparkling sea and unique
atmosphere that exists here.

**WHAT IS IT**
One of the prettiest of a group of 140
islands off the south-west coast of
Cornwall.
**ALSO KNOWN AS**
In legend it is said that Tresco was
part of the 'land across the sea' and
also King Arthur's resting place.
**WHAT IS THERE TO SEE**
St Mary's, Bryther, St Martin's,
St Agnes.
**WHAT IS THERE TO DO**
Visit the Abbey Gardens, which
contain 20,000 exotic plants from all
over the world.

*Tresco, the second largest island
of the Scilly Isles.*

# The Dingle Peninsula

The Dingle Peninsula in south-west Ireland is the northernmost of five peninsulas that jut into the Atlantic like the fingers of a hand and Dunmore Head has the distinction of being the far western point of mainland Ireland. Each peninsula has a ridge of mountains, and the Dingle's are the Slieve Mish mountains. The highest peak, Brandon, at 953 m (3,127 ft), is Ireland's second highest mountain.

The peninsula is known for its spectacular scenery and its incomparable early Christian monuments, Iron-Age fortifications and beehive huts. Dingle itself is a beautifully situated village lying at the foot of Mt Ballysitteragh. It still has a fishing fleet in its almost land-locked harbour and is an excellent base from which to explore the antiquities on the peninsula. Its own major attraction is Fungie the dolphin, who has lived in the harbour since 1984.

The Oratory of Gallarus is a tiny, eighth-century, drystone Christian church – the best-preserved example in Ireland – and looks like an upturned boat. Nearby stands the fifteenth-century Gallerus Castle and a group of ruined beehive huts, one of which has been restored. Kilmalkedar, has a ruined twelfth-century Romanesque church, with interesting stone carvings, and an Ogham stone. Ogham is a script used between the fourth and ninth centuries and is made up of notches or lines that represent 20 letters of the Latin alphabet. At Riasc are the excavated remains of a seventh-century monastery, which include several crosses and a carved pillar stone. Due west of Dingle is the Iron-Age promontory fort of Dunbeg, which stands on the edge of the cliffs, and farther west still, more than 400 beehive huts, in varying states of preservation, stand on the lower slopes of Mt Eagle.

*The rocky cliffs of the Dingle Peninsula.*

# Killary Harbour and Connemara

*Sunset in Killary Harbour.*

Connemara is a unique and beautiful part of western Ireland, in County Galway, and Killary Harbour, which separates Galway from County Mayo, is Ireland's only fjord. Enclosed by mountains on either side, this 16-km (10-mi) long deep-water inlet boasts some of Ireland's most spectacular scenery and fabulous opportunities for boating.

This area of Connemara was seriously affected by the potato famine, which was sparked by the failure of the potato crop in 1845/6 and 1848. Most of rural Ireland relied on potatoes as the staple diet, and more than a million people died from starvation and disease during this period. More than 2.5 million others were forced to emigrate in order to survive. You can walk the famine relief road that was built in 1846 by local people in exchange for food. Nowadays there are mussel farms in the fjord and plenty of opportunities to taste them. You can even harvest your own mussels from the shoreline and cook them yourself if you want.

North Connemara contains the National Park, which covers 5,000 acres of wild countryside and includes bogland, moorland, lakes and mountains. Plants and wildlife abound, including rare bog and heathland plants such as St Dabeoc's heath, a species of heather. Peregrine falcons and merlins can be seen, as can otters, red deer, Connemara ponies and grey seals around the rocky coastline.

**WHAT IS IT**
Ireland's only fjord.
**WHAT IS THERE TO SEE**
A variety of of wildlife can be seen in the area.
**WHAT IS THERE TO DO**
Visit Leenane, Kylemore, Killary Adventure Centre and Lough Inagh.
**DO NOT MISS**
Harvesting and cooking your own mussels in Connemara.
**HOW DO I GET THERE**
By car.

*Black Lake in the Gap of Dunloe.*

# The Gap of Dunloe

The Gap of Dunloe lies to the east of Killarney, within the Killarney National Park. Killarney itself is the most visited tourist attraction in Ireland and is the main town from where visitors can explore the sights around the lakes, and walk, cycle or ride through the Gap of Dunloe. This area has been praised by visitors since the middle of the eighteenth century; the climate is benign, the heather-clad mountains are dramatic and there are ruined castles and churches and glorious views of lakes and islands to be seen.

From Killarney you can walk along a ridge that overlooks Lough Leane. This is the largest of the lakes of Killarney and it contains 30 small islands. On the largest of these islands, Innisfallen, you can see the ruins of a seventh-century abbey founded by St Finan Lobhar. As you walk on you will find Dunloe Castle. Built in 1215 and now a hotel, it has a group of Ogham stones in the grounds. Just before you reach the Gap of Dunloe, you pass Kate Kearney's Cottage. Now a bar, this was the home of a nineteenth-century beauty who sold illegally distilled whiskey, 'poteen', to passers by.

The gap itself was carved by glaciers and the route through it has extraordinary views of the three small lakes within it and the boulder-strewn gorge that cuts between Purple Mountain and the MacGillycuddy Reeks – the highest mountain range in Ireland.

**YOU SHOULD KNOW**
Killarney is the most visited tourist attraction in Ireland.
**WHAT IS THERE TO SEE**
Ross Castle, Tralee.
**WHAT IS THERE TO DO**
Hike through Gap of Dunloe for incredible views of the surrounding scenery.
**HOW DO I GET THERE**
Travel by car, but once you are there it is easy to get around by bike.

# Dublin's Pubs

Dublin is the capital of the Emerald Isle, as Ireland is known, and it lies roughly halfway down the east coast, in the lovely Dublin bay. It is a compact little city, divided by the River Liffey into the north and south sides. Public transport is excellent, but the best way of seeing Dublin is on foot, which is particularly useful if you wish to sample either of the country's most famous exports – Guinness and Jameson whiskey.

Dublin's pubs are famous the world over, and since Arthur Guinness founded his brewery at St James's Gate in 1759, they have been a focal point of the city's social life, the place to go to talk politics and literature, philosophy and sport. Music has also played a large part in Dublin's pub life, and you can still enjoy authentic traditional Irish music in many an old watering hole.

Dublin has been, and still is, home to an astonishing array of literary giants, three of whom, Samuel Beckett, George Bernard Shaw and WB Yeats, received the Nobel Prize. Many more are world famous, and are known to have spent a great deal of their time in various pubs and bars around the city. Today you can join an award-winning literary pub crawl that is both informative and entertaining, although you might want to drink your first pint of Guinness in the Gravity Bar on the top floor of the Guinness Hop Store. This houses the World of Guinness exhibition, which will educate you in the finer points of Ireland's most famous drink.

**ALSO KNOWN AS**
The capital of the Emerald Isle.
**WHAT IS THERE TO SEE**
Many pubs have live performances of traditional music.
**WHAT IS THERE TO DO**
Have a drink in one of the best pubs, including The Dawson Lounge, Davey Byrne's, Toners, Doheny and Nesbitt's, Jonnie Fox's Pub.
**YOU SHOULD KNOW**
Dublin is really easy to get around on foot.

*John Mulligan's – one of the oldest and most characterful pubs in Dublin.*

# Mir Castle

**WHAT IS IT**
A sixteenth-century castle 85 km (53 mi) south-west of Minsk.
**WHAT IS THERE TO SEE**
Dudutki Open Air Museum, Njasvizh and Minsk.
**YOU SHOULD KNOW**
The castle is a UNESCO World Heritage Site.
**HOW DO I GET THERE**
Travel by bus from Minsk.

Some 85 km (53 mi) south-west of Minsk lies the small town of Mir, and its sixteenth century castle. Founded by Duke Ilinich, it subsequently belonged to the powerful Radzivil family, who completed the originally Gothic construction in fine Renaissance style, adding a three-storey palace along the north and east walls. Its plastered façades are punctuated by limestone doorways and window embrasures.

The castle is surrounded by defensive earthworks and bastions, and its walls are 13 m (43 ft) high and 75 m (245 ft) long. Despite these precautions it was damaged by war several times during its history, particularly during the Napoleonic period. Some restoration occurred at the end of the nineteenth century, when the surrounding area was landscaped.

Built predominantly of stone and red brick, the original castle forms a square, with a tower at each corner. The fifth tower, in the centre of the western wall, has a drawbridge that leads over the moat to the entrance arch. The five towers differ in design and decoration, including the number and design of the embrasures.

Since 1994, when the castle was listed as a UNESCO World Heritage Site, further restoration work has taken place – and a museum, with an interesting display of weapons and costumes, has been opened in one of the towers. The history of the castle is rich and colourful and it is well worth taking a guided tour in order to fully appreciate it.

*Mir Castle.*

# Rock-Hewn Churches of Ivanovo

A UNESCO World Heritage Site situated in the Rusenski Lom National Park, 20 km (12 mi) south of Ruse, in northern Bulgaria, high on the rocky banks of the Rusenski Lom river, this is an area full of natural caves. From the thirteenth century hermits and monks carved some 40 churches chapels and monasteries and about 300 cells out of the limestone rock, on both sides of the river, using some of the natural caves as their starting point. In the fourteenth century wonderful murals were painted on the walls, and well-preserved examples can still be seen today in five sites. They testify to the exceptional talent and skill of the artists of the Tarnovo school. The caves remained inhabited until the seventeenth century.

The Church of the Holy Virgin is the foremost of the churches, and contains a splendid portrait of Tsar Ivan Alexander. In the so-called 'Demolished Church' is a portrait of the Tsar's first wife, Teodora, who later became a nun, and Tsar Ivan Asen II appears in the 'Buried Under Church'. The Second Bulgarian Empire was established by two brothers, Asen and Petar, in 1185 and their descendants ruled until 1396. During this period the Tsars often made donations to the rock monastery, which is why they are depicted in this way.

The Rusenski Lom is prone to flooding and the caves were affected in both 1979 and 2005.

*Murals on the walls and ceiling of one of the monasteries.*

**WHAT IS IT**
Churches carved into the limestone rock and natural caves of the area, dating back to the thirteenth century.
**WHERE IS IT**
The monastery is on the banks of the Rusenski Lom River, 20 km (12 mi) south of Ruse in northern Bulgaria.
**WHAT IS THERE TO SEE**
Belogradchik and Ruse.
**HOW DO I GET THERE**
Travel By bus or train from Sofia to Ruse, then by bus.

*Fishing boats at sunset.*

# Sozopol

The Black Sea coast of Bulgaria has long been the most popular tourist destination in the country, both for northern Europeans in search of the sun and for Bulgarians themselves. Sozopol, which is about 30 km (19 mi) south of Burgas, is the oldest of the Black Sea towns, and was first settled in 610 BC by the ancient Greeks. It was known as Apollonia Pontica. The Romans arrived in the first century BC, and the town became prosperous. It came under Turkish rule in 1453 after a long siege and its importance waned. During the nineteenth century Sozopol gradually became a major fishing port and, finally, a tourist destination. The Archaeological Museum gives a glimpse of the town's rich cultural heritage and the various civilizations that moulded it.

Sozopol's old town lies on a small, rocky peninsula that is connected to the mainland by a narrow strip of land which is now a pretty park. There are some 45 architectural monuments in the town, including several interesting churches. The Renaissance St Zossima Chapel was built in the thirteenth century in honour of the patron saint of sailors. The fifteenth-century church of St Bogoroditsa contains gorgeous wooden screens, embellished with ranks of icons, that separate the sanctuary from the nave.

The old town is criss-crossed by narrow, cobbled lanes and, together with its old wooden houses, has an atmosphere that is both tranquil and romantic. There are two good, sandy beaches and plenty of restaurants and cafés overlooking the sea. The town has been a favourite with artists for many years, and in September the Apollonia Festival of Arts attracts visitors from all over the world.

**WHAT IS IT**
The oldest town on the BlackSea, dating back to 610 BC.
**WHAT ELSE IS THERE TO SEE**
Ivan Island and Nesebar, Varna.
**WHEN SHOULD I VISIT**
The Apollonia Festival of Arts takes place each September and is worth visiting.
**HOW DO I GET THERE**
Travel by air or train from Sofia to Burgas, then by bus from Burgas.

# Prague

Prague lies on a bend in the River Vltava, almost exactly half-way between Berlin and Vienna. It is set on seven hills surmounted by castles and churches, with Prague Castle (Pražský hrad), on the west bank, dominating the city.

Under the rule of Charles IV, Holy Roman Emperor and King of Germany, fabulous Gothic palaces and churches were built. In the recent past, Prague remained undamaged throughout World War II, and undeveloped during Communist rule. Since the end of Communism Prague has become a hugely popular destination, particularly with young people who come to enjoy the café culture and vibrant nightlife in the most beautiful surroundings.

The castle complex is home to the city's finest churches and museums. Founded in the ninth century, it has always been the seat of power. Outside the gate is the eighteenth-century Sternberg Palace (Sternberský palác), home to the National Gallery with its superb collection of Old Masters. The second courtyard contains the lovely Royal Gardens and in the third courtyard is St Vitus's Cathedral, a wonderful Gothic structure begun in 1344. The walls of the chapel containing the tomb of St Wenceslas are covered with precious stones and paintings of his life story.

Below the castle walls lies Malá Strana, the Little Quarter, which contains the impressive St Nicholas Cathedral and many beautiful old buildings. Crossing the Charles Bridge is a must for anyone visiting the city. This footbridge was built in 1357 and has towers at either end with fabulous views. Staré Město, the Old Town, is a fascinating tangle of atmospheric alleyways and narrow cobbled streets. Eight towers surround the enormous stone square at its heart, and there are superb churches and palaces to be visited.

**WHERE IS IT**
Prague is almost exactly halfway between Berlin and Vienna.
**WHAT IS THERE TO SEE**
The Old Town Hall, the synagogues of Josefov, Wallenstein Garden, Troja, John Lennon Wall, Vysehrad castle, Nové Město, the astronomical clock.
**DON'T MISS**
Crossing the Charles Bridge is a must for spectacular views over the river and city.
**YOU SHOULD KNOW**
Entrance fees are payable at most tourist attractions.

*The Charles Bridge and city buildings in winter.*

# Český Krumlov

**WHERE IS IT**
In the southern Czech Republic close to the border with Austria.
**WHAT IS THERE TO DO**
Take one of the tours around the chateau.
**WHAT IS THERE TO SEE**
Egon Schiele Art Centre, the Eggenberg Brewery, St Vitus's Church, Zlatá Koruna monastery, the castle at Hluboká nad Vltavou.
**HOW DO I GET THERE**
Travel by train or bus from Prague.

Český Krumlov is set on a winding stretch of the Vltava River. It is a gorgeous, small medieval town in the southern Czech Republic, not far from the Sumava Hills and the border with Austria. Its magnificent Gothic castle was built in the thirteenth century, and revamped as a Renaissance chateau in the sixteenth century.

The chateau stands on the west bank of the river, opposite the old town centre, and is entered through the Red Gate. Crossing a bridge over a moated bearpit you reach the oldest part of the castle, which has round towers and Renaissance frescoes. The complex is so large, with more than 40 separate buildings, that there are three separate tours.

The tours include the older, Renaissance rooms, as well as the Masquerade Hall with its superb eighteenth-century murals. You can learn about the history of those who lived here: the Rosenberg family, who ruled the town for 300 years from 1302 and were followed by the Eggenbergs, and finally the Schwarzenbergs, who lived here from 1719 until 1945. You will see the extraordinary Rococo theatre, complete with original scenery and props – a Baroque opera is performed here once a year. Among the highlights are the seventeenth-century coach, made of 24-carat gold and only used once, and the Rococo marble Chapel of St George. The beautiful gardens are well worth exploring.

The pretty old town centre lies within a horseshoe bend of the river and dates from between the fourteenth to the seventeenth centuries, and is in an excellent state of preservation.

*The town from the castle.*

# Tokaj wine region

Tokaj, with its population of less than 5,000, is a picturesque little place at the foot of the Kopasz Mountains with the Zemplén Hills to the north and the Tisza and Bodrog rivers to the south. The Zemplén Hills are volcanic and the autumns are mild, which may go some way towards explaining why this area produces such fine wines and has done so continuously since the seventeenth century.

*Tokaj sits below this hillside vineyard.*

Unlike Eger, the main city in northern Hungary which is famous for its red wines, including the well-known Bull's Blood, Tokaj, farther to the north-east, produces only white wines. It is known throughout the world, however, for its sweet dessert wines – Louis XIV said of Tokaj that it was 'the wine of kings and the king of wines'.

In fact Tokaj produces various different types of white wine. Hárslevelü is probably the driest, but Furmint is the basic dry white, which is found on every wine list. Szamorodni can be dry or sweet and is a more complex wine, something like a sherry. Aszú is made from the grapes that ripen most quickly in a bunch. Legend has it that in 1630 a farmer fled the area fearing an invasion, leaving his grapes unharvested. On his return he found they had rotted on the vine and sugar had concentrated within them, producing this honeyed wine. There are four levels of sweetness available. Aszú Esszencia is the king of wines itself – an unimaginably delicious flavour that should be drunk by itself, and every last drop savoured.

In all, there are 28 villages and towns in the Tokaj wine-growing region, which stretches along the southern and eastern foothills of the Zemplén range. Everywhere you go around the region you will see private cellars and vineyards offering wine-tastings.

**WHAT IS IT**
Hungary's best-known wine region.
**WHAT IS IT KNOWN FOR**
Tokaj is known throughout the world for white wine, and particularly for its sweet dessert wines.
**WHAT IS THERE TO SEE**
Rákóczi Pince cellars, the Tokaj Museum, the Tokaj Himesudvar Winery.
**INTERESTING TRIVIA**
Louis XIV said Tokaj was 'the wine of kings and the king of wines'.
**HOW DO I GET THERE**
By train from Budapest.

*The Parliament Building sits on the Pest side of the Danube.*

# Budapest

Budapest is really three distinct towns set on either side of the Danube, and linked by bridges. In 1873, the three towns merged. Óbuda and Buda (the historic medieval city on Castle Hill with the Buda Hills ranged beyond) are on the west bank, and Pest (the administrative and commercial city) is on the east. Large parts of the city are listed as a UNESCO World Heritage Site because of their architectural, archaeological and cultural importance.

Budapest's history is long and full of strife, with invasions by Celts, Romans, Huns and other tribes, Ottoman Turks and Austrians, it suffered bombing and invasion during World War II and the violence of the uprising in 1956. Since the break-up of the Soviet Union, Budapest has once again become a thriving, lovely city.

Castle Hill, the heart of Budapest, is a beautiful area. It has suffered many times over the centuries from the ravages of war – but the Hungarians have painstakingly rebuilt their city and once again it stands proud. The neo-Gothic Mathias Church has a multi-coloured, tiled roof, and a wonderful interior, and the castle itself is now home to some excellent museums in various wings, displaying marvellous paintings, including those of Eastern European and Hungarian artists as well as modern artists such as Picasso and Lichtenstein.

Pest too has some marvellous museums – including the National Museum – and churches, of which St Stephen's Basilica is the city's largest. Its neo-Renaissance dome shelters a glorious interior, and the balcony of its Panorama Tower provides 360-degree views of the city and surrounding area. The National Opera House is a spectacular building in Andrassy Ut, the grandest boulevard in the city built during the glory days of the Austro-Hungarian Empire. The Parliament building dominates the river bank and its spectacular interior is worth seeing, as are the Hungarian crown jewels, including St Stephen's crown, that are housed here.

The legacy of the Turks' 145-year domination is chiefly seen today in the many thermal spas and Turkish baths that survive.

**WHAT IS IT**
Originally Budapest was three towns that merged in 1873.
**WHAT IS THERE TO SEE**
The Great Synagogue and the Jewish Museum, Parliament, Gellert Hill, Heroes' Square, Esztergom and Szekesfehervar.
**DO NOT MISS**
The views of the city from the Panorama Tower of St Stephen's Basilica.
**WHAT IS THERE TO DO**
Spend a day at the thermal baths.

# Auschwitz Concentration Camp

Auschwitz I, with its sister camp Auschwitz II-Birkenau, was the largest Nazi concentration camp. It is *c*.60 km (40 mi) west of Kraków, on the site of a Polish army barracks outside the town of Oswiecim. It was originally intended to house Polish political prisoners, but was instead developed into an enormous death factory, exterminating between 1.5 and 2 million 'undesirables', about 90 per cent of whom were Jews.

Over the camp's gate is the chilling legend *Arbeit Macht Frei* ('work will make you free'). The camp authority's attempt to destroy the evidence of genocide before they fled the advancing Soviet army did not succeed and about 30 prison blocks remain, some of which house part of the Auschwitz-Birkenau State Museum.

The Visitor Centre screens a bleak, 15-minute documentary about the camp's liberation in 1945. Auschwitz-Birkenau, just 3 km (2 mi) away, was where most of the exterminations took place. At the height of its operation it could hold 200,000 people at once. It enclosed 300 prison barracks, five huge gas chambers, each built to hold 2,000 people, and crematoria. The ruins are haunting and utterly shocking.

The site is well worth visiting, although it is not for the faint of heart. The unspeakable horror of the sight of thousands and thousands of toys, shoes, spectacles and bundles of human hair, heaped up in neat mounds, makes an impression that will never leave you.

**WHAT IS IT**
The infamous Nazi concentration camp where between 1.5 and 2 million 'undesirables' were exterminated during WWII.
**WHAT IS THERE TO SEE**
Ruins of the concentration camp and memorial to the horrors perpetrated there.
**WHAT SHOULD I KNOW**
It is not for the faint hearted. The horrific nature of some of the images and installations will remain with you long after you have left.
**HOW DO I GET THERE**
Travel by train, bus or taxi from Kraków.

*The phrase over the front gate, Arbeit Macht Frei, translates as 'Work will make you free'.*

# Bialowieza National Park

**WHERE IS IT**
The national park is located on the border with Belarus, 200 km (120 mi) east of Warsaw.
**WHAT IS THERE TO SEE**
Palace Park and its museum; Bialowieza village.
**HOW DO I GET THERE**
Train, bus or car from Warsaw.
**YOU SHOULD KNOW**
It is a UNESCO Biosphere Reserve and World Heritage Site. The park is off-limits without a licensed guide.

*European Bison roam the snowy Bialowieza Forest. Once near extinction, the bison were reintroduced into the forest and this is the last wild herd in Europe.*

Bialowieza National Park is situated some 200 km (120 mi) east of Warsaw, on the border with Belarus, which also has protected areas. It is one of the last virgin forests left in Europe, a remnant of the primeval forest that once covered much of the European plain, and was once a favourite hunting spot for the kings of Poland, and the site of the former residence of Tsar Nicholas I, in the Palace Park.

The ancient forest's huge trees and pockets of dense vegetation provide shelter for a wealth of biodiversity. It is home to some 11,000 species of flora and fauna rarely seen elsewhere in Europe, including 120 species of breeding birds, 7 species of reptiles, 11 species of amphibians and 8,500 species of insects.

This is the last habitat of the European Bison, (in Polish, *ubr*). The national park is also home to semi-wild konik ponies, which are being bred in an effort to bring back from extinction the tarpan, a breed of horse popular all over Europe in the Middle Ages, and zubrons, a cross between bison and cows. Among the 54 species of mamals living here are wolves, red deer, roe deer, lynx, beaver, elk and wild boar. The European Bison Reserve enables you to see some of these animals within the confines of a small park, or you can tour around the Strict Nature Reserve, really the main attraction here, with a licensed guide, either on foot or by horse-drawn cart. This is a real paradise for nature lovers.

# Gdańsk

Gdańsk is a beautiful, old port city on the Baltic Sea, in the north of Poland. First settled in the ninth century, it became the thriving city of Danzig after being conquered by the Teutonic Knights in the early fourteenth century. By the middle of the sixteenth century it was the most important Baltic port, and Poland's largest city.

It was here that World War II started in September 1939, when the German battleship *Schleswig-Holstein* fired on the Polish naval fort at Westerplatte. The city was devastated during the war, but almost all of its historic centre has been painstakingly restored. It was also in Gdańsk that the Soviet Empire began to crack when Lech Walesa jumped over the shipyard fence, organized Solidarity and proclaimed a general strike. The monuments to the Polish defenders of Westerplatte, and to the shipyard strikers of Solidarity are not far apart.

Gdańsk used to be one of the richest port-cities in Northern Europe and it shows – the buildings are bigger and the streets are broader than in other medieval cities. St Mary's Church is possibly the largest brick church in the world. Dlugi Targ is the splendid main square at the heart of Glone Miasto, Main Town. From here you can easily walk to the huge, fourteenth-century town hall and many other architectural gems, such as the unique, seventeenth-century houses lining St. Mary's Street. You can stroll for hours along the picturesque old streets and river banks of the ancient port that has been so significant in European history.

*Gdańsk Town Hall dates from the fourteenth century. The city was largely destroyed in World War II and later reconstructed.*

**WHAT IT IS IT**
A beautiful old port city on Poland's Baltic coast.
**WHAT IS IT KNOWN FOR**
World War II started here.
**WHAT IS THERE TO SEE**
The National Museum, the seaside town of Sopot, Oliwa Cathedral and Monastery.
**WHAT IS THERE TO DO**
Wander around the picturesque streets.

# Grunwald

South-west of Olsztyn, in north-east Poland, stands the Monument of the Grunwald Battlefield, in an area of gently rolling meadows. This monument, unveiled in 1960, celebrates the Polish victory over the Teutonic Knights in 1410, in what was the largest battle in medieval Europe.

The Polish forces, numbering about 39,000 men, were helped by regiments from Russia, Czechoslovakia and Lithuania, as well as by the Tartars. They were commanded by King Wladyslaw Jagiello, and led by his brother Witold, the Grand Duke of Lithuania. The Teutonic Knights, were mainly Germans but were aided by mercenaries from all over Western Europe who were supported by infantry and cannon.

The battle was won by the stratagems and cunning employed by the Polish king, who had been fighting the Tartars, Turks and Cossacks since his early childhood. To him the rows of noble knights in heavy armour marching into battle resembled cattle led to slaughter. They proved to be no match for the lightly armed and highly mobile Polish, Lithuanian and Tartar cavalrymen. After ten hours of carnage, half of the 27,000 Teutonic Knights were dead or captured and the rest routed. In World War I, on this same spot, the Germans took their revenge and beat the Russians at the Battle of Tannenberg.

The victory at Grunwald is widely regarded as a turning point in Polish history, and the battlefield and the small museum about the battle are frequently visited. Standing on the hill, beneath the monument, where the king stood, one can imagine this clash of civilizations, and looking out over the grassland and forests below there is a certain sense of eeriness.

*The monument marks the site of a battle in 1410 between the Polish allied forces against the Teutonic Knights.*

**WHAT IS IT**
The site of the largest battle in medieval Europe.
**WHAT ELSE IS THERE TO SEE**
Olsztyn.
**HOW DO I GET THERE**
By train or bus to Olsztyn, then by road.
**WHEN SHOULD I GO**
The best weather is from May to September.

# Ketrzyn

Ketrzyn is a charming village in north-eastern Poland, dominated by a fourteenth-century castle, which houses an interesting regional museum. However, the main reason visitors make their way here is the 'Wolfsschanze', Adolf Hitler's wartime military headquarters. The so-called Wolf's Lair is located in the forest east of the town, and what remains of it, after it was blown up by the retreating Germans in 1945, is both historically important and a major tourist attraction well worth seeing.

It was here, in July 1944, that a group of high-ranking German officers headed by Baron Claus von Stauffenberg tried to kill Hitler. Arriving for a meeting, von Stauffenberg placed his briefcase, which contained a bomb, close to the Führer's seat, and then left the room to take a pre-arranged phone call. The explosion killed two members of staff and badly wounded others, but Hitler, who unfortunately arrived late for the meeting, merely suffered minor injuries. The conspirators were left to die hanging from butcher's hooks and several thousand others who were suspected of involvement in the plot were also executed.

The ruins of 'Wolfsschanze', with 2–3-m (6–10-ft) thick concrete walls, endless fortified underground corridors, conference rooms and living quarters, all bear witness to Hitler's paranoia, and leave a lasting impression, especially in contrast to the surrounding pristine forest and meadows covered with delicate wildflowers.

**WHAT IS IT**
The site of the 'Wolfsschanze', Adolf Hitler's wartime headquarters.
**WHAT IS IT KNOWN FOR**
The attempted assassination of Adolf Hitler happened here.
**WHAT IS THERE TO SEE**
The Great Masurian Lakes, Olsztyn.
**HOW DO I GET THERE**
Take a train or bus from Warsaw.

*Hitler's wartime military headquarters was the site of an attempt to assassinate him.*

# Kraków

Kraków is in southern Poland. It was first mentioned by a Jewish merchant, Jakob ben Abraham, in 966, and by 1038 had become the medieval capital of Poland. The city was built on the Vistula river, beneath the Royal Castle on Wawel Hill. Legend has it that the castle was built on the lair of a ravenous dragon, which demanded a virgin every two weeks but was finally slain by Prince Krak, the founder of Kraków. Tourists can visit the dragon's cave beneath the castle.

Kraków is the only large city in Poland that remained intact during World War II and today it is a well-preserved, charming, medieval city, with picturesque cobbled streets, numerous churches, museums, cafés, restaurants and bars, some of which still serve mead – the medieval drink made of fermented honey and herbs. It boasts an impressive central square with the fourteenth-century St Mary's church, and a sixteenth-century Renaissance cloth hall. The square is filled with countless stalls, selling numerous products from local artisans.

The painstakingly restored Jewish quarter Kazimierz feels eerie and haunted – here is a Jewish neighbourhood without Jewish residents. At the start of World War II 65,000 Jews lived here, but they were exterminated in the nearby Plaszów Concentration Camp, made famous in Steven Speilberg's film *Schindler's List*.

South of the Old Town the splendid royal castle and cathedral crown Wawel Hill. The tenth-century castle was extended and restored in the sixteenth century and contains the royal apartments and magnificent contemporary tapestries. The cathedral saw the coronation and burial of Polish royalty for 400 years, and its golden domed chapel is considered to be the finest Renaissance example in the country.

*Wawel Cathedral is Poland's national sanctuary and was the coronation site of Polish monarchs.*

# Marienburg Castle

Marienburg Castle is the ancient seat of the Grand Master of the Teutonic Knights. It is situated in Malbork on the Nogat River, a branch of the Vistula River, about 50 km (30 mi) from Gdańsk and 250 km (155 mi) from Warsaw. The Marienberg Castle is a classic example of a Gothic medieval fortress, one of the best of its kind in Europe, and the largest brick castle in the world. Together with a system of multiple defensive walls with gates and towers, it covers over 32 ha (80 acres).

Built in 1276, Marienburg Castle became the seat of the Grand Master of the Teutonic Knights in 1309. Badly damaged during World War II, when it housed the prisoner-of-war camp Stalag XXB, it has since been superbly restored. The castle is divided into three major parts; the oldest section is the rectangular High Castle with an arcaded courtyard containing a refectory, chapterhouse, treasury and St Mary's Chapel. In the fourteenth century, the old forecastle was converted into the Mid Castle, the Grand Refectory, the Knights' Hall and the Palace of the Grand Master. The Lower Castle held the armoury and St Lawrence's Church.

The interior houses several exhibitions, including a permanent exhibition detailing the castle's history, together with collections of medieval sculpture, stained-glass windows, coins and medals, weaponry, iron and foundry work, pottery, tapestries and a priceless collection of amber art. In the summer, *son et lumière* spectacles are held in the castle courtyards.

*Marienburg Castle, the largest brick castle in the world, sits on the Nogat River.*

**WHERE IS IT**
On the Nogat River, a branch of the Vistula River between Gdańsk and Warsaw in northern Poland.
**WHAT IS THERE TO SEE**
Gdańsk, Slowinski National Park.
**YOU SHOULD KNOW**
There is an entrance fee.
**HOW SHOULD I GET THERE**
Travel by train or car from Warsaw or Gdańsk.

433

*Chandeliers hang in the dark St Kinga Chapel at the Wieliczka salt mine.*

# Wieliczka Salt Mine

The Wieliczka Salt Mine has been worked for some 900 years and reaches a depth of about 327 m (1,000 ft) below ground level. It is virtually on the south-eastern outskirts of the city of Kraków and, during the Middle Ages, was one of the world's biggest and most profitable industrial establishments, as common salt was, commercially, the medieval equivalent of today's oil.

One well-travelled Frenchman observed in the eighteenth century that Kraków's Wieliczka Salt Mine was no less magnificent than the Egyptian pyramids. Millions of visitors, crowned heads and celebrities such as Goethe and Sarah Bernhardt among them, have appeared to share his enthusiasm when exploring the subterranean world of labyrinthine passages, giant caverns, underground lakes and sculptures of Polish heroes, all carved from the crystalline rock salt. They have also marvelled at the ingenuity of the ancient mining equipment.

The mine is fully operational and produces about 20 tonnes of salt each day. Increasingly, since the mid-eighteenth century, it has become a tourist attraction. Every last inch of it has been carved out and fashioned by hand and the chapel, measuring 54 by 17 m (177 by 56 ft) and rising to 12 m (39 ft) in height, took 32 years to make, entailing the removal of 20,000 tonnes of salt. The chapel is richly ornamented, and everything is made of salt. The altarpiece, the chandeliers and the sculptures and other religious artefacts are incredibly beautiful. The unique acoustics of the place make listening to music here an exceptional experience.

**WHAT IS IT**
A fully operational salt mine, dating back 900 years.
**WHAT IS THERE TO SEE**
Wieliczka Salt Mine Museum.
**YOU SHOULD KNOW**
There is an entrance fee.
**HOW DO I GET THERE**
Travel by train or bus from Kraków.

# Zakopane

Zakopane is a beautiful mountain resort nestled in the Tatras, the highest range in the 1,000-km (620-mi) long Carpathian Mountains, not far from the border with Slovakia, in southern Poland. Towering above the town is Giewont, a mountain in the shape of a sleeping giant, topped by an enormous cross.

Zakopane is popular both in the summer and in the winter – during the two high seasons it enjoys, the population swells from 33,000 to more than 100,000. It is a great place for both outdoor activities and for a more relaxed contemplation of nature. The main summertime activity is hiking in the mountains of the magnificent Tatra National Park area, with its many fine peaks and alpine meadows. Here you can see a good variety of birds and animals – even the rare brown bear!

The symbol of Zakopane is the *szarotka*, a hardy little white flower, better known as edelweiss, which can grow anywhere and withstand any weather. If you prefer to be a little less active, you can take the cable-car to the summit of Kasprowy Wierch. Here you can stand, surrounded by fantastic, panoramic views, with one foot in Poland and one foot in Slovakia.

In winter, the skiing is excellent, with four major ski areas and more than 50 ski lifts to transport you from peak to peak. Laid-back apres-ski spots are numerous and lively. This is also the capital of Podhale folklore, a culturally distinct area where the native 'Highlanders' still wear colourful local costumes. The Highlander culture extends to its food, and there are several specialities including the local smoked, sheeps' cheese – *oscypek* – which is carved into various designs.

**WHAT IS IT**
A beautiful mountain resort in the Carpathian Mountains.
**WHAT IS THERE TO SEE**
The Tatra Mountains Museum, Mt Gubalówka, Lake Morskie Oko.
**HOW DO I GET THERE**
Travel by train or bus from Warsaw, or Kraków.
**WHEN SHOULD I VISIT**
In summer to enjoy hiking in the mountains and the abundant wildlife, or in winter for skiing.

*Zakopane in the Tatra Mountains.*

# The Great Masurian Lakes

**WHAT IS IT**
The largest lake system in Poland with 45 lakes, 12 canals and 8 rivers.
**WHAT IS THERE TO SEE**
Pisz Forest, Swieta Lipka Monastery and the towns of Gizycko, Mikolajki and Sztynort.
**HOW DO I GET THERE**
By train or bus from Warsaw or Gdańsk.
**YOU SHOULD KNOW**
This is a UNESCO World Biosphere Reserve.

*Lake Narty, one of the 45 lakes in the area.*

North-east Poland's Great Masurian Lakes are the most extensive system of lakes in the country. The region is a beautiful landscape of hills, forests, farms and lakes, many of which are connected by a network of canals and rivers. Altogether there are 45 lakes, 12 canals and eight rivers, making up the most extensive stretch of water in Europe, and the area is extremely popular for sailing and canoeing as well as hiking, mountain biking and fishing.

Lake Sniardwy is the largest lake in the country, covering 110 sq km (42 sq mi). The whole area is home to an extraordinary range of plants and animals and includes several nature reserves, including Lake Luknajo Reserve, the largest Central European breeding ground for mute swans. There are fabulous water birds to be seen – bitterns, herons and rare black storks, as well as raptors such as eagles and kites.

The Augustow Forest is one of the most extensive in Poland and is mainly covered in ancient pines and spruces. It is home to many birds and mammals including European bison, elk, wild boar, wolves and beavers. The town of Augustow makes a good base for summer visitors as it is very close to three of the lakes. There are various other towns dotted around the region, all of which become busy during the summer.

If you are not a sailor, it is easy to travel the lakes in comfort on a pleasure boat from any of the lake ports, or take a trip on the Elblag Canal. This was built some 150 years ago and is still much admired for its hydraulic-powered rail lifts that allow heavy vessels to be transported overland between separate waterways.

# Sighisoara

*Birthplace of Vlad the Impaler.*

Sighisoara is an exquisite, fortified medieval town set in the Tarnarva Mare River valley in Transylvania. Once a Roman fort, it was founded by craftsmen and merchants, known as the Saxons of Transylvania, in the twelfth century, and was the birthplace of Vlad the Impaler, Count Dracula – his house is now a restaurant.

The medieval citadel is entered through the Clock Tower, one of nine remaining towers out of the original 14. It was built in 1360 to defend the main gate, and in 1604 was topped with a wooden clock. This was remade by Johann Kirschel, who constructed two groups of limewood figures beside the two large dials. The clock mechanism moves the figures, for example, a soldier, representing Mars, and the angel of the night who carries two candles. The Sighisoara towers were built by craftsmen's guilds between the fourteenth and sixteenth centuries and each bears the name of its trade, such as Blacksmiths and Shoemakers.

At the southern end of the citadel is the Gothic Bergkirche, with a beautiful interior that includes remnants of fifteenth-century frescoes. It is reached by a covered, wooden stairway, which was built in 1642 to help people reach both the church and the school on the hill. The streets and houses within the citadel, which is still lived and worked in, are all wonderfully preserved. Narrow, cobbled streets wind past tiny craftsmen's cottages and wealthy merchants' houses, painted in pink, green and yellow ochre. Sighisoara richly deserves its title of 'the pearl of Transylvania'.

**WHERE IS IT**
Sighisoara is in Translyvania, central Romania in the Tarnava Mare River valley.
**WHAT IS IT KNOWN FOR**
Being the birthplace of Vlad the Impaler, or Count Dracula.
**WHAT IS THERE TO SEE**
The Monastery Church, the Tailors' Tower, the Venetian House, the Medieval Art and Theatre Festival, Biertan.
**HOW DO I GET THERE**
By train or road from Bucharest.
**YOU SHOULD KNOW**
Sighisoara is a UNESCO World Heritage Site.

437

*The Winter Palace.*

# St Petersburg

Tsar Peter the Great of Russia founded St Petersburg in 1703. He had a vision of a great city dedicated to art and culture, providing a 'window on the west', and decided to build it on what was then a large, Finnish swamp, the delta of the Neva River, on the edge of the Baltic Sea's Gulf of Finland.

St Petersburg is unlike any other Russian city. Dominated by the Winter Palace, which stretches for 200 m (660 ft) along the river front, it is imbued with a sense of Russian imperial history. The Baroque palace was commissioned by the Tsarina Elizabeth for use by the imperial family during the winter, and its lavish interior gives an insight into the opulent lives of the tsars. Catherine the Great added the Hermitage in 1764 to house her private art collection, which has now grown so large that it is housed in five beautiful buildings and is second only in size to that of the Louvre's.

There are dozens of Baroque and Neoclassical palaces within the old centre of St Petersburg and the area was declared a UNESCO World Heritage Site in 1990.

The city is also known for its amazing array of churches, among which the Cathedral of Peter and Paul in Palace Square contains the tombs of Peter the Great and his successors, and the astonishing St Isaac's Cathedral's enormous dome is covered with 100 kg (220 lb) of gold. The Kazan Cathedral on Nevsky Prospekt is modelled on St Peter's in Rome.

St Petersburg is a beautiful city, with a rich history, and an absolute must for lovers of art and architecture.

**WHAT IS IT**
The former capital and cultural centre of the Russian Empire.
**WHERE IS IT**
On the Gulf of Finland in northern Russia.
**WHAT IS THERE TO SEE**
Nevsky Prospekt, the Russian Museum, the Steiglitz Museum and Yusupov's Palace.
**WHAT IS THERE TO DO**
Visit the Alexander Nevsky Monastery.

# Lake Baikal

Lake Baikal is special. Very special. It is the deepest, purest, oldest and, in volume, the biggest lake in the world. It holds 20 per cent of the world's unfrozen fresh water. It is so large that all the rivers in the world combined would take a year to fill it. It is in an active continental rift, which is spreading by about 2 cm (¾ in) a year and earthquakes occur regularly.

No fewer than 336 rivers and streams flow into the lake, while only one, the Angara, drains out of it. About 636 by 80 km (395 by 50 mi), with a coastline of about 2,100 km (1,305 mi) and containing 30 islands, Lake Baikal is in an immense area of breathtaking physical beauty, surrounded by mountains and forests in southern Siberia close to the Mongolian border. Wildlife in the national park surrounding the lake includes bear and deer, but it is the flora and fauna within the lake that make it really special. Baikal is home to more species of plants and animals that occur in only one place than any other lake in the world, including the world's only fresh water seal, the nerpa (Baikal seal). There is also a huge variety of edible fish from pike and perch to sturgeon and salmon.

Lake Baikal's deep waters are well oxygenated – unlike the dead waters found in the lower depths of other deep lakes – and are therefore rich in aquatic life. The water is so clear that in most parts of the lake you can see to a depth of 50 m (165 ft), although, as in so many places, human activity has begun to damage the lake, chiefly through the construction of the Irkutsk Dam and a wood pulp plant that pours effluent into the southern end of the lake.

**WHAT IS IT**
The biggest lake in the world, holding a rich variety of aquatic life.
**HOW DO I GET THERE**
Fly from Moscow to Irkutsk, then by bus, car or ferry to Listvyanka.
**WHAT IS THERE TO DO**
Take a boat trip on the lake or spend a few days on Olkhon Island.
**DON'T MISS**
The Circum-Baikal railway from Slyudyanka to Port Baikal; the hot springs in Arshan; hiking in the Sayan Mountains.
**ALSO KNOWN AS**
The Blue Eye of Siberia, *Ozero Baykal* and *Dalai-Nor*.

*The Trans-Siberian Express passes by Lake Baikal.*

# The Kremlin and Red Square

**WHERE IS IT**
The Kremlin and Red Square are in
the centre of Moscow.
**WHAT IS IT KNOWN FOR**
The colourful domes of St Basil's
Cathedral are an iconic image of
Red Square.
**WHAT IS THERE TO SEE**
Assumption Cathedral, Archangel
Cathedral, Theatre Square
and the KGB Museum.
**WHAT IS THERE TO DO**
Visit the Annunciation Cathedral and
see some of the most beautiful
iconostases in the land.

*The gilded domes of the
Annunciation Cathedral
with the Cathedral of the
Assumption behind.*

The Kremlin is a vast, fortified, roughly triangular complex of buildings at the heart of Moscow, and its name conjures up visions of Stalinism and KGB agents. Today, however, Moscow is at the centre of post-Communist capitalism, and is buzzing with enterprise and energy.

The Kremlin is surrounded by gardens to the west, the Moscow River to the south and Red Square to the east. In the fourteenth century it became the headquarters of the Russian Orthodox Church, and three great cathedrals were built here during the fifteenth and sixteenth centuries. There is a great deal to be seen! The Annunciation Cathedral contains some superb icons and a most beautiful iconostasis; Ivan the Great Bell Tower, with its two golden domes, can be seen from up to 30 km (20 mi) away, and stands next to the Assumption belfry which contains the Kremlin's biggest bell; the Armoury contains a multitude of treasures, including the royal regalia. Among other things you can also see the Poteshny Palace, where Stalin lived, and the Senate, which houses the offices of the President.

The 700-m (2,300-ft) Red Square (*Krasnaya ploschad*) is dominated by the glory that is St Basil's Cathedral, its fabulously colourful onion domes topped by golden needles and its main tower topped with a smaller, golden dome of its own, the epitome of a Russian church. Lenin's tomb is at the foot of the Kremlin wall, and queues still form to walk past his embalmed body. Red Square's sheer scale and the contrast between the beautiful churches and palaces and the stark Kremlin wall create a lasting, if unsettling, impression.

# The Moscow Metro

The Moscow Metro was designed as a hymn of praise to socialism. The beauty of the stations is renowned, and their sumptuous décor should be seen and enjoyed by everyone visiting the city.

The original line was opened in 1935, although plans for its construction had existed since before the Russian Revolution. The first plan was rejected but in 1912 a second proposition was approved. The outbreak of World War I, followed by the revolution delayed its construction until 1931.

This line originally had 13 stations, the most interesting of which is Kropotkinskaya. The walls and columns of the station were faced with marble taken from the demolished Cathedral of Christ the Saviour, and the columns themselves, which support the vaulted ceiling, were designed as five-pointed stars.

Ploshad Revolutsii, on the second line, is symbolic of the new socialist world – there are 76 bronzes depicting farm workers, athletes, soldiers and sailors. Mayakovskaya station, on the third line, represents a day in the land of socialism. The ceiling of the hall is covered in mosaic panels, made of opaque glass, representing the day from morning to night, and back to dawn.

In 1950 the ring line was opened and its Komsomolskaya station (1952) is the best of all. Designed by Shchusev, its underground pavilion is topped with a steeple crowned with a five-pointed star and the interior is sumptuous, full of astonishing mosaics depicting military victories and Russian heroes, marble, granite, multicoloured glass and chandeliers.

The Moscow Metro carries an average of 8.1 million passengers each day, making it one of the busiest in the world. Visitors should not miss this gorgeous underground art gallery-cum-museum – and you can travel on it too!

*A tunnel at Arbatskaya Station.*

**WHAT IS IT KNOWN FOR**
The Moscow Metro is known throughout the world for its lavish décor and beauty.
**WHAT IS THERE TO SEE**
Novokuznetskaya, Kievskaya, Krasnye Vorota and Park Kultury.
**DON'T MISS**
Komsomolskaya, the most beautiful of all the stations.
**YOU SHOULD KNOW**
The metro is open from 5.35 am–1.04 am daily.

*The houses and churches of Levoča.*

# Levoča

The Spiš region is generally regarded as the most beautiful part of Slovakia and Levoča, one of the finest walled towns in the whole country, is often known as the 'jewel in the Spiš crown'. Dating from the thirteenth century, the town enjoyed several hundred years of great prosperity because of its key position on a number of important trade routes and to a clever local law that forced merchants to stay in Levoča until they had sold all their goods.

The wealth of Renaissance structures that the town possesses today is mainly the result of extensive and elaborate construction work that followed a major fire in 1550, in which many of the town's buildings were destroyed. One that did survive however is the magnificent fourteenth-century St Jacob's Church, home to the world's tallest (over 18.5 m/60 ft) Gothic wooden altar which was hand-carved over a period of ten years by the great carver and sculptor Majster Pavol, after whom the town's splendid medieval main square is named. Other notable buildings include the town hall, the trade house, the theatre and more than 60 burghers' houses, mostly from the fourteenth and fifteenth centuries, in the main square.

With its medieval walls, its fine collection of well-preserved old buildings, its attractive setting and interesting history, Levoča – long a source of pride to the local Slovak population – has over recent decades begun to attract an increasing number of admirers from many other countries.

**WHAT IS IT**
A town in the most beautiful part of Slovakia, in the south-west.
**ALSO KNOWN AS**
The 'jewel in the Spiš crown'.
**HOW DO I GET THERE**
By road or rail from Košice or by rail from Bratislava via Spišské Podhradie.
**DON'T MISS**
Central Europe's largest castle at Spišské Podhradie; the cathedral and Gothic houses at Spišské Kapitula; the murals in the church at Zehra.
**WHAT IS THERE TO DO**
Spend a day hiking in nearby Slovenský Raj national park.

# Bled

Known in Slovenia as the 'alpine pearl', Bled is a particularly attractive small town in a fairy-tale location. Set against the backdrop of the forested slopes of the Julian Alps in north-west Slovenia, and the peaks of the Karavanke Mountains, it sits beside a beautiful emerald-green lake with an island in the middle and looming over all, perched high up on the rocky cliff on the northern side of town is the awe-inspiring red-and-white Castle of Bled, the origins of which date back to the eleventh century. It was rebuilt in the seventeenth century, renovated and remodelled in the 1950s and now houses a museum.

Once home to the Yugoslav royal family, famous as a health spa at the beginning of the twentieth century and later the summer residence of President Tito, Bled has naturally always been something of a magnet for visitors – from the pilgrims of many centuries ago to the honeymooners of today.

On the island in Lake Bled there is a picturesque little white seventeenth-century church complete with a wishing bell. Legend has it that a husband who can carry his new bride up the 99 stone steps from the dock to the church will enjoy a happy marriage and ringing the bell will make the couple's dreams come true.

**ALSO KNOWN AS**
The 'alpine pearl'.
**DON'T MISS**
Take a horse-drawn carriage ride around the lake.
**WHEN SHOULD I GO**
Arrive in July for Rikli's festival, when thousands of lighted candles float on the lake.
**HOW DO I GET THERE**
By road or rail from Ljubljana.
**DO NOT MISS**
Lake Bohinj – 30 km (19 mi) south-west of Bled, hiking in Triglav National Park, wandering around the Old Town in Ljubljana.

*A popular trip on Lake Bled is to the island by 'pletna', Bled's version of a gondola.*

# St Sophia Cathedral

**WHAT IS IT**
Kiev's most famous landmark.
**WHERE IS IT**
In Kiev, the Ukraine's capital in the north of the country.
**WHAT IS THERE TO SEE**
The tomb of Yaroslav the Wise, the cycle of frescoes in the lofts, the Golden Gate and St Michael's Monastery.
**YOU SHOULD KNOW**
It is a UNESCO World Heritage Site.

Kiev is the capital city of the Ukraine, and Saint Sophia's Cathedral is its best-known landmark. The monastery complex is large and elaborate. It was built between 1017 and 1031 in honour of prince Yaroslav the Wise, to commemorate his victory over the nomadic Asian Pecheneg tribe, but has been added to and renewed over the centuries. The cathedral was named after the Aya Sophia cathedral in Constantinople, and was surrounded by other churches dedicated to patron saints. The exterior that we see today dates from the seventeenth and eighteenth centuries, when Baroque modifications were made to conceal the original structure.

The cathedral, has 13 golden onion domes, five naves and five apses, with two-tiered galleries on three sides. The interior walls are covered with frescoes and mosaics of the highest order, dating back to the eleventh century, but including work from the seventeenth and eighteenth centuries as well. The mosaics in the cathedral are notable for their rich tones, made up of 177 different shades against a gold background. Possibly the most magnificent example is the 6-m (20-ft) high image of the Virgin Mary at prayer. The 21 shades of blue in her clothing convey the folds and flow of the fabric.

South of the cathedral stands what was the refectory and is now the Baroque Little Sophia Church, the Metropolitan Residence, the church seminary and the superb, four-storey, azure-and-white Bell Tower. This last stands 76 m (250 ft) high and is richly embellished with stucco.

*Mosiac of the Virgin Mary at prayer in St Sophia Cathedral.*

# Kiev Pechersk Lavra

The Kiev Pechersk Lavra (Kiev Cave Monastery) is built over wooded slopes above the Dnieper River. The name Pechersk refers to caves in the rocky banks of the river, where two monks founded the monastery in the eleventh century. Lavra comes from Greek and means a monastery of the Eastern church, living communally but inhabiting detached cells, or, as in this case, caves. This complex, believed to have been erected on a site chosen by God, is the spiritual home of the Ukranian people. Today some of the buildings are museums, but it is also a functioning monastery.

The original few inhabited caves grew into two independent cave systems, each of which has three underground churches lit by candles and displaying wonderful icons. The monastery grew to cover several hectares and was surrounded by walls and towers within which the monks built beautiful churches with spires and golden domes.

In the thirteenth century it suffered damage from invading Tartars, and although it remained in use it was not until the seventeenth and eighteenth centuries that its great revival occurred. Most of the glorious buildings seen today date from this period although one, the Holy Trinity Church above the main entrance gate remains virtually unchanged since the twelfth century. It contains some superb frescoes. The Great Bell Tower, which at 96.5 m (317 ft) was the tallest structure in Kiev for 200 years, gives marvellous views over the city.

The interior of the nineteenth-century Refectory Church is almost completely decorated with murals and the exterior is crowned by a gold-striped dome.

The most important building, the Dormition Cathedral was blown up in 1941 but restored to exquisite glory in 1998–2000.

*The rich decoration of the Dormition Cathedral.*

*The old town and the harbour.*

# Dubrovnik

The former city-republic of Dubrovnik stands on the coast of South Dalmatia, the most southerly region of Croatia. Behind it rise the Dinaric Alps, limestone peaks that form the border with Bosnia-Hercegovina, and facing the city are the blue waters of the Adriatic. Its ancient city walls, reinforced with towers in the fifteenth century, surround and protect a wonderfully preserved historic city centre, that was designated a UNESCO World Heritage Site in 1979.

Known as Ragusa from the twelfth century until 1918, it became a rich and powerful republic thanks to its location. By the sixteenth century it had a huge fleet of merchant ships, carrying goods to western Europe, but its decline began after a terrible earthquake in 1667, which razed many Gothic buildings and killed some 5,000 people. New Baroque buildings were erected, and to this day those fortified medieval walls have largely protected the city from the wars that have raged around it. In the early 1990s the Yugoslav People's Army besieged Dubrovnik and ruined many of its famous terracotta tiled rooftops. However careful restoration work since then has returned the city to its former glory.

The old city is pedestrianized, but it is small enough to be able to visit all the sights easily and is a joy to stroll around. The main street, Placa, is paved with gleaming white limestone dating from the 1460s, although the buildings to either side were erected after the earthquake. The Sponza Palace dates from the 1520s and is one of the few buildings not to have been damaged by the earthquake. Other important buildings are the Rector's Palace, the Cathedral, the Dominican Monastery with its lovely fifteenth-century cloister, and the Franciscan Monastery.

**WHAT IS THERE TO SEE**
The city walls, the Orthodox Church, the Synagogue and the Summer Festival.

**IF YOU DARE**
Get involved with the water sports in the area, including diving and sea kayaking.

**DO NOT MISS**
Do some island hopping on the Elafiti Islands for secluded sandy beaches and beautiful scenery.

**HOW DO I GET THERE**
Travel by air from elsewhere in Europe, ferry from Bari (Italy) or bus from Split.

# Hvar Island

Hvar is a long and narrow island, which in 1997 was nominated as one of the ten most beautiful islands in the world by *Traveller* magazine. It is a perfect place to escape to from the mainland, an island of lavender fields and vineyards and hills giving fabulous views to the mainland mountains. The island has many pretty Venetian villages, and if you just want to relax, head for the south-east, which is still largely untouched.

The Venetians brought prosperity to Hvar in the fifteenth and sixteenth centuries, using it as a base for their Adriatic fleet. In 1571 Turkish troops laid waste to Hvar town. The buildings you see today were mainly erected in the late sixteenth century or later.

St Stephen's Square is the largest in Dalmatia. It is lined with shops and cafes, with one end opening onto a small harbour and the other occupied by the magnificent sixteenth century cathedral. On the southern corner of the square is the former Arsenal, which now houses an art gallery that leads to the old theatre. The arched vault beneath the gallery used to allow Venetian ships to anchor safely while undergoing repair. In 1610 a democratic agreement was signed giving all citizens equal rights and for a short time the years were counted from that date, and the Latin inscription over the door reads 'the second year of peace'.

South of the square, there is an impressive fifteenth century Franciscan monastery, now a museum, where concerts are performed during summer, and north of the square a footpath leads you up to the sixteenth-century fortress.

**WHAT IS IT**
One of the ten most beautiful islands in the world.
**WHAT IS IT KNOWN FOR**
Pretty Venetian villages and lavender fields.
**WHAT IS THERE TO SEE**
Stari Grad, Church of St Lawrence at Vrboska, vineyard of Zlatan Otok at Sveta Nedjelja.
**HOW DO I GET THERE**
Take a ferry from Split.

*A village on the coast of Hvar Island.*

# Korcula Island

Korcula is a long, narrow island, situated just south of the Peljesac Peninsula of South Dalmatia. The island is thought to have got its name from the Greek *korkyra melaina* after the dense pine forests that once covered it. It is a just a short ferry ride away from the mainland and was first settled in 6,500 BC.

The town of Korčula, on the north-east coast, is often described as being like a mini-Dubrovnik because of its roofs of terracotta tiles set above the sea on a small, fortified peninsula. The island has changed hands several times over the centuries, but the architectural legacy left by the Venetians between 1420 and 1779 is second to none.

The Land Gate is the main entrance to the old, fortified town, and the symbol of Venice, the winged lion of St Mark, can be seen above the arch. The Gothic-Renaissance Cathedral of St Mark stands on the main square. The doorway built by Bonino of Milan in 1412 has Adam and Eve to either side, and St Mark above. There is a lovely rose window in the centre of the façade. The Renaissance interior was carved by a local stonemason, and contains treasures such as an early Tintoretto.

Next to the cathedral is the seventeenth-century Bishop's Palace, which holds the town's treasury, and opposite it is the museum, housed in the sixteenth-century Renaissance Gabrielli's Palace. The island is famous for the Moreska, a medieval sword dance that originated in Spain and is now performed during the summer in a garden next to the Land Gate.

*The marina beside the old stone houses on the island of Korcula.*

# Split

Set on a peninsula jutting out into the Adriatic, Split is the second largest of Croatia's cities, with a fascinating history. In 295 AD the Roman Emperor, Diocletian, ordered an enormous palace to be built here, and the heart of the city still lies within its ancient walls.

During the Middle Ages many new buildings were erected inside these walls, incorporating parts of the Roman structure and obscuring the original layout. For almost 400 years, from 1420, Split came under the authority of Venice, and became a wealthy trading port. Gorgeous Venetian-Gothic palaces were built and the resulting mixture of architecture is unique.

The Bronze Gate, one of four, leads from the seafront into the Podrum, a series of underground halls said to have been Diocletian's prison. His mausoleum, guarded by an ancient Egyptian sphinx, is now the site of one of the oldest Catholic cathedrals in the world, dedicated to St Domnius whose remains replaced those of Diocletian in the seventh century. The circular interior has eight columns supporting the dome, and a thirteenth-century hexagonal pulpit of superbly worked stone. The wooden doors, now protected, were made in 1214 and are magnificently carved with scenes from Christ's life. If you can face climbing the steps of the bell tower, you will have an amazing view of the whole area.

The City Museum is a marvellous piece of Venetian-Gothic architecture, built as a palace for the Papalic family in the fifteenth century. The Iron Gate, to the west, leads to the white-marble-paved Narodni Trg (People's Square), in which a Gothic building with three arches, built in 1443, now holds the Ethnographic Museum.

*Split from the top of Marjan Hill.*

**WHAT IS IT**
The second largest of Croatia's cities.
**WHAT IS THERE TO SEE**
The Bronze Gate, Jupiter's Temple, Marjan Hill, Diocletian's Mausoleum, Mestrovic Gallery and the Archaeological Museum.
**WHEN SHOULD I GO**
Arrive in the summer and soak up the atmosphere at Split Summer Festival.

449

*Visitors enter the Blue Cave on the islet of Bisevo, near Vis.*

# The Blue Cave

The coast of Dalmatia is scattered with islands across its entire length. There are more than 1,100 of them, of which fewer than 100 are inhabited. Vis Island is the farthest inhabited island from the mainland, and until 1989 it was a base for the Yugoslav navy. This fact, combined with its relative isolation, has enabled Vis to remain fairly unspoiled despite the rugged natural beauty of its interior and sixteenth-century Venetian fortress and monasteries.

Just 5 km (3.1 mi) south-west of Komiza, Vis's second town, on the west coast lies the tiny island of Bisevo. Formed from limestone, the island is less than 6 sq km (2.5 sq mi) in area and has a permanent population of only about 20 people. To the east, Bisevo rises to 240 m (790 ft) and in the centre is an area of olive groves and vineyards, but what it is most famous for is its coastal caves. There are 26 caves around the coastline, all of which can be visited by boat, and the Blue Cave (*Modra Spilja*) in Balun Cove is by far the best known, and is often favourably compared to Capri's Blue Grotto.

The Blue Cave is some 24 m by 12 m (80 by 40 ft), its waters reaching to 20 m (66 ft) in depth. The best time to see it is between 11 am and 12 noon, on a sunny day when the sea is calm. This is when the sunlight sneaks through a submerged opening in the rock and, reflecting off the white sandy floor, floods the cave with a superb shade of blue – a sublime, once-in-a-lifetime experience.

**WHERE IS IT**
On the shore of Bisevo, an island near Vis in Croatia's Dalmatian islands.
**WHAT ELSE IS THERE TO SEE**
Medvidina Cave, the Green Cave, Ravnik Island, the Church of Our Lady of the Pirates, Vis Island, the Town Museum.
**WHAT IS THERE TO DO**
Island hopping.
**HOW DO I GET THERE**
Take a catamaran from Split or a boat from Komiza town.

# Zagreb

Zagreb is a lovely Austro-Hungarian style city, full of glorious churches, museums and art galleries. It is divided into an upper and lower town, each with its own distinctive character, which meet at the vast, paved main square, Trg Bana Jelacica.

The upper town, Gornji Grad, is the oldest part of the city, and is set on two hills. It is easy to spend time wandering through the winding cobbled streets that lead you from one splendid building to another. Starting from the main square you pass the city's main market on your way to the cathedral. First built in 1217, this has been rebuilt and added to over the centuries – its neo-Gothic façade and twin steeples were added in the 1880s. The interior is an ornate masterpiece, and the north wall carries the Ten Commandments written in a twelfth-century script. St Mark's Church, dating from the thirteenth century and restored in the 1880s, is famous for the red, white and blue tiles on its roof arranged in the coats of arms of Zagreb and the kingdoms of Croatia, Dalmatia and Slavonia. The Lotrscak Tower, which is part of the thirteenth-century fortifications, affords spectacular views over the city, and every day at noon a cannon is fired in remembrance of its past role in warning the citizens of imminent attack.

A funicular railway goes down to the lower town (*Donji Grad*), which was built to a grid design in the late nineteenth century and is made up of handsome squares set around central gardens, wide boulevards and parks. Most of the museums are here, including the Mimara Museum and the Strossmayer Gallery of Old Masters.

*St Mark's Church, Zagreb.*

**WHAT IS IT**
The capital of Croatia, with beautiful old buildings and teeming with museums.
**WHAT IS THERE TO SEE**
St. Catherine's Church, Mirogoj Cemetery, Maksimir Park.
**WHAT IS THERE TO DO**
Take a stroll round Medvednica Nature Park and get away from the bustle of the city.

# The Acropolis

**WHAT IS IT**
The Acropolis is a limestone outcrop that stands above Athens, Greece's capital.
**WHAT IS IT KNOWN FOR**
The Parthenon, which is considered the most famous building in the world.
**ALSO KNOWN AS**
Acropolis means 'high city'.
**WHAT IS THERE TO SEE**
The Acropolis Museum, the Theatre of Dionysus Eleuthereus, the Panathenaic Way, the ancient Agora.

The word 'Acropolis', is synonymous with Athens in the minds of many people. In fact 'acropolis' means 'high city', and there are many other towns and cities in Greece built around a mount or peak. The Acropolis in Athens is a limestone outcrop surmounted by the distinctive shape of the Parthenon, a constant reminder of the glory of Ancient Greece.

The Propylaea is the superb marble entrance gate to the Acropolis, built in about 430 BC, and considered by many to be architecturally the equal of the Parthenon. Built on a slope, it has five gates with enormous doors and wings to either side.

The Parthenon, a Doric temple constructed between 447 and 432 BC, is made of about 13,500 blocks of marble, no two the same. It is a masterpiece of design, using sophisticated techniques to counteract optical effects that would have made the columns look too thin and the building squat. The outer colonnade consists of 46 columns supporting 96 metopes (carved panels) with battle scenes. The inner, Ionic, frieze was a majestic 160-m (524 ft) long but was removed and taken to Britain by Lord Elgin in the early nineteenth century.

The building held a statue of Athena that was over 11 m (36 ft) high and covered in gold. The extraordinary marble roof was cut so thinly that light filtered through onto the statue. Sadly, neither exists today, but the aura of this extraordinary place is redolent with the weight of the history of civilization.

The Ionic Erechtheum is perched at the north edge of the Acropolis overlooking the city. Its original caryatid statues are the the museum.

*The Acropolis and Parthenon.*

# Delphi

The ruins of the great complex of Delphi are situated in a suitably awe-inspiring position on a ledge beneath the towering cliff face, with the clear waters of the Gulf of Corinth sparkling 600 m (1,970 ft) below. When consulted, Apollo's priestess was believed to deliver the god's response in the form of esoteric riddles. The Ancient Greeks considered Delphi to be the centre of the world, and it is mentioned in almost every Greek myth.

*The Tholos in the Sanctuary of Athena Pronaia at Delphi.*

The site consists of two separate sacred areas, little more than 1 km (0.5 mi) apart. The Sanctuary of Athena Pronaia has two ruined temples, ruined altars and treasuries and the Tholos. The old Temple of Athena Pronaia was built in the seventh century BC, but suffered from landslides and earthquakes and only two columns and a piece of wall remain. The superb Tholos, built in the early fourth century BC, is a rotunda encircled by two circles of 20 columns, three of which were reconstructed with a small section of entablature and frieze in the 1930s. The New Temple of Athena was built following an earthquake that destroyed the Archaic Temple of Athena in 370 BC. A gymnasium of the same era is nearby.

The Sanctuary of Apollo is more extensive and is covered with an astonishing collection of ruins, monuments, friezes and altars linked by the paved Sacred Way, which leads to the Temple of Apollo. To the west, Roman steps lead to the well-preserved theatre, which has 35 tiers of seats. Right at the top of Delphi is the stadium, which is also wonderfully preserved, and has stands cut into the rock face capable of seating 7,000 spectators, and a triumphal arch at the end. Here the Delphic games took place every four years.

**WHERE IS IT**
About 160 km (100 mi) north-west of Athens.
**WHAT IS THERE TO SEE**
The Museum, the Treasury of the Athenians, the Sanctuary of Gaia-Themes, Mount Parnassos.
**WHAT IS THERE TO DO**
The Sanctuary of Apollo has a vast collection of ruins, altars and monuments.
**DID YOU KNOW**
In ancient times the Greeks considered Delphi to be the centre of the world.

# Mt Athos

Mount Athos (Agio Oros) is situated on the most northerly, and most beautiful, peninsula of the three that spread out like fingers from Halkidiki, in the Macedonian region of north-eastern Greece, some 140 km (90 mi) south-east of Thessaloniki. Known as the Holy Mount, it is the treasury of the Greek Orthodox faith, and the entire peninsula is dedicated to the worship of God.

It is the oldest monastic republic in existence and among its rules, which have been enforced for more than 1,000 years, are those stating that no women are premitted within 500 m (1,650 ft) and that no images of women are allowed.

*Monastery on Mount Athos.*

The Holy Mount covers an area of 350 sq km (135 sq mi) and is a self-governing part of Greevr state. It is divided into 20 self-governing monasteries and a number of smaller monastic communities known as 'sketae'. These communities operate three different forms of monastic rule, *coenobitic*, where the monks live and worship together, *idiorrhythmic*, where the monks organize their own time and only come together on Sundays and Holy Days and solitary, where monks live as hermits in caves in the cliffs.

The peninsula has an extraordinary natural beauty. The slopes of the mountain are clothed with ancient evergreens that stretch towards the highest point, which is above the treeline at 2,033 m (6,700 ft). According to the legend, the Virgin was travelling to Cyprus with St John the Divine when a storm forced them to take refuge at what is now the Holy Monastery of Ivira. The Virgin was so impressed by the beauty of the place that God gave her the mountain saying, 'Let this place be your lot, your garden and your paradise, as well as a salvation, a haven for those who seek salvation'.

**WHAT IS IT**
A self-governing monastic republic dedicated to the worship of God.
**HOW DO I GET THERE**
By boat from Ouranopoulis to Daphne.
**WHAT SHOULD I KNOW**
Only men can apply to visit and must do so via the Mt Athos Pilgrim's Office in Thessaloniki at least six months in advance. Only ten non-Orthodox pilgrims are allowed per day and only one night is allowed at any one monastery.

# Mt Olympus

At 2,919 m (9,570 ft), Mt Olympus is the highest mountain in Greece, its rugged precipices rising to a broad summit covered in snow. It is on the east coast of mainland Greece, looking over the Aegean Sea. Mt Olympus is part of a mountain chain that runs north into Bulgaria and south into Turkey and it straddles the border between Thessaly and Macedonia.

According to Greek mythology, Mt Olympus was where Gaia gave birth to the Titans. They were so enormous that they used the Greek mountains as their thrones, and Cronos, the most powerful Titan, sat on Mt Olympus itself. It was later the home of the principal gods in the Greek pantheon who, according to Homer, lived in palaces of crystal on the summit, eating nectar and ambrosia, the food of the gods, which reinforced their immortality. Alexander the Great came to make sacrifices at ancient Dion, at the foot of Olympus, before he went to war, and today you can visit the museum and archaeological park there.

The town of Litochoro, which means City of the Gods is the normal place to start any hike on Mt Olympus. It takes two days to make the climb and return again – although experienced hikers can do it in one. There are refuges along the way in which to spend the night. This beautiful, wild area is rich in flora, having 1,700 species of plants, several of which occur nowhere else.

*Hikers climbing towards Mytikas on Mt Olympus.*

**WHAT IS IT**
The highest mountain in Greece.
**WHERE IS IT**
Near the east coast of Greece, straddling the border between Thessaly and Macedonia.
**WHEN SHOULD I VISIT**
The best months for climbing are April, May and June.
**HOW DO I GET THERE**
By road or rail from Athens or Thessaloniki to Litochoro.

# The Samaria Gorge

**WHAT IS IT**
A 16-km (10-mi) gorge in Crete's only national park.
**WHAT ELSE IS THERE TO SEE**
Knossos and Chania.
**HOW DO I GET THERE**
By bus to Omalos from Chania. After the descent, most people get a boat back to Chania.
**WHEN SHOULD I GO**
Late spring is the best time.
**WHAT SHOULD I KNOW**
There are guards to help walkers and make sure they are safe. There is an entrance fee.

The Samaria Gorge is in one of the national parks of Greece, and the only one situated on Crete. Set in the White Mountains of western Crete, the gorge is 16 km (10 mi) long, starting from Omalos at an altitude of 1,250 m (4,100 ft) and dropping all the way down to sea level, at the village of Agia Roumeli. It is a hike that can take anything from between four and seven hours and it is best to start early in the morning to avoid too much of the midday heat, as well as the crowds.

The first mile is a steep drop of 1,000 m (3,300 ft) that follows a tricky trail called the Wooden Stairs – this is the hardest part of the trek after which the slope is gentler. The path follows the river bed, so the park is only open from late spring when the river is dry. The vegetation is at its best in spring, when there is a mass of wildflowers, and the scent of mountain thyme and oregano fills the air. This is one of the last areas still inhabited by the rare, horned wild mountain goat known as *kri-kri*, and hikers occasionally report a sighting.

Half-way through the gorge lies the deserted village of Samaria, now a resting place for tired walkers, and towards the end of the gorge the rock walls narrow to a 3-m (10-ft) gap, known as the Iron Gates, and rise dramatically on either side to some 650 m (2,130 ft). For thousands of years, up to and including as recently as World War II, this gorge has been the last refuge of Cretans escaping from, and defending themselves against, invaders.

*View over the Samaria Gorge.*

# Patmos

Patmos is the most northerly island of the Dodecanese. The islands lie strung out, like jewels in a necklace, between Samos and Rhodes off the south-west coast of Turkey. Patmos is where St John the Divine wrote the Book of Revelation and is also known as the 'Jerusalem of the Aegean'. The island has a mystical, otherworldly atmosphere, and many visitors report having extraordinarily vivid dreams here.

In 1088, the Emperor Alexius I Comnenus granted Patmos to St. Christodoulos, so he could found a monastery here in honour of St John. He chose a spectacular site that dominates the whole island, and the Greek Orthodox rituals still practised here are virtually unchanged from the eleventh century.

The fortified monastery consists of a complex of buildings. Apart from the main church, in which Christodoulos's sarcophagus can be found, the Chapel of the Theotokos contains Byzantine frescos of the Virgin Mary which were only discovered in 1958 as the result of an earthquake. Other treasures are in the Library and the Treasury.

The Cave of the Apocalypse is also a place of pilgrimage – in it St John wrote the Book of Revelation after God spoke directly to him from a crevice in the rock face. At the mouth of the cave is the late eleventh-century chapel of St Anne. The nearby Patmian School was first established in 1713 as a seminary, and its students have risen to the highest ranks of the Greek Orthodox Church.

Patmos and the surrounding islets also have splendid secluded bays for swimming and sunbathing far away from the crowds.

*The fortified Monastery of St John dominates Khora (Patmos town).*

**WHERE IS IT**
This is the most northerly of the Dodecanese Islands off the west coast of Turkey.
**WHAT IS THERE TO SEE**
The Monastery of St John, Patmian School, Ecclesiastical Museum and the Cave of the Apocalypse.
**HOW DO I GET THERE**
By hydrofoil from Samos or ferry from Kos to Skala port.
**WHEN SHOULD I VISIT**
The best weather is from April to October.

*The Temple of Poseidon
at Sounion.*

# Temple of Poseidon

Cape Sounion is the southernmost tip of the region of Attica, 65 km (40 mi) south-east of Athens. The Temple of Poseidon is dramatically poised on a 60-m (200-ft) cliff, with stunning views over the Aegean Sea and islands beyond.

The temple was built about 440 BC, to replace an earlier temple that had been destroyed by the Persians. Numerous archaeological finds on the promontory prove the area was in use as long ago as 700 BC and the existence of a sanctuary here was mentioned in the *Odyssey*. The classical temple seen today is thought to have been built by the architect of the Theseum in Athens, and is made of Agrileza marble. Fifteen columns still remain, standing on an imposing base, but much of the west side of the temple has been destroyed. The Propylon, or entrance gate, was added a little later.

Cape Sounion was fortified in 412 BC, during the Peloponnesian War, with the temple positioned at the south-eastern end of the fortress. Since 1994, the Athens Archaeological Society has been excavating the area and has found part of the central street and the remains of houses. On a small hill to the north-east of the temple, the remains of the Sanctuary of Athena can be seen, but it is the Temple of Poseidon that has always drawn visitors – Lord Byron passed this way and carved his name on one of the stones here. Today the site is a favourite spot for Athenians and foreigners alike, who come to watch the glorious sunsets from this classically beautiful place.

**WHAT IS THERE TO SEE**
The coastal resorts of Glyfada, Vouliagmeni and Lagonisi.
**INTERESTING FACT**
A sanctuary here was mentioned in the *Odyssey*.
**DO NOT MISS**
Watch a spectacular sunset.
**WHEN SHOULD I VISIT**
The best weather is from May to September.

# Santorini

**WHERE IS IT**
In the southern Cyclades, south-east of the Greek mainland.
**WHAT IS THERE TO SEE**
The Historical and Cultural Museum of Santorini in Phira, the traditional village of Oia, the Prehistoric Thera Museumand the excavations at Akrotiri.
**ALSO KNOWN AS**
The classical name of the island was Thera, and Santorini comes from the patron saint of the island, Santa Irina.
**WHAT IS IT KNOWN FOR**
Santorini is famous for its grapes.
**HOW DO I GET THERE**
Travel by ferry, catamaran, cruise ship or plane from Athens.
**WHEN SHOULD I VISIT**
The best weather is from April to October.

Santorini is the epitome of a Greek island, reached through a huge circular bay, which once was covered by an enormous volcano. At some point around 1650 BC the volcano erupted with such force that 30 cubic km (7 cubic miles) of magma was ejected so the top of the mountain collapsed and the 8-km (5-mi) wide bay was formed from the sunken crater. It is thought that this eruption also destroyed Knossos, in Crete.

The island's classical name was Thera, and it was not until the thirteenth century that it became known as Santorini, a corruption of Santa Irina, the name of the patron saint of the island. One popular theory is that the island is what remains of Plato's lost kingdom of Atlantis, although it does not match the geographical location. The cliffs are formed of bands of multi-coloured rock and your first view of the island, with its sheer cliffs curving around the bay and rising almost 350 m (1,150 ft) from the sea, is breathtaking.

Thanks to the volcanic nature of the island, the soil is extraordinarily fertile, and Santorini is famous for its grapes. Unusually, the vines are grown low to the ground and trained in circles to protect them from strong winds from the north. The white wine produced here is some of the best in Greece.

On the south-western peninsula of the island lies the Bronze Age city of Akrotiri. This fascinating place is slowly being excavated from the ashes of the eruption, and it is in a state of preservation that equals Pompeii. Some of the finest frescoes of the ancient world have been found here.

*Church in Oia on Santorini.*

# Symi

The lovely, mountainous, island of Symi lies 41 km (25 mi) from Rhodes. Part of the Dodecanese group, the island is small, only 57 sq km (22 sq mi), with a rocky coastline with small coves and sandy beaches.

In 1309, Symi was conquered by the Knights of St John, who developed both a boat-building industry, and the sponge diving trade. In the 1830s it came under Turkish rule, followed in 1912 by Italian rule. Then the capital of the Dodecanese, it was home to the world's largest sponge fishing fleet, and had a population of 30,000. The decline of sponge fishing and damage during World War II led to Symi's decline, and today the population is about 2,500.

The town is divided into upper and lower parts, dominated by the fortress of the Knights of St John and linked by 500 steps lined with Neoclassical, pastel houses with flower-filled courtyards. The harbour is utterly beautiful, surrounded by hills forming a natural theatre. On a still day, in the upper town, it is possible to hear conversations taking place right down on the waterfront.

The Archaeological and Folklore Museum and Hatziagapitos Mansion in Chorio are worth a visit. Set in a bay to the south-west of the island is the monastery of Archangel Michael Panormitis. Built in the early eighteenth century on the site of a much older monastery, it contains a wonderful iconostasis, fine Byzantine frescoes, and two museums with a fascinating library.

A great many visitors discover Symi on a day trip from Rhodes, but the island is so relaxing and has such natural charm and beauty that some of them return year after year to stay for as long as they can.

**WHAT IS THERE TO SEE**
Monastery of Megalos Sotiris, Monastery of Roukouniotis, Rhodes.
**WHAT IS THERE TO DO**
Hire a boat to a secluded beach or hike across the beautiful countryside to any of the isolated chapels.
**HOW DO I GET THERE**
By boat or hydrofoil from Rhodes or Piraeus.
**WHEN SHOULD I GO**
The best weather is from May to October.

*The town of Gialos.*

# Vatican City

Although the Vatican City covers less than 1 sq km (0.4 sk mi) in Rome, it is in fact a sovereign state governed by the pope. It is the administrative headquarters of the Roman Catholic Church.

Stroll across the gigantic, seventeenth-century St Peter's Square towards the basilica, passing Bernini's quadruple rows of Tuscan columns crowned with statues of the saints, and the Egyptian obelisk, brought to Rome from Heliopolis by Caligula.

St Peter's Basilica is enormous and can hold 60,000 people. Its spectacular interior is unbelievably opulent. The extraordinary dome, designed by Michelangelo, is 119 m (390 ft) high, its balconies decorated with reliefs. Make the effort to go up to the top and you will be rewarded with the finest possible views of the Vatican City and Rome itself. Inside the basilica Bernini's Baroque canopy towers over the altar, Michelangelo's *Pieta* is exquisite, and everywhere you look there are works of art by the Italian masters.

As if this were not enough, the Vatican Museums, housed in a collection of sumptuously adorned wings, boast one of the finest and most extensive collections of art in the world, including Michelangelo's Sistine Chapel frescoes, the suite of rooms Raphael painted for Pope Julius II and Fra Angelico's exquisite chapel for Nicholas V, as well as staggering amounts of Egyptian, Etruscan, Roman and Renaissance sculpture, paintings and porcelain.

*St. Peter's Basilica and St. Peter's Square in Vatican City.*

# Rome

Rome is two cities – ancient and modern – and it is hard not to be awestruck by its blend of noise, excitement and bustle threaded with sudden calms of tranquil reflection. Some 2,500 years as a political and economic centre have defined its insouciant but passionate sophistication. Whether they have shopping on the Via Veneto, ancient ruins, historic churches, art or the *dolce vita* in mind, no visitors ever go away disappointed.

The rich Roman ruins range from the remains of the sumptuous imperial palaces on the Palatine Hill and the temples in the forum to the arresting simplicity of Augustus's *Ara Pacis* (altar of peace), the huge Baths of Diocletian, the exquisite beauty of the Pantheon, the eeriness of the catacombs and the chill of the Colosseum where, like the Circus Maximus, a discontented population was kept in check by often bloodthirsty public spectacle.

As the centre for centuries of the Christian world, Rome has more than 900 churches and basilicas, among the most important of which are San Giovanni in Laterano (St John Lateran, the pope's church as Bishop of Rome), Santa Maria Maggiore and San Lorenzo Fuori le Mura. Amongst other churches popular with visitors are Santa Maria Sopra Minerva, San Luigi dei Francesi, Santa Maria del Popolo and Santa Maria in Cosmedin, where the brave can put their hand into the Bocca della Verità to see if they are telling the truth.

The city has a wealth of treasures and notable galleries include the Galleria Borghese, the Palazzo Doria Pamphili, the Capitoline museums, the Museo Nazionale delle Terme, the Galleria Colonna, and the Palazzo Barberini with its National Gallery of Antique Art.

Among the multitide of monuments in Rome are the dozens of fountains in leafy squares, where the footsore visitor can sip cappuccino while being soothed by the sound of running water.

*The Colosseum in Rome.*

**WHAT IS THERE TO SEE**
The Palatine Hill, Trajan's Forum, the Castel Sant'Angelo, the Spanish Steps, the Borghese Gardens.
**WHAT IS THERE TO DO**
Take in the atmosphere and architectural gems as you stroll around this beautiful city.
**DO NOT MISS**
Cerveteri up the coast – these are the best Etruscan tombs anywhere.
**YOU SHOULD KNOW**
Most tourist attractions have entrance fees.

# Venice

*Sunset at the Doge's Palace and the Basilica of St Mark.*

Venice shimmers in the middle of a huge lagoon on the north-western edge of the Adriatic. Built on wooden piles dug into a series of mud flats and islets, it appears to float on water. Its realities – looming through a winter mist or sparkling in sunshine – are more beautiful even than its myths and legends.

The Grand Canal, at the heart of Venice, sweeps in a majestic S-shape through its centre. On either side, the shabby grandeur of more than 300 palaces bears witness to Venice's 1,000-year-old blend of Europe and Byzantium. Their collective elegance and richness of detail make a powerful reminder of the wealth and confidence of Venice in its imperial heyday, culminating in the Doge's Palace and St Mark's Square (Piazza San Marco). The palace dominates Venice in every direction – as befits the ducal home and seat of a government for 700 years. A vaporetto (water-bus) trip from San Marco to Piazzale Roma and back again is a good introduction to the city.

Save your gondola ride to explore some of the 177 canals spanned by 450 bridges linking Venice's six districts or lose yourself in the narrow alleys away from the super-smart shops and hotels, where the only noise is of water slapping walls and washing flapping overhead.

For two weeks before Lent, during Carnevale the city is a swirl of outrageously glamorous masked decadence, but if that does not appeal, the spectacular basilica of St Mark, the Doge's Palace, the glassworkers on the island of Murano and the beautiful buildings are more than enough to keep anyone occupied. For those of an artistic bent, the best galleries are the Accademia, the Galleria Giorgio Franchetti in the Gothic Ca' d'Oro and the Peggy Guggenheim Collection.

# Florence

Florence is the soul of Italy. Its centre, closed to traffic, still looks and feels like the late-medieval city state it once was. It resonates with the historical impact of its contribution to the cultural and political development of all Europe. It has an almost overwhelming range of galleries, fabulous buildings and treasures crammed into and between its churches. Its heart is the Duomo, dedicated to Santa Maria del Fiore, a perfect Gothic masterpiece, topped by Brunelleschi's dome and full of frescoes by some of Italy's greatest artists. Next door, the baptistery is a re-used Roman temple, with three sets of bronze doors that were among the earliest large bronze castings in the Renaissance.

Renaissance Florence is dominated by the Medici and the works of the artists they patronized. Florence's two major art galleries – the Uffizi and the Palazzo Pitti – were built for their art collections. The third major gallery, the Accademia, houses Michelangelo's monumental statue of David (the one outside the Uffizi is a copy).

Florence is the birthplace of Renaissance architecture, and such monuments as Brunelleschi's Ospedale degli Innocenti (foundling hospice) and the Pazzi chapel in the church of Santa Croce, and Michelangelo's work at San Lorenzo in the Medici Chapel and Laurentian Library are perfect examples of their type.

A stroll along the banks of the Arno offers an opportunity to enjoy Florence's unspoiled skyline of russet domes and towers. It also offers you the Ponte Vecchio, the only surviving original bridge, with its houses and shops, still bustling with people. But wherever you are, the duomo dominates the skyline from every direction. It is truly exquisite, and its subtlety and beauty remain the hallmark of Florentine sensibility.

**WHERE IS IT**
In Tuscany, in the north of Italy.
**WHAT IS THERE TO SEE**
The loggia dei Lanzi's open-air sculptures and the churches of San Miniato al Monte, Santa Maria Novella, Santo Spirito and Orsanmichele.
**WHAT IS THERE TO DO**
Have a picnic in the Boboli Gardens, explore the wine-growing regions of Tuscany.
**ALSO KNOWN AS**
The soul of Italy.
**DO NOT MISS**
The cathedral, or duomo, Florence's most beautiful building.
**WHAT SHOULD I KNOW.**
The city centre is a UNESCO World Heritage Site.

*The Duomo dominates the skyline of Florence.*

*The cathedral in the old town of Siena. It has a magnificent carved roof.*

# Siena

Siena is the classic image of Tuscany. About an hour's drive south of Florence, it sits on the northern edge of the Crete Senese, a landscape of soft, rounded hills bathed in warm, golden light, the random geometry of glowing grainfields dotted with cypress-shrouded farmsteads, fortified, medieval hilltop villages and isolated ruins. Ruled by Etruscans, then Romans, controlled by the Milanese Visconti family, then the Spanish and finally by Cosimo I de Medici, Siena's history has been turbulent. Today, however, its tranquil air of antiquity makes exploring it a delight.

Dominated by the Romanasque duomo (cathedral) at the top of the hill, the city's historic centre is a maze of little alleyways. Carved shadows mark every twist, opening suddenly onto sunny squares and ancient churches. But everything radiates from the enormous, scallop-shaped, Piazza del Campo in the centre. One of the greatest squares in the world, it is overlooked by the Palazzo Pubblico and the soaring Torre del Mangia. Collectively, they are a UNESCO World Heritage Site and represent a millenium of Siena's cherished aspiration of independence and (not always successful) democracy.

Twice a year, the Piazza del Campo hosts the Palio, a frantic, bareback horse race round the cobbled streets between the 17 wards of the city. Habitual calm is shattered by rival processions, each a kaleidoscope of colourful medieval dress, screeching bands driven by remorseless drums, and flags, tossed twisting high above packed crowds. The furious excitement surrounding the tribal rivalry of races is purely Sienese. These races have been run continuously for at least 500 years, but based on earlier traditions, they are part of Siena's living history.

**WHAT IS THERE TO SEE**
The Palazzo Pubblico and the Torre del Mangia, the duomo and the Museo dell'Opera del Duomo, the Pinacoteca Nazionale, the church of San Domenico.
**DO NOT MISS**
The Piazza del Campo – one of the greatest squares in the world.
**WHAT IS THERE TO DO**
Enjoy the Palio which takes place twice a year.
**YOU SHOULD KNOW**
There are entrance charges for most historic sites.
**HOW DO I GET THERE**
By bus or rail from Florence, Rome or Milan.

# Pompeii

Pompeii is a city frozen in time. It was destroyed by a volcanic eruption in 79 AD, caught between Vesuvius and the sea. The eruption was two days old when a sudden change of wind brought a huge cloud of burning hot ash crashing down without warning – catching most of the population. Aristocrat and slave died together.

It is a city, not a village, and is known to have been where many wealthy Romans had holiday villas. You can walk through its streets and see its shops, houses, theatre, gladiator school, forums and markets. In the haunting Garden of the Fugitives you can even see its people: 17 casts made from the pockets of air found during excavation. There is a woman with her arms stretched forward to ward off her fate; others, mouths open, uselessly shielding children; even making love.

The human detail is best seen in the House of Vettii, the home of two merchant brothers. Even the flowers in the garden left botanically exact impressions in the ash, as did the dripping water feeding the cooling system in the atrium. Remarkably intact frescoes were found in some rooms.

Throughout the city, some of the best revelations are public and private frescoes, which give clues to daily life in Pompeii, its festivals and routines. Nowhere can this be seen more effectively than in the brothel, where above each doorway is a mini-fresco showing the occupant's specialities.

**WHERE IS IT**
On the Bay of Naples in the Region of Campania in south-west Italy.
**WHAT IS IT**
One of Italy's most famous cities, frozen in time.
**DON'T MISS**
The House of Vettii as it is the best example of human life in Pompeii.
**WHAT IS THERE TO SEE**
The Temple of Venus, the basilica, the theatre, the gladiator's barracks, the Villa of the Misteries.
**HOW DO I GET THERE**
By train or bus from Naples or Sorrento.

*The ruins of Pompeii with Vesuvius on the horizon.*

# Herculaneum

Ercolano is a modern town just south of Naples. Herculaneum is the Roman resort town destroyed by Vesuvius in 79 AD, at the same time as neighbouring Pompeii. Only a quarter of the site has been excavated so far – and this is enough to exhaust even the most determined visitor.

All the evidence confirms that Herculaneum was an upmarket seaside resort. It feels different to Pompeii, because people were there to enjoy themselves, or to provide services for those on holiday. Appearances mattered to Roman visitors who were comfortable but not wealthy. For example, many of the columns were made of brick, then rendered to approximate fluted marble that resembled the real thing found in Pompeii.

You can see metal bathtubs whose shape proves that there is no need to change a good design over 2,000 years, an early immersion heater in the men's communal baths; a price list painted on a wall, a poster advertising a shop's range of wines and a fast-food restaurant where the counter is set with fixed earthenware pots that would have kept the food hot. All the shops and houses used brightly coloured, extensive mosaics and frescoes to foster a holiday atmosphere, and many have survived.

The paintings and mosaics are humourous and suggestive but many of the very best artefacts are held in museums elsewhere, because they have been considered too sexually explicit, or in some cases, pornographic to be on general display. They were briefly on display in the Secret Museum of the National Museum of Naples in the 1960s, but were finally opened to the public in 2000, with a warning about the contents.

*Bathing room in the public baths at Herculaneum.*

# Torre Annunziata

Torre Annunziata is a modern seaport in the shadow of Vesuvius, between Pompeii and Herculaneum. In 1842, the remains of three buildings were discovered and identified from a thirteenth-century map of Roman roads as the hamlet of Oplontis. This is the name sometimes given to the third and smallest of the amazing excavations of the ruins caused by the volcanic eruption of 79 AD.

The discovery included a bath house, a rustic villa crowded with victims of the eruption (and a hoard of gold coins and jewellery), and possibly the greatest of all the finds associated with the Pompeii area. This is a huge residential villa, now fully excavated and partly restored, that was part of the Imperial family's estates. It is believed to have belonged to Poppaea Sabina, the slave mistress of the Emperor Nero, who became his second wife, so the house is often called the Villa Poppaea.

The villa has three principal sections, the owner's domain, the servants' quarters, and a 'production area' that managed the estate, doing everything necessary for the upkeep of both a great house and a farm. It offers a first-class insight into the lives of élite Romans. The long colonnaded walks, the *trompe l'oeil* and perspective in the frescoes (which survive in many of the rooms) and the internal courtyard decorated with landscapes – all reeks of luxury and excess. What a place it must have been!

Even the villa's demise under a hail of pumice and ash clouds has contributed to the feeling – you can see an exquisite little bird, petrified while pecking at a fallen fig. At any rate, the Villa Poppaea has a beauty and grandeur unequalled elsewhere in the Pompeii complex.

**WHAT ELSE IS THERE TO SEE**
Sorrento, Caserta, Baia, Cuma.
**DON'T MISS**
Villa Poppaea for an unparalleled insight into the lives of wealthy Romans.
**HOW DO I GET THERE**
By train or bus from Naples or Sorrento.
**YOU SHOULD KNOW**
This is a UNESCO World Heritage Site.

*Fresco at the Villa Poppaea in ancient Oplontis.*

*The fifteenth-century Renaissance Palazzo Ducale, in Urbino.*

# Urbino

Urbino is a pinnacle of Renaissance art and architecture. It is a hilltown in the Marche region of central Italy that achieved cultural importance for a short period and then fell back into obscurity, which had the happy effect of preserving its harmonious sixteenth-century appearance. The centre of the city is a UNESCO World Heritage Site.

The Palazzo Ducale dominates the city. It provided a standard for all Renaissance palaces that followed it and is still a worthy setting for one of the greatest collections of Renaissance paintings in the world, the Galleria Nazionale delle Marche. It is appropriate that the duke who built it was the legendary *condottiere* (aristocratic mercenary soldier), Federico II da Montefeltro, honoured throughout Europe as a diplomat and patron of art and literature. His court attracted outstanding humanist scholars and artists, such as Piero della Francesca, whose *Flagellation of Christ* is one of the gallery's highlights. The scale of the palace is not obvious from the city, its 500 or so rooms are human in scale and the duke's *studiolo* is a masterpiece of *trompe-l'eil* in inlaid wood. There is a warren of tunnels and caves under the palace, which used to house the servants' quarters, kitchens, laundries and stables.

The city was also home to the painter Raphael and his family home is now a museum. On one wall there is a fresco that has been attributed to him. Raphael even influenced the majolica pottery for which Urbino is still known 500 years later.

Urbino remains a favourite with many visitors because of its fairy-tale skyline and the harmonious blend of the medieval cityscape and the Renaissance palace, which was designed to complement its surroundings, not to dominate them.

**WHAT IS IT KNOWN FOR**
The Galleria Nazionale delle Marche, one of the greatest collections of Renaissance paintings in the world.
**WHEN SHOULD I GO**
Visit Urbino's flower festival in May or the Jazz festival in June.
**WHAT IS THERE TO SEE**
The museum in Raphael's childhood home, the medieval city centre.
**WHAT IS THERE TO DO**
Visit the Oratorio di San Giovanni Battista e San Giuseppe and the Church of San Bernardino.

# The Amalfi Coast

The Amalfi Coast (Costiera Amalfitana) stretches for just 40 km (25 mi) along the south side of the Sorrentine Peninsula, between Positano and Vietri sul Mare, south of the Bay of Naples. It is stunningly beautiful. Backed by the spine of the harsh Lattari mountains, it consists of vertiginous slopes plunging 210 m (700 ft) into the deep, intensely blue Tyhrrenian Sea. Broken by rocky spurs and ravines into tiny bays and secret coves, it appears to be completely wild and even hostile. But every twist and turn of the switchback coast road reveals a dramatic new vista of ancient fishing villages clinging to the mountainside, tumbling down to quayside huddles of colourful boats and café awnings.

Positano is becoming the resort of choice for the rich, powerful and famous. Its multi-coloured houses crowd together, interwoven by a million steps, arcades, and arched passages full of shops, lively bars and excellent restaurants. It is both the prettiest of, and a blueprint for, the other communities dotting the area. Amalfi itself, in the middle of the coast, is still the largest and most influential town here. Only modern tourism has restored to it some of the colossal wealth it used to command. But though Amalfi is as historically fascinating as any of its neighbours (it was once a major naval power with a population of 70,000), its perfect setting now attracts people seeking pleasure and recreation.

The Amalfi Coast's communities look seawards. The switchback coast road was only built in 1850. But whether you see this section of the coast from land or sea, its loveliness is a romantic fantasy come true.

**WHAT IS IT**
The Amalfi Coast is a beautiful stretch of coastline 40 km (25 mi) long that runs along the south side of the Sorrentine Peninsula.
**WHAT IS THERE TO DO**
Explore the 'Path of the Gods' and walk from Positano to Praiano.
**WHEN SHOULD I GO**
Spring and Autumn is best as the area is really crowded in Summer.
**WHAT IS THERE TO SEE**
The gardens of the Villa Cimbrone and Villa Rufolo in Ravello, the old paper mill in Amalfi, Capri.

*Houses and hotels cling to the cliffside in Positano.*

# Assisi

Assisi is an exceptional Umbrian hill town whose development since the thirteenth century has been guided by an idea. As the birthplace of St Francis (in 1182), and site of his most significant revelations and works, the town has ever since been the repository of masterpieces of art and architecture created to honour his legacy.

The process began only two years after his death and swift canonization. Assisi had flourished under the Umbrians, Etruscans and Romans – but only now did it expand beyond its Roman walls. The lower church of the Basilica of St Francis, a monastery for the new order of Franciscans, has frescoes by Giotto and Cimabue among others, while the upper church has more frescoes by Giotto depicting scenes from St Francis's life. A bad earthquake in 1997 damaged some of the frescoes. Nearly all of Assisi's art and architecture, through the Renaissance and later centuries, reflects St Francis's precepts of simplicity, humility and tolerance of differing beliefs. The church of Santa Chiara (St Clare, founder of the Poor Clares Order of nuns) heads the list with its simple Gothic interior; the Renaissance finds some of its most harmonious expression in the Basilica of Santa Maria degli Angeli (1569), and (remarkably in an age of flamboyance) the peaceful ambience of the seventeenth-century palaces of the Bernabei and Giacobetti. This basilica houses the Porziuncola, Assisi's most moving treasure, the little chapel ('of the Angels') that Francis restored, and in which he died.

The only major exceptions to successive generations' attempts to create a city of peace and harmony are the twin medieval castles on either side of town. Today Assisi attracts many groups and individuals looking to share the town's beauty, simplicity and tranquillity.

*The Monastery of St Francis.*

# The Aeolian Islands

Greek and Roman mythology and the ancient history of the world itself converge 25–50 km (15–30 mi) off the north-eastern coast of Sicily, at the Aeolian Islands (Isole Eolie), whose natural and man-made wonders range from the ancient citadel (*castello*) of Lipari, with its acropolis and unbroken history of the island's inhabitants from Neolithic times, to the extraordinary red, ochre and yellow shoreline of Vulcano.

*Lipari in the Tyrrhenian Sea.*

The now sparsely populated Aeolian Islands (Lipari, Panarea, Salina, Vulcano, Stromboli, Filicudi and Alicudi) are a volcanic archipelago. The earliest settlers, the Cnidians, (580 BC) named the islands after Aeolus, the keeper of the winds and Homer's Odysseus faced the mighty Cyclops here. More recently, Rossellini's 1950 film, *Stromboli*, was inspired by the active volcano of the same name, where regular eruptions still send special-effect, red, molten lava down the scarred rocks. The charming *Il Postino* was filmed on Salina in the 1990s. The archipelago was designated a UNESCO World Heritage Site in 2000 because of its importance to the fields of geology and vulcanology, in particular because Stromboli and Vulcano are the archetypes of two different forms of eruption and have been studied for more than 200 years.

The islands offer the restless traveller the white sandy beaches and pale blue sea of Lipari; the tranquillity of the garden island of Salina, with its fresh capers, delicious fish and octopus and soft, sweet, golden dessert wine, Malvasia; extraordinary rock formations; and the Bay of Fumarole whose waters, warmed by bubbles of sulphurous steam, lap the volcanic black beaches. Buoyant pumice and smooth black obsidian litter the beaches of Lipari. Panarea, with its treacherous underwater rocks, and rocky Filicudi with its basalt shoreline, both boast ancient settlements. Alicudi, the most remote island, promises panoramic views and an unspoiled way of life.

**WHAT ARE THEY**
A volcanic archipelago off the north-east coast of Sicily.
**WHAT IS THERE TO SEE**
The archeological museum in Lipari, the lighthouse with the horses's head on Strombolicchio, night trips up Stromboli, the Valley of the Monsters.
**NOTABLE GEOGRAPHY**
The Bay of Fumarole offers incredible rock formations and black beaches.
**HOW DO I GET THERE**
By boat, ferry or hydrofoil from Milazzo, Sicily or Naples.
**WHEN SHOULD I GO**
The best times are spring and autumn.

*The town of towers,
San Gimignano.*

# San Gimignano

The astonishing and beautiful old walled hilltop town of San Gimignano 'delle Belle Torri' in Southern Tuscany displays one of the best-known skylines in Italy. Set amongst cornfields, olive groves and vineyards in the verdant Val d'Elsa with its 14 remaining towers (there were once 72), symbols of the wealth of the town's medieval families, the place took its name from the Bishop of Modena who is said to have repelled Atilla and his Huns.

To walk into San Gimignano on a pulsatingly hot July afternoon, when the shutters are down as people take their siestas, is an extraordinary experience. The tallest tower, at 54 m (177 ft), and the only one that can be climbed, is the Torre Grossa, which has spectacular panoramic views. The Palazzo del Popolo has a charming courtyard with frescoes on the walls and in the museum upstairs you can enjoy Memmo di Filipuccio's wedding scene frescoes.

The thirteenth-century church of Sant'Agostino has a beautiful fresco cycle by Benozzo Gozzoli, depicting the life of the saint, as well as an altarpiece by Pollaiuolo.

Wander through the town to the Rocca, the old ruined fortress, and walk up the valley to the Balze, a deep ravine where, since the middle ages, churches and other buildings have fallen into the depths.

**WHERE IS IT**
North-west of Siena and south-west of Florence.
**ALSO KNOWN AS**
San Gimignano delle Belle Torri.
**WHAT IS THERE TO SEE**
The Collegiata (the former cathedral), Palazzo del Podestà, the Museum of Wine, the Archaeological Museum.
**DO NOT MISS**
Climbing the Torre Grossa for stunning panoramic views.
**HOW DO I GET THERE**
By bus from Florence or Siena.
**WHAT SHOULD I KNOW**
The historic centre is a UNESCO World Heritage Site.

# Orvieto

Orvieto is a particularly charming Umbrian hill-town. It perches on a huge outcrop of soft volcanic tufa, with its steep cliff served by a funicular railway that isolates the spectacular Etruscan and medieval centre at the top from the modern area of Orvieto Scalo at the bottom. Its small historic area and easy accessibility make it a magnet for both day-visitors and for people seeking a special base from which to explore the region.

Orvieto's political importance throughout history is legendary. It was *primus inter pares* (first among equals) of the original Etruscan Federation. It resisted every attack – the Etruscans dug a honeycomb of deep wells (Pozzo della Cava is amazing), underground chambers, passages and openings looking out over the plain into the soft tufa. Later residents, ever threatened by siege, added underground mills and stables. In 1527, during the sack of Rome, Pope Clement VII took refuge here and had a spectacular well, with a double ramp to allow easy access, constructed.

Above ground, the twelfth-century black-and-white cathedral dominates the winding lanes. It is Orvieto's most dramatic attraction, and has some fantastic frescoes by Luca Signorelli and Fra Angelico, but scarcely less so are the myriad pretty churches and palazzos crowding round it. Orvieto is a byword for good restaurants and fine wine, and you can enjoy both in sumptuous medieval surroundings. In fact, even 1,500 years ago, Orvieto earned the nickname *Oinarea*, 'where wine flows'.

**WHAT IS IT KNOWN FOR**
Being the last Etruscan city to fall to the Romans.
**ALSO KNOWN AS**
Oinarea, or 'where the wine flows'.
**WHAT IS THERE TO SEE**
The Civic and Claudio Faina Museum, Moor's Tower, the Church of San Giovenale, Orvieto Underground, the Etruscan necropolis outside the town.
**HOW DO I GET THERE**
By train from Rome, Florence or Perugia.

*Orvieto and the surrounding area.*

# Gubbio

Gubbio's historic centre is a crash course in medieval architecture. It is a town of Gothic austerity, dark-grey stone and narrow streets; developed to defend the wealth and power acquired as a city state. The Romans constructed the second largest theatre in the empire just outside the walls. Within them, the number and richness of merchants' houses are just as inspirational as the twelfth-century cathedral with its striking rose window and symbols of the Evangelists, or the Palazzo Ducale, built in 1470 with the most extravagant flourishes late medieval craftsmen could make, to show the grandeur and status of Federico II di Montefeltro, Gubbio's new conqueror. The palazzo's Inner Court is reminiscent of the same patron's Palazzo Ducale in Urbino.

Gubbio is home to the Eugubine Tables, a set of bronze tablets that constitute the largest surviving text in the ancient Umbrian language. They are housed in the massive, early fourteenth-century Palazzo dei Consoli, itself a statement of how Gubbio prospered in the Middle Ages.

Among the city's other treasures are the basilica of Sant'Ubaldo (which has remnants of beautiful fifteenth-century frescoes), a Roman mausoleum, the late thirteenth-century church of San Francesco, Santa Maria Nuova and the Pallazzo and Torre Gabrielli.

On 15 May, the city's palio, the Corsa dei Ceri takes place. Three teams devoted to saints, each carrying a statue on an octagonal plinth weighing 400 kg (880 lb) and 5 m (16.5 ft) tall, race from the Palazzo dei Consoli to the basilica of Sant'Ubaldo. The teams wear distinctive costumes of yellow, blue or black tunics, white trousers and red belts and neckbands. The race is followed by a raucous throng of supporters supporting their own city district. The race is one of Italy's best examples of living folk tradition.

*The Palazzo dei Consoli.*

# Castel del Monte

Castel del Monte is a unique masterpiece of medieval military architecture and a strong statement of imperial might. Standing proud on the top of a hill and visible from kilometres around, it was built in about 1240 near Bari, in the south-eastern Italian region of Puglia. Castel del Monte is a successful blend of elements from classical antiquity, the Islamic Orient and north European Cistercian Gothic. It is a UNESCO World Heritage Site.

The castle, which may not ever have been intended as a defensive structure, was the inspiration of the Holy Roman Emperor Frederick II Barbarossa on his return from the Crusades, where he had seen the octagonal base of the Dome of the Rock, although he could equally have been inspired by the imperial example of Charlemagne's chapel in the cathedral at Aachen. Each of the eight corners has an octagonal bastion, the idea for which may come from buildings he had seen in the Near East.

Barbarossa enjoyed using the castle for only a few years before his death in 1250, and after some time it became a prison, then a refuge for plague victims, before being abandoned. Only recently has Italy rediscovered its enormous symbolic potency. Today the Castel del Monte has been restored and it now graces the reverse of the Italian 1 cent coin.

*Steps to the Castel del Monte.*

**WHAT IS IT**
A thirteenth-century castle 16 km (10 mi) from Andria, built for the Emperor Frederick II Barbarossa.
**INTERESTING FACT**
Castle del Monte appears on the reverse of the Italian 1 cent coin.
**WHAT ELSE IS THERE TO SEE**
Bari, Barletta, the Castellana Grottoes.
**HOW DO I GET THERE**
By car or bus from Andria.

*View over the grounds of the Villa d'Este in Tivoli.*

# Hadrian's Villa and Villa d'Este

Hadrian's Villa (the Villa Adriana) is in spectacular ruins, yet it is still the greatest example of a Roman garden. Built by Hadrian at Tivoli, near Rome, early in the second century, its 30 buildings cover some 100 ha (250 acres) of pools, grottos and wonderfully contrived settings and vistas. It recreates a sacred landscape that can still inspire – and which is still traceable despite Cardinal Ippolito d'Este, Lucrezia Borgia's son stripping most of its marble to build his own gardens at the Villa d'Este nearby in the 1550s. Both villas have UNESCO World Heritage Site status.

Hadrian drew on his extensive travels for the design of his imperial palace. By combining Greek, Egyptian and Roman architectural orders he turned the beautiful buildings into a personal statement and many of the structures have symbolic meaning. As well as the residential palace, there are bath complexes, pools, a Greek theatre, a Temple of Venus and barracks for the Imperial Guard.

The Villa d'Este is another masterpiece. Cardinal d'Este used the greatest architects, artists and engineers to create a palace surrounded by a fantastic terraced garden in the late-Renaissance Mannerist style. Hadrian was his muse, but the cardinal appropriated recent technologies for his fantasy garden. Its blend of architectural elements and water features (the sequence of fountains is breathtaking) had, and still has, an enormous influence on European landscape design. The villa has also been celebrated in poetry, painting and music like Franz Liszt's evocative *Les Jeux d'Eaux à la Villa d'Este*.

**WHAT IS IT**
Two villas and gardens about 30 km (20 mi) east of Rome.
**WHAT IS THERE TO SEE**
Medieval Tivoli, with several tower houses, the temples of Hercules and the Tiburtine Sybil, the papal fortress of Rocca Pia, the beautiful waterfalls.
**YOU SHOULD KNOW**
There are entrance fees.
**DO NOT MISS**
The fountains and water features of the Villa d'Este.
**HOW DO I GET THERE**
Travel by train or bus from Rome.

# Mt Etna

Mt Etna is Europe's highest active volcano, at 3,323 m (10,900 ft), and Sicily's greatest natural attraction. To the ancient Greeks, it was the realm of Hephaestus, the god of fire, and home to the one-eyed Cyclops. Now it is a paradise for skiers in winter, and for hikers all year round. Although there are towns clustered around its base, there has been little building on the mountain itself because it has numerous vents and it is impossible to predict where the next eruption will be, whether it will produce large amounts of lava or just steam and ash. Today, its wilderness is protected by law.

Etna has several smaller peaks on its flanks that are beautiful places to walk. The hike up the Monte Gallo, on the western side, leads to the *Rifugio della Galverina*, an outpost in the heart of the oak, pine, beech and birch forest that surrounds much of the volcano. From Case Pirao on the north slope, climb to the dazzling beechwood of Monte Spagnolo, pausing to explore some of the caves that pepper the Etna complex.

Away from the popular routes, nature trails offer a chance to see lizards, weasels, hare, porcupine, snakes and even wild cats. The spectacular landscape is also home to raptors such as falcons and golden eagles, as well as owls and shyer birds such as partridges.

Climbing to the top of the volcano is strictly forbidden, and if it is going through an active phase, or is showing signs of activity, routes lower down will be restricted and closures may change from day to day depending on the wind direction.

**WHAT ELSE IS THERE TO SEE**
Alcantara Gorge, Adrano, Bronte, Randazzo.
**WHAT IS THERE TO DO**
Arrive in winter and enjoy hiking and skiing on the mountain.
**YOU SHOULD KNOW**
Some of the trails lie along steep cliffs and extra care should be taken.
**HOW DO I GET THERE**
By bus or the Ferrovia Circumetnea railway from Catania.

*View from Taormina, Sicily, to the Bay of Giardini Naxos, with Mt Etna in the background.*

*The Sicilian resort of Taormina.*

# Taormina

Taormina has long been Sicily's most famous resort. Set high above the Ionian Sea, it was for centuries a major crossroads of the ancient world. It is a gem of interlocked Greek, Roman and medieval styles – influenced by Phoenician, Carthaginian, Arab and Bourbon tastes, as each ruled the city in turn. Taormina's consequent reputation for lavish adornment in art and architecture is matched by the wealth and luxury enjoyed by its inhabitants. The maze of streets, alleyways and staircases harbours hidden squares, terraces looking out to sea, and a profound sense of balmy enchantment.

Taormina's splendour and sensuality has inspired visitors for more than 2,000 years. Ovid loved the local fish, while Pliny the Elder praised the wine. Elizabeth Taylor first partied with Richard Burton here; Goethe and Pirandello came to admire the staggering Roman theatre (known as the *teatro greco*) that dominates the city; and DH Lawrence wrote several works while staying here. The town is still a playground for the rich, famous and beautiful and the sophisticated buzz reaches its height during the film festival, one of several to take advantage of Taormina's special blend of beauty and history.

The blend extends far beyond the city walls. As well as nearby beaches, the water itself is one of the best diving sites in the Mediterranean. You can even swim among the stones and broken columns of Greek temples. Above the water, ruins of long-gone cultures still hug the corners of the fields. And the backdrop to all this is Mt Etna, often smoking, and occasionally bursting into nocturnal fire along snow-covered slopes, leaving a trail of steam and light in its wake.

**WHAT IS IT**
Sicily's most famous resort.
**WHAT IS THERE TO SEE**
Torre dell'Orologia, Church of San Giuseppe, Villa Comunale, Isola Bella nature reserve, Alcantara Gorge.
**YOU SHOULD KNOW**
There is an entrance fee for the Roman theatre.
**HOW DO I GET THERE**
By bus or train from Messina or Catania.

# Noto

Noto is the Baroque city of Sicily. The ancient city was totally destroyed by an earthquake in 1693; so Noto was rebuilt 13 km (20 mi) away in the then-popular Baroque style. Noto is the place to see Baroque art and architecture not just in its grand expressions of palaces or great churches, but in lesser, domestic and secular forms. Even the smallest details are harmonious: if you walk down Noto's grand main street, Corso Vittorio Emanuele, it feels like you are entering a period film set.

Of course, the grandest buildings are still the most interesting and most beautiful. The best are concentrated in the Piazza Municipio, Noto's main square, where the cathedral of San Nicolò de Mira (which has been undergoing repairs after a recent, less severe earthquake) is

**WHERE IS IT**
In south-east Sicily.
**ALSO KNOWN AS**
The Baroque city of Sicily.
**WHAT IS THERE TO SEE**
Syracuse, Modica, Ragusa.
**DO NOT MISS**
If you are short of time, make sure you see Piazza Municipo.
**HOW DO I GET THERE**
By train from Syracuse, or by bus from Syracuse or Catania.

flanked to its left by the Palazzo Alfano and the Palazzo Villadorta, a fantastic froth of late Baroque at its most fanciful: it is covered in wrought-iron balconies and fabulous lions, nymphs, ogres and mythical creatures. To the right of the cathedral is the Palazzo Vescovile, and opposite is the Town Hall, known as the Palazzo Ducezio. The latter is famous for its portico, and both buildings represent a more restrained form of Baroque decoration than some buildings here.

If all the Baroque style has not become too much, farther down the Corso is Noto's other important piazza, the Piazza XVI Maggio, which features the Vittorio Emanuele theatre and the church of San Domenico, with its spectacular, elegant curving façade, which was built in 1727.

*The church of San Francesco d'Assisi.*

# Pantalica

Pantalica is one of Sicily's special hidden surprises. Just west of Syracuse, the rivers Anapo and Calcinara converge in a spectacular limestone gorge in the Monti Iblei hills. Admire it from the road along its upper edge before clambering down through the trees to follow the disused railway track on the valley floor.

Coming from Sortino, pass a wonderful, clear pool in the Calcinara, shortly before it joins the Anapo at the wildest and most beautiful part of the gorge, where eagles soar above. The gorge widens out to lush fields and orchards of citrus, almonds, walnuts and even persimmon.

The spectacular, but harder way to explore Pantalica is to take the straggling road from Ferla. Just before it ends in a precipice, a rough track tumbles downhill to the Anaktoron – the remnants of the ancient capital of King Hyblon, a king of the Sikels – Sicily's original inhabitants.

And this is Pantalica's real secret, for you will pass over 5,000 tombs cut into the limestone, part of a vast necropolis developed between the thirteenth and eighth centuries BC. The tombs were re-used in the Byzantine era by refugees, who carved deep into the rock to build the church of San Micidario nearby.

Pantalica feels other-worldly and it is hard to leave the breathtaking beauty that frames the secrets of almost forgotten civilizations.

**WHAT IS THERE TO SEE**
Syracuse.
**WHAT IS THERE TO DO**
Follow the trails through Anaktoron and see the rock tombs.
**HOW DO I GET THERE**
Travel by car or bus from Syracuse or Ferla.
**YOU SHOULD KNOW**
This is a UNESCO World Heritage Site.

*The Rocky Necropolis of Pantalica.*

# Agrigento

**WHAT IS THERE TO SEE**
The Temple of Concord, the Temple of Juno and other monuments of ancient Akragas.
**WHAT IS THERE TO DO**
Visit the Archaeological Museum, explore the medieval town.
**WHEN SHOULD I GO**
The best times are spring or autumn.
**DO NOT MISS**
The sight of the Temple of Concord lit up at night.

Agrigento lies on Sicily's south coast, the modern city spreading untidily from its medieval core. Its real treasures lie a few kilometres away, in the site known as the Valley of the Temples, where the ruins of Agrigento's Greek, Carthaginian and Roman past are testimony to its earlier importance and glory.

Founded in about 582 BC, the wealthy and important Greek colony of Akragas had some of the best public monuments outside Greece itself. The colony was destroyed and rebuilt on several occasions, particularly during the Punic Wars between Carthage and Rome. Surrounded by olive groves and almond orchards, the city's ruins include necropoli, houses, streets, auditoria and a small theatre. However, it is best known for its group of seven Doric temples on the acropolis (high ground) above the colony. Standing proud above the vast site is the Temple of Concord (a name given to it later – its original dedication is not known), which was constructed in about 450 BC, and is in excellent condition despite its missing roof, chiefly because it was adopted as a Christian church in the late sixth century.

Dating from about ten years later is the Temple of Juno, which has not survived so well, but was built in the same form as the older building.

The largest temple on the site was that of Olympian Zeus, which was built in celebration of a military victory some time after 480 BC, but sadly little of it survives because of earthquake damage and the quarrying of its stones to help create the harbour of Porto Empedocle nearby. Other temples here were dedicated to Hephaestus, Hercules and Asclepius.

The best time of the year to visit is in spring when the almond trees in the nearby orchards are in bloom.

*Temple of Concord, Agrigento.*

# La Scala

Even if you are not that fond of opera, if you miss the opportunity to visit La Scala (officially, the *Teatro alla Scala*), you will regret it. Here, Rossini made his name and Puccini's magnificent *Madame Butterfly* made her debut.

In 1776, the Regio Teatro Ducale was destroyed by fire and the great Neoclassical architect Giuseppe Piermarini was commissioned by Empress Maria Theresa of Austria to build a theatre to replace it. He chose the site of a demolished church, Santa Maria alla Scala. Piermarini must have had phenomenal builders because what is probably the most perfect theatre in the world was completed in under two years. It opened on 3 August 1778 with a performance of Antonio Salieri's *l'Europa Riconosciuta*.

In the intervening years, La Scala has been dark three times, firstly during World War I. It was reopened after Arturo Toscanini led an independent, autonomous council to raise the money to reopen it in 1920. La Scala was bombed again during World War II, and again, Toscanini helped raise the funds to reconstruct and reopen it in 1946, with a series of benefit concerts. Finally in 2001 the theatre went dark for extensive renovations. At a cost of around US $70 million , Mario Botta, the architect, was responsible for the work and in December 2004 La Scala reopened, again with a performance of Salieri's *l'Europa Riconosciuta*.

La Scala is sumptuous from its plush, red velvet seating and chandeliers to the emotion and appreciation with which its patrons greet performances of ballet and opera and its conductors cast and rehearse the varied repertoire. Do not miss it; it is the epitome of architectural, acoustic and musical passion and excellence.

*The auditorium of La Scala Opera House.*

**WHAT IS THERE TO SEE**
The theatre museum, the cathedral.
**WHAT IS THERE TO DO**
Make sure you visit the refectory of Santa Maria della Grazia, containing Leonardo da Vinci's *Last Supper* – you will need to book in advance.
**DO NOT MISS**
Make sure you see an opera while you are here.
**VITAL STATISTICS**
Total capacity 2,200 people: 678 orchestra seats, 409 seats, first and second galleries, 155 boxes on four levels.

*Feriolo on Lake Maggiore.*

# Lake Maggiore

Like many of the world's most fascinating places, Lake Maggiore, the most westerly and second largest of the pre-alpine lakes of Europe is a place where history, cultures and regions meet. To the west, its banks are in Piedmont, to the east in Lombardy and to the north in Switzerland. Before the unification of Italy, Piedmont and Lombardy were separate nation states, guarding their lands from the greedy designs of their neighbours. At Ornavasso you can still see the medieval watchtower with its spectacular views over the Ossolo valley and the peaks of the Corni di Nibbio alongside the octagonal Baroque church of the Madonna della Guardia, built between 1674 and 1772.

This stunning waterscape boasts the perfect semi-Mediterranean climate, mild in both summer and winter, encouraging glorious lush and exotic flora such as the orchids to be seen on the Borromeo islands, Isola Madre, and Isola Bella, which also boasts an exquisite palace. The Borromeo islands are visible from almost every part of the shore and can be reached by the frequent ferries and water taxis that cross and recross the lake. Visit Swiss Locarno in spring for the magnificent camelias, mimosa and forsythia.

Leggiuno has the sanctuary of Santa Caterina del Sasso, a Dominican monastery begun in the thirteenth century, which is perched high on a rock over the lake. Arona's giant bronze statue of St Charles Borromeo is hollow and the energetic can climb up inside to gaze at the view through the saint's eyes.

At Ornavasso visitors can reach the sanctuary of the Madonna del Boden by following a muletrack, while Stresa's cable-car will take you 1,370 m (4,500 ft) up the mountainside. The last-named village is a charming patchwork of cobbled streets and square – but then there are so many charming villages in this pretty area.

**WHERE IS IT**
Straddling the border between north-east Italy and southern Switzerland.
**WHAT IS THERE TO SEE**
The Alpine Botanic Garden in Stresa, the Palazzo Borromeo on Isola Bella, Palazzo Madre on Isola Madre.
**DO NOT MISS**
Stresa's cable-car for stunning views.
**CLIMATE**
Here you can enjoy the perfect semi-Mediterranean climate, with mild summers and winters.
**HOW DO I GET THERE**
By bus or train from Milan.

# Lake Trasimeno

Lake Trasimeno is a place of contrast and contradiction. Surrounded on three sides by hills, its tranquil green waters are home to an abundance of fish and breathtaking birdlife, from wild swans to herons, cormorants, widgeon, stilts and wild geese. This, the largest lake in peninsular Italy, is a haven of peace. Conversely, the medieval fortifications of Passignano, Monte del Lago and Castiglione del Lago and the remains of castles on the Polvese and Maggiore islands proudly bear testimony to its turbulent military history. Legend has it that when one of the most decisive battles of the Punic War was fought here in 217 BC and Hannibal of Carthage defeated Gaius Flaminius of the Roman Republic, the fighting was so fierce that neither side noticed an earthquake, which happened in the heat of battle.

Nowadays, the luxuriant waterside flora is rarely disturbed except by wild boar and coypu. Olives and pines grow on the Perugian islands of Polvese; Isola Maggiore and Isola Minore, the last of which has been uninhabited for centuries. Frequent boat trips take visitors to the islands. The inhabitants along the shores still earn their living from the abundant fish in its waters, and Lake Trasimeno is a popular sport fishing destination. The waters are replaced naturally every 22 years. Visitors also come to enjoy the fortified towns and examine the remains of Etruscan civilization to be seen here.

**WHAT IS IT**
The longest lake in peninsular Italy.
**WHAT IS THERE TO SEE**
Castiglione del Lago's Rocca del Leone (1247) and the nearby palace of Ascanio della Cornia, Palazzo Casali 12 km (7.5 mi) from Cortona.
**WHAT IS THERE TO DO**
Take a boat over to the islands and get a closer look at the scenery.
**HOW DO I GET THERE**
By train or bus from Perugia, or hire a car.

*Lake Trasimeno, Perugia.*

# The Royal Palace at Caserta

**WHERE IS IT**
North-east of Naples.
**WHAT IS IT**
An eighteenth-century royal palace considered by many to be the last great example of Italian Baroque architecture.
**WHAT IS THERE TO SEE**
The gardens feature a series of fountains and an 80 m (260 ft) waterfall fed by the specially built aqueduct. They are said to rival the gardens of Versailles.
**YOU SHOULD KNOW**
It is closed on major holidays and there is a entrance fee.
**HOW DO I GET THERE**
Travel by train from Naples, or hire a car.

The eighteenth-century royal palace (*palazzo reale*) at Caserta with its park, aqueduct and the San Leucio complex, in the region of Campania, was declared a UNESCO World Heritage Site in 1996. It was conceived by King Charles IV, later Charles III of Spain, as a majestic statement of the power, wealth and prestige of the Bourbon dynasty, and it was built outside the teeming city of Naples, with its discontented inhabitants, just as his ancestor Louis XIV had built Versailles outside Paris to escape the Parisians. Charles had much to live up to, as did his architect Luigi Vanvitelli. And they succeeded!

The palace at Caserta most nearly rivals the palace at Versailles. It has been said that it is the last great building of the Italian Baroque. The main palace has 1,200 exquisite rooms, 25 magnificent royal apartments and a main staircase that boasts 116 steps carved from one piece of stone. Vanvitelli designed and built a magnificent aqueduct to provide the water for the many fountains, and pools, most of which featured glorious statues. The little theatre is modelled on Naples' Teatro San Carlo and the whole is set in vast, enchanting parkland with graceful Italianate gardens, including the English Garden.

The whole included a barracks and the San Leucio complex, a royal silk factory disguised as a pavilion. The inhabitants of the area were forcibly picked up and moved 10 km (6 mi) to make way for Caserta. Construction began in 1752, but the architect died before it was complete. The work was carried on by his son Carlo. Charles IV never spent a night here, because he became king of Spain but the palace was completed for his son, Ferdinand IV of Naples.

*The throne room of the royal palace.*

*The rooftops and towers of Bologna.*

# Bologna

Bologna is the capital city of Emilia-Romagna in northern Italy. Since ancient times, this has been Italy's most fertile wheat and dairy region, and it is famous for its fine food and wine. Europe's oldest university was founded here in 1088 when Bologna was a wealthy, independent commune. In an effort to outdo each other, every family of note erected a tower in their own honour. There were once more than 170 of them, but only a handful remain today.

The two towers that rise above the Piazza di Porta Ravegnana are well-known landmarks. Leaning precariously they have both managed to defy gravity for hundreds of years. The Garisenda tower is 49 m (160 ft) high, but originally it was considerably taller. Unfortunately, the Garisenda family did not bother much with foundations for their tower – they were trying to out-do the neighbouring Asinelli family's tower, which is an astonishing 97 m (318 ft) high. Garisenda leans 3.2 m (10 ft) from the vertical, and as long ago as 1360 the top half was taken down as it was considered to be dangerous. It is still closed to the public to this day.

The Asinelli tower also leans, although not as much. Completed in 1119, it has 498 steps that you can climb in order to see the most breath-taking view of the red-tiled roofs of the city and the verdant countryside beyond. On a clear day you can see as far as the Adriatic and the Alps.

The historic centre of Bologna is beautiful and among its highlights is the church of San Domenico, which has the saint's shrine, made by Nicola Pisano, and some early sculptures by Michelangelo.

**WHAT IS IT KNOWN FOR**
Bologna is famous for its food and wine.
**WHAT IS THERE TO SEE**
Piazza Maggiore and Piazza del Nettuno, Palazzo Comunale, Basilica of San Petronio, Basilica of Santo Stefano.
**WHAT IS THERE TO DO**
Climb the Asinelli tower for a spectacular view of the city.
**YOU SHOULD KNOW**
The Museo Civico Archaeologico has one of the best Etruscan collections in Italy.

# The Leaning Tower of Pisa

The Leaning Tower of Pisa is one of the Seven Wonders of the World, but would probably be so anyway, even if it was vertical. The tower is the bell tower (*campanile*) of the cathedral with which it shares the Campo dei Miracoli. The unusual design of the tower resembles that of the Tower of Babel as described by the Greek writer Herodotus. There are 294 steps in the bell tower and seven bells tuned to a musical scale.

Construction began in 1173, and by the time the third level was added in 1178, the lean was already noticeable. Work stopped for almost a century because of Pisa's almost constant wars with the neighbouring city state of Florence and began again in 1272 under the direction of Giovanni di Simone. Four further floors were added, at a different angle to the lower ones, but construction had to stop again in 1284 when Pisa was defeated in battle by Genoa. The bell-chamber was finally started in 1372, fully 199 years after building work had begun.

It is now known that the tilt is caused by the inadequate foundations sinking into the weak subsoil, but before this was understood various attempts to correct the problem, such as digging out the walkway round the bottom or Mussolini's project in which concrete was poured into the foundations, simply made matters worse.

Work started in 1999 to strengthen the foundations and remove some of the subsoil on the high side, and the tower was brought back to a lean of 13 degrees. It is now hoped that it will remain a monument to the vision of its designer and a testament to the twelfth century prestige and wealth of the city of Pisa.

**WHAT IS IT**
One of the Seven Wonders of the World.
**WHAT IS THERE TO SEE**
The cathedral, bapistery and museum, the Church of Santa Catharina, the National Museum of San Matteo.
**YOU SHOULD KNOW**
There is an entrance fee. Numbers are strictly limited, and queues for the timed tickets are very long.
**HOW DO I GET THERE**
By air to Pisa or rail or bus from Florence.

*The Leaning Tower and the cathedral on the Campo dei Miracoli.*

# Padua

Padua (Padova) lies 37 km (23 mi) west of Venice, on the River Brenta. There has been a town here since before Roman times, but the Middle Ages were its glory days. The university, founded in 1222, is the second oldest in Italy, and boasts many venerable figures such as Galileo, Petrarch and Dante amongst its professors and alumni.

Modern Padua is a lively city but is something of an urban sprawl surrounding a lovely medieval centre, which holds a remarkable treasure – the Arena Chapel. Enrico Scrovegni fearing for the soul of his father, a money lender, used his ill-gotten gains to build this chapel, dedicated to the Virgin Mary. In 1305, he commissioned Giotto to paint a series of frescoes upon the walls, and the results are magnificent, illustrating the life of Christ and his Mother. One of the best-known images is the Kiss of Judas, and the series ends with the Last Supper. Visitors must book at least one day in advance to visit the chapel, and can only spend 15 minutes there. It is, however, an experience not to be missed.

The other main site of interest is the basilica that houses the shrine of St Antony, which has a wealth of art. Outside is Donatello's giant bronze equestrian statue of Gattamelata, the Venetian general Erasmo da Narni.

The historic centre holds other treats, as well as a tragedy – the Chiesa degli Eremitani, built in the fourteenth century, was full of marvellous frescoes by Mantegna, most of which were destroyed during World War II. There are, however, splendid Palladian villas, some of which may be visited, dotted around the area.

**WHERE IS IT**
37 km (23 mi) west of Venice on the River Brenta.
**WHAT IS THERE TO SEE**
The Museo Civici agli Eremitani, the Basilica del Santo, Palazzo della Ragione.
**DON'T MISS**
The frescoes in the Arena Chapel.
**YOU SHOULD KNOW**
You need to book at least one day in advance of your visit to the Arena Chapel and you can only spend 15 minutes inside. Entry fees payable
**HOW DO I GET THERE**
By train from Venice, Bologna or Milan.

*The Basilica in Padua.*

# Ostia Antica

Ostia Antica is a 20-minute train ride from Rome, and a world away. Its 10,000 acres of excavations reveal more details of ancient Roman life than any other single site. The ruins are beautifully preserved – often up to the second storey of whole streets – and because it is impossible to glimpse any modern contrivances and the site is almost always nearly empty, Ostia is the perfect place to imagine what being a citizen of ancient Rome was really like.

Ostia began as a military post guarding the Tiber estuary into the Tyrrhenian Sea in about 450 BC. As Rome grew in size and power, so did its port, filling the surrounding meadows until it was both a major naval base, and perhaps the most important trading centre in the Empire. When the Tiber silted up and was no longer navigable, Ostia was simply abandoned.

At its peak, Ostia was a flourishing commercial centre with a population of more than 100,000, whose apartment buildings, taverns, grocery shops and baths are still intact. The main street, *Decumanus Maximus*, is more than 2 km (1 mi) long – you can drag your feet in the deep ruts left by the long-gone four-wheeled carts that were the main means of ferrying merchandise and baggage between Rome and the sea.

Visitors are free to wander. There are mosaics and columns everywhere, but the highlights are such domestic details as the fishmonger's marble slab and the communal toilets that seated 20 at a time. Behind the 3,500-seat theatre, where live performances are held in summer, is the forum with the Temple of Ceres at its centre. In addition to temples, public baths and grand public spaces, you can explore the houses of the poor and the typical street plan and shops, and be a Roman for a day!

*One of the many mosaics in Ostia Antica. This depicts hybrid sea creatures including a bull-serpent with rider.*

# Paestum

The three glorious temples at Paestum are the most important Greek monuments south of Naples. The town was founded in the sixth century BC, and, being near the coast, was named Poseidonia, in honour of Poseidon, the god of the sea. By the first century BC it had become an important Roman trading port, but was abandoned because of the decline of the Empire, Saracen raids and outbreaks of malaria. The temples were not rediscovered until the twentieth century, and today they are a UNESCO World Heritage Site.

The Temple of Ceres (now known to have been dedicated to Athena) is the smallest, and the first you come to before strolling through the ruined city, which has several other buildings to explore. The Basilica, dedicated to the goddess Hera, is the oldest monument, with nine Doric columns along the front and 18 along the sides. The Temple of Neptune (in fact dedicated to Apollo) which dates from around 450 BC, is both the best preserved and the largest of the three temples, missing only its roof and some of its interior walls.

The museum contains many finds from both the town and the temples – bas-relief friezes, tomb paintings and treasures, including the diver's tomb, a marvellous example of fifth-century BC art. If you should find yourself in southern Italy, make the effort to visit Paestum for the rewards are great.

*Exterior of the Temple of Neptune.*

**WHAT IS IT**
Paestum contains the three most important Greek monuments south of Naples.
**WHAT IS THERE TO SEE**
the National Park of Cilento and its cave systems, the Monastery of San Lorenzo at Padula and Salerno.
**WHAT IS THERE TO DO**
Visit the temple of Neptune for a look at the best-preserved temple.
**YOU SHOULD KNOW**
A visit to Southern Italy would not be complete without a visit to Paestum.
**HOW DO I GET THERE**
By bus from Salerno, train from Naples or Salerno or by car.

*Buildings lining the
waterfront in Portofino.*

# Portofino

If you are looking for the high life, come to Portofino, one of Liguria's most exclusive seaside resorts, and also one of its most beautiful. It is situated on an idyllic promontory, its harbour is full of the elegant yachts of the international jet-set and its calm waters reflect the lovely ochre and yellow houses ringed around the water's edge.

The village has long been a favourite with celebrities – Truman Capote and Guy de Maupassant both wrote here; Hollywood stars such as Greta Garbo, Clark Gable, Elizabeth Taylor and Rex Harrison stayed here, the Duke and Duchess of Windsor honeymooned here and Aristotle Onassis arrived on his yacht. Today the rich and famous tend to holiday in private villas up in the hills behind the town but you never know who you might spot hiding behind sunglasses and sipping a Campari and soda at a waterfront bar.

Take the steps up to the Castello Brown, bought by an English diplomat in the 1860s and transformed into a family home. The gardens are lovely and offer great views of the harbour below. A little farther on the lighthouse has even more spectacular views.

Take a boat trip or a walk across the promontory to the eleventh-century Abbazia di San Fruttuoso, set amongst pine trees and olive groves. Nearby, but out to sea, is a bronze statue of Christ, placed on the sea-bed in 1954 to protect sailors. You can either take a boat to see this, on a calm day, or dive down for a close-up look, if you are not too busy shopping in one of the expensive little boutiques around town.

**WHAT IS IT**
One of Liguria's most exclusive seaside resorts, east of Genoa, and a draw for the jet-set.
**WHAT IS THERE TO SEE**
Rapallo, the church of San Giorgio, Santa Margherita, the five villages of Cinque Terra.
**WHAT IS THERE TO DO**
Enjoy the café culture and partake in an afternoon of celebrity spotting.
**HOW DO I GET THERE**
Travel by bus or ferry from Santa Margherita.

# Capri

The enchanting island of Capri, in the bay of Naples, is one of Italy's loveliest resorts. This small island rises sharply from the sea and is a beautiful jumble of tumbling purple, pink and white bougainvillea, lemon trees, narrow, winding lanes, and pastel houses.

Capri was the playground of emperors. Augustus, who loved to party here, supposedly founded the world's first paleontological museum in the Villa Augustus, to display the Stone-Age artefacts found by his builders. Tiberius retired here in 27 AD, and built various villas. Nowadays Capri town and Anacapri, the island's second town, are full of holiday makers, but the countryside between and around them is hilly, beautiful and much more peaceful.

Visit the gardens of Caesar Augustus and admire the astonishing views across the sea to Faraglioni Rocks. Walk along the Via Tiberio to the Villa Jovis, the best and largest of the Roman villas, where both Tiberius and Caligula were reported to indulge in orgies and torture, although this rumour may have been anti-imperial propaganda. At Anacapri you can explore the Villa San Michele, and its superb gardens, built by Axel Munthe, a Swedish doctor, on the ruins of another Roman villa.

Whatever you do, do not forget to visit the world famous Blue Grotto, one of several sea caves along the rocky coast. The sunlight reflecting off the white sandy floor turns the water an astonishing, iridescent blue. There are not too many places to swim from these craggy cliffs, but Capri is a splendid place for water sports and diving or just sitting back with a Limoncello to enjoy the view.

**WHAT IS THERE TO SEE**
The Monastery of San Giacomo, Mount Solaro, the islands of Ischia and Procida.
**WHAT IS THERE TO DO**
Ensure you visit the gardens of Augustus, take the chairlift up to Monte Solaro.
**DO NOT MISS**
The Blue Grotto.
**HOW DO I GET THERE**
Take a ferry or hydrofoil from Naples, Sorrento, Salerno, Positano or Amalfi.

*The Faraglioni Rocks stand in the water off the coast of Capri.*

# Skopje

In 1963 a dreadful earthquake almost annihilated the town of Skopje, killing over 1,000 inhabitants and pulverizing their homes. Happily the Old Bazaar and the ancient churches and mosques of the old town, north of the Vardar River, were spared.

At first glance Macedonia's capital city looks entirely modern, but in fact it has been inhabited since at least 3,500 BC. In 148 BC it came under Roman rule and subsequently passed into the hands of the Byzantine Empire. In 1392 it was conquered by the Turks and remained part of the Ottoman Empire for 500 years. A fifteenth-century stone bridge with 11 arches leads over the Vardar to the old city where you will find the Daut Pasha hamam, an extensive public bath complex that now houses the National Art Gallery's special collection, and the fascinating Old Bazaar, one of the largest of its kind in Europe. Here too is the fifteenth-century Mustafa Pasha's Mosque. At the top of the hill stand the ruins of the fifth-century Kale fortress.

The little church of Sveti Spas (the Holy Saviour), was built in the seventeenth century, and boasts a wonderful iconostasis carved from walnut wood. This beautifully realized high-relief work depicts plants, animals and the figures of various saints, all in traditional, local costume. In the courtyard stands the sarcophagus of Goce Delcev, a leader of the national liberation movement who was killed in 1903.

Skopje is a welcoming city that has a great deal of interesting historical monuments to see, as well as a burgeoning arts scene and vibrant nightlife.

*St Panteleimon in the nearby tiny village of Nerezi.*

# Ohrid

The town of Ohrid is probably the most beautiful town in Macedonia, situated on the shores of Lake Ohrid in the south-west of the country, with steep, cobbled streets that wind through the old town beneath the tenth-century citadel of Tsar Samuil, which may be on the site of one built by Alexander the Great's father, Philip II of Macedon. The town became Christian early on – its first known bishop was Zosimus, in about 344 AD. Many fine churches and monasteries were built, though most are Byzantine, some are from the late Middle Ages, when the town was known as the 'Slavic Jerusalem'.

There is a wealth of exquisite religious artwork here – fabulous icons, frescoes, mosaics and iconostases created in different eras. The thirteenth-century church of St Clement has beautiful frescoes, while the monastery of St Panteleimon has more than 800 icons from the eleventh to fourteenth centuries. It is said that by the fifteenth century there was a chapel for each day of the year, and those that have survived stand as a testament to the superb artists who have been drawn here over the course of 1,000 years.

The region's more distant past can be seen in the National Museum of Ohrid, which has some of the stunning grave goods found in the ancient Greek cemetery in nearby Trebenishta and more recent discoveries from Gorna Porta including a fifth-century BC golden death mask and glove, and the Roman theatre.

Ohrid is a popular summer resort with both Macedonians and those from farther afield because of its rich cultural heritage and beautiful setting and a popular alternative to cultural sightseeing is to relax in one of the cafés that line the lakeshore promenade, and admire the translucent waters and forested mountains.

*Frescoes inside the church of St Naum.*

**WHAT IS IT**
One of the most beautiful towns in Macedonia, set on the shore of Lake Ohrid.
**ALSO KNOWN AS**
Slavic Jerusalem.
**WHAT IS THERE TO SEE**
Church of St Sophia, Church of St Naum, Church of St Clement, Church of St John the Divine, the Roman theatre.
**HOW DO I GET THERE**
By air from Ljubljana or Zurich or by bus from Skopje.
**YOU SHOULD KNOW**
This is a UNESCO World Heritage Site.

# Valletta

*One of Valletta's 365 churches.*

The Baroque, fortified city of Valletta is built on the high, rocky Sceberras Peninsula, on Malta's north-east coast, and is surrounded on three sides by two of the most beautiful natural harbours in Europe, the Grand Harbour and Marsamxett harbour. A panoramic harbour view can be seen from the Upper Barracca Gardens.

In 1530 the Knights of St John came to Malta and soon realized the strategic importance of the peninsula. They began to build their fortress in 1566 and completed it just 15 years later. It is named after its founder, the Grand Master Jean Parisot de la Valette, but was designed on a grid pattern by an Italian military engineer, Francesco Laparelli, who provided a sewage system and piped fresh water in case the fortress was ever besieged.

Explore the ancient fortifications, then wander through the narrow city streets and you will see statues and fountains and parapets above you sporting coats of arms as well as splendid Baroque architecture. St John's Co-Cathedral is magnificent. Its severe façade shelters an interior of lavish Baroque extravagance, with painted ceiling vaults, intricately carved stone walls and superb marble tombstones set in the floor. Among its many works of art is Caravaggio's late masterpiece, *The Beheading of John the Baptist*, while there are other important works in the museum next door. The Manoel Theatre, with its sumptuous interior, was built in 1731 and is one of the oldest theatres in Europe still in use, and can be seen on a guided tour. Valetta is not a museum-piece, as well as a tourist destination, it is a busy, working city with a lively arts programme and offers something for everyone.

# Kotor

*The village of Kotor.*

First settled during Roman times, when it was part of the province of Dalmatia, and later becoming the ancient maritime centre of Montenegro, Kotor lies some 22 km (14 mi) up the Adriatic coast from the busy beach resort of Budva. The attractions of the town owe much to its beautiful setting at the end of the Gulf of Kotor, a submerged river valley, surrounded by cliffs and steep-sloped hills.

Despite being hit by earthquakes, most recently in the 1970s, Kotor is a particularly well-preserved medieval town, with no fewer than six Romanesque churches dating from the twelfth and thirteenth centuries and a wealth of fine old buildings, from palaces to small private houses, all in a labyrinth of narrow cobbled streets and squares. Kotor and its surroundings were under the rule of the Republic of Venice for nearly 400 years and the Venetian influence is clearly visible in much of the town's architecture.

Kotor's city walls, parts of which date back to the ninth century, are one of the finest examples of fortifications in Europe. Reaching up to 20 m (66 ft) high and over 10 m (33 ft) wide in places, they wind for 5 km (3 mi) around the city and up to the top of the steep rocky cliff to the Fortress of St John where you will be met with spectacular views of the town and across the entire bay.

Unlike some ancient cities and towns in Europe which, for much of the year at least, can seem like museum pieces overrun by tourists, Kotor is very much alive, with locals thronging the many shops, bars, nightclubs and restaurants, often until late in the evenings.

**YOU SHOULD KNOW**
Kotor has been a UNESCO Heritage site since 1979.
**HOW DO I GET THERE**
Travel by road from Podgorica or Budva.
**WHAT IS THERE TO SEE**
The view from the Fortress of St John and the city walls.
**DON'T MISS**
The mountain road from Kotor to Cetinje, Durmitor National Park.

# The Alhambra

The city of Granada is set on and around three low hills against the backdrop of the Sierra Nevada mountains and is dominated by the Alhambra palace.

In 1238, when Muhammad I took control of Granada, the Christians were regaining ground across the Iberian peninsula, and Granada became a Moorish vassal state of Spain. Under these unpromising circumstances, the caliphs of the Nasrid dynasty produced the finest flowering of their art and architecture ever to be seen.

The Alcazaba is the oldest part of the site, dating from the mid-thirteenth century, and was built on the foundations of the original nineth-century Moorish fortress. From the watchtower of the Alcazaba you can see the Alhambra proper, a spectacular series of courtyards and halls decorated with carved wood, ornate stucco, fantastic ceiling paintings, horseshoe arches and the fabulous complex patterns of multicoloured glazed tiles. There are many fountains and pools throughout the site and the delightful sounds of water can be heard where ever you go. The pool in the Court of Myrtles is a perfect example of Moorish architecture, surrounded as it is by graceful columns and arches that are reflected in the water.

The Hall of Kings is a vast banqueting hall in which sumptuous feasts were held and the ceiling boasts marvellous hunting scenes painted on leather. At the centre of the palace is the famous Court of the Lions. Built by Muhammad V, the courtyard is lined with arcades supported on alternating paired and single marble columns.

The Moorish parts of the Alhambra are a beautiful reminder of the rich legacy and sophisticated culture of the almost forgotten Muslim inhabitants of western Europe.

*The Alhambra with the Sierra Nevada beyond.*

# Barcelona

Sitting on Spain's north-east Mediterranean coast, the Catalan capital, Barcelona, is a great European city which, despite having a splendid medieval centre including the well known Las Ramblas, is best known for the extraordinary Modernist buildings created by Antoni Gaudí (1852–1926) and other architects. Most of these buildings are to be found in the Eixample area.

The Casa Milà, known by the locals as La Pedrera is perhaps the most famous example of Gaudí's domestic architecture – an apartment block whose undulating façade, supposedly inspired by the rock face of Montserrat, Catalonia's sacred mountain, appears to flow around the corner, and whose rooftop chimneys and air vents form a sculpture garden.

It is Gaudí's still unfinished church, however, that is his greatest achievement. From 1884 la Sagrada Família became Gaudí's obsession and he even lived on the site for 16 years. It has four spires, each over 100 m (330 ft) high and topped with coloured ceramics, and stone porches that look as though they are made of dripping wax or a weird stalactite formation. The Nativity façade is the most complete part of Gaudí's church, with doorways that represent faith, hope and charity.

Other Gaudí works include the Casa Batlló and the Palau and Park Güell. Other UNESCO World Heritage Sites in Barcelona are Lluis Domènech i Montaner's Palau de la Música Catalana and Hospital de Sant Pau.

Barcelona has a wealth of museums, including the Fundació Joan Miró, the Museu Picasso and several dedicated to different aspects of Catalan art and history.

**WHAT IS THERE TO SEE**
Palau and Park Güell, Palau de la Música Catalana, Museu Picasso, Las Ramblas and Illa de la Discordia.
**DO NOT MISS**
Spend an evening on Las Ramblas soaking up the atmosphere and enjoying the street performances.
**WHAT IS THERE TO DO**
Visit the Museu Picasso and see original works in an extensive installation.

*Casa Batlló by Gaudí.*

*St James stands over the doorway of the cathedral.*

**WHAT IS IT**
The third most important place of Christian pilgrimage after St Peter's in Rome and Jerusalem.
**WHAT ELSE IS THERE TO SEE**
The convent of San Martino Pinario, the Obradoiro façade, Raxoi's Palace.
**YOU SHOULD KNOW**
There is an entrance fee for the museum and cloisters.

# Santiago de Compostela

In the ninth century, a tomb supposed to be that of St James the Apostle was discovered at Santiago de Compostela, and by the Middle Ages this had become the third most important place of Christian pilgrimage after St Peter's in Rome and Jerusalem. Today, both pilgrims and tourists still follow the ancient route across northern Spain to the towering cathedral.

Santiago Cathedral was built on the site of a ninth-century basilica between the eleventh and thirteenth centuries. Although there have been additions such as the Baroque Obradoiro façade, the interior remains as it was almost 800 years ago. Behind the Obradoiro façade stands the superb twelfth-century Portico de la Gloria with its three decorated arches. Christ, flanked by four apostles and eight angels, dominates the central arch, and St James stands directly below him on a column carved with the Tree of Jesse.

Inside the cathedral the extremely ornate gilt and silver confection of the altar contrasts strongly with the cool, dark simplicity of the rest of the interior.

During the Middle Ages, as many as two million visitors made their way here on foot each year, and in the twelfth century a monk named Aymery Picaud wrote the first guide book in the world in order to help them, describing in detail the best routes through France and Spain and the best places to stay. Today, visitor numbers have not changed, but although many people choose to walk at least part of the way, it is not strictly necessary.

# A Coruña

A Coruña (La Coruña or Corunna) is built on a narrow peninsula in the north-west of Spain at the tip of which stands the Torre de Hercules – the oldest working lighthouse in the world. Originally built by Gaius Sevius Lupus it has stood and served for 1,900 years. It appears in many medieval manuscripts, including the Hereford *Mappa Mundi*, which dates back to about 1285. The naval architect Don Eustaquio Giannini completely overhauled it in 1785, in a very sensitive reconstruction that echoed the Roman design he found within. The tower, which had fallen into disrepair, was raised again in 1847 and stands 49 m (161 ft) high. Today the lighthouse has been fully modernized and its beacon has a range of 37 km (23 mi). Climb the 242 steps to the top for a panoramic ocean view.

Other sights in the city include the fortress of San Antón, on an island in the bay, which now serves as the town's museum of archaeology and history and has exhibits dating back to the Bronze Age on. The fine arts museum is housed in the old Capuchin convent.

*The Tower of Hercules is the world's oldest functioning lighthouse.*

The Plaza Maria Pita, named after a woman who raised the alarm about Sir Francis Drake's attack in 1589, has the colossal Palacio Municipal, whose ornate façade and bronze-clad domes disguise the fact that it was built in the early twentieth century. The church of San Jorge is also well worth a visit.

**WHAT IS IT**
A town in north-west Spain with the world's oldest working lighthouse.
**DON'T MISS**
Climbing to the top of the Tower of Hercules for an amazing panoramic view of the ocean.

# Pamplona

Pamplona has been the capital of Navarre (Navarra) in northern Spain since the ninth century and is believed to have been founded by the Roman general, Pompey.

Ernest Hemingway put Pamplona and its 'fiesta' firmly on the map when he published his book *The Sun Also Rises*. At midday on 6 July the fiesta gets going with a bang as a rocket explodes outside the town hall, and the crowd tie their red handkerchiefs around their necks, singing and shouting 'Viva San Fermín!' On the last night, 14 July, the party comes to an end with crowds of people holding candles and singing Basque songs in the main square.

The eight-day fiesta of San Fermín is a week of non-stop riotous parties, fireworks, parades, music, dancing and, at 8.00 am each day, the *encierro* (running of the bulls). Six bulls are released to run through the old town's cobbled streets, on their way to the bull-ring for the evening's bull-fight. Every day, too, men take the opportunity to run through the streets with the bulls, risking injury, even death.

If this sounds too dangerous for you, Pamplona also has Spain's best medieval military architecture in the form of the star-shaped citadel and city walls that Philip II had built in order to defend against the depredations of the French.

**WHAT IS THERE TO SEE**
The Museo de Navarra, the citadel, the cathedral.
**WHEN SHOULD I VISIT**
The festival runs from 6–14 July.
**YOU SHOULD KNOW**
Every year there are serious injuries sustained in the *encierro*.

*The bulls take the bend on Calla Estafeta during the bull-run*

# Guggenheim Museum

**WHAT IS IT**
A world renowned art gallery.
**WHAT TO SEE**
The wide range of art from the last 40 years of the twentieth century, the medieval city centre.
**DO NOT MISS**
Louise Bourgeois' *Maman*, Yves Klein's *Fire Fountain*.
**YOU SHOULD KNOW**
There is an entrance fee.

Bilbao is in the Basque Country of northern Spain and since the nineteenth century has been Spain's leading commercial port. An urban development scheme was introduced to regenerate the industrial sprawl, complete with futuristic buildings and a stylish metro system, and the port was moved to the coast. In 1991 the Basque authorities and the Guggenheim Foundation agreed to found a new Guggenheim Museum as part of the revitalization of Bilbao. In 1993 Frank O. Gehry's design was accepted, the foundation stone laid and in October 1997 the museum opened. By October 1998, the museum had received more than 1.3 million visitors.

The building is a piece of art in its own right. Built in limestone, glass and titanium it covers a 3.25 ha (8 acre) site that runs down to the river, 16 m (55 ft) below the level of the rest of

*Guggenheim Museum in Bilbao.*

Bilbao. Outside it are several fantastic installations by contemporary artists. Inside, the spectacular atrium, with its flower-shaped skylight, is the centrepiece of Gehry's vision and is surrounded by 19 galleries on three levels, connected by curving walkways suspended from the roof.

# Santa María de Guadalupe

The monastery of Guadalupe was founded in 1340, by Alfonso XI, in gratitude to the Virgin Mary, who had helped him to win an important battle. Legend has it that the religious significance of the site came about thanks to a peasant who, whilst out searching for a missing cow, had a vision and discovered a statue of the Virgin, carved by St Luke.

Over time, three hospitals and a school of medicine were built and a pharmacy, where monks made remedies from herbs picked in the sierras, and one of the largest libraries in Spain were added. However, it was when the Conquistadors chose Guadalupe as their shrine and brought treasure to it from the New World, that it became the sumptuous building that it is today. In Latin America Our Lady of Guadalupe is held in great reverence – she is the patron saint of Mexico.

The stone monastery, with its battlements and towers, is magnificent. From its hill-top vantage-point it completely dominates the village that has grown up around it. Today, the monastery is a Franciscan foundation and is still visited by thousands of pilgrims each year. Take a guided tour and admire the illuminated manuscripts, embroidered vestments, painting and sculptures and the cloister with its Moorish horseshoe arches. The simple wooden statue of Our Lady of Guadelupe, with her smoke-blackened face, adorned with a ceremonial crown and gorgeously embroidered robes.

**WHAT IS IT**
An revered monastery founded in 1340 by Alfonso XI.
**WHY IS IT IMPORTANT**
The monastery is still visited by thousands of Catholic pilgrims each year.
**WHAT TO SEE**
The Baroque sacristy; the church; the Ermita del Humilladero.
**YOU SHOULD KNOW**
The entrance fee to the monastery is waived on Fridays.

*Ornamental window surrounds of the monastery.*

# Montserrat National Park

**WHAT IS IT**
Spain's first national park.
**WHAT IS THERE TO SEE**
Spectacular natural scenery, the
basilica, the statue of the Moreneta,
the hermits' dwellings.
**WHAT IS THERE TO DO**
Listen to the boys' choir sing the
Montserrat hymn daily except during
July and at Christmas.
**DO NOT MISS**
The mountain views and
hermits' dwellings.
**HOW DO I GET THERE**
By rail from Barcelona, then up the
mountain in the cable car or the
Montserrat Rack Railway, or by car.
Funiculars railways lead from the
monastery almost to the
mountain top.

The small wooden statue of The Black Virgin of Montserrat, revered locally as La Moreneta, is at the heart of Catalonia's most holy site, the basilica, monastery and hermitage of Montserrat. The complex is near the top of the spectacular saw-toothed mountain of the same name, which was designated as Spain's first national park, about a century ago.

Whichever way you approach the monastery, on foot, by car, rack railway or cable car, the mountain views are marvellous. Drivers approaching from the north get a particularly wonderful view of the sierra at Manresa. The monastery, which is surrounded by small chapels and hermit's caves, was founded in 880 and enlarged in the eleventh century. In the fifteenth century it gained independence from Rome and its fame spread. In the early nineteenth century it was badly damaged when the French attacked Catalonia, but was rebuilt in 1844. Today it is a Benedictine monastery, which holds a marvellous collection of art in its museum. El Greco, Caravaggio and Zurbaran's religious paintings are featured, as well as modern works including some early Picassos, and some pieces from ancient Egyptian and the near east.

The combination of the Catalan cult of La Moreneta, combined with visitors who wish to visit the monastery and hermitage, means that this is a big tourist attraction, and unsurprisingly there is a large commercial element here. However the whole area is so beautiful that it is still worth visiting.

*Montserrat monastery
near Barcelona.*

# Córdoba

In 711 the Moors entered Spain and by the middle of the century Córdoba was ruled by Abd Ar-Rahman, a charismatic leader who set in train a building programme that dramatically raised Córdoba's profile. By the tenth century it was the most important city west of Constantinople, home to Andalucia's first university and a library of more than 4,000 books.

The Great Mosque, known as the Mezquita, was originally built by Abd Ar-Rahman, who was a great believer in religious tolerance. This is particularly interesting in view of the fact that some 500 years later, after the reconquest, Alfonso X decided to add a royal chapel. A little over 100 years later, a second chapel was added, and about 150 years after that, the Church decided to build a cathedral within the mosque as well, destroying part of the original building.

Entering the mosque through the bronze-covered gateway, you find yourself in the Patio de los Naranjos, a courtyard full of orange trees around a pool where the faithful washed ritually before praying. Inside, the ranks of terracotta-and-white striped arches march into the distance and the beautifully decorated cupolas take your breath away. Make sure you see the superb *mihrab*, or sacred prayer niche, with its amazing mosaic arch and stone cupola shaped like a shell.

Walking away from the gateway, you will find yourself in the Juderia, the medieval Jewish quarter, where the cobbled alleys are far too narrow to accommodate cars. You can see little whitewashed houses and workshops with beautiful wrought-ironwork and tiny fountains with water splashing into beautiful basins of glazed ceramic tiles set in lovely patios.

*Cupola in the Mezquita in Córdoba.*

**WHERE IS IT**
Andalucia, southern Spain.
**WHAT IS THERE TO SEE**
The Torre del Alminar, the stunning interior of the mosque, the Alcázar de los Reyes Cristianos, the Synagogue.
**WHY IS IT IMPORTANT**
Córdoba was home to Europe's first university.
**YOU SHOULD KNOW**
There is an entrance fee.

*The palace and monastery of the Escorial.*

# The Escorial

Phillip II built the Escorial to fulfil a vow he had made after a hermitage dedicated to St Lawrence was demolished during a Spanish victory over the French in 1557. Previously his father had made a wish on his deathbed for a church with a royal mausoleum to be built, and the Escorial (*Real Monasterio de San Lorenzo de El Escorial*) accomplished both desires.

The palace stands in the foothills of the Sierra Guadarrama, and its vast grey, granite walls and austere appearance began a vogue for an architectural style known as *desornamentado*, meaning unadorned. The bleak basilica and simple royal apartments belie the wealth of the Habsburg art collection, which is largely housed in other buildings on the site such as the library and the royal pantheon.

The highlights of the basilica are the sumptuous altar and, in the chapel, Benvenuto Cellini's astonishing crucifix. The library, with its barrel-vaulted ceiling decorated with Tibaldi's frescoes, contains 40,000 books and manuscripts and the museum houses works by Titian, Tintoretto and Bosch. An impressive fresco by Giordano stands above the main staircase of the Augustinian monastery. The royal pantheon is somewhat unnerving. A flight of stairs leads down to the octagonal room, passing the *pudridero* a room where royal corpses were left to decompose for several years before being placed in the gilt and marble coffins that line the walls of the mausoleum.

**WHERE IS IT**
In the foothills of the Sierra Guadarrama, 45 km (28 mi) north-west of Madrid.
**WHAT IS THERE TO SEE**
The Museum of Art, the library, the royal pantheon, the chapter houses.
**YOU SHOULD KNOW**
There is an entrance fee but EU citizens get in free on Wednesdays.
**HOW DO I GET THERE**
By train or bus from Madrid.

# The Prado

*One of the galleries in
the Prado.*

The Prado was originally built by Juan de Villanueva for Charles III,
as a natural history museum. Later, Napoleon's brother Joseph
decided it should be an art museum, and by the time it opened in
1819, under Fernando VII, it housed the royal art collection. There
is no doubt that the Prado is one of the world's finest museums,
holding more than 9,000 works of art by, among others Velázquez,
Goya, El Greco, Raphael, Titian, Botticelli, Caravaggio, Veronese,
Fra Angelico, Bosch, Rubens, Dürer, Rembrandt and the Brueghels.

Queen Isabella began the royal collection in the sixteenth
century, and this was added to by her successors until the
nineteenth century. The Prado displays some 1,500 works of art,
mainly paintings, at any one time. Some of these are on permanent
display and the rest are shown on a rotation system. Try to see both
the Goya and the Velázquez collections. The museum has had some
major renovations in the last few years, the most recent being an
underground link joining the main building to the Jerónimos
building and the refurbishment of the Casón del Buen Retiro, with
its collection of nineteenth-century Spanish art. Nearby are the
Museo Reina Sofía, which has twentieth-century art, the Palacio de
Villahermosa, which houses the Thyssen-Bornemisza Museum and
the Museo Arqueológico, which has the Egyptian, Mesopotamian,
Greek and Roman collections that used to be in the Prado.

**WHERE IS IT**
In the centre of Madrid.
**WHAT IS IT**
One of the world's finest museums.
**WHAT IS THERE TO SEE**
Fra Angelico's *Annunciation*,
Bosch's *Garden of Earthly Delights*,
Rubens' *The Three Graces*,
Velázquez's *Las Meninas*.
**DON'T MISS**
The Goya and Velázquez collections.
**YOU SHOULD KNOW**
The Prado displays about 1,500
works, some of which are on
permanent display and others
on a rotation system. It is closed
on Mondays.

# Los Jameos del Agua

**WHERE IS IT**
North-eastern Lanzarote in the
Canary Islands.
**WHAT IS IT**
A spectacular series of underground
volcanic caves that now house a
restaurant, garden and auditorium.
**WHAT ELSE IS THERE TO SEE**
Cueva de los Verdes.
**HOW TO I GET THERE**
By air to Lanzarote and then by car
via Arrieta or Orzola.

Los Jameos del Agua, (meaning 'the water hollows'), is a section of a long volcanic tube that formed within the lava flow of the extensive eruption of the Corona volcano which occurred about 3,000 years ago. It is part of the large Atlantida volcanic cave system in north-eastern Lanzarote.

In 1965, a local artist, César Manrique, was inspired to landscape this volcanic tube with its caverns and hollows that were formed where parts of the volcanic roof collapsed. Opened to the public by the island administration in 1968 as a series of unique entertainment venues, it was finally completed in 1987 with the construction of a superb natural auditorium with a capacity of about 600 seats.

Steps lead down to an extraordinary underground restaurant, complete with dance floor and bar. A 100-m (330-ft) long path leads the visitor to the Jameo Grande, an enormous cavern, 62 m (200 ft) long, 19 m (62 ft) wide and 21 m (69 ft) high. The path crosses a crystal-clear, saltwater, tidal lagoon in which a rare species of almost blind albino crab lives. This cave has been transformed into a lush tropical garden planted around an emerald green, man-made pool.

At the far end of the Jameo Grande, a marvellous underground auditorium opens up. Famous for its excellent acoustics it is regularly used for concerts and shows such as the prestigious Festival of Visual Music of Lanzarote. Nearby, a scientific institution devoted to studying the volcanic nature of the island has a good exhibition for visitors interested in the island's geology, flora and fauna.

*The auditorium in los Jameos del Agua.*

# Lisbon

Lisbon (Lisboa) lies snuggled between seven hills on the northern side of the mouth of the River Tagus (Tejo). The Praca do Comercio by the harbour is one of the most distinguished squares in Europe with three sides of handsome buildings over arcaded galleries and the fourth formed by the riverfront.

For at least 3,000 years this harbour has been in use by different powers, but Lisbon's heyday was between the fifteenth and seventeenth centuries, when Portugal was a wealthy and powerful empire-building nation. Vasco de Gama discovered the sea route to India in 1498 and enormous profits were made from trading in spices and precious stones. In the seventeenth century gold was discovered in Brazil, but by the mid-century Portugal's empire was in decline. In 1755 Lisbon was severely damaged by an earthquake, and never regained its former glory. Nowadays, however, it is a successful European capital city, and a great place to visit.

Lisbon is a lovely place, full of contrasts, from modern high rises to Art Nouveau buildings, wonderful mosaic pavements, brightly tiled buildings and the medieval Moorish area of the Alfama. There are fabulous buildings, museums, monasteries and parks to see. Look out over the city from the top of any of the hills – the Castello de São Jorge has panoramic views, and don't miss the façade of the church of Nossa Senhora da Conceição Velha or the unique Manveline (Portuguese late Gothic) architecture of the Jerónimos Monastery, with its delightful clouster, and the Belem Tower.

**WHAT IS THERE TO SEE**
The National Museum of Ancient Art, the Museum Calouste Gulbenkian, the monastery of São Vicente de Fora and the church of São Roque.
**DON'T MISS**
The panoramic views of the city from Castello de São Jorge.
**YOU SHOULD KNOW**
There are entrance fees for museums.

*The monastery of São Vicente de Fora sits above Lisbon.*

*The Douro River flows
through Oporto.*

# Oporto

Oporto, known in Portugal as simply 'Porto', is the second largest city in the country, and stands at the mouth of the Douro River.

Since the 1850s port wine producers have matured and stored their wine in warehouses in Vila Nova de Gaia across the river, and about 60 establishments scramble up the hill from the waterfront. It is possible to tour about half of them, and sample their wares. In the 1980s five dams with locks in were constructed along the Douro enabling small cruise ships to sail through to the heartland, where port wine grapes are grown on hot, steeply terraced hillsides.

Beside the huge two-storey bridge of Dom Luis I (there are five others, including Gustav Eiffel's 1877 Dona Maria Pia railway bridge) is the austere sixteenth-century Augustinian monastery of Serra do Pilar. The centre of Porto is dominated by the twelfth-century Cathedral of Se, with its Romanesque rose window and Gothic cloister. Other buildings of note are the Neoclassical Palacio da Bolsa with its magnificent Arabic ballroom, the Manueline Church of Santa Clara, which has an unbelievably opulent interior, and the fourteenth-century São Francisco, with its baroque interior decoration and carved Tree of Jesse. Porto also has a wealth of other architecture: the São Bento railway station has painted tiles by Jorge Colaço that show early forms of transport and other interesting scenes. Old areas of the city, such as round the cathedral are a maze of twisting streets and pretty, if crumbling, buildings.

The people of Porto have always prided themselves on their work ethic, but the lively restaurant and bar scene in the evenings show that they also know when to play.

**WHAT IS IT KNOWN FOR**
This is the centre of the port wine industry, from which the city was given its name.
**WHAT IS THERE TO SEE**
The Ribeira district, the Douro Valley and its vineyards, Amarante.
**DON'T MISS**
The Cathedral of Se.
**YOU SHOULD KNOW**
This is a UNESCO World Heritage Site.

# Coimbra

Coimbra is the seat of Portugal's oldest university, which was founded in 1290 in Lisbon but moved here in 1537 on the top of a hill by the River Mondego. The old town is built around and beneath it, while the new town is around the base of the hill and along the riverfront. The university is built around a large square, beneath which is the entrance to a Baroque chapel. The Library of João V is the main draw – a fabulous decorative space holding more than 300,000 books, with a frescoed ceiling and beautiful tables made of fine woods. The cathedral, Se Velha, is a stark late twelfth-century Romanesque building; its plain interior is lit up by a gilded sixteenth-century altar.

Other highlights within the city are the University's eighteenth-century botanic garden and the Machado de Castro Museum, which is housed in the former bishops' palace. Portugal dos Pequeninos Park is a collection of child-sized scale models of important Portuguese buildings.

South-west of Coimbra, just 16 km (10 mi) away, are the Roman ruins of Conimbriga, settled in the first century AD. Some 300 years later Conimbriga's inhabitants fled to Coimbra to escape invasion, leaving behind what are now Portugal's most important Roman remains. The Villa of Cantaber with its underground heating system, the wonderful mosaic floors of the House of Fountains, and the remains of an aqueduct and a forum are fascinating.

**WHERE IS IT**
195 km (120 mi) north of Lisbon.
**WHY IS IT IMPORTANT**
Portugal's oldest university is here and is still considered to be the main seat of learning in the country.
**WHAT IS THERE TO SEE**
Museo Nacional Machado de Castro, the monastery church of Santa Cruz, the city museum in the Edificio Chiado, the *azulejos* (glazed tiles) of Coimbra.
**HOW DO I GET THERE**
By train or bus from Lisbon or Oporto.

*Coimbra University library.*

509

# Évora

Évora stands upon a gentle hill at the heart of the Alentejo plain, some 150 km (93 mi) south-east of Lisbon. Its historic centre is protected by a ring of fortified walls and dominated by an imposing, fortress cathedral. Évora is the best example of Portugal's 'Golden Age' because, unlike many other towns and cities, it was unaffected by the terrible earthquake of 1755.

Évora's history spans 2,000 years. Under Roman rule it was known as Liberalitas Julia, and both a Roman aqueduct and a temple can still be seen. In 715, it was conquered by the Moors, who also left their mark architecturally. In the twelfth century it was returned to Portuguese rule, and flourished during the Middle Ages, when several kings made it their home.

The Gothic cathedral was completed in the thirteenth century, but the cloisters and the doorway are fourteenth-century additions. The dome above the transept is uncommon in Portuguese churches and the baroque altar is an eighteenth century reconstruction.

Nearby stands the Roman Imperial Temple with its 14 Corinthian columns and part of the entablature – the best-preserved Roman monument in the country. Facing the temple is the gorgeous Gothic church of São João Evangelista, which was founded in 1485. The nave is lined with the most beautiful hand-painted tiles, produced by one of Portugal's master tile-makers in 1711.

There are some 4,000 buildings of historical interest within the city walls: churches, palaces, gates and squares, yet it is a lively, university town, surrounded by vineyards and beautiful, rural scenery. The Alentejo plain is one of the country's poorer regions, but it is rich in history.

*The inner courtyard of the São João Evangelista convent.*

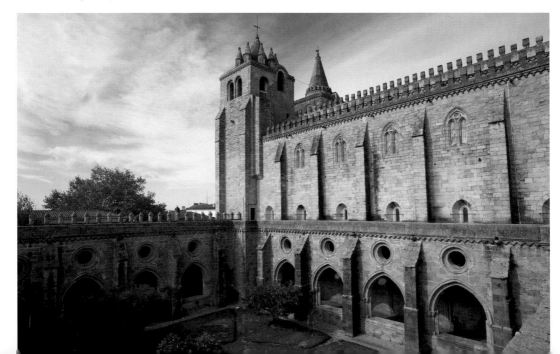

# Sintra

Sintra stands on the northern slopes of the wooded hills of Serra de Sintra, 30 km (20 mi) north-west of Lisbon, and only 12 km (7.5 mi) from the sea.

In the centre of the town is Pena National Palace, dominated by two huge towers. The palace, surrounded by a beautifully landscaped park, was rebuilt in 1839 and is among the most notable examples of royal architecture in the country. The old Hieronymite monastery, which had been added to and extended over the centuries and had elements of Moorish, Gothic, Manueline and Renaissance architecture appealed to King Consort Ferdinand Saxe-Coburg Gotha's taste for the Romantic. He had this extraordinary Bavarian-inspired building constructed around the ruins to serve as the royal family's summer palace. Many of the halls and patios boast glorious *azulejos*, hand-painted glazed tiles, from the fifteenth and sixteenth centuries. The chapel and cloister are part of the original monastery, the rest is a delightful fantasy land of pastel-coloured turrets and battlements, with elements of Gothic, Manueline and Renaissance architecture thrown in. The landscaped park around it is beautifully designed, and contains a sixteenth-century cross marking the highest point of the Serra de Sinta, and offering fantastic, panoramic views.

The nearby Quinta da Regaliera is a stunning villa built at the turn of the twentieth century. It is decorated with symbols of alchemy, the Knights Templar and Portuguese mythology, and the garden is full of lakes, fountains and grottos. Pathways lead to the Initiation Well, with its spiral staircase descending to mysterious underground caverns.

*Pena National Palace.*

**WHERE IS IT**
Sintra is 30 km (20 mi) north-west of Lisbon and 12 km (7.5 mi) from the sea.
**WHAT IS IT KNOWN FOR**
The varying types of architecture from very different eras.
**WHAT IS THERE TO SEE**
Castelo dos Mouros, Cappuchin Monastery, Queluz Palace.
**DO NOT MISS**
The amazing panoramic views from the park.

*A dried fruit stand in Istanbul's Grand Bazaar.*

# The Grand Bazaar

The Kapaliçarsi, or Grand Bazaar, of Istanbul, is the largest covered market in the world. It spreads over 20 ha (50 acres) and contains some 4,000 shops on 65 streets. The whole bazaar is surrounded by a wall, and can be entered by any of eleven gates. Once inside, you will find that the vast array of goods for sale, the noise and excitement of being in such exotic surroundings will give you enough energy to walk around for hours.

Mehmet the Conqueror took the city, then Constantinople, from the Christians in 1453, and began the building of the bazaar in order to boost trade. Over the centuries it has suffered from terrible fires and even an earthquake, but its original grid pattern design of streets with arched roofs, linked by a maze of narrow passages, remains the same.

As with most ancient medinas, the Kapaliçarsi is divided into separate areas that trade in specific goods, such as antiques, leather, jewellery, spices and carpets, but when you are deep inside you seem to be in a fantastic maze from which there is no way out. In fact, although it can be both hot and full of people, you are never far from a small café or stall selling cold drinks, and there are tiled water fountains at regular intervals. The merchants are often very friendly and it can be highly enjoyable to drink glasses of tea with them while discussing world affairs and haggling over some desirable object.

**WHAT IS IT**
The largest covered market in the world.
**YOU SHOULD KNOW**
The Kapaliçarsi (Grand Bazaar) is open all day from Monday–Saturday.
**HOW BIG IS IT**
The Kapaliçarsi spreads over an impressive 20 ha (50 acres) and includes 4,000 shops.
**WHAT IS THERE TO SEE**
Keçeciler Caddesi for carpet shops, Ic Bedesten for jewellery and leather goods, the hamam (Turkish baths) on Yerebatan Caddesi.

# Topkapi Palace

The Topkapi Palace (*Topkapi Sarayi*) stands on a promontory called Seraglio Point, at the eastern end of the Old City of Istanbul, looking out over the Bosphorus and the Sea of Marmara. The extensive palace complex covers about 70 ha (175 acres), and was once home to 40,000 people. Mehmet II began the building in 1462, and the Ottoman empire was ruled from here for nearly 400 years.

Today, visitors enter the palace through the Middle Gate, which leads into the Second Court, or Divan Court, where the Council of State assembled, presided over by the Grand Vizir. The Sultan was able to eavesdrop on the proceedings from behind a latticed window. To one side of the Divan Court is the harem – a maze of almost 400 apartments, rooms, halls and terraces grouped around two large chambers. The eunuch's quarters are near the entrance, and consist of uncomfortable little rooms no better than those of the lesser concubines. The eunuchs decided which of the concubines were presented to the Sultan, and his favourites walked the 'golden way' to his private apartments. Each of his four wives had her own quarters, but only the Sultan's mother had a whole floor to herself.

The Third Court contains the magnificently decorated throne room, the library of Ahmet III, with its incomparable collection of Greek and Arabic manuscripts, and the amazing collection of robes, covered with precious stones and made of silver and gold thread, that were worn by the sultans. All of these pale before the magnificence of the Treasury itself – four rooms full of jewels including the emerald Topkapi dagger, the Spoonmaker's diamond, which is the fifth largest in the world, and two enormous uncut emeralds.

**WHY IS IT IMPORTANT**
This was the centre of the Ottoman Empire for 400 years.
**YOU SHOULD KNOW**
There is an entrance fee.
**WHAT TO SEE**
The Mehmet II pavilion, the Bagdad pavilion, the Dolmabahçe Palace.
**HOW BIG IS IT**
The entire palace complex spans 70 ha (175 acres).

*Harem in the Topkapi Palace.*

# The Blue Mosque

The *Sultanahmet Camii* (the Sultan Ahmet Mosque or Blue Mosque) was begun in 1609 and took seven years to complete. This magnificent building, with its six graceful minarets, overlooks the Sea of Marmara, the Golden Horn and the Bosphorus, and its silhouette dominates the skyline of the old city.

The Blue Mosque was commissioned by Sultan Ahmet I and designed by Mehmet Aga. The interior of the domes, and the arches, are covered with decorative calligraphy but it is the 20,000 or more blue Iznik tiles that cover the interior walls that have given it its name. The huge central dome is 33 m (100 ft) wide and, together with the smaller domes and half domes, rests on four enormous 'elephant's foot' pillars, each one of which is 4.5 m (15 ft) thick. The vast enclosed interior is surrounded by 260 stained glass windows through which daylight floods, enhancing the blue tiles within. Sadly, the stained glass is not original – that glass was shattered long ago in an earthquake.

When they were first erected the six minarets caused a huge furore, as the only other mosque with six minarets was at Mecca, and so it appeared to some that the sultan was being presumptuous. He, thinking laterally, had a seventh minaret built at Mecca, thus neatly avoiding the problem. The Blue Mosque is open daily for visits, except during prayers, and men and women are welcome as long as they remove their shoes and are dressed modestly. The floor is covered by a splendid carpet, and scattered with ancient and beautiful prayer rugs.

*The Blue Mosque in Istanbul.*

# Hagia Sophia

Hagia Sophia, the Church of Holy Wisdom, is a former Orthodox church, across from the Blue Mosque. It is one of the largest enclosed spaces in the world, and an astonishing architectural feat. The first basilica was completed in 360, but burned to the ground in 532, and subsequently rebuilt by Emperor Justinian as the finest Christian church in the Roman Empire.

Justinian almost emptied the empire's coffers in the lavish construction. He brought marble and other building materials from Asia and Egypt, and looted columns from Ephesus. The vast central dome which spans a good 30 m (100 ft), rests on two half domes and the huge buttress around it, forming an overwhelmingly large space inside. The Weeping Column, made of porous stone, leaches water from the cistern beneath and is said to have curative properties.

In 1453, after the fall of the city to the Turks, Aya Sofya became a mosque and the four minarets that surround it were added later – the brick minaret by Mehmet the Conqueror, the most slender by Bayezit II and the two broader ones by Selim II. Most of the sultans added something to the church, in particular Mahmut II who, amongst other things built a beautiful library. Many of its treasures have been looted over the centuries, the Crusaders even took the carved, gilt bronze doors as well as the gold and silver throne. Both the original mosaics and their early replacements have largely gone, but of those that remain, the finest are in the women's gallery and even in their current condition, those such as Christ Pantocrator are awe-inspiring. It has been a museum since Mustafa Kemal Atatürk had it reclassified in 1935.

**WHAT IS IT**
One of the largest enclosed spaces in the world.
**WHAT IS THERE TO SEE**
The eighteenth-century fountain, the tombs of the sultans, the alabaster urns from Pergamon.
**YOU SHOULD KNOW**
The Hagia Sophia is open daily except Monday.

*Sun setting behind the Hagia Sophia.*

*Ruins of the ancient city of Troy.*

# Troy

The city of Troy is known throughout the world, thanks to Homer's epic poem, *The Iliad*, in which the Greeks, led by Agamemnon, laid siege to the city of Troy for ten years in order to retrieve his brother Menelaus's wife, Helen, who had been been abducted by King Priam's younger son, Paris. According to *The Odyssey*, the Greeks achieved victory by hiding soldiers inside a wooden horse and sailing away, apparently defeated. The Trojans brought the horse inside the city, and while they were sleeping off their celebrations, the soldiers crept out, opened the gates for their comrades who had secretly returned, and laid waste to the city.

This story was thought to be a myth until the 1870s, when German amateur archaeologist, Heinrich Schliemann, used his fortune to finance a massive dig at his chosen site, the hill known as Hisarlik. Eventually nine successive settlements were uncovered, each one on top of the last. The oldest dated back 5,000 years. Schliemann's methods damaged parts of the city, and the site is compact and perhaps not as impressive as many visitors expect, although recent evidence suggests that there was an extensive settlement outside the citadel wall. However, substantial ares of walls remain and there are fragments of buildings stewn about the site. In any case, the history and legend that are attached to the ruins make this a remarkable and fascinating place.

Among the unsolved mysteries about Troy is Schliemann's discovery of 'King Priam's treasure', most of which is now in the Pushkin Museum in Russia. Not only did it come from the wrong layer of the city, but the discovery may have been faked.

**WHERE IS IT**
In Çanakkale province in western Turkey, not far inland from the Sea of Marmara.
**WHAT IS IT KNOWN FOR**
The site is steeped in history and legend, made famous by Homer's epic, *The Iliad*.
**WHAT IS THERE TO DO**
The Troy Festival in August is worth visiting.
**WHAT IS THERE TO SEE**
Heinrich Schliemann's house, Ancient Pergamon.
**WHEN SHOULD I VISIT**
The climate is best in spring or autumn.

# Mt Ararat

Mt Ararat (*Buyuk Agri Dagi*) is the highest peak in Turkey, at 5,137 m (16,854 ft). It is a dormant volcano that stands on an arid plain, its permanently snow-covered summit visible for miles around. It is situated in the far north-east of the country, 16 km (10 mi) west of Iran and 32 km (20 mi) south of Armenia.

The area has belonged to several coutries over the years: chiefly the Ottoman Empire, although it also featured in the centre of the Armenian coat of arms. It was part of the Soviet Union for a few decades until being returned to Turkey in 1923.

Mt Ararat is of great interest to both archaeologists and religious groups because of its importance in the Book of Genesis. Noah and his family supposedly found themselves here after the Great Flood. In 70 AD Josephus mentions that the Ark is on Ararat for all to see, as did Marco Polo in 1300, although both reports were second-hand. A text on tablets found at Nineveh, known as the Epic of Gilgamesh, which dates from the seventh century BC, tells the same story and both may be derived from an earlier Babylonian version. In the Epic of Gilgamesh, the hero is called Utnapishtim, and it was the god of wisdom, Ea, who commanded him to build the ark.

In 2004, the area was designated as the Kackar Mountains National Park, in an effort to attract tourists. This has made visiting the area easier for foreign visitors, but permits must still be applied for at least two months before a proposed visit, because this is a politically sensitive region.

**WHAT IS THERE TO SEE**
The Ishakpasha Palace and the prehistoric ruins that dot the area are definitely worth a look.
**WHAT IS THERE TO DO**
Book a local guide for the four-day trip and climb Mount Ararat.
**HOW DO I GET THERE**
Hire a 4 x 4 drive from Dogubayazit.
**WHEN SHOULD I VISIT**
The best temperatures are in late August.

*A perfect cloud cap covers the summit of Mt Ararat.*

# Karapinar Crater Lakes

**WHERE IS IT**
On the central Anatolian plateau,
100 km (60 mi) east of Konya.
**WHAT IS IT KNOWN FOR**
The lake at the Meke crater is said
to be the world's 'blue bead to avert
the evil eye'.
**WHEN SHOULD I VISIT**
The best weather is May to
September, the Anatolian plateau is
very cold in winter.
**HOW DO I GET THERE**
By air to Konya, then by car or on a
coach trip.

The crater lake of Meke (Mekegölü, meaning 'smelling lake') sits in a caldera formed millions of years ago when the top of the volcano was blown off and the cinder cone in the middle (Mekedagi) formed in a smaller eruption about 9,000 years ago. The earliest known representation of a volcanic eruption – a wall painting in a shrine found during the excavations of the excellent Neolithic site at Çatalhöyük about 50 km (30 mi) away – has been dated to about 6200 BC and may represent a phase of activity here.

The lake is said to be the *Nazar Boncugu* (a blue glass bead that you will see all over Turkey, which is said to avert the evil eye) of the world. It lies at 981 m (3,219 ft) above sea level, is 4 km (2.5 mi) in circumference and up to 12 m (40 ft) deep in places.

The cinder cone is about 300 m (1,000 ft) high. The blue-green, saltwater lake sits in an eerie volcanic landscape, and is a haven for many migratory birds and home to a variety of waders, ducks and flamingoes.

The Karapinar volcanic field was formed by intense volcanic activity, and there are several other craters as well as five cinder cones and two lava fields. Just 3 km (2 mi) north-west of Meke is a second lake – the Aci crater lake (Acigölü), which has fewer birds. At night the water sparkles as though with phosphorescence, but this too is a feature of volcanic geology.

*Meke crater lake and volcano.*

# Cappadocia

Cappadocia is a huge, isolated plateau in central Turkey, dominated by the extinct volcano of Erciyesdagi. Frequent eruptions that occurred over millions of years covered large parts of the plateau with tufa, a soft rock formed by volcanic ash, which in turn has been eroded over the centuries into bizarre conical hills in an amazing range of colours – off-white, yellow, violet, red and pink. These hills have been sculpted by the wind, rain and snow into an extraordinary variety of forms, some as high as 50 m (165 ft). The fairy chimneys form because harder rock above the tufa prevents erosion at the top but not at the sides. Eventually the cap falls off and then the rest of the chimney soon erodes. Because of their thick walls, they are cool in summer and warm in winter.

For centuries people have carved dwellings ino the rock. The Hittites are believed to have begun the underground city of Derinkuyu some time after 2000 BC. It is many storeys deep and has stones that could be rolled into place to block doorways and a sophisticated ventilation system. It is thought that as many as 20,000 people could take refuge here. In Christian times churches and monasteries were also carved from the rocks and many thousands of people sheltered in the underground cities during the Arab invasions of the seventh century. The Göreme and Ilhara valleys in particular had a large number of churches, chapels and monasteries dug out of the rock, sometimes below ground and sometimes above, and many of these retain their Byzantine decoration.

*The cave dwellings of
Cappadocia.*

# Ephesus

The ancient city of Ephesus is the jewel in the crown of Turkey's archaeological sites. Founded in the thirteenth century BC, by the end of the first century BC it had become a major Aegean port with a population of more than 300,000. By the time of Augustus Caesar it was the capital of Roman Asia, but as the port silted up the city waned, and finally it was abandoned altogether. This is no doubt why it remains in such good condition, because despite all the wars that went on around it, there was no need to sack an already deserted city.

The site is large, and takes a day to see. At the top of the Marble Avenue, a road paved with marble and worn by chariot wheels, stands the restored, two-storey library of Celcus. Built in 135 AD it has a beautiful, pillared façade and an intricately carved interior. Rolls of papyrus can still be seen in the Reading Room across the courtyard. The library adjoins a huge square where buildings were grouped around a water clock, with a brothel standing on a nearby corner.

The first-century stadium is entered through a huge, vaulted arch, large enough to allow horses and chariots to drive through. The 217-m (712- ft) track was where the races were held, and where gladiators battled to the death in front of an audience of 70,000. The Arcadian Way is lined with columns and leads from the port to the theatre, which stands with Mount Pion at its back. Its 66 tiers of seating, which held 25,000 spectators, are carved into the mountain. The Temple of Artemis, one of the Seven Wonders of the World, was destroyed centuries ago. The last version is represented by a single column.

**WHERE IS IT**
Next to Selçuk, on the west coast of Turkey 70 km (45 mi) south of Izmir.
**WHAT IS THERE TO SEE**
The Virgin Mary's House, the Basilica of St John, the Archaeological Museum, the Isa Bey Mosque.
**WHEN SHOULD I GO**
Enjoy the Ephesus Festival in early May.
**HOW DO I GET THERE**
By air or boat to Kusadasi, then by bus.
**HOW LONG SHOULD I SPEND THERE**
The site takes a whole day to see.

*The reconstructed façade of the library of Celcus.*

*Portal of the Great Mosque.*

# Divrigi

Situated in central Anatolia, the Great Mosque and Hospital of Divrigi were commissioned in 1228 by Ahmet Shah Mengusoglu and his wife, Turan Malik and are one of the most important early works of Islamic architecture in the whole region. The mosque and the adjoining hospital, which was later converted into a *medrese* (school) were built in pale yellow stone and stand a short distance from the town. Both buildings are fabulously carved and sculpted.

The mosque consists of a single prayer room crowned by two cupolas. The one over the centre of the mosque has a lantern, and the other, over the *mihrab* (the niche that indicates the direction of Mecca) is larger with an eight-sided, ribbed cupola topped with a pointed roof. The mosque has three massive, beautifully decorated doorways: the one to the east is no longer operational, while the northern one was obviously the original main entrance. The inside is divided into five aisles, each of which has five bays, by 16 pillars carrying the stellate vaulting. The stone and ebony *minbars* (staircase-pulpits) are beautifully carved. The style of carving in both buildings has been influenced by Armenian manuscript decoration.

The entrance to the hospital is through a small door set within a magnificent arched doorway that dominates the western façade of the building. The doorway rises to the full height of the walls that are taller than those of the mosque. It has two arches, one within the other, that stand proud of the wall. The central door is set into a rectangular recess surrounded by superb carvings in relief, and a window above has human figures representing the Sun and Moon.

**WHERE IS IT**
Central Anatolia, 140 km (90 mi) south-east of Sivas.
**WHY IS IT IMPORTANT**
The Great Mosque is an important early work of Islamic architecture.
**WHAT IS THERE TO SEE**
The Castle Mosque, the tomb of Sitte Melik.

# Sumela Monastery

The Monastery of the Black Virgin of Sumela is carved into a hollow in the sheer rock face of a mountain, some 350 m (1,150 ft) above the valley floor. Often shrouded in mist, it appears to cling to the mountain above a steep gorge in an impossibly inaccessible situation, surrounded by tall, dark pine trees.

The monastery was founded in the fourth century by the Blessed Barnabas, a Greek monk who brought with him a miraculous icon of the Virgin Mary, thought to have been painted by St Luke. In 1340 the shrine was rebuilt and added to by Emperor Alexios III, and there are frescoes in the main church that tell the story of his coronation here. Over the centuries more treasures were brought to this sacred shrine, and more frescoes were painted. It continued to be one of the most important centres of the Byzantine Church.

After World War I and the Graeco-Turkish conflict that followed, the Greeks were expelled from Turkey and the Orthodox monks hid as much as they could before their departure, including the icon. In 1931, the Turkish government allowed the icon to be retrieved and taken back to Greece. The abandoned monastery and its glorious frescoes began to fall into crumbling disrepair, until serious restoration began in the 1990s. A 40-minute hike up the mountain brings you to the steps of the monastery, which is a complex of dormitories, courtyards, corridors and chapels around the main church.

*The fourteenth-century Sumela monastery clings to its cliff face.*

**WHERE IS IT**
Near Trabzon on the Black Sea coast of north-east Turkey.
**YOU SHOULD KNOW**
The monastery is open daily and there is an entrance fee.
**WHAT IS THERE TO SEE**
Trabzon, the Black Sea coast, Amasya's rock tombs.
**HOW DO I GET THERE**
By air or ferry to Trabzon.

# Kekova

**WHERE IS IT**
On the Mediterranean coast
of Turkey.
**WHAT IS THERE TO DO**
Take a tour of the islands of Kekova,
visit Kas and ancient Xanthos or walk
on part of the ancient Lycian Way.
**WHAT IS IT KNOWN FOR**
The beautiful underwater city
of Apollonia.
**HOW DO I GET THERE**
By boat from Kas.
**WHEN SHOULD I VISIST**
Spring, summer and autumn have
the best weather.

Kekova is a lovely island on the Mediterranean coast, and it gives its name to the whole group of picturesque islands in this area. Earthquakes have shaken the ground so often that the larger part of ancient Apollonia on the north shore of Kekova island itself has slid into the sea, creating an amazing sunken city that can be seen through the clear blue water. You can swim here amongst the marble halls, columns and stone steps of buildings that date back to the fifth century BC. On the shore of the Bay of Tersane, the remains of a frescoed Byzantine church can be seen.

The survivors of the earthquake moved across the water to the mainland and established the ancient cities of Simena (which today is the site of the small fishing village of Kale), Theimussa and Aperlai. Simena was founded in 3000 BC and once was a thriving city, minting its first coin in the fourth century BC. It did not begin to decline until the ninth century AD, when an earthquake caused severe damage to the city. The ruined fortress, Kalekoy Castle, features the pointed arches of the Lycian period (168 BC–fourth century AD), and the walls show signs of having been repaired during the Byzantine era. Inside is a small theatre with room for 400, an orchestra pit and a changing room for the performers.

Outside the walls, overlooking the sea with wonderful views of the whole area and its bays, islands and inlets, are the ruins of the Temple of Poseidon, and farther down towards the sea there are the remains of houses, tombs and a bath house.

*A sunken Lycian tomb off the shore.*

# Bitlis

The town of Bitlis stands in the middle of the region of the same name, in the midst of a green oasis, on a tributary of the Tigris River and nestled amongst the mountains in eastern Anatolia. Situated at about 1,500 m (4,900 ft) above sea level, the town is surrounded by walnut trees, and is also an important centre for tobacco and honey production.

The most visible monument in the town itself is the Byzantine castle, the polygonal towers of which rise above the twelfth-century Ulu Mosque, the Serefhan Medrese, Serefi Mosque and the Bayindir Kumbet mausoleum, all built in the local dark stone. There are many old buildings in the town with Armenian inscriptions above the doors, and the Seljuk cemetery has tombstones with inscriptions from the twelfth century.

There is much to be seen nearby: Lake Van (Van Gölü), Turkey's largest lake, which is almost the size of Luxembourg, has no outlet so the sulphur springs within the lake make the water highly saline. This area is the home of the famous Van cats. They have long white fur and one blue and one yellow eye. They enjoy swimming in the lake, where they hunt for a rare form of small carp.

Ahlat, a little to the north, was, in the twelfth century, the capital of a Seljuk principality. The old town is now deserted and has the appearance of an open-air museum with the remains of several Seljuk buildings and inscribed mausoleums and tombstones. Farther on are the remains of the ancient city of Adilcevaz where many important finds have been made, and to the west is Kef Castle. The island of Akdamar Adasi, in the south-east corner of the lake is the site of an exquisite tenth-century Armenian church.

*A mountain village in Bitlis province.*

**WHAT IS THERE TO SEE**
Mount Süphan and the Rock of Van fortress.
**WHERE IS IT**
Bitlis is located 1,500 m (4,900 ft) above sea level, nestled in the mountains of Eastern Anatolia.
**WHEN SHOULD I VISIT**
Arrive in spring and late summer for sightseeing or winter for skiing.
**DO NOT MISS**
Lake Van, the largest lake in Turkey, is almost the size of Luxemborg.
**HOW DO I GET THERE**
By air to Van.
**LOOK OUT FOR**
The famous Van cats.

*The travertine terraces in Pamukkale.*

# Pamukkale

The pools and terraces of Pamukkale are one of the wonders of the natural world, situated about 20 km (13 mi) north of Denizli. The name means 'Cotton Fortress' and legend has it that this was where the Titans spread out their cotton crop to dry. Visitors are no longer allowed to clamber around Pammukale, but can still swim in the warm-water pools of nearby hotels.

In reality, this is a huge, dazzling white cliff that drops some 100 m (330 ft) from a volcanic plateau from which water gushes in every direction. Hot streams of milky water, full of calcium carbonate and other minerals, flow from the plateau and down the cliff, creating terraces and overflowing basins as they go, covering everything in their path with white mineral deposits. Over the centuries the cliff has come to look like solid, gleaming waterfalls and great curtains of water apparently frozen in mid-air. The sound of water bubbling and splashing can be heard everywhere.

Ancient Greeks and Romans believed the water had curative properties – and built the city of Hierapolis here from 190 BC. It is a vast complex of arches, columns, hot baths, temples, churches and a fascinating necropolis. The theatre is well preserved and restored, with stone seating for up to 15,000 people. The city was struck by several earthquakes and was finally abandoned during the fourteenth century, but its extensive ruins are well worth a visit.

**WHY IS IT IMPORTANT**
The pools and terraces are one of the wonders of the natural world.
**WHAT IS THERE TO DO**
Swim in the warm, milky pools at nearby hotels.
**WHAT IS THERE TO SEE**
Ancient Aphrodisias is an hour and a half away by car.
**HOW DO I GET THERE**
By air to Izmir, train to Denizli, coach tour or private car.

# Nemrut Dag

The cone shaped pinnacle of Nemrut Dag rises to 2,150 m (7,054 ft) in a remote area of south-eastern Turkey, not far from the town of Adiyaman. This monument was the brainchild of King Antiochus I and was erected during the first century BC.

Antiochus conceived the idea of a majestic burial chamber for himself, hidden within the mountain and topped with colossal statues of Greek and Persian gods and goddesses. His inscription reads 'I, Antiochos, caused this monument to be erected in commemoration of my own glory and of that of the gods'. The burial mound on the summit is 50 m (165 ft) high and 150 m (500 ft) in diameter and is formed from fist-sized stones. The whole area is littered with stone panels, carved in relief, and the heads of gigantic statues that have been decapitated by earthquakes and the passage of time.

The three vast terraces contain two rows of enormous torsos sitting on thrones. Each figure was carved from a 5-tonne block of stone, and they are all between 8–10 m (26–33 ft) high. The detached heads, which include that of Antiochus' own statue, have fine Greek features topped by Persian-style headwear. A sandstone panel depicting a life-size lion together with stars, the crescent Moon and planets, has convinced some historians that it is the oldest known horoscope in the world.

This monument was not discovered until 1881. Excavations and restoration work have been continuing since 1984, and in 1989 Nemrut Dag was declared a national park. Recently, a team of archaeologists has discovered the location of the burial chamber though it has not yet been reached.

**WHERE IS IT**
90km (56 miles) north-east of Adiyaman in eastern Anatolia.
**DO NOT MISS**
Seeing the sunrise from the peak.
**WHAT IS THERE TO SEE**
The rock carving of Mithradites and Hercules shaking hands at Eski Kale.
**WHEN SHOULD I VISIT**
Late spring or early autumn.
**HOW DO I GET THERE**
By air to Adiyaman.
**YOU SHOULD KNOW**
This is a UNESCO World Heritage Site.

*Colossal heads at the burial site of Antiochus I.*

# Petra

World famous as the 'rose-red city half as old as time', Petra is one of the most spectacular sites in the Middle East and many regard it as the most impressive ancient city remaining in the modern world. Archaeologists believe that Petra has been inhabited since prehistoric times – the remains of a 9,000-year-old city have been discovered, making it one of the earliest known settlements in the Middle East.

Surrounded by mountains riddled with passages and gorges, Petra was constructed by the Nabateans, who dominated the lands of Jordan during pre-Roman times, in order to command the trade route from Damascus to the Arabian Peninsula. They half-built, half-carved into the solid rock to create this wonderland of temples, tombs and elaborate buildings. From its origins as a fortress city, Petra became a wealthy commercial crossroads between Arabia, Assyria, Egypt, Greece and Rome. Later it was incorporated into the Roman empire and is thought to have been home to some 30,000 people in its heyday.

Most visitors approach Petra – either by foot or on horseback – through the Siq, a cleft in the rock that sometimes narrows to less than 5 m (16 ft) wide.

After winding around for 1.5 km (1 mi), the Siq suddenly opens upon the most impressive of all Petra's monuments, the Treasury. Carved out of solid rock in the side of the mountain and standing over 40 m (130 ft) high, it is one of the most elegant remains of antiquity.

*The Treasury, Petra's most impressive monument.*

**WHEN WAS IT FOUND**
Petra's existence was known only to a few local Bedouins and Arab tradesmen until 1812, when a young Swiss explorer rediscovered it to finally reveal its glories to the west.
**YOU SHOULD KNOW**
You will need to pay an entrance fee and you can get one, two or three day passes.
**WHAT IS THERE TO SEE**
The High Place of Sacrifice, the Roman theatre, the Monastery, the rock-cut tombs.
**HOW DO I GET THERE**
Travel by road from Amman.
**DON'T MISS**
The desert scenery at Wadi Rum, about 70 km to the south, Dana Nature Reserve, the Crusader fortresses at Shobak and Karak.

# Baalbek

One of the world's great historical sites, Baalbek (Heliopolis), some 85 km (52 mi) north-east of Beirut, is a place of superlatives: it is the largest complex of Roman temples ever built, some of its columns are the tallest ever erected and its stones – some weighing nearly 1,000 tonnes – are the largest ever used in any construction. The site is on a high plateau in the fertile Bekaa valley and lies against the impressive backdrop of the parallel ranges of the Lebanon and Anti-Lebanon mountains.

The great period of construction of this vast temple complex began with the building of the Temple of Jupiter by Julius Caesar in 15 BC. This was followed by the Temple of Venus and the Temple of Bacchus, which has long been the best preserved Roman temple in the world, depite suffering serious damage in 2006.

The temples functioned as important places of worship until Christianity became the official religion of the Roman empire, and by the end of the fourth century many of the most significant statues and buildings, including much of the Temple of Jupiter, had been destroyed. The origins of Baalbek are in fact thought to predate the Roman conquest by at least 3,000 years. The Phoenicians chose the site of Baalbek for a temple to their god Baal-Hadad and the massive stones here are evidence of an earlier civilization.

At the time of its inclusion on the UNESCO World Heritage list, Baalbek was acclaimed as 'one of the finest examples of Imperial Roman architecture at its apogee'.

*The entrance to the Temple of Bacchus.*

**ALSO KNOWN AS**
Heliopolis (city of the Sun).
**HOW DO I GET THERE**
By road from Beirut.
**WHEN SHOULD I GO**
March–May, September–November
**WHAT SHOULD I DO**
Check with the Foreign Office about the advisability of visiting the area.

*Houses in Damascus usually have plain exteriors but are highly decorated and lavish inside.*

# Damascus

The capital of Syria, with an estimated population of between four and five million, Damascus is said to be the oldest continuously inhabited city in the world and excavations on the outskirts indicate that people were possibly living here as long ago as 10,000 BC. Often referred to as the 'Pearl of the East', Damascus lies on the Barada river, which makes the area fertile enough for a wealth of fruit and crops to be grown and livestock to be reared.

Today, in large parts of Damascus you will find yourself surrounded by the cacophany, concrete and apparent chaos that typifies many large cities in the Middle East, so the old city seems tranquil and calm in comparison. Encircled by a seven-gated Roman wall, which has been rebuilt many times, the old city is divided into the market area, Muslim area, Christian area and the Jewish area.

At one time the centre of Islam, and still the Muslim world's third most important site after Mecca and Medina, the Umayyad Mosque, dating from the beginning of the eighth century, is the most famous of the old city's many architectural glories, with its splendid minarets and courtyard adorned with golden mosaics. Next door is the red-domed Mausoleum of Saladin, containing the remains of the great hero of Arab history.

Another of the joys of being in the old city is shopping in the Souq al-Hamidiya. Damascus used to be the trading capital of the Arab world, and after a few hours seeing just some of the thousands of stalls and shops and taking in the atmosphere and the colourful sights of the souq, you might think it still is.

**WHY IS IT IMPORTANT**
Damascus is said to be the oldest continuously inhabited city in the world and was once the centre of Islam.
**WHAT IS THERE TO SEE**
Azem Palace, Chapel of Ananias and Al Nouri, Damascus's most famous hamam (Turkish baths).
**IF YOU HAVE TIME**
The Roman theatre at Bosra, about 140 km (85 mi) south of Damascus and Palmyra (Tadmor) – about 180 km (110 mi) to the north-east.

# Krak des Chevaliers

Krak des Chevaliers was acclaimed by TE Lawrence ('Lawrence of Arabia') as the greatest of the Crusader castles and 'the most wholly admirable castle in the world'. Looking like a child's fantasy castle brought to life, it sits on a 650-m (2,130-ft) cliff along what was the only route from Antioch to Beirut and the Mediterranean Sea.

In 1144 the Krak was given to the Knights Hospitaller as their headquarters in Syria to enable them to control and guard this important strategic corridor. The Hospitallers rebuilt and expanded it into the largest Crusader fortress in the Holy Land, adding an outer wall 30 m (100 ft) thick with guard towers 8–10 m (26–33 ft) thick, to create this concentric castle, which, today, is one of the best-preserved fortresses in the world. The castle encompasses an area of 3,000 sq m (32,300 sq ft) and has 13 huge towers, as well as many stores, cisterns, corridors, bridges and stables. It is thought that it could accommodate 5,000 soldiers with their horses, equipment and enough provisions to withstand a siege of five years. The fortress is one of the few sites where Crusader art, in the form of frescoes, has been preserved. The English king Edward I, while on the Ninth Crusade, saw the fortress and used it as a basis for his own castles in England and Wales.

The Krak des Chevaliers (which means 'Fortress of the Knights', in a mixture of French and Arabic) is without doubt one of the world's greatest masterpieces of military architecture. The view from its towers is stunning, covering a vast area extending from Mt Lebanon to the Homs Gap and the Mediterranean can be seen sparkling in the sunshine.

**WHERE IS IT**
East of Tripoli on the road from Antioch to Beirut.
**WHAT IS IT**
One of the best preserved fortresses in the world.
**HOW DO I GET THERE**
By road from Damascus via Homs which takes about four hours.
**WHAT IS THERE TO SEE**
Qala'at Saladin, near Lattakia.

*The Krak des Chevaliers.*

# Sana'a

**WHEN SHOULD I GO**
October to March.
**IF YOU HAVE TIME**
Do not miss the rock palace of Dar al-Hajar 14 km (21 mi) to the north-west, the mosque at Shibam 27 km (17 mi) farther on and Husn Thula fortress and the town of Amran about 55 km (34 mi) north of Sanaa.
**WHAT SHOULD I KNOW**
The old city is a UNESCO World Heritage Site

The capital of Yemen, Sana'a is situated 2,200 m (7,200 ft) above sea level on the Arabian Peninsula about 320 km (200 mi) north of Aden and was one of several settlements that grew up on the ancient trading routes from the south to the north. Surrounded by mountains of basalt, and situated in a relatively flat plain, Sana'a was, according to legend, built by the son of Noah, and throughout history has always been one of the major cities in Yemen.

The old walled city is one of the biggest and best-preserved medinas in the Arab world and has some 50,000 inhabitants, many of whom live in homes that are more than 400 years old. The world's first high-rise houses were built here – six- and seven-storey houses built of dark basalt stone and sun-dried mud-bricks. Their window surrounds are intricately decorated with elaborate friezes and are a complex infrastructure of round and angular shapes. Together with their panes, which were until recently made of thin slices of alabaster, they represent a unique architectural heritage.

The old, walled city contains a wealth of architectural gems, including the Great Mosque, which was built at the time of the Prophet Muhammed. The souq, a vast maze of narrow alley-ways and winding streets, is one of the oldest in Arabia. Known as Souq al-Milh (or Salt Market), it has an astonishing and colourful variety of goods on sale from spices and every kind of foodstuff to copper, woodwork and clothing. Early morning or early evening are the best times to visit.

*The houses of Sana'a.*

# Socotra

Situated 170 km (100 mi) east of the Horn of Africa, the isolated and wonderful island of Socotra is actually part of Yemen, which lies some 500 km (300 mi) to the north. Sometimes called the Galapagos of the Indian Ocean, it boasts an astonishing variety of plant and animal species that are unique to the island. There are no fewer than 300 plant species, 113 insect species, 24 reptile species and six bird species that you will find nowhere else in the world.

If you are intrepid enough to go here (only 400 tourists visited in 2005), you will find yourself experiencing a culture very different from the ways of the modern world. Until 1990 the island had a barter economy, witches are said to have been tried as recently as the 1960s and most people in the mountainous areas still live in caves and light fires by rubbing sticks together. The 40,000 inhabitants of Socotra are thought mostly to be descended from the settlers who arrived some 3,000 years ago from the Queen of Sheba's ancient city state of Saba on the south Arabian peninsula. Yet the pale skin and green and hazel eyes of others would seem to be evidence of the Greeks, Romans, Portuguese and ancient Egyptians who have arrived over the centuries.

According to botanists, the island of Socotra ranks among the top-ten endangered islands in the world. Indeed it seems unlikely that the island's culture and geography can remain so unspoiled and unaffected by the modern globalized world for much longer. So if you are tempted to go there for the trip of a lifetime, go soon!

**HOW DO I GET THERE**
Fly from Sana'a or Al-Mukalla.
**WHEN SHOULD I GO**
October to February.
**WHAT IS THERE TO SEE**
The enormous cave at Huq, the dragon's blood trees and the desert roses, the deserted golden sandy beaches.
**YOU SHOULD KNOW**
Socotra is among the top-ten endangered islands in the world, and is known as the Galapagos of the Indian Ocean. The island's tourist infrastructure is a pioneering example of ecotourism and In order to protect the island's unique heritage, visitor numbers are limited.

*A grove of Dragon's Blood Trees.*

# Jerusalem

From the sky, Jerusalem is a mass of white stone dwellings, spread over hilltops, with the walled old city as a centre point. Jerusalem is a city rich in history – from its foundation 5,000 years ago and King David's rule 3,000 years ago, to the presence of Jesus 2,000 years ago, the capital of modern Israel has experienced a tumultuous past. Over the centuries the Egyptians, Assyrians, Babylonians, Persians, Greeks, Romans, Byzantines, Arabs, Crusaders, Mamaluks, Ottomans and the British have all fought for, ruled over and lost Jerusalem.

An archaeologist's paradise, Jerusalem is home to relics dating back as far as 3000 BC. Relics discovered before 1948 are housed in the Rockefeller Museum, and those excavated after this time are housed in the Israel Museum's Samuel Bronfman Archaeology Wing, which has sections on prehistory, the Canaanites, Israelites and Second Temple, Roman and Byzantine periods.

Within a matter of a few kilometres you can switch from the history and intensity of the old city, to the cosmopolitan buzz of downtown, from the hubbub of an outdoor market to the serenity of a panoramic lookout, from hearing Arabic on Salah al-Din Street to Hebrew in Malha Mall, from the tradition of Mea Shearim to the dance club culture of Talpiot.

The walled Old City is the centre of Jerusalem, with Jewish West Jerusalem on one side and Arab East Jerusalem on the other. The old city is made up of several different areas: the Muslim, Christian, Armenian and Jewish quarters as well as the highly contested Temple Mount, where Abraham is said to have prepared his son for sacrifice. The First and Second Temples were subsequently built on this site, and it is from here that Muhammad ascended to heaven. The gleaming gold-covered Dome of the Rock, dominating the skyline, stands in this compound as does Al-Aqsa Mosque.

The only remaining wall of the Holy Temple, which was otherwise destroyed in 70 AD, provides the border between the Temple Mount and the Jewish quarter. This is known as the Western, or Wailing, Wall and is Judaism's holiest site. For thousands of years, Jews in all parts of the world have built their temples facing west, in order to pray towards the Western Wall. Here worshippers pray aloud and by pushing written prayers into the cracks between the ancient stones.

The Jewish quarter also contains numerous religious institutions, museums, and archaeological sites, such as the Cardo, an ancient Roman thoroughfare.

Bordering the other side of the Temple Mount is the Muslim quarter, which is reached through the main Damascus Gate. Rich in architecture from the Mamluk period (1250 to 1516), the Muslim souq, winding through a labyrinth of alleys, offers a treat for the senses.

Jaffa Gate is the entrance to the Armenian and Christian quarters. On your way in, you will pass the Tower of David Museum. Home to more than 1,000 Armenian residents, much of the life of this community goes on behind the high walls of the Armenian compound. Within the Christian quarter is the Holy Sepulchre, where Christ was crucified. Many pilgrims follow his last footsteps to this church along the 500-m (1,640-ft) Via Dolorosa, best approached from Lion's Gate.

The old city and its ramparts make a wonderful place to get lost in by day and to marvel at the fairytale-like beauty when floodlit at night.

Just 1 km (0.5 mi) outside the walls of the ancient city are more historically important religious sites and scenic vistas including the Mount of Olives, home to the convent of St Mary Magdalene with its golden rooftop, the Chapel of the Ascension where Jesus rose to heaven and the Tomb of the Virgin Mary.

Western Jerusalem's Mea Shearim, inhabited by strictly Orthodox Jews living a life devoted to the Torah and dressing in the same way as they have for hundreds of years, is another place you should visit, although walk around with respect in modest dress and refrain from taking photographs (this also applies if you visit Arab East Jerusalem).

There are so many attractions and sites here that it is impossible to list them all, although another one not to be missed is the Haas Promenade high on the hills of East Talpiot, from where you can get views of the entire Jerusalem landscape, including the old city and walls as well as the skyline of the new city.

*The Dome of the Rock.*

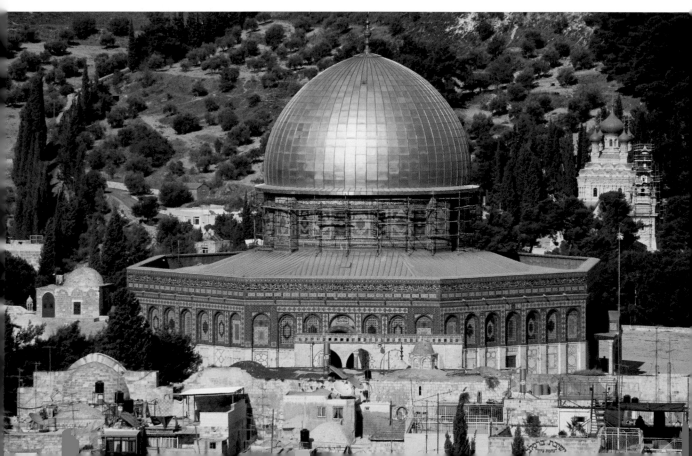

# The Dead Sea

The Dead Sea on the border between the West Bank, Israel and Jordan in the Jordan Valley, is the deepest hypersaline lake in the world, located at the lowest exposed point on the Earth's surface.

The Dead Sea has attracted visitors from around the world for thousands of years. The saline waters and mud on the shores of the Dead Sea contain many minerals believed to have medicinal and theraputic benefits. Many visitors cover their bodies with the dark mud to try to benefit from the restorative effects.

The other common activity for visitors is to try to sink, but it is futile. The unusually high salt concentration means that the water is denser than the human body so it is impossible not to float.

The sea is called 'dead' because its high salinity means no fish or other aquatic organisms of any size can live in it, although minuscule quantities of bacteria and microbial fungi are present. The surrounding mountains, however, are host to a variety of species including camels, ibexes, hares, hyraxes, jackals, foxes and even leopards. Hundreds of bird species inhabit the zone as well.

The human history of the Dead Sea dates back to remote antiquity. North of the Dead Sea lies Jericho, one of the many candidates for the oldest continually occupied town in the world.

Sodom and Gomorra, mentioned in the Book of Genesis and destroyed in the times of Abraham, and the three other 'Cities of the Plain' are believed to be nearby.

Because of the geology of the underlying rift below the bottom of the lake (which is an extension of the Rift Valley in Africa), lumps of asphalt are squeezed out of the ground and bob up to the surface and this was a valuable product for trade with the Egyptians, who used it, among other things, for preserving mummies.

Herod the Great, Jesus, and John the Baptist were also closely linked with the Dead Sea and its surroundings. In Roman times the Essenes settled in Qumran on the Dead Sea's northern shore. There, in the soft marl of the Dead Sea area, they carved out storage caves for their holy texts, and 2,000 years later the cache was found and given the name 'the Dead Sea Scrolls'.

The Dead Sea is naturally endorheic, meaning it has no outlet, and its main source of water is the River Jordan. The northern part of the Dead Sea receives scarcely 100 mm (4 in) of rain a year, while the southern section receives even less – a mere 50 mm (2 in). The reduction in the flow of the River Jordan, combined with the high evaporation rate of the Dead Sea, means that the surface area is shrinking and it is becoming less deep. The waters of the southern end of the sea have already drained and have become salt flats.

*Floating around in the Dead Sea.*

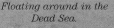

# Persepolis

*A parade of bearded figures,
bearing tributes to the king of
Persia, ascend a
stone staircase.*

Persepolis, the magnificent palace complex founded by Darius the
Great in about 518 BC, was built over a century as the seat of
government for the kings of the Achaemenid Empire as well as a
centre for ceremonial events and festivities. Erected at the foot of
Kh-Rahmat, or 'Mountain of Mercy', or 'Mountain of Grace' in the
Marv Dasht plain, 644 km (400 mi) from modern-day Teheran, the
site was burned, looted and destroyed by Alexander the Great.

The ancient hub of the Persian empire, now a UNESCO World
Heritage Site, was built of dark grey marble from the adjacent
mountain, on an immense half-artificial-half-natural terrace. The
wealth of the city was reflected in the extravagant construction of
the buildings, inspired by Mesopotamian models.

The largest and most complex building was the audience hall, or
*Apadana*, marked by a large terrace, whose east side adjoined the
Kh-Rahmat, while the other three sides were formed by a retaining
wall. The terrace, dotted with more than 36 enormous columns,
some of which are still
standing, was accessed
via two monumental
stairways.

Following their
destruction in 331–330
BC, the ruins were left
hidden beneath their
own rubble until their
eventual excavation by
archeologists from the
Oriental Institute of the
University of Chicago
from 1931 to 1939. In
addition to the audience
hall, archeologists also
uncovered three
ornamented sepulchres,
the stairs of the Council
Hall and the Harem of
Xerxes among other
monuments.

Even after 2,500
years, the ruins of
Persepolis are still
awe-inspiring.

# Isfahan

Isfahan, or Esfahan, is the capital of Isfahan Province, and Iran's third-largest city. Located in the lush Zayandeh Rud plain, at the foot of the Zagros mountain range, Isfahan is located on the main north-south and east-west routes crossing Iran. Designated a UNESCO World Heritage City, it contains various Islamic architectural sites ranging from the eleventh century to the nineteenth.

Shah Abbas the Great brought the Golden Age to Isfahan when he made it the new capital of the Safavid dynasty during his reign in the sixteenth century. Under his rule, Isfahan became known by Persians as *Nesf-e-Jahan*, or 'half of the world', because it held so many riches – in wealth, geography, architecture, religion and culture – that to see it was to see half the world! In its heyday, Isfahan had some of the most impressive parks, libraries, religious schools, shops, public baths and mosques of any city in the world. With a population of 1 million, it was also one of the largest.

Isfahan is located at an oasis, and so its people are able to produce wheat, barley, rice, cotton, grapes, melons and alfalfa, as well as keep herds of cattle, goats, sheep and donkeys, and this lush area is in marked comparison to the arid surrounding desert.

The city's monumental architecture, one of the most impressive aspects of Isfahan, is made up of eight traditional elements: gardens, platforms, porches, gateways, domes, arched chambers and minarets. Many of the great buildings still in existence are located in the Imam Square, a vast rectangular area spanning 512 m (1,700 ft) long by 159 m (522 ft) across. Highlights include the fabulous Imam Mosque, a masterpiece of Chahar-iwan style and the Sheikh Lotf Allah Mosque. Both are well regarded for their coloured arabesque tiles, their domes and their Safavid-style decoration. At the northern edge of the square is the entrance to the bazaar, the Dahrvasa-e-Qaysariya, and to the west is the entrance to the Royal Palace, or Ali Qapu. Although the square has undergone some renovations throughout history, the majority of the fundamental structures remain much as they were in the sixteenth century, which makes this a truly special, atmospheric place.

*The roof of the arched entrance to the Sheikh Lotf Allah Mosque.*

**WHAT IS IT**
A UNESCO World Heritage Site containing a variety of Islamic architectural treasures.
**WHERE IS IT**
340 km (211 mi) south of Teheran.
**WHEN SHOULD I GO**
Spring and autumn.
**WORTH A SPLURGE**
While you're there, pick up an Isfahan carpet.
**MUSICAL ASSOCIATIONS**
Duke Ellington once wrote a song, *Isfahan*, in honour of the city.

# DESTINATIONS

4Corners Images/Cozzi Guido 153

Alamy 367; /John Angerson 393; /Jon Arnold Images 445; /Claudio H. Artman 431 /Tibor Bognar 231; /G. P. Bowater 498 bottom left; /britishcolumbiaphotos.com 132; /Sean Burke 64; /Pat Canova/Bruce Coleman Inc. 495; /Frank Chmura 486; /Nic Cleave 229; /Gary Crabbe 195; /Jan Csernoch 98; /Tristan Deschamps 65; /Ianni Dimitrov 422; /Johan Elzenga 41; /Robert Estall Photo Agency 93; /Expuesto-Nicolas Randall 31; /Michel Friang 226; /Alfio Garozzo/CuboImages srl 479 bottom right; /David Halbakken 288 inset; /Barrie Harwood 383; /Robert Harding World Imagery 27, 442; /Steffan Hill 301; /Jeremy Hogan 420; /Andrew Holt 85; /Images&Stories 525; /David Keith Jones/Images of Africa Photobank 16; /JTB Photo 202 right, 213, 223, 230, 233, 234; /Michael Juno 66 top right, 66 bottom; /Khaled Kassem 270; /Christian Kober 531; /Zute Lightfoot 28; /LookGaleria 436; /Celia Mannings 8 left, 88 ; /Isabella Mary 396-397; /Barry Mason 285; /Neil McAllister 336; /Philipp Mohr 478; /Andrew Morse 516; /Profimedia. CZ s.r.o. 506; /Mick Rock/Cephas Picture Library 425; /David Sanger Photography 100; /David South 273; /Jon Sparks 333; /Jane Sweeney 235; /Ulana Switucha 284; /Tom Till 312; /Angelo Tondini/CuboImages 483; /Ariadne Van Zandbergen/Robert Estall Photo Agency 25

Caroline Babler 331

Bluegreen/Roberto Rinaldi 97; /Rick Tomlinson 114

www.byron-bay.com 306

Corbis UK Ltd 2 left, 7 picture 6, 50, 60, 69, 148, 177, 194, 323, 462, 538; /Peter Adams 239 bottom/zefa 107, 202 left, 283; /Alinari Archives 460; /Theo Allofs 7 picture 1, 269/zefa 79, 81; /James L. Amos 171, 174, 317; /Jonathan Andrew 416; /Bernard Annebicque 51; /Archivo Iconografico, S.A. 493; /Maher Attar/Sygma 529; /Craig Aurness 162, 191; /David Ball 302; /Anthony Bannister 26, 36; /Dave Bartruff 326, 402; /Neil Beer 127; /Annie Griffiths Belt 406; /Nathan Benn 169; /Yann Arthus-Bertrand 5 centre, 17, 19, 72, 78, 157, 296-297, 310, 454, 457, 487, 520; /Richard Bickel 112; /Kristi J. Black 512; /Tibor Bognar 5 centre top, 9 centre, 40, 49, 75, 108, 380, 384-385; /Regis Bossu 360; /Andrew Brown 387; /B.S.P.I. 94 centre right, 121; /Kevin Burke 433; /Michael Busselle 401, 496-497, 501; /Ralph A. Clevenger 417; /Shelan Collins 252; /Dean Conger 444; /John Conrad 147; /Ashley Cooper 391; /Claro Cortes IV/Reuters 286; /Philip James Corwin 200; /Daniel J. Cox 214 left; /Alissa Crandall 37; /Tony Craddock/zefa 528; /Richard Cummins 178, 418; /Jeff Curtes 377; /Fridmar Damm 84/zefa 359, 366, 453; /Jay Dickman 471; /Bruno Domingos/Reuters 94 centre left, 110; /Despotovic Dusko/Sygma 505; /Reinhard Eisele 103; /Abbie Enock/Travel Ink 282; /Ric Ergenbright 39, 212, 364, 394, 404; /Macduff Everton 409, 476; /Expuesto-Nicolas Randall 8 right; /John Farmar/Cordaiy Photo Library Ltd. 414-415; /Kevin Fleming 176, 187; /Werner Forman 57, 316; /Franz-Marc Frei 347, 370; /Free Agents Limited 204, 220; /Gerald French 196; /Michael Freeman 70, 240, 241, 244, 266-267; /Free Agents Limited 224; /Michael Freeman 293; /Rick Friedman 144-145; /Stephen Frink 7 picture 3, 104, 268; /Maurizio Gambarini/dpa 250; /Andreas Gebert 332; /Raymond Gehman 135, 322 right, 428; /Walter Geierspeger 325; /Philippe Giraud 430; /Rainer Hackenberg/zefa 451, 182; /Karl-Heinz Haenel 507; /Richard Hamilton 515; /Blaine Harrington

III 474; /Martin Harvey 13, 14-15, 62; /Robert Harding World Imagery 314, 343, 424, 485; /John Van Hasselt/Sygma 372; /Dallas & John Heaton/Free Agents Limited 489; /Lindsay Hebberd 95 left, 137, 251, 256; /Chris Hellier 522, 533; /John Heseltine 473, 508; /Jon Hicks 329, 427, 449; /Robert Holmes 45, 139, 341, 342; /Angelo Hornak 337, 468; /Jeremy Horner 6 picture 4, 119, 123, 239 top, 247, 265; /David Hosking 386; /Eric and David Hosking 80; /Dave G. Houser/Post-Houserstock 320; /Jan Butchofsky-Houser 163; /Rob Howard 54; /Hanan Isachar 53, 536-537; /Mimmo Jodice 466, 467; /Mark A. Johnson 2 centre, 120; /Peter Johnson 43; /Martin Jones 389, 410; /Ray Juno 368, 469; /K. Imamura/zefa 146; /Wolfgang Kaehler 9 left, 24, 58, 115, 141, 264, 439, 521; /Catherine Karnow 166; /David Katzenstein 423; /Herbert Kehrer/zefa 464; /Layne Kennedy 161; /Richard Klune 382, 399; /Earl & Nazima Kowall 11; /Bob Krist 189; /Kim Kulish 180; /Frans Lanting 3 centre, 125, 192; /; /Danny Lehman 154, 446, 490; /Frans Lemmens/zefa 44, 82-83, 255; /Charles Lenars 346; /George D. Lepp 168; /Barry Lewis 339, 426, 440; /Liu Liqun 206; /Chris Lisle 253, 330, 335, 344, 345, 375, 434, 527, 532; /Massimo Listri 419, 484; /Yang Liu 202 centre, 207; /Christophe Loviny 279; /Araldo de Luca 488; /Ludovic Maisant 259; /William Manning 172; /Gunter Marx Photography 129; /Stephanie Maze 117; /Joe McDonald 29; /Will & Deni McIntyre 6 picture 5, 94 left, 158; /Wolfgang Meier/zefa 21; /Gideon Mendel 227; /John and Lisa Merrill 67; /Momatiuk - Eastcott 2-3 centre, 20; /Gail Mooney 165, 351, 352, 354; /Kevin R. Morris 290; /David Muench 159; /Charlie Munsey 249; /Amos Nachoum 87; /Mike Nelson 55; /Michael Nicholson 362, 400, 413; /John Noble 296 centre left, 303; /Kazuyoshi Nomachi 5 top, 32, 38, 46, 48; /Jack Novak 361; /Richard T. Nowitz 167, 373, 441; /Pat O'Hara 160, 170; /Roques-Rogery Olivier/Sygma 322 left, 324; /Charles O'Rear 86, 304 ; /Diego Lezama Orezzoli 539; /Christine Osborne 8 centre, 68; /Tim Page 254; /Sigit Pamungkas 262; /David Paterson 397; /Jacques Pavlovsky/Sygma 322 centre right, 498 top left; /Caroline Penn 10; /Paul C. Pet/zefa 238; /Photowood Inc. 365; /Bryan Pickering 348; /Sergio Pitamitz 30, 59, 202-203, 459 top right, 480/zefa 101, 482; /Michael Pole 313; /Louie Psihoyos 321; /Ann Purcell 8-9, 18; /Carl & Ann Purcell 7 picture 2, 407; /Carl Purcell 35; /Neil Rabinowitz 173, 181; /Jose Fuste Raga 6 picture 2, 6 picture 1, 184-185, 205, 288-289, 318, 443, 500-501/zefa 73, 190, 502, 511; /James Randklev 186; /Vittoriano Rastelli 503; /Steve Raymer 291, 294, 295, 358, 438; /Carmen Redondo 228, 379; /David Reed 42; /Roger Ressmeyer 465/NASA 151; /Reuters 22, 450; /Reza/Webistan 517; /David Samuel Robbins 216, 497; /Joel W. Rogers 130-131; /Hugh Rooney/Eye Ubiquitous 491; /Bill Ross 7 picture 4, 155, 463; /Guenter Rossenbach/zefa 71, 74, 470, 477; /Hans Georg Roth 448, 510; /Galen Rowell 197, 198, 296 right, 311; /Suhaib Salem/Reuters 323 centre, 499; /Kevin Schafer 322-323, 452; /Matthias Schrader 322 centre left, 369; /Ute & Juergen Schimmelpfennig/zefa 456; /Paul Seheult 398; /P.J. Sharpe/zefa 494; /ML Sinibaldi 203 right, 292, 371; /Richard Hamilton Smith 183; /Lee Snider/Photo Images 338; /Joseph Sohm 193; /Paul A. Souders 272, 297 centre, 308, 376; /Herbert Spichtinger/zefa 6 picture 6, 296 centre right, 307, 458, 514; /Hubert Stadler 479 top right; /Paul Steel 297 left, 300-301, 319; /Eberhard Streichan/zefa 381; /Keren Su 260, 340, 374, 432, 435; /David Sutherland 429; /Sygma 408; /Murat Taner/zefa 175, 357; /Arthur Thevenart 237, 530; /Roger Tidman 415; /Penny Tweedie 296 left, 299; /Jeff Vanuga 199; /Ruggero Vanni 76, 492, 504; /Sandro Vannini 421, 437, 475, 535; /Brian A. Vikander 34, 217, 242; /Patrick

Ward 61, 392; /Ron Watts 142, 143; /Karl Weatherly 5 centre bottom, 133; /Ronald W. Weir/zefa 6 picture 3, 388; /Nik Wheeler 33, 92, 99, 134, 140, 152, 271, 274, 275, 280, 287, 315, 403, 405, 447, 513; /Joy Whiting/Cordaiy Photo Library Ltd. 395; /Staffan Widstrand 95 centre, 124; /Larry Williams 298, 461; /Peter M. Wilson 327, 509; /WildCountry 363; /Adam Woolfitt 390, 412, 523; /Roger Wood 5 bottom, 47, 52; /Alison Wright 203 left, 236, 248, 309; /Michael S. Yamashita 219, 225, 232, 246; /Jim Zuckermann 245; /Zuma 481

Fortidsminneforeningen 378 top right, 378 bottom left

Marco Fulle 518-519

Getty Images 209/Roger Antrobus 472; /Christopher Arnesen 222; /Raphael Van Butsele 353; /Cosmo Condina 138; /Mark Daffey 455; /Greg Elms 257; /Jill Gocher 261; /Jean-Pierre Pieuchot 350; /Rudolf Pigneter 63; /Simon Plant 459 bottom right; /Steve Satushek 526; /Chris Simpson 94-95, 105; /David Tipling 355; /Ruth Tomlinson 334

High Impact Stock Photography/Ian Lauder 136

Hong Kong Tourism Board/www.discoverhongkong.co.uk 7 picture 5, 214-215 right

Lonely Planet Images/Krzysztof Dydynski 122; /Greg Elms 356; /David Else 12; /Greg Johnston 96; /Izzet Keribar 524; /Martin Moos 218

Polly Manguel 89, 90, 91, 106

Alfred Molon Photo Galleries 77, 276 bottom, 276-277, 278

Musee Toulouse-Lautrec, Albi, Tarn, France 349

Photolibrary Group/Dr. Derek Bromhall 23; /JTB Photo 211, 263

www.santafe.org 179

South American Pictures/Steve Harrison 94 right, 109; /Frank Nowikowski 156

Tourist Office Alpbach Valley & Tyrolean Lake District 328

www.turismo.gov.br/Brazil Ministry of Tourism 116

www.visitbath.co.uk 411

www.visitmorningtonpeninsula.org 305

Wikipedia/Michel Y.G. Meunier 111

Cover photography: Alpbach Valley & Tyrolean Lake District Tourist Office back image 5.www.visitbath.co.uk back image 7.www.byron-bay.com back image 4. Corbis UK Ltd/B.S.P.I. back main; /K. Imamura/Zefa front image 5; /Frans Lemmens front image 6; /Gail Mooney front image 2; /Sergio Pitamitz/Zefa front cover image 1; /Carmen Redondo front image 3; /Keren Su front image 4; /Brian A. Vikander front main picture.Getty Images/Jill Gocher front image 7. Polly Manguel back image 1.Musee Toulouse-Lautrec, Albi, Tarn, France back image 6. Wikipedia/Michel Y.G. Meunier back image 2.

- [ ] Mekong Delta, Vietnam
- [ ] Mercantour National Park, France
- [ ] Mesa Verde, USA
- [ ] Miami South Beach, USA
- [ ] Milford Sound, New Zealand
- [ ] Mir Castle, Belarus
- [ ] Mogao Caves, China
- [ ] Monasteries of Popocatepetl, Mexico
- [ ] Monet's Garden at Giverny, France
- [ ] Monte Verde, Brazil
- [ ] Montreal, Canada
- [ ] Montserrat National Park, Spain
- [ ] Mont-St-Michel, France
- [ ] Monument Valley USA
- [ ] Mornington Peninsular, Australia
- [ ] Moscow Metro, Russia
- [ ] Mount Ararat
- [ ] Mount Athos, Greece
- [ ] Mount Bromo, Indonesia
- [ ] Mount Elgon National Park, Kenya
- [ ] Mount Etna, Italy
- [ ] Mount Fuji, Japan
- [ ] Mount Kenya, Kenya
- [ ] Mount Kilimanjaro, Tanzania
- [ ] Mount Olympus, Greece
- [ ] Mount Rushmore, South Dakota, USA
- [ ] Mount Sinai, Egypt
- [ ] Mount St Helens, USA
- [ ] Mozambique, Island of
- [ ] Murchison Falls, Uganda
- [ ] Museum of Modern Art, New York City, USA

- [ ] Namib Desert, Namibia
- [ ] National Air and Space Museum, Washington, DC, USA
- [ ] Nemrut Dag, Turkey
- [ ] Neuschwanstein, Germany
- [ ] New England, autumn colours of, USA
- [ ] Ngorongoro Conservation Area, Tanzania
- [ ] Niagara Falls, Canada
- [ ] Niger Delta, Mali
- [ ] Nikko, Japan
- [ ] Niort, France
- [ ] Noosa, Australia
- [ ] Noto, Italy
- [ ] Notre Dame Cathedral, France

- [ ] Oaxaca, Mexico
- [ ] Ogasawara Islands, Japan
- [ ] Ohrid, Macedonia
- [ ] Okanagan Valley, Canada
- [ ] Okavango Delta, Botswana
- [ ] Oktoberfest, Germany
- [ ] Old Man of Hoy, UK
- [ ] Old Town Lijiang and Dali, China
- [ ] Olduvai Gorge, Tanzania
- [ ] Oporto, Portugal
- [ ] Orange, France
- [ ] Orchha, India
- [ ] Orvieto, Italy
- [ ] Ostia Antica, Italy
- [ ] Oxford, UK

- [ ] Padua, Italy
- [ ] Paestum, Italy
- [ ] Painted Desert, USA
- [ ] Palawan Island, Philippines
- [ ] Pamplona, Spain
- [ ] Pamukkale, Turkey
- [ ] Panang Hill, Malaysia
- [ ] Pantalica, Italy
- [ ] Patagonia, Argentina
- [ ] Patmos, Greece
- [ ] Pembrokeshire Coast, UK
- [ ] Perito Moreno, Argentina
- [ ] Persepolis, Iran
- [ ] Petra, Jordan
- [ ] Phang-Nga Bay, Thailand
- [ ] Pingyao, China
- [ ] Place des Vosges, France
- [ ] Plain of Jars, Laos
- [ ] Polonnaruwa, Sri Lanka
- [ ] Pompeii, Italy
- [ ] Port Antonio, Jamaica
- [ ] Portmeirion, UK
- [ ] Portofino, Italy
- [ ] Prado museum, Spain
- [ ] Prague, Czech Republic
- [ ] Puerto Angel, Mexico
- [ ] Pyramid of Kukulcán, Mexico

- [ ] Quebec City Winter Carnival, Canada

- [ ] Quebec, Canada
- [ ] Queen Charlotte Islands
- [ ] Queenstown, New Zealand

- [ ] Raft Cove, Vancouver Island, Canada
- [ ] Rangiroa, French Polynesia
- [ ] Rebun Island, Japan
- [ ] Reichenau, monastic island of, Germany
- [ ] Rhine Valley, Germany
- [ ] Rift Valley, Kenya
- [ ] Riga, Latvia
- [ ] Rijksmuseum, Netherlands
- [ ] Rio de Janeiro, Brazil
- [ ] Rock carvings of Tanum, Sweden
- [ ] Rome, Italy
- [ ] Rotorua, New Zealand
- [ ] Rottnest Island, Australia
- [ ] Rwanda National Park, Rwanda
- [ ] Rwenzori Mountains National Park, Uganda

- [ ] Saba, Leeward Islands
- [ ] St Augustine, USA
- [ ] Sainte-Chapelle, France
- [ ] Saint-Louis, Senegal
- [ ] St Petersburg, Russia
- [ ] St Sophia Cathedral, Ukraine
- [ ] St-Tropez, France
- [ ] Salisbury Cathedral, UK
- [ ] Saltaire, UK
- [ ] Salvador, Brazil
- [ ] Salzburg, Austria
- [ ] Samaria Gorge, Greece
- [ ] Samarkand, Uzbekistan
- [ ] San Antonia, USA
- [ ] San Augustín Archaeological Park, Columbia
- [ ] San Diego, USA
- [ ] San Francisco, USA
- [ ] San Gimignano, Italy
- [ ] Sana'a, Yemen
- [ ] Santa Cruz Carnival, Bolivia
- [ ] Santa Fe, USA
- [ ] Santa María de Guadalupe, Spain